A History of Economic Thought

ECONOMICS HANDBOOK SERIES

SEYMOUR E. HARRIS, Editor

Burns · SOCIAL SECURITY AND PUBLIC POLICY

Duesenberry · BUSINESS CYCLES AND ECONOMIC GROWTH

Hansen · A GUIDE TO KEYNES

Hansen · MONETARY THEORY AND FISCAL POLICY

Hansen · THE AMERICAN ECONOMY

Harris · INTERNATIONAL AND INTERREGIONAL ECONOMICS

Henderson and Quandt · MICROECONOMIC THEORY

Hoover · THE LOCATION OF ECONOMIC ACTIVITY

Johnston · STATISTICAL COST ANALYSIS

Kindleberger · ECONOMIC DEVELOPMENT

Lerner · ECONOMICS OF EMPLOYMENT

Taylor · A HISTORY OF ECONOMIC THOUGHT

Valavanis · ECONOMETRICS

SOCIAL IDEALS
AND ECONOMIC THEORIES
FROM QUESNAY TO KEYNES

A HISTORY OF ECONOMIC THOUGHT

Overton H. Taylor
HARVARD UNIVERSITY

NEW YORK
TORONTO
LONDON

McGRAW-HILL BOOK COMPANY 1960

A HISTORY OF ECONOMIC THOUGHT

 Library of Congress Catalog Card Number 60–8042

9 10 11 12 13 14 15 16 - MAMM - 7 5 4 3 2 1 0

62930

Editor's Introduction

For many years teachers of economics and other professional economists have felt the need of a series of books on economic subjects which is not filled by the usual textbook, or by the highly technical treatise.

This present series, published under the general title of *Economics Handbook Series,* was planned with this need in mind. Designed first of all for students, the volumes are useful in the ever-growing field of adult education and also are of interest to the informed general reader.

The volumes present a distillate of accepted theory and practice, without the detailed approach of the technical treatise. Each volume is a unit, standing on its own.

The authors are scholars, each writing on an economic subject on which he is an authority. In this series the author's first task is not to make important contributions to knowledge—although many of them do—but so to present his subject matter that his work as a scholar will carry its maximum influence outside as well as inside the classroom. The time has come to redress the balance between the energies spent on the creation of new ideas and on their dissemination. Economic ideas are unproductive if they do not spread beyond the world of scholars. Popularizers without technical competence, unqualified textbook writers, and sometimes even charlatans control too large a part of the market for economic ideas.

In the classroom the *Economics Handbook Series* will serve, it is hoped, as brief surveys in one-semester courses, and as supplementary reading in introductory courses and other courses in which the subject is related.

Seymour E. Harris

Editor's Preface

O. H. Taylor's *A History of Economic Thought: Social Ideals and Economic Theories from Quesnay to Keynes* is a book that embodies the fruits of his life-long studies and reflections, concerned with the history of economic theory *and* the relations of its main developments with the broad, general patterns of philosophical and over-all social, moral, and political thought, which have been their wider intellectual backgrounds or contexts.

The book opens with a chapter which first surveys the general outlook and mode of thought (in all fields) of the eighteenth-century Enlightenment; and then considers in that setting, the social-and-moral philosophy *and* contributions to economic theory of Quesnay and the Physiocrats. In a series of three chapters all designed to illuminate Adam Smith's thought, there is first a review of the earlier theories of psychology-and-ethics, of Smith's forerunners in that field: Lord Shaftesbury, Bernard Mandeville, and Francis Hutcheson; next a study of Smith's philosophy of science (expressed in his essay on the history of astronomy) and of his *Theory of the Moral Sentiments;* and finally, a full study of Adam Smith's ideal-and-theory of the self-adjusting, liberal economy, as elaborated in the *Wealth of Nations.*

The next chapters consider, in succession, the entire system of thought of Jeremy Bentham and his followers, the English Utilitarians; the work of Malthus on the population problem, in its relations to the utopian socialist-and-anarchist philosophy of Godwin, to the Utilitarian system, and to classical economics as a whole; and the Ricardian theory of economics and political economy. The study of John Stuart Mill's thought is divided between two chapters, the first dealing with his views in philosophy, ethics, politics, and logic, and the second with his economics. Taylor then examines intellectual Marxism as a whole and in its parts—philosophical, socio-historical, and economic-theoretical—and in its relations to earlier socialist thought, the philosophy of Hegel, and Ricardian economics.

Turning back to the main line of development of economic theory, as that continued through the late nineteenth into the twentieth century, the author surveys the late-Victorian conservative liberalism as the ruling climate of political thought in its epoch, and the growth and character of neo-classical economic theory, or marginal analysis, within that climate; and then studies fully Alfred Marshall's system of economic theory, as the most important single, particular product of that general movement. Finally, coming down to the most recent and now still current period, the book discusses the ideologies of Communism, fascism, modern democratic socialism, and the new modern brand of liberalism associated with the American, Rooseveltian New Deal; and the main recent developments of economic theory, having important bearings on general problems of public policy. Taylor selects for special treatment in this period Keynes and Keynesian economics and E. H. Chamberlin's theory of monopolistic competition.

This is a book that should interest a rather wide variety of readers: economists, political scientists, philosophers, historians, university students (undergraduate and graduate) in all those fields, and mature, educated, and thoughtful citizens in all walks of life, beyond as well as within academic walls.

The editor believes that others will be as impressed by this splendid volume as he has been. Taylor's command not only of economic thought but of related disciplines is unique. I know no other volume in economics dealing with controversial issues which is as objective as this one. This volume truly represents a lifetime of thought.

Seymour E. Harris

Preface

The "scope" of this book is more limited in one direction, and broader in another, than the abbreviated title on its cover—*A History of Economic Thought*—may lead the reader to expect. On the one hand, this is not a complete or comprehensive history of economic thought; only a part, although a major part, of that subject matter is surveyed herein. And on the other hand, another portion—about one-half—of the space and attention in this book is devoted to some parts of another, quite different subject matter—history of philosophical and over-all social, ethical, and political thought—the social philosophies that have been associated with different, main developments, systems, and varieties of economic theory, as their wider intellectual backgrounds or contexts. Let me further explain these two points, in turn.

The accounts and discussions, included in this book, of some major parts of the past development of economic theory—from Quesnay and Adam Smith to Keynes—add up to a much less than all-inclusive history within that field. The developments which occurred *before* the time of the Physiocrats and Adam Smith—in antiquity, the Middle Ages, and the age of mercantilism—are entirely omitted; the reason is not that I regard them as unimportant or lack interest in them—the contrary is true—but solely that I had to exclude them, to reduce the book to a manageable size. Further, the book's coverage even of its modern period is highly selective, i.e., it is far indeed from complete. Only main elements—and not all of those—of the contributions of a certain number of great economists are included. Quesnay and Smith, Malthus and Ricardo, and J. S. Mill and Karl Marx have been selected from the earlier part of the period. Then the "neo-classical" development of the late nineteenth century, or marginal analysis, or the revolution in value and distribution theory, is dealt with in another way: through, first, a general survey of this movement as a whole, and then a more detailed study of Alfred Marshall's particular theoretical system. And the final chapters consider only E. H. Chamberlin's theory of monopolistic competition, and the Keynesian system.

On the other hand, all of *that* material makes up only about one-half of the book. Alternating with the parts devoted to developments of economic theory are others dealing with the "social philosophies" which have tended to be "associated" with them. Thus, the structure of economic theory erected by Quesnay is considered after and along with —in relation to its background in—not only his entire philosophy but also the entire ruling philosophy or climate of opinion about everything of the eighteenth-century Enlightenment. Then the study of Adam Smith's economics is led up to through a prior study of the "line" of thought in moral philosophy, or psychology-and-ethics, of Smith's "forerunners" in this other field (Lord Shaftesbury and Francis Hutcheson, and the intervening critic with a different outlook, Bernard Mandeville); and Smith's own completion of that line of thought in his almost forgotten other book which preceded the *Wealth of Nations*—his *Theory of the Moral Sentiments*. Again, Benthamism in its entirety is discussed in a chapter which follows that on Smith's economics and precedes the chapters on Malthus and Ricardo. The first of the two chapters on John Stuart Mill's thought deals with his work and views in the fields of philosophy, ethics, politics, and logic; and the second deals with his economics and political economy. The chapter on Marx considers the entire background and substance of intellectual Marxism as a whole, and includes discussion of Marx's work in economic theory, as one part of that. And so on. Even the later parts of the book, pertaining to more modern or recent times in which formal political philosophies have been of declining importance, and declining relevance to the newer developments of economic theory, include chapters on the broad, vague, widespread "ideologies"—late-Victorian conservative liberalism, and twentieth-century Communism, fascism, democratic socialism, and New Deal liberalism—which I think are worth discussing as factors in the intellectual environment around the modern developments of economic theory. In sum, the book as a whole is concerned in about equal measures with these two very different and never strictly connected but I think always significantly, loosely interrelated subject matters: history of economic theory *and* history of political theory in the age-old "broad" meaning of the latter term, or "social philosophies."

Some readers will no doubt regard this intermingling of discussions of two different subject matters in the same book as queer and objectionable. I will not defend it here at any length; an argument striving to convince all potential critics of the propriety and desirability of this character or feature of the book would become interminable and remain inconclusive, for the basic questions and conflicting viewpoints at issue run too deep to be resolved by any amount of argument. But let me say a few words, only, in very partial "reply" to each of the two different "objections" which may be felt, in the same or in different quarters. The first of these refers merely to the simple fact that I am violating the ideal of strict specialization of some modern scholars: sticking narrowly or strictly to one's specialty or special field, becoming thoroughly competent in that, and not spreading one's attention and efforts over so wide an area as to make one's achievement or performance, as a whole and in every part, superficial. Can one who is, by profession and training, an economist and student of the history of economics, possibly be or become qualified to do properly thorough work in that field *and also* in the very different and equally vast field of philosophical, social, and political thought and *its* history?

The task that I have undertaken is indeed immense; and I can only say that I have done my best, and I know very well that the accomplished results, presented in this book, have great limitations. But I believe that the universe of all knowledge, thought, inquiry, or intellectual discourse, with all its internal diversity, has a unity whereby its different parts illuminate each other; so that spreading out one's efforts over a wide area, involving more than one discipline, *can* lead to achievements having special values, worth or compensating their inevitable shortcomings. The "narrowness" of outlook which is the penalty or price of "thorough" mastery of a single discipline or branch of knowledge seems to me as serious a deficiency as the other kind of "superficiality" of knowledge of the matters of relative detail within each specialty, which is the penalty or price of greater breadth of outlook or perspective; and pursuit of the latter, at its own accepted and acknowledged cost, seems to me as well worthwhile as pursuit of the former at *its* own cost. In particular, I think that the histories of economic theory and of political theory, in the sense I have indicated, *are* related, mutually relevant, or mutually illuminating studies, and a work endeavoring to treat (parts of) both together *may* have merits sufficient to "offset" its inevitable limitations within each field.

The other, second and different "objection," which is likely to be felt by some economists, raises more profound issues, about which I will say very little. Economics, it may be said, is in some degree at least a science; and the history of economic theory is a history of progressive, scientific-theoretical investigations and discoveries, or work producing an ever-growing and improving body of real knowledge and understanding of its subject matter. But in utter contrast with that, all political theories or philosophies, or all-embracing cosmic and social and ethical philosophies, or "ideologies," are mere expressions of the local and transitory, subjective moods of individual "thinkers" or/and social and political movements, parties, cults, etc., in particular times and countries. They are purely speculative, void of demonstrable or verifiable truth or validity, as largely emotional as intellectual in content or substance, and intent not purely on discovering truth or understanding actualities but largely on inspiring and directing political action toward particular goals and along particular paths. And they are always biased, partisan, fervent, and dogmatic—in short, they are in every way antithetical in spirit and nature to all science. Hence—so runs the conclusion from this contrast—economic theory and political theory of this kind are not only radically unlike each other, but are incompatible; and to study their histories together and assume and look for genuine, positive relations between the two, or reciprocal debts and contributions to each other, is a proceeding that must start from false premises and make no sense and produce only intellectual confusions.

Now I do myself partly, but only partly, agree with the point of view that I have just stated. Economics—the economic inquiry—is, and long has been, *in some degree* a science, though I emphasize the qualifying phrase. And the parts of this book which deal with developments of economic theory deal with them *as* phases of the progress of a science, *not* as mere integral parts of the political or social-and-moral philosophies that are separately examined along with them, or parts just like, and dominated by, the latter in their own entireties. But I do not think that economic science, or theoretical work in it, is or has been or can be so perfectly or absolutely scientific—objective, unbiased, neutral, and throughout secure as opposed to "speculative"—as to make it possible to say, generally, that the great contributions which have been made to its development by great economists have been wholly uninfluenced by the political philosophies shared, and often partly created, by those economists in their other roles as more than that—human thinkers, in their human environments, about human life and affairs in general. Nor do I see any point in avoiding recognition and study, or lack of point in trying fully to understand and appraise, the influences exerted by the social philosophies upon the economic theories of the great economists, and vice versa. The economist's proper effort to make his own work and thinking within economics as scientific and objective as possible can I think be aided best, not by trying to shun or avoid broad, social-philosophic thinking and concern also with that and its history, but by a procedure of a contrary kind. Precisely in his effort to achieve objectivity, one should try to make his own social, moral, and political outlook or philosophy as fully explicit, conscious, clear, and self-critically examined as possible; and study and compare with it the diverse political philosophies of great economists of the past, and the effects thereof on their achievements within economics; and learn how to profit by and avoid their mistakes in this matter, or parallel mistakes, or any improper control of his own economic thinking by his political opinions.

Moreover, although I recognize the difference of the natures of this book's two subject matters—the relatively more scientific nature of economic theory and essentially non- or extrascientific nature of all systems of philosophical political thought—I do not at all share the inclination toward contemptuous dismissal of the latter as not worth serious, participating study, which often accompanies insistence on that contrast. For I do not share the positivistic point of view, widely prevalent today in our culture and among economists and other scholars, which leads them to value, as intellectual productions, *only* the strict sciences, and despise, as sterile and illusory, all efforts to think or inquire, as rationally as possible, about all the great questions of vital moment for human civilization, which do not admit of or cannot be given scientific answers. I am convinced that civilizations, and civilized men, cannot live by or upon scientific knowledge alone, in the sum of all its varieties or branches, however fully developed they may become. I believe that in addition to that, all-comprehensive "faiths," which ideally should be informed by, and consistent with, the sciences as far as the latter go, but must go beyond the limits of them all and affirm answers to the greater questions which they cannot answer—that these too are indispensable and, for the good of their adherents and of mankind, need imperatively to be made as well informed and reasoned, reasonable, or relatively rational, and not arrogantly but humbly although firmly held, as possible. The sciences alone yield only knowledge of the causes of effects, that is, of means to ends—the knowledge that is power—not wisdom about values, or to guide and civilize men's choices of their ends. Hence in the measure in which intellectual life and culture come to be dominated by the scientific studies only, they make men and societies increasingly efficient and potent but at the same time increasingly barbarous. Philosophy in the ancient sense—the pursuit of wisdom, or a relatively complete set of all value-judgments, mutually consistent and consistent with all known or knowable and all most likely truth and reality, and the needs and capacities of all human beings—this other and different intellectual pursuit or activity, though unlike science and not to be confused with it or allowed to dominate or control and distort it, is by no means inferior to it in worth, dignity, or importance, or proper appeal to inquiring minds. That philosophy cannot attain its goals, is never-ending discussion forever inconclusive and scarcely progressive, can never establish "the Truth" in its sphere and lead to prevailing agreement among all upon that, but remains always a rivalry of many discordant philosophies—all this is true but beside the point. The *pursuit,* if carried on in the right spirit, is of infinite value, despite all the dubiousness that forever attaches to all the results attained. And political philosophy is philosophy applied to or in consideration of all the general affairs and problems of politically organized societies. Like pure or general philosophy, it is plural by nature—produces a variety of diverse and warring political philosophies—and they all play their important roles in the developments and functionings of the civilizations within which they flourish, in uneasy, complex, in neither direction purely beneficial or purely injurious, interrelations and interactions with all social sciences, including economics. Holding these views, I have tried to produce a balanced, critical study of a historic panorama of composite patterns of thought made up of structures of economic theory and the political philosophies that were "allied" with them, in the minds of their exponents and receptive publics; and in each case I have tried to discuss both parts of the composite whole, and the interrelation or interaction between them, with equal interest.

Then further, of course, being interested in political philosophies and the problems or issues they are about, I am not impartial or neutral among them all, but have my own point of view in this field, or "bias"; and avowal of this is due in fairness to the reader. As anyone who reads the book will soon discover, my own attachment is to what, in the book, I call the classical liberalism—the philosophy or vision of societies of largely free individuals, under limited governments (having limited spheres of authority and activity), of the liberal-democratic kind, and with economic activities and relations organized mainly in systems of free, private enterprises and competitive markets. As very much of the history or development of economic theory, through the period of nearly two centuries surveyed in this book, has occurred or gone forward in loose association with the forms or variants of the classical liberalism shared, as their political outlooks, by the economists concerned, it is natural, and not entirely a reflection of my "bias," that the history of "liberal" thought in that sense fills a particularly large part of this book. And I can only hope that my own sympathy with it has not made me too uncritical of the expressions of it, which are reported and discussed in the book, or of its often partly unfortunate or questionable effects on the economic theories of economists devoted to it, or made me grossly unfair, e.g., to Marx and other socialist thinkers, or others not in the same liberal tradition, in my accounts, discussions, and evaluations of their philosophies and economic theories.

This book is an outgrowth from, or reduction to book form of, a part of the course of lectures, covering the same ground, which I have given annually for many years at Harvard University. Actually, I have been giving two different courses, adapted to the different interests and capacities of different groups of students and, though the courses are much alike in substance, I have been treating the materials in different ways. In my undergraduate course, for college juniors and seniors, majoring in either economics, political science, history, or philosophy, and generally having interests and (some slight) attainments in all or several of those studies, I have tried simply to make this course contribute to education for enlightened citizenship; I have kept the parts concerned with "scientific, technical" economic theory and its history, on a rather simple, elementary level, and expanded and stressed the parts concerned with history of philosophical, social, and political thought, somewhat more than I have in the other, advanced course, given to graduate students of economics. The latter has been given as a course in the history of economic theory and the wider "backgrounds" of that in general intellectual history; with the aim of helping these young, future, professional economists to become equipped for the tasks of modern economic research and analysis, not only with the kinds of equipment acquired in their other, more strictly professional training courses, but also with this kind of historical knowledge, literacy, and perspective. Naturally, the history of development of the "conceptual tools" of economic "science" has been treated more fully and on a more advanced level in this graduate course than in my undergraduate course, but the differences between the two courses, although substantial, have been limited, and are perhaps hardly as pronounced as their similarity. The character of the book reflects something of the characters of both courses, and is perhaps "intermediate" between them.

Although not specifically designed or written as a textbook or book for use in university courses, the volume may be usable in courses in history of economic theory or/and of political theory; and the "selected bibliography" at its end may be useful to instructors and students in such courses—consisting as it does largely of the reading lists I have used in my own courses. And of course I hope that other readers, of all types, may find that list of books for further reading useful, also.

I am hopeful that a rather wide variety of lay readers, as well as professional economists, other kinds of professional scholars, and university students may all alike find this book readable and of some interest and value. Although it includes often fairly full and not purely "elementary" accounts and explanations or expositions of more or less "technical" economic theories and whole, logical "systems" of such theory, I hope and believe that I have presented these in language that all generally educated readers, whether previously familiar with economic theory or not, can readily understand. And besides hoping that even those parts of the book will interest readers who may initially be mainly interested in its other parts, I also hope that even those primarily concerned with economic theory and its history will find my discussions of the broader social philosophies of the great political economists of former times of interest also; and that a fair number at least of my colleagues—fellow economists—will read the entire book, and find it worth reading, throughout. Perhaps I have a desire to be a "missionary" in both directions—to convert as many noneconomist or lay readers as I can into interested students of economic theory and its history, *and* to convert more fellow-economists into interested students, also, of the diverse, general views or perspectives on all human affairs which formerly concerned all philosophical political economists.

I gratefully acknowledge the help I have had in the production of this book: from numerous former students, discussions with whom have helped to form, improve, and clarify my own ideas; from my friend and colleague, Seymour Harris, who read the book in manuscript and made a number of most helpful suggestions, by accepting which I have considerably improved it; and from the Ford Foundation, which through a small grant has helped me in meeting the expenses of preparation and publication of the book.

Overton H. Taylor

Contents

CHAPTER 1

The Eighteenth Century; Locke and Newton; the Natural Order; and the Physiocrats

THE ENLIGHTENMENT

The intellectual revolution of the seventeenth century, which established the new foundations of modern thought in philosophy, the natural sciences (chiefly physics), and the "moral (social-and-moral) sciences," was followed by a wide popularization and continuing, further development of the new way of thinking—in all of these areas, but especially in the one last mentioned—which is commonly and appropriately called the eighteenth-century "Enlightenment." Although this name was first firmly affixed to the latter movement as a whole by nineteenth-century historians, the word *Enlightenment* was already in common use, and a favorite term, in the eighteenth century itself, and describes exactly what its intellectuals generally, confidently thought of as going on, and of themselves as taking part in or contributing to. The "light" of the new advancing understanding of all nature and human affairs, and of reasoned moral wisdom, was being spread abroad to "enlighten" the minds of more and more of the people everywhere, and was growing continually "brighter" in the meantime; and the lingering "darkness" of formerly prevailing, age-old ignorance and errors, superstitions, and hoary, stupid traditions and prejudices of all kinds, was being progressively dispelled—abolished.

The somewhat excessive, naïve, and complacent optimism that prevailed widely among the eighteenth century's intellectuals had several sources. One main root of this optimism was their belief, containing much truth but exaggerating it into serious error, that all "sciences"—the social-and-moral sciences as well and surely as the natural sciences—

had now at last become equipped with the right, fully sound, and effective method and fundamental concepts; and were certain not only to go on advancing rapidly and securely, but finally in some not extremely distant future to attain complete and perfect knowledge of the general patterns of all nature, and all human life, societies, and history, and the true morality which, when universally understood and obeyed, would make the human world either entirely or rather nearly a perfect, happy society, or "heaven on earth."

Then there was also, along with this overestimation of the new intellectual advances as such, an immense overestimation of the potential, universal, "natural," intellectual and moral capacities of all human beings for entirely "rational" thought and behavior, including "moral reasonableness"; and hence, of the power of all "scientific" truth or knowledge to become, as achieved and communicated to the people, effective in controlling (guiding) their activities and conduct, and reshaping all human societies, institutions, and practices into conformity with or realization of a "rational" plan. And finally, to the century's optimism a different, third contribution was made by its remnant of religious faith, which took the form of a belief—not set over against but blended with all that was thought of as scientific knowledge—that a wise and benevolent God had "designed" the system of nature and (or including) the faculties and fundamental inherent propensities of human nature. In its blend with the epoch's scientific thought, that religious belief made it seem that natural science was finding in and throughout all nature, apart from mankind, an admirable "harmony"; or showing that the cosmos is a whole of parts all "spontaneously" and reliably performing their appropriate functions in the over-all smooth working of the system as a whole. And the social-and-moral sciences were thought to be finding in the world of men and all their voluntary doings, full indications of the possibility, and the reforms needed for realization, of a similarly harmonious, human-social cosmos—a world of free individuals, rationally pursuing satisfactions of all their "natural" desires, *and in so doing,* always acting in the ways that would fit in as appropriate parts of an orderly system of "natural" social processes, on the whole conducive to the highest attainable collective welfare of all mankind.

Of course, the reader must be cautioned not to conclude, from this too simple summary account of that epoch's ruling climate of opinion, that there was anything like a complete uniformity or unanimity of all eighteenth-century thought about everything or indeed about anything. In fact, the century knew a wide variety, and countless conflicts, of particular views on particular questions, and even of the entire overall perspectives of different minds and groups. Perhaps the common or very widely shared, general climate of opinion really was little more than a common or current, abstract, intellectual "language," or frame of reference, which was throughout sufficiently vague to accommodate the whole wide range of differing and disagreeing, more specific views and creeds.

Yet the common climate, or language, or whatever we call it, did and does have much importance. It did signify Western culture's achievement and possession, within that epoch, of *a degree of nearness, rare in its history, to agreement* of all leading minds on the fundamentals of one all-embracing, almost unified or coherent, and simple, attractive, widely popular "philosophy." That philosophy does still need and repay careful, at once sympathetic and critical, study in the world of today, which owes much to it and yet has moved rather far away from it. Many true, realistic and wise, practical insights, and other elements (notions) which must be described as utopian, idealistic illusions were blended together in it all, in diverse proportions in the different variants of the whole "philosophy" evolved by different thinkers and groups, or in different quarters. And today our culture, though in many ways much altered from its state in that epoch, is full of both kinds of elements, still often similarly blended or confused together. The needed critical revision of our whole, still basic inheritance from the Enlightenment never has been carried out completely; and progress in achieving this can be aided by direct study of eighteenth-century thought itself, because in that thought the basic insights, illusions, and confusions all stand out far more simply and clearly than they do in the more sophisticated and complex intellectual productions that are current in our time.

In its main, immediate, antecedent sources and its general character, most (and all typical) eighteenth-century thought was both Lockeian and Newtonian, i.e., was deeply influenced in philosophy, ethics, and politics by Locke, and in both the natural and the social sciences by the "example" and the fundamental concepts of Newtonian, or classical, physics. We may consider the results of these mingled influences under the two headings of *method* and *substance*. In epistemology and methodology, or theory of knowledge and scientific method, or philosophy of science, both the "empiricism" expounded by Locke and that practiced by the physical scientists *were beginning* to produce real effects or evoke more than lip service generally, in all kinds of inquiries; but they still were somewhat inconsistently mingled or blended with a rather large remainder of, or carry-over from, the ancient, unempirical, or absolute, speculative-and-logical "rationalism." And in metaphysics, or theory of reality, or philosophy of the character of all that is and all that ought to be, the prevailing, over-all conception was that of a "natural order," or a system of systems of natural-scientific, ethical, and social-scientific "natural laws," ordained by a wise and benevolent God, the "designer" of all nature and human nature, to ensure a harmonious, orderly functioning of both the nonhuman natural universe, and all human societies. The ideas of the natural order and the system of natural law which profoundly affected the substance of eighteenth-century thought in all fields is the central subject of this chapter. But first a few things must be said about the mixture (in varying proportions) of declining "rationalism" and rising "empiricism" that prevailed in the century's way or ways of thinking about or approaching all kinds of problems.

There is much truth, but a plurality of partial (limited) truths rather than any one simple and absolute truth, in the references that are often made to "eighteenth-century rationalism," to the "Age of Enlightenment," and to the "Age of Reason." There did prevail then, in a measure perhaps hardly equaled at any other time since the classic age of ancient Greek thought, and certainly not often at all nearly approached today, a high, ardent faith in the power of the human faculty or instrument of "reason" to solve all problems, refute and abolish all erroneous beliefs and practices, and achieve and diffuse into all minds, in time, all of the true knowledge, understanding, and wisdom needed to "guide" all men and societies to attainment of the highest levels of wealth, welfare, and happiness made possible by their environments, natures, and abilities. But to a great extent in theory, at least, and usually to some extent—in varying degrees in the cases of different thinkers—in practice also, the object of this high and even excessive faith in reason, was reason *applied to or in analysis of all human experience; not* "pure" reason working without experimental or empirical data, or at mere deduction of the logical results of its own primary, supposed, general insights, or purely speculative constructs or assumptions. The usually professed and to some extent practiced "method" of inquiry, in other words, was tending to become that of "rational empiricism," rather than that of simple, pure, or absolute "rationalism."

Yet my qualifications, included in those statements, must be emphasized. There were still some exponents, i.e., defenders as well as practitioners, of the absolute "rationalism" which tried to set up a few "self-evident" primary truths and deduce all others, on all subjects, from them. And even the more numerous and more typical inquirers of the time, who sincerely professed their adherence to the Lockeian "empiricism" and the natural-science method of observing facts and testing theories for agreement with them, generally fell very far short of actually performing, or even realizing or conceiving, all that was needed in the way of thorough, careful, systematic, empirical research, and critical testing of their plausible, "rational" theories for agreement with "experience." What they really did as a rule was to "reason" from or upon simple, plausible, general assumptions arising from or suggested by their limited amounts of informal, casual, "everyday" experience and observation and their "common sense," i.e., the currently, commonly accepted, general ideas or concepts with which they construed and organized all such experience, and which *seemed* to have the full and conclusive support of it all. And this, of course, really differed less than they often supposed from the avowed method of the all-out "rationalists," who regarded their "common sense" beliefs not as summaries of everyday experience, but rather as "self-evident" intuitions of pure reason.

It also must be said, however, that eighteenth-century minds could thus blend, without any sense of being inconsistent, tendencies toward the contrary "methods" of all-out "rationalism" and full-fledged "empiricism," because in and for that age the appeals to "reason" and to "experience" were in the main not rivals but allies, in the general, common opposition to all uncritical, reverent acceptance of views supported merely by tradition and authority.[1] Men were to use their free, independent, individual reasoning minds *and* the facts experienced or observed with their own senses, to criticize or test all traditionally received, authoritative doctrines, refute and discard all the errors and nonsense included in them, and advance beyond them to new, more clearly and cogently conceived and reasoned, and securely grounded truth or knowledge on all subjects. And this intellectual liberalism—assertion of the universal individual right and duty of free, skeptical or critical and innovative inquiry, thought, expression, and discussion—was the basic side of the many-sided liberalism of eighteenth-century thought throughout the ethical or normative sphere, and the link directly connecting its liberal with its scientific spirit and outlook. Distrusting all tradition and authority, and trusting that all minds when emancipated from them would be able to reason correctly from truths borne out as such by the experiences of all to a new, common, true, and all-sufficient wisdom; the men of the Enlightenment tended to expect, too hopefully, that the on-going progress of all free and progressive sciences, and of popular education, would in time bring into being a new world of rationally reconstructed societies of free, enlightened individuals all severally both thinking and behaving "rationally" and in line with their own best interests as individuals and with those of all mankind.

One of the roots of the excess of optimism in that much too hopeful outlook was the defect of the usual "method" of eighteenth-century thought already noticed here—excessive reliance on mere reasoning or logical, speculative theorizing, not accompanied, controlled, and fed by sufficiently extensive and thorough empirical research. This deficiency or one-sidedness—relative excess in the direction of pure "ra-

[1] Cf. Morris Cohen, *Reason and Nature: An Essay on the Meaning of Scientific Method,* 2d ed. (Glencoe, Ill.: Free Press, 1953), p. 5.

tionalism" in the presupposed philosophy of science—contributed to excessive optimism because it meant deficient awareness of the endless variety and complexity in or throughout the real, empirical world, and the consequent, necessary endlessness of the temporal process of increasing and improving all human knowledge; or the folly of hoping for mankind's eventual attainment of the complete and perfect knowledge in all fields, which through its applications would perfect the human world or all human practices. The dreams of utopia, fostered by the Enlightenment, involved the false belief that the sum or complete pattern of all truth is simple or finite, and can all become known as just the full set of the implications of a small group of simple elementary propositions sanctioned by the "common sense" of one culture and epoch.

Yet it is as easy to be too severe as to be too lenient in judging this feature of eighteenth-century thought. The use in thought of relatively simple, manageable, abstract, conceptual and theoretical "models" of reality, which oversimplify it, is always necessary for any attainment of even partial understanding of it. And the best theoretical visions of this kind—yielding the best or greatest degree of understanding of their real, empirical subject matters—are not the most elaborate, complex, or intricate schemes; but those which manage, in the simplest ways in which this is possible, to come nearest to representing, fully and truly, all the main or more important features of the real, empirical subject matters. Very simple structures of theory can be contemptibly superficial, or be works of genius full of penetrating insight; and impressive, elaborate, or complex structures can be still better than the best simple ones, getting nearer to full, true "realism," or be worse than the worst simple ones, containing as little true insight and obscuring that little with unnecessarily complex formulations. The eighteenth century, of course, had its superficial thinkers, but it also produced *many* inquirers, including some workers in natural science and even more in the social-and-moral studies, who really were men of genius, and made their simple, theoretical visions—versions or developments of all or parts of the prevalent vision of "the natural order," *in* the universe *and for* all human societies and conduct—vehicles of much true knowledge, understanding, and wisdom.

They all indeed fell short, by widely varying, great distances, of adequate awareness of the limitations of their own achievements; the infinite complexity of the complete-real subject matters and mazes of problems which they only very partially illuminated; and the need for literally endless, further progress beyond their attainments, and the permanent impossibility of any human attainment of the omniscience that would be required to realize utopia or a perfect society. But, of course, only the superficial thinkers of the time were flagrant utopians; the inquirers who produced solid achievements displayed only the limited degrees of overoptimism resulting from their degrees of failure to sense sufficiently the still unfathomed complexity of *all* truth in contrast with the bits of it included in their simple visions.

There was also, however, another way and field in which exaggerated notions of the powers of "reason" tended to prevail in much (by no means all) eighteenth-century social-and-moral thought, and infect it with degrees of overoptimism or utopianism. That is, besides the too nearly, only "rational" or not adequately "empirical" *method* of inquiry, there often occurred, as a *substantive* element (assumption) of theoretical systems in this area, the *psychological* "rationalism" or intellectualism which grossly exaggerated the potential, universal role of "reason" in determining the lines or patterns of all human behavior. This ancient idealizing conception of "human nature" and the psychological processes through which human conduct is engendered and determined, imputed to everyman's "reason" the decisive role in directing his behavior; and to everyman himself a great—potentially perfect—capacity and tendency to make the conduct of his life and all his activities ideally "rational." In other words, it imputed to man a tendency—which his achievement of adequate knowledge could make perfect—to choose correctly in every situation, among all the courses of action open to him, the course logically required by or best adapted to the situation and his well-considered and arranged set of ends or objectives; or required to maximize the resulting total satisfaction of the total constellation of his (definite and self-known) "natural" desires. All this might be a notion simply of *expedient* behavior, involving "rational" choice of ways and means, but to ends determined not by (ethical) "reason" but by nonrational, simply factual (psychological), human-natural desires. But there usually was also present as a further modifying element the (vague and difficult) notion of a power of "reason" to control or modify all desires themselves and make them "morally reasonable," i.e., to make all the desires of each individual not only mutually consistent but also consistent with the likewise reasonable desires of all other men; and in short, to make the over-all result a prevailing, "rational" pursuit by all of morally *proper* ends only, or a greatest, true welfare of all severally, in perfect harmony with their greatest collective or common welfare. This last idea will be noticed again below as the main substance of the usual form of the century's notion of the system or code of ethical "natural law."

In any case, in all forms the belief in the power and tendency of the "reason" of all men to make all their actions and behavior-patterns fully "rational" was, of course, a main source of the universal tendency to confuse, or blend together, *normative* theories of *right* behavior and *positive* (in aim, descriptive, explanatory, and predictive) theories of *actual* behavior. And, of course, it strongly contributed to the prevailing optimism or utopianism; in a world of potentially, "naturally," ideally "rational" human beings, the progress and spread of knowledge and "enlightenment" would be certain to result in progress toward a realized "heaven on earth."

Finally, this seriously mistaken idea of human psychology had still another serious result for and in all social sciences affected by it, and especially for economics, in which it gained its strongest hold and has too largely persisted to the present day. It has helped to perpetuate the sway of excessive "rationalism," or has hindered advance toward adequate "empiricism," in method of inquiry in this field, by supporting the convenient but fallacious substitution of logic for empirical psychology; that is, the substitution of mere elaboration of "the logic of choice" in rational behavior, to maximize total satisfaction of the wants of the actors, for investigation of the actual psychological factors and processes through which actual behavior is determined. So long as a social science, e.g., economics, remains content to theorize about "rational" behavior, instead of investigating the actual human behavior in its field of interest, it can at best become only partially an empirical as well as a rational science; i.e., its empirical research can develop only in the spheres of study of the objective situations to which the human actors in its subject matter "react," and study of the results of their (observed but not explained) mass behavior. All this is good, but the central field for empirical research—detailed study of the actual causation and character of the actual behavior itself—remains empty or filled only with the unempirical figments of "the logic of choice."

Yet it is significant that, as we shall see, the greatest eighteenth-century economist, Adam Smith, was emphatically one of the minority of his epoch's workers in the social-and-moral sciences who did *not* exaggerate the role of "reason" in the genesis and determination of human behavior; but who, on the contrary, were fond of attributing all kinds of behavior mainly to various, nonrational, instinctive propensities, and "natural," but socially influenced, psychological (emotional) forces; and who were pioneers in the scientific study of the psychology and social psychology of human emotional life and its results in the spheres of all culture and all individual and collective behavior. It was not from Adam Smith but from other sources that his nineteenth-century successors acquired or carried on and developed the "psychological rationalism" described and criticized above, which they made a basic ingredient of their own, and of most subsequent, systems of economic theory. Yet again, it seems a further paradox that the latter did not therefore reach conclusions diverging notably at all from those arrived at by Adam Smith on the basis of his different, *not* overrationalistic views in psychology.

That fact indeed poses a problem which we shall have to deal with later in this book; and may lead us to some mitigation of the above critical remarks on the harm done to economic science by its frequent dalliance with ideas of "rational" behavior. But it must be said here, on the other side, that while Adam Smith's thought was free of that particular illusion—belief in the potential power of "reason" to control or direct all human conduct—it did contain or involve, along with good insights into psychological truths about human emotional life, illusions of another kind in that field, which were common or prevalent in eighteenth-century thought generally and could easily be all the more pronounced wherever "psychological rationalism" was rejected, and could replace that as an alternative source or ground of broadly similar, partly wrong conclusions.

I speak now of the (again) overoptimistic notion of the "natural goodness" of mankind, or the fitness of the Providentially designed faculties and fundamental instincts of human nature to engender a harmony of the spontaneous mental functionings and behavior of free men with the real conditions of proper functioning of their societies and their common welfare. That there are real, "natural," psychological and social processes of adaptation or adjustment of individual and collective habits of feeling, thought, and action, to the real environments concerned and the real conditions of tolerably adequate satisfaction of "human nature's" strong demands, was the basic general, true insight of eighteenth-century social science. But there was a common proneness to exaggerate that insight or the relative perfection of those "natural" processes, and develop theories of a highly, socially beneficent, natural functioning of the psyches of all men, and of the social systems either deliberately, jointly constructed and operated by them, or evolving and functioning with but little conscious, over-all, human "planning." And when and in so far as such overoptimistic theories did not rely on exaggerated notions of the role of reason in directing all human conduct, they relied instead on one-sided notions of the more or less purely "good" or socially fortunate constitution of the nonrational, emotional part of human nature.

But I have gone beyond discussion of the "method," only, of eighteenth-century thought, and have begun to touch also upon (one part of it) its "substance"; I must now turn to a more systematic survey of the latter's over-all pattern, i.e., the common conception of the all-embracing system of "natural law" and the "natural order."

In a sense the most fundamental part of that conception was the part that has since been most widely discarded in the on-going development of modern thought, and is least readily understood today, i.e., the idea of a system or code of *normative, ethical* "natural law" prescribing the right patterns for all human societies and conduct. This was a very old idea, which had played important roles, in earlier forms, in ancient-classical and mediaeval thought; but a last revival and revision of the notion flourished in this epoch. Essentially, it was Locke's idea of the "natural" moral law or code and the "natural rights" of all men under it, which prevailed on through the eighteenth century. It continued to seem "obvious" to the "common sense" of the men of the Enlightenment, as it had seemed to Locke's, that all men, alike sharing or representing the same "human nature," are alike entitled in justice to the same rights and liberties; and obliged, in justice to each other, to make their conduct always consistent with these rights of all—the rights and liberties required to enable all to develop and exercise their "natural" abilities, toward attainment of full satisfactions of their "natural" desires.[2] Of course, the elements or terms even of this conception were quite broad or vague; and there were other, differing conceptions, less fully in line with Locke's, of the code of "natural" law or justice, which still more widely extended the range of diverse, more specific moral visions that could be and were expressed in this common "language." Thus the complete range of these conceptions came to extend all the way from the conservatism of a Blackstone—which regarded English common law as a practically perfect embodiment of all "natural" law or justice—to the most radical socialist and anarchist visions that emerged on the left-wing fringe of the French Revolution. But the central, main body of eighteenth-century social-and-moral thought evolved on or along the liberal "middle way" between those extremes toward full developments of the Lockeian, liberal vision of the "naturally" right form for human societies—best adapted to the "human nature" of their members—as that of societies of freely competing-and-cooperating, free individuals, all severally both asserting and exercising their own, and at the same time fully respecting one another's, "natural rights."

In its eventual full development this line of thought was to lead to both the ideal-and-theory of liberal democracy in the political sphere, and the ideal-and-theory of the liberal economy—an economic system of free and competitive enterprises and markets. But within the

[2] Cf. Locke, *Two Treatises of Civil Government*, any edition, book 2 (or *Second Treatise*), chap. 2, p. 5. In this passage, Locke conveys his central doctrine, of the equal rights of and reciprocal duties among all men under ethical natural law, through his long, approving quotation from "the judicious Hooker"—the sixteenth-century English writer, Richard Hooker, *Ecclesiastical Polity*. Hooker had merely reproduced, in the passage here quoted by Locke, the mediaeval "argument" originated by St. Thomas Aquinas—that, because all men alike have the same human nature, they all ought in reason to love one another, and respect as each other's all the rights they would severally claim for themselves. Note the union in this "argument" of (1) the Aristotelian-Scholastic idea of the common or universal "nature" of the species, (2) the Christian idea of everyone's ethical duty to "love" all his fellows, and (3) the classical Roman law idea of each individual's just rights.

eighteenth century it was the latter ideal-and-theory, much more than the former, which attained quite full and definite elaborations and began to win widespread acceptance and practical influence. Liberal-democratic political thought (not to speak of practice) was to become mature and ascendant—at any rate in Europe, including England—only in the nineteenth century. The one exception to be made under that statement concerns the United States, of which the eighteenth-century "founding fathers" did work out a quite mature, complete, detailed, and very impressive liberal and *somewhat* democratic political philosophy. There is much to be said in support of the claim that liberal democracy originated in this country—though as a product of the European or all-Western Enlightenment, and a logical development of the ideas of Locke. The Rousseauistic philosophy of democracy, of the French Revolution, was not liberal nor in line with the idea of ethical "natural law"; for its doctrine of an absolute sovereignty or unlimited authority of the so-called "general will" of the entire community involved a collectivistic subjectivism, voluntarism, and "totalitarian" authoritarianism in conflict with the liberal ideal of restraint of *all* authority (even that of democracy, i.e., of the popular majority) and protection of the liberties of *all* individuals, by principles of justice regarded as objective, i.e., not "made" by human desires or wills at all, but only "found," discerned, or grasped by the "reason" common to all men as the really valid, impartial norms which must restrain all for the sake of all.

We must now consider, however, in addition to and along with that idea of *ethical* "natural law," the ideas of natural-scientific and social-scientific "natural laws" (of successions of events and their causal connections or processes), which also pervaded eighteenth-century thought and its vision of "the natural order" existing in the universe and to be achieved in all human societies. These ideas made their own contributions, along with that of the ethical "natural law" conception, to the theories of the requisite structures and potential, "natural" functionings of the liberal economy and of liberal democracy. There is no doubt that Newtonian or classical theoretical physics, with its conception of the physical universe as a mechanical system, and its theory of the "natural laws" of the motions of bodies and the "working" of that system, profoundly influenced the basic concepts and assumptions commonly involved in eighteenth-century theorizings, not only in the "natural" sciences but also in psychology and economic, political, and all social science. Not only the inanimate world and all nonhuman living organisms, but also human beings (their minds as well as their bodies) and human, economic and political societies, came to be generally conceived or thought of as (either literally or by analogy) "mechanisms" or "mechanical" systems, operating or functioning through internal processes conforming to or exemplifying discoverable "natural laws," i.e., either those of physics (mechanics) or others like them. As the great historian of the science of mechanics, Ernest Mach, has said, there came into vogue among the French Encyclopedists a belief that "they were not far from a final explanation of the world by physical and mechanical principles." And as Mach adds, their "joyful overestimation" of the scope of the new ideas of physics and mechanics amounted to "a substitution of a mechanical mythology for the animistic of the old religions." [3]

Mach's use of the word *mythology* may rightly suggest that there were (and are) no adequate grounds for confidence in the full validity of the purely mechanistic view of all processes; but to a large extent this result of the influence of mechanics on all modern scientific thought, in all sciences, has continued to flourish and develop to the present day. Within eighteenth-century thought, however, the mechanistic view as then understood—even in physical science itself, and above all in the "sciences" concerned with human life and affairs—was not yet the grim outlook that it was to become, or to seem at least to many minds, in its later, more modern developments, when it came to be entertained *alone* in full "purity" and stringency, and apparent conflict with religion and ethics.[4] On the contrary, it was still combined and interfused with religion and with ethics. In all fields it was blended with the belief in a harmony and beneficence for mankind, of the system of all "natural" processes, proving that it all must have been designed by a wise and benevolent God; and in the "moral science" fields, also with belief in the code of ethical "natural law," and the "free wills" and responsibilities of all men for voluntary obedience to that code, as the only way in which they could achieve the *potential,* "natural," harmoniously and beneficently operating, human societies or social, political, and economic systems.

THE PHILOSOPHY OF THE PHYSIOCRATS

Let us now, finally, consider one particular, emphatic and somewhat special version and development of that entire vision of "the natural order," viz, the system of (combined) social-moral philosophy and economic theory of the group of late eighteenth-century French economists who are called the "Physiocrats." The members of this small group

[3] Ernst Mach, *The Science of Mechanics: A Critical and Historical Account of Its Development,* T. J. McCormack, trans. (Chicago: The Open Court, 1919), pp. 463–464.

[4] On the grimness of the nineteenth century's deterministic idea of the mechanistic universe and its natural laws—and the reactions of romantic thinkers and poets against this, see A. N. Whitehead, *Science and the Modern World* (New York: The Macmillan Company, 1925), chap. 5.

or "sect"—the latter word is appropriate—called themselves simply the "economists"; but the other descriptive and distinctive name for them at once came into and has remained in universal use because their over-all message, strongly stressed in all their writings, was indeed their advocacy and theory of "physiocracy," i.e., "government" of all human societies entirely by or through the system of "natural law"—meaning both (1) the principles of "natural justice" and (2) the "natural laws" of economics, as expounded by them.

They were the first exponents of a comprehensive, systematic, thorough, and consistent philosophy of "economic liberalism"—universal liberty or freedom of individual enterprise, competition, and trade—and the writers who first gave wide currency to the maxim or slogan *laissez faire, laissez passer*—let all men *do* the parts of the world's demanded economic work which their situations, markets, abilities, facilities, and interests make it "natural" for them to do, and let every current of trade and every sequence of economic events or developments take its "natural" course. But in their interpretation of it, this "gospel" did *not* mean that governments would have no work to do, or should be inactive; nor did it mean—above all, not this!—that all established, traditional institutions, practices, etc., should be "let alone" or left unchanged. On the contrary they were reformers, decidedly, with a program for "enlightened" reformation first of their country's (and every nation's) government, and then of the laws and the economy of France (and of every country) by a vigorous, reforming government. Everywhere there must be "enlightened" and vigorous public action to create, develop, and maintain the ideally just legal order, fully formulating and enforcing the true principles of ethical "natural law," right, or justice; and then only, within that legal framework, the "natural laws" of the "automatic" working of the (each) national economy would ensure continuous, full use and the best possible uses of the resources and abilities of all its members, to maximize their mutual services and collective or aggregate economic output—the sum of the realized satisfactions of the needs of all.

The Physiocrats were slightly earlier or older contemporaries of Adam Smith, who knew them and their work and views but did not fully agree with them and was not greatly influenced by them. Nor did their entire, exact, special system of thought or doctrine, as such, ever enjoy a *very* wide vogue, or *greatly* influence or contribute to the subsequent, general development of economic thought. But it is possible and usual to analyze their total system into two quite different parts or components and ascribe to these two "things" widely different amounts of merit, historic influence, and importance in every sense. From the standpoint of modern economics, the core of their system was a real, substantial, by no means flawless but in and for its time brilliant contribution to economic analysis. This has been highly praised and diversely used, improved, and built upon by more modern economists; and among present-day economists, familiar with it as a part of the entire, general history of their science, it is generally regarded as having been in its time a great step forward in the progress of economic thought. I will soon hereafter return to, and briefly explain the nature and value of, this central "scientific" part of the work of the Physiocrats—their economics proper; but first I must further describe and discuss the other part of their total system—the wider context of other ideas within which they themselves developed and presented their economic analysis—their cosmic-and-ethical and normative political and legal philosophy. For although it has long been the usual practice of modern economists and historians of economics to dismiss *this* lightly, as neither really connected with economics proper nor of any serious interest on its own account, I cannot fully concur in either view.

The broad philosophy of the Physiocrats as presented in their writing was fully embraced by few and adversely criticized by many even among their contemporaries. It soon came into very general disrepute, because it made fully explicit, in terms too unreticent, bold, and bald for the taste of an already increasingly cautious, skeptical, almost positivistic time, the metaphysical-and-moral faith which most minds, though in fact still largely retaining its substance, were becoming ashamed to hold so firmly and avow so brashly. But this very fact makes the writings of the Physiocrats highly useful to the student of all liberal-and-economic thought in its general development through and beyond that time, as with due care one can use their fully, clearly expressed, fundamental philosophy as a guide to full understanding of the more or less similar but discreetly guarded, half-latent presuppositions involved in the views and arguments presented in the writings of other, more typical, liberal economists. And I think this philosophy, as presented by the Physiocrats, is relevant for understanding that phase of the general development of economic theory, and is also very interesting in itself.

The essentials of both the philosophy and the economics of the "sect" were worked out and presented best by its leader and sole important original thinker, François Quesnay. He came from rather lowly and obscure, lower-middle-class French provincial origins, and always retained rural, agrarian sympathies, which affected one famous feature of his economics (see below). But he was by profession a physician or medical man, and court physician at Versailles; his knowledge of biology and medicine also probably affected the cast of his social-economic thought which may be described as a study of the conditions of "health" in the social-economic "organism." Not his vocation, however, but his avocation or role of self-made philosopher and economist, absorbed his main energies and led to his main achievements. He was active in this role in the 1750s, 1760s and 1770s—the time when all French intellectuals (*les philosophes*) were most busily analyzing and criticizing the condition of their country and the faults of its *ancien régime,* and contributing to the trend of thought and public opinion that was to produce the great French Revolution. But Quesnay and his disciples, the Physiocrats, were moderate reformers, not revolutionists, and belonged, when the Revolution came, to the moderate faction that lost out or got "swamped" by the radical-democratic tide with which they had no particular sympathy. On the fringe of the "sect," not a full member of it but an independent figure largely in agreement with its general position, stood the eminent economist Turgot, in his own way fully as great a man as Quesnay; and Turgot tried but failed to reform and save the "old regime" by introducing as a minister, too late and against still fatally effective opposition, some of the long-needed, "enlightened" economic and fiscal policies. But we are concerned now with the elements of Quesnay's—the Physiocratic—general philosophy, which are all well presented in his essay on *Droit Naturel*—natural law, right, or justice.[5]

This essay begins with the observation that previous writers on its subject had failed to produce any large or substantial body of generally agreed-on, definite principles, because—in Quesnay's view—they had not adopted or formed the right "method" of inquiry, empirical as well as rational, for use in this field. It is clear as we read the essay that Quesnay himself retained much of the French Cartesian spirit of pure rationalism as to method, with its stress on "clear and distinct ideas" and frequent appeal to "self-evident" axioms; yet his way of thinking, though half-Cartesian, was also half-Lockeian, and he claimed and tried to give his theory of natural justice an empirical as well as a rational foundation. One must, he goes on to say, proceed through observation of the facts about actual human situations and relations; how particular individuals are placed, what services they need from and are in positions to render to each other, and what reciprocal rights and duties they must recognize if all, severally and jointly, are to enjoy the fullest possible prosperity and happiness. And he illustrates his meaning by discussing, on this basis, rights and duties between parents and their children. Young children, as yet unable to provide for their own needs, require various parental services; their parents are the persons generally best situated and able to provide these services; *hence* the children have "natural rights" to the services in question, and the parents have the corresponding "natural duties" to their children. Then years later, as a rule, these relationships become reversed; aged parents have needs which their grown-up children can best meet, and consequently, rights

[5] Quesnay's essay *Droit Naturel* can be found in Auguste Oncken (ed.), *Oeuvres de Quesnay* (Paris: Jules Peelman and Company, 1888), pp. 359–377.

to the services which now are the duties of the latter. In short, Quesnay's moral principles really are those of "utilitarianism," though he still identifies them with or as the rules of ethical "natural law." What "nature" prescribes is always whatever is necessary or required to maximize the happiness—all-around fulfillment of the needs—of all concerned, under the basic conditions that exist and cannot be altered.

A still broader philosophy, however, of the order and laws of nature as a cosmic system, is connected in Quesnay's mind with his approach to the rules of *droit naturel* (natural justice), and expounded later on in the same essay. He speaks of two kinds or groups of "natural laws," physical and moral—*les lois naturelles physiques,* and *les lois naturelles morales.* And in his characterization of the former, what stands out is that religious-optimistic sense of the (relative) harmony and beneficence of physical nature as a system of events or processes, which was described above as ingredient in nearly all eighteenth-century thought, and is here expressed and supported (argued) by Quesnay in a simple, homely, but quite interesting way. I don't know whether Quesnay had ever read or become acquainted with the famous argument on this matter of the great philosopher, Leibniz—the Leibnizian thesis and "proof," which Voltaire had ridiculed in the story of *Candide,* that the actual world (which God has made) is the best of all possible worlds (which He could have made); but I think Quesnay's simple "argument" is identical in substance on the crucial point with that of Leibniz, and can be understood best if I first say a word about the latter.

The key to the Leibnizian argument is the quite orthodox Christian theological and mediaeval Scholastic idea, retained by Leibniz, that although God is "omnipotent," He is above all "rational" in His nature, and is therefore bound or limited by the laws of logic, i.e., He cannot do or make contradictory or inconsistent things; not even God can make 2 plus 2 equal 3 or 5 or anything but 4, or make rain both wet and dry. Now any rational or self-consistent, complex or multiple universe—whole or system of many parts—must be, as Leibniz said, a system of *com-possibilities,* mutually compatible entities, properties, events, and processes. And it is then argued further, that *any such* universe would be certain to contain some "evils" from the human standpoint—things or properties of things or events obnoxious to human desires and sensibilities—as inevitable concomitants of the "good" items or features, inseparable from them—the "price," so to speak, of any creation or existence or occurrence of the latter. And then the concluding Leibnizian thesis was that in the actual universe the "evils," though many and serious, are the fewest and in their sum the smallest possible, relative to the far greater (in aggregate value) flood of "good" things and events, all necessarily and logically entailing the associated "evils" as their minimal "prices."

Quesnay's train of thought, then, is the same but expressed very simply. He flatly asserts that the physical laws of nature are "the laws of the trains of events as favorable as possible to the happiness of all sentient beings"; and provides a homely illustration of his thought. "The rainstorm which inconveniences the traveler, waters the fields"; and the benefits conferred on all life by the storms, which water the fields, far outweigh the injuries without which the benefits could not be had. One may, of course, smile at all of this, if he is so inclined; the thesis, of course, never was or could be really proved, but it also cannot be disproved, and does not seem to me pure nonsense. Anyway, it was a typical eighteenth-century belief, and one integral part of Quesnay's philosophy.

But when Quesnay goes on to speak about the natural moral laws—*les lois naturelles morales*—he uses similar language to cover other, additional, and different ideas and problems. *These* laws are said to be those of the human actions and resulting trains of events in human societies, "as favorable as possible to the happiness" of all members of the latter. But the human actors are said to have "free wills" and rational minds to use in deciding upon their actions; and the concept, *lois naturelles morales,* clearly is meant to cover or include both rules or standards of ideal conduct, which men ought to obey but can disobey, and social-scientific laws of the social processes consequent and contingent upon consistent, actual obedience by all actors concerned, to those standards. Hence there is not here, as in the preceding statements about nature's physical laws, simply the idea of an optimal, inevitable, actual course or pattern of events; but instead there is the idea that all men as free and rational moral agents ought to, and can, always so act that the results of their actions will be or make up a system of social processes "as favorable as possible" to their common welfare.

In fact, a fuller analysis of this part of the essay reveals *three* ideas in Quesnay's theory of the system of *lois naturelles morales:* (1) the rules of *prudent* individual conduct, "rational" for each actor in his actual circumstances, or correct for maximizing the long-run over-all satisfaction of his own desires; (2) the rules of *justice* (*droit naturel*) among men in their mutual relations and dealings, which ought to be enforced where necessary, impartially upon all men alike, by an ideal legal system, leaving open to all only those prudent or rational, self-interested actions which at the same time are just to all affected persons and thus conducive also to maximal social welfare; and (3) the quasi-mechanical laws of the social-economic processes that will go on *if* both the rules of prudence and those of justice are universally obeyed.

There is, I think, no doubt that Quesnay and his disciples assumed the universal, spontaneous tendency of men to be or become, with the growth and spread of knowledge or "enlightenment," adequately prudent or rational in their own interests, in conducting or managing their own private resources, affairs, and lives. But it was to be the business of "enlightened" government to make them all invariably just to one another, or protect the "natural rights" of all, in their mutual dealings, by developing and enforcing a system of positive law, having as its substance or contents the true principles of *droit naturel.* And Quesnay and his disciples advocated as the form of government best fitted for this task, a regime which they oddly called "legal despotism"—the "enlightened despotism" often idealized in the eighteenth century, with stress on the point that it should be "legal," i.e., bound by its constitution always to obey, and enforce upon its subjects only, the principles of valid, ideal law or justice—*droit naturel.* What they actually envisaged was a constitutional monarchy, with an active but law-abiding executive "government" and a representative, deliberative, and consultative national assembly to help this executive government to develop the legal order in accordance with a national consensus as to what its provisions must be. But the third and unique organ in their ideal system, much stressed by them, was to be a supreme tribunal of nine (!) wise old men, selected and trained throughout their lives to be the best judges of all that *droit naturel* commands, forbids, and permits, and having a veto over all decisions of the executive government and assembly, to keep them in line with *droit naturel.* It is impossible not to be struck by the resemblance between this part of the Physiocratic blueprint and the later, familiar, American institution, our Federal Supreme Court with its power of "judicial review." And although I know of no solid evidence of a real historic connection of the two, there is the fact that one prominent Physiocrat, the first du Pont de Nemours (an ancestor of the later American, great industrial-capitalist family of the same name) was a friend and correspondent of our Thomas Jefferson, who indeed came near to being a Physiocrat himself in his economic and related social-moral (though not political) philosophy.

The Physiocrats, then, believed: (1) that the laws of physics make all the processes of nature at large "as favorable as possible to the happiness" of all living things including human beings; (2) that human beings have the ability and duty to discover and obey the "rational," normative rules of a code of ethical "natural law," synonymous with the requirements for universal, maximal prosperity and happiness, and consisting of (*a*) the rules of prudent conduct of their private affairs by individuals and (*b*) the rules of justice in dealings among individuals, to be enforced by a reformed government; and (3) that *when* human societies achieve conformity of their institutions and the conduct of their members to that code, their economic systems will thereafter operate or function as harmonious self-adjusting mechanisms on exactly the lines required to maximize the prosperity and happiness of all concerned. I have still to indicate, however, what they conceived to be the main contents of the rules of justice—*droit naturel*. Although they did not get beyond a few high abstractions or broad generalities, they did regard this code as sanctioning private property in land and movables, general freedom of contract, and freedom of all economic enterprise, competition, and trade from legally or socially supported obstacles designed to benefit favored groups by denying equal opportunities to other groups.

The controlling general idea in this whole matter was that of equal freedom for all individuals, i.e., not unlimited freedom for anyone, but all the freedom for everyone consistent with the same freedom for everyone else. And the reciprocity of rights and duties among all—identity of A's natural rights as against B with B's natural duties to A and vice versa—was a point they always stressed. Also the utilitarian identification of these rights and duties with the conditions of maximal happiness—satisfaction of needs—for all concerned, must be borne in mind. If the Physiocrats had really gone far at all toward carrying out the empirical studies suggested or called for by that identification, they would have been forced to recognize the inadequacy—or real vagueness, indeterminateness—of their simple, general vision of an ideal harmonious society of "free" individuals. They were under the illusion that their simple, abstract, "rational" blueprint fully specified all necessary features of the legal framework within which the (otherwise) "free" economy would automatically function optimally for the economic welfare of the entire population. But I must now briefly describe their different, central, and more solid, real "scientific" achievement—or scheme of real economic analysis—viz., Quesnay's analysis of the social-economic process as a pattern of interrelated flows of inputs of work and resources in economic production, outputs and sales of products, incomes, and outlays or expenditures (for consumption and for new inputs in production) in the continuing operation of the national economy and the connected segments into which this analysis divided it.

THE ECONOMICS OF THE PHYSIOCRATS

The gist of that scheme of analysis was summed up in Quesnay's justly famous "economic table"—*tableau economique*—which his disciples regarded as one of the greatest discoveries or inventions in the history of all science, and which does hold an important place in the history of economic science.[6] As originally published, the table was a

[6] See Quesnay, *Analyse du Tableau Economique,* in *op. cit.,* pp. 305–328. The *Tableau* itself, in one form or version, is presented within this essay or text explaining it (see p. 316).

rather cryptic-looking diagram of zigzag lines connecting different hypothetical numbers and saying in effect this kind of thing: if in one year the nation's producers of wealth invest this total amount of money, and sell the resulting products for this other total amount, and divide and use the proceeds thus and thus, then the following incomes will be realized by these different groups of people; and the year's consumption by the nation or its population can be this much, and the total savings for investment next year, this much, and so on. In other words, the table was an early pioneering step toward the two overlapping and related kinds of investigative work that many economists *now* carry on (of course in far more advanced and sophisticated forms) and call "national income analysis" and "mathematical economics."

Through a long period after its first appearance, Quesnay's economic table was not understood by most other economists. Though it really was or is simple and clear enough, the kind of work represented by it was not familiar or attractive to most economists until a more recent time; and prejudices against it, hindering the intensive, intelligent study of it which would have led to full understanding, were created by the extravagant praises lavished upon it by Quesnay's disciples, and the common dislike of his and their rather high-flown, doctrinaire, and dogmatic general philosophy. But a few able nineteenth-century economists did fully appreciate it; one among these, interestingly, was Karl Marx, who, in spite of the wide and deep philosophical or ideological gulf dividing his mind from Quesnay's, justly esteemed the latter as a great economist and developed avowedly from this table, or with the help of its suggestions, his own similar-and-different analysis of the flows and divisions of inputs and outputs, incomes and spendings, savings and investments in the "capitalist" economy.[7] Still later and, of course, in no connection at all with Marx, the English economist Henry Higgs revived the study of Quesnay's table and properly explained it to the profession.[8] Finally, in recent decades the modern developments of income analysis and all mathematical and statistical economic studies have brought into being a general recognition of Quesnay and his table as having tried long ago to start the science upon this track.[9]

[7] For Marx's praise of Quesnay and his *Tableau,* see K. Marx, *Theories of Surplus Value, Selections* (New York: International Publishers, 1952), pp. 71, 72. And on the relation of Marx's own "tables" of the income-flows, etc., in the "capitalist" economy to Quesnay's *Tableau,* see Appendix A (by Shigeto Tsuru) in P. M. Sweezy's *Theory of Capitalist Development* (New York: Oxford University Press, 1942), pp. 365–371.

[8] See Henry Higgs, *The Physiocrats* (London and New York: The Macmillan Company, 1897), especially chap. 2, pp. 26–48.

[9] For what is perhaps the best brief, modern account and appreciation of Quesnay's contributions to economic analysis and their relations to very modern work, see J. A. Schumpeter's *History of Economic Analysis* (New York: Oxford

The scientific value of Quesnay's table lay entirely in its rudimentary and limited, but clear and significant grasp and display of three simple general truths which every more advanced analysis of the same general kind also grasps and displays and tries to illuminate and specify in much fuller detail. The first general point is that the economic universe, exemplified in every "economy," is or contains a system of interdependent, variable quantities, all so interrelated that when any of them change, all are (in time) bound to change together in more or less determinate relationships. The second point is that there is always in (throughout) a social "economy" or economic "body" a "circular flow" of wealth (income and expenditure), which *may* be thought of—and no doubt *was* thought of by Quesnay with his biological-medical background—as remotely analogous to the circulation of blood in an animal organism; i.e., expenditures by producers upon production become the incomes of consumers which, when spent by them, buy the products and become the producers' revenues, the sources of their new expenditures on new productions, etc. And the third point is that there is within an "economy" some discoverable set of "conditions of a general equilibrium" of all the related, variable quantities and "forces" causing them to change; i.e., some unique set or pattern of relative values of all the variables as compared among themselves, such that, when or if they all come into this set of relations, no economic actor will any longer have any motives or incentives to further change his behavior-pattern so as to bring about further changes of any of those quantities; all economic actors will then already have attained their relative optimal or best attainable (incomes—or gains—or satisfactions—maximizing) economic situations or positions. Quesnay made a beginning at the work of analyzing the consolidated income and expense accounts (not known or available to him empirically but conceived and illustrated with hypothetical figures) of an economic society or all its members together; and the interrelations of the economic quantities and their changes, which would appear in such a system of accounts; and the "circular flow" of income (or expenditure) out from and back to producing enterprises; and the conditions or requisites of a healthy general equilibrium of the economic system.

Quesnay's *particular* analysis, however, *also* embodied, in no real connection with any of those true and useful ideas but as a fundamental

---

University Press, 1954), pp. 223–243; pages 239–243 deal specifically with the *Tableau*. And note especially Schumpeter's reference—p. 241, last lines, and n. 11—to the most important modern (now still recent) work having a clear and avowed "relation" or indebtedness to Quesnay's *Tableau*, viz., Wassily Leontief's system of "input-output" analysis, developed in the latter's *The Structure of American Economy* (Cambridge, Mass.: Harvard University Press, 1941; rev. ed., New York: Oxford University Press, 1951).

doctrine in his system, a peculiar, mistaken notion which expressed his "agrarian bias." This doctrine ran to the effect that a nation's agricultural land and labor—its farms and working farmers—are the sole producers of its annual *produit net,* i.e., the (small) part of its annual gross output of wealth which is surplus over and above the (main) part which must be used up in consumption by the people and replacement, maintenance, or upkeep of the previously existing stock of capital. Quesnay conceived the French national economic society of his time as made up of three parts, classes, or groups of people: (1) the proprietary class—aristocratic owners of the nation's soil, in their great estates; (2) the producing class—the peasant cultivators of the soil; and (3) the "unproductive" or "sterile" class—the entire urban population of artisans, merchants, etc. In applying those seemingly derogatory adjectives to the last group, he did not, he explained, mean to stigmatize it as useless or parasitic. Its members lived, he admitted, by doing the useful and necessary work of transporting, processing, and marketing the land's raw produce, and this work (he further agreed) considerably added to or increased the total value of all that produce; but this additional value, he maintained, was only equal to that of the group's necessary or proper consumption plus the upkeep of its capital—there could be no *net* product or surplus above mere "support" of the group and its activities, attributable to the latter.

Only the country's farms and farmers could produce, besides "support" of the farm families and upkeep of their working capital, a *produit net,* which was all included in the rent paid to or received by the proprietary (landlord) class, and *should* be used by the latter to (1) support the state or pay the only tax (single tax, *impôt unique*) which the state ought to levy, and (2) accumulate all new capital and make all the long-term investments needed to improve the land and its productivity. In more detail, Quesnay analyzed the annual flow of newly produced wealth out from and (in part only) back to the producing farms, in the following way. He supposed the farmers to retain on the farms, in kind, one fraction of their output (of its total value) for direct consumption by their families and replenishment of their working capital (seed, fertilizer, etc.) for use in producing the *next* year's crops. Another fraction would go into their exchange with the townspeople, i.e., be sold to the latter for money with which the farmers, in return, would buy urban products of the same total value, also for use on the farms, partly in consumption there and partly to maintain farm capital (tools, etc.). The rest would go as rent to the landlords, who would use a part of this rent in their consumption of farm and urban products, and have the remaining, final part—the *produit net*—as their, and the country's, only "net" income (net or surplus after provision for all private consumption and capital-replacement needs); and the only possible real or ultimate source of (1) all public revenues and (2) all net growth over time of the country's stock of wealth or capital.

It seems best to postpone for a moment the hard question, why and how—on what (to them) apparent grounds or through what mistakes—Quesnay and his followers arrived at that strange doctrine—their belief in the sole responsibility of agriculture for the entire "net" national income in that sense. We must consider first the doctrine's *meaning* for them as brought out by the reform proposals—"radical" in one but not in another sense—which they based upon it, and their way of arguing *from* the doctrine *for* these reforms. Their *single tax* proposal was indeed "radical" in the France of that time; it called for a great change—a complete reversal—of the very bad fiscal practices and situation which existed and were helping to bring on the country's imminent, great revolution. The regime's extravagance and heritage of debt from the expensive wars of Louis XIV were supported by a heavy profusion and confusion of taxes, which were—or at least were meant and thought to be—paid (either directly or through purchases of taxed and therefore high-priced goods and services) by virtually all of the people *except* the members of the privileged, landowning aristocracy—Quesnay's "proprietary class"—whose privileges included *exemption from* all taxes. And the queer little doctor at the royal court and his few disciples advocated nothing less than abolition of all existing taxes and replacement of them with a wholly new and shocking, substantial, single direct tax on the land-rent incomes accruing to the noble lords from their great estates!

Yet the advocates of this reform did not themselves regard or represent it as radical or revolutionary in its real (according to them) prospective consequences; nor did they appeal to any radical or revolutionary sentiments in arguing for it. Unlike their much later and wholly independent American successor in this matter, Henry George, the founder of the more modern and well-known but different land-rent–single-tax movement, the Physiocrats did *not* regard legal private ownership of land and appropriation of land-rent income as unjust, i.e., involving "exploitation" of the "landless" majority of the people by the "landlords"; nor did they preach governmental confiscation for public uses, of all land-rent income, and abolition of all other taxes, *as* a righteous measure against a wicked, rich minority, for the (just) benefit of the suffering majority, and to abolish poverty. The Physiocrats did not associate justice with any redistribution of wealth from the few rich to the many poor; they did not dream of abolishing all poverty (raising the incomes of the masses far above a "subsistence" level), or have any animus against the nobles who, in their great estates, owned the soil of France. They argued that the real effects of their tax reform plan—their single tax—would not cost these nobles anything but would instead actually benefit them, in the long run, along with the entire nation. According to their analysis of the sources and required uses of all incomes in the national economy, the nobles had in their "net" incomes from their lands or estates—"net" over upkeep of their estates and households at the *status quo ante* levels—the *only* "net" incomes in the country, wherewith any public taxes (of whatever kinds) *could* be paid in the last analysis. And, the Physiocrats argued, the nobles *already were really* paying *all* taxes—and a larger sum than necessary, in consequence of the wasteful and expensive nature of the existing complex array of taxes and the whole fiscal system—via the tax-raised prices of all or most of the goods and services they had to buy.

The peasants, artisans, and merchants generally or as aggregate groups needed—so this argument asserted—their entire incomes merely to cover their expenses, live, and maintain their capitals with no increase over time. Hence whatever taxes these groups had to pay in the first instance, they would necessarily pass on or shift as burdens to their customers by adding them as costs to the prices charged. And among the customers, all those likewise getting only incomes barely sufficient for their needs would again shift the burdens in the same manner to *their* customers, etc. Thus all tax burdens of all kinds must, through repeated shifting, finally come to rest upon the only incomes able to afford them, i.e., the net incomes of the owners of the agricultural estates. A single direct tax then, upon the landowners in the first instance, would merely recognize the inevitable facts, immensely simplify the fiscal system, and save the estate owners the unnecessary additional amounts they had been paying in reality, in consequence of (1) the excessive expenses and losses incurred by the state in trying to collect all the taxes levied in the existing system, and (2) the tendencies of all tax shifters to increase their prices by *more than* the amounts of their tax payments, to recoup also all their cost increases indirectly due to the tax system, and profits on their increased investment outlays. Moreover, when freed of the depressing effects of the existing wrongly placed tax burdens and the struggles to shift or recoup them, etc., the entire national economy would work more freely and efficiently, the *produit net* and net incomes of the estate owners would increase, and they could pay a tax sufficient for all needs of the state and still be much better off.

In that argument, then, the advocates of the single tax made clear the meaning they attached to their underlying doctrine, that only the agricultural branch of the national economy could produce or engender a net income over and above the part of gross income absorbed in paying for the costs of production of the products involved—including the producers' costs of living and the upkeep of their capitals; and that all of this net income, arising only in agriculture, went into the rent-incomes of the owners of the farm lands, who therefore *must* or alone *could* financially support the government. And on the ground of the same doctrine the group arrived at a second proposal or piece of advice to the landowning nobility: that this wealthy group or class should recognize and accept also, besides its unique ability and consequent obligation to finance the government, its similar unique ability and consequent obligation to finance the economy's needs for capital growth or expansion and development, i.e., to save and invest, in permanent or durable improvements of and on the estates of its members, the amounts needed to enable the peasant farmers to make the land as productive as possible. The rest of the population was held to be as unable to do net saving and investing, i.e., contribute to an increase as distinct from mere replacement or maintenance of existing capital, as to contribute (really) to the public revenues; all but the landowners, sole recipients of the *produit net,* could produce and earn or acquire only enough to "keep going" or continue their parts of the *status quo.* But we have still to ask, what features of the scene they surveyed—and/or of their outlook upon it—led Quesnay and his followers to this odd fundamental doctrine; what portions of truth and of error did it contain, and how may we account for the mistake it involved?

As the doctrine was asserted with very little explanation or defense, every student's answers to those questions must be largely conjectural, and I offer my own conjectures for whatever they may be worth. Had the doctrine been presented as only a guess at the facts—the relevant, nonexistent, statistical aggregates—in or for the France of that time, then I think we might say that it probably was not *very* far from correct; what alone was *wholly* wrong and unfounded was the doctrine's claim to be or state a universal "necessary" truth. Surely it was true about *most* of the ordinary or humble French people of that time—and has been true of most similar people, small peasant farmers and town workingmen, in most societies and times all through human history—that as a rule they could barely earn enough to make ends meet, and could not have been final, uncompensated payers of much in the way of taxes or any other "extra" charges, or been able to do much saving for investment, without declining into deep and wretched poverty. What, of course, does seem odd, however, is the apparent failure of the Physiocrats to recognize that there were even then, and within their country, quite a few quite prosperous urban capitalists, i.e., merchants, bankers, and the like, normally receiving substantial "net" incomes in the Physiocratic sense and clearly able, while living well, both to pay substantial taxes and to save, invest, and expand their enterprises. Yet it may have been true for this class as a whole, in the whole economy, that the profits of some were about offset by the losses of others; that even the *bourgeoisie* or business class as a whole (counting in all the petty shopkeepers, etc.) generally had a group income hardly more than sufficient to continue its part of the *status quo*. The class of owners of the great agricultural estates *did* then receive most of the economy's "surplus" output or income above that needed for current use to preserve the *status quo;* and in that economy at that time, probably, any very generous financing of the state *and* of national economic growth, development, or progress *would have* required large direct or indirect drafts upon the land-rent income of the aristocracy for these purposes. The traditions and attitudes of that aristocracy indeed were such that it was not a psychologically, sociologically, or politically realistic or feasible project to try to convert it into a thrifty, enterprising, progressive, and enlightened-patriotic "capitalist" class, willing and eager to use its great income for those purposes. But the blind optimism of the Physiocrats in *this* matter did not signify that anything was wrong with their *economic* analysis as such.

Where they went wrong in their economics was in supposing (1) that the apparent connection of most—all, they thought—of the economy's "net" income, with agriculture, signified or resulted from a uniquely high or great productivity inherent in the latter as a special branch of all economic (productive) activity; and (2) that this imagined, superior productivity, i.e., sole "net" productivity of agriculture was a universal, permanent, "natural" fact or "law" which would always, in all societies, make farm-land rent the all-important, only possible source of all public revenues and of all new capital for economic progress. In all still mainly agricultural economic societies, having three-fourths or more of their total populations and resources employed within their agricultural sectors, *and* having land-tenure systems concentrating ownership of their farm lands in small numbers of very large estates owned by the few richest families, the latter of course get the main large incomes and together get most of the national "net" incomes. But all this reflects local and temporary combinations of facts: (1) of limited economic development as yet achieved, and (2) of existing property arrangements and social structure—not a law of nature whereby only the agricultural part of all economic activity can ever, anywhere produce a surplus above its own current upkeep requirements and the bare-living costs of the working people employed in it. In fact in every such situation it is the still *low* productivity of agriculture which makes necessary its absorption of most of the society's manpower and resources, and restricts the growth of industry and commerce and of *their* productivity. At the same time it is true—the reverse side of the truth just stated—that within an economy the ability of an agricultural sector, smaller than the whole economy, to produce a surplus over what must be used up within that sector, is necessary for the existence of the rest of the economy; and that growth of this surplus productivity of agriculture is necessary for growth of the rest of the economy. But the other sectors of an economy also can develop productivities beyond their own requirements and contribute to each other's progress and to that of agriculture. The Physiocratic view of this whole matter was strangely one-sided, containing much insight but also a definite error.

That error may have been rooted, possibly, in the notion included in their general philosophy of the Providential beneficence of nature. This connection is suggested by a statement of Adam Smith's, reflecting a very partial agreement on his part with them on this point, that "in agriculture nature labors along with man." [10] So long as most nonagricultural, industrial production—manufacturing—was human handwork unaided by power-driven machinery, it was perhaps plausible to think of the fertility of soil and the natural processes favorable to life that go on in it, and the fecundity of plant and animal life as representing the sole contributions made by nature assisting and supplementing human efforts in economic production—uniquely in agriculture; and to think of the "surplus" output of agriculture, appearing in its value-form chiefly as farm-land rent, as explained thereby.

[10] Adam Smith, *Wealth of Nations,* E. Cannan (ed.), vol. I, p. 343.

CHAPTER 2

Adam Smith's Forerunners in Moral Philosophy

INTRODUCTORY

The present chapter is the first of a series of three chapters, together presenting what is perhaps—as compared with the "scales" of other parts of this book—an exceptionally full or extended discussion of Adam Smith's thought and writings *and* all that may help us to understand them: the main, immediately antecedent sources, and his own development, of his views in philosophy and ethics, *and* his great work on the *Wealth of Nations*. Extended discussion of all this is called for, I think, by the unity-in-variety of Adam Smith's intellectual output as a whole, its complexity and richness, the merit or interest of each part in itself, and its relevance to other parts of the whole; for full understanding of his entire outlook, the works and ideas of those predecessors who most influenced his philosophy and ethics are also to be considered in this chapter.

Smith's contributions to the special science of economics may not deserve in all respects quite as high or preeminent a place in the history of that science as it long was customary to assign to them. Some of the best modern "authorities" on this matter—eminent economists and historians of economics, writing in our time—have gone rather far—indeed in the extreme cases too far in my own opinion—in the direction of "deflating" his old reputation in that field. To this question I shall return, in the chapter on Smith's economics. It still is true, and generally recognized, that Adam Smith's famous work on the *Wealth of Nations* is one of the world's, or all history's, truly great books, and a rich mine of wisdom on a very wide range of subjects—economic, psychological, and sociological, and historical, moral, and political. Accordingly, the last or "culminating" one in my series of three chapters in the titles of which Smith's name appears, will outline and discuss the *Wealth of Nations* and (or including) the theory of economics elaborated in it. But I think it desirable to lead up to that with the present and the immediately following chapter.

In the world after Smith's time, the wide public which (very properly) so highly esteemed his work on the *Wealth of Nations* very quickly, completely forgot, or became and thereafter remained oblivious to, his very different earlier work, *A Theory of the Moral Sentiments* —which indeed was not nearly so great or important but which, I think, had and still has much interest and value. This almost universal neglect of Smith's other main work has entailed the loss or lack by his successors and the general public, of the benefit of an essential part of his total system of thought, a part which is not only interesting and valuable in itself, but is also in need of study by all who wish fully to understand the point of view—the economic liberalism—of the *Wealth of Nations*. Hence I shall take up, in the second in this series of three chapters, Adam Smith's *Theory of the Moral Sentiments* or theory of the "natural" basis of ethics and of free societies; and even the discussion of that will be preceded (within the same chapter) by a brief look at still another of Smith's writings—the first of his three very early, "juvenile" (as he himself came to call them) "philosophical essays." This essay deals with the history of astronomy and will give us, I think, a glimpse of Smith's philosophy of science and of "nature," which can be illuminating in the study of his two great books. But first of all, in the present chapter, I intend to survey the previous development, down to the entry upon the stage of Adam Smith himself, of the "line" of thought in psychology-and-ethics which found its culminating development in his own *Theory of the Moral Sentiments.*

THE "SENTIMENTAL" MORALISTS

The "line" or "school" of eighteenth-century British "moralists" to which Adam Smith belonged was known to contemporaries and to subsequent historians of ethical thought as "the sentimental school." But that appellation was never meant as a jeering epithet; the word *sentimental* in this application was used not in the opprobrious sense, but solely or simply to indicate the fact that these "moralists"—i.e., "scientific" students of the origins, development, and substance of (sound) morality as a "natural" product of human experience and reflection—conceived all morality as made up not of purely rational principles but rather of "sentiments," i.e., joint products of human emotions *and* reason. In other words, the members of this school turned away from the age-old, main-traditional, and still in their times widely prevalent, pure rationalism in ethical theory—the effort to deduce all valid moral laws or principles from a few self-evident axioms; they sought instead to develop their own peculiar kind of "empiricism" (?) in this field, i.e., an effort to find in the study of human emotional life and experience the basic data—value-feelings, if I may use this more modern expression—from which rational, ethical reflection could arrive at the "natural" moral laws, as inductive generalizations from experience.

As it was conceived and carried out by these writers this was to a great extent a new, original approach to ethics and, I think, a very interesting and significant, largely or at least partly sound one, involving and leading to important insights. But the problems involved are extremely difficult, and the total structures of thought produced by these thinkers, though full of good insights, were also full of illusions and/or at best doubtful speculations, and left much to be desired. In the subsequent development of modern thought, the eighteenth-century climate of opinion within which the distinctive outlook of this "sentimental school" could arise and flourish, has been succeeded by a growing number of changing, separating, and diverging, rival climates of opinion in different quarters; and *none* of them has fostered or allowed any widespread, continuing, advancing work on the same lines —or lines nearly the same, with the needed corrections or improvements —which might have continued and improved and added to the insights achieved by that sentimental school. It is difficult for most modern minds to understand and appraise the writings of these moralists altogether fairly; but I think there is still much of great interest and value which can be learned from them.

SHAFTESBURY

The founder of this "school," or earliest figure in this line of thinkers, was the Lord Shaftesbury who flourished in the late seventeenth and early eighteenth centuries—the third Earl of Shaftesbury, by name Anthony Ashley Cooper. This noble gentleman was a somewhat dilettantish dabbler in various sciences and fine arts and in all philosophy and humanistic studies; but he was also an able and important thinker who exerted much influence on many of the later, leading figures of the eighteenth-century Enlightenment. In particular he *may* have influenced Rousseau a good deal and in any case certainly anticipated or preceded Rousseau in asserting the native "natural goodness" of mankind, and attributing this more to "good, natural" emotional dispositions than to "reason," and regarding mankind as all too easily corrupted by misuse of the latter on the higher levels of its cultivation and achievements. In defending his optimistic view of the innate and potential qualities—high moral capacities—of human nature, he fought a two-front war against the two great seventeenth-century English bodies of deeply pessimistic doctrine on this question—Puritanism and "Hobbism." The gloomy Calvinists, and the gloomy materialist Hobbes, alike aroused his ire as false "defamers of our human nature." [1]

In the sphere of religious thought, Lord Shaftesbury was a leading Deist, one of the first and principal members of the small group of Deists, in the true, strict sense of the word, who rejected Christianity in all its official or churchly forms entirely, and all its ideas of a strictly supernatural realm, miracles and mysteries, the special Christian Revelation of religious and moral truths beyond those "evident" to the "natural reason" of mankind, and original sin and supernatural salvation; but believed, on grounds held to be within the reach of everyday experience and reason, in a wise and benevolent God or Supreme Being, the original "Designer" of all nature and (or including) human nature. But the Deism of Shaftesbury, while it divided him sharply from the Puritans and all such groups of fervent, orthodox Christians, did not seriously divide him from Christians of the "liberal, enlightened" type which became the most common in the eighteenth century. As we shall see in a moment, it did not at all concern or trouble his mid-eighteenth-century Presbyterian disciple Francis Hutcheson, who taught Adam Smith and was the link between Lord Shaftesbury and the latter. The important elements of Shaftesbury's thought, expressed in his discursive essays on *Men, Manners, Opinions, and Times,* came on the whole rather more from secular or nonreligious and philosophical sources than from any strictly religious or theological sources.

One chief source was the philosophy of Locke, who was to Shaftesbury an elder, personal friend and the tutor of his childhood. And it was in part—though another partial source will be mentioned in a moment—from Locke's idea of "the internal sense, or power of reflection" in the human mind, that Shaftesbury developed his own, not entirely similar, idea of "the moral sense"; the central faculty within every person, through or with which he can continually "observe," and instinctively or intuitively judge and regulate, his "passions" or "affections" and therefore his conduct. As is well known, Locke had thought of "the internal sense" rather as the mind's power of introspective "observation" of its own current *thoughts or ideas* and the *logical relations* among them; and hence as also the source, or architect, of all purely rational or logical (i.e., not also, in the ordinary sense, empirical) science, e.g., pure mathematics, and perhaps also ethics conceived likewise as a purely general or formal science, arranging and reciprocally adjust-

[1] To check this and everything said in this chapter about Shaftesbury's views, see his *Characteristics of Men, Manners, Opinions and Times,* 6th ed., 1737, vol. II, *Inquiry Concerning Virtue and Merit.*

ing and relating all ethical ideas and propositions into a self-consistent, logical system.[2] But Shaftesbury changed Locke's "internal" into his own "moral" sense, so to speak, by or through a shift of emphasis which made this faculty as he conceived it the "observer" (and judge) mainly not of the intellectual but rather of the emotional or affective part or side of one's current stream of consciousness, i.e., the current states or characters, changes, and relations of all the included feelings or emotions, desires and aversions, etc. In other words, the emphasis was shifted to this other aspect of man's (every person's) continuous, involuntary self-awareness and self-criticism; to one's awareness at each moment, not of what he is thinking but of the feelings he is "having"—and the feeling, present within this awareness, of approval or disapproval of those (other) feelings which are its objects, and of one's self for "having" them. Of course, this notion also is a special or modified description of what in Christian (?) thought is called one's "conscience"; but our attention here must be upon the special, exact nuances of Shaftesbury's particular conception of a sixth or internal "sense" or receptor of primary, immediate, direct experiences or perceptions—perceptions, in this case, of one's current emotional states, and their ethically "beautiful" or "ugly" characters.

Those last words, however, indicate a feature of the conception and of Shaftesbury's thought which must be traced not to Locke but to other sources. This writer and, after him, Hutcheson and Adam Smith (when thinking and writing about matters in this universe of discourse) had marked tendencies to associate ethics with aesthetics, or (often) consider these two subjects together, and as somewhat similar and related. In Shaftesbury's case his own artistic interests no doubt contributed to this; but in further explanation of the genesis and meaning of his whole conception of "the moral sense," so central in his psychology-and-ethics, I must refer to—besides Locke's "internal sense"—another, different ancestor of that conception. This was the notion which had been developed by Henry More, one of the Cambridge Platonists and a friend of Sir Isaac Newton, of what he (More) called "the boniform faculty"—aesthetic-ethical "sense" of "good form"(!). The reader must forgive or indulge, at this point, the necessary brief digression on or about the Cambridge Platonists and Henry More as one of them.

The Cambridge Platonists were a famous group of late-seventeenth-century English scholars, thinkers, writers, and preachers—Anglican

[2] For Locke's idea of "reflection" or the "internal sense," see his *Essay Concerning Human Understanding,* any edition, book 2, chap. 1, sec. 4; and for his discussion of the nature of mathematics, and the possibility of making ethics a demonstrative science *like* mathematics, see the same work, book 4, chap. 3, sec. 18–20; book 4, chap. 4, sec. 6–9.

divines and dons at Cambridge University—who were first brought up as Puritans but then revolted intellectually from or against strict Calvinism, and became exponents of an interesting type of liberal, "broad" or "latitudinarian" Christian religious, philosophical, and ethical thought.[3] They indeed owed much, intellectually, to Platonism and to other, modern (post-Renaissance) philosophies; and contributed much, I believe, to an important and pervasive feature of the later, common eighteenth-century outlook, i.e., to its cheerful faith in the strong attractions of all beauty and goodness for the rational-and-emotional "nature" of mankind. It is likely, I think, that a widespread revulsion and overreaction against Calvinism's exaggeration of the general Christian doctrine of "original sin" into its own extreme doctrine of the "total depravity" of mankind apart from God's supernatural grace, did much to produce the swing to that opposite extreme view which became a foundation stone of eighteenth-century liberalism, i.e., a belief in the predominant and perhaps potentially perfect "goodness" of the "natural" dispositions of mankind. At all events the Cambridge Platonists in *their* reaction away from Puritanical distrust of the senses, all sense-pleasures, and all human emotions, *and* distrust of any free use of "reason" in dealing with religious and moral problems, went all the way to the other pole. They held that in their essentials truly Christian faith and morality are identical with the purely "natural" religion and morality which all human beings tend to be led to embrace spontaneously, simply by the joint activity of their powers of reason and all their finest "natural" human feelings and desires or aspirations.

On the epistemological question of *how* men are led to the true religious and moral insights as a part of their knowledge, the "Platonists" as a group were in formal disagreement with Locke; believing in the doctrine, which he attacked, of "innate ideas" or intuitive-rational, "self-evident," a priori knowledge of "first principles," and rejecting his doctrine that the primary sources of all true knowledge lie exclusively in "experience," i.e., in sense-perceptions. But there were bridges from both sides over the apparent gap between the two positions; Locke's own belief in "the internal sense, or power of reflection," did much of the work, in his system, which the belief in "innate ideas" was made to do in other philosophies, including that of these "Platonists"; and the latter could stress, along with or instead of intuitive-rational insights, intuitive feelings that could be included, with

[3] For a brief discussion of this group's philosophy, see James Seth, *English Philosophers and Schools of Philosophy* (London: J. M. Dent & Sons Ltd., 1912). For a full discussion, see John Tulloch, *Rational Theology and Christian Philosophy in England in the Seventeenth Century,* 2 vols. (Edinburgh and London: 1872); vol. 2 is devoted to the Cambridge Platonists. As to the influence of the group on Shaftesbury, see Sir Leslie Stephen, *History of English Thought in the Eighteenth Century,* 3d ed. (London: Smith, Elder, and Co., 1902), vol. 2, p. 23.

a little stretching of this, in the Lockeian concept of "experience." And among the "Platonists," Henry More in particular appears to have gone far in the latter direction, transferring emphasis from the role of intuitive "reason" to that of intuitive aesthetic and ethical "feelings" considered as ingredients in "experience." More held such feelings to be the sources of man's potential, "natural" knowledge of *and* delight in the realm of all real, objective values and the possibilities of ideal harmony as the goals of all the fine arts and—the supreme one among them —the ethical art of living the good life. And he conceived man's, or human nature's, quasi-instinctive discernment and love of (both actual and potential) harmonious forms or patterns, as a special human "faculty" which he called "the boniform faculty."

Then also, More's theory of the work or functioning of this "faculty" included a further point, which had significance for Shaftesbury also, and reflected More's friendship and intellectual intercourse with Newton, the great physicist. To Newton—himself a religious man and philosopher as well as a scientist—and to nearly all thinkers in that epoch, the Newtonian system of the physical universe seemed a revelation of a beautiful and marvelous, self-maintaining, harmonious order of physical laws and processes, confirming faith in the wise and admirable artistry of God, the "Designer" of all nature. And to More, who shared that appreciation and interpretation of Newtonian physics, his own "discovery" of man's "boniform faculty" seemed part of an extension of the Newtonian vision, so to speak, into the sphere of human life and affairs. God had designed human nature also and endowed all men with a specific, innate ability and desire to envision, love, seek, and achieve harmony in their lives and societies. All this, then, entered also into Shaftesbury's doctrine of man's "moral sense"—a concept evolved, in the way just described, both from Locke's "internal sense" *and* from Henry More's "boniform faculty."

Shaftesbury's complete view, however, of psychology-and-ethics included more than just his theory of the character and function of the "moral sense." In addition to describing this "faculty" as everyman's internal observer and judge of his own "passions" or "affections," he went on to describe the latter—all human emotions—as of three kinds. In one category, he placed all "self-regarding" or self-centered feelings, desires, and ambitions, summed up as or in "self-love" and "self-interest," and regarded (by Shaftesbury) as ethically *neutral,* i.e., neither virtuous nor vicious, but—if held within the proper bounds or limits *and* unmixed with any hostilities toward others—entirely, ethically acceptable; harmless (even useful to society) and blameless. But then he set over against this, and stressed especially, his second category of "natural affections"—unselfish, altruistic, or benevolent feelings and desires to benefit, serve, or aid one's fellow men; and applied the adjective "natural" *especially* to these benevolent emotions, to emphasize his view that they are fully *as* "innate" in everyman's "nature" *as* the "self-affections" involved in "self-interest," and are independent of and coordinate with them, and "naturally" quite equal to them in number or abundance, strength or intensity, etc. And finally, he recognized as all too frequently present in men as they were and had been in all existing and historic societies, emotions of a third, vicious kind—malevolent or malignant feelings of pleasure in hurting or harming others; but he called these "un-natural," insisting that they represented not anything inherent in human nature but only some externally caused, partial, and remediable distortions or perversions of that, due to the influences upon men of bad environments or social conditions, historically created and continued through ages of prevailing ignorance and errors, superstitions, etc., which had produced and supported institutions, customs, and conditions unsuited to human nature and divergent from those required for its healthy development.

That last contention of Shaftesbury's, obviously, was an early assertion of two important, related, optimistic assumptions of the liberal Enlightenment: its complete denial of "original sin," or confident belief in the original and recoverable "natural goodness" of mankind; and its "environmentalism," explaining all unethical impulses and behavior as results of bad social conditions, and supporting a full faith in the power of "enlightened" social reform to cure all evils. But in order not to misinterpret all this we must bear in mind along with it Shaftesbury's—and the entire Enlightenment's—view assigning a large, *legitimate* place and role in all human life and affairs to everyman's human-natural "self-interest." In the total historic change from the traditional Christian outlook to that of the Enlightenment, the quiet abandonment of the radical and unworldly Christian ideal of absolute unselfishness or self-forgetting, all-absorbing "love" for all fellow men was fully as important as, and profoundly modified the meaning of, the explicit change from belief in the "natural sinfulness" of men to belief in their "natural goodness." For as it involved the former, the latter change was only in a small part a (slight) alteration of the old view *of the facts;* in a greater part it was rather a change of standards and revaluation of almost agreed-on facts, leading to acceptance of much of the "selfish" motivation and behavior which had been regarded as "sinful" as ethically quite all right and entirely consistent with "natural goodness."

Thus the "optimism" in the new outlook was less extreme than we might suppose, being combined with and modified by a good deal of "realism." And the extent of all that was held to be due only to past, ignorant mistakes in society-building and the malign influence (on individual conduct) of bad social environments, and to be curable through social reform, was limited by the acceptance of a large role of "self-interest" in affecting the behavior of all individuals severally, as universally and permanently inevitable *and* not deplorable at all, inherent in human nature, and capable of playing a useful, necessary, and acceptable part in the building and the working of adequately good societies. It is only, then, in the beliefs that in everyman's nature as it can develop under the right, appropriate social conditions there will be (1) entire absence of malevolent feelings or impulses toward his fellows, and (2) adequate presence of benevolent feelings or impulses serving to supplement and to counterbalance, moderate, or limit his "self-interest" to the extent required to make him a good member of a good society—it is only in these two beliefs that we may see the measure of the certainly questionable, and probably excessive, idealistic optimism in the outlook of Lord Shaftesbury.

In Shaftesbury's theory as a whole, then, the "moral sense" had these functions in the on-going life-experience of each individual: (1) in existing, imperfect societies and men, to cause or enable each man to notice as they arise within him, and dislike, and if possible suppress, his malevolent feelings toward others, i.e., not allow them to affect his conduct; and (2) in all possible societies and men, to cause or enable each man to "sense" and maintain the appropriate "balance" or equilibrium between and among his "self-affections" and his "benevolent, natural affections"—or all his self-favoring and all his others-favoring desires or motives. The central doctrine was that the special feelings *about* one's (other) feelings, involuntarily experienced through the "moral sense," are feelings of the repulsive "ugliness" of all malevolent feelings, and the attractive "beauty" of all benevolent feelings, and the neutral but innocent, acceptable qualities of all self-centered feelings and desires *when* these are untainted with hostilities to others *and* sufficiently moderate and so directed as to be consistent or compatible with adequate good will toward others. Man's ethical task, then, is to allow only those of his feelings (and resulting impulses) which please or do not displease his "moral sense," to affect his actions; and to keep in the over-all "balance" of relative intensities most satisfactory to his "moral sense," all the feelings-and-impulses it does not repudiate, as joint determinants of his behavior-pattern. Among his final conclusions Shaftesbury stressed above all this idea of the proper "balance of the passions"; and declared that if all men would sufficiently attend to and maintain *this* "balance" in their souls and lives, then "the balance of trade in commerce, and the balance of power in politics, of which we hear so much, would take care of themselves."(!)

MANDEVILLE

We have next to notice the contrasting ideas of a writer who was not in the sentimental school of Shaftesbury's followers but who, as a critic of Shaftesbury's thought, *may* have influenced the views of his (the latter's) later followers and especially those of Adam Smith, on some points, considerably; and who, in any case, presented views some attention to which will help us, later, in the study of theirs. This was Bernard Mandeville, author of the famous or notorious pamphlet in doggerel verse entitled *A Fable of the Bees, or Private Vices, Public Benefits;* which embodied a satirical attack upon Lord Shaftesbury and his views, and a reassertion of the "cynical" views that he had opposed, viz., Hobbesian (?) or Puritanical (?) and mercantilistic views about human nature and the state and the economy.

At the basis of the "argument" of this "fable," in support of the paradox expressed in its subtitle—that "private vices" are indispensable sources of "public benefits" in all human societies—lay the extreme *ascetic* definitions of "virtue" and "vice" that were presupposed. According to this underlying view, all self-indulgences in satisfactions of one's bodily appetites and worldly ambitions, beyond acquisition and use of what is necessary for just staying alive, are by definition "vices"; and the only virtuous or nonvicious motivation and conduct is that of the ascetic saint who embraces poverty and the lowest or no social status, shuns all worldly enterprise and competition, and seeks only the salvation of his soul. Obviously then, if the conduct of all men conformed to this ideal there would be no adequate markets for the economic output of a growing, fully employed, busy population, and no growth of wealth, refinement, and civilization.

Societies can have these "public benefits" only if and because the statesmen who rule them cleverly bring into and maintain in existence laws and customs which stimulate in all men in the right degrees, and regulate, and direct into socially useful channels, the wants and ambitions which are—from the moral standpoint assumed—"private vices." Attractive rewards and deterrent penalties must be so contrived, adjusted, and applied as to induce the members of all classes to behave, steadily, in the moderately "vicious" ways that are socially expedient. The working people, of the lower classes, must be made and kept ambitious for better incomes but obedient, industrious, sober, etc., mainly by threats and fears of punishment for nonconformity with these standards—discharge from their jobs and unemployment if they do not satisfy their employers, and fines, jail sentences, or worse if they break public laws or ordinances. But gentlemen, of the upper classes, generally can be induced to serve the public well through "flattery," with all the praises and rewards that can elicit, feed, and utilize their main "vice," their "vanity" or thirst for the self-esteem that rises with and depends upon the public esteem one knows he is held in.

And of that last point, Lord Shaftesbury was held up as a shining example; *he* had been so well flattered, by general praise as a public benefactor, that he had come to regard himself as a very good man; and then, generously generalizing from himself to all other men, he had attributed to human nature the fine balance of (not too) self-indulgent and (amply) benevolent dispositions, and the fine moral sense directing an unfailing maintenance of this balance, which he found in himself but did not realize that society and the state had created there through the art of "flattery."

Now it should be clear that Mandeville's entire position, although presented thus with ridicule of Shaftesbury's and as in direct, full opposition to the latter, really differed *not* completely but only on some points from the latter. What gave to Mandeville's thesis the form of the piquant paradox, that "private vices" can and must be made the sources of essential "public benefits," was his simultaneous acceptance of two mutually inconsistent ethical standards: the ascetic standard involved in stigmatizing all expansive economic wants and ambitions—however harmless and useful to society—as "vices"; and the contrary, worldly, "social utility" standard involved in approving as desirable and indeed essential, the "public benefits" shown to be attainable by societies only as results of sufficient prevalence and intensity in their members, and appropriate control, channeling, and utilization by the societies, of precisely those so-called "vicious," human-natural motive forces.[4] But the ascetic standard had no place or recognition whatever in the thought of Shaftesbury or in that of his successors—of all or any members of the sentimental school. Theirs was throughout a self-consistent, "worldly" ethic, viewing with no disapproval but entire approval the private motives comprised in "economic self-interest" and called "vices" by Mandeville, *as well as* the "public benefits" which they *like Mandeville* saw as connected with and dependent on those motives. *Thus far* then, their position differed from his *not* as to facts but only in adding to the same conception of these facts a partly different because self-consistent set of value-judgments.

In another part, however, of the common total field of inquiry, there was disagreement as to facts (about human nature); i.e., Shaftesbury asserted, and Mandeville denied, the existence in men generally of "natural benevolent" dispositions and an innate "moral sense" which, along with and as concomitants and modifiers of their "selfish, worldly"

[4] To check my interpretation, and for its own interest, the reader should get from a good library and read—it is not very long—*The Fable of the Bees*, 3d ed. (London: 1724).

wants and ambitions, could further help a great deal to make their "natural" spontaneous conduct generally beneficial to their fellows and society. And this difference of views entailed another one. Mandeville, like Hobbes before him, assumed that the "natural" man is *completely* selfish, i.e., that his selfish, worldly wants and ambitions are his *only* motives. Therefore, he concluded logically, again as Hobbes had done, that all the work of creating and maintaining social cooperation, or a harmony of men's private with their common or public interests, or a general "harnessing" of the former into service to the latter, is work that must be done by the state and the arts of statesmen, through an "artificial" system of social pressures upon and bribes held out to the basically and "naturally" un- and antisocial, or in that sense, immoral individuals. In considerable contrast with *that* view, Shaftesbury and his successors held—but developed, among them, different theories of this matter—that there is inherent in human nature a "natural" source of a socially useful and adequate "natural" morality which, as a set of spontaneous attitudes in the people, can both support the state in performing its proper, important, but limited role or functions, and, apart from its work, engender directly among the people much spontaneous cooperation and reciprocal adjustment. Yet we shall have new occasions, in discussing the new schemes of thought of Shaftesbury's successors, and especially in discussing Adam Smith's scheme, to compare them not only with Shaftesbury's but also with Mandeville's theory of the psychological and social factors and processes involved in harmonizing the motives and actions of individuals with society's proper and inevitable requirements.

HUTCHESON

Francis Hutcheson, who in the generation between Shaftesbury and Adam Smith was the former's most important avowed disciple (though more original than that word suggests) and the latter's admired and beloved teacher, was an outstanding, mid-eighteenth-century leader in the lively and important Scottish part of the Enlightenment, and a very attractive, engaging figure. Originally an Ulsterman or Scot from Northern Ireland, he was of course a Presbyterian, and, in his way, a devout Christian, but as to the character of his faith and theology, comparable only with the most "liberal" or "modernist"—nonorthodox, perhaps Unitarian—Christians of today. Apparently, he saw no significant difference between his own religious outlook and Shaftesbury's Deism. Not a clergyman but only a layman in his church, and not a professional (Christian) theologian, he was a "polymath" or wide-ranging, learned, and brilliant scholar-classicist, humanist, and moral philosopher or student of all the social-and-moral "sciences" of his time—and no doubt had also, as men of his kind then generally had, a respectable though nonprofessional knowledge and understanding of physical science.

Though he came from Northern Ireland, he spent most of his mature life and had his main career in Scotland, at the University of Glasgow. The details of his career there need not concern us. He soon became and long remained an influential member of the faculty, and played a part in helping to bring about much of the progress that went on in that period in renovating, modernizing, and improving the University's intellectual life and activities. Throughout, his position was the professorship which Adam Smith was to hold after him—of "natural religion, ethics, and civil policy." Smith as an undergraduate was a pupil in his class, became a personal friend, and later always referred to him as "the admirable and never to be forgotten Hutcheson." In his major, large, comprehensive treatise on "the principles of moral philosophy" (virtually all social-and-moral "science"), and no doubt in the course of lectures Smith attended, Hutcheson dealt with, among other subjects, extensive parts of economics—theory of value and prices, etc. But I shall describe and discuss here only, as alone commandingly important for our purpose, the general argument of his small book with a very significant, long title: *An Inquiry into the Original of Our Ideas of Beauty and Virtue*.[5]

That title reflects both Hutcheson's adherence to, and a problem presented to his mind by, Locke's epistemology. According to Locke's theory, all knowledge is made up of ideas developed from and supported by sense-perceptions; but the latter themselves are only mental images or "copies" of their objects and sources or "originals" in the external world. Now it may be easy to locate or specify the "originals," in that sense, of all those ordinary sense-perceptions which are the data of—as we might say now—all the purely descriptive or not (also) evaluative and normative or prescriptive "sciences." But what objective items or configurations, existing in "the external world," i.e., not only in the observers' minds, can be the "originals," in the same sense, of those special perceptions, impressions, feelings, or experiences which, in turn, engender and support "our ideas of beauty and virtue," i.e., the (objectively valid) ideas of aesthetic and ethical values required in the "sciences" of aesthetics and ethics? This little book of Hutcheson's, then, was his effort to answer that question or solve that problem and thus to establish the true foundations of aesthetics and ethics.

His solution involved the contention that man's outfit of "senses" includes, in addition to the familiar five (sight, hearing, etc.), both an aesthetic sense or sense of beauty and a (further and different) moral sense or sense of virtue. But his careful definitions of these concepts

[5] Francis Hutcheson, *An Inquiry into the Original of Our Ideas of Beauty and Virtue* (London: 1725).

made them mean, in his usage, nothing mysterious or objectionable, and perhaps "nothing much." He began by insisting on a sharp distinction between every "sense" as a *mental* "capacity," and the bodily sense organ which serves it merely as a tool or roadway in from the external world. Each "sense," by his definition, is "a capacity of the mind to experience sensations" of a certain kind or character, when affected *through* the sense organ(s) and nervous system by the appropriate external stimuli. Given this separation of senses from their organs, there can be more senses than organs; the extra senses can be served by the same bodily organs which serve the others. Man's aesthetic sense, then, is his mind's capacity to experience—to perceive and enjoy—the beauties of all those objects or configurations produced by nature or by human arts, which are beautiful, i.e., which do engender this kind of experience. Thus the question, what are the objective "originals" of human subjective experiences and ideas of beauty becomes this question: what characteristics in object-sources of human sense-perceptions are the necessary and sufficient conditions of their being perceived and enjoyed as beautiful? And Hutcheson's answer—the core of his simple, classical, aesthetic theory—was his phrase, "uniformity amidst variety." Whatever has both a pleasing orderly shape or form—symmetry—and enough variety or richness of different aspects to be not oversimple and dull or monotonous but interesting, appeals to the human aesthetic sense as being beautiful. He then developed this theme somewhat, with illustrations in such fields as sculpture, architecture, and music.

The part of this little book concerned with aesthetics—a prelude only to the part on ethics—concludes with a foray out from and beyond aesthetics, into the psychology and philosophy of (natural) science as a human activity, and the philosophy of nature as the field explored by science, and "natural theology." It is both a bridge to his theory of ethics and a forerunner of Adam Smith's similar discussion of these topics in his essay on the history of astronomy, which we shall take up later.

Here Hutcheson argues as follows. It is man's aesthetic sense and love of aesthetic experience—delight in discovering and exploring "uniformity amidst variety"—together with the fact that all nature is full of precisely that combination, which leads and has led to the development of all natural science, i.e., "pure" science, pursued for its own sake—for the sake of the intellectual (aesthetic) pleasure of discovering new uniformities or laws in the endless variety of natural phenomena. And this in turn leads to the endless output of useful by-products—the achievements of applied science or technology—which generally are not foreseen or aimed at by the pure scientists who make the basic discoveries which lead to them, but which never could be achieved, through purely practical effort and intelligence, by the inventors who do aim at them, without the aid of those prior discoveries. Here, then—the inevitable, final conclusion for this religious and typical eighteenth-century mind!—is another proof of the wisdom and benevolence of God, the Author of all nature and of human nature; He has made nature a system pervaded by "uniformity amidst variety" *and* endowed human nature with an aesthetic sense for which exploration of that is delightful; and has thus ensured the production and enjoyment by mankind of both progressive pure science and its not humanly foreseen or intended but useful and welcome by-products in the other, dependent sphere of progressive technology.

Now the theory of ethics worked out in the second half of this same little book is linked by analogies with *both* the author's (basic, general) theory of aesthetics *and* that theory of the aesthetic aim and the unforeseeable, utilitarian results of science. Let me first bring out the analogy with the latter. As man the scientist, lured on and guided in his studies by his aesthetic sense, contributes to *knowledge of* the order and harmony in the variety of nature, *and thereby also contributes unknowingly to later useful inventions* and thus to the welfare and happiness of mankind; so also, man the (good) citizen, lured on and guided in all good conduct by his moral sense, contributes to *creation and maintenance of* (moral) order and harmony in the variety of his own life and other lives and that of his entire society, *and thereby also contributes, in the main unknowingly, to all the useful results* of such order and harmony for the welfare and happiness of all concerned.

In other words, the character of Hutcheson's theory of ethics—and as we shall see in the next chapter, also that of Adam Smith's different theory—involved a peculiar blend of one aspect (only) of utilitarianism with a different thesis, antithetical to and replacing the other aspect of that—an intuitionism. In one sense these authors accepted as the ultimate criterion of goodness or ethical correctness in human conduct, the utilitarian (social utility) criterion—the view that good conduct is or means conduct as conducive as possible, through all its consequences, to the happiness of all (in any way affected) members of the society one lives in, and of all mankind. But they insisted that this cannot be men's daily working criterion, guiding them in all their moral decisions, because men cannot have or attain enough knowledge and foresight of all the consequences of all their possible actions, to be able to choose, deliberately, the actions best calculated to promote universal happiness. And at this point both authors fell back, in different ways, on faith in the "guiding hand" of Providence which, they held, had endowed or equipped human nature with certain *other* powers and propensities besides practical intelligence. These powers were "designed" to lead men to quasi-instinctive moral decisions and actions, only *felt* by the actors to be "good" *intrinsically*, i.e., in a nonutilitarian sense but *in fact* generally having, in the main beyond the horizons of their limited foresight, the right, favorable consequences for social order and harmony, and thus for universal human welfare and happiness.

Hutcheson did not develop this part of the theory nearly *so* fully or clearly as did Adam Smith; he did not begin to equal Smith's later achievement by working out a comparably complete, definite, detailed, and systematic theory of the psychological and social factors and processes which together make men's moral attitudes and actions and their consequences generally, though *not* intentionally, conducive to a universal common good, the conditions of which men cannot know or understand completely enough to be able to fulfill them as well, deliberately. Hutcheson's standpoint in fact was probably *less* far removed than was Adam Smith's from full-fledged utilitarianism. Since the non-utilitarian, intuitionist side of Hutcheson's thought was so much less explicit, it can too easily remain unnoticed and is not very easily grasped and explained. Thus in what is to be said next I may *seem* to be describing a simple, fully utilitarian theory; but if that impression is conveyed it will be corrected later.

The reader will recall that for Hutcheson the first task of the ethical inquiry is to find "the original of the idea of virtue." As we saw, "the original of the idea of beauty" is every structure of order and harmony "amidst variety," which is present and perceived as such in any part of nature or work of art; it is this which always gives to any observer with a normal aesthetic sense the experience or feeling that he can express only by exclaiming, "That is beautiful!" The parallel question then is, what is it that, when present and perceived in any "piece" of human conduct and its motivation, is experienced or felt through the observer's or self-observer's moral sense as being morally admirable, good, or virtuous? Hutcheson's surprising, simple answer to this question is the single word, *benevolence*. With high enthusiasm on this point he follows Shaftesbury, and even seems to go beyond or outdo Shaftesbury in stressing and exalting this human propensity. On the question of fact, he contends that men in general are *not* dominated entirely or mainly by "self-interest," but have it also in their natures to be spontaneously, abundantly, *and purely* benevolent toward their fellows, endeavoring only to aid, serve, or benefit the latter, with no thought or hope of any resulting benefit or pleasure for themselves. And on the question of ethical value, he contends that *only* motivation and conduct of *this* kind strikes the moral sense as admirable and worthy to be called good or virtuous.

An early commentator may have been right in suggesting that Hutcheson had been led to his extra emphasis on those contentions by or in his indignant reaction against Mandeville's, and the rather widespread eighteenth-century, revival or continuation of the Hobbesian theory of man's (every individual's) total selfishness, and the fondness for ascribing all, even the most laudable, actions to open or secret selfish motives. But I think the deeper root, in any case, of Hutcheson's stand upon these matters was his own "sweetly" Christian character. He described the ideal or summit of virtue as the constant attitude of "universal, calm benevolence" toward all mankind; and this I think was his way of describing "Christian love" for all mankind, in the different language of his "age of reason." As he saw the matter, all men know in themselves at least sporadic, fluctuating feelings and impulses of pure benevolence toward other particular persons they are "fond of"; but it is the moral function of man's "reason" to make those feelings constant, stable, and consistent, and to extend or generalize them into a universal and impartial principle or purpose of pure, complete good will toward all; and it is the function of his moral sense to make him feel the goodness or attraction of that potential state of his mind and feelings, character, and behavior, and thus to inspire his efforts to attain and maintain it. Yet our author insisted that in taking this line he was not implying that the good man is benevolent for the sake of the "selfish" pleasure of self-approval. He does or may have that pleasure as a by-product, but only on the condition of not seeking it; any conscious aim at self-gratification even in this sense would spoil the benevolence, the virtue, and the pleasure of the moral sense. Truly good or virtuous (praiseworthy) conduct must be *purely* benevolent, self-forgetting, or outgoing, and attentive only to the needs, desires, and welfare of others.

Yet in spite of this stress on "benevolence" as the only virtuous (admirable) motive in human conduct, Hutcheson after all followed Shaftesbury *also* in conceding a large *legitimate* place and role to "self-interest." Pursuit and enjoyment of satisfactions of one's own ordinary wants and ambitions, if kept consistent and "in balance" with entire good will toward all other persons, can be a large legitimate part of life, not indeed deserving any moral credit but also not deserving any censure. In particular, Hutcheson explicitly rejected the ascetic principle assumed by Mandeville and others, and insisted that pursuit and enjoyment of wealth, comfort, and even many (all innocent) luxuries could be entirely innocent, in no way improper, if always combined and harmonized with adequate, sincere, and active benevolence. Thus, although his special stress on benevolence tended to obscure this fact, he really agreed with Shaftesbury in conceiving an impartial "balance" of all the "self-affections" *and* "benevolent affections" as the (total complex) source or motivation of most fully morally acceptable conduct. Behind his special stress on benevolence, as alone virtuous, i.e., delightful to the moral sense and needing special emphasis and cultivation to achieve and maintain it in sufficient vigor and purity, there may have been a remnant of the Christian sense of human "sinfulness" or proneness to err (only) in the other direction of excessive "selfishness"; a belief that men could maintain the "balance" only through single-minded effort to be as benevolent as possible.

In any event, however, this entire ethical theory as *thus far* described here may well seem not to differ at all from the theory that is known as utilitarianism. Surely, "universal, calm benevolence" can be translated, with no change of meaning, as the aim or purpose always to act in the ways that will have on the whole the best results for the happiness of mankind; and legitimate, intelligent self-interest must mean the aim, allowable when not in conflict with that higher aim, to act in one's private affairs in the ways that will have the best results for one's own happiness. The function of Hutcheson's moral sense seems to be only to approve, inspire or incite, and fortify the former, virtuous aim, and to accept the latter when consistent with it. Happiness of one's self and for others—universal happiness—seems to be the goal.

From all I have said thus far it would seem that the moral sense figures only as a regulator of the two aims or motives; it does not, as a substitute for or a supplement to practical intelligence, supply intuitive knowledge to guide choice of "good" actions, in the place of insufficient ordinary knowledge as to which actions will have the best results for happiness. Moreover, it is true, as I have said, that Hutcheson did have *much* in common with utilitarianism. Not only did he in a way make universal happiness the moral goal, but he was one of the earliest promulgators of the not too fortunate—the logically ambiguous and in other ways unsatisfactory—utilitarian formula, "the greatest happiness of the greatest number" of men, to more fully describe that goal. Yet he did also insist upon the valid point, which I think is fatal to the *utility* of utilitarianism as a guide for daily, personal conduct, viz., the point that it is far beyond human power to attain and apply all the predictive knowledge, of all the consequences of all possible actions, required for choice of those best calculated to maximize happiness in general. And I think the apparent discrepancy means not that he was inconsistent but that his theory involved another idea which must now be explained.

Let us go back to the starting point—the analogy between the experiences and functions of the moral sense and the aesthetic sense. In the mental activities or functionings leading respectively to creation of beautiful works of arts, to new discoveries in pure science, and to all good human conduct, the most important part of the "knowledge" employed is not of the nature of applied scientific or technical knowledge of the effects and efficacies of means to the ends being sought. The creative arts do indeed have their exacting techniques, and science has methods it must use correctly, and good conduct likewise depends partly on all that is possible in the way of intelligent, informed choice of means to its ends. But the even more vital factor in all these cases is, rather, intuitive knowledge—the "sense" or feeling—of the harmonies to be created or embodied in the works of art, or looked for in nature, or created and/or sustained (by good conduct) in one's own and other men's lives and circumstances. Assuming that the meaning of this statement in the first two applications is clear, let me further explain the last, or ethical, application of it.

In a sense the goal sought by the moral agent or good-man-acting is something like the all-around and continuing "greatest happiness"—balanced, optimal, or fullest possible satisfaction of all the human-natural needs—of himself *and* others—of *all* the persons upon or for whose experiences in that respect his conduct may have important consequences. But as a process, his groping pursuit of the goal is generally (necessarily) far from being a purely rational maximizing of the summed results-for-happiness, of his actions, involving choice of his actions simply in the light of his (never adequate) predictive knowledge and "measurements" or estimates of the trains or patterns and sums of the results of alternative possible actions. Something of that kind may be in some degree possible and requisite, but as a rule one's main reliance must be upon intuitive knowledge—sense or feeling—of the kind or kinds of harmonious, over-all patterns for one's life and other lives and their environments which, if achieved or realized and continued therein, would be or "feel" most conducive on the whole to continuing, all-around fulfillment of all the human needs of all concerned. Hence it is less accurate or realistic to describe the proper, conscious, ethical aim as an aim at "maximizing happiness," than to describe it as an aim toward realizing intuitive ethical visions of internally and mutually harmonious lives—with "maximal happiness" for all resulting more as a by-product of those harmonies than as the goal initially, precisely conceived and deliberately sought. The art of proper conduct of human life is less a technical art or applied science of most efficient choice and use of means and steps to attain exactly specified ends, than a fine or creative art of realizing modes or styles of living so ordered as to be in "felt" harmony with the constellations of "felt" human needs concerned.

This view is my own, but it was, I think, also involved in or required as a part of Hutcheson's theory of ethics, though not so distinctly expressed by him. Now let me further apply and develop this view in the spheres of the legitimate self-interest and the virtuous benevolence contemplated in Hutcheson's theory. Even in the sphere of good management of one's own private economic affairs and resources, where in a sense the aim is to maximize the over-all and over-the-long-run satisfaction of one's present and future economic wants, the kind of "intuition" that I have been speaking of, of the appropriate "pattern" to be maintained, has its part to play, as an important supplement to all the possible and needed—but necessarily incomplete and insufficient—precise calculations.

Keeping good accounts of one's income, expenditures, and savings, budgeting, economizing, etc., are important; but the task of "estimating" one's current and future wants, and the satisfactions prospectively attainable through alternative uses of resources, cannot be entirely a matter of precise, detailed, predictive knowledge and comparative measurements. In a substantial part one has to rely on his vague intuitive sense or feeling of the kind of over-all pattern or "balance" that it probably is wise on the whole to maintain. And in the sphere of "benevolent" concern for the welfare of others, it is still more largely true as a rule that one cannot sufficiently know, in detail, all their current and prospective needs and wants, and all the likely direct and indirect effects of one's own alternative possible actions upon their satisfactions and frustrations, and thus be able to make fully informed and logical choices of the actions likely to result in the largest contributions to their happiness. In wise "benevolence," practical intelligence and all the available, relevant, definite knowledge of course must be used as far as they will go; but the still more vital factor is intuitive, sensitive, or sympathetic response to the feelings manifested by the other persons as to what elements they most want and lack in the over-all patterns of their environments and lives; and intuitive decision making as to which if any of those elements one can most properly, acceptably, and effectively help them to achieve, and how one's help can best be rendered.

Then as to the main part of what Hutcheson meant by "*universal* benevolence"—the proper attitude and behavior of each individual, not toward the other "near" persons within his range of more or less intimate contacts, knowledge, and responsibilities, but toward all the distant, unknown persons in the total mass of all mankind—I am sure that he meant only the kind of general good will signifying chiefly the desire that all men should have the essential forms and degrees of freedom, opportunity, and security required to enable them to achieve for themselves—with the help, when needed, of their own "near" associates—proper satisfactions of their human needs. And I'm sure it is in line with the whole tenor of his thought to say that the main result in overt (public or citizens') behavior is joint development and support, by common consent, of the class of social, political, and legal systems and public policies required to ensure the proper liberties, opportunities, etc., to all men alike. Then, within such institutional frameworks—"natural" products of the native moral decency of mankind—and the moral "climate" of general and reciprocal good will among all, the legitimate "self-interest" of each individual would play the principal remaining role in prompting and directing most of his ordinary, everyday behavior. The "benevolence" of each individual, however, toward his "near" associates would so limit and modify his "self-interest" as to make its results (or the joint results) in his conduct never injurious but instead generally beneficial to them also; and his "universal benevolence" or general good will toward all the rest of mankind, would further restrain him from excessive partiality, not only to himself, but even to those "near" associates, as against all or any other men beyond his group.

And finally, I think it is not "reading back" too much of Adam Smith's (more fully explicit) vision into his teacher's, to attribute to Hutcheson—who made contributions of his own to "liberal" economic theory—something of the special vision of the way in which, together with the moral and institutional controls already referred to here, a competitive economic society's "market mechanisms" can make the "self-interests" of its members unconscious but effective servants of the economic welfare of the entire society.

In sum, then, Hutcheson's theory of the factors in human nature, experience, reflection, and motivation, operating to make men's actions "good," i.e., conducive to their common, general welfare and happiness, was a complex theory which, although it assigned fairly important roles to "universal benevolence" and to "reason" and thus to deliberate and as far as possible informed and rational efforts by all good men severally, to act in line with the requirements of "the greatest happiness" of all men collectively; yet also assigned an even more important role, in helping to bring about the same end-result, to the intuitive, ethical, judgmental feelings of a human-natural "moral sense" which enables men to apprehend (sense or feel) and create or realize the "natural" moral order in their lives and societies, as their "aesthetic sense" enables them to create and appreciate aesthetically well-ordered works of fine art, and in pure science to grasp the pattern of the order in all nature.

CHAPTER 3

Adam Smith's Philosophy of Science and Theory of Social Psychology and Ethics

SMITH'S BIOGRAPHY

Adam Smith was a gentle, amiable, learned, meditative, shrewd, and wise philosopher and scholar who rose quietly from rather simple and humble origins to his great achievements and well-earned fame. He was born and grew to young manhood in the small Scottish village of Kirkaldy, near Glasgow; the only son of a soon-widowed mother of small means, he lived with her until her death, and never married. After being graduated from Glasgow University, where his forerunner, Hutcheson, was one of his teachers, he spent six years in independent study in the library at Oxford University. He reported in letters to his friends that the University was intellectually dead; and although there was little to be learned from his teachers and fellow students, he laid there the foundations of his own wide and deep learning or scholarship "on his own." [1] Intellectual life in England as a whole was rather sluggish in the eighteenth century; although the Enlightenment was largely a continuing growth from and beyond the very great activity and achievements of seventeenth-century English thought, it was going forward mainly in France (Paris) and Scotland (Edinburgh and Glasgow) and various other European centers, much more than in England.

Returning in 1746 to Scotland from Oxford, Smith a bit later spent some time—from 1748 to 1750—in Edinburgh, giving lectures there on literature (*belles lettres*) and logic, rhetoric, and literary criticism. In this field he shared the tastes which prevailed in his century—agreeing, for example, with Voltaire's low opinion of Shakespeare and preference for

[1] My authority for this and all of the biographical information on Adam Smith herein presented is John Rae, *The Life of Adam Smith* (London: Macmillan & Co. Ltd., 1895).

the "classical" dramatic works of Racine and others. Probably it was at this time also that he wrote the "philosophical essays," of which I will speak further, though these were never published until after his death when his executors found them among his papers.

In 1751 Smith entered into his professorship at Glasgow, serving at first, for one year, as Professor of Logic, and thereafter in the chair of Moral Philosophy which he held until 1764. Undoubtedly both of his two great books were largely outgrowths of his courses of lectures to his Glasgow students, but while his *Theory of the Moral Sentiments* was published in 1759, in the midst of his period as professor there, it was not until 1776—long after the end of that period—that he finished and published his greater work, the *Wealth of Nations*. Among his friends in the Glasgow college community, during his time there, were James Watt, "mathematical instrument maker" for the university and "inventor of the steam engine," and Hutton, the "founder" of the modern science of geology. He also made some friends among the businessmen of Glasgow and perhaps acquired from them some of his extensive, realistic knowledge of business.

Resigning his professorship in 1764, Smith spent the next three years and a bit more as tutor of the young Duke of Bucchleuch, travelling with him on the Continent; during a part of the time they spent in Paris, Smith met Quesnay and several of the Physiocrats, as well as other French intellectuals. Years later he returned to his home in Kirkcaldy, where he did the main writing of the *Wealth of Nations;* and after completing that, he held for a time the public office of Commissioner of the Customs for Scotland.

Smith's range of active intellectual interests and studies was always very—by present-day standards, quite incredibly—wide, embracing philosophy, extending in some degree into the physical and natural sciences, and ranging and probing *most* widely and deeply in the broad area of the social-and-moral studies—general and social psychology and ethics, jurisprudence, economics, and much of what now is called sociology, much of history, and most of the public policy problems confronting national states and governments.

SMITH'S PHILOSOPHY OF SCIENCE AND OF "NATURE"

Our survey of Smith's principal writings and ideas can best begin with the first in his group of three "philosophical essays," which apparently were written at a time near the outset of his adult intellectual life and career.[2] The titles of these three essays are, respectively: (1) *The*

[2] See Adam Smith, *Works,* vol. V, *Essays on Philosophical Subjects* (London: 1822); or any of the numerous separate editions of Adam Smith's *Philosophical Essays.*

Principles Which Lead and Direct Philosophical Inquiries, Illustrated by the History of Astronomy; (2) *The Ancient and the Modern Logic and Metaphysics;* (3) *The Ancient Physics.* All three are very interesting, but it will be necessary and sufficient to confine our attention here to the history of astronomy. As its full title indicates, this essay—about a hundred pages in length—presents a philosophy of the nature and development of science in general *and* illustrates this from the history of astronomy.

The first few pages present a theory of the aesthetic character and attraction and the psychological (emotional) motivation of all scientific intellectual work. Specifically, Smith's theory of this matter speaks of a sequence of three different emotions—"surprise, wonder, and admiration"—which succeed each other in that order in the mind of the observer and student of initially unfamiliar and unexpected natural phenomena, as he advances from ignorance to understanding of the relations which connect them with previously known and familiar parts of the system of all natural phenomena.

In our common experience of the long familiar, ever-recurring events in nature, we learn to expect them to go on recurring in their uniform, familiar, temporal order, and in fact come to think of them as so linked together by causal connections that "of course" they "must" recur in that order. But any "new," i.e., never previously observed, event, appearing unexpectedly in a vacant spot in the familiar sequence, is observed for the first time with a feeling of "surprise." And this surprise at once leads to or arouses "wonder," i.e., curiosity and speculation—an eager effort of the imagination to explain or account for the surprising event. Now here is the crux of Smith's theory of how science develops: this effort, he says, takes the form of imagining a set of possible "connecting links," i.e., still other, never yet observed, intervening events or trains of them *such that, if they* can be verified as actually occurring in the intervals just before and after the event to be explained, and "connecting" it with the last preceding and first succeeding parts of the long familiar sequence, *then the entire sequence including the entire newly discovered part within it will be felt to be understood as coherent* and "natural."

Note that this theory says (1) that all scientific hypotheses originate as works or products of the creative human imagination; (2) that they are about—are imaginative or conceptual visions of—"connecting links" which make events that otherwise would seem detached or isolated seem to be included in, and connected with, the rest of the coherent, patterned process of nature; and (3) that to gain acceptance, such hypotheses *not only* must be verified or be successful in that sense *but also* must be subjectively satisfying to the human mind. When they have been formed, developed (had their implications worked out or made explicit), and successfully verified, satisfactory hypotheses of this kind end the first feelings of "surprise" and the subsequent "wonderings" which led to them, and restore and enhance the feeling of understanding *and* "admiration" of the order of nature, by showing that and how that order includes the newly discovered events and relations as a part coherent with the parts previously known and familiar.

A good many other points are made in this essay and I will in a moment continue this account of it; but I pause to note how the essay's opening and main thesis, already described here, illuminates the nature of Smith's two later great works in social science. He conceived all natural science as working to form, develop, and verify theories of "connecting links," joining events that seem isolated to nonscientific observation together into a coherent, ordered system of all events, all mutually connected; and his own later works endeavored to do the same thing in social science—to form, elaborate, and confirm theories of the "connecting links" among the seemingly separate mental and emotional lives and behavior-patterns of the different individual members of a human society, which in fact "link" them all together as connected parts of coherent, orderly, or systematic social processes.

As we shall see later, his *Theory of the Moral Sentiments* endeavors to show that *one set* of "connecting links" among the men in a society, i.e., their mutual "sympathies" and desires for each other's "sympathies," interconnect and thus control the evaluations in their minds, and the make-ups of their individual systems of "moral sentiments," which control their conduct, in such a way that they tend to evolve a moral consensus and a legal order expressing and supported by it, which more or less impartially defines and protects a consistent system of rights and liberties for all and reciprocal duties among all. And then as a later achievement his theory of economic life, in the *Wealth of Nations,* endeavors to show that, *within* the moral climate and legal framework evolved in the manner explained in the earlier work, *a different, additional set* of "connecting links" among the wealth-seeking behavior-patterns of the individuals, i.e., those involved in the competitive market process, so interconnect and control those behavior-patterns that, although they result from and serve the acquisitive "self-interests" of the individuals, they fit together and make up a social-economic process of unconscious cooperation which tends to maximize the aggregate wealth and economic welfare of the entire society or population. Here I am, of course, only pointing ahead to these Smithian theories of the moral and the economic "natural order" in human societies of free individuals; but I wanted to indicate, at this point, how they carry out in their fields the conception of all science as a search for "connecting links" among events, which was presented in Smith's essay on the history of astronomy. And now let me return to that essay and the further points made in it.

There we next get a theory—incidentally suggestive of something like an "economic interpretation" of intellectual history—of the *different kinds* of "connecting links" among the events of nature, which peoples in past times or in different stages of the advance from savagery to civilization have been prone to imagine and believe in. In early, primitive, poor, ignorant, and wretched societies, Smith says, the naturally prevailing pessimism and abject fears of the mysterious menacing forces of nature disposed the people to imagine and believe in a multitude of capricious, interfering gods or demons. When angered by events, including human actions, displeasing to them, these gods or demons reacted by producing such terrible events as eclipses, lightning bolts, etc., and thus functioned as the "connecting links" between the initial provoking and those subsequent events. But in later, more advanced and prosperous, comfortable, secure and confident, and enlightened societies, says Smith, a more cheerful, calm, and rational outlook became prevalent, and led men to form the conception of all nature as a single, coherent, reliable, and generally or mainly beneficent system, which must have been designed and made originally by a single, wise, and benevolent God, who, after setting up the world-machine and setting it in motion, never interfered with it. "Thus," he says, "science gave birth to the first theism," i.e., philosophical monotheism in contrast with primitive, superstitious polytheism. And thereafter, the development of science was a progressive growth of knowledge and understanding of more and more of the internal "connecting links"—of a natural, not supernatural kind—among the more obvious parts of nature as a system, machine, or mechanism.

This entire passage has, I think, two rather remarkable features for an essay written in the eighteenth century. One is the suggestion, by this young philosopher and historian of science who was not yet an economist at all, of something like the idea of "economic determinism" in intellectual history—or at least an idea of the controlling influence of social conditions upon what might be called intellectual fashions, in each part of history—and the resulting idea of "historical relativity" of received "truth" in each epoch to the transient social and psychological conditions disposing men to think in that way. Smith does not say that the later-achieved view of nature as a single, coherent, mechanical system was or is, in any absolute sense, superior to or truer than the primitive belief in a world of disparate events "connected" only by the capricious wills of interfering spirits; he says only that each outlook was the "natural" result of the social and psychological situation which produced it—prevailing misery, pessimism, fear, etc., in the primitive case, and prosperity, comfort, optimism, etc., in the later, civilized communities which first developed the "scientific" point of view.

The other remarkable feature of the passage is *the way* in which the deistic belief in a wise and benevolent "Author of Nature" is brought in—not as a certain truth or a premise held to underlie the conception of nature as a well-ordered system, but only as a psychologically "natural" inference from, or hypothesis to account for, the over-all character of the system of nature as described by scientific theories and observations—and a "natural" product, along with science, of the optimistic temper of a prosperous and comfortable society. We shall see, moreover, that all Smith's writings generally bear out the impression we get here, of the author as a nondogmatic, humble, skeptical, or cautious thinker, aware of the impossibility of human attainment of final absolute truth, and the socially and culturally conditioned character and uncertain validity of his own and all men's ultimate or fundamental beliefs. He did, I think, "believe in" both the science and the Deism of his epoch, but with a quality or degree of "belief" that was less than "absolute."

But now, going on with his account of the nature and history or development of science, we come at last to the point where he takes up the special history of astronomy and treats that as illustrating some further important points about all science. The next general point he makes is that as a science advances, and multiplies its observations of facts or accumulates a great mass of empirical knowledge, the system of theory or set of hypotheses and deductions from them which it has been developing and using, i.e., its theoretical account of the system of relations or connections among all the observed events, becomes increasingly complex, and *may* in time become *too* complex and cumbersome, hardly manageable or usable any longer, and intellectually, economically, and aesthetically unsatisfactory. When such a point is reached, a "revolutionary" reconstruction and simplification of the science's whole system or structure of theory is needed—the discovery or invention of some new, more simple and general, fundamental hypothesis leading logically to a new way of relating and thus explaining all the old and many new observations much more simply. And this was what Copernicus supplied for astronomy.

The pre-Copernican, Ptolemaic system of theory in astronomy, as developed to fit and "explain" a long-growing number of observations of the relative motions of the heavenly bodies, had become excessively complex and cumbersome. The hypothesis of a stationary, central earth with the moon, planets, sun, and stars at various distances revolving around it at differing speeds, etc., had been and remained consistent or reconcilable with all observations. But as the observations multiplied and the conceived system of the orbits and motions of the other bodies relative to each other and the earth had to be extended and amended to agree with the new as well as the old observations, this theoretic system, necessitated by the geocentric hypothesis, became too complicated to be satisfactory to the keenest minds. And then Copernicus showed that, by assuming the sun to be in the center of the solar system, with the earth and other planets revolving around it, it was possible to construct a very much simpler body of theory which would equally well fit and account for all the known facts; and the acceptance of this new idea produced a great advance in the science of astronomy. Here again it seems to me, though of course I can speak only as an ignorant layman in this field, that as an eighteenth-century production this, Adam Smith's appraisal of the significance and merit of the Copernican discovery, must be regarded as remarkably "modern." It very clearly presented not the naïve view that in an absolute sense Copernicus was "right" and the older theory was "wrong," but instead the very modern —relativistic?—view that as *both* theories fitted the facts, the superior merit of the Copernican theory lay simply in its greater simplicity.

Apparently in Smith's mind the ground for preferring as best the scientific theories which interrelate or account for their data in the simplest ways was not the advantage of intellectual "economy," i.e., accomplishing the task with a minimum of intellectual labor, but the *aesthetic value* or attraction of the simple theory, or what mathematicians still call "elegance." At least, his next point has to do with this matter, of the role—not always wholly beneficial, as he points out —which aesthetic preferences often play in the actual development of scientific theories. His forerunner and teacher, Hutcheson, as we have seen, thought of the search for beautiful harmonies in the pattern of nature as the whole essence of pure science and as always successful—assuming that in every part of nature the *real* pattern *is* the one with the greatest aesthetic appeal to the human mind; but Smith describes a famous episode in the history of astronomy to show that complete reliance on that assumption can lead scientists to form hypotheses which subsequent observations do not bear out, but oblige them to modify.

The astronomer Kepler was led by his faith in Pythagorean-Platonic ideas of the harmony or beauty in the pattern of nature, and of the supreme beauty, among geometric figures or forms, of the perfect circle, to believe at first that the orbits, in which the earth and planets move around the sun, must be perfect circles. Tycho Brahe, who in their observatory and with their telescope made the observations to test this hypothesis, had much difficulty in convincing Kepler that in fact the planetary orbits were *not* circles but ellipses. Smith's essay correctly describes this episode and, I think, draws the correct general conclusion or moral from it. Aesthetic predilections which play a role in shaping scientific hypotheses can be helpful within limits or lead to *nearly* correct (successfully verifiable) hypotheses, but if trusted too fully they can be misleading; the actual forms in the pattern of empirical nature cannot be counted on to conform exactly, or more than approximately, to the expectations suggested by such human predilections.

I have now substantially, and sufficiently for my purpose, reported the substance of Smith's essay on the history of astronomy. That it includes nothing about the Newtonian theory of the "gravitational" mechanics of the solar system is surprising and disappointing—the more so in view of the fact that, as we shall see, there is an unmistakable analogy between that and Smith's economic theory of the quasi-gravitational mechanics of a competitive economic system. By a useful metaphor labor and capital can be said to "gravitate" to their most remunerative locations and employments in the system, and products to "graviate" to their best markets, etc., with resulting adjustments of all strictly competitive wage rates and profit rates to uniform levels, of product prices to levels equalizing supplies and demands with each other and just covering necessary production costs, and in short of all the variables in the system to "equilibrium" values. But in spite of Smith's surprising failure to include discussion of the crowning Newtonian contribution to the development surveyed, enough is included to show us that he had much knowledge and understanding of the nature and history of this natural science, and a very perceptive and interesting philosophy of science in general. In his own creative work he applied both his understanding of the nature of natural science, and a good understanding of the necessary adaptations of ideas and methods in social science, to the different nature of the human-psychological-social subject matter. But we must now turn our attention to the first of his two large studies in this area—his *Theory of the Moral Sentiments.*

PSYCHOLOGY AND ETHICS

It is very difficult to summarize the long, complex, elaborate, intricate, subtle and elusive, systematic theory presented in this book, and make one's summary convey even a remotely adequate and just idea of the whole or of all its most essential parts. The book is large, discursive, and diffuse, and its argument is clearly reasoned and has throughout—to my mind, at least—a clear and cogent logical structure. But each step in that argument, to be appreciated, needs the illustration and support provided in the book through extensive, detailed descriptions of the common human mental and emotional reactions to and in different kinds of social situations, which the reader who has been in such situations and has good introspective powers can observe or remember in his own experience. The bare abstract scheme of theory is, by itself, so extensive and complex that in a short summary all that supporting material must be omitted, though as summarized without it the scheme of theory is less fully intelligible and convincing.

Of course, the degrees in which different, thorough students of the entire book itself have found or will find it all convincing to their minds, always have varied and will vary through a wide range. And while it is difficult enough merely to summarize the book's argument, it is still more difficult to appraise it or estimate its merits, and to make one's summary enable the reader to understand and appraise one's appraisal. At the end of this chapter I shall notice a few of the widely different appraisals which have been made, and sum up my own. But let me first try to summarize or outline the book's argument or scheme of theory —with due warning to the reader that if he wants more understanding than my very imperfect outline can convey, he must read the book.[3]

The book is about the formation in the minds of the individual members of a human society, by their mental and emotional faculties and propensities and their social contacts and experiences, of the shared moral sentiments which become the regulators of their conduct and of the institutions they agree to develop and support. It also includes the presentation of Smith's view of the character and contents of those moral sentiments *when* they are sound or valid; and his view of the causes, in features of men's social situations and experiences, which tend to make their moral sentiments sound or unsound. And the whole work's implicit view of the social function of the moral sentiments, and final criterion of their soundness, is that they should make the spontaneous behavior of each individual—although he cannot foresee or intend this end-result—as conducive as possible to the common welfare and happiness of the entire society.

As a general matter it is humanly impossible, in Smith's view, for men to be so fully "rational," informed, and able to foresee all or many of the consequences of their own and other's actions for the welfare of society, that they can or could or ever do, in any large part, work out their moral principles and judgments and decisions on their actions with a view to deliberate, intelligent promotion of the welfare of society. In its social-psychological basis the morality that grows up and becomes prevalent in a society is always, by Smith's account, a mass and pattern of com-

[3] I do seriously recommend reading the entire book—Adam Smith, *A Theory of the Moral Sentiments*, 6th ed. (London: 1790), or any later edition available in the best libraries—as well worthwhile for the interested reader and required to make him a competent critic of my condensed account of its main substance. My account is not documented with page references to the many passages that I discuss because the separate passages cannot be well understood apart from the entire context, i.e., without reading the book or a great part of it. But a fairly good short cut is to read the extract or selections reproduced in L. A. Selby-Bigge, *The British Moralists* (Oxford: Clarendon Press, 1897).

mon or prevalent, nonrational, emotional attitudes or feelings imputing simply intrinsic rightness or wrongness, goodness or badness, to different, specific kinds of conduct in specific kinds of social situations or human relations. But Smith believed—with a measure of optimism which we shall have to examine and appraise hereafter—that human nature is so constituted and leads to such interactions of the minds of men in a society, so modifying each other's emotional attitudes, that the moral consensus they "naturally" develop *under the right conditions* tends to produce the kind of conduct and institutions *in fact* most conducive to their common welfare. What we have to try to grasp is his theory of the process—in the emotional lives of associated, interacting men—by or through which their moral sentiments are engendered and formed.

In his choice of the basic idea out of which he developed this theory, Smith discarded what had been the basic idea of his forerunners, Shaftesbury and Hutcheson, and made, I think, beyond doubt, a real and great advance in "scientific" analysis. Instead of assuming as they did, with no solid warrant, that every man is endowed "by nature" with a simply innate "moral sense" which can be his infallible guide, Smith dug deeper or began farther back with a more fundamental and verifiable set of "innate" propensities—of associated men to "sympathize" with, or imagine and share, each other's feelings and impulses, when and as far as they can, and to try to win and hold each other's "sympathies" with their own emotions. And he undertook to show in detail how, through the operation of these propensities, the "consciences" in men develop as not innate but socially formed or acquired, internal monitors, building up from their sympathetic and unsympathetic judgments on the feelings—and actions—of their fellows, and from knowledge of their fellows' judgments on their own, the standards ultimately formulated and applied also in moral self-criticism and self-control.

It is important to realize at the outset that *sympathy,* in Smith's use and meaning of this word, is *not* synonymous with benevolence or altriusm; *nor* is it inconsistent with the quite large role that he assigned, in both of his two great books, to "self-interest" as a major factor in the production of each individual's attitudes and actions. Nor is "sympathy," in Smith's conception of it, simply "pity" or sympathy (only) with the sufferings of others. It is "fellow feeling" or an imaginative, vicarious sharing of another's feelings—or the feelings imputed to him—of *all* kinds, which occurs when and in so far as the subject, in observing the other person's conduct and inferring the feelings which that seems to express or manifest, imagines himself (the subject or observer) to be in that acting person's place or situation; and feels that in that situation he (the observer) would be impelled to feel and act just as the actual actor is acting and (apparently) feeling. In short, this "sympathy" is an acquisition into one's self—one's own feelings—of a kind of echo or reflection of the other, observed, active person's apparent feelings, which results from a successful, imaginative "identification" of the self with that other person. I think it is that which a more modern psychological theory calls *empathy;* at all events, by Smith's account, it is participation, through imagination, in the feelings of one's more or less intimate associates, who become in a sense one's alter egos. Further, he calls it "concord of feelings" and says that as such it is always desired and agreeable—among associates, any "discord" or discrepancy of feelings about the same matters is always disagreeable. There is in everyone—this is his basic thesis—an instinct or propensity *to* sympathize in this sense with one's fellows as fully as one can, *and* to so modify or control one's own feelings and behavior as to win and hold their sympathy or "fellow feeling" with one's self.

Now the next point or step in Smith's argument is that, with reference to any observed "piece" of human conduct, the observer's or spectator's ability to sympathize with the feelings or emotions that appear to prompt or produce it, or be manifested in it, is the necessary and sufficient, immediate basis of his (the spectator's) *moral approval* of the conduct in question; though we shall see in a moment how this is qualified in a sense in view of the complications that arise when conflicting sympathies with diverse parties come into play. If the passive spectator of an acting person's situation and action achieves a full "concord of feelings" with the actor, or says to himself: "I know just what and how that fellow is feeling, and why he is doing that, and if I were in his place my feelings and conduct would be just what his are"—then the spectator automatically *approves* the conduct he observes. But if the spectator is unable to sympathize, and instead feels that the actor's feelings appear to be and must be either much stronger or much weaker, or of a different kind, than he thinks his own in the actor's place would be, then disapproval is as automatic as approval where full sympathy is present.

In explaining our moral judgments on the conduct of others, however, Smith generally works with a "triangle"—the spectator, the actor, *and* a third party who may be injured or benefited by the actor's action. For in Smith's view the total complex question of the all-around goodness of an action involves two different questions: the "propriety" of the actor's emotional and resulting active response to his own situation, and the "merit" of his action which has to do with its effects upon other people and their emotional responses to it. If the actor's response to his own situation or provocations as seen by the spectator wins the latter's full sympathy and consequent approval of the action *as* entirely "proper" in that situation; *but* the party on the receiving end, so to speak, is injured by the action, resents it, and shows his resentment, *and* the spectator on imagining himself in *this* person's position, sympathetically shares and approves his resentment; then the "mixed" result is that in the spectator's judgment the action, although it has "propriety," also has "demerit" or must be disapproved on the latter ground, in spite of being approved as far as the former is concerned. To win complete approval an action must strike the spectator as having *both* "propriety" *and* "merit," i.e., as both expressing a suitable response to the occasion which prompts it on the actor's part, and benefiting the affected person or persons and evoking on his or their parts a gratitude with which the spectator also sympathizes; so that, sympathizing with both or all of the parties concerned, he is pleased with the action in all its aspects. A beneficial but improper action is only half good, like one that is proper but injurious. And if some of the persons affected by a proper action are benefited and grateful, but others are injured and resentful, and the "impartial spectator" has sympathies with both groups, then he judges the action as good in two aspects but bad in the third aspect, and thus morally imperfect to that extent.

This formation, however, of the moral judgments of the spectators upon particular actions occurring in particular contexts, is only the beginning of the process which Smith is describing and analyzing. He goes on to describe an interaction and reciprocal adjustment of feelings between the spectators and the actors, which results from the initial differences of strength or intensity of the feelings on the two sides—discrepancies or gaps between the stronger feelings impelling the actors to their actions and the generally weaker, even if similar, sympathetic feelings of the passive spectators—and from desires and involuntary efforts on both sides to close or narrow these gaps and achieve fuller "concord of feelings." This type of interaction, he holds, leads to modifications of the (future) conduct of the actors, in the directions dictated by the feelings of the spectators, which may in the meantime also change a little in the other way or become more sympathetic. The feelings, responsive to the stimuli which prompt men's actions, are often overexcited and too strong or vivid to permit, at the moment, adequate reflection, awareness of the impressions likely to be made on passive, calm, disinterested spectators, and self-control. On the other hand, the mere faint echoes or pale reflections of those feelings in the minds of even the most sympathetic or least unsympathetic spectators are as likely to be in a sense too weak, i.e., inadequately appreciative of the provocations or incitements experienced by the actors and the measures of real justification there may be for their strong feelings and resulting actions. But this very discrepancy and the instinctive efforts of the actor and the spectator to overcome it have a moral function, of producing convergence toward the mean or medium intensity of feeling that would lead to performance and approval of the right, appropriate reaction to the actor's stimuli and situation.

One commentator on Smith's theory has rightly noted the resemblance between this idea and Aristotle's theory that (every) virtue lies in a mean between two extremes of feeling and behavior—which in turn of course had behind it the general ancient Greek ideal of "moderation in all things" or "nothing in excess." But Smith goes beyond that Greek and Aristotelian outlook; he adds his theory *of a social-psychological process operating to produce* convergence of the feelings of men in a society, as actors and spectators of each other's actions, toward agreement in the "mean" or appropriately moderate, neither too much nor too little excited states, productive of the right, appropriate reactions to all situations, and prevailing, sympathetic approval of them. And this may be described as a theory of a process of adjustment of the feelings of all concerned, as "forces," into a moral or healthy state of "equilibrium." When any event or development in one part of a society initially concerns and excites some members greatly and others much less or not at all, and the former tend to react with a violence of which the latter disapprove, the social contacts and emotional interactions among all and their common desire for "concord of feelings" cause the hot and the cool feelings, so to speak, to become diffused into all minds and to modify each other; so that all approach the intermediate emotional temperature, which generally is more conducive than either extreme to the right, appropriate behavior in response to the original event.

There is still much more to come, however, in Smith's theory of the total process he is analyzing. Let us next proceed with him, from and beyond his analysis of the formation and the influence of our sympathetic and unsympathetic judgments, as external spectators, upon the conduct of our associates, and of theirs as external spectators of our conduct, to his analysis of the way in which we arrive at our own judgments upon and standards for our own conduct. As a product of all his experiences of judging others and of being judged by them, everyone develops or acquires a "conscience"—called by Smith "the internal spectator or man within the breast." This acquired inward monitor has the function of judging and controlling one's own feelings and resulting actions, by the standards derived from or implicit in all of that underlying experience; but it is able to apply those standards to the self in a more accurate and exacting way, because it has the benefit of fuller and more certain and accurate knowledge of one's own feelings than is available to the external spectators.

Were Smith's whole theory of the human-natural basis of morality *only* one of an instinct to win and hold others' sympathies or comply with their judgments, it would lead to no better or other morality or ethics than that of simple, expedient conformity with public opinion; and some critics have accused him, falsely, of leading up to just that and no more. But he says explicitly that human nature is such that a man cannot be satisfied with having, simply, the good opinions of his fellows, of his character and conduct, if within himself he knows that those good opinions depend in part upon elements of ignorance and error and would be changed for the worse if others knew the whole truth about him as fully as he knows it himself. There is in everyone not only a desire for praise from others, the external spectators, but also a desire for inward knowledge of one's own praiseworthiness; the better-placed and informed internal spectator also must be satisfied. Hence everyone tends to watch and control or modify his own feelings, impulses, and actions, in a manner guided by all his memories of the censures and approvals he has felt in observing the behavior of others, and encountered as theirs upon his own past behavior; but with the advantage of the unique fullness of self-knowledge, and a view to gaining and retaining not only the respect of others but also his own full self-respect. We still have not reached the culminating point of this analysis, however. So far, it has been focused solely upon human feelings or emotions; we have next to see how Smith conceived the limited but important ethical function or role of "reason."

Our fleeting, specific, or "atomic" feelings of the moral qualities—the powers to win or attract the sympathy of the ideal, fully informed, and impartial spectator—*of* the feelings that produce our actions, cannot by themselves be sufficient, reliable, moral guides, because they are unstable or variable—subject to new distortions in each new moment or interval of time by one's special situation, stimuli, and mood or emotional state at that time. When one is under the pressure of any strong excitement, enthusiasm, or temptation, even one's "internal spectator" is affected in the sense that its current or temporary, mere feelings of the moral qualities of the object-self's excited feelings and contemplated actions, tend to be unduly biased in their favor. Only in one's later and best moments of calm, detached reflection and sober, retrospective self-examination do his internal spectator's verdict-feelings on particular past feelings-and-actions in their contexts, become reliable. Hence we learn, Smith says, to use such good moments of reflective insight also to form or work out for ourselves *general rules or principles* of good or "praiseworthy" conduct in *all* situations of particular kinds; and to make strong resolutions to try always to live up to these rules, even and especially at the times when our momentary feelings incline us to deviate from them. Eventually we may work out a full code or system of such rules of conduct for all important kinds of frequently recurring situations and moral problems. But, according to Smith, all such rules are arrived at as *inductive generalizations from* our countless particular experiences or moral feelings on particular occasions: of sympathies and nonsympathies in our roles as spectators of other's actions; of knowledge of their verdicts as spectators of our actions; and of our own self-judgments in our best, detached, reflective moments. And the rules of conduct *thus* arrived at, Smith immediately adds, *are the celebrated moral laws of nature.*

In a sense, I have now completed this bare outline of Smith's theory *of the process of formation of* "the moral sentiments"—feelings and whole classes of feelings generalized into principles that are still, as principles, "felt" as having normative or constraining force. But I must notice the points made in two or three further passages, which throw additional light upon that theory, before going on to the *substance* of Smith's ethics. In the passage that I take up first, he dissents from and criticizes the explanation which his friend, the great philosopher David Hume, had put forward, of the source or root of the human "sense of justice," i.e., the tendency of any witness of any deed of injustice or injury, committed by one man against another, to feel indignation at the deed and want to see it punished or see justice enforced by the state.

Hume also employed a concept of "sympathy" as a cornerstone of his theory of ethics, but he did not use this concept in the same way in which Smith used it. Hume merely assumed that each individual is led by "sympathy" with his fellow men in general to desire to see all the conditions that affect their happiness made and kept as favorable as possible to a general, continuing prevalence of happiness throughout society. In other words, Hume used the postulate of "sympathy" among men only as a stepping stone to a simple utilitarian theory of ethics, according to which every moral sentiment or feeling, such as the one against all unjust actions and in favor of laws to punish them, *arises from foresight of and desire for the social utility,* for human happiness in general, of a regime of legally enforced justice among all. But Adam Smith rejects this view as psychologically unrealistic; he argues that in any typical, particular, actual case the feeling that immediately arises in the spectator of a deed of injury of one man by another—the spectator's feeling of sympathy with the victim and indignation at the deed and the doer of it—*is too instantaneous and unreflective* to be the product of any foresight of the social consequences of general toleration or nonrestraint of this kind of behavior, and the social utility of laws and punishments designed to restrain it. Any close, accurate, introspective observation, he insists, of the feeling at its point of origin in an actual case, will show that it is not a reasoning sympathy with the general desire of all men for happiness, but an unreasoning, purely instinctive or automatic, instantaneous, and specific sympathy with the victim in that case, or sharing *of the latter's* automatic resentment or indignation and desire for vengeance. And although the propensity in men to react thus does have the socially useful *result* of leading them to develop and support, in organized societies, legal systems which enforce justice and thus protect happiness in general; the primary source of this development—the propensity in question—is not itself an achievement of human, rational wisdom, but a fortunate element in the constitution of the nonrational, emotional part of human nature.

And now I come to the most interesting and important part of this critical discussion of Hume's theory of the origin of "the sense of justice." Hume, Smith goes on to charge, has here been guilty of the unscientific procedure of trying to "explain" this natural human emotional reaction (in the spectators) to unjust actions, by referring only to its "final cause" or socially useful end result, instead of ascertaining and describing correctly its "efficient cause," i.e., the instinct to sympathize with the victims of injustice or share their resentments and desires for vengeance. And he regards this error of Hume's as a typical case of a common fault of the social as compared with the natural sciences! In the natural sciences the lesson has been learned that the real scientific task is to understand not merely the good purposes that events and processes serve or accomplish, but the mechanisms through which they are brought about. Thus we know, for example, that a scientific explanation of the performance of that timekeeping instrument, a watch, must not merely refer to keeping time as its purpose or function, but must also explain *how* the structure and working of its inner mechanism of wheels and springs brings about the result; and we impute the conscious purpose, planning, and wisdom involved not to the watch but to the watchmaker who designed its mechanism. In our efforts to explain how human beings and societies operate or function, however, we are still too prone to think of the *ends* toward which they function as sufficiently explaining *how* they function and attain those ends, and not to study with sufficient, detailed thoroughness and realism the psychological and social mechanisms which are at work. We tend to exaggerate greatly the extent and the role of the human, conscious, or deliberate purposes, foresight, and planning involved; or to impute to the wisdom of men too much of what in fact is more largely due to the wisdom of God, the Designer of the psychological and social mechanisms which make men in much of their behavior *unconscious* servants of their common welfare. We may reject this whole argument's deistic conclusion and suspect it of overoptimism, but I think we must recognize the valid and important insights in it.

Now I turn to a different passage which throws light in another way upon Smith's general theory. In *this* passage he compares his theory of the way in which an individual's sympathies with others can affect or modify his self-interest, and all his relative evaluations of events affecting his own and others' interests, with the theory of perspective in the science of optics. If I see a very small hill rising at only a short distance from where I stand, and at the same time see a very distant, high mountain, my retinal image of the former may be as large and high as that of the latter, or (even) much larger and higher; but having learned by past experience to allow for the effect of distance in diminishing the apparent size of a visual object, I instantly, automatically, and unconsciously make an approximately correct allowance, and mentally *see* the two elevations as having something like their true, relative heights. In a similar way, then, says Smith, if I accidentally prick my finger and feel a slight pain there, and at the same time read or hear about a great famine and starving millions of people in far-off China; were it not for the factor of sympathy, the pain in my finger would seem to me far more important—a greater tragedy—than that terrible famine. But through my natural capacity for an imaginative sympathy with those distant and unknown but human people, I can instantly, automatically, and unconsciously correct the tendency of their remoteness from me and my own concerns to make me indifferent to their fate; and I can instead *feel* the relative magnitudes of these two evils in something like their real proportion.

This very interesting analogy brings out an aspect or facet, in a sense unlike the others mainly emphasized in Smith's whole theory, of the roles of men's sympathies and other related feelings in the production of morality. Here the stress is not upon the more reliable (universally effective) than inspiring role of sympathy with associates and desire for their sympathy, in producing a rather mediocre morality of little more than social conformity within a group. The theory of moral "perspective," in the passage now under consideration, suggests the possibility of life on a higher moral plane. If men could generally and consistently achieve and maintain universal, full, and well-balanced sympathies with all fellow human beings everywhere on earth, which would fully correct their extreme partialities to themselves and the small numbers of persons "near and dear" to them; if everyone could thus achieve the same true sense of proportion in the scheme of his felt appraisals of his own and of all men's greater and lesser joys and sorrows; then the full harmony among all men, of which all-out "idealists" have always dreamed, might be realized. Although Adam Smith in this one exceptional passage pointed toward this possibility, he very clearly did not think of it as likely ever to be realized generally or at all widely, in better than quite remote approximations.

In fact, in the next and last (in my order) of the three illuminating passages that I am describing here, he goes rather far in just the opposite direction, of the "realism" or pessimism of the man with no illusions. He describes (and censures) the very common tendency of men to associate and sympathize with each other only within many different, separate, narrow, and rival groups, and hence to develop as many different, narrow, diversely biased and conflicting codes of morality or moral sentiments. His first example of this is the narrow nationalism which distorts the moral feelings of the people of each country or makes them regard as "right" whatever they believe is to their country's interest or advantage. Because we associate with our fellow countrymen much more than with foreigners, we tend to sympathize with the former only and not with the latter, and thus come to have as a national group of people a shared, warped feeling of the self-evident, perfect goodness, rightness, or justice of all that is wanted by or will benefit "us," the people of this superior country. He then speaks of other examples: within a country, each of the many occupational, regional, class, and other "interest" groups develops a special set of warped "moral" feelings on all matters touching the special interests common to its members, and fully sanctions that set of interests as against the opposed interests of every other rival group.

It is plain that Smith did not by any means hold or think that the interplay of sympathies and desires for sympathy produces, under all conditions or under those that commonly exist, any one universal and/or entirely sound or valid system of moral sentiments, prescribing and producing altogether truly ethical conduct, i.e., the conduct most conducive to the common welfare of all mankind or of all the members of any one great, e.g., national society. For he regarded sympathy or identification with—imaginative sharing of—the value-feelings and desires of others, and the resulting ability to "weigh" them fairly against one's own "selfish" desires and all others (also sympathized with) in conflict with them, and arrive at objective or impartial value-judgments, "just to" *all* the desires at stake—he regarded all this as conditioned and limited by the range of one's frequent, intimate associations with others, which alone enable the ordinary, unimaginative person to appreciate their attitudes and sympathize with them. Associating only or mainly with those whose situations, interests, and attitudes already are largely similar to one's own, results in but little correction of the bias of one's attitudes; on the contrary, it results in the formation of a narrow and biased set of sympathies and moral sentiments unduly partial to the desires of one's limited group.

Though Smith himself nowhere makes the connection explicit, it is impossible not to see in this feature of his theory of the process of formation of men's moral sentiments, an important part of the ground or basis of his own *liberal individualism and internationalism;* i.e., his belief in the desirability of a world of free, detached, highly mobile, and cosmopolitan individuals, who would all severally form or acquire very wide ranges of friendships and sympathies with countless people of all kinds everywhere, and thus be led toward the kind of universal and well-balanced sympathies, or true moral perspective, productive of agreement in a sound, impartial morality. At the same time, I repeat, he clearly never expected that such an ideal situation and result would be fully realized. Although he regarded as highly imperfect the patterns of actual moral sentiments which do develop and operate in men's minds and conduct, in their actual societies and groups, he yet also regarded these sentiments as generally or normally, fairly good on the whole, socially useful and indeed indispensable, hard to improve or change, and so in the main to be accepted, with philosophic resignation, as nearly the best that can be hoped for; the *mainly* beneficent "natural" products, in this sphere, of men's natures and social experiences as they are, and "natural" roots of their social institutions and regulators of their private actions. But we have still to look at his account of the substance of this human-natural morality or ethics—taken in what he thought to be its best really possible or widely, humanly attainable state or form. I shall now summarize this rather briefly, and add, at the end, remarks on two quite different appraisals, and my own concluding appraisal, of the book as a whole.

The "natural" morality, according to Smith, prescribes or "recommends" three cardinal virtues—"prudence, justice, and benevolence." He defines "prudence" as "the intelligent care of one's own health, wealth, and happiness"; in other words, this concept is clearly the same as that of enlightened or rational self-interest which was to figure in the *Wealth of Nations,* and has figured throughout modern times in nearly all economic theory, as the principal motive-force directly involved in the production and determination of men's economic activities and decisions. Thus it is of great interest, not only in general but also in connection with our coming study of Smith's economics, that we find this kind or quality of behavior treated here, under the name of "prudence," *as a moral virtue*. But as we shall see, his treatment, in this work on ethics, of the other two virtues along with this one, is of equal interest, also, in connection with his economics (as well as in general). Even though his theory of the socially well-working competitive economy of free and mobile individuals "prudently" pursuing and protecting their private interests had less to say about "justice" and "benevolence," we shall find that it *presupposed* the presence and effectiveness, in (throughout) the society and upon the economy, of a moral climate and legal order ensuring "justice" and encouraging "benevolence" among the individuals, *along with* their "prudence" in conducting their own private affairs. Moreover, we shall see that his theory of ethical behavior treated prudence in the management of one's own affairs, and justice to others, as *connected* virtues, or regarded the latter as almost a part of the former. But first we must notice, in addition to the definition of prudence already quoted, his definitions of justice and benevolence.

Justice, as a quality of an individual's attitudes and behavior toward others, is defined by Smith as "a scrupulous refusal ever to hurt or injure anyone else, in the pursuit of one's own interest or advantage." Of course, the crucial part of this—"refusal . . . to . . . injure . . . ," i.e., to do injustice to another—makes the definition circular and question-begging; justice is defined only as refraining from injustice. But I think we can say with ample warrant and some useful effect, that Smith's idea of justice involved a conception, similar to Locke's, of *the equal natural rights* of all individuals—rights which, being equal or alike for all, mutually limit one another and thus form a consistent system which imposes upon each individual *a duty to respect,* i.e., never to violate or infringe the rights of his fellows—to be measured in the case of each one of them as equal to his own. For Locke, that duty to confine the pursuit of self-interest within the limits or bounds of due regard for the rights of others was a dictate of the "reason" which tells every man that all other men, being human like himself, have the same human rights that he has. For Smith, it was a dictate and result of the proper "sympathy" with others through which one can "feel with" them to the extent of "feeling" their just rights as equal to and as limiting one's own. But for these two writers, I think, the content of justice itself was substantially the same. And the "negative" character of Smith's definition—of justice to others as noninjury of them—served to sharpen his distinction between "justice" and "benevolence," which he defined as going beyond this bare justice to others, into positive efforts to assist or benefit them.

Finally, it is very significant and revealing that Smith explicitly ranked this last virtue in his list well below the other two, and especially far below justice, in importance. General prevalence of tolerable approximations, at least, to justice among a society's members is, he held, indispensable for the society's continuing existence; and the members generally must conduct their own affairs with tolerable prudence if the society is to flourish. But the addition of a degree of mutual benevolence among the members, although desirable, will, he said, only make it a more "agreeable" society; benevolence is not, like justice, indispensable; nor is it as important as prevailing prudence.

Now let us consider the passage already alluded to, in which Smith links "prudence" or enlightened self-interest and "justice" to others together, or explains why and how the former in its own best development *includes* the latter, even though the latter also has its own independent basis and supreme importance on its own account. The spectators, he says, of the conduct of each individual, instinctively sympathize with and applaud his efforts to rise in the world or increase (improve) his income, wealth, and social status, unless they see him climbing to success by trampling down his fellows. If they suspect him of doing the latter, they sympathize not with him but instead with his victims, and vigorously and indignantly condemn his behavior. And since everyone desires to avoid the disapproval of the spectators and to win, instead, their sympathy and approval, both for its own sake and as an asset of value to him in his efforts to rise in the world, it follows that just, i.e., never unjust, behavior toward others is a part or counsel of prudence itself. This idea is of course precisely parallel with the maxim of Benjamin Franklin's Poor Richard, that "honesty is the best policy." Smith is saying in effect that justice to others, in the course of one's efforts to rise in the world, is the best policy. But the reader who has followed what was said above about Smith's earlier account of the origin of "the sense of justice," will not accuse him of holding, or intending to suggest, that either men's obligations or their tendencies to be just to their fellows have as grounds or motives *only* those of policy, expediency, or prudence. He regarded justice among men as supremely, morally imperative and socially indispensable in its own right; as having its own independent source of support in men's "natural" feelings and social interactions; and as limiting the sphere of the legitimate ends and means of all courses of action arising from self-interest; and yet he regarded it *also* as generally supported or reinforced by enlightened self-interest or prudence, itself.

And now it must be said, further, that the conception thus developed here, in Smith's *Theory of the Moral Sentiments,* of the ideal prudent, i.e., prudent-and-just man, is the nearest thing to be found in any of his writings, to the concept "economic man." Commonly and erroneously imputed to Smith the economist, but in fact never, in its generally understood meaning, held by him, that concept was invented by some of his minor nineteenth-century successors. As we shall see in the next chapter, the conception of the "normal" or "natural" behavior of men in their economic activities, which Smith was to utilize in his work on the *Wealth of Nations,* was not the notion of behavior dictated solely by "the desire for wealth" and uninfluenced by any moral considerations, but instead was that of the behavior, on the part of each individual in his economic situation at each moment, which is at once "prudent" in his own interest and just to all or not unjust to any of the persons with whom he is dealing or competing.

It is surely not too difficult, then, to understand that Smith could hold that such behavior by the individuals within a society—behavior mainly impelled and directed by their self-interests but regulated both by their socially engendered and prevailing moral sentiments and by the competitive market system—generally would be in fact positively beneficial, not merely to themselves, but to each other and the common welfare of all, despite the assumed nonexistence in the individuals of intentions to benefit each other and society or to do more than act in their own interests without injuring anyone.

I must now speak of another passage, near the end of the *Theory of the Moral Sentiments,* which brings out a very interesting and significant part of the further positive basis of Smith's conception of "nature" as using men's "selfish" ambitions to make them unconscious contributors to the welfare of their fellows and society. In this odd passage we get a theory of the source and result of a common illusion which leads the most able and ambitious individuals to go on striving to enlarge their private fortunes *beyond* the point of any real advantage or benefit to themselves (in terms of happiness), with the result of really benefiting large numbers of poor, working people, and society at large. A modest income is really all that anyone needs, as far as economic requirements are concerned, for his greatest happiness. Great wealth is not a boon to its owner at all; required expenditures, harassing obligations and responsibilities of many kinds, and anxieties, make the lot of the rich man really not enviable; the carefree beggar has, in reality, a security which kings crave in vain. But great wealth—a palatial residence, retinue of servants, and the whole apparatus of elegant living—appears to be a well-designed "machine for producing happiness," and so arouses in every able and ambitious man a human and natural, although deceptive or deceived, admiration of it, and a determination to acquire a splendid happiness-machine of this kind for himself. And in his strenuous efforts to achieve this aim, he develops enterprises, earnings, savings, and investments, which create employment and wages for a host of working people, and useful products which many people buy, use, and enjoy, and so really benefits all those other people more truly and substantially than he benefits himself. The goal of his selfish ambition is a chimera with which cunning "nature" lures him into serving others better than he serves himself.

It is time now to return to a point that I passed over earlier, in Smith's discussion of the three moral virtues of his list—prudence, justice, and benevolence. A comment of his reveals still another part of the basis of his advocacy, as likely to work best for the common good, of a society of free individuals and a limited role, only, for the state or government. Of the three virtues and the groups of rules of conduct connected with them, he says that the rules of justice are relatively exact, like the rules of grammar, but the rules of prudence and those of benevolence are more inexact, like the rules of rhetoric. The requirements of justice among men can be spelled out in uniform, general, and definite rules or principles, which therefore can and should be promulgated and enforced by the state, as law—a body of just law enforced through the courts. But the rules of prudence, which should guide each individual in the conduct of his own affairs, are more inexact or imprecise, intuitive, and relative to the different circumstances and sets of desires of the different individuals, and therefore are best left to each one of them, to work out and apply by the free use of his own judgment. The rules of proper benevolence, also, elude precise or fixed formulations and vary with particular cases and relationships of the persons concerned; and are generally unfit for this and also for another reason to be publicly prescribed or made obligatory. Benevolence must be voluntary, or it ceases to be benevolence and to be a virtue; compulsory benevolence is a contradiction in terms.

Yet in saying this, Smith characteristically adds a qualification which opens the way, after all, to a somewhat larger role for the state than that of enforcing bare ordinary justice, only, among its citizens or subjects. Wherever certain persons, such as employers, are in positions of special responsibility for the welfare of certain other persons or groups, such as their employees, something more than bare negative and impersonal justice from the former to the latter—some positive, humane attention to their needs, going beyond mere noninfringement of the ordinary legal rights which are those of *all* men—may be properly required. But the state, in imposing such "extra" obligations upon persons in such special positions, should be careful not to require from any of them more than the small amount of "benevolence" to those other persons, at his own expense, which he can be expected in the normal case to accept and render willingly, or which the community's "natural" moral consensus regards as appropriate in all situations or cases of that kind. This significant passage plainly indicates, I think, that if Smith had been living and writing a century later, but with his fundamental views unaltered, he would have been *not* an advocate of the strict or extreme and harsh version of the *laissez-faire* gospel, but instead a moderate or cautious advocate of much very modern, humane, or protective "social legislation" in its limited, moderate, or conservative forms.

There is, finally, one more passage in the *Theory of the Moral Sentiments* which reveals still another facet of the quality and basis of Smith's liberalism or individualism in social philosophy. Too often, he says, the ambitious social "plans of statesmen or projectors" assume that men—the individual subjects of the state—"can be moved about at will, like the pieces on a chessboard"; but the framers of such plans "forget that" on the human chessboard "every piece has a principle of motion of its own." It is plain that, for this reason, he felt that all such plans would in practice fail to work as expected, and that they must be rejected as morally wrong because in conflict with the human right of every individual to move about and behave as impelled and directed by his own internal "principle of motion," in so far as this freedom or spontaneity of all can be made consistent with their common welfare.

We have now surveyed one half, and in the next chapter will survey the other half, of Smith's theory of the "automatic" social processes tending to ensure, to a great extent, such harmony of the free or spontaneous behavior of all with the requirements of their common welfare. The social-psychological process—the interplay of sympathies and desires for sympathy—which generates and shapes the communal pattern of the moral sentiments of a society of free men, makes that pattern and the just legal order or system supported by it, a set of generally spontaneously approved or accepted norms confining each individual's behavior in pursuit of his own ends or interests, within the bounds of justice to his fellows. And the economic process (competitive market process) described in the *Weath of Nations* and to be studied in our next chapter, when it operates within the climate and framework of that set of ethical and legal norms, causes the self-interests of the individuals to lie in contributing as fully and efficiently as they can, through the markets, to the satisfaction of each other's needs and wants and to the common wealth and welfare of all.

As we have seen and will see more fully, Smith never held that either process, in general, works *perfectly;* in his at once moderately optimistic and moderately pessimistic outlook, all dreams of perfection were to be dismissed as foolish illusions. That in civilized societies the two processes together could work on the whole quite well, and better than any system of public controls in conflict with them and unduly restricting individual freedom, is the fundamental thesis that his two great books together embody. But in working out and coordinating these processes, the state as one agency involved has a very essential, yet limited, role to play—mainly though not quite exclusively that of developing and enforcing a general system of just law or legal justice which expresses the society's or public's "natural" moral sentiments within that field.

At the end of his *Theory of the Moral Sentiments,* Smith indicated his intention to write and publish another book, on "the principles of natural justice, which ought to underlie and be the foundation of the laws of all nations." It is regrettable that, for reasons unknown to us, he never wrote this promised treatise on the principles of jurisprudence. But a modern economist and student of his work, Professor Edwin Cannan, discovered years ago in a country house in England a well-preserved copy of a student's (one of Adam Smith's pupils) notes of his course of lectures on "Justice, Police, Revenue, and Arms"; and it is clear that the first part of this, on justice, could have been expanded and developed into the promised work on jurisprudence, and that the other parts together *did* become, with extensive revisions and additions, the *Wealth of Nations.* The section on police, as Cannan's historical scholarship established, meant and was about the part of public or governmental policy which aims to ensure at all times "plenty and cheapness of commodities" for the people as consumers—the main theme of the *Wealth of Nations*. And the other sections, on revenue and arms, i.e., public finance and national defense, are also included, in improved forms, in the *Wealth of Nations*. But I must now conclude this chapter with a few remarks on the small and varying success of Smith's *Theory of the Moral Sentiments* in impressing readers in his own time and in later times; the diverse impressions it has made on different judges; and my own judgment about its merits.

Apparently the book had at first, for a short time, a considerable though never *very* great success or popularity in contemporary clerical and religious circles and some others, but has never been at all widely read, or highly esteemed except by rare, individual readers, since about the end of the eighteenth century. I can only explain this as resulting from the difficulty or subtlety of its subject and substance; the qualities of its style and tone which very much "date" it and have seemed quaint and unattractive to most more modern readers; the subsequent changes and divergent trends of modern currents or modes of thought in its field; and the fact that the success of its author's later and greater book in a different field not only overshadowed it, but made Smith for most people only the great economist and one whom they could hardly think of as likely to have been a great moral philosopher. Perhaps I may add two further points or parts to that explanation. When in later times the inaccurate popular impression of the central message of the *Wealth of Nations* gained general currency or favor in the business community and corresponding disfavor among the moralists, social reformers, and prophets hostile to that community, few members of either group retained any disposition to study, with open minds, this earlier work whose message was not in line with their presuppositions about Smith's views. And finally, there has been, I think, a long, modern decline of really widespread, great, intellectual interest in study of or reflection upon the foundations of ethics; a growth and spread of disbelief in the possibility of significant intellectual achievements in this field, and of tendencies among the growing number and percentage of proudly "tough-minded" people to relegate this inquiry to the province only of the "tender-minded." Yet I must admit that not even the sum of all these considerations can fully explain the largely adverse appraisals of the book by some able scholars and serious students of it, or the favor it has occasionally found in other unexpected quarters.

An outstanding example under the first of these headings is the appraisal that was made by the nineteenth-century English free-lance scholar, Sir Leslie Stephen. His *History of English Thought in the Eighteenth Century*, a standard and first-rate work, described and discussed Smith's contribution to ethical theory along with the contributions made by other British writers in his century, including Shaftesbury,

Hutcheson, Butler, and Hume; but rated Smith's work in this field far below most of the others considered—describing it as "superficial" and as supporting only the rather contemptible morality or ethics of mere conformity with public opinion.[4] The completeness and the grounds of my own disagreement with this view have already been made clear, and I can only say that I think Leslie Stephen "slipped" strangely in this connection, or misread, misunderstood, and misjudged the book. But a most interesting contrast is provided by the highly favorable opinion that was reached, surprisingly, by T. H. Huxley, the famous biologist and champion, before the lay public, of Darwin's theory of evolution, in the period of attacks upon that theory in religious circles.

In a published lecture by Huxley on *Evolution and Ethics,* Smith's *Theory of the Moral Sentiments* was praised as the nearest thing Huxley knew of to "a scientific treatment of the subject of ethics."[5] The context or background of this opinion, in Huxley's lecture, is of great interest. Here the champion of Darwinism was denouncing, as a product of a misunderstanding and perversion of his hero's scientific theory, the tendency of much thought in the human-social sciences or studies to conclude that, since the forces and laws of "nature" as they operate in the subhuman, biological world appear to be ruthless and amoral, but to bring about "progress" to better-adapted forms of life through a ruthless struggle for survival; it must be proper for human beings and groups, also, to engage in such all-out struggle, and to suppress their "sentimental" or sympathetic, humane, ethical feelings and inhibitions which tend to bring about departure from the healthy, rugged ways of "nature," help the "unfit" to survive, and thus hamper evolutionary social "progress" through unrestrained competition. The general theme of this lecture by Huxley is that human imitation of nonhuman "nature" is an absurd, ancient, nonscientific ideal or notion with no definite meaning, which when construed in this way with the alleged sanction of Darwinism misuses the latter and leads to pure, pernicious nonsense. "Nature's" processes are not the same in all spheres or at all levels of existence; the organic realm as a whole has laws which do not operate in the inanimate realm; and civilized human societies require and develop modes and norms of behavior unlike those prevailing in the greater part of the organic realm, below the human level. Cooperation as well as competition has its role in the evolutionary process; in human life the role of the former becomes peculiarly important, and involves the growth and operation of a uniquely human, vital factor—

[4] Sir Leslie Stephen, *History of English Thought in the Eighteenth Century,* 3d ed. (London: Smith, Elder, and Co., 1902), vol. 2, pp. 71–77.

[5] T. H. Huxley, *Evolution and Ethics, and Other Essays* (New York: Appleton-Century-Croft, Inc., 1894) pp. 26–33.

ethical culture or civilization. This factor has its "natural" basis not in "nature" at large but in *human* nature; and we need a science of its basis there, to be the source, which general biology cannot be, of the real contributions which science can make to ethics. It was as a step—the best one that he knew of—toward the building of this needed science of the human-natural foundations of ethics, that Huxley praised Adam Smith's *Theory of the Moral Sentiments*.

The book's deistic "piety," or attribution of the elements of human nature which underlie morality to Providential "design" instead of to "evolution," apparently did not disturb the agnostic and evolutionist Huxley. No doubt he knew that the pre-Darwinian, admiring studies, under deistic influence, of the "adaptations" of the parts of organisms for their vital functions, which seemed to be "evidences of design," had contributed to biological science; and that Darwin's theory, in providing an alternative explanation of the origins of those "adaptations," by no means discarded but only added to the previously achieved understanding of those adaptations. And he could see that Adam Smith's analysis of the human propensities which make man a social and moral being, "by nature" adapted for his functioning as such in human societies, would retain its value even if further studies, discarding Smith's Deism, should replace that with an explanation of the "evolution" of those same human propensities. I would not in advance expect Huxley to surpass Leslie Stephen as a discerning judge of a book of this kind, but in this case I think he did.

Let me not end this chapter, however, on a note of apparently pure adulation of Smith's book. Of course the *Theory of the Moral Sentiments* has many faults or deficiencies. Although, as we have seen, its optimism, or concentration on the socially fortunate part of the emotional make-up and functioning of the human being, is by no means unqualified, it is, I think, considerably excessive or one-sided. There is too much contrast with the modern Freudian picture of the human lusts or passions, and the frightful difficulty of developing the savage infant into a moral, civilized, and socially "adjusted" adult, without destroying his mental health and inner integrity! But perhaps it is permissible to opine that the latter picture is commonly exaggerated or one-sided in its way, and that Smith's picture contained a part of the truth which the Freudians do not always adequately recognize. Smith also, I think, overdid his belittlement of the role of reason or intelligence or the need for it to achieve, and its power to achieve, revisions or improvements of intuitive-emotional morality in the direction of a code more in harmony with the understood requirements or conditions of social welfare. But criticism of this kind could be endless and need not be further developed here. Our principal concern is not to evaluate

Smith's theory of the formation and substance of a good, free society's morality, but to understand it as the complement and background of his theory of the way in which, given such a society and morality, the former's economy or economic system would operate or function in producing and distributing its wealth or prosperity. Assuming that we now understand this complement and background, let us go on to study, in the next chapter, the essentials of Smith's economic theory.

CHAPTER 4

Adam Smith's Ideal and Theory of the Self-adjusting Liberal Economy

SMITH'S ETHICS AND HIS ECONOMICS

Seventeen years after the appearance of his *Theory of the Moral Sentiments,* Adam Smith completed and published the very different and much greater book on which his fame rests—his *Inquiry into the Nature and Causes of the Wealth of Nations.* As a reader turns from that earlier to this later book, he is certain to notice a slight but striking change of tone—to fewer and less lavish expressions of sentiment and piety and a fuller display of hardheaded realism—which naturally goes with the transfer of attention to a different subject matter, or aspect of human life and affairs. As compared with the psychology of the ethical emotions, the economics of the production, exchange, distribution, and growth of a nation's outputs of material goods or wealth evokes another mood; it is a "drier" subject. This difference indeed may not fully explain the slighter prominence of "piety" in the later book; but it is a fact of interest, however we explain it, that although "the unseen hand" of Providence is *once* referred to in the *Wealth of Nations,* in a famous passage that will be discussed in its place, this theme is much less prominent here than it was in the *Theory of the Moral Sentiments.* But the dissimilarity of the two books should not be overstressed or regarded as evidence of a change, in that interval of seventeen years, of Smith's general outlook or philosophy.

Above all there is no foundation, I think, for the view that arose among some nineteenth-century German scholars who thought they saw a puzzling conflict between the central theses of the two books and engaged in much discussion of what they called "the Adam Smith problem"—how to reconcile, or understand as compatible, the earlier work's stress on "sympathy" among men as the basis of the common morality in a sense constitutive of each human community, and the later work's stress on each individual's "self-interest" as the principal motive-force directly involved in economic behavior as such.[1] I have already, in the foregoing chapter, explained my view of this matter—that the central themes of the two books respectively are not in conflict, but complement each other. Moral control (limitation) of the play of "self-interest" in economic life, by the moral climate and legal framework engendered by men's mutual "sympathies" in the manner explained in the earlier work, is presupposed in the ideal-and-theory of economic life presented in the *Wealth of Nations*, though it is not discussed in the latter to any great extent. Some new evidence on this point, however, does appear directly in the *Wealth;* and I must discuss this and another related point about Smith's *economic liberalism* before taking up his economic *analysis*, or theory of the "nature" (definition) and the "causes" (conditions and process of free growth and diffusion) of national wealth.

Smith's great economic treatise contains *both* his "preaching" of his "gospel" of economic liberalism, i.e., economic freedom for all individuals, *and* his "scientific" theory or account (general description and explanation) of the operating processes of the economic systems of (national) societies, and the effects upon those processes and their results of the ways and degrees in which the societies do or/and do not accept and realize the liberal ideal in developing their institutions and public policies. And these two parts—the ethical-normative and the positive-scientific (descriptive-explanatory) parts—of the book's total message are partly interdependent or bound together, and yet are largely independent of each other. There is one—largely implicit, by no means fully explicit—"dual" structure of thought, in which the ideal or advocated regime is assumed as the (fully realized) setting, enabling the economic processes to work out on the best possible lines for the economic welfare of the society or all its members; and the explanatory theory, in this form or on these assumptions, is a demonstration of the beneficial results to be expected from the perfect liberal regime and the economic processes as they would be under it. But the main explicit structure of thought in the *Wealth of Nations* is descriptive-and-explanatory and quite "realistic," though moral-and-economic criticisms are added at various points to the account of facts. Smith *generally* did *not* assume that actual societies do or can or (at all probably) ever will fully realize his ideal regime, and he was more interested in understanding or explaining (and secondarily, judging) actual patterns of behavior and events than in working out a full sys-

[1] For the best summary and resolution of that German discussion in a scholarly work, which reaches a conclusion similar to my own, see W. Hasbach, *Untersuchungen über Adam Smith und die Entwicklung der politischen Ökonomie* (Leipzig: Dunker und Humboldt, 1891).

tematic theory of an unreal, ideal world. And he never, I think, allowed his vision of what "ought to be" to obscure, distort, or confuse his grasp of the current actualities which he sought to ascertain, describe, and explain.

His ethical-and-economic ideal vision of "the system of natural liberty" for all individuals seemed to him to be in a sense implicit or potential in the "nature" of the universe and of mankind, and to have much real power and a "tendency" to get itself *approximately* realized, through the working out of men's "natural" propensities and uses of their intelligence, experience, and growing knowledge, to adjust their conduct to the real conditions of attainment of their fullest welfare. But he had an excellent realistic awareness of the fallibility and endless foibles of mankind (including himself), and the permanent imperfection of all things human, and did not expect that the reforms which he advocated and believed to be "recommended by nature," would be *fully* carried out in practice, anywhere. Thus, for example, though he advocated international "free trade," he said with characteristic, resigned and good-humored, moderate pessimism—in this case not foreseeing what would happen in mid-nineteenth-century England—that it would be as foolish to expect Great Britain ever to "free" its foreign trade completely from any customs tariff against imports, as "to expect to see Lord Bacon's Atlantis established in these islands." [2]

The more nearly each nation or people could be persuaded to make its actual institutions, policies, and conduct conform to or realize the liberal ideal, the better its economy would function and develop, economically and ethically, for the welfare, in every sense, of all concerned. But no very near approach to perfection could be expected; and the main tasks would always be to advance knowledge and understanding of the ever-changing, current realities and real possibilities, to point out the defects of current practices and their results, and to work patiently for the small improvements which might be or become attainable. Still, when all is said, Smith's normative philosophy of economic liberalism remains as one important part or component of the total message of the *Wealth of Nations;* and a little more must be said about this philosophy before we turn to the book's contributions to economics as a "positive science."

ON THE HISTORICAL BACKGROUNDS OF ECONOMIC LIBERALISM

As conceived by Adam Smith, the liberal vision of the good, "free" society and economy had its grounds in both his economics and his ethics; or drew its support and its contents or meaning not only from his theory of the functioning, and conditions of best (economic) func-

[2] See *Wealth of Nations,* E. Cannan (ed.), 5th ed. (London: 1930), p. 435.

tioning, of the economic system, but also from his earlier-published theory of psychology-and-ethics. Freedom for all and justice among all would both conform to the "natural" moral law as grasped by all men with well-balanced sympathies, and enable the "natural" (spontaneous) processes of the economic system to work at their best for the growth of national wealth and its wide diffusion among all the people. However, a long-standing and very widespread misconception of the character and meaning of Smith's economic liberalism has arisen from (1) neglect and ignorance of its real, joint basis in his *ethics and* his economics, and (2) the tendency to confuse or fully identify it with the more modern, crude and loose, "free-enterprise" ideology of modern businessmen, which is in a measure historically indebted to it but is not the same or in full agreement with it.

During the nineteenth century the latter grew up as a class-interest-biased political "gospel," popular among businessmen and unpopular in other quarters; and it came to be supposed, widely but erroneously, that the same constellations of desires and opinions in the same or corresponding quarters had existed in Adam Smith's time and world, and that he had been an exponent of the views and desires of businessmen. But in fact Adam Smith, as he expressed himself in the *Wealth of Nations,* was consistently and most severely, morally critical of the businessmen of his time and their usual attitudes. He spoke in scolding terms of "the wretched spirit of greed and monopoly, so prevalent among our merchants and manufacturers." [3] He asserted that businessmen "in the same trade seldom meet together—but the conversation ends in a conspiracy against the public." [4] Further, about labor and wages he remarked that "everyone complains about the conspiracies among working men to obtain higher wages, but no one notices the fact that their employers are everywhere and always engaged in a tacit conspiracy to hold wages down." [5] And finally, his most favorable reference to any social "class" was that to "the country gentlemen of Great Britain, the class of men least infected with the wretched spirit of greed and monopoly." [6] Now I want to make several points about these passages.

In the first place, it is clear that "the wretched spirit of greed and monopoly," alleged by Smith to be too common in the businessmen of his time, *was not* what his theory of the processes of the tolerably liberal and well-working economy assumed and approved of as the "self-interest" which, under the institutions and conditions involved in the character of that system, would generally prompt each individual to actions

[3] See *op. cit.*, pp. 426–427.
[4] *Ibid.*, p. 130.
[5] *Ibid.*, pp. 68–69.
[6] *Ibid.*, p. 476.

that in fact (although without his foresight of this fact) would also have good results for the economic welfare of society at large. The kind of "self-interest" assumed in his theory of the well-working liberal economy was conceived as operating always (1) only within the limits of or allowed by a legal and moral code of justice to others; (2) under the regulative constraints or pressures of a universally, fully effective competition (absence of monopoly power in anyone's hands) which would make everyone dependent for his private gains on serving the public at least as well and cheaply as any of his numerous competitors would serve it; and (3) only in economic action responsive to market demands, *not* in political action, in concert with others sharing the same special interest, to win public favors at the expense of other rival groups.

In the second place, in reading Smith's censures on the group selfishness described as leading businessmen to "conspire against the public interest," or leading workingmen to conspire to raise wages and their employers to conspire to lower them, it is pertinent to recall the point made in the *Theory of the Moral Sentiments* about the narrow or exclusive sympathies, within but not among interest groups, which tend to develop and imbue such groups with diverse, distorted patterns of moral sentiments, partial to their special interests and in conflict with the general interest of society at large. And in the third place, Smith's expressed view that in his time and world "the wretched spirit of greed and monopoly" was *most* prevalent and intense among or in "merchants and manufacturers" and *least* so among or in "country gentlemen," is, I think, to be explained largely by the following important fact about that time and world. The public policies of mercantilism—the direct antithesis of Smith's economic liberalism—then had (still) their numerous beneficiaries and supporters mainly among the "merchants and manufacturers," and their opponents mainly in agrarian circles or among "country gentlemen." In the general argument that I am making here, this last point is particularly important and needs some further elaboration.

There is little doubt that Smith's knowledge of the desires and efforts of many businessmen to retain and increase the public favors—including restraints on their would-be competitors—which mercantilist policies conferred upon them, was the principal ground for his rebuke to their "wretched spirit of greed and monopoly"; or that his relative commendation of the "country gentlemen" had behind it his sense of their more frequent readiness to accept the policy program he was advocating, of freedom and justice for all and no special favors to any individuals or groups. But I must now refer briefly to the background of all this, and of later changes of conditions and attitudes in those different quarters after Smith's time, in the course of economic and political history.

Behind the vogue of mercantilism in the seventeenth and eighteenth centuries lay the fact that the early, still mainly commercial, or pre-industrial-revolution "capitalism" of that epoch was not yet so well developed, strong, and self-sufficient as to have, or want, much independence in relation to the national states and their central governments. It was not yet ready to be or become the *laissez-faire* "capitalism" of a later epoch; instead, within each country, it was being nurtured, assisted in many ways, and controlled and utilized by that country's government—with the hearty approval of the main (the favored) groups of businessmen concerned, who sought and welcomed state assistance to their enterprises and accepted the controls going with that assistance as a small price to pay for it. In that epoch indeed, the main over-all purpose of each country's government, in its efforts to stimulate and direct or guide the country's commerce and handicraft industries, was to foster growth of national wealth *mainly for the sake of* national diplomatic and military power and security. The main concern of each nation's policy was for growth of the relative wealth-and-power of the nation-state as such and as compared with rival, foreign nation-states; and not, as in the subsequent liberal era, for elevation of the absolute level of the wealth-and-welfare of the nation's people. But the leading businessmen of the time, or many of them, found their private interests in full harmony with the former interpretation of the public (national) interest, and very well served by the public policies which in fact were jointly inspired and shaped by that public purpose and their private interests. And behind all this there was another fundamental feature of the economic situation which must now be noticed.

Before the industrial revolution got under way, industrial technology and productivity were *almost* "static"—advancing only very slowly. The main potential sources of large new increments of wealth, both private and national, lay not in efforts simply to increase production, but rather in invention and use of stratagems to control or manipulate, to the advantage of a country and its merchants and producers and the disadvantage of their foreign rivals, the terms of exchange of their products for money, and of the money for other needed products and means of production. The world's economic life was a struggle among men and among nations to wrest from each other the largest possible shares of a nearly fixed total output; and each nation's government had to play a large, vital role, and use all its power and ingenuity, to subdue or compose the internal struggle and to help the nation's "traders" to win gains for it and themselves at the expense of foreign nations and their "traders." Each businessman tended to see growth of his private wealth as depending largely on growth of his country's national wealth. He viewed the latter as depending on success of the government's efforts, through various devices of policy, to stimulate expansion of domestic industries, commerce, and exports, and to limit imports; to maintain a favorable balance of foreign trade, and net inflow of "treasure" or the money metals; to keep within the country a large, growing, and actively circulating supply of money, i.e., a large and growing flow of spending and demand for all domestic products, ensuring fullest use of the country's manpower and productive resources; and to maintain at high levels, for the country's businessmen, both their selling prices and sales volumes, while holding down their costs for wages, interest, and raw materials, and thus enhancing their profits and accumulations of new capital.

Though there were some fallacies in this body of theory of the way to make a nation wealthy—the criticisms made by Adam Smith and the other liberal economists of his and a later time were not wholly wrong—there were in it also, in relation to the conditions of its own time, real insights and merits which the later liberal critics failed to recognize. But whatever its real relation to the purpose to increase national wealth, the mercantilist scheme of policy well suited the private interests of most leading businessmen of the epoch and had their allegiance. And to Adam Smith it all appeared to be a mere reflection of those private interests—of "the wretched spirit of greed and monopoly" in the benefited merchants and manufacturers—rationalized in the bad sense by a wholly fallacious body of theory, falsely purporting to prove it to be well conceived in the general interest of the nation as a whole.

Mercantilism, however, with its concentration on policies of aid to industry and commerce, tended to neglect and hamper agriculture, which was still the main or largest productive sector of every national economy, employing the greater part of its people and resources. Manufacturing (handicraft) industries were favored as leading to finished, high-value exports, and replacements for expensive imports; as most easily expansible in such a way as to aid attainment of domestic full employment; and with a view to retaining for domestic use most of the nation's output of food and raw materials, to keep these goods abundant within the country, and to keep down the cost of living and necessary wages of the working people (as costs to businessmen) and the costs of raw materials. All this, however, tended to have a detrimental effect on the prosperity of agriculture—especially in the eighteenth century.

In the last few decades just *before* the *industrial* revolution really got under way, there was a considerable growth, and some spread into actual use, of many new and sound ideas of more efficient and productive farming practices and methods. And this in turn led to a development, among enlightened country gentlemen, scientific farmers, and their friends in the ranks of "intellectuals," of two new attitudes or views. One of these was a sense of the either growing or impending need of one's country's agriculture for "free trade"—unhampered access for agricultural products to their best markets anywhere in the world, and unhampered access by all farmers to the world's best and cheapest sources of supply of seeds and plants, fertilizers, farming tools, etc.—and other public policies designed to encourage adoption and use throughout the nation's agriculture of the most productive farming practices. The other result was a whole new view of the best or true way to foster growth of national wealth in general: the view that every nation could do more to this end, in no conflict with the similar efforts of other nations, simply by encouraging its farmers to make their farms as productive as possible, than it could accomplish through all the policies designed merely to win marginal commercial gains, at the cost of, and against the counterefforts of, foreign nations. Production-mindedness as opposed to market-strategy-mindedness had its earliest growth in these agrarian circles, rather than in urban business (commercial and industrial) circles, because (at least visibly potential) productivity was rising faster in agriculture than it was, as yet, in manufacturing. And this production-mindedness was largely a new attitude of mind, which harmonized with the universally humane-liberal ethical outlook and the religious belief in an ultimate harmony of the real, best interests of all men and all nations—ideas which were becoming generally prevalent in this age of "enlightenment," though they were as yet less prevalent among businessmen than in most other quarters.

We have seen already in a previous chapter that the Physiocrats, who best illustrate all that I have been saying here, argued that a nation's agriculture is the *sole* source of *all* net growth of national wealth over time—the only branch of a national economy which can produce a surplus over necessary current consumption and upkeep costs—and that they built around this belief their entire (closely blended) system of economic theory and philosophy of economic liberalism for the benefit of agriculture and therefore of the nation. The Physiocrats did not stand alone; but I will cite here only one other exponent of agrarian-liberal-economic views—the American one, Thomas Jefferson. As is generally known, of course, Jefferson was a typical Enlightenment figure, acquainted with and influenced by the ideas of the Physiocrats but adding others of his own. He was himself a country gentleman and scientific farmer, and an advocate of a mainly agrarian-liberal democracy and *laissez-faire* economy; he had a moral aversion to urban businessmen and the public policies they then generally stood for, and a general dislike of industrial, commercial, and urban growth as, in his view, a menace to the moral and political health of society. It would be a gross error to suggest that the Physiocrats and Jefferson, or the Physiocrats and Smith, or Jefferson and Smith, were in complete agreement on all matters; but a glance at the main points of *partial* similarity of their views can help us to understand Smith's thought in the context of its time.

Neither the Physiocrats nor Smith shared Jefferson's belief and/or interest in political democracy; but in spite of this difference and its importance, they all shared the same basic, humane-liberal, ethical outlook, or impartially sympathetic concern for the ample and equal freedoms and rights and the welfare of all men, which is the main part of true liberal-democratic "idealism." And they all derived from this basic attitude their visions of a good economy or economic society; i.e., they conceived that society as a system in which all individuals would freely maximize their own economic welfares *by* maximizing their productive contributions to each other's welfares and their common welfare. Just laws governing their mutual dealings, and the economic "natural laws" of a competitive market mechanism, would ensure "automatic" responses and adjustments of the supplies of all goods and services to public (market) demands for them; and determination of their prices by their necessary costs of production by efficient methods; and determination of the incomes of all individuals by the competitive market values of the services which they or their properties performed for others.

And finally, in all three of these patterns of economic-liberal thought—the Physiocratic, the Jeffersonian, and the Smithian—one finds *more or less of* "agrarian bias"; though Adam Smith had much *less* of this bias than did the Physiocrats and/or Jefferson. Smith did *not* share the Physiocratic belief that only agricultural production contributes to the growth of national wealth by yielding a "surplus" over necessary current consumption and upkeep-costs; though he *did* say that in agriculture, "nature labors along with man," and that this accounts for the *special* "surplus" which appears as the rent of agricultural land.[7] His general view, however, was that the growth of national wealth arises from the increase of efficiency in *all* production, industrial as well as agricultural, which depends on the advance of "division of labor" or specializations on particular tasks, which in turn depends on the growth of wider markets and more adequate supplies of capital. Nor did Smith share Jefferson's emphatic fear of the moral and political effects of industrial and urban growth, or his belief that the civic virtues could flourish only in a mainly agrarian society; though he did regard the "country gentlemen" as morally superior to the "merchants and manufacturers" of his time and country, i.e., as having more of the liberal spirit and the production-mindedness going with that spirit in the economic sphere, or less of market-strategy-mindedness and the narrow-interest pressure-group spirit or "wretched spirit of greed and monopoly."

Adam Smith lived and wrote, however, rather unsuspectingly, on

[7] See *ibid.*, p. 343.

the eve of a great transformation of Great Britain's economy and of the circumstances and resulting attitudes of its agricultural landlords and urban businessmen. This transformation reversed or interchanged the roles of the landlords and businessmen, and caused Smith's successor, the next great British liberal economist, David Ricardo, to reverse Smith's judgments about them. With the advance of the country's industrial revolution, the leadership of and predominant weight in its business community passed from the merchants to the factory owners or industrial capitalists; and these newly risen, commonly self-made and very individualistic, self-reliant "captains of industry" generally tended to rely for their profits on their own abilities to win out in free competition in efficient production, and ask the government only to keep out of their way or let them alone in that endeavor. It was now the "country gentlemen" who needed and sought, and used their still great political power to gain and hold, special favor or assistance from the government, in the shape of an agricultural protective tariff, or "the Corn Laws," to shelter and shore up their declining sector of the national economy.

The rising efficiency and expansion of British manufacturing entailed a contraction of British agriculture. And the relative cheapening of agricultural production in, and of transportation from, other parts of the world, and the growing advantage for Britain of exchanging exports of manufactured products for imports of food and raw materials instead of producing the latter at home, were all working to enforce the contraction of the country's agriculture, by lowering the prices and profits obtained by its farmers and the rents they could pay to their landlords. The farmers and landlords sought *via* the Corn Laws, or protective import duties on food, to check or resist this "natural" readjustment. But the industrial capitalists—*and* Ricardo, Adam Smith's successor as the leading liberal economist—saw that effort to protect agricultural prices, profits, and rents (by making food scarce and dear) as increasing the cost of living for industrial workers (hence the wages their employers must pay them, and the cost of producing and difficulty of exporting manufactured goods), and so as retarding the country's "natural" and desirable economic progress. Thus between Adam Smith's time and Ricardo's day the situation had changed so completely that Ricardo's economic liberalism aligned him generally *with* the business and *against* the agrarian community. Yet Ricardo's economic liberalism was identical with Smith's; the change was not in the relatively impartial, consistent, and stable outlook of these liberal economists, but in the circumstances and resulting attitudes of those broad groups in the general population, whose "principles" varied with their situations and the dictates of their selfish interests.

The "conversion" of the nineteenth-century British business community to economic liberalism was due less to the influence of the teachings of the country's liberal economists than to the currently existing situation for its industrial capitalists which made those teachings acceptable to them, i.e., in accord with their self-interests as long as that was their situation. Soon after Ricardo's time, "the Manchester School" of leaders of economic and political opinion in that business community—Richard Cobden, John Bright, and company—really created and spread abroad the business-class ideology of liberalism, which embodied both their interpretation of Adam Smith's and Ricardo's teachings and their own ideas of the public policies that businessmen should favor as "best for business." Although in a sense this ideology in time became and long remained widely prevalent among businessmen in all countries, its extension beyond England into other countries, and beyond the middle portion of the nineteenth century into more recent times, has all been variously partial or qualified; i.e., it has been less complete, less self-consistent, and less nearly equivalent to the economic liberalism of the classical economists than was the original mid-nineteenth-century British version.

For as the industrial revolution occurred in other countries later than in England, and as its results everywhere went on developing, the effects on the interests and views of the local populations and successive generations of businessmen concerned were never again in all respects the same as in the original British case. "Free" international trade, which suited the self-interests of the pioneer British industrialists whom it did not expose to any foreign competition they could fear, did *not* suit the self-interests of their more belated and initially handicapped German, American, and other competitors when those came on the scene. Hence this vital tenet of the economic liberalism of the classical economists has by no means had the universal or enduring support of the world's businessmen. Nor has that other, even more central tenet of the true or classical economic liberalism, i.e., that every national economy should be and remain fully competitive throughout, or should be "free" from private-monopoly controls in or of any of its parts, had anything like the full, genuine support of all businessmen in any country since the arrival on the scene everywhere of modern "big business."

Moreover, in all recent times the business-class ideology, which often claims descent from and agreement with the classical economic liberalism, has become reoriented against new modern alternatives which are very unlike the mercantilism in opposition to which the latter was developed. Freedom *for* business as such *from* the public controls and burdens which become its lot in a democratic "welfare state" is not at all the same as the ideal of Adam Smith and all the other great liberal economists of the past; their ideal included *equal* freedom *for all* individuals *of access to all opportunities* (for gain through service) in the world, in contrast with any regime excluding multitudes from opportunities, for the benefit of favored, established enterprises regarded by the state as most helpful to growth of its own wealth-and-power vis-à-vis rival foreign states. The modern debate about the relative merits of "free enterprise," as conceived by our businessmen, and "the welfare state" raises or involves new modern issues which were never contemplated or conceived by Adam Smith and/or the other founders of the old or classical economic liberalism; and without new modifications of the latter it is hardly possible to derive from it wise and adequate solutions of these modern problems. But whatever position(s) on the problems of today may be implied in the old economic liberalism, certainly no such position is by any means wholly identical with that of our typical, present-day, conservative businessmen.

THE QUALITY OF SMITH'S ECONOMIC THEORY

We must now turn our attention, however, away from Smith's economic liberalism and related matters, to consideration of just his economics proper, as presented in the *Wealth of Nations*—that work's description and analysis of the "natural" growth and operation of a nation's economy or economic system, and its normally growing, annual output of national wealth. We shall not agree with either the once common excessive admiration of Smith's work in this field, or the severe adverse criticisms that have been directed against it by a few modern economists.[8] Smith's economic analysis was by no means, throughout, original or novel; much of its substance and/or equally good or even better solutions of many problems had been worked out and presented by earlier economists. All his work is pervaded by one general defect which annoys some modern critics, I think, excessively; but which does, I grant, deserve some adverse criticism, even though it is in a way "the price of," and is outweighed by, a connected merit of another kind.

Smith's scientific-theoretical work, as such, or economic *reasoning*, is everywhere a bit loose, vague, or fuzzy, or falls short of the very strict conceptual precision and logical rigor which later became, for many economic theorists, an all-important intellectual ideal. But precision and rigor are most easily and commonly achieved by clear but simple and narrow minds with very limited, inadequate knowledge and awareness of the infinite diversity and complexity of the real, empirical world, i.e., minds that can contentedly choose and strictly adhere to a few clear and simple abstract assumptions, rigorously develop or deduce

[8] See, e.g., the more critical than admiring treatment of Smith's economics in J. A. Schumpeter, *History of Economic Analysis* (New York: Oxford University Press, 1954).

their logical implications, and accept the resulting systematic theory as an *adequate* analysis and representation *of* a real social economy. For a mind with both a relatively very full knowledge and awareness of the rich content of reality, and a strong sense of the importance of truth-to-facts and not truth only about logical implications, it is always very difficult and often impossible to formulate or spell out all that is "felt" to be probably true about the real, empirical subject matter, in a fully precise and rigorous, logical theoretical system. Fuzzy reasoning is, of course, by no means necessarily or always a result or sign of its author's possession of abundant realistic knowledge and awareness; but as a rule any investigator-and-author who *does* attain such knowledge and awareness in unusual abundance is very likely to be unable, for that reason, to attain also the highest level or degree of precision and rigor in his theoretical system; and I think there is no doubt that this rule accounts for Adam Smith's case.

Good systematic theory in a science *should*, of course, have *both* attributes together in the highest attainable degrees—precision-and-rigor *and* "adequacy" to the entire rich mass of empirical subject matter. But a perfect combination of both qualities generally is unattainable in a science with a *very* complex subject matter; and I think the greater scientific excellence generally should be ascribed to works that excel in realistic "adequacy" but are (in consequence) somewhat deficient in the virtue of precision-and-rigor, rather than to those which excel in the latter but are correspondingly deficient in the former respect. On this view, the *Wealth of Nations* deserves to rank very high indeed in the entire list of general treatises in economics that have thus far been produced. Nor is its greatness very much diminished, in my view, by its lack of very great originality in one sense, i.e., by the fact that many, perhaps most, of the insights to be found in it on different particular problems had been attained and expressed before by earlier economists. Construction of a comprehensive, well-balanced, and coherent synthesis of previous contributions to the understanding of different parts of a subject can be a scientific achievement as difficult, admirable, and valuable as any other; and as a supreme achievement largely of this kind, the *Wealth of Nations* became and long remained the outstandingly rich source of suggestions for most of the subsequent development of economic science.

Unfortunately it is possible to consider here only the main points of the major chapters in the first two of the work's five "books." This means omitting entirely the parts concerned respectively with economic history—the historic "progress of opulence," through related developments in and of commerce, industry, and agriculture—international trade and economic relations, and public finance. Our attention must be confined to just the work's basic general structure of economic theory—of the definition or composition of a nation's annual income or output of wealth, and the fundamental causes or conditions of its growth through time; the work of the market system in the pricing of different products and allocation of the nation's productive labor and resources among different employments; the division of the national income into the class-incomes, wages, profits, and (land) rent; and the roles of money, credit, and capital in the operation of the national economy.

Any effort to summarize, interpret, and discuss Smith's treatments of these topics is hampered by the already-mentioned degree of fuzziness of his concepts, definitions, and explanatory theories. But we shall be able to grasp his main points clearly enough if we take care not to get lost in the details of a too meticulous search for entirely precise and consistent ideas and arguments, which are not there. A more serious and inevitable defect of the condensed account I am about to offer is that it cannot begin to convey the wealth of wisdom in the full text itself; the reader who wants to absorb what he can of that must himself read and study the *Wealth of Nations,* not what I say about it. The substance tends to be dry or dull, even as presented in full by Adam Smith, in his good literary style, with many touches of wit and humor, and shrewd comments or asides on human ways; and the "bare bones" to be served up here may seem *very* dry. But I hope at least to bring into view the main "skeleton" of the work's general theory of economic life—which still in a way is that of all modern economic theory. It will be necessary at some points to interrupt or complicate our step-by-step advance through the text, with side excursions into comparative discussions of Smith's more "antiquated" notions and the now more familiar concepts, which have replaced them in our current thinking; but the reader should try to follow, throughout, the entire, consecutive argument as such, and I will try to help him to do so.

THE NATIONAL OUTPUT AND CONDITIONS OF ITS GROWTH

Adam Smith's development of his theory of economics begins with his answer to his first question: what is the "nature"—i.e., the proper concept—of the real substance, composition, and amount of the "wealth" that a nation during any period is acquiring or achieving—the true determinant of its current degree of wealthiness or "opulence" (an eighteenth-century word often used by Smith); the word we would now use is, of course, "prosperity." And the answer is that this is the nation's current annual output or production of "the necessaries, comforts and conveniences of life"; which he also says is "the annual produce of the land and laboı of the people." [9] Now what these statements give us is a rudimentary, rough idea of what we now call "the national

[9] See *Wealth of Nations,* pp. 1, 4.

income," or rather, "gross national product"—in "real," not money, terms. But as compared with Smith's, the latter, modern concept has become far more elaborate and refined; for with the modern availability of statistical data and techniques, mostly not available in Smith's time, modern economists at least try to make comparative measurements of the total "real" incomes or outputs produced in successive years by many different national economies. And in order to do this as well as possible, they have had to go far beyond the point reached by Adam Smith, in elaborating and clarifying the concept itself.

Very little can be said here about these modern refinements, which will be discussed mainly in a chapter near the end of this book; but one or two points must be indicated now for the sake of full understanding of Adam Smith's own concept. The root of the difficulty of measuring—or rather, first, defining with full clarity, with a view to measuring—the variations, growths, and changes of annual national total outputs of "real" wealth is the fact that these total outputs are composite, heterogeneous collections of physical volumes of production of countless diverse kinds of goods or items. There can be no meaningful adding up of, e.g., given numbers of bushels of wheat, tons of iron, yards of cloth, etc.! It can make no sense to try to measure the absolute "total" output of goods of all kinds produced in a given year in a given nation; but we can try to determine how any two such composite outputs compare, i.e., how much larger or smaller than one the other is, by some such—at best rather arbitrary—criterion as the average percentage difference of the included outputs of all the separate single items included alike in both collections. But then there is another difficulty which usually dictates, after all, a different procedure. What we usually have the fullest available data about, or can best estimate and have to start with, are *not* the physical volumes of production of (all) the separate kinds of goods, but the total money-values, at the prices (of all the separate items) current in the countries and years concerned, of the total composite outputs—the national money-incomes, earned through production and sale of, and spent in consumption plus investment outlays for, all the goods produced. These money-value totals we *can* estimate as absolute amounts, for particular national economies and populations in particular years; the "sums" of the physical volumes of production of all the diverse items included is a meaningless notion, but money-value is a, and the only available, common denominator. But then—if we agree as we must with Adam Smith's basic idea, that "real" wealth or wealthiness means abundance of all useful goods, *not* of money—we must, in comparing the national incomes or outputs of any two nations or of any one of them in two different years, *correct* our total money-value figures by removing the part of the difference or change accounted for by the average percentage difference or change of the prices of units of the diverse goods included, so as to have left the part reflecting only the differences or changes of the actual physical volumes of production.

The modern statistical devices used in performing that last operation —"index numbers" of "price-level" changes—had not been invented in Adam Smith's time, but they and that use of them are in line with his ideas. For his concept of, and stress on, a nation's output or supply of "real" wealth—all the "necessaries, comforts, and conveniences of life"—involved his rejection, as fallacious, of the view that he imputed (with some unfairness) to earlier, mercantilist writers, that a nation is wealthy in proportion to the amount of its "treasure" or supply of money. If at a later as compared with an earlier time, the people of a nation are receiving, holding, and spending more money, but are paying correspondingly higher prices for the goods they buy—as they will be, if no larger supplies of the latter are available—then their greater "nominal" wealthiness in *money terms* will *not* make them really any more wealthy or better off. What really matters is not the supply of money but the supplies of goods being produced and made available to the people in the markets; and the growth of national wealth depends at bottom simply on the rise or advance of productivity—efficiency in producing, and distributing through the markets to the people, "the necessaries, comforts, and conveniences of life."

This was Adam Smith's first principle of economics and point of departure in his search for all its further principles. But before going on to the next steps in his analysis, we must linger a moment on his partial unfairness to, and too complete rejection of, the different ideas and approach of his mercantilist predecessors. Thus we may have in mind, in our further study of his scheme of theory, a true understanding of theirs, and be in a position to discover and appreciate both the (major) points of superiority of his analysis as compared with theirs and the (minor) points of inferiority that resulted from the bias against all their views which led him to reject their special, true insights along with their mistakes and shortcomings.

The mercantilist writers in general were not wholly "guilty," as Adam Smith thought they were, of the radical, simple error of confusing (identifying) a nation's "treasure" or supply of the money metals with its total "wealth." Nor did their (excessive) concern for protection and increase of the former arise only or entirely from their *tendencies* to fall into that confusion; to a considerable extent it had real grounds, of more than one kind, which cannot be simply condemned and dismissed. For one thing, it is relevant in this connection that, as I have said already, the economists of the mercantilist epoch and persuasion, in a measure of contrast with their "liberal" successors, thought of a nation's wealth *less* as the basis of the economic welfare of its population and *more* as the basis of its military power and preparedness for war. And in that epoch, a large internally owned stock of the money metals had much direct value as a "war chest," ensuring that the government would always be able at any time, whenever the need arose, to commandeer a sufficient amount of the internationally, i.e., universally acceptable, means of payment, and pay well for an ample number of foreign mercenary soldiers and ample quantities of military supplies obtainable anywhere in the world.

But beyond that point and of far more importance are the other points to be emphasized here. In some ways the best of the mercantilist economists actually surpassed Adam Smith and his followers, in degree of understanding of the complexity of the role or roles of money in a commercial economy, and the ways in which variations of the stock and flow of money in a nation can stimulate or depress all its economic activities and thus affect its output of "real" wealth or goods of all kinds. At least, as we shall see at the end of this book, the now widely accepted, modern, "Keynesian" view of these matters involves a partial rejection of the Smithian and "classical" view and a partial return to, or a new, more favorable interpretation of, the old mercantilist views which Smith and his followers entirely rejected. To discuss these questions of monetary theory at this point is to jump ahead to book 2 of the *Wealth of Nations,* where Smith presents his views upon them; but we need to do this, in order to evaluate the very first contention of his treatise—that a nation's wealthiness depends *only* on the quantities of goods it can produce and is *not* affected by the variations of its stock or supply and flow of money.

The "classical" theory of money, of Smith and his followers, went beyond the truth in laying down its basic tenet that money is *only* a "medium of exchange," i.e., a device to obviate direct barter or to greatly facilitate the exchanges of different particular goods for each other, which were thought of as the sole, final objective of all commerce. In other words, this theory of money insisted that money as such has no utility or economic significance of its own—is not in itself "wealth" at all, even in one form, or anything ever worth holding or keeping for any length of time, unexchanged for other things—but is only a symbol of and "ticket" for, or means of acquiring, other directly useful goods, which alone are "wealth." This strong contention is an overstatement; it denies the truth discerned, and perhaps overstressed in mercantilist, and now again in much modern thought, that money is not only a medium of exchange but also a "store of value" or generalized form of wealth, having not, like other specific goods, just a few limited, specific uses but (because it is always readily exchangeable for whatever else is wanted) in effect the complete range of all possible uses, of all forms of wealth. Therefore it *is* often worth accumulating and retaining (hoarding) for a time *as* money until the right opportunities occur to exchange it, to the greatest advantage, for other specific goods.

Moreover, the Smithian and classical view, in thus (too fully or radically) denying that money is in any degree "real wealth," also missed or failed to perceive or unduly minimized the important possible *effects of* expansions and contractions of the stock and flow of money in a national economy *upon* its actual outputs of all the specific goods thought of as making up its "real wealth." For the contention that money is useless until exchanged for other goods led to the unrealistic assumption that receivers of money will never tend to hoard it even temporarily, but will always promptly spend all they get, for either consumption or investment (producer's) goods. In this way, the circulation or flow of money through an economy will, according to this contention, be always continuous, uninterrupted, and (for each unit-period of time) a constant multiple of the amount or stock of money existing in it; and a national population's aggregate (consumption plus investment) spending, or demand for goods of all kinds, will always exactly equal the aggregate money-value, at appropriate prices, of all the goods that it can produce.

Then finally, *another* unrealistic assumption in this theory of money completed the basis of its "demonstration" of the total unimportance of a nation's supply of money for its level of "real wealth." This was the assumption—which would be true in the ideal liberal, competitive economy—that all prices are completely flexible, and always promptly adjust to whatever level is required to make the current flow of money, or demand for goods, just equal to the current flow of goods to market, times their current prices. Logically on these assumptions, then, Smith and his followers reasoned their way to conclusions which overminimized—perhaps almost as seriously as mercantilist thought had exaggerated—the importance of all monetary events and policies for, or in affecting, the "real" wealth or prosperity of nations; and which regarded the latter as depending essentially, not on developments in the sphere of money, but *only* on those affecting the levels of achievement of agricultural and industrial productivity, or power to produce in abundance all "the necessaries, comforts and conveniences of life." The new, emphatic distinction between a nation's monetary and "nominal" wealth ("treasure" plus other wealth measured or valued in the current money) and its "real" wealth was a great advance in economic analysis; but an advance that was marred and diminished, somewhat, by the too simple and extreme doctrines—overcorrections of the previous, opposite, mercantilist errors—in which it was clothed.

Let us now go on with Smith's discussion of "the causes" or determinants of a nation's annual output of "real" wealth. The first determinant of that, he says, is the proportion of the nation's labor force or working population which is employed in "productive labor," as compared with the remaining part employed in "unproductive labor."[10] Now here we encounter an idea or a group of ideas which played an important role in the structures of economic theory erected by Adam Smith and his immediate successors, but which *modern* economic theory has long since discarded. At the basis of the "classical" ideas of "productive" and "unproductive" labor lay what is now regarded as a too narrow "materialistic" idea of "wealth" as a category including *only salable, tangible, or material goods,* and *not* including any mere services from persons to other persons, which are not "embodied" in material goods. Workers producing material goods were regarded as "productive," and all those only rendering (other) services were regarded as "unproductive." There was no intention to stigmatize the work of the latter as socially useless, or less important, necessarily, than production of material goods; the idea was only to distinguish it from the latter. Thus the work of farmers, artisans, and factory workers, etc., was called "productive"; and the work of most government officials and employees, and many other people, was called "unproductive." Relying on these definitions, then, Smith was asserting tautologically that, other things being equal, the greater the percentage of its population engaging in "productive labor," the greater will be a nation's output of "wealth" (things). In passing, let us notice one of the practical bearings of this point of view; viz., it helped to lead Smith and his followers, in appraising public policies, to hold that for growth of national wealth, strict limitation of governmental spending and employment is important. Since by their definitions most of the latter was "unproductive," and entailed diversion of labor and resources from private uses in producing goods to public use in "producing" (rendering) services only, it would surely reduce the nation's output of goods. Let me pause to comment on this point of view and on the opposed modern view which has replaced it.

In the latter part of the nineteenth century, as we shall see in a later chapter, the early classical, narrow, materialistic idea of "wealth" as only material goods, was replaced in professional economic thought by the much broader idea of wealth as all items (goods or services) having any "utility" or power to satisfy any human "wants." "Wealth" came to mean *all* want-satisfying items of whatever kinds, material or immaterial, tangible or intangible, durable or ephemeral; and "productive" acts, to mean *all* acts that anyone would pay for. Moreover it was pointed out—already by John Stuart Mill—that *no* human "productive" activities ever increase the amount of "matter" in existence. The activities that are said to "produce" material goods only alter their forms and properties in ways that make them more useful as means of satisfying

[10] See *ibid.*, pp. 1, 313–315.

human wants; and so other activities—transporting goods to the places in which they are most useful, or storing and preserving them up to the times when they are most wanted, or contributing to want-satisfactions in whatever other ways—are "productive" in the same sense. All that can be increased is the flow of "utilities" or want-satisfactions enjoyed by consumers; and all that contributes in any way to this is "productive." In short, the late-nineteenth-century "utility economics" replaced the early, classical, narrow, *physical* ideas of "wealth" and "production," with all-embracing *psychological* ideas or concepts.

Now the logic behind the latter concepts is impeccable, and they are on the whole to be preferred, but the former still can be understood as making sense to some extent, in some connections. The modern view tends to broaden the idea of the economic sphere or part of life to the point of including within it much that—while indeed it all has its economic aspect—is mainly noneconomic. And the older view, for all its difficulties, had behind it the not entirely mistaken "common-sense" notion that it belongs to "economy" (as opposed to waste or extravagance) to give priority in the use of labor and resources to production of substantial, enduring wealth, and not divert them too freely or largely from that into production merely of ephemeral services or satisfactions. Especially in economically little-developed, still poor societies, inadequately supplied with the basic material goods that people need, it makes sense to regard any large relative expansion of purely "service" activities and expenditures as poor economy, which those societies can ill afford. But my main concern here is not to settle or decide these questions, but only to enable readers to understand the point of view of Adam Smith and his immediate successors. To them "wealth" meant material goods, and "productive labor" meant the part of the labor force employed in producing material goods; hence the more people thus employed, the greater their output of wealth could be.

And now we come to a second point in Smith's discussion of the conditions of a large national output of wealth. If most of the people are to be employed in productive labor, the nation must first have a large or adequate supply of capital—Smith's word is "stock"—previously produced but not yet consumed, rather saved and invested, or accumulated wealth. For Smith argued that while all "unproductive labor" is paid from or with its employers' "revenues" or disposable current incomes, expended by them on their personal consumption, all "productive labor" on the contrary is and must be paid from or with accumulated capital or "stock," to be replaced by reinvesting the profits from the sale of the productive labor's products. If a wealthy man has both a fine house in the country, staffed with a large force of domestic servants, and a factory or workshop in town where he employs a set of productive workers who turn out goods that he sells, then he pays his domestic servants out of his net income, i.e., their wages are a part of his outlay on his own consumption; but he pays his productive workers in his place of business out of the working capital used to run the business, and expects later to replace the capital so used, by saving and reinvesting the expected profits, or a substantial part of them. "Unproductive" labor, rendering services which are immediately, finally consumed or enjoyed, is paid directly with expenditures from people's incomes upon their consumption. But "productive" labor in the fields and workshops, producing goods which will become consumers' goods and be finally consumed only at various later times, and must in the meantime be carried as capital investments, must itself be paid for with or from capital investments. Thus only a nation in which much capital has been accumulated can employ its people mainly in productive labor, and have a large annual per capita output of new goods or wealth.[11]

We are here at the starting point of the long and obscure, historical development of the theory of capital and its formation and role in the economy, and will have to consider this subject further in future chapters. Just now we need only to emphasize the fact that all Adam Smith's points about the conditions of high national productivity lead back to this point—the need for abundant capital, and hence for conditions and policies favorable to saving, investment, and growth of the supply of capital.

Although this too will lead us back to that point in the end, we have next to notice Smith's *most* emphasized and famous condition of high national production, viz., a highly developed division of labor (of all "productive" labor) among many diverse, interdependent, specialized occupations. In the primitive, undeveloped economy of a self-sufficient household or small local community supplying all its own needs, everyone must be a "Jack of all trades" and cannot become very efficient or productive in any of them. But in a well-developed, large, complex, and efficient market-organized economy, the sum of the work to be done is divided up into a great many different kinds of work, each carried on by workers specializing entirely in it, and using their income from the sale of their output to the other groups, to buy what they need of the products of the other groups of specialists. And there tends to be, as Smith was aware, an endless, continuing evolution in this direction—growth of an ever more elaborate pattern of more and more finely divided labor or subdividing, multiplying specialties or occupations, with a consequent progressive rise of productivity or output per man-hour. Advancing specialization leads to advancing efficiency of the workers in each field, for the reasons discussed in Smith's famous passage—reduction of the variety of tasks to be learned and performed by each worker, saving of the time lost in shifting about among different tasks,

[11] See *ibid.*, p. 316, and book 2, chap. 3.

acquisition of more skill by continuous practice of the same few operations, etc. We need not review in detail his entire treatment of this topic; but we must note his general conclusion that advancing division of labor is *the main* cause of economic progress (rising productivity), and then examine some general features of his view of the matter.

It is unfortunate that the illustration he uses—the superior productivity of a pin factory he had observed, in which the making of a pin was divided into twenty different operations, each continually and solely performed by a different group of workers, over that of the simpler method of letting each worker make a whole pin—illustrates only one small facet of his whole, real, many-sided conception. Under "division of labor" he included not only this division of the work within one establishment, making one whole product, into different tasks for different groups of workers employed therein; but he also included all other parts of the division of the whole economy's work, among diverse, specializing industries, firms, and plants, and regions or localities, etc. And so he failed to make a really complete analysis of all the ways in which specialization, in all its forms, contributes to efficiency. Then as to why, in general, it does so, Smith paid little or no attention to the reason which many people think of first, viz., the variety of the native aptitudes of different people and the advantage of making each kind of work the exclusive specialty of those best fitted for it by their native gifts. For one of the beliefs prevalent in his epoch, which Smith shared, was the optimistic environmentalism which holds that in native endowments most men are substantially alike or equal—all potentially capable in all directions—and that most human differences result from differences of environmental influence, opportunity, education, and experience. The philosopher and the street cleaner, Smith asserted, differ mostly for the latter reasons only.[12] Thus his view of division of labor or specialization was that it increases everyone's efficiency, primarily by leading all to acquire higher skills through practice. And so the general concept meant to him, not a hierarchy of human types, abilities, activities, and social classes, but a society of equals, all highly productive in their diverse specialties, and living well by obtaining from each other ample supplies of all kinds of products, through multiple exchanges (sales and purchases) in their common market.

It remains to notice one further part of his explanation of the rise of productivity along with the rise of specialization. Smith lived at about the beginning of his country's first "industrial revolution"—the great outburst of mechanical inventions which heralded the end of the old system of handicrafts and ushered in, in their place, the modern age of factories equipped with power-driven machinery. And he tried to use his theory about division of labor to explain this newest industrial

[12] See *ibid.*, p. 17.

phenomenon of his time, also, suggesting that, as advancing specialization progressively isolates operations simple enough to be done by machines, intelligent workmen skilled in those operations see the possibilities and invent the required machines.[13] This idea, of course, though not devoid of truth, is far from being an adequate theory of the history of inventions. All in all, Adam Smith probably exaggerated the role of division of labor in economic history, in making its progress *the main* cause of all economic progress. But beyond doubt it has been very important indeed in all times both before and since the industrial revolution, though its interrelations with technological progress have been more complex, and the latter in our modern times has become far more important in itself, than Smith could realize.

According to Smith's theory, then, the productivity of a nation's economy depends mainly on how far division of labor or specialization has advanced within it. And he next went on to say that the advance of the latter depends in turn, in great part, on the *widening of markets;*[14] the first precondition for existence of finely divided or highly specialized labor is the presence or availability of markets large enough to absorb the large outputs which then can and must be produced. Until there is a large free-trade area, politically unified and free of internal customs barriers, having an efficient transportation system connecting all its parts, and well populated with consumers enjoying good incomes and living standards—in other words, so long as the products of each producing firm or unit can reach only a small, local, and poor market—it will not "pay" any such organization to have a work force of many diverse kinds of highly specialized and productive workers. Though its cost of production per unit of output would be much lower if it could thus produce and sell the resulting total output, it cannot sell enough to make this feasible. Growth of markets, then, and of the scale of production or sizes of producing units along with their markets, makes possible and tends to bring about the advance of division of labor or specialization, which raises productivity and lowers costs.

This principle, expressed by Adam Smith in the statement that the extent of division of labor depends on the extent of the market, was the "germ" of the economic "law" of decreasing unit-cost of production with increasing output, first fully expounded over a century later by Smith's late English successor, Alfred Marshall. And in the meantime, the idea or point involved played its part as one ingredient both in the "classical" argument (of Smith and his immediate successors) for international "free trade," and also in the seemingly opposed argument, advanced a bit later in other quarters, for tariff protection to "infant industries." "Free" international trade, by causing the trading coun-

[13] *Ibid.*, pp. 10–11.
[14] See *ibid.*, book 1, chap. 3.

tries, in developing their industries, to take full advantage of the possibilities of the best international or geographical division of labor—with each country specializing in producing, for all the countries together as one vast market, just those products which it is able to produce most efficiently—can as a rule raise productivity and lower costs in all the countries and industries concerned, and make all better off. But within any one (large) country, which in a given period of its history is just beginning to develop certain particular industries—in which it can become highly efficient in the long run, but which as "infant industries" within that country are at first unable to meet foreign competition because their as yet small markets and small-scale operations do not permit the best internal divisions of labor—it may well be true, and consistent with the "classical" argument just stated above, that a temporary protective tariff, by giving those national industries a monopoly of the entire national or internal market for the products concerned, can stimulate their growth and the evolution of more efficient methods in use within them, to the point of lowering their costs so far that they can become parts of an ideally efficient, international, free-trade economy.

Advancing productivity depends on advancing specialization, which depends *for one thing* on expanding markets. Let us return now to this line of Adam Smith's thought and follow him still farther along it. With his next point, he brings up again the need for growth of the supply of capital. High specialization requires not only a wide market; it requires also, he argues, abundant capital. Not only is capital needed in any case, as we have seen already, to employ and support or pay all "productive" labor; but, he now adds, *more* of it is needed for this purpose, per worker, the more advanced is the division of labor in the economy concerned. For one aspect of a (national) system of finely divided labor or highly specialized production is division of the total work of making each complete consumer's good into a long series of separated "stages," from production of the initial raw materials and tools required, through many different steps of processing and intervening acts of transportation, merchandising, etc., to the final delivery of the finished product from the retailer's shelf to the ultimate consumer; and with separate firms and their staffs of employees, specializing in the many different stages of the total process. Now in that long series of firms, from the one that provides the basic raw material to the retailer in contact with the final consumer, each firm must "advance" the wages it pays to its employees out of its working capital, and later replenish that from the proceeds of its sales of the still unfinished products to the next firm in the series. Only the last step—the final consumer's purchase of the finished product—is or can be "financed" with or from current income, as contrasted with previously accumulated capital; up to that point, there must be capital enough to finance everything, at every step. Growing division of labor or specialization lengthens the series of separate enterprises and groups of workers representing the successive stages of the production process; increases the average time-distance from performance of an act of productive labor to the receipt of the finished product by the final consumer; and hence increases the amount of capital required in the economy, relative to the number of its workers, to meet the needs for investments at all points in the lengthy process.[15]

In making this argument, Adam Smith anticipated a good deal of the much later and far more elaborate theory about capital and its role in the economy, which the late-nineteenth-century Austrian economist, Eugene Bohm-Bawerk, was to develop; and we may here postpone the question of the validity of this line of thought about capital, until we take up its later and fuller developments, including Bohm-Bawerk's. At the present point the reader should try only to understand as well as he can, but not to judge, this special thesis and supporting argument of Adam Smith's, to the effect that an economy can advance to higher levels of specialization and productivity only if it achieves, along with expanding markets, also a growth of its supply of capital, outstripping that of its labor force. We are back once more at his main, basic precondition for economic growth and development or progress: extensive saving, investment, and new capital formation by all the people who receive incomes large enough to enable them to contribute to this.

"VALUE" AND THE PRICE SYSTEM

Let us now go on, however, beyond Adam Smith's theory of the "real" national income or output as a whole, and the conditions of its growth, into the second and central, general part of his total system of economic theory—his theory of the functioning of the economy's market system, for "exchange" of the products of its different industries and occupations. This involves the causes and effects of the changing relative values and prices of those different products, the processes of adjustment of supplies to demands and of prices to their appropriate levels, and the work of the price system in allocating all units of labor, land, and capital into their most productive-and-demanded and most remunerative employments. Smith indeed did not make this one "central" part of all economic theory—just the "theory of value" and of the working of the market or price system—by any means as (relatively) large or predominant a part of his entire work, as many of his nineteenth-century successors were to make it, of *their* works. As we shall see later, it was Ricardo, not Smith, who established the tradi-

[15] See *ibid.*, pp. 258–260; book 2, "Introduction."

tion of conceiving "economic theory" as a narrow inquiry concerned with little more than just the "laws" which, in a competitive economy, "control" the prices of products and the division of the national income into the "shares" going respectively to the workers in wages, to the capitalists in interest and profits, and to the landlords in ground-rents. Adam Smith's first and main interest was not in these topics for their own sakes, but in the broad study of the aggregate national income or output as a whole, and the conditions of its growth—"the causes" or conditions of a generally efficient functioning and development of national economies, which would lead to high and rising levels of per capita production and wealth. But he saw in the progressively advancing division of labor, not only the main cause of rising productivity, but also a development inseparably conjoined with that of a system of markets, for "exchange" of the products of the different groups of specialized producers. And he was led to include in his work a substantial analysis of the "natural" functioning, and conditions of best functioning, of the system of markets and prices, as "natural" regulators of the allocation of all units of labor, land, and capital into their most productive-and-demanded uses or employments. It was in this part of his work, moreover, that his economic liberalism and his economic science were most fully united. The equal freedom for all men of access to and choice among all opportunities, and free competition among all, which his liberal conscience felt to be a moral imperative, was, in his economic analysis, the main condition for best economic functioning of the system of markets and prices. This condition he felt, would keep the pattern or balance of all uses of labor and resources and that of the resulting supplies of all products properly adjusted so as to maximize the national output and the satisfaction of the public's wants. Thus Adam Smith's theory of value, etc., is, though a small, an integral and central part of his whole, much broader theory of the best possible development and functioning of the economic systems of nations and the world. And we must now examine this part of his work with some care, for it sketches out in rough outline the whole body of theory or reasoned analysis which most of the nineteenth century's economists sought to develop and refine into their far more elaborate, detailed, precise, and rigorous systems.

In approaching the question of what underlies and determines the "value" of a good, Smith begins by distinguishing two different meanings of the word "value." One meaning is the good's value-in-use—what economists of a later time were to call utility—the good's degree of importance to its user, his degree of esteem for it, or its subjective value in his mind. And the other meaning is value-in-exchange—the good's "power to command" other goods in exchange in the market, or the quantities of other goods which other people are willing to offer in exchange for a unit-quantity of the good in question. And then Smith went on to say—mistakenly, as was later proved—that value-in-use has no regular correlation with value-in-exchange, and hence cannot be the foundation of the latter. To show this, he used as illustrations, water and diamonds. The former, he said, has a very high value-in-use—is among all commodities one of the most useful, even indispensable for the support of life—but usually, in most places, times, and circumstances, has little or no market value, or value-in-exchange; whereas diamonds, though they have only a trivial or insignificant value-in-use, always have a very high market or exchange value.[16]

As we shall see, it was to be or seem one of the "great discoveries" of a later time—although one that had been more or less fully anticipated by various acute but little known writers even during and before Smith's time—that this apparent "paradox of value" admits of a simple explanation which dissolves it. Water-in-general may be said to have immense utility or value-in-use, i.e., *some* water is a necessity for everyone, and wherever it is or becomes sufficiently scarce or in short supply, relative to the demand for it, it acquires a market price or value-in-exchange commensurate with the intensities of consumers' needs and wants for the quantities they lack and require. Water or anything else can be cheap or costless—have little or no market value or exchange value—only if it is available to everyone in amounts so nearly or fully sufficient that more than he has already will have little or no value-in-use for anyone, and therefore, little or no exchange value; and wherever this condition is satisfied, these results follow, for any good whatever. Diamonds may be judged in a general way to have little value-in-use; but the number available is less than the number rather keenly wanted by rich or well-off people who in fact esteem them highly enough, and are able and willing enough to pay well for "one more" in each case than they already have, so that each one on the market can be sold for a high price, which never exceeds its subjective value in the buyer's mind at the time of his purchase.

In short, the apparent discrepancies or disproportions between the exchange values of things and their use values (as estimated by their buyers) disappear as soon as we realize that the use-value estimates which count, or motivate the buyers, are not vague notions of the general utility of each *kind* of good under all conditions, but in every case —for each buyer and user of each good—the "marginal" or differential utility of the last additional unit which he chooses to buy at the good's current price. We shall see more fully in a later chapter, how the "founders" of the modern theory of value in economics thus correctly explained the determination of the market prices (exchange values) of goods by their available supplies and the utility estimates, desires, and

[16] See *ibid.*, p. 30.

demands of the potential buyers. But because Adam Smith and his immediate followers lacked or missed the essential clue to this relation, they mistakenly put aside the idea of value-in-use as not important for their purpose, i.e., *not* the basis of value-in-exchange. Hence they developed peculiar, one-sided (but not entirely erroneous) theories of the latter as "governed" only—under conditions of competitive production, which they generally assumed—either by the full "necessary" cost of production or by something in that sphere.

We shall soon need to ask why and how one special, major but not all-inclusive part or component of production cost—the "quantity of labor" or number of man-hours of work required to produce a thing—came to be singled out and regarded as "the fundamental" cause and determinant of the thing's value-in-exchange. But we are not yet quite ready to discuss this famous "labor theory of value"; for the common opinion that Adam Smith himself adopted or sponsored it is incorrect. As we shall see, he says explicitly that it could have been true only in and for a primitive economy (as he conceived that) in which there were only laborers, owning their ultrasimple means of production, exchanging their products with each other, and hence getting the whole benefit of all production, not having to "share" it with "landlords and capitalists." For the economy of his own time and country, in which he was mainly interested, Smith discarded "the labor theory of value" as not valid. Instead he regarded the "natural prices" of goods as determined by and equal to their complete costs of production per unit, i.e., the wages the (capitalist) producers must pay for the labor, plus the rent they must pay for use of the land, plus the profit they must earn on the capital, required per unit of output.

But we have still, first, to unravel Smith's long, complex, and in some parts confused, discussion of the whole subject of value, to see how he reached those conclusions and what they meant to him, and what other ideas he considered and accepted also or rejected, along the way.

After laying aside use value as not the basis of exchange value, but before proceeding further in the search for the basis of the latter, Smith first takes up the different question of *the true measure* of exchange value. In this connection he brings forward *a* "labor theory" which is *not,* however, *the* "labor theory" that I have been speaking of—of what *determines* exchange values—but is a different idea, to be distinguished from that. Not the labor-embodied determinant, but the labor-commanded measure of value, is alone in question at this point. Smith says that the amount of money a thing will "command" in the market, i.e., its market price in money, is only the "nominal price" of the thing and not its "real price." Here his meaning is that, since money itself is capriciously variable in its own value or buying power per unit, from one locality to another and one time to another, it is not a fixed or reliable yardstick or measuring rod with which to measure the values of things other than money. He sought for some thing having a constant or invariable value in itself, so that the numbers of units of this which other things would exchange for would *truly* measure or express *their* values; and he argued that the amount of men's labor which a thing will "command" or exchange for, is or affords this ideal, stable, or reliable measure of the thing's exchange value. What a good really signifies to its possessor (apart from its use value to him) is the amount of other men's labor it enables him to purchase or command. This is the "real price" of the good, in contrast with the often illusory or illusion-breeding "nominal price" in money. Then Smith offers, in support of this idea of the fixed value of labor-time "commanded," the very dubious argument that a given amount of "toil and trouble" undergone by a worker in performing labor, has a fixed or uniform subjective value in the minds or feelings of the worker himself.[17]

In the end, however, Smith gives up his labor-commanded measure of values as, though ideal in theory, not usable in practice, since there is no fund of homogeneous labor, divisible into a certain number of uniform or equal, objective units.[18] And then, still continuing his search for a less variable or elastic measuring rod than money, he turns to a more practical, second-best measuring rod, in the place of labor—"corn, the staple food of labor," which, he argues, and shows by an excursion into economic history and statistics, has among all commodities an exceptionally high relative stability of its own exchange value (for other goods generally). His theory to account for this long-run average stability of the value of grain, the great food staple, is a very interesting anticipation of the later Malthusian theory about food supplies and population growth. As Smith puts it, whenever food (grain) is temporarily plentiful and cheap, the large laboring class, the bulk of the population, is well off and develops a higher birth rate and lower death rate. Since the population grows faster than usual, the demand for grain grows fast and soon equals the supply at a higher price, and this raises the price of grain back up to its long-run average level. And conversely, whenever grain is scarce and costly, population growth is slowed and the demand for grain slackens relative to the normally growing supply, and allows the price to fall back to the average level. It is interesting and typical, too, that Smith not only presents this piece of theory but "backs it up" with empirical, i.e., historical-statistical evidence, chiefly about the relative stability, over a previous long period, of the corn-rents of farms, which he shows to have fluctuated and risen much less than their money-rents.[19] But finally,

[17] For the entire paragraph in the text above, see *ibid.*, book 1, chap. 5.

[18] *Ibid.*, p. 33.

[19] See *ibid.*, pp. 36–38.

after all this discussion, he really makes no use, in his general theory of exchange values and prices, of his corn-measure, any more than of his labor-commanded measure of values generally. He ends instead with a theory or explanation simply of the money-prices of competitively produced goods, as determined in the long run by their money-costs of production.

Still we are not ready for that, his final theory. Let us now examine in more detail his conception and theory of what he imagined as the primitive economy, in which different goods would exchange for each other in the ratios obtaining between the amounts of labor-time required to produce them. He supposes that two primitive hunters go into the forest in pursuit of game; one kills and brings back deer, and the other, beavers; and they exchange or barter deer for beavers and vice versa, with each other. If it generally requires an hour of hunting time to get one deer, but in the same length of time one can catch two beavers, then the "natural" exchange ratio between the two "products" is two beavers for one deer. For at any other ratio, all hunters would prefer to hunt only deer, or only beavers. The primitive economy is in equilibrium, i.e., the distribution of effort among its different activities is stable, only when the different products exchange on the terms that make the alternative employments equally remunerative.[20] The conception of a primitive economy in which all labor is perfectly mobile among all occupations, and every individual makes the choices or decisions required to maximize his gains, as they work and trade with each other in a competitive market—all this of course is historical nonsense; but as a methodological device or construct for "getting at" the simplest essential elements of the theoretical problem of exchange-equilibrium in a (modern) competitive market economy, the idea makes perfect sense and deserves high admiration.

Moreover, Adam Smith, unlike his successor Ricardo, fully recognized the great limitations of the classical "labor theory of value," arrived at as the result of that "mental experiment": that it would hold true *only under* the extremely simple conditions thus conceived or assumed. In Adam Smith's words—only in that primitive state which (he supposed) "preceded the appropriation of land and the accumulation of capital stock in private hands, when the laborers did not have to share [any of the value of output] with landlords and capitalists," could their respective products have, in equilibrium, exchange values or relative prices strictly proportioned to and simply determined by the relative amounts of labor-time, alone, "embodied" in them.[21] In any economy having all three classes of participants in production and in the proceeds from it, and having competition of all employments for

[20] See *ibid.*, p. 49.
[21] See *ibid.*, pp. 49–52.

land and for capital as well as for labor, the equilibrium set of the relative prices of the different products must just enable each industry —all the producers of each product—to attract and retain all needed labor, land, and capital by paying, from the total value of the total output of that product, wages *and* rents *and* profits as high as those obtainable by the recipients in or from any other industry. And it follows that, except in the possible, rare cases of production of two different products by enterprises using exactly the same proportions of labor, land, and capital, the equilibrium (full-cost) prices of the exchanging products never can be exactly proportional simply to the required input-quantities of labor alone.

We shall see in a later chapter, why and how Smith's able but (in this matter) misguided successor, Ricardo, strove to argue away or minimize the force of that demonstration of "the labor theory's" inapplicability to a complex economy, and to justify and reinstate that theory (with minor qualifications) in or for such application. We shall also see that Ricardo thus facilitated Karl Marx's different and still more untenable development and use of the same theory. But it is a gross, though a common, error to attribute either Ricardo's or Marx's "labor theory of value" to Adam Smith.

It may seem, indeed, that Smith anticipated or agreed with Marx and even went beyond Ricardo's position on *this* matter, *if* we take Smith's phrase about the laborers "having to share with the landlords and capitalists" to imply that the laborers alone *produce* all wealth or all of its "value" but get only a part of *their* output, the rest going to the landlords and capitalists. But I think this interpretation of Smith's phrase is unnecessary and unwarranted. He nowhere says that what the laborers "have to share" with the other classes is produced by the former alone; and I cannot reconcile the supposition that he meant this, *together with* the fact that his cool, passing use of this phrase gives no indication that he felt any moral indignation against the landlords and capitalists, with all or any of the evidence that we have about his character and moral attitudes. It seems to me more natural, and in keeping with the context, to understand him as meaning only that—in contrast with the situation in the simple, "primitive" society of his conception, containing only working people, who owned their simple means of production and received the entire output—the workers in the more "advanced" society and economy "have to share" *its* greater output; and this greater output is made possible by the economy's more advanced division of labor *and* division of functions (in production) between the laboring and the owning-and-managing classes.

It is true, however, that neither Smith nor his immediate successors fully, or altogether clearly, explained or analyzed the productive functions and contributions of the non-wage-earning classes, and the causes and/or ethical justifications of the "property" or non-wage incomes—rents and profits. At times they appeared to think of all production as performed or carried on *by* labor, as the sole *active* agent, only passively assisted by land and capital as inanimate material means of production owned by their employers. And Ricardo even, as we shall see, explicitly held the landlords (but not other capitalists) to be only the receivers of a "surplus" unearned by them. Their "rent" reflected, indeed, productive contributions by their lands but not by themselves; or it resulted only from the fertility and scarcity of good land, the control of the price of produce by the high "marginal" cost of production (including no rent) on the poorest land in use, society's need for the use of the better lands, and the ability of the legal owners thereof to charge "rents" equal to the values of their "surplus" outputs over that of the "marginal" land. This "rent" doctrine of Ricardo's may be viewed as another of his steps going part of the way toward the position of Marx, i.e., singling out and disparaging *one special* class of property owners as, if not "exploiters" of labor (and of urban capitalists), at least receivers of an "unearned" share of the national output. But Ricardo clearly did not regard in this same light, his nonlandlord "capitalist" friends, the saving-and-investing people who by or through that highly useful activity increased the economy's supply of capital and its productivity. He failed, however, to lay explicit stress on that as their productive function, and the cause and justification of their profit-income. And by regarding "real capital" or "capital goods," e.g., machinery as only "stored up labor"—the continuing "embodiment" of the past work of the wage earners who "made" the machinery—he once more opened a doorway for Marx.

In spite of all that, however, I think that Ricardo's "labor theory of value" as such meant only that, in a competitive economy in which the supplies of goods get adjusted to the demands for them, the relative prices or reciprocal exchange values of such goods tend to be or become (roughly) *proportional to* the amounts of labor-time directly and indirectly involved in their production; and these amounts of labor-time are the main, predominant ingredients and determinants of the total production costs which must be "covered." *This* proposition—the *proportionality* of relative values to relative labor-inputs in production—is consistent with the view that the profit-additions included with wage-costs in the absolute prices of all goods, which (if they are equal percentage additions) do not alter or affect relative prices or exchange values, are additions "earned" by the capitalists who get them through the productive service of saving-and-investing, and not subtractions from amounts of valuc thought of as created solely by labor. The different, Marxian proposition is that the "values" of goods are not merely proportional to, but equal to and indeed identical with, the amounts of labor-time "embodied" in them; and the frequent ascription of *this* notion to Ricardo and even to Adam Smith is, I think, preposterous.

It is easy to understand why many of the early, grossly incomplete, or but little-developed analyses of economic life saw mainly the large role of labor in creating most wealth, and the rough relations which must generally exist between the values of goods and the amounts of labor represented by them; and why they failed to see, and explain as clearly, the contributory roles or productive services of other groups, and the nonlabor elements of costs and values. But the disservice of Marx to the progress of analysis was even greater or worse than that of simply crystallizing and perpetuating—in the thinking of his followers—a primitive and inadequate theory of value. He exaggerated and distorted even that primitive theory—or vague tendency of much earlier thought—into an absolute dogma, explicitly and completely identifying all "values" with labor-quantity costs alone, and representing the class of wage-earning laborers (in "capitalist" societies) as the *sole* producers of all wealth. This representation was not even consistent with his own explicit and emphatic recognitions, at other points in his writings, of the great role of capital-accumulation by the "capitalist" class, in raising the economy's productivity to new, higher levels! And all this nonsense could have been avoided if Adam Smith's successors had fully understood and accepted his early proof that "the labor theory," even in the mild form in which Ricardo tried to reassert it, could not be valid except under the simple conditions which he thought had prevailed in and only in a prehistoric, primitive society.

We must now go on, however, beyond Adam Smith's initial discussions of the true measure and the foundations of value, to his final theory of the process which determines and is, in turn, affected by the actual prices of goods in the market place. Here we leave "the labor theory" behind us, and turn to Smith's theory of the process or processes which—in the liberal or free, competitive economy—are forever adjusting and readjusting the supplies of all goods to the (changing) demands for them, and their prices to the levels of their costs of production conceived as made up of the wages, profits, and rents which must be paid for the needed labor, capital, and land, for each unit of output.

This theory of the pricing process has two parts: the first explains the determination of current, temporary "market prices," and the second, that of the long-run equilibrium or "natural" prices, which are "norms" from which the actual, temporary "market prices" can depart but to or toward which they are in time brought back by the forces activated by their deviations. Now on the first topic—current actual prices at any time and the immediately underlying current demand-

and-supply situation—Smith's analysis was in one respect at least more advanced than that of his immediate successors. He saw, as they did not, that as a rule "the demand" for any good is not for any fixed amount of it regardless of the price charged, but is rather an array of many potential demands for different quantities, each ready to materialize at the appropriate price; and that in the same general demand situation, the quantity demanded may be expected to increase as the price falls, or decrease as it rises. In other words, he rather clearly anticipated the later modern idea that market demands are generally more or less elastic (reponsive to or variable with price) and can best be represented by appropriately shaped "demand curves." But instead of using exactly that language and device, Smith uses the term "the effectual demand" to designate the quantity demanded at the "natural" or cost price, and notes that less will be demanded at temporary prices above, and more at those below, that level.[22] If the supply on the market is small and only equals the amount demanded at a high price, the price will rise to that level, i.e., the sellers will charge all they can get and still sell all that is for sale; but if the supply is large and can all be sold only at a low price, the competition of the sellers to win sales will drive the price down to that lower level. All this is commonplace now and seems obvious but, although Smith saw and said it, his immediate successors missed the point and had a more primitive and muddled theory of demand, supply and market price, based on the false notion of demand as single-valued or quite inelastic.

But it was the second and main part of Smith's theory of the competitive price system's and economy's functioning—his theory of the long-run adjustments tending to bring about and maintain the "natural" pattern of employments of all labor, land, and capital, and outputs or supplies and prices of all products—which became and remained, with much further development, the great centerpiece of most subsequent economic theory, and the core of the demonstration of the great merits, for the common welfare, of the liberal or free and competitive economy. If the output of any product is temporarily too small, i.e., less than "the effectual demand" for it, and its price accordingly is high, above the "natural" or cost level, then either the wages, the profits, or the land-rents (or any two or all three of these) obtainable in this industry will be higher than in others. This will, in turn, attract or draw more of the needed factor or factors of production out of lower-paid employments into this one, until the output of this product has been increased sufficiently to bring its price down to the "natural" level. And conversely, if any product is being overproduced and its market price therefore is below the full cost-of-production level, there will be a movement of the adversely affected workers, capital, or/and land out of this

[22] See *ibid.*, pp. 58–59.

into other employments, until the output of the product shrinks and its price rises to the point of "natural" equilibrium with the rest of the economy.

This argument assumes the existence throughout the economy, of full and effective "mobility" of all factors of production, out of less and into the most remunerative industries, occupations, and locations; of universal absence of all and any publicly or privately created and maintained barriers or obstacles impeding such transfers; and of freedom and opportunity for everyone to leave his former field or line of activity if it ceases to reward him at the generally going rate, and to enter whatever field or line is offering the greatest rewards or attractions. And this assumption, or conception of a very free and flexible or fluid, self-adjusting system, of highly mobile and adaptable people and resources, all having access at all times to all opportunities and sure to respond to the most attractive ones, was and is the essence of the classical liberal ideal for every economy. It has never been a very realistic conceptual picture of any actual economy or, perhaps, of any really possible or attainable one, and Smith knew this very well, as all his discussions of facets of the problem show. But it was his central thesis that the more nearly this ideal is realized, the better the economy will function both in the private interests of all men severally and in their common or collective interest.

Smith's belief in the harmony of all private interests with the public interest, in or under his ideal system, was the belief which found expression in his famous or notorious, often misunderstood sentence about "the invisible hand" of Providence which works in, through, or behind that system where and in so far as it is realized. The key role in the system's processes of adjustment is played by the businessmen or capitalist employers of the other factors of production, who by transferring capital out of the less into the most profitable industries, bring about resulting transfers of labor and of land-uses. Hence the sentence in question refers especially to the public consequences of the private interests and decisions of those central figures, though it is understood that the workers and the landowners also act freely in their own best interests, and in so doing best serve the public interest. The idea is simply that, where nothing is monopolized, protected, or privileged but everything is open to the competition of all comers, and all the competition is to best serve the public and thus gain its patronage, the most remunerative activities and locations for and methods in them will be those best combining high physical productivity and responsiveness to urgent public wants and demands. And Smith, having shown this, was merely restating it in saying that thus the capitalist, though aiming only at his own profit, "is . . . led . . . by an invisible hand" to invest his capital where and so that it will make the largest contribution to the wealth (output or income) of the nation.[23] Under the right liberal institutions and public policies, conforming to the "natural" moral law of equal freedom for and justice among all men, the self-interest of each individual will be best served by, and will tend to produce, the decisions and actions which also best serve his fellows and community. The "guiding hand" *immediately* at work is that of the liberal institutions and public policies and the market mechanism as conditioned in its working by them. But behind all this, Smith's deistic piety saw at work "the guiding hand" of Providence, the ultimate "Author" of all those capacities and propensities of human nature which direct men toward formation, acceptance, and realization of the liberal ideal.

WAGES AND PROFITS

I have now sufficiently described Smith's theory of the national output or income as a whole, and the conditions of its greatest growth; as well as his theory of the "natural" processes of adjustment, in the liberal economy, of the supplies of particular products to the demands for them, and of their prices to the "natural" levels. It remains to describe, or say a little about, his theory of the "natural" division of the total national income from all activities into the wages of the workers, the profits of the capitalists, and the rent of the landlords; or the forces and processes which determine those shares or the relative general levels of those three kinds of incomes. But because this chapter is already long and this was the least well developed and satisfactory part of Smith's structure of theory, I shall only touch very briefly on a few of his main points about these matters, and chiefly about wages and profits; his theory of land-rents is so confused that there is little point in trying to discuss it.

Smith's theory of the prevailing levels of these factor-rewards throughout the economy is divided from his theory of the pricing (and supply adjustments) of particular products by the fact that the latter includes, as far as the factor-rewards (e.g., wages and profits) are concerned, only the idea that mobility and competition tend to bring about *the same* wage rate for each kind of labor, and *the same* (net average) rate of return on the invested capital, in all industries or parts of the economy. The outputs and prices of all products can be in equilibrium, i.e., the incentives for movement of more labor and/or capital out of some into other employments can be zero, only when the rewards or attractions offered by all employments have been equalized. How *the levels* are determined *at which* wage rates and profit rates tend to be equalized—the levels which, in equilibrium, prevail all over the economy—is the question now to be considered.

[23] See *ibid.*, p. 421.

But in jumping directly into this I am omitting—with reluctance—the part of Smith's discussion of wages and profits which deals with the persisting differences or inequalities that he saw as resulting, chiefly, from practices and deliberately maintained conditions, in the real world around him, that were *not* in accord with his liberal ideals. These were remnants of feudal and of mercantilist arrangements, monopoly-maintaining rules of local guilds or corporations of merchants and of craftsmen, provisions of the old Elizabethan Poor Law, etc., which prevented or impeded the free migrations and transfers of labor and capital out of old, declining into new, growing industries and localities, and which maintained high wage rates and profit rates in some parts of the economy at the cost of perpetuating abnormally low ones in other areas. And a reader can see, especially clearly in Smith's critical discussion of these practices and their results, the at once economic and ethical grounds of his liberal outlook. He condemned all ways of creating and maintaining inequalities of wealth and status by monopolizing opportunities for some and denying them to others—all "artificial" restraints on the free flow of men and resources into their most useful and gainful employments—as both (socially) uneconomic and unjust. Such restraints reduce the aggregate national wealth below what it would be if all workers and resources were used as productively as possible, and preserve exceptional gains for some through unjust restrictions of the opportunities of others.[24] But I must now go on to my final comments on Smith's theories of the causes of generally high or low wages or/and profits throughout a national economy.

In his theory of wages in that sense, Smith's main point is that their level in a country depends essentially upon whether its economy is advancing (growing), stationary, or declining; or to be more definite, upon the relation between its rate of economic growth and that of the growth of its population and supply of labor. If new capital is being formed and invested and in consequence the national output and demand for labor is growing, ahead of and no less than the growth of the available supply of labor, then a good level of real wages can be maintained. But if economic growth ends or slows down too much, the population and labor supply will tend to continue to grow until the competition of too many workers for too few jobs forces wages down to the low level of mere subsistence for the existing numbers, and checks further population growth. And in the worst case, of the retrograde or declining economy, the same kind of process will work toward "starvation" wages and an eventual corresponding shrinkage of its population. In this simple theory of wages there are implicit both of the two main ideas on the subject of Smith's immediate successors—their "wages-fund" doctrine of dependence of the demand for labor on the

[24] See *ibid.*, book 1, chap. 10, part 2.

supply of capital, and their (the Malthusian) theory of population growth as the long-run controller of the level of wages, through the supply of labor. But Smith was more optimistic or less pessimistic than Malthus and Ricardo; he envisioned as possible a rate of continuing economic growth sufficient to match population growth and maintain better-than-subsistence wages. And he put the whole matter in an especially fruitful and suggestive way by stressing the point that the condition of stable high, or good wages (maintained in spite of population growth) is a sufficient rate of growth of new investment, production, and employment.[25]

Smith (and also his immediate successors) used the word *profit* to refer to the entire net personal income of the owner-manager of a business enterprise, who invested in it his own capital (and often, also, some borrowed capital), and, in addition, actively directed the enterprise. But they thought of "profit" as mainly (though they recognized the presence of other elements in it) the owning capitalist's return on his own or equity capital—which modern economic theory calls "interest"—and always related the entire sum of "profit" in their sense to the amount of equity capital; i.e., they computed it as such-and-such a percentage return on the latter, or "rate" of profit. They used the word *interest* as applying *only* to interest on borrowed capital; and Smith as an observer of the world around him judged the usual average "rate of profit" to be "about double" the rate of interest on well-secured loans.[26] He further suggested that the difference was due mainly to the risks borne by the owner-manager but not by his creditors; and thus indicated, though he did not develop this thought, the presence in "profit" of a large element (in addition to the pure—in the modern sense—interest or return on the equity capital as such) of something one might call a risk, or uncertainty-premium, to compensate or induce investment of one's capital in the hazardous way, in one's own business, with no guarantee of any return on it or even against loss of the principal. Finally, a third recognized element of this composite income, "profit," was the owner-manager's "wages of superintendence" for his "labor" in directing the business. But Smith rather minimized the importance of this element, arguing that "profit" as a whole could not be *mainly* of this nature, because observation showed the *amount* of "profit" to vary generally, about proportionally, with the amount of (equity) capital invested; i.e., large and small enterprises (by that criterion) tended to earn about the same *rate* of profit, and the amount of work of superintendence required to run the business, Smith thought, did *not* vary in that same proportion—was not doubled when the capital was doubled.

[25] See *ibid.*, pp. 71–75.
[26] See *ibid.*, p. 99.

All this, of course, was a primitive or rudimentary, inadequately analyzed and developed concept of "profit," going little beyond the current every-day business usage and ideas in a world of mainly unincorporated personal proprietorship enterprises. The modern idea of "the entrepreneur" as performing a function distinct from that of the "capitalist" or saver-and-investor, and earning or receiving "pure profit" as a form of income distinct from interest or the return on capital as such, did not appear in the development of economic theory until much later (rather late in the nineteenth century). All the "classical" economists thought of most "capitalists" as active, "enterprising," owner-managers of firms, but as *mainly* performing in the economy the all-important function of accumulating and investing or providing capital; and thought of "profits" as in main essence the percentage returns on or from capital although as increased, beyond the rate of interest on secured loans obtained by idle capitalists, by additions of risk premia and of "wages of management."

Not only, however, were Smith's and his early successors' *concepts,* or uses and definitions of terms, in this field, unsatisfactory; their *theory* of "profit" or of what they mainly meant by the term—the return on, from, and to capital as such—was even more seriously deficient. It contained or offered little or no explanation of, or answer to, the question of why any such return exists; they had only a theory, or theories, to explain variations of the *rate,* by relating this to certain other variables, but not to explain or account for the phenomenon itself. And as I have noted before, this deficiency or lack, together with their tendencies to emphasize the role of "labor" in all production (including, of course, production of the capital goods in which the capitalists invest) and in the formation or determination of the values of all products, left the way open for Marx and others to "explain" all "profit" or return on capital as obtained only by "exploiting" (underpaying) labor—returning to the wage earners less than the value of *their* output. Yet it really is clear enough, at the same time, that Smith and his early followers regarded the saving-and-investing or capital-forming-and-providing service of the capitalists as a real and great productive service, involving much commendable and socially useful "parsimony" or self-denial in consumption. This service was indispensable, *in addition to* all the work of the laborers, to enable society as a whole not only to produce enough but to limit its consumption and direct its production, not excessively into that of luxuries to be consumed by the idle rich, but sufficiently also into that of wage-goods to support, and buildings, machines, and tools to equip, productive workers, i.e., a large net output of new, real capital for use in continuing, and efficient production. That continuing capital accumulation was, for Adam Smith, the basic condition of continuing growth of the national output, we have seen already; and this implies that the capitalists by accumulating and providing new capital, contribute to that growth of output and thus "earn" their profits. In fact, it may be that Smith (and his early followers) failed to develop a more explicit theory of the source of profits only because that answer seemed to them obvious and not in need of any further statement or elaboration.

On the question, finally, of what determines the rate of profit, Smith's theory, I think, reduces to this simple answer—the degree of scarcity or abundance of capital relative to the economy's need for it. He saw the rate as tending to decline with the progress of accumulation, or growth of the supply, of capital relative to the supply of labor. Population growth would increase the latter; but unless or until the capital supply increased sufficiently, there would be only a limited demand for labor, and a limited productivity of the labor employed. There would be, however, a high variability of that productivity with each small variation of the capital supply, and hence low wages and high profits. But if capital became really abundant, the keener competition among the capitalists, both for labor and to sell their outputs, would both raise wages and lower the prices to consumers of the final products, and thus in both ways reduce or lower the prevailing rate of profit.[27]

Smith did not explicitly develop or state, or perhaps grasp, the great principle or "law" of "diminishing returns"—decreasing additions to output by successive, equal additions to the supplies of labor and capital employed on the available, fixed supply of land—which Ricardo was to use to explain why the profit rate would fall in the course of economic growth and development. But Smith also held that the profit rate would fall, and his own explanation was not far short of agreement with or anticipation of Ricardo's. Moreover, in his passage about the different divisions of the total national outputs into wages, profits, and rents, in old, fully populated and developed and new, sparsely populated and capital-poor and underdeveloped countries—the Europe and North America of the late eighteenth century—Smith suggests a general view of the causes governing income-distribution which foreshadows not only Ricardo's theory of "the effects of progress" on that distribution but also, in a vague way, the much later "marginal productivity" theory of this whole subject.

As Smith noted, in the old world where population growth and capital accumulation had gone far in relation to the local supplies of land and natural resources, so that labor and capital were abundant but land was scarce, both wages and profits were rather low while land-rents were high and absorbed large parts of the national incomes; but in North America with its great abundance of good land, sparse population, and (then) small supply of capital, both wages and profits were high,

[27] See *ibid.*, pp. 89; 93–96.

while land-rents and values were as yet very low.[28] Implicit at least in these simple observations were (1) the prediction that future growth of population and capital relative to land in North America would in time bring about there an approach to the European pattern of income-distribution; and (2) discernment of the principle that in competitive economies the workers, capitalists, and landowners severally tend to receive incomes proportional to the values of their differential contributions, or those of their properties, to the total outputs of those economies—differential contributions which are high where the "factors of production" concerned are "scarce," and additional units of them are badly needed to enable production to be increased substantially, and which will decline if the "factors" concerned become more abundant as compared with others. I, of course, do not mean that Adam Smith fully anticipated or worked out this important insight of much later theorists; but in this discussion of wages, profits, and rents in old and new countries he came close to anticipating the main general substance of the modern analysis. As we have seen, he did this in nearly all parts of his economic theory. His analysis of national wealth, the conditions of its growth, and the development and functioning of national competitive business economies contained or implied at least the starting points for subsequent development of most of the insights that have since been achieved into most parts of this vast subject.

[28] See *ibid.*, p. 94.

CHAPTER 5

Benthamism

INTRODUCTORY

At this point in the unfolding of the story that we follow in this book as a whole, we must now again turn away from our recent preoccupation with economics to study a new development in the wider field of (general and social, moral, and) political philosophy; the development, namely, of the body of ideas known as "Benthamism" or "English Utilitarianism." This was an outgrowth from the eighteenth-century Enlightenment, which revised the earlier formulations and foundations of its "liberalism," and played a great role in the on-going development of civic thought and life or practice in the nineteenth century. It stood in a loose but significant relationship, which we shall need to examine, to the economics of Ricardo and his collaborators and disciples, which revised some parts of, and further developed, Adam Smith's economics. Adam Smith himself, as we have seen, was not only an economist but also a social and moral philosopher with a very wide vision and field of interests, though he was hardly, in the full sense of this term, a *political* philosopher. But some of his successors, and among them Ricardo especially, had a much narrower concern with economics only, and left to others the work of formulating and elaborating the basic general points of view and the more inclusive visions of the actual and the desirable patterns of all human life and affairs which, however, their structures of economic theory continued to presuppose, and require as supplements. Thus as Ricardo and Bentham were or became friends and, in a sense, intellectual collaborators, the latter's "broad" system of thought has to Ricardian economics a relationship somewhat similar to that of Adam Smith's psychology-and-ethics to *his* economics; though it made a difference that Ricardo and Bentham were two quite different individuals, while Adam Smith as an economist and a social-moral philosopher was in both roles one and the same man.

But the importance of Benthamism goes far beyond that of its loose relationship to Ricardian economics. It became the main or most important statement of the intellectual foundations of British democratic thought; the main British source, after Adam Smith's work, of the *laissez-faire* philosophy of economic policy (and yet also the main source of the later and seemingly opposite ideas of the British Fabian socialists); a great source of humanitarian, social-reform ideas and movements of many kinds in various fields; and a principal source of the entire outlook of the British Liberal party in its heyday. Also in the field of the law and legal studies—which was from the outset the central field of Bentham's own interests—his work and that of his disciple Austin came to exert a great influence, over a long period, upon the "legal science" taught in English and American law schools, and applied by the lawyers and judges trained by them. There was also a still more widespread, but less profound and lasting, influence of Benthamism as a whole, beyond the English-speaking world, upon much Continental European thought. Bentham's own intellectual antecedents lay very largely in a part of the eighteenth-century *French* Enlightenment (particularly in the writings of Helvetius, one of the Encyclopedists); and all his (Bentham's) voluminous writings were immediately translated into and published in French, and were for a time widely read and admired all over Europe.

The simplicity and crudity of Bentham's system of philosophy, psychology and ethics, jurisprudence, sociology, and political theory stand in a degree of contrast with the greater subtlety, refinement, and profundity of the best thought of earlier times in the same fields. His few and simple basic ideas were very ancient, but he stripped away and discarded many of the refinements, qualifications, and supplements that had usually accompanied them, and stated them in a new, bald or bare, and sweeping, direct, and forceful way, which made them and their corollaries seem all-sufficient for solving the problems of practical life. In a way Benthamism represented a culmination of the simplifying, superficializing trend of thought of much of the Enlightenment, and exactly suited the pragmatic temper and outlook characteristic of the long-rising and now dominant business and middle-class people, who demanded from their intellectual servitors and leaders more practicality and less depth than the older, aristocratic, ruling classes had accepted from *their* mentors. The idea that in business life, as such, intelligent pursuit by each individual of the greatest financial gain for himself could be made to harmonize with the greatest general growth of the wealth or prosperity of all men collectively, had long been an "axiom" of business-community thought and of much economic theory. And the essence of Benthamism was a wider generalization or extension of this idea, applying it not to economic life alone but to *all* life, and replacing the calculation of economic gains or benefits from contemplated actions, with attempted, broader calculations of all gains or benefits for human "happiness." There is truth in the jibe that was uttered by the German romantic philosopher, Schopenhauer: "The English Utilitarians talk about happiness, but they mean money."

The simple core of all Benthamism consisted of just this series of propositions: (1) all that human beings, universally, want from life can be summed up as the greatest obtainable amount of happiness, or sum of pleasures, and avoidance, as fully as possible, of unhappiness, pains, or displeasures; (2) the good or right or ideal conduct of life is simply its intelligent conduct, to maximize the pleasure and minimize the pain experienced in or from all the results of all one's actions, choices, or decisions; (3) the social problem is simply that of so arranging society's institutions and laws and the relations and interactions among its members, that for everyone the course of action most beneficial to himself will be always the one most beneficial to his fellows also, and deterrent penalties of self-injury will be attached to all courses injurious to others; and, finally, (4) all this can be achieved by creating and applying an exact science of ethics, jurisprudence, and politics, using as its master tool a (Bentham's) "felicific calculus," of the relative quantities of pleasure and pain to be expected as results of different private and public actions, and so of the pattern of all actions required to bring about "the greatest happiness of the greatest number."

It is worthwhile to glance back, however, at earlier pre-Benthamite forms of utilitarianism—the type of ethical theory identifying the moral "goodness" of actions with their "utility" for or in the production of human "happiness"—before taking up, in more detail, the special development given to this creed by Bentham and his followers. Most of the social thought of the Enlightenment had been more or less strongly tinctured by or with this general idea, though it usually had been combined or blended with the more absolutistic or less relativistic ethical "natural law" ideas which Bentham, as we shall see, professedly rejected. That is, there had been a prevailing faith that "The Wise Author" of all nature and human nature had so "designed" them that, by a planned coincidence, the intrinsically right or good actions, prescribed by the divine-and-natural moral law or code, would also always turn out to be the actions most "useful" in or through their results for the "happiness" of the actors and of society at large. So it eventually became a "natural" further step to drop the insistence on—independently and intuitively cognizable—intrinsic or absolute "right and wrong" or ethical "natural law," and accept the study, simply, of the results of all actions for the happiness of mankind, as sufficient to determine their degrees of "goodness" or "badness."

But about the earliest important form of or transition toward this new doctrine to develop in a part of English thought—before Bentham's time—was the "theological utilitarianism" of a number of eighteenth-century divines who taught that God had so perfectly arranged the rewards of pleasure and penalties of pain for the actor, which invariably follow all possible actions—in this life *or* in the next or afterlife—that the best behavior, most conducive to the happiness of one's fellows generally, is always and alone expedient for everyone in his own self-interest.[1] Other more secular, and political, philosophies could easily transform this, or develop independently on a line parallel with it, by putting the State in the place of God, i.e., by holding it to be not the already accomplished work of the latter but the task or function of the former, thus to so arrange deterrents and incentives—all fully effective within this world—as to lead each citizen, in best serving himself, to best serve society. It was this last development of the basic line of thought, first carried out in France by some of *les philosophes*—intellectuals contributing to the ideology of the French Revolution—which Bentham took over especially from his French forerunner within that group, Helvetius, and made his own and the basis of his system.[2] And with it, he also took from Helvetius (and the Enlightenment generally) an associated, still more general doctrine or conception that we have already noticed—that of the "mechanical" or "mechanistic" structure or pattern of all nature or existence including all human life, as a system of relations (scientific "natural laws") connecting all events, including all human experiences, thoughts, and actions, into one endless chain of causes and effects. It was a basic assumption of Bentham's thought that every man is a reasoning and happiness-seeking "machine," reacting to his stimuli on the lines required to maximize his happiness, and thus capable of being manipulated, by applied-scientific statecraft and legislation, so that he will always maximize both his own and his contributions to all mankind's happiness.

Let us now look for a moment, however, not at Bentham's intellectual antecedents and basic ideas, but rather at his odd personality, early situation and career, and first practical aims; since all these factors greatly affected what he did with the ideas that he absorbed and those of his own which he added to them. Jeremy Bentham was a queer, eccentric individual, who has seemed unattractive, even repulsive, to many students. Many word-portraits of him have been unfair caricatures, but he was in himself almost a caricature of "the intellectual" —generally overserious to the point of ridiculous solemnity, conceited, given to "pontificating" on all occasions, and to mistaking the simple

[1] See Ernest Albee, *A History of English Utilitarianism* (New York: The Macmillan Company, 1902), pp. xiii–xv and chap. 4.

[2] See Sir Leslie Stephen, *The English Utilitarians* (London: 1900); vol. 1, p. 177.

and plausible abstract, general theories which appealed to him, for all-important, universal, and eternal truths. Although his blood was purely English, his mind was in one sense or way peculiarly un-English, or at least had a bent which seems the opposite of that which is commonly imputed to "the English mind." The latter is generally said to have little use for abstract, general ideas and theories, even less for all-comprehensive, architectonic, logical systems of them, and least of all for attempts to formulate in this way, or make fully and clearly explicit, the most basic assumptions underlying all its views or convictions; it is said to prefer concrete experience to abstract theory, rough and flexible rules of thumb to precise and rigid principles or doctrines, and the test of results to that of logic.

Now in a way *the substance* of Benthamism *does* conform to that English recipe. Utilitarianism *is* the principle of having no (moral) principles except those found by experience, in actual situations, to lead in practice to the most "useful" results, i.e., the greatest (personal and) general "happiness." But *the intellectual method* employed by Bentham and his disciples to elaborate and support this point of view—by deducing a complete system of both theorems to explain all human behavior, and precepts to control it, from a few initial propositions held to be universally agreed upon and indisputable—was "un-English," and more in line with the main traditions of French and Continental European thought—if the usual generalizations about these matters have any validity. Bentham tried to give a logical and systematic intellectual formulation to the "common-sense" beliefs which he, and most or many other Englishmen of his time, held; and the resulting discrepancy or tension between the substance and the method of his thought makes it very difficult to achieve a fair description and evaluation of it. His "system" as a whole, I think, contains both a great deal of shrewd, good sense and a great deal of nonsense. The good sense resides in the intrinsically imprecise or vague elements of the "common-sense" substance, and the nonsense enters through the unwise effort to formulate them with entire precision. It was in the highest degree "useful" and salutary to admonish governments that the function of all laws and public policies is to be "useful" for or conducive to the general happiness or welfare of the governed. But it was in the highest degree chimerical, useless or futile, and in many indirect results mischievous, instead of salutary, to believe and propagate belief in the possibility of working out exact rules for maximizing a social sum of individual sums of happiness—rules that would do this and be the rules of an applied, *exact science* or scientific art of "social engineering."

Bentham's foible in that direction, however, was very prevalent in his generation, and his personal eccentricities and bent of mind only led him to carry it further than did most of his contemporaries. Born well back in the eighteenth century, and fully launched upon his career by its end, he became, however, the adored and highly influential leader of a band of able disciples only in his full maturity and old age, i.e., in the first three decades of the nineteenth century. Having some inherited wealth—enough to make him financially independent—he was a free-lance thinker, writer, and reformer with no other profession or connections. He devoted his life and abundant energies, from his early youth on, wholly to his self-conceived mission of discovering, and teaching and proving to all who would listen to him, the true principles of good-and-wise legislation and human conduct. Holding the law—the body of laws enforced in each state—to be terribly important as the mass of rules by or through which all men are governed, he made the study and reform of law, or legal systems, his first and continuing, central field of work; and developed the other parts of his total system of thought—his views in psychology, ethics, political theory, and political economy—as auxiliary parts either contributing to or supplementing his jurisprudence or philosophy of law.

He had, however, no use or respect for the professional body or guild of lawyers, and held their traditions of thought to be peculiarly stupid, irrational, rigid, unprogressive, and in general effect inhumane or barbarous. In particular, he despised the cherished character of English common law. The accumulation of all past judicial decisions, and their use as precedents to guide each new generation of judges in deciding similar disputes or cases, seemed to him to yield merely an unordered heap or hodgepodge of mutually conflicting and mostly antiquated, no longer relevant, implicit rules of law, which derived their authority from nothing better than mere blind tradition, and were peculiarly resistant to rational, progressive, and humane reform with the progress of "enlightenment." The law, he thought, ought to be a rational science or logical system of all the general rules or principles, and sanctions to ensure obedience to them, which are needed to direct all human conduct (or the part of it needing and properly subject to legal control) onto and along the paths conducive to the greatest general or universal happiness. And to make it that, or with that in view as the ideal goal, there must be a radical break with all mere tradition or old precedents, and a thorough, complete, systematic rational revision of all existing law, which then, as revised, should be codified. A bit later on in this chapter, I shall return to, and describe in somewhat more detail, some of Bentham's principal ideas about the character and basic elements of the ideal body of law or legal system. But at this point I must detour into the development of his political theory of the form or kind or system of government which would be required and able to produce, develop, maintain, and enforce his ideal system or code of law.

Understandably, in view of his conception of the latter, he at first—

in his youth, still within the eighteenth century—inclined toward the then widespread ideal of government by an "enlightened despot," who should as nearly as possible realize the ancient ideal of the perfect lawgiver. But it is very interesting to follow and understand the evolution of his political thought from that starting point to the extremely different position he finally arrived at, which made him and his disciples in early-nineteenth-century England the leading advocates of full-fledged, radical, political democracy. From first to last, his interest in political theory, as such, was subsidiary to his primary interest in the philosophy and reformation of the law; and what he sought to conceive and bring about was the form of government that would be, on the whole, best fitted to function as the agency that would in time remake all law into what it should be. He began with efforts to work through or upon the existing government of England as it stood in the late eighteenth century; i.e., he sought to "enlighten" a few leading members of the aristocratic governing group, or to convert them, through argument, to his ideas of the needed legal reforms, and perhaps, by making these powerful men his active disciples, he hoped gradually to transform the existing government, as far as this should prove necessary for the purpose, into one more nearly realizing the ideal of "enlightened despotism"—or "enlightened" oligarchy, which might serve as well. But he made no headway at all in these efforts to find or make converts within the ranks of the ruling noble lords, and soon became fully disillusioned with this program. And he came to see that on his own theories about the mainsprings of all actual human thinking and behavior, he had no logical ground for expecting anything else but the failure he had met with in this quarter.

Every man is necessarily directed in all his feelings, thoughts, and actions by his own self-interest—the (to him apparent) conditions of his own greatest happiness. Coincidence of the self-interest of each with the common interest of all—of the conditions of each one's own with those of universal happiness—does not by any means fully exist in existing societies, but has to be realized or brought into (complete) existence through all the requisite institutional reforms. In aristocratic states, the selfish interests of members of the ruling class in retaining their positions and privileges are in conflict with the interests of the main body of the people, and make them (the aristocrats) incapable of wanting, or of being led or persuaded to want, to support or aid any carrying out of the reforms that are needed in the interests or for the benefit of "the greatest number" of the people. If a government is to be expected to remake all law into what it should be, i.e., to make and administer all and only the laws required to advance the happiness of the people generally, then this must be a government so framed as to fully align the self-interest of each legislator and official *with* the interests or desires of the people or of the majority among them. And this means that it must be a political democracy, in which only the governors who best serve the governed can both gain and retain their powers.

It was by this line of reasoning that Bentham was led to advocate political democracy, and in consequence his theory or ideal conception of the latter was and remained the purely "mechanistic" vision of a self-equilibrating system of interest pressures operating on and through the government, and mechanically producing the legislation most strongly desired by the popular majority. There were some stipulations intended to ensure that the potencies and balance or resultant of the forces at work would be such as to produce that democratic outcome: there must be universal, equal suffrage—all adult citizens must have equal voting rights; all the legislators must represent equal constituencies, and need election and reelection by majorities of those voting on them; the representative legislature must have full control of the executive government and, indirectly at least, of the selection, powers, and conduct of all officials; and all the people as voters must, in time, be educated to the point of being able to vote in line with their true interests always, and be immune to the propagandas and pressures directed at them by interest pressure groups attempting to mislead them. The countless difficult problems not really solved by this crude theory of democracy are fairly obvious; but despite its rather utopian character and all its gross defects, the Benthamite conception of and program and argument for political democracy was on the whole an admirable and great achievement in and for its time.

It would be going too far afield here to go into detail about the actual, gradual growth or realization of political democracy in nineteenth-century England, and the part that was played in that process by the politically active members or adherents of the Benthamite circle. They of course were by no means the only, and perhaps were not the most influential, contributors to that development in the world of practice; but they supplied a good part of the intellectual leadership of the movement, and were far in advance of it in the sense of being very early advocates of the full-fledged democracy that was not achieved until a much later time. They supported and aided the first great step that was taken toward the goal, the passage of the Reform Bill of 1832, which made the House of Commons more representative of a larger fraction of the English people, but which went much less far than they wanted to go. And the later reforms which together gradually went the rest of the way owed something at least to the lingering aftereffects of their early writings, speeches, and agitations. In their early time their bold advocacy of a complete democracy, which was a frightening idea to most upper-class Englishmen, was perhaps *one* of the causes of the fact that, besides being called "the Utilitarians" and "the Benthamites," they were also called "the Philosophical Radicals."

They were "radicals," however, not only on that question but on *all* questions—though not in the sense in which we use the word *radical* today, meaning extreme, revolutionary, and often violent, but rather in the word's original and proper and then current sense, in which it was applied to all fully "rationalist" and antitraditionalist thinkers-and-reformers whose visions, analyses, and programs tried to deal especially with the "roots" of all human practices and institutions, and aimed at (though often only eventual and gradual) "root-and-branch" reform or reconstruction of society. Most or many of the quite early nineteenth-century "radicals" in English and European and all Western politics were in or from the middle or bourgeois, not the laboring, class and were "radical" or thoroughgoing individualists or libertarians, not socialists or collectivists like the people who are mainly thought of as "radicals" today; though there *were* some ("utopian" and other) socialists among the "radicals" of that early time, too—as we shall see later on in this book. There was in England in the time of the Benthamites a Radical party with that name which later coalesced with the older Whig party to form the Liberal party; and the Benthamites were "philosophical radicals," supplying much of the intellectual leadership of the Radical party, and a bit later, of the Liberal party. Political democracy was only one part, though it was an important part, of all that they stood for and worked for.

But I must now return to the logical starting point of intellectual Benthamism as a whole and, proceeding through it from that point, describe and discuss in a more detailed and systematic way—taking these up in a logical sequence—all the main divisions or parts of it as a body of doctrines in the fields of all the human, social, or moral "sciences"—psychology and ethics, the science and art of education, politics and jurisprudence, and (the strictly Benthamite, not the Ricardian) economics and political economy, or positive and normative theory of the economy and the role of the state and the law in relation to it.

THE SYSTEM OF DOCTRINES

"Nature has placed mankind under the governance of two sovereign masters, pain and pleasure. It is for them alone to point out what we ought to do, as well as to determine what we shall do." [3] That sentence, which opens one of Bentham's many books, his lengthy *Introduction to the Principles of Morals and Legislation,* succinctly states

[3] Jeremy Bentham, *An Introduction to the Principles of Morals and Legislation* (New York: Hafner Publishing Company, 1948), p. 1.

the twin propositions which formed the foundation of his whole edifice of thought. He believed that—together with their reasoning minds—men's impulses to seek pleasures and avoid pains are both the mainsprings of their actual behavior and their potential, true guides to all good behavior. And it is necessary at the outset to grasp clearly the distinction and the relation between the positive and the normative—the psychological and the ethical—part or member of this "pair" of doctrines. Men *do* seek to maximize their pleasures—satisfactions of their wants or desires—and minimize their pains—dissatisfactions or frustrations. But they generally accomplish this only very imperfectly because their knowledge (foreknowledge of the actual consequences of their choices for their later realized enjoyments and sufferings) is too limited and otherwise imperfect or mixed with illusions, superstitions, prejudices, etc.; because they use too little reflection and/or faulty reasoning; and because their societies are so badly organized that in striving, as individuals, to fulfill their own desires, they become involved in mutual conflicts and defeat or frustrate each other's efforts. The *goal* to be sought then—through universal education and social reconstruction—is a society of men who *will really,* always, make and carry out the right decisions, i.e., those really required, in the actual circumstances, to bring about the best possible results for their own *and* each other's happiness. The gap between what human behavior is and what it ought to be is attributed in Benthamism not to any "wrong" or "evil" basic human desires; the idea that there are any such desires is rejected as self-contradictory, for under Bentham's definitions "good" *means* simply "pleasant" which in turn simply means "desired," while "evil" means "painful" which means "undesired." Rather, the gap between actual and ideal behavior is attributed entirely to (1) the deficiencies of men's knowledge and reasoning (about the factual conditions of success in attaining their ends), and (2) the defects of their ill-organized societies, which often make injury or frustration of each other a condition of their fullest successes as individuals, instead of making the latter always dependent upon the best service to each other.

But I must still further stress a few points about Bentham's easily confusing uses of his basic terms, "pleasure" and "pain." He did *not* use these as they are often used, in the narrow sense of physical sensations (only) signifying satisfactions or nonsatisfactions of the bodily appetites (alone); instead he used them always in the broadest possible sense, of *all* experiences felt by the experiencers as pleasing or displeasing, i.e., as signifying fulfillments or nonfulfillments of *any* of their desires, of whatever kinds. Satisfactions and frustrations of intellectual, aesthetic, religious, moral, and all "high" aspirations were included *equally with* those of "base, animal" desires. Thus it is *not true* that Benthamism either assumed as prevalent in fact, or approved as ethically adequate, the kind of conduct which results from aiming only to satisfy the latter, or running toward "pleasures" and away from "pains" in the narrow and "low" sense. Instead the most devastating valid criticism of the creed's basic notions is that it defines those key words *so* broadly as to make its psychological and ethical "first principles" mere truisms or tautologies—assertions that include and agree with all the possible facts and views, and thus convey no information. To say that all desires are and should be desires for "pleasures" or ingredients of "happiness," *and* define these words as meaning the goals of all or any desires whatever, is to say only that men desire whatever they desire, and should desire whatever they should desire; to include all the possible answers in a blanket formula, and thus beg all the crucial questions.

The real significance, however, of this way of thinking is that it tries *to start out by* formulating a fully general or all-inclusive *approach to* the problems of human life or conduct, so that all of the particular facts, relations, and possibilities can then be examined with the aid of, and be fitted into, this conceptual framework. Also, Bentham aimed or hoped—the belief in this possibility was his great illusion—to make psychology and ethics quantitative, mathematical sciences by working out a method of measuring or weighing the relative strengths or intensities of all human desires and aversions and the relative magnitudes or degrees of importance of all satisfactions and dissatisfactions, and arriving at *formulas* that would specify the conditions of simultaneous attainment by all men of their "optimal" or best possible patterns of behavior, maximizing their (properly weighted) aggregates of achieved satisfaction of all their needs and wants, in their real situations. Actual behavior would then be explained as all the resulting actions, roughly tending toward those "optimal" sets of results that in the world as it is are too blindly aimed at. The extreme generality of Bentham's thought and its "quantifying" bent account for his refusal to accept any ranking of different kinds of desires and pleasures in a moral hierarchy, or any *qualitative* distinctions of that kind. It was his contention that the "lower" pleasures are so regarded only because common experience shows them to be, all things considered, the *smaller* pleasures; and that full, exact understanding of the entire spectrum could best be achieved by reducing all qualitative distinctions and gradations to quantitative ones. But further, he insisted that each individual must be his own judge in thus ordering and evaluating his own experiences; if anyone prefers pinochle to poetry—gets more pleasure from the former than from the latter—then the former is for him the "better."

And yet, finally, Bentham could thus think that he accepted all the desires existing in anyone as legitimate—or as deserving some degrees of satisfaction and capable of receiving them along with concurrent attainment of adequate or proper satisfactions of all the other desires of the same and all men—only because he in fact, although unconsciously, imputed value-judgments and desires like his own, and those of other decent contemporary Englishmen, to all men; he could not imagine all or many of the "hellish" desires and perverse "pleasures" which in fact are prevalent in this wicked world. This too explains why he thought that his really neutral or empty—purely general, nonspecific—basic theory of life as pursuit by all men of their "greatest happiness" or fullest satisfaction of their actual desires, was a theory leading with logical necessity to his fairly specific, liberal-democratic vision of the good society. What in fact led him to the latter was not the former but the set of more specific, implicit value-judgments which he read into and confused with it. What regime and set of public policies in a particular society will make "the greatest number" of its members "happiest" depends on the qualities of the desires that are most strong and prevalent among them. If those are of the right (or wrong) sort, they may be much more fully satisfied by or under a bellicose despotism than by or under a pacific liberal democracy. Bentham really assumed a universal nonexistence in mankind of any other desires than those which —however varied—are all potentially compatible with or adjustable to one another; or capable of being reconciled (to the point of foregoing any violent aggressiveness) to the only partial satisfactions consistent with as fair measures of satisfaction of all other existing desires. And this assumption helped him, also, to retain the age-old overconfidence in the power of the "reason" in all men to control or determine all their choices of means to their ends in their situations, or make all of their conduct in that sense fully "rational." His was indeed a far too simple, innocent "psychology" containing no real perception or suspicion of the wild dark jungle of the human passions, their frequent power to overwhelm weak "reason," and the stubborn irrationality of much human behavior.

I have not yet sufficiently spelled out and/or emphasized one vital difference between the first premise of Bentham's psychology and that of his ethics. His basic psychological principle was that of *egoistic* hedonism—that everyone's actual behavior is determined entirely by "self-interest" or the aim at *his own* "greatest happiness." And yet at the same time his basic ethical principle was that of *universalistic* hedonism—that the proper ethical goal is the greatest happiness *of all mankind*. It was *this* discrepancy between the positive and the normative side of this system of thought which made the concept and problem of "the harmony of interests" within society crucial and central for it. The individual members of society who were assumed to be inherently selfish could be expected or be led to behave generally in the ways most conducive to the common welfare of the entire society only if it could either be shown to be true, or be made true (by the requisite reforms), that all the self-interests are in harmony, i.e., that each in best serving himself will always also best serve all and *vice versa.* But the confused, equivocal sense in which the self-interest assumption really was made and used, is reflected in Bentham's statement about himself, that he was as selfish as all other men but so fortunately constituted that he found his own greatest happiness in doing his utmost to promote that of all mankind. In other words, even ideal "benevolence" or "altruism" is only a special form of "selfishness," since anyone who tries to help or benefit others does so because he wants to, and is acting to satisfy this want of his own or to increase his own happiness. This ambiguity is another result of the tautological way of equating pursuit of happiness or pleasures for one's self with that of satisfactions of whatever are one's desires or interests. And there is in this result a confusion of or between the two different relations of the self to (all or some of) its interests—as their subject and as their object. In other words, there is a confusion of the harmless truism that all actions necessarily result from interests of (felt by) the self, with the different, restrictive, and partly false proposition that all must result from interests solely *in* the self or in winning benefits for it alone. At the same time there probably was in Benthamism in this connection—among its more truly realistic insights—the insight, only somewhat exaggerated by or through the mistake just described, that in fact a great deal of "selfishness" in the everyday sense is a very prevalent and stubborn trait in (most) human beings. And yet while the creed was in one way overpessimistic on this point, it was overoptimistic, almost utopian, in its confidence that, in a properly organized society of properly educated people, the "self-interests" of all could be made to yield the same results (behavior) as would flow from perfect universal "altruism"—because there would then be a perfected and universally perceived harmony among all the "interests" at work as motive-forces. It is, then, the development of this last conception—exhaustively traced by the great French scholar, Élie Halévy, in his large work analyzing Benthamism, *The Growth of Philosophical Radicalism*[4]—which I must now, with some indebtedness to him but in my own way, summarily describe.

It is *not* true that Bentham *simply* carried on the common, naïvely optimistic, and vague eighteenth-century belief in the Providential "design" of, and resulting "harmony" throughout, the entire cosmic "system of nature" including (each) human society in its "natural" form and state. The tendency of Bentham's thought was more purely secular, anticlerical, agnostic, and pragmatic than metaphysical; and his notion was not that of a preestablished or inherent, universal, timeless, and perfect "harmony" of or among all the forces of "nature" in-

[4] Élie Halévy, *The Growth of Philosophical Radicalism,* Mary Morris (trans.) (New York: The Macmillan Company, 1928).

cluding all human, psychological, and social forces. Instead, his idea was that of a "harmony" of the "interests" of the members of any tolerably well-organized society, already *partly* and *imperfectly* in being, *and to be more fully achieved,* created, or perfected by deliberate reforms. The part of the optimism generated by the Enlightenment which Bentham fully shared was not its deistic faith in a wisely planned universe, but its faith inspired by advancing science, in the power of human "reason" to plan and reshape human societies so that all their members, in exchanging services, would best serve each other and themselves. There was even much more in Bentham's than, e.g., in Adam Smith's thought, of this notion of "rational" planning and reconstruction of societies, to *make* them more fully harmonious. But he did conceive as already existing, e.g., in the England of his time, *a partial or imperfect* harmony of the interests of the society's different members, factually based in their division of labor and resulting interdependence, which entailed for everyone an interest in performing services for others in order to obtain *their* services, and a general interest in earning and retaining the good will of others as a condition of his own well-being. To *perfect this* harmony, partly through improved and universal education of the people to make them all more fully aware of their true interests or to "enlighten" and socialize them, and partly through all the needed reforms of or in the society's political, legal, and economic system, became the great aim of Bentham and his followers.

To explain, now, the ideas involved in the *educational* aspect of that program, I must first turn to a further part of the group's (not primarily Bentham's own) work or thinking in the field of *psychology,* which I have not yet touched upon. The already explained and discussed "hedonism," or pleasure-pain theory of all behavior, was not by itself the whole of the Benthamite theory of psychology, though it was fundamental. The other, no less important, part of the whole—this was developed mostly by Bentham's great disciple and lieutenant James Mill, the father of John Stuart Mill—was a special, quite elaborate, and in its day and way an impressive development of "associationism" in psychological theory. It was an effort to analyze all mental life—the sequential formation, flow, and pattern, in every mind, of all its sensations, perceptions, memories, imaginings, concepts, reasonings, emotions, and volitions—as a process conforming to or exemplifying a set of scientific laws of the "associations" of or among particular experiences and mental states, whereby each one as it occurs suggests, evokes, or generates as immediate successors the others that have become "associated" with it. This general idea is very ancient and had a many-centuries-long history of limited, partial development by diverse writers; in the eighteenth century it was much more fully developed on somewhat differing lines by David Hartley, Condillac, and others. James Mill avowedly built upon Hartley's work, and produced, in his book *An Analysis of the Phenomena of the Human Mind,* a treatise which deserves to rank well among the historic classics of "scientific" psychological theory.[5] "Associationism" may perhaps be called the introspectionist forerunner of modern "behaviorism" in psychology; or the latter's central notion of "conditioned reflexes" may be called a physiological translation or equivalent of the former's notion of "associations." If for a time whenever you feed your dog you ring a bell, the dog will learn to expect and seek its food whenever it hears the bell; sensations which repeatedly occur together build up linked thoughts or responses—one becomes a "sign" of the other. And if all mental life and/or behavior is but a fabric of such formed linkages, then—as both these schools of psychological theorists have tended with similar optimism to conclude—almost any mind and character can be molded or developed into one having almost any set of abilities and "bents," by or through (from its infancy on) proper "conditioning" of the organism's "reflexes," or education to form the mind's association-patterns.

This then was James Mill's central idea in psychology and the theory of education that he based upon it. The minds, characters, and conduct of men as citizens are made what they are by the association-patterns formed in their streams of consciousness by their experiences and educations; and the task or function of education—in the broadest sense—is to so form these patterns, in the minds of all, that all will be model citizens.[6] And in combining this idea with the principle of "hedonism" which he shared with Bentham, he bridged the gap between the assumption of each man's innate, total selfishness—disposition to seek only pleasures for himself—and the ideal of conduct conducive to the greatest general happiness throughout society. His argument was that universal, proper, social experience and education, from birth through life, would cause everyone always to associate expectations of pleasure or pleasant consequences for himself exclusively with actions beneficial to his fellows—and painful consequences for himself with all actions injurious to them. Thus by what he called "the chemistry of the human mind," pure selfishness could become in effect pure altruism. Though men would remain at bottom simply seekers of pleasures for themselves, i.e., selfish pleasures would really remain their ultimate ends, their efforts to give pleasures to others would become (1) the sole means or routes used toward their final ends, hence (2) always their imme-

[5] See the good account of the scope of this work and its intellectual antecedents in J. S. Mill's Preface to his "new edition" of his father's book: James Mill, *An Analysis of the Phenomena of the Human Mind,* J. S. Mill (ed.) (London: Longmans Green & Co., Inc., 1869).

[6] *Ibid.*, vol. 2, chaps. 22–25.

diate or proximate ends, and even (3) their sole *conscious* aims, in all their conduct.[7]

Now to a considerable extent, in a rough, imperfect way, young children in existing societies already are "brought up" by parental discipline and that of group life and experience, in that manner and with that result. The crudely, directly selfish, animallike infant learns, as it grows up, that actions injurious to and punished or resented by others—elders or contemporaries—result in more pains than pleasures for itself, and that only all actions which benefit and please others and win approval and rewards from them, are in fact safe routes to its own happiness. And the mental "associations" thus formed, by oft-repeated experiences of what leads to what, become the components of the child's and young adult's character or "second nature." What is needed, then, to produce the good society made up entirely of good citizens, is simply a full, deliberate, scientific perfecting of the socializing or civilizing educations—personality-forming, complete, planned experience-patterns—given to all individuals from birth onward, to and into their adult lives. I will not use any of my limited space here to say more about Mill's or the Benthamite group's development and applications of this part of their scheme of thought—their philosophy of, and program to reform, all education. They did not in fact develop the idea very far beyond the starting point already sketched although it was an important and revealing part of their total system of ideas. I must return now to other parts of their thought which they did more with or made more out of, and above all and first, to Bentham's philosophy of and program to reform all law—the legal system of society.

In moving on to this, however, I am not moving as far away from the ideas in psychology and about education, just described, as might be thought. For Bentham's ideal legal system was to do, in its own sphere and way, more of the same work which James Mill's ideal educational system would do in *its* sphere of operation upon the young. That is, the right legal system would continue, for all adults, the same channeling of the pursuit by each of his own success and happiness, into best promotion of the common welfare of all, by (again) attaching deterrent penalties to antisocial behavior, and attractive rewards or incentives only to socially useful behavior; though in the main, as we shall see, the latter (rewards) were to be offered not directly by the law or the state but rather by or through the competitive market system operating *within* the right legal framework. In a sense the educational process alone was not fully trusted to endow the citizens as individuals with socially ideal characters (association-patterns) firm enough to remain intact even when or if continually exposed to adult experience-patterns of a contrary kind. The right association-patterns in the mental lives of

[7] *Ibid.*, vol. 2, chaps. 22–25 *passim.*

adult citizens must be *kept* intact by making the legal system one that would cause their experience-patterns to continue to conform to and reinforce them.

The best starting point, however, in considering Bentham's philosophy of law, the state, and the economy, is his rejection of the age-old and in his time (though already declining) still prevalent belief in a system of "natural" law, right, or justice and "natural rights" for all individuals; and the nature or presuppositions and bearings of his effort *to substitute for* that ethical-juristic "natural law" tradition, his own (as he thought) different and superior "principle of utility." He found—correctly enough—that the "natural law" idea had been and was being so diversely used and construed in different quarters that it must be regarded as, in itself, meaningless. Since everyone could give it any meaning he pleased, or appeal to it to sanction his own moral-and-political ideas, whatever their color, Bentham concluded that it should be universally discarded as a mass of empty jargon, a vehicle for all opinions, and a source of confusion. On the one hand the great eighteenth-century English, ultraconservative legal writer, Blackstone, in summarizing and eulogizing the body of English common law, had declared it to be, as it stood, a practically perfect embodiment or expression of the true principles of "natural" law, right, or justice. And at the other pole, some extremists among the supporters of the French Revolution had appealed to the principles of "natural law," as conceived by them, to sanction their really or virtually anarchistic ideas of "the rights of man" as nature-given rights of all individuals to absolute liberties not to be curbed by any state or other human authority. The "natural law" conception, then, was equally a cloak for the worst reactionary prejudices and for the worst anarchical fallacies.

All this is quite true as far as it goes; what must be questioned is the validity of Bentham's faith that his own "principle of utility"—setting up as the test of good law (legislation) its "utility" for or conduciveness to "the greatest happiness of the greatest number"—was itself really a determinate principle, free of such ambiguity. There is not only the obvious ambiguity of that carelessly worded phrase or formula with its two superlative terms, leaving unanswered the question *which* is really to be maximized, the number or percentage of (more or less) happy people, or the intensity of the happiness of those most largely benefited. Beyond and apart from that there is the more fundamental ambiguity arising from the fact that the specific desires, and constellations of them, of different human beings, differ endlessly, and hence so do their ideas of "happiness" or the word's meanings for them, and the conditions or requisites of fullest realization of their diverse and often incompatible kinds of "happiness." Bentham's belief in the possibility of creating and using a true, logical-and-empirical science of the real conditions of attainment of a maximal social aggregate of "happiness" or satisfactions of the needs and wants of the people generally, was his great delusion. Were such a science really possible, its achievement would, of course, give to the "utilitarian" test of "good" law and government—"utility" for the happiness of the governed—a clarity or fixity of meaning not to be found in the old, supposed test of agreement or conformity with "natural law" or ideal "justice" (as conceived by each person appealing to that imaginary standard). But since in fact Bentham's projected "science" of the laws required to best serve the people's "happiness" was an impossible figment and bound to remain that, his "new principle" was really as vulnerable as the "natural law" idea, to his own chief criticism of the latter.

Ambiguity, however, or openness to diverse and conflicting interpretations, is not necessarily so fatal a defect in a system of ethical, juridical, and political thought, as it is held to be by scorners of "all but" the kind of "exact science" which simply is not attainable in these fields. Any "philosophy" of this kind—asserting and arguing that such-and-such are the basic principles of "natural law," *or* conditions of best growth and prevalence of human happiness, or whatever—*may* be, in spite of all its inevitable intellectual defects, an achievement of very great intellectual, moral, and practical value, if it has both a good measure of internal logical consistency and much of the relative wisdom that is the fruit of mature reflection or meditation upon a wide range of relevant experience. Thus neither Bentham's criticism of the "natural law" tradition, nor the similar criticism which applies as truly to his own "utilitarian" philosophy, really justifies any complete or very severe condemnation of either one, or "settles" any appropriate question about its merits or about how they compare with those of the other. The "natural law" philosophy *in* its best developments before Bentham's time *in* the tradition of liberal thought which he in his way continued, had on the whole very much to commend it; and his own liberal development of his "utilitarian" philosophy was—to my mind—in some ways superior and in other ways inferior to the "natural rights" philosophy of his forerunners.

Nor were the two by any means so completely different in real substance as he thought they were; he did not really abandon the whole of the earlier "natural rights" philosophy so completely as he thought he did. The notion of a set of rules so directing men's conduct in their mutual dealings that they would fulfill the conditions of their own and each other's welfare or happiness, always had been a large, inherent part of the meaning of the notion of the code or system of "natural law." Some at least of the further elements that were *also* included in the liberal conception of that system—involving, e.g., notions of particular essentials of "true" human happiness or fulfillments of the "real needs" of "human nature," *and* an impartial, equal concern for the liberties, rights, opportunities, and happiness of *all* individuals—in fact remained implicit also in Bentham's thought, even though its explicit formulations appeared to exclude them. Thus for example, in laying down his dictum—quite unsupported by his basic formal principles—that in the computation of the social aggregate of happiness, every individual within the society was to count as one and only one unit, Bentham was simply in substance repeating that assertion of *the equality of the natural rights of all* individuals which was a very important tenet of the liberal "natural law" philosophy of Locke and others. On the whole, the differences between the older liberalism employing the language of the "natural law" tradition, and the new "utilitarian" liberalism, were only different distributions of emphasis among the several ideals contained in both. The utilitarian version shifted the main emphasis away from belief in individual liberty (for all men alike), as a final *end* or good in itself, to belief in the social utility or expediency of (much) liberty for all severally, as one of the main conditions of their greatest common or collective welfare or prosperity and happiness; and away from belief in a fixed set of liberties, decreed by "nature" and limiting the authority of the political state, to belief in an active, "rationally" or "scientifically" planning and managing state, which should grant and secure the proper liberties to all *and* act to realize and maintain *all* the conditions of their greatest welfare. And these alterations, though they strengthened liberalism as a creative and progressive force and helped it to develop a more adequate program, weakened the convictions underlying its most fundamental ideal—liberty for everyone—and opened a way toward utopian and potentially illiberal, authoritarian visions of an omnicompetent "welfare state."

We must now consider, however, some of Bentham's more specific ideas of the lines on which different parts of the body of English law, as it stood in his time, should be reformed to make them ideal instruments for causing men to act in the ways most conducive to their common welfare. The field in which he most fully and clearly developed his ideas, and in which his critical and reforming work and influence brought about much improvement, was that of criminal law. Bentham was an important contributor to the modern progress of scientific and humane criminology, criminal jurisprudence, and penology. English criminal law in his time was still full of survivals from more barbarous ages—useless, cruel, and excessive punishments for petty crimes and misdemeanors, and other provisions reflecting irrational popular emotional attitudes. Bentham insisted that the sole purpose of legal punishments for crimes should be, not to express or gratify the public's desires for revenge upon the criminals, but only to deter men from committing crimes by causing them to foresee as certain results for themselves, pains severe enough to outweigh all the pleasures they could hope to gain.[8] The prescribed punishments should not be any more severe than necessary to make them effective as deterrents; and, besides *enough* severity in the prescribed penalties, the other all-important requirement was invariable certainty and promptness of conviction and actual punishment. Bentham made those points and then went beyond them, using his hedonistic ethics and his "felicific calculus" to argue that the penalties for particular crimes should be scientifically calculated and adjusted to make them represent or threaten *the minimal, just sufficient* pains required for the deterrent purpose. For in themselves all pains are evil, as all pleasures are good; good = pleasant, and painful = evil. The sole purpose of the law should be to do all it can to increase the sum of the pleasures enjoyed and decrease the sum of the pains suffered in society as a whole by making it not pay any individual, in resulting pleasure for himself, to destroy the pleasures of his fellows or increase their pains; and the pains inflicted or threatened for this purpose must be the least severe ones capable of doing the job, if the over-all purpose is to be best served.

Criticism of that line of thought must be mitigated by recognition of the greatly useful work that Bentham accomplished by applying it thoughout his analysis and proposed reformation of all criminal law; but a good deal of criticism is still in order. His belief in the possibility of exact measurements and calculations of amounts of pleasure and pain added its fringe of fantasy to the sounder elements of his thought in this as in every field. And his belief in the possibility of making appropriate punishments for crimes always highly effective as deterrents, in the cases of all types of crimes and of potential criminals alike, was, of course, a result of the worst mistake in his theory of psychology: his assumption that all human behavior is essentially "rational," i.e., results from foresight and comparison of the pleasant and painful consequences for one's self, and therefore can be controlled by controlling those consequences.

But I must now bring into view the relative positions in his wider scheme of thought of his treatments of (1) criminal law, (2) one topic in the field of civil law—the institution and law of private property—and (3) political economy. In general, he envisaged a division of functions between the state and the economy. The state as the maker and enforcer of all law should *largely* confine itself to the negative part of the task of perfecting the harmony of private interests with the public interest, i.e., the task of defining, prohibiting, penalizing, and thus preventing all antisocial actions—making the actions that are contrary to the public interest also contrary to all private interests. And the other, positive part of the same general or total task—rewarding and

[8] Jeremy Bentham, *The Rationale of Punishment* (London: 1830), chap. 1.

thereby evoking socially useful actions by individuals—should in the main be performed by or rather through the competitive market system or economy. Let the state, through the law and the deterrent penalties for violations of its rules, make all deeds injurious to others unprofitable for the doers; and then let the people, as individuals, acting within the law and through the market system, reward each other for and thus elicit from each other all desired or useful services. Rewards and punishments—incentives and deterrents—represent the two ways of aligning men's self-interests with their common interest. Although the state is required for the work of developing and applying all the requisite deterrents—the task of attracting men and their resources into different lines of socially useful work, with incentives properly adjusted to the public's demands for different kinds of work and the abilities and alternative opportunities for the doers of them, can (in the main) be done far better through a competitive market economy operating within the framework of the law.

I shall return in a moment to Bentham's argument in support of that *laissez-faire* thesis, as presented in his *Manual of Political Economy*, a small work or essay also published (in French by the translator Dumont) as Part Four of another work of Bentham's, *The Rationale of Reward.*[9] But punishing and thus preventing crimes is not, he recognized, the only work which the state must do. There must be, besides the body of criminal law, also a body of civil law including the law of property and contract, which enables men to carry on their businesses and dealings and to know what belongs to whom, and on what conditions their promises to and claims on each other will be valid and binding. Bentham's ideal economy required a system of private property rights as its legal foundation; and his view of the ground of moral justification of private property rights must now be considered before we go on to further consideration of his views in economics.

Property rights, of course, were not for Bentham "natural rights," for he repudiated that conception. Like all rights in his system, they were purely state-created legal rights, to be justified, if at all, only on the ground of their social utility or expediency—conduciveness on the whole, through the sum of their consequences, to "the greatest happiness of the greatest number" of the people. And he recognized, at the outset of his discussion of private property, a set of *unfavorable* consequences arguing, as far as they go, *against* the institution. It results in a society having a highly uneven distribution of wealth and income—containing a few very rich, more only moderately rich, and many poor

[9] Jeremy Bentham, *The Rationale of Reward* (London: 1830). In this edition—a retranslation from the French edition of all Bentham's works by the French translator Dumont—part 4 was added by Dumont from an originally separate essay by Bentham, called *A Manual of Political Economy.*

people. And Bentham's "felicific calculus" included or led him to an anticipation of one part of the later "utility economics"—the principle of the "diminishing utility" to anyone of further additions to his wealth, beyond the amount required to satisfy his most urgent needs and wants. Public measures, then, to confiscate and redistribute wealth or lessen economic inequality—transfer income from the rich to the poor—would in the first instance increase the social aggregate of happiness, want-satisfactions, or economic welfare, by taking from the rich only trivial satisfactions and giving important new ones to the poor. Bentham granted the validity of this argument within its own terms or field of reference, but held it to be outweighed by a counterargument concerned with other considerations. A private-property system, by making everyone "secure" in the knowledge that he himself would own and enjoy the fruits of his own productive efforts and achievements, would set up strong incentives causing all to strive to maximize their own productive contributions. And the probable result, in Bentham's judgment, would be a national output of wealth, to be distributed, so much larger than could be obtained otherwise that, despite unequal distribution, even the poor would be (in the long run) richer or less poor than they would come to be under any regime *not* providing the strong incentives to full productive effort by all, which only a private-property system could provide. Thus Bentham originated both the main argument that has ever since been used by socialists and egalitarian reformers of all kinds, *and* the main counterargument used by defenders of the system of property rights at the basis of pure "capitalism," in the debate as to which kind of regime offers the greater promise of leading toward abolition of poverty. And it was typical of Bentham's thought thus to state the grounds of both views, *and* decide between them only on the basis of a judgment about probabilities to be verified or not by subsequent experience.

In Bentham's over-all conception, then, of the well-arranged and hence well-functioning society and economy, the state through the law would do two things (mainly) to enable the economy to function on the lines determined by a full harmony of all men's self-interests with their common interest. The state, through the criminal law, would close (make actually disadvantageous for all individuals) all roads (which would otherwise be such) to private gains through acts injurious to others or the public, thus leaving open as roads to private gains only all types of services to others. And through the law of property, the state would further tie all private gains to public services by making whatever others (the market) would pay for the productive services of each individual and/or of his possessions, the source and measure of his income. The remaining work (in perfecting the harmony of interests), would be to so adjust the relative magnitudes of the rewards or incentives for different services—contributions to the outputs or supplies of different goods or products—as to lead all severally, in choosing the activities and courses most advantageous for themselves, to choose those most beneficial to the public, *i.e.,* most productive of things most in demand; and *this* could be done best by or through the automatic working of the competitive market or price system, operating under the general conditions thus created by the state through its legal system. This view of the proper functions of the state, and the functions capable of being *better* performed by a market system "free" from state "interference" in its sphere, was what the counsel of *laissez faire* as to economic policy meant, as a part of Benthamism. And Bentham presented his general argument for this position most clearly and fully in the tract already mentioned above—his *Manual of Political Economy,* also appearing as Part Four of *The Rationale of Reward.*

The Rationale of Reward, apart from that added fourth part, deals with the "principles" to be observed by governments in acting directly to reward and encourage—e.g., contributions to science and inventions —socially useful private achievements not sure to be adequately in demand in the markets. But our main interest here is in the argument of Part Four or the *Manual,* directed against state subsidies, loans, and aids to favored industries and enterprises, restrictive regulations of those *not* favored by the government in power, protective tariffs, and all devices to make the pattern or balance of production of different goods and services—the allocation of society's manpower and resources among various activities—different from that which the "free" automatic operation of the market or price system would bring about. And the essence of this argument is very simple: that the judgments of public authorities as to which activities should be especially rewarded and encouraged, and what the pattern of relative rewards should be to bring about the socially most useful pattern of activities, cannot be as fully informed, impartial, and accurate as the set of judgments (reflecting those of all the people as consumers) which are formed and registered and made effective in the markets and through the price system.

BENTHAMISM AND ECONOMICS

I regret that I cannot take up in this chapter any of Bentham's other contributions, in other writings, to economics. He made in all a good many substantial ones, and was in his own right an economist of no mean abilities and achievements. His main historic importance, however, is based on his work and intellectual output in other fields already surveyed here; and for all its interest, his work in economics had and has far *less* importance than that of Ricardo, who became *the* great authority on economics in and for the circles or receptive public made up of both his own and Bentham's followers. The two men were not by any means in complete agreement on all questions in the field of economics; but they seem never to have discussed their points of disagreement, or even paid much attention to each other's writings or opinions in this field. Since Bentham was mainly absorbed in developing his whole, broader system of thought, he left the expressions of his views in economics—a minor part of the total field of his interests—so scattered about in various parts of his writings, generally concerned more or as much with other subjects, that they may scarcely have come to the attention of Ricardo, whose interests were concentrated in economics only. Ricardo's prestige and influence in all economic discussions, throughout the overlapping circles that were his *and* Bentham's, became so great that on economic questions Bentham's views, when they differed from Ricardo's, got little attention; and apparently Bentham himself hardly ventured to argue with Ricardo. In any case, their differences on various special points or questions, though numerous and often significant, were minor as compared with their broad general agreement, as advocates and theorists of a liberal competitive economy and as at once admiring and critical students of Adam Smith's *Wealth of Nations*. There remains a problem, however, as to why Bentham did *not* develop the fundamentally different, un-Ricardian theory of value and of all economics, which was logically implied in his pleasure-pain psychology and "felicific calculus," and was to be developed at a later time by the economists who reconstructed their science on the basis of their "utility" concepts. I must say a few words about this problem, before ending this chapter with my final remarks about Benthamism as a whole.

If the view which has been expressed by various writers is accepted, that Bentham's conception of all human behavior as pleasure-maximizing is the both logical and historical source of the conception (in all economic theories built around this) of economic behavior as gain-maximizing, then it is very difficult to understand Ricardo's, and of course still more Bentham's own, failure to work out the fully and directly hedonistic theory of economic behavior in the same kind of thorough, detailed, and systematic way in which that was done later by the more modern "utility" economists. But in fact the assumption that economic, i.e., business, behavior is or tends to be gain-maximizing, which had been the familiar, accepted, matter-of-course assumption in most economic theory for centuries before Bentham's time, had its original roots, beyond question I think, not in the hedonistic or any formal psychology, but simply in the common experience of businessmen and observations of their doings by economists, to the effect that business activities are carried on "to make money," and to succeed in their aim must be guided by profit and loss calculations or estimates of comparative, prospective costs and returns. And the costs and returns were usually thought of, not only by businessmen but also by most economic theorists—until long after Ricardo's and Bentham's time—not in the psychological and subjective terms of pain-costs and rewards of pleasure or want-satisfaction, but in objective terms—either monetary, as in the conduct of business itself, or in "real" as opposed to monetary but still objective terms, i.e., as required inputs of labor-time and materials used up in production, and resulting outputs of products (in physical quantities).

Economists learned, fairly early, to go beyond the common way of thinking familiar to businessmen, to the extent of analyzing the pursuit of wealth as the effort to maximize not simply the ratios of money receipts to money costs or outlays, but the ratios of the quantities of goods (desired ones of course) obtained, to the quantities of labor-time and material resources expended to produce them or exchanged for them. The quantities-of-labor-and-goods calculus went a step nearer to the "ultimates" involved than the pure and simple money-expenses-and-returns calculus, but still was concerned with physical or objective, not psychological or subjective quantities, and thus was not in the same realm of discourse with Bentham's "felicific calculus." And the latter as used by its author was not a new tool for economics, set up to supersede the former in that field, but a way of generalizing and adapting the economic conception of rational or most useful behavior, for use in analyzing and reforming or improving *the other* departments of human life and affairs. The idea of all intelligent living as happiness-maximizing, though itself very ancient in the literature of philosophy, psychology, and ethics, was never I think the source of the more or less equally ancient idea of business behavior as wealth-maximizing. But in this epoch and partly through Bentham's work, it acquired or borrowed *from* the latter's already more precise elaborations and their common currency, a new, apparent precision and very widespread appeal or persuasiveness, within the culture of modern capitalism. Economic life as the pursuit of wealth was already becoming rationally organized in efforts to maximize the economic outputs, incomes, and wealth of all men and society; let all the rest of life or the pursuit of happiness become more rationally organized also, in appropriate institutions and behavior in all fields, to maximize the happiness of all men individually and collectively! But the full working out of the repercussion of the hedonistic theory of life in its entirety, upon economic theory as the special theory of one part of life, was a later development, and was not much more largely or nearly carried out or anticipated in Bentham's own work than in Ricardo's.

No doubt another part of the explanation of that fact is that neither Ricardo's nor Bentham's "calculus," or anything of the kind then widely known or available within either economics or the other social, moral, or human "sciences," had any benefit of or connection with the branch of higher mathematics which is now called "calculus," and which came to play an essential role in the development of the modern economic "utility analysis" and all modern economic theory. Ricardo and Bentham came very close to the way or ways of thinking about their subject matters which *needed* the mathematical tool of "calculus" in the technical sense for easy, full, and clear expression and development of the ideas and reasonings involved. Ricardo's "law of diminishing returns" of additional produce from use of additional labor and capital on given land pointed toward modern "mathematical economics," and so did Bentham's anticipation, already noticed above, of the "law of diminishing utility" of the modern "utility economists"—yet neither man had any of the mathematical equipment which would have enabled him to work out fully all the latent implications of his lines of thought. It was their colleague Malthus, to be taken up in the next chapter, who predicted that "fluxions," as calculus was then called, would some day come into use in economic science and help to solve its problems, as it long had been solving those in the physical sciences. Bentham's lack of this set of conceptual tools no doubt helps to explain why he did not transform economic theory, or reject Ricardo's labor-and-goods approach and replace it with a wants-and-satisfactions or "utility" approach, as the later utility economists were to do. His crude or rudimentary "felicific calculus"—a mere "table" of most common (as he thought) kinds or sources of human "pleasures" and "pains," and the features and relationships likely to make them relatively great or small in magnitude—was hardly a tool that he could have used to do the work of reconstructing economic theory. Yet it is hard to be confident of the validity or great importance of this explanation, in view of the fact that among the founders of the modern utility economics, while Jevons, Walras, and Marshall (in different degrees) all had and used the mathematical equipment which Bentham lacked, the no less original and effective and important "Austrian School" of Menger and his followers did a full and thorough job of the same kind *without* any such equipment. Hence I am the more inclined to stress mainly the other point which I first made above—that in Bentham's time and world economic theory was still firmly on its own mainly objective, not subjective, basis, and seemed to be doing all right on that basis. Besides, Bentham's main interests lay in other directions and did not lead him to think of analyzing economic life as such in terms of pain-costs and returns of want-satisfaction instead of in the Ricardian terms of physically required and measured man-hours of work, and physical amounts of products produced and exchanged for each other in the markets.

Nor was it, to my mind, *wholly* regrettable or a defect of his work that he did not do this; nor (later on) *wholly* a gain or an unalloyed gain for economics when others did do what he failed to do. Economics was already, in Bentham's time, a bit more advanced toward the status of an "exact science" than were the other "moral sciences" equally within the wide field of his interests; and was so *partly because* it (economics) had available to it and was working with a more nearly sufficient body of manageable, objective, and thus empirically measurable data. Psychology, ethics, education, jurisprudence, and politics perforce had, and have, to work largely with their tenuous, elusive, unmeasurable, subjective data, and Bentham's efforts to reduce them to exact sciences with the aid of his "felicific calculus" were in an essential part illusory and productive of much nonsense.

I think the later "intellectual revolution" in economic theory, which brought the subjective elements of its subject matter into the exclusive foreground of attention and pushed the objective elements, focused on in Ricardo's thought, into a neglected background, went too far and did harm as well as good to economic theory. But of course the early belief in the full sufficiency of the objective elements and data alone, or the virtually physical-science character of economic science, had its large component of illusion also. Not even economics can be wholly an exact science, precisely because as a human science it too has in its subject matter an essential part which is subjective and beyond the reach of truly scientific observation, measurement, description, and analysis. The early tendency to pay little attention to this part was a mistake, but so was the later belief that it—this subjective terrain—could be conquered by and for exact science, and made the basic part of strictly scientific economics. To these questions, however, we shall return in future chapters.

There is perhaps no great need to say much more, in concluding this chapter about Benthamism, than I have said already. In spite of all the great intellectual weaknesses in it, which I have pointed out, it was on the whole in its time and world a very "useful," comprehensive, at least superficially clear and cogent, and constructive vision of the possibilities of, and the lines of effort needed to achieve, a rationally organized and functioning liberal society of free, enlightened seekers of more wealth and happiness, cooperating to attain them by building and operating a democratic state, a rational legal order, and a free market economy. The tinge of utopian optimism in the creed was not much more pronounced than was needed to make it, as it was, widely and highly effective or influential in spurring men to confident, hopeful, and zestful efforts along the lines it pointed out. At the same time it contained a good measure of down-to-earth "realism." Its recognition and acceptance of (most) men's simple, selfish, worldly aims or propensities as facts which education and statecraft or public life must take as data and try to cope with, and its stress on the need for a social order designed and fitted to utilize these psychological and social forces and make them as far as possible conducive to the common welfare, alleviated the utopian optimism and directed the efforts inspired by that, on largely sound and truly useful lines.

Yet the entire structure of thought or doctrine *was* superficial and glaringly deficient at important points, and one can sympathize to no small extent with the contempt expressed for it a few decades later by Carlyle, Ruskin, and others. The common association or linkage at the time, in the public mind, of all of Benthamism with the "classical"—mainly Ricardian—"political economy" has or had some paradoxical aspects not yet noticed here, but to be taken up hereafter. One may be mentioned now: the Benthamite vision as a whole *was* optimistic, not to say utopian, but the Malthusian-and-Ricardian economics as we shall see in the next three chapters had in it a strong strain or strand of pessimism about England's, and every country's, long-range economic and general future or potentialities. But this as we shall see was not quite as grim or unalleviated, really, as it often has been thought to be; and in many minds at the time the two bodies of thought or doctrine seem to have blended well and in some ways mitigated each other's defects. The "classical" economics was on the whole I think a more solid "science," more nearly deserving that designation, than the very much broader and (despite its pretended precision) vaguer system of thought about everything of Bentham and his followers. But the latter in its way expressed the wider context of ideals and assumptions within which the "classical" theory of the "laws" of the economy was in fact conceived and can best be understood; and I go on now to the task of describing the growth and elements of that special economic theory, and helping the reader to understand it.

CHAPTER 6

Malthus; Population Growth and Poverty; and Classical Economics

It might seem logical to go on immediately from our story of Benthamism as the new, revised version of the classical liberalism in over-all social and moral philosophy, into study of Ricardo's work as the main architect of the classical theory of political economy. But it seems advisable at this point to take up, first, the important, special contribution that was made to Ricardo's work by his friend and (on other questions) intellectual opponent, the Reverend T. R. Malthus, through his (Malthus') essay on human population growth as affected by and affecting economic conditions. The "Malthusian" theory about population growth, which Ricardo accepted and incorporated into his own system of economic theory, was an element of the latter of such importance that it needs to be studied before we study Ricardo's theory as a whole. Also, the Malthusian theory is of great interest in itself; it has its own significant place in the general history of science, and historic connections with conflicting social-moral-and-political philosophies. We shall find much of interest in another, different part of Malthus' work and views in economics on questions on which he disagreed with Ricardo; but we must defer these matters until we meet them at the end of Chapter 8, on Ricardo's system.

The present chapter is concerned only with the famous Malthusian "law" of population growth and its economic causes and effects. This "law" has been the subject of so much controversy, and is so widely familiar but still often misunderstood, that the reader may well think it a hackneyed subject and yet, perhaps, find here some unexpected new light upon it. But let me begin with a few words about the man, Malthus; who and what he was; his general outlook and place among (?) or relations with the Utilitarians; and his place in the history of thought on this special subject (population growth), and the interests and point of view which he brought to it.

MALTHUS AND THE UTILITARIANS

The Reverend Thomas R. Malthus was in several ways an odd member—in so far as he was a member—of the Utilitarian group or circle. Most Utilitarians tended to be anticlerical or at least cool toward the established church, but he was an Anglican clergyman in good standing. Again, the group in general was "radical," opposed to all aspects of the traditional order in English society, and optimistic about the future—of forever on-going, universal growth of human happiness—which its members thought would get under way with the carrying out of their program of sweeping reforms. But Malthus was a very conservative, in some ways almost "reactionary" thinker, inclined, e.g., to defend the traditional class structure of English society and the very classes—aristocracy and gentry—of which the Utilitarians were as a rule severely critical. To a great extent—although the tradition about this exaggerates it somewhat—he was a "pessimist" who held that realization of the hopes of reformers, for improvement of the lot of the main mass of mankind, always would be *severely limited* by the inexorable operation of (1) a biological and (2) an economic "natural law," which their theories failed to take into account. Yet to include him in the Utilitarian group, as is generally done, is not entirely wrong, in spite of all those important points which thus made him a far from typical member of the group. For of course the Utilitarians did not all agree completely among themselves about everything or indeed about anything—full uniformity of views is never found in (throughout) any such group—and even the especially pronounced departures of Malthus from the norm were still matters of degree. He was associated in a mutually friendly way with the Utilitarians and was regarded, apparently, by himself and by most of them, as one of them; and he did have much in common with them. Let me further explain this rather briefly.

In the first place, although Malthus was a clergyman, he was also and above all a full-fledged economist and social scientist, not noticeably differentiated from other such scholars in his time by his rather incidental clerical profession; there was then still nothing unusual about that, as there would be today. Of more importance than his clerical position was another which he held—he was the first "Professor of Political Economy" in any English, and perhaps in any, university or college—at the East India College, founded to train administrators sent to India, at Haileybury, in Hertfordshire. And he did his main work not in theology nor as a preacher, but in secular economic and social science; nor did his work or output in this field have any peculiar overt or pronounced quality or religious flavor. It is true and important, however, that there was in his fundamental views a "Christian" element, in some conflict with a central feature of the common outlook carried on from the Enlightenment and shared by most Utilitarians. That is, in contrast with their more one-sided or pure and simple cosmic optimism and utopian tendency—belief in the harmony of the natural universe and potentially perfect harmony of human lives and societies propelled and directed only by the natural desires and intelligence of mankind—the outlook of Malthus had in the "Christian" way another, "pessimistic" side or aspect, which conceived everything "natural" as infected with "evil" or disharmony. "Human nature" (apart from supernatural grace) especially was by no means wholly "good" or "rational," but, rather, was dominated by strong "passions" which the "reason" in most men is hardly able to restrain sufficiently to preserve their welfare.

But the Christian theological source of this outlook (or realistic, true insight) appears nowhere explicitly in the writings of Malthus, and may have been only unconsciously present in his mind. And on the whole his approach to the population problem and all the problems in economic and social science which he studied, was strictly scientific in the modern sense. His scientific empiricism—attention to empirical research as well as to theorizing—marked him as superior in this respect to Ricardo and most other economists of their time. And it was Malthus who first, with remarkable insight and foresight, predicted the modern development of "mathematical economics"; i.e., he expressed the belief that "fluxions," as calculus was then called, would some day come into common use in economics as the kind of tool it already was and long had been in the science of physics. Intellectually then, this clergyman had a full, intelligent devotion to science, at least, in common with the other leading Utilitarians. As to the political question of or about the national, state, or established church—which most Utilitarians felt ideally should be disestablished, though they did not strongly urge or press the issue—Malthus never actively defended the establishment or discussed the question. Altogether then, Malthus the clergyman was set apart from the Utilitarians generally somewhat, but not so far as we might expect.

He was much more seriously divided from them by the facts that he was among them a conservative among radicals, and a pessimist among optimists. But his limited or moderate although distinct conservatism had a character and basis such that its distance from the also limited or moderate radicalism of the more typical Utilitarians was not immense, and involved mainly, amicably discussable differences of intellectual judgments rather than wholly incompatible fundamental ideals and emotional attitudes. Malthus saw much more of social utility for the general welfare *in* the traditional institutions, which he defended and the radicals attacked, than *they* could see in them—and *less* utility of that kind in their reform proposals than they claimed for them; but he agreed with them in appealing, always, to that same Utilitarian criterion. And finally, as neither his pessimism nor their optimism was unlimited, so neither was the width of the gulf between them. The Malthusian pessimism was indeed rather grim but, as I have said, the usual account of this somewhat exaggerates it; and the excessive part of it had its immediate—supposedly empirical-scientific—source or ground in a defective part of his theory (of the comparative potential growth rates of food production and population) which can be corrected without affecting the main substance of his theory. In any case this pessimism could be and soon came to be avoided altogether via the post-Malthusian advocacy of universal birth control as the way to solve the problem which his theory posed. And on the other side, though Utilitarians generally tended to be optimists they were ready to be realists, i.e., to accept all "hard facts" convincingly brought to their attention; and in this were unlike the very different, all-out utopian radicals against whose outlook, only, Malthus argued in developing his theory.

THE POPULATION PROBLEM

The study of the possibilities and history of population growth and its variations with and effects upon economic changes and conditions, had a long history before Malthus took it up; and the previously existing (but never widespread) body of knowledge and ideas on the subject included many at least partial anticipations of the conclusions which he reached independently, as well as other views of different tenors. But this lack of complete novelty in his new study of the subject and his findings does not much reduce the proper estimate of the merit of his *Essay*,[1] or justify belittlement of its great significance and influence. The older, similar, and other relevant knowledge and ideas had made no lasting and widespread impression, and were before he wrote mostly unknown to him and, certainly, entirely unknown to most members of the very wide public which received the message of his powerful *Essay* as a new and momentous revelation. Nor did he *only* reproduce (independently in the main at least) and communicate effectively to a much wider public, *just* what had been known or thought and said before on the subject. He produced a new combination of old bits of knowledge and insights, never previously combined in just the same way, added a few new discoveries and insights of his own, made

[1] T. R. Malthus, *An Essay on Population*. A good modern edition, from the original 7th edition, is (London: J. M. Dent & Sons, Ltd.; and New York: E. P. Dutton and Co., Inc., 1933).

the whole a (within its limits) complete and unified, coherent, penetrating theory, and made clear its important bearings on great social problems, as no one had done before.[2]

But of course, as Malthus by no means said the first, he also by no means said the last, words on the subject; the research in this field, which began long before his time, has continued and gone on making further new advances ever since; so that now in the light of the best modern knowledge the old Malthusian theory is seen to have been very crude, rudimentary, and defective in many ways. As we shall see at a later point, the task of evaluating it as a contribution to or toward full, true understanding of its subject is not an easy task; but it is safe to say that with all its faults, it was in and for its time a quite substantial scientific achievement in that direction. It holds a place of honor in the more general history of science, i.e., of biology as well as of social science, because Charles Darwin, by his own account, was led or helped by his reading of Malthus' *Essay on Population* to conceive and develop the Darwinian theory of biological evolution.[3] Darwin generalized or extended, beyond the human species to all living species, the Malthusian picture of fecund life—fast-growing populations where and while the foods they need are available in ample or easily produced supplies; lagging growths of those food supplies; growing severity of the struggle for survival; rising death rates approaching equality with the stable or constant, high birth rates generally found in nature and much of human history, and assumed in both theories; and reduction in this way of the growth rates of populations to those of their food supplies. And on this basis, Darwin built up the rest of his theory of the evolution of new species, using the further ideas of heredity, variations of the traits of offspring from the parental types, and "natural selection," in the struggle for survival, of the variant strains or types with the new traits best adapting them for success in their environments. There is truth, along with exaggeration, in the statement made by a modern economist, that Darwin's theory originated as simply a vast generalization from and beyond the competitive economics of Malthus and Ricardo.

THE IDEOLOGICAL BACKGROUND: MALTHUS VERSUS GODWIN

We are, however, here concerned, not with Darwin's theory at all, but only with that of Malthus, about growths of human populations

[2] See, however, for a review of the earlier contributions on the subject, made before Malthus' time, and a much less favorable estimate than mine of the merit of Malthus' contribution, Schumpeter, *History of Economic Analysis* (New York: Oxford University Press, 1954), pp. 250–258.

[3] See *Charles Darwin's Autobiography*, Sir Francis Darwin (ed.) (New York: Henry Schuman, Inc., Publishers, 1950), p. 54.

and of their powers to produce or obtain economic support for themselves. Before I take up in detail the scientific substance of this theory, I want first to notice—as distinguished from it—the social-philosophic (conservative) outlook, and opposition to a certain utopian radical creed that came to Malthus' attention, and led him into his study and theory of population growth and "pressure on subsistence" as the true "natural" cause of the widespread poverty which the radical utopians dreamed of abolishing. For without a prior separate understanding of the views and controversies of the social-philosophic kind, which stimulated the work of Malthus in developing his scientific theory, formed the wider context within which he presented it, and controlled the applications which he and, after him, other conservatives made of it to contemporary problems of public policy—we would not be in a position to disentangle the scientific theory itself from those concomitants, understand and appraise it properly in its own sphere, and understand and discount the diverse prejudices which too often have distorted popular discussions of it. The initial formation in the mind of Malthus, in his youth, of his interest in the study of population growth, was an indirect result of arguments with his father about a body of ideas or doctrines then arousing interest in some English intellectual circles. This creed or cult, which attracted the elder Malthus but repelled his son—*our* Malthus—was a form of the combined utopian socialism and "philosophical" anarchism which had grown up first in France on the left-wing fringe of the French Revolution, and appeared later in England in the writings of that odd and interesting figure, William Godwin, father-in-law of the poet Shelley.

The main essentials of this visionary creed were the following beliefs. (1) Human nature is "perfectible," i.e., with the progress of "enlightenment" all human beings can, and will in time, become intellectually and morally "perfect" individuals and citizens, spontaneously thinking, feeling, and acting always and only in the ways that are best for the individual and collective welfare of them all. (2) In all historic and existing imperfect societies, the main roots of the evils afflicting them have been and are the institutions of private property, the family, and inheritance of wealth or property in families, which work to engender and perpetuate economic, social, and political inequality, or division (stratification) of every society into upper and lower classes—the rich and mighty few and the poor, humble, and miserable many—in perpetual conflict with each other; and as a further consequence of all that and the crowning evil, the coercive state, which exists to protect the property of the rich, to repress the rebellious poor, and generally to control the conflicts among men and groups which all result essentially from their inequality, or failures to give and receive "natural justice" in their dealings with each other. And (3) in the attainable ideal society of the more or less distant future, all those institutions and all coercion of some by other human beings will have been abolished; and all, as completely free, equal, and fraternal individuals, will live together in spontaneous, perfect harmony, or mutual cooperation for their common good; and the poverty and misery or wretchedness that have always been the lot of the majority will vanish from the earth.

Now unlike his father who felt only the allurements of this vision, our Malthus as strongly felt or sensed what seemed to him its unrealism or incompatibility with universal, permanent, hard facts, or "natural laws," or features of the world and human nature and behavior as they really were and always would be. And among all the many elements of the creed which he might have attacked as unrealistic, he selected one and concentrated on refuting it: the belief that the poverty of the many poor people in old, densely populated countries was a condition caused by the institutions and the inequality condemned by the Godwinians (and defended by our Malthus), and would be forever eliminated in the envisioned socialist-and-anarchist utopia. Malthus suspected, and set out to prove in his study of population growth, that the existence of widespread poverty in old, mature societies is a hardly entirely curable, or preventable, "natural" result of a strong tendency of the fecundity of the species to produce in the long run, in every territory or environment, more people than the greatest possible growth of economic production therein can adequately supply with food and economic support; and further, that as far as the (limited) power of social systems and institutions to affect the matter is concerned, precisely the social order attacked by the Godwinians and supported by his own views was best able to do all that could be done to ameliorate the evil, while their utopia, if ever realized, would in the end make it worse than ever.[4]

Let me now only lightly sketch the entire argument, in support of those conclusions, of our author's famous *Essay*—including the parts which do not, as well as that which does belong to his more strictly scientific (biological and economic) theory; and later, I shall return to a more thorough examination of the latter only. Taken as a whole and as directed against the Godwinian creed, the argument elaborated by Malthus in his *Essay* undertook to prove that the true fundamental

[4] The familiar story of the origin of Malthus' work on the population problem, in his arguments with his father about the Godwinian gospel, is retold succinctly and well—with references to the original sources—in J. M. Keynes' essay on Malthus, in his *Essays in Biography* (New York: Harcourt, Brace and Company, Inc., 1933), p. 116. This essay by Keynes is as a whole commended to the reader; a short, readable, and delightful essay, it confirms and further illuminates much of all that I say in this chapter, and adds other information, not here presented, about Malthus and his work and views in economics generally.

cause of mass poverty lies not in alterable, man-made, social institutions but in two universal and permanent "laws" of "nature" itself—a biological and an economic "natural law."

On the one hand there is the strong sexual desire inherent in human nature and the consequent tendency of mankind to multiply—of the human population of the world and of every country to grow—*as long as the additional people can be fed and can survive, at a high and accelerating* "geometrical" (his word) or exponential rate. (Since—in a population that has long been growing, and as long as its continuing growth is not restrained by any external "checks"—the numbers of new babies born in successive years are continually increased by the previous increases of the numbers of adults of both sexes in the childbearing age range; the series of population sizes at successive dates twenty-five or thirty or some such number of years apart, will be not of the form 2-4-6-8-10, etc., but rather of the form 2-4-8-16-32, etc.) And on the other hand there is—so Malthus argued—the long-run impossibility of a continuing rate of growth of production of food, and other necessary life-supporting goods, sufficient to equal and support continuing growth of population at anything like such an otherwise "natural," potential rate, or to enable the latter to go on being realized in fact. Under any and all kinds of institutions and social systems, human populations will in time tend strongly to outgrow the limited powers of the available land areas, and the labor applied or applicable on them, to feed and support the growing populations—*until* the growths of the latter are checked, as eventually they must be, by the coming into play of some or all of the various checks necessitated by the "natural" excess of the "natural" rate of unchecked population growth, over the highest maintainable rate of growth of food production.

Let me still postpone the necessary full examination of our author's central "scientific" argument and evidence, about those unequal potential growth rates of population and of food production, and take up now his ideas and argument about the two kinds of checks on population growth which together (in some proportion) must in the long run reduce its rate to that of the increase of "subsistence." For his reply to the utopians is contained in this part of his theory, about the better and worse checks and the way in which, within limits, a society's choice of its institutions and public policies will affect the method, timing, and ulterior results of the necessary checking of population growth, or the speed of arrival and the degrees of prevalence and severity of the poverty that will be entailed as a factor in that process.

The realized rate of growth of a population depends, of course, upon the extent of the excess of its annual birth rate—the number of babies born each year, per thousand members of the preexisting population—over its annual death rate—the number of individuals who die each year, per thousand members of the preexisting population. Hence there are two ways in which the ultimately necessary restraint or adjustment of a population's rate of growth to that of the obtainable amount of food and economic support for it, can be accomplished. In so far as this adjustment is *not* brought about, *while* there is still a favorable ratio of obtainable "subsistence" to population, *by* growth of prevalent sufficient use or practice of "the preventive check," or reduction of the birth rate, it *will* be brought about instead, inevitably, in the long run, *by* a growth of dire conditions—overpopulation, scarcity of "subsistence," and widespread poverty—bringing strongly into play "the positive checks," which increase the death rate. Malthus indeed discussed as "positive checks" *all* factors operating to increase the death rate—growing degrees of frequency and severity of wars, epidemics, murders, accidents, etc., *as well as* growth and spread of the poverty which entails undernourishment and lack of proper housing, sanitation, medical care, etc.—and argued, rightly, that growth of excessive populations of countries relative to their areas and resources, tends to bring about rising death rates in *all* these ways. But he stressed as the main part of this grim picture, the widespread severe poverty among the masses in every much too populous country, which plays the main role in making its death rate nearly equal to its persisting high birth rate and thus slowing its still on-going population growth to that which can be supported—barely, on the same low inadequate standard of living—by its limited or slow continuing growth of food production and/or production of other products and acquisition of "subsistence" in exchange for them. And he saw this grim state of affairs as the eventual destiny of every country unless its people could achieve, earlier and sufficiently, a general use of "the preventive check" reducing its birth rate to a level so low that, even with a good standard of living for all and a low death rate, the population would thereafter grow no faster than the total obtainable supply of "subsistence" and additional comforts, and the good standard of living for all would thus be maintained.

Our "pessimist," however, did not believe in the possibility of more than a limited, partial achievement—in the only way of which he could approve—of that latter, happier solution of the problem. Being a conservative moralist, he could not advocate, suggest, or consider encouragement of the general use of contraceptives or birth control, in that sense, as the way to bring about the much-to-be-desired reduction of the birth rate, for that would have meant encouragement of immorality. A bit later, the movement advocating birth control in that sense was to get under way, in part as a result of the influence of his theory and with such stress upon his theory in its arguments that it has been called "neo-Malthusian"; but Malthus himself would have disowned it. For him "the preventive check," which he favored, meant only what he called "moral" or "prudential restraint," i.e., general practice, by potential parents, of deliberate abstinence from more than a limited, strictly controlled, amount or frequency of sexual intercourse. Good or moral men and women would, of course, indulge in sexual intercourse only within marriage, *and* the good married couples would not have intercourse so often as to have unwanted, or too many, children; and the moral-and-prudent ones would not want to have more children than their current or assured prospective incomes would enable them to support and bring up properly. As a moralist Malthus held all of this self-control to be obligatory; as a "pessimist" he regarded this as rather too much to expect from weak human nature, and did not think it ever would or could be more than partially achieved. The strength of the sexual desire is generally too great to be more than partially controlled by the little of moral-and-prudent "reason" and will power which most people have. What he did mainly urge and hope for was somewhat longer postponements of marriage (with, of course, no sexual intercourse until after marriage)—especially by young and as yet poor workingmen. Let them wait until they could attain good steady jobs and incomes and, making later starts, they would produce in all fewer children and, as far as possible, hold down the sizes of their families and thus remain able to support them well with their earnings. In so far as a country could induce the (at least relatively) poor majority of its people to do this in every generation, there would be a reduction of its birth rate and annual excess of births over deaths, which would slow down its population growth enough to both postpone and alleviate the not completely avoidable, grim, future situation (of too many people and too little "subsistence" to support them all properly, widespread, serious poverty in the lower classes, and belated slowing of further population growth at that stage only by the consequent higher death rate).

At this point we come to the argument about the effects of diverse social systems. Since the fundamental cause of mass poverty is "pressure of population upon subsistence," the task of designing the best social system for preventing poverty (as far as it can be prevented) is that of designing a system calculated to give the people and especially the poorer people the strongest possible incentives to use or practice "the preventive check." And this can be done best, Malthus argued, precisely by a system having, as its main institutions and resulting features, those condemned by the utopian radicals: private property, the family, responsibility of parents for all economic support of their children, inheritance or bequests of property in family lines, *and* economic inequality or social stratification—*if* the system also provides good opportunities for all able and ambitious, young poor men to rise by their own efforts in the economic and social scale. In a society having *all* those features *including* that last one, there is *not only* protection of the better-off minority of its members from having to share, fully, what would otherwise eventually come to be *universal* poverty; and the unequal division of the wealth is *not only* no cause at all of the (at least relative) poverty of the masses; but on the contrary, in such a society, that inequality plays its part in the good work which *all* the features of the society, together, do, of limiting as much as possible the intensification of the poverty of the poorer majority by excessive increase of their numbers. All the features of this best system work together to discourage reckless multiplication of the already poor, by making them bear the full burden of the consequence—intensification of their own poverty; and to encourage them to limit their families in the hope of achieving better economic positions for themselves and the few children they are or can become well able to provide for. *If* there is enough "vertical social mobility" in the modern phrase—an essential feature of the good, stratified but free, individualistic society which Malthus was defending—the existence of the richer middle and upper classes *and* the attractive chances for those "below" of climbing into them, is *no* cause of the initial poverty of the latter *but* the potent stimulus they need to inspire their efforts to rise above it, and not burden themselves with too many children to support and in that way also contribute to the basic cause of poverty in general. In the socialistic society envisioned and desired by the Godwinians, the tendency of population to outgrow its sources of economic support, and depress all in time into dismal poverty, would be unrestrained and at its worst; equality would mean equal poverty for all. There would be no visible hills to be climbed; and the communal guarantees of support for all children, and equal shares for all regardless of their efforts, would destroy all deterrents to reckless multiplication or incentives to prudent restraint of that, and all incentives to ambition, industry, enterprise, and high and rising economic productivity.

Now it should be clear that in the *whole* argument of Malthus, which I have now outlined, there are different, separable, and dissimilar parts, which call for individual evaluation. Taken by itself, his basic general biological-and-economic theory of the tendency of unchecked population growth to proceed more rapidly than production of food and support for the multiplying people can be increased; the eventually necessary emergence and operation of the checks on population growth, reducing its rate to that of growth of support for it; and the point that avoidance of overpopulation and mass poverty depends on doing the checking early and sufficiently through "the preventive check" instead of later through "the positive checks"—all this is entirely of the nature of a scientific theory; however imperfect it may be as a solution of the complete complex of all the relevant scientific problems.

But the rest of the whole, broader argument, added on to just that group of propositions, has a different and more dubious, nonscientific character and belongs rather to the history of social philosophies than to that of science. The exclusion from consideration, on moral grounds, of birth control through contraceptives as a way of making "the preventive check" effective is not scientific. And the argument about the alleged-to-be certain or predictable effects of different social systems on the "incentives" and behavior of the people has little if any scientific value and more of the quality of a "rationalization" of our author's feelings against socialism and in favor of the liberal-conservative social order which had his allegiance. The Utilitarian character of *this* argument is, of course, apparent, and it belongs as much or as little as all Benthamism does to psychological-and-social science; that is to say, hardly at all by the more modern and stricter standards that are becoming applicable even in this field. As against the naïve Godwinians, Malthus indeed had at least the better "common sense" on his side, not only in holding that the mass poverty which aroused his humane concern as well as theirs was caused by "pressure of population on subsistence" and not by the set of institutions they attacked; but also in imputing to those institutions and the resulting "incentives" for the people, tendencies to stimulate production of an ever-growing output of "subsistence" and a restraint of population growth through some degree of widespread use of "the preventive check"—and in arguing that the ideal regime of the Godwinians, if ever realized, would lack those tendencies.

But the relatively better case that he made for those opinions, as compared with the one they made for theirs, of course, did not by any means amount to truly scientific proof of the former, or (still less) of these still broader propositions easily confused with them: that the institutions he was defending had never anywhere played any part in the causation or aggravation of mass poverty, or that the latter could never have any other cause than population "pressure"; that exactly the set of institutions or social system which he favored would always, everywhere, not only work entirely to reduce and not at all to increase poverty, but would serve as the only or best possible system for minimizing the amount and depth of it; or that socialism in any form would necessarily always, in the long run, lead to extreme and universal poverty, by overstimulating population growth and failing to achieve enough growth of production.

We can therefore, from this point onward, put aside—with the final comment, "not proved nor provable"—the entire "ideological" or political part or appendage of Malthus' study and discussion of the population problem and its wider bearings. And we shall turn to an intensive consideration solely of his (at least more) scientific analysis of that problem itself—that is, of the potential rates and long-run tendencies of growth of population and of production of food and support for it, and the possible and probable developments of the different checks on population growth and their results. For it is possible to examine and appraise the Malthusian theory proper, alone and apart from the background or context of its author's social philosophy or political opinions. Malthus developed it as a basis for, and mistakenly believed that it conclusively supported, the latter. But his narrower "scientific" theory itself was and is logically independent of the broader political views which he thus attached to it, and demands an appraisal, unaffected by our judgments of them, within its own field and by scientific standards.

THE SCIENTIFIC CORE OF THE "MALTHUSIAN THEORY"

Now in the effort to become equipped to make that appraisal, it is not irrelevant to recall the historic linkage of this Malthusian theory, of the tendencies of *human* population to grow up to and "press upon" the limits of the powers of their environment to support them, with the Darwinian theory of the evolution of all forms of life, involving at its own basis Darwin's notice of the unmistakable fact that what Malthus asserted to be true of human populations is certainly true, generally, of populations of other kinds of living creatures. But in order to be not more (or less) impressed by this linkage than we should be, in favor of the Malthusian theory and its claim to scientific validity in its own narrower and special field, we need to compare and contrast the human situation and historic changes in it—including the great change that has come about in the Western world *since* the time of Malthus—with the (universal and constant) situation in the rest of the living world, or biological universe. Also we need to consider the human situation that Malthus saw around him, and its place in the historic course of change of the variables and relations among them, examined in his theory, if we are to account for, understand, and be able to appreciate and criticize justly the features of his theory which have seemed to be disproved by more recent Western experience.

Broadly speaking, the pessimistic, grim picture which Malthus drew applies with substantially full truth not only (as Darwin saw) to other forms of life beyond or apart from mankind, but also to (probably) *most* of the human societies and epochs that would be surveyed in a full study of all human history, *including* present-day Oriental and other economically "underdeveloped" societies. That is, in most societies and times *apart from* the modern Western world as affected by all the gradually maturing consequences of the industrial revolution (which was young or new in Malthus' day), human populations generally *have* adjusted to their sources and possibilities of economic support in about or nearly the same way or manner which is characteristic of the populations of living creatures of all other kinds, and which Malthus supposed would be permanent in the human world. This means the adjustment of the number of people living in a region or environment to the power, and any changes of the power, of the environment to support them, through the process involving (1) a relatively stable or steady high birth rate and (2) a more variable death rate depending on economic conditions, i.e., the current ratio at every time of the population's size to its greatest total obtainable supply of food and all necessary life-supporting goods.

In detail, that process goes on as follows. As long as economic conditions for all or most or a major part of the population are at all good or easy, the population grows, i.e., most families can obtain enough life-supporting goods to preserve or extend the lives of the parents and at least more than two children per family, and the death rate is at least a little less, though not necessarily very much less, than the birth rate. But the possibility of obtaining from its environment ever-increasing supplies of all life-supporting goods—in a society without, or almost without, the knowledge, means, and attitudes required for technological and economic progress—is or in time becomes very limited. So as the population grows, its total output of life-supporting goods can grow only slowly, and this latter growth will eventually slow down further, to or toward a complete halt, as the population becomes too large and dense relative to the available supply of fertile land and all life-supporting natural resources. Then, with growing poverty, the death rate rises to approximate equality with the still high birth rate, and the "adjustment" is completed—population growth ceases until new economic growth occurs and, by lowering the death rate, renews the cycle. Wherever (human or other) living creatures multiply, and can only within strict limits get additional means of supporting the additional volume of life, and have a birth rate determined only by their instincts and not by effective foresight and planning, prudence and self-control; the size of the population is adjusted in the long run, through variations of the death rate, to about the maximum number of individuals which the environment and its resources can support or enable to survive. Thus the normal state of things includes the fixed high birth rate, population growth always fully matching whatever economic growth occurs, prevailing poverty or intense "struggle for existence," and a death rate never long far below the birth rate.

The human species, however, has always possessed unique potential powers to alter all that in its own case or to escape from that grim situation, universal in the rest of living nature and generally also in the human lot. There emerged, in the Western world just after Malthus' time, a far greater development of those human powers and the results of their exercise than he foresaw or allowed for in his theory. The human powers here referred to are of two kinds: to control the environment and make it yield, through increasingly efficient economic production, ever more rapidly and greatly increasing outputs of "subsistence" plus multiplying comforts for more and more human beings; and to contol the number of new human beings born, or replace control of this variable merely by the sexual desires of potential parents and the fecundity of the species, with joint control of it by all human desires and intelligent forethought employed in their service. Without a good measure of achievement of the second, however, no amount of the first kind alone would in the long run "solve the population problem." Malthus was unanswerably right in his simple fundamental point, that if there could be indefinite continuance of unchecked population growth on its cumulative, percentagewise, or accelerating course, it would in a finite time surpass any possible growth of production of "subsistence," and fill up all of the standing room on earth. And he further saw rightly that, as long as birth rates remained rigid at high levels, each (temporary) increase of prosperity would only, by lowering death rates, correspondingly, further accelerate population growth and be dissipated without any permanent rise of living standards. It is true that he was far too pessimistic, as subsequent events have shown, about the possibility of increasing production of all goods including all human foods. Or he did not at all sufficiently foresee how fast and far the economic-technological revolution, in his time already under way but still in its early stages, would go, and how it would raise the productivities of land and labor in all branches of production. But the more important cause of the failure of his theory to remain fully valid in application to our modern situation was his excess of pessimism on a different point: his underestimate of the extent of the possible and subsequent development of "the preventive check" and decline of the birth rates of modern nations to levels far below those which were normal in past ages and are normal today in the not yet modernized parts of the world.

There still does not exist, however, any complete knowledge and understanding of all the factors that have helped to bring about, in our Western world since the time of Malthus, those two great, general changes—the immense, continuing growth of all economic productivity and production, and especially the decline of birth rates—which have together produced our modern, happier, un-Malthusian situation. There is as yet no complete assurance that what now lies in the future is to be a full extension of both changes throughout all the rest of the world, and no reversal of them or of either of them, ever, anywhere, and thus an eventual permanent release of all mankind from the grip of the grim Malthusian "laws." We do know the main general causes or conditions of the economic progress that is one part of the story; and the prospect now appears good for a gradual, world-wide extension and continuance of this progress, though the difficulties still to be overcome in many parts of the world are greater and more numerous, complex, and profound than most people realize. Steady or relatively steady, rapid, ever-on-going, and all-around or well-balanced economic progress can be achieved, wherever all these requirements are met. There must be scientific and technological progress—ever-new discoveries and inventions; growth of saving and investment or capital formation; education of whole peoples in all the needed ever-changing skills and essential basic attitudes and habits; and the emergence also in sufficiently growing numbers, and into positions of full respect and influence in their countries, of at once ambitious, able, morally decent, and socially responsible leaders and administrators of all kinds of progressive, productive enterprises. There must be adequate, ever-new improvements of the methods and organization of all economic activities; and the growth of market or/and economic planning systems able to bring about all badly needed adjustments of each national economy's over-all pattern of expansions and developments of its different industries or branches, to the changing wants and demands of the people.

But how fast and fully all of those requirements can or will be met, in all the vast parts of the world that as yet have hardly begun to meet them, we of course do not know. Nor can we be entirely certain that even our Western countries will go on meeting them as well as or better than they have been doing in the recent past. The race of economic progress with population growth, which the former must win everywhere if dire mass poverty is to be abolished everywhere, is by no means certain to win that success universally, or go on winning it forever, anywhere. Malthus was entirely right about the general nature of the problem, and not far wrong about its degree of difficulty. Also as that "race" gets under way now in the "underdeveloped" countries, their experiences are bearing Malthus out on *this* point: the *first* effects of the first new achievements of some economic progress, or rise and spread of better living standards, invariably show up chiefly in a decline of the death rate and increase of the gap between it and the birth rate. This *speeds up* population growth, which in turn tends to cancel out all the gains as far as living standards are concerned, or again makes extreme poverty as prevalent and severe as it was before. Achievement everywhere of a large general reduction of the birth rate, as soon as possible, is imperatively necessary *along with* immense, general, and sustained economic progress, if the latter is really to "win the race."

In this connection there is special need for better knowledge than as yet exists, of all that has been involved in or "behind" the declines of the birth rates of the Western nations, which began not long after Malthus' time, went beyond his highest hopes, and have played an essential part in making possible the progress so far achieved by these nations toward eliminating mass poverty within their territories or improving, and sustaining the improvements of, the living standards of their peoples generally. I shall return to this problem in a moment, but first we need to consider a little more closely the strictly economic side or part of the Malthusian theory. This includes the limitations that Malthus thought would always restrict the increase of the world's and every nation's output or obtainable supply of "subsistence" for its people; and some especially important aspects and contributing causes of the more recent gradual lifting of these limitations by or in the modern Western economic progress, which Malthus in his time could not fully foresee.

It is necessary to realize that not every kind or part of general economic progress has the same direct relation to the task of meeting a growing population's need for more "subsistence," and relieving the "pressure on subsistence" which Malthus saw as the cause of mass poverty. *Industrial* progress in the narrow sense of "industrial"—rising efficiency in, and expansion of, manufacturing industries—can by itself enlarge the total amounts of employment and (money) income for the people, and of manufactured goods available to them; but without a sufficient concurrent growth of the supply of *food,* from *agricultural* production—either in the same (industrial) country or countries or in others able and willing to produce for export growing *surplus* amounts of food beyond their own consumption of it—without this, industrial progress alone and the accompanying growth of the industrial population and its total income and demand for food, would *increase* the relative scarcity and cost or price level of the latter, and thus fail to relieve poverty. What is necessary to support—keep alive all members of—a growing population, is growth not simply of the total output of goods of no matter what kinds, but growth specifically of the output of food and all truly necessary life-supporting goods; and a large, essential part of this must be increase of production of food on and from the land or soil—of which there is, on the earth as a whole and within the territory of each country, only a finite and ultimately, approximately fixed or unincreasable amount. Thus, what Malthus rightly tried to compare with the potential amount of population growth, in the absence of checks on this, through a given time interval, was the potential amount of growth through the same time interval, not of general or over-all economic production, but of food production from the land or soil.

Now the *great* advances that were being made *in his* time and world, in increasing the efficiency of production, were being made not in agriculture but in industry. There had been earlier, significant improvements of methods and efficiency in agriculture, as we saw in a previous chapter, and some further ones of course were coming along; but the major advances that were then going on in the technology of production were confined to industry (including transportation, but not agriculture). Malthus lived in the midst of an early phase of what was later appropriately named the *industrial* revolution. The comparable revolution in the technology of agriculture—yielding *immense* increases of food-harvests per acre of farm land and per man-hour of farm labor—was to be delayed until very nearly our present time, and was not remotely conceivable as possible in Malthus' time. He therefore naturally assumed that the growth of food supplies to feed the growing populations of his country and all countries would have to come from (1) more intensive cultivation of the more fertile land already in use, and (2) the extension of cultivation onto previously unused, because inferior, land—with only a little help from new improvements of farming techniques, methods, and efficiency or productivity.

The industrial revolution that was going on around him was already causing rapid growth of industrial employment and total wage income, a slight current improvement of the always before and still low standard of living of the working people, a fall of their death rate, encouragement of early marriages and large families (the prevalence of child labor played a part here), and thus full continuation (a slight rise, even) of their high birth rate. He witnessed a spurt of fast population growth, which increased the supply of labor in a not much delayed response to the increase of demand for it and allowed only the slight rise of wage rates, and tended to aggravate the scarcity and cost of food and thus keep widespread poverty in existence, in spite of all the industrial progress and expansion. How long would it remain possible to go on increasing the food supply enough to match the population's growth, or prevent the latter from making the former increasingly insufficient, further spreading and intensifying poverty, raising the death rate, and *thus only* restraining itself (the population's further growth) to equality with that of its food supply? This was the question which Malthus asked and to which he gave the imprecise or vague but pessimistic answers that we must now consider.

He sought to formulate a comparison of the most rapid, continuing increase of food production, which it could be realistic to expect, with the rate at which the population would continue to increase as long as the existing degree of excess of its birth rate over its death rate remained unchanged. On the mathematical nature of the latter rate of growth he was right of course beyond any question; as we have seen, it would be some "exponential" rate, i.e., from each year to the next the population would increase by some fixed *percentage,* hence the successive *absolute* increases would themselves be increasing over time—in the long run, rapidly. Now in the first edition of his *Essay,*[5] Malthus *simply* set over against that the idea that food production could not be expected to go on increasing by more than some constant *absolute* amount from each year to the next; the series of annual food outputs would at the best have the form 2-4-6-8-10, etc., as against a series of population sizes of the form 2-4-8-16-32, etc. But in the second and later editions, while unfortunately always retaining that too rigid contrast of the assumed potential rates of growth of population and of food production, he offered a gradually expanding and improving discussion of the reason why the latter could not increase sufficiently, bringing into use—though never too clearly—the classical "economic law" of which he was one of the several original "discoverers"—the "law of diminishing returns" of additional produce from applications of additional labor on the available farm land. If a growing country, with a fixed area of tillable soil, went on growing, and increasing its agricultural output, after all its most fertile soil was already under fairly intensive cultivation, then with given, unchanging agricultural techniques or methods, the further increases of the amounts of manpower and farming capital employed, partly in more intensive cultivation of the best land and partly in extension of cultivation onto poorer land, would yield only decreasing increases of the total output, i.e., a decreasing ratio of the total output to the required total input of efforts and resources.

This true proposition may seem to imply an even more pessimistic conclusion about the potential growth rate of food production than the idea of the "arithmetical ratio" or series of successive, equal, absolute increases, until we remember the proviso about no technical progress in agriculture, and realize the consequence—that where such progress does go on, unless we can predict its rate, we cannot draw *any* conclusion about the rate of increase of food production over time, from "the law of diminishing returns" alone. The approach to the problem by way of the latter was more valid than the idea of the "arithmetical ratio," but was analytically a partial approach only and quite inadequate to solve the problem. It could yield Malthus' "pessimistic" judgment on the matter only with the aid of the further assumption that while there would be improvements of agricultural techniques and practices which would delay or modify full operation of "the law of dimin-

[5] The first edition of Malthus' *Essay,* privately printed in 1798, is a rare book or collector's item. The many successive later editions—which are quite accessible—progressively grew in size and underwent many changes in character and contents, beyond the one vital change noted in my text above. The first edition only briefly, boldly elaborated Malthus' general theory; the later ones both added more and more supporting, empirical evidence, and introduced many careful qualifications or modifications of the theory. See Keynes' essay on Malthus, *op. cit.*

ishing returns," they would never be important enough to reverse or completely nullify or counteract it. With the help of that assumption then, his final conclusion was not very different from his first one; while population growth would go on at an accelerating (absolute) rate until new checks to it came into play, the growth of food production could not be expected to go on at much if any more than a constant absolute rate—and so in time there would be inevitable growth of food scarcity and poverty and a rise of the death rate, slowing population growth to equality with the growth of the food supply.

WHY IN THE MODERN WEST THE PREDICTIONS OF MALTHUS HAVE NOT BEEN FULFILLED

Now as I implied earlier, the assumption of absence from the scene of any occurrence or any prospect of a real "revolution" in the technology of food production was in fact valid enough in the time of Malthus and remained valid a good way beyond his time; yet the experience of the Western world of the nineteenth century did not bear out his gloomy predictions, and we must continue our search for the answer to the question of why it did not. As the *industrial* "revolution" went on developing, the totals of employment, income, and output in the Western national economies grew immensely; the living standards of the masses and all classes slowly improved; death rates fell lower and lower; and there was a vast, unprecedented growth of population. Eventually, for reasons we have yet to consider, birth rates also declined enough to more than offset the decline of death rates, and to again slow the population growth and allow the improvement of mass living standards to continue. But before that change occurred, the early, fast growth of population had already gone so far that we must ask how the required, immense increase of total food production was achieved, or where it came from, and what happened in this sphere to falsify the Malthusian forecast of growing poverty and rising death rates due to growing scarcity of foods? The real "revolution" in agricultural technology did not come early enough to bring about the great increase of the food supply necessary for the "zooming" populations of the fast-industrializing Western countries in the middle and late decades of the nineteenth century. Nor was any significant amount of food obtained through trade or exchange with the not yet industrializing, or still almost purely agricultural, Oriental and other far-distant countries or regions that we then called "backward" and now call "underdeveloped." For in all *those* areas the primitive and unprogressive agricultural techniques, the teeming, dense populations, extremely low mass living standards, etc., meant that food production there could in general barely meet the minimal needs of the native populations. The West did get from them industrial raw materials, and sell them manufactured goods to some extent, but they could do very little to meet the West's needs for increasing food supplies. That those needs *were* met was due to a fortunate circumstance in or feature of the Western situation in that epoch, which Malthus perhaps could and should have foreseen, but did not.

The fortunate occurrence was the opening up, for settlement and cultivation by people of European descent, of vast new areas of fertile land in central and western North America, parts of South America, Australia etc.; and the creation of facilities for adequately efficient, rapid, and inexpensive transportation of people and goods of all kinds, in immense quantities, between those regions and the already industrialized and densely populated ones on or near the European and American shores of the Atlantic Ocean. The newly opened regions or vast areas of fertile land had previously been almost vacant or uninhabited; and the people who moved into them in great numbers, from the eastern parts of the United States and Canada and from the British Isles and Europe, took with them the best farming and other economically productive skills, "know-how," and equipment that had so far been developed anywhere. In these new, vast regions, they were long able, even with continuing growth of their numbers, to find, occupy, and cultivate so very much very good land per family or per person, that the ratios of the food-harvests they produced to the numbers of farm workers involved were very much higher than such ratios had been, were, or could be in the old, densely populated farming areas where "the law of diminishing returns" was in full operation. What for a time went into operation, so to speak, with and after the sudden increase of the total area of fertile land available for the growing population of the North Atlantic region to spread out over and be fed from, was *the reverse aspect* of that economic "law." That is, just as with a growing ratio of the supply of farm labor to a fixed supply of farm land, the output per farm worker must eventually fall, so also, if it is the land supply which increases, relative to the labor supply, the output per worker rises.

Thus the opening up of the new, vast land areas and abundant, rapid, and cheap transportation to and from them, prolonged the period of time through which there could be, along with continuing, fast growth of the total population of the European stocks, fully adequate growth also of the total production and supply of food for it all. And with no rise of food costs and—due to the on-going industrial revolution—a continual cheapening, and growing abundance, of all other goods, and the rise of the incomes of people of all classes, there went on a continuing rise of their standards of living. And before the growth of population could again surpass the growth of food production from the enlarged food-producing area, there occurred, first, a decline of birth rates sufficient (in spite of also falling death rates) to slow down further population growth, and then later, the onset of the recent and current revolutionary advances of agricultural technology and productivity.

The former of those two new fortunate developments or chapters in the story of the modern West's "escape from" the Malthusian dilemma, now calls for the discussion which I promised earlier. The marked decline of birth rates in all countries sharing the modern Western culture, which went on as a new "trend" through the last decade of the nineteenth and first three decades of the twentieth centuries, was indeed a fortunate development for these countries. By causing their populations to grow, from 1890 to the present, *much less* than they would have grown otherwise, the decline of birth rates has played a large, indispensable role in the continuing advances of these countries in improving the living standards of their people generally. Thanks to that lowering of their birth rates and the slowing down of population growth, these countries have been able to use their growing productive powers and total outputs of all economic goods to support, not inordinately growing populations on the old low living standards always (for the masses) at or near the level of grim poverty, but instead moderately growing populations *and* continually rising living standards, progressively spreading as such to more and more of their people.

Now as I have said before we still lack anything like full knowledge of all the causes that have together brought about this crucially important, highly beneficial change of birth rates to low levels, probably unique in human history. Some growth and spread of the practice of birth control or use of contraceptives has no doubt played its part, but—though of course adequate, reliable knowledge on this point is nonexistent—hardly can have played more than a rather small part in accounting for the total change which has occurred. Probably a larger part of the change has been due rather to a rise and spread of the use or exercise of what Malthus meant by "the preventive check"—deliberate self-restraint by men and women, in the matter of sexual intercourse, in order not to have too many children. But it is likely that the *main* causes of the change have been factors which hardly fit in that category either, though they work to reinforce "the preventive check" in that sense, and reduce the difficulty of its exercise, as well as to supplement it or bring about the same result in a larger, further part in other ways.

What I speak of now is the rise and spread of new interests, attitudes, and habits, uniquely prevalent and strong (thus far) in modern Western populations, which in various ways divert more of the ardors and energies of both husbands and wives into other channels. In our mobile and ambitious, busy populations, great numbers of husbands and wives spend frequently recurring intervals of time apart from each other and, though "living" together, are largely oriented to or absorbed in their own respective demanding activities away from each other and their homes and families. Perhaps there is enough more of physical (spatial) separation of the sexes than in other cultures, to have some effect; and of far more importance probably, the greater variety and intensities of the other competing interests or desires of most men and of many women, and their other energy-consuming, physical, mental, and emotional activities, may reduce the vigor of their sexual desires or the frequency of the times when those desires become too insistent to be denied. But if all this is true—and it is uncertain speculation—it is probably important mainly or largely in the way of facilitating a very widespread, intentional limitation of the sizes of families or the numbers of children born per married couple; a limitation desired and practiced for both economic and other reasons. And this point brings us back to "the preventive check" as conceived by Malthus, and his views about the desirability of making it generally and strongly effective, the impossibility of doing enough or very much in that direction, and the social institutions, policies, conditions, and "incentives" for the people that would best do all that *could* be done.

In spite of what I said earlier about the nonscientific, political or polemical, and dubious nature of this part of the argument advanced by Malthus in his *Essay,* I will say now that there *may* be *much* truth in the following general explanation of the subsequent, actual development—the great decline of birth rates—which we are discussing: that it has (perhaps) shown that Malthus was right about the conditions or required causes of a development of this kind, and wrong only in his pessimistic underestimate of their potential strength. Our modern Western societies do have—and had especially in the period of the great decline of birth rates—even more fully than the English society of his time had—the features that he saw as best calculated to induce most people to restrict the numbers of their children. The great decline of birth rates occurred in the context of the following conditions in every Western society. There was general prevalence of much "vertical mobility" for all able and ambitious individuals, within a "stratified" society or hierarchy of income-levels or economic classes, and general prevalence of the ambition to "rise" in the scale and provide one's children with the economic means for "rising" further. Also, there was a property system and economic system generally enabling individuals and families to prosper in measures roughly proportionate to their amounts of ability, ambition, effort, enterprise, and thrift; and the economic support of children and their (increasingly extensive and expensive) educations had to be provided mainly by their parents. There was, finally, a general, on-going growth of the economic wants and ambitions of most parents, for themselves and their children, and consequently a rise of the minimal ratios of their incomes to the sizes of their families, which they felt to be "necessary" for "decent" support of the latter, and to be the minima they "must" achieve and at least maintain through efforts both to increase their incomes and to avoid too early or too great enlargements of their families. Surely *all* that has operated, as Malthus argued that it would, to strongly motivate and help (at least) to cause both the modern growth of all economic production and the spreading growth of "prudent restraint" of the production of children. Moreover, it might be said that perhaps many of the *most* modern changes of or in the public policies and institutions of our Western nations—phases of the trend toward "socialism" or "the welfare state"—have helped to cause the recent tendency of birth rates to *rise* again, as well as (according to the common view of modern conservatives) reducing the "incentives" for and relaxing the efforts of millions to perform their economic or productive tasks ever more efficiently and "rise" to higher levels of economic success.

Yet I would caution those readers who incline toward conservative views but wish to think about these problems as objectively as possible, *not* to "run away with" the line of argument expressed in the foregoing paragraph; and decide too confidently that what produced the Western situation in happy contrast with the grim Malthusian forecast was *simply* adherence to the advice of Malthus or the realization, for a time, of a social order and "way of life" conforming to his precepts. It is probable, I think, but not provable, that the "incentives" to economic ambition and productive effort, and restraint of childbearing, on the parts of millions, which perhaps were maximal in that social order and "way of life" *did play some substantial part* in helping to bring about both the speeding up of economic progress and the slowing down of population growth through the fall of birth rates, which together banished the Malthusian specter.

But the *complete,* true explanations of both parts of that achievement or process must be much more complex. The speed and extent of the West's economic progress from the time of Malthus to the present surely have been due *mainly* to the great advances—vastly exceeding all that he anticipated—of science and technology and their applications in all branches of economic production. Even if we are convinced that in this part of history competitive capitalism, through its special "incentives," has greatly helped to foster those advances and full utilization of them, and to make them fully effective by stimulating the productive efforts of the people generally, we must recognize another possibility at least. And that possibility is that, hereafter in other parts of the world, societies with different economic, social, and political systems, cultures, and "ways of life" may yet prove able to equal or surpass our civilization's past and future scientific, technological, and economic-production achievements, with the aid of other systems of "incentives" unlike those in our tradition but no less effective. Nor is the needed restraint or moderation of birth rates and population growth a development which has been brought about in the Western case *entirely*, and can be brought about in other cases *only*, through the "incentives" to general use of "the preventive check" approved by Malthus and most fully realized in the Western "way of life" at a later time.

Economic considerations in the minds of parents against having large families—desires to save expenses and to achieve and maintain high living standards—unquestionably did play an important part in helping to reduce the normal size of the family in the West from eight or ten to two or three children. But I think it also is certain that that is by no means the whole story. Besides those economic considerations and deliberate decisions, many, varied, and changing circumstances and non-economic, often less deliberate and less conscious, attitudes or feelings also were important contributory causes. And other societies and cultures may evolve within themselves different but equally effective sets of causes of the same result.

We must now turn our attention, however, away from consideration of just the Malthusian theory and the population problem, and go on to consider, in the next chapters, the entire "classical" system of economic theory—as created mainly by Ricardo—in which the Malthusian theory became one basic element. As we shall see, this special element contributed by Malthus entered, above all, the "classical" economic "theory of wages," or doctrine about the long-run "natural" level of the real-wage incomes of working-class families: that although there would be on-going growth of the national economy's total output, profits, new savings and investments or new capital, and demand for labor, the growth of its population and therefore of its supply of labor would in the long run "tend" to exceed the greatest possible growth of demand for it, and would force and hold real wages in general down to a "subsistence" level, i.e., barely enough to "support" the working population.

The complete role of the Malthusian element, however, was larger than just its role as the basis of that theory of wages. It formed an essential part of the background of Ricardo's theory of all economic growth and of all its consequences, for all shares or parts of the national income—profits and land-rents as well as wages for labor—and his gloomy theory that all economic growth would some day come to an end in "the stationary state." The crowding of the land and the great difficulty of further increasing production from it would, according to this theory, reduce the wages and the profits resulting from new investments to the point of ending all growth of population and of capital, i.e., all economic growth whatever. At the same time, although the population *Essay* of Malthus thus very greatly affected Ricardo's economics, the latter included much more besides; and to it—Ricardo's economics—we now proceed.

CHAPTER 7

Ricardo: Introductory

RICARDO AND SMITH, A CONTRAST; THE MERITS OF RICARDO'S THEORETIC SYSTEM; AND THE EXCESSIVE DOGMATISM OF ITS DEVOTEES

We must now take up the difficult but interesting and important task of understanding—mastering—the ideas and arguments of David Ricardo, the brilliant English-Jewish stockbroker and economist, M.P., and widely respected public figure of his time—immediately after the Napoleonic Wars—who was the leading expert on England's then current problems of monetary, fiscal, and commercial policy, *and* the principal creator of the "classical" science of political economy. This system of economic theory *and* canons of "sound" governmental economic policy was the ruling "orthodoxy" in this field—above all in England but also to a great extent, at least among professional economists, in all or most Western countries—from the 1820s to the 1870s. As a former teacher of mine used to say, Adam Smith was not the father but only the grandfather of the classical theory of economics and political economy; its father was Ricardo. Ricardo made, though a duly respectful, a thorough and critical study of Adam Smith's great treatise on the *Wealth of Nations,* or rather of its views and reasonings on problems in which he (Ricardo) was interested. Finding those views and reasonings suggestive, but on some vital points confused and unsatisfactory, he set out to clarify, revise, improve, and further develop them, and to add his own new insights to them.

Ricardo's brilliant mind was of a very different type from Smith's, and very differently equipped, by his background of experience, for intellectual work in his much more narrowly circumscribed field of interest. Unlike the Scottish professor whose work nevertheless taught him much, Ricardo was no wide-ranging and thorough "bookish" scholar, and had no well-meditated and articulate, all-embracing social-and-moral philosophy. Ricardo was first of all a businessman—a stockbroker—who, after making his moderate but substantial fortune rather early in life, retired from business, bought a country estate, and went into public life. He became an active member of Parliament, the country's leading expert on its currently acute problems of economic policy, *and* a keen economic theorist, intent upon solving a limited number or group of logical problems which seemed to him to be the fundamental problems of the science. Though he brought to this work an excellent background of practical experience and realistic knowledge which, undoubtedly, fully affected and benefited his theoretical work as such, he omitted all that empirical knowledge from his written presentations and expressed only his deductive reasonings from or upon a few deliberately unrealistic, reality-simplifying, abstract assumptions. To this character of Ricardo's work and its contrast with Smith's—and the seeming paradox that as between the two it is the professor's work that is rich in realistic details but lacks theoretical precision and rigor, and the work of the practical man that never mentions any specific facts but is all pure, rigorous, abstract theory—to all this we may perhaps find a clue in a seventeenth-century writer's—Dudley North's—remark, to the effect that men with abundant practical experience learn to abstract from all nonessential details and concentrate or focus sharply on essential, general truths or principles.[1]

It is important to approach the study of Ricardo's work with a mind as free as possible both from the awe or excessive respect which his great reputation long inspired (in a time now far in the past), *and* from the adverse prejudices and "debunking" attitude which later grew up with and after the widespread reaction against, and turn of more modern economic theory away from, the Ricardian dogmas. Within the total history of the general development of economic theory, the true or deserved place of the Ricardian-classical system of doctrines, which had immense prestige for a time, is indeed far less important than it seemed to its devotees within that time, but also is far more important than some modern critics would have us think. Among the latter I would name especially the late Professor J. A. Schumpeter—one of the most eminent of modern economists *and* historians of economic science, but in my humble judgment an unduly severe and unfair critic of Ricardo and the Ricardian-classical ideas and doctrines. Viewing the latter in relation to the total course of the earlier, and concurrent, and subsequent development of all economic theory, Schumpeter called the Ricardian system or special structure of theory and its special history, a "detour" away from the main highway along which the science, throughout its history, has advanced.[2] And toward support of that

[1] Sir Dudley North, *Discourse Upon Trade,* 1691; Hollander reprint (Baltimore, Maryland: Lord Baltimore Press, 1907), preface, *passim.*

[2] J. A. Schumpeter, *History of Economic Analysis* (New York: Oxford University Press, 1954); pp. 469–480 and *passim.*

characterization, Schumpeter had and offered much evidence and acute analysis; but I think the characterization is, nevertheless, a great exaggeration of the valid point involved.

It is true that before and during, as well as after, the period of the Ricardian-classical system's (never universal) vogue, there were other important insights and lines of development of theory in the field, which lay beyond the mental horizons of Ricardo and his followers. At the end of its heyday or time of dominance, its major tenets had to be opposed and subjected to (at least) large revisions before those other contributions could come into their own or be generally accepted. I think the Ricardian system, all the same, was no (entirely or mainly) false, barren, or wasteful "detour," but a construction of lasting value, embodying (approximate) truths or insights or discoveries, fully as important as those which it failed to grasp and appreciate. It needed only to be adjusted to and combined with those other *also* true and important principles in a consistent and coherent synthesis.

As will be explained later on in this book, I think the late nineteenth-century exponents of the Jevonian, Austrian, and Walrasian "revolution" in economic theory, against or away from the Ricardian-classical tradition, indeed made very valuable new contributions and on the whole advanced the science far beyond the, by comparison, rudimentary state in which Ricardo left it. They went too far, however, as leaders and followers of "revolutions" always do, in their wholesale rejection of the Ricardian structure and exclusive claims for their own un-Ricardian insights. Their better-balanced contemporary, Alfred Marshall, who took the wiser course, refused to accept or share the "revolutionary" view of the new advance in which he fully participated along with them, and instead retained, with revisions, much of the Ricardian structure, and worked to construct exactly the "synthesis" referred to above. To this we shall return in later chapters; at this point I have wanted only to say that the now widespread underappreciation of Ricardo's achievement in economic theory and of its not only historic but enduring value is, in my opinion, as seriously mistaken and as harmful to the on-going search for all truth in the field as was the once widespread "worship" of just his system of ideas and aversion to all others known or thought to be in any degree inconsistent with it.

About the origins of that latter attitude, it should be said first of all that little if any of the "blame" for its development can justly be laid at the door of Ricardo himself. In the main at least it was later, inferior exponents of Ricardian-classical economic theory who in their formulations gave it the dogmatic form and tone and appearance of claiming virtual completeness, perfection, or finality. But certain features of the character inherent in this system of thought, as it came from the mind of Ricardo himself, no doubt facilitated the later growth, in the second-rate minds of the mass of its adherents, of such uncritical and all-criticism-resisting devotion. It was an impressive abstract theoretical system, deriving its general principles or "laws" with compelling logic from assumptions highly congenial to the "common sense" of that culture and epoch. And it combined two things which gave it a very strong appeal to many minds. In one aspect it was a set of explanatory "laws" or principles to explain the over-all general pattern of the current operation of the real economy, its on-going growth, and the main resulting changes of its structure—a theory of all that which did, to many minds, satisfactorily explain a great array of continually observable phenomena. And with that it combined a further set of normative principles or precepts—mistakenly regarded and represented as simply the logically proved and necessary corollaries of the explanatory theory—to guide or govern governmental economic policy and to direct that policy on just the lines which at the same time were strongly and emotionally desired, on (partly) different grounds, by different groups. The policy program was desired on idealistic grounds by the classical economists (Ricardo and his followers) *and* a great many other intellectuals of the time—all heirs of the liberal Enlightenment—*and,* on grounds of *both* moral conviction and economic self-interest, by growing multitudes of members of the English business community and of the entire, dominant middle-class public of the time.

It is hardly to be wondered at that such a body of doctrine—which could thus seem to its votaries to give them both a clear, convincing, and full explanation or understanding of the course of events in the world around them, and "scientific proof" of the moral and practical necessity or imperativeness of the public policies to which they were emotionally committed anyway, along with a great part of the society around them—tended to become "The Truth" in its field, to be not so much developed and improved by further critical inquiry, as simply taught to the young and the public, and defended against all attempts to criticize and alter it. But as we are seeing throughout this book, this same kind of thing has always tended to happen, in the same way and for the same reasons, throughout the history of economic-and-political thought, to *all* at once explanatory and normative systematic theories of political economy and the typical moods of their groups of adherents, in their times and areas of prevalence. The case of the Ricardian-classical system is in no way unique in this respect, and indeed is far from being the *worst* case of the kind on record. As we shall see, Marxism, for example, has become in *its* own circles a far more extremely rigid, static, and self-enclosed dogmatism than the Ricardian-classical-liberal political economy ever was. Moreover, we may, I think, be led to appreciate the relative freedom of the mind of Ricardo himself from all such "ideological" bias and dogmatism if we now look (1) at his special position in the general history of economic-and-liberal thought, and (2) at the link leading from Ricardo's to Marx's theoretical system.

RICARDO'S REALISM AND RELATIVE PESSIMISM VERSUS THE USUAL ECONOMIC-LIBERAL OPTIMISM

The "normative," political, or policy-precepts component of the Ricardian system was essentially the same "economic liberalism" which had been supported earlier by the Physiocrats, Adam Smith, and others, and was being supported in Ricardo's day in England also by his friends the Benthamites. It was beginning to win general or widespread support in the English business community, and in fact to win the political power that it was to have and hold widely in the Western world throughout the nineteenth century and well into the twentieth. Also this same policy-gospel was to be supported, as a rule very fully and strongly, by those leading nineteenth- and early-twentieth-century economic theorists who were otherwise—in the field of technical, positive-scientific economic theory—participants in the above-mentioned "revolution" against or away from Ricardo's ideas and influence. As we know, the "economic liberalism" that is here in question has always meant advocacy or support of a largely "free" (from direct and detailed control by governments) competitive "capitalism," or economic system of "free" private enterprises and competitive markets. And the usual tendency—except in the case of Ricardo's system of thought—of unions of this "gospel" with structures of economic theory, as such, has been to give the latter a dogmatic, optimistic bias about that economic system's "automatic" processes and results for the economic and general welfare of societies accepting, realizing, and maintaining it. But Ricardo, although he too was devoted to "economic liberalism," was objective enough as an economic theorist to adhere to his logic and assumptions—assumptions controlled not by his ideals but by his realistic knowledge even though the assumptions departed from the latter in the way of "simplifying" it—and let all this lead him, as it did, to a set of conclusions which on the whole was rather more pessimistic than optimistic, and must have been very disappointing to his dearest wishes. And he thus created a theoretical system of which some main elements were to aid Karl Marx—who indeed changed what he took from Ricardo, developed it in his own way, and added much else of his own—to create *his* "damning" analysis of all "capitalism," and alleged "scientific proof" that *not* economic liberalism but its extreme antithesis, complete socialism, was destined to become the only regime able to meet the needs of mankind, and survive.

Although the full meaning and basis of all that I am saying here can be made clear to the reader only gradually, and in the course of this entire chapter and several later chapters of this book, let me try here and now to explain my present point a bit more fully and exactly, and guard it from the most likely misunderstandings. Between the Ricardian and Marxian systems of economic theory, the only very partial similarity and historic connection has, beyond doubt, a certain degree of real significance, though I think too much is often made of it. As I will argue later on, the Marxian account of the matter grossly exaggerates the degree of resemblance and logical connection between the two systems. The elements, moreover, of Ricardo's system which Marx built upon were by no means flawless or entirely valid in themselves, even when understood as Ricardo meant them, and they became more false than true in Marx's version, involving his distortions and additions. But the general point that I want to suggest here can be summarized in the following way.

Most developments of economic theory carried out by devotees of economic liberalism have been seriously infected with the liberal-optimistic bias or departure from full objectivity. They have been perceptive only or mainly of the more attractive, harmonious, and generally beneficial aspects of the potential functioning and development of "free" or unfettered competitive capitalism, and relatively blind to that system's weaknesses, disharmonies, and internal difficulties. On the other hand or at the other pole, the Marxian development of economic theory is even more seriously infected with bias of the opposite, extremely pessimistic kind (pessimistic from the "capitalist" standpoint of course), or blind to those (by no means wholly unreal) "good" features of the same real system which the liberal economists have been too prone to see as its only ones and as more perfect than they are. But Marxian theory (as we shall see later) does yield insights of real value into the features of "capitalism" which account for both its "dynamism" and its difficulties or tendencies to develop malfunctionings endangering its power to endure as a system. The Marxian insights into all this both stand alone and exaggerate it, grossly, in order to produce the pretended "proof" that the system is fated to destroy itself and, in dying, give birth to the world's predestined, eventual socialist utopia. But finally—and *this* is my point here—Ricardo, in about equal measures of contrast with most other liberal economists *and* with Marx, was decidedly no pure optimist about the economic system which he favored (as relatively the best, really possible one in his world and time), but on the whole he was a remarkably objective, well-balanced realist. That is, he was able to carry on and develop—without the usual overoptimistic exaggerations and one-sidedness—the line of thought and class of insights evolving in the liberal tradition, *and* go *part* of the way toward the very different, later views and insights of Marx; he anticipated and supplied much of the valid part of the content of the latter—along with, even, some partly mistaken, unduly pessimistic notions, in a measure contributory to Marx's plunge *beyond* true objective realism into his own black fantasy or nightmare.

No doubt the characters in this respect of the theoretical systems produced by different economists have been much affected by the current states of or conditions in the real societies around them, and by the ruling climates of opinion in their times and circles. In the eighteenth-century world of the Physiocrats and Adam Smith, there was no obvious, flagrant unrealism in their vision of the potential harmonious and beneficent functioning and development of the liberal national economic systems which they advocated and conceived as ready to emerge into actual existence with removal of the then still existing traditional public restraints, of mediaeval and/or mercantilist origins, upon the mobility and rights of free choice and the private labors, investments, enterprises, trade, and competition of the mass of individuals. The greater parts at least of the populations of France and Great Britain at that time were relatively prosperous or well off by then current standards; and the prospects of substantial improvement of most people's circumstances through the emancipations or libertarian reforms proposed by those economists were real. The structures and degrees of stability of those national economies or economic societies —the numbers and sizes of the actually or potentially competitive enterprises and producing units in the different industries, the markets and marketing facilities that existed or could easily be developed, the potential, widespread, genuine competitiveness or relative absence of very powerful monopolies, and the slowness then of great changes through time of technology and cost, supply, and demand conditions for different goods and services, and the relative adequacy of the slow adjustments to such changes, which general economic freedom for all individuals would ensure—all gave much realism, in relation to that setting, to the optimistic theory of the potential functioning of the advocated liberal or "free" economy, as a self-adjusting, smoothly working, harmonious system, enabling all to best serve themselves by serving each other.

Also, of course, as I have explained in earlier chapters, the prevailing philosophy of that epoch and the only limited development of empirical research and knowledge were further important factors helping to account for the optimism in the Physiocratic and Smithian theoretical systems, which was no doubt somewhat excessive even in relation to the real possibilities actually inherent in their real environments. Although their relative (in that time inevitable) empirical ignorance, and the too idealistic optimism of their Enlightenment philosophies, gave a touch or tinge of utopianism to their economic-liberal-and-economic-theoretical visions, still I think it also is true that the (transitory) characters of their real environments helped to cause, engender, or suggest those visions, and give them much support or *relative* "realism." Above all, those real environments had not yet begun to feel the profoundly disturbing impact of the imminent or incipient industrial revolution which—in its early stages, while most of its eventual benefits to the people generally were still in the future and the most prominent current results were the strains and distresses of the transition—was to make the real world around Ricardo and still more, a bit later, that around Marx, conducive to their more pessimistic theoretical visions.

One important part of the pessimism in Ricardo's vision resulted, as we know, from its inclusion of the Malthusian theory of population growth and "pressure on subsistence" and the resulting inevitability of mass poverty at the bottom of society. But we also have seen in our study of that theory, that the current real situation helped to suggest and support it, and gave it a fuller measure of validity in application to that situation than it was to retain in a later, more fortunate epoch. And so we can largely attribute this part of the Ricardian (relative) pessimism not simply to the Malthusian theory, as such, but rather to that aspect of the contemporary, real environment which made that theory so convincing to Malthus and to Ricardo alike, and to all their followers. There were other aspects of that real environment—and the resulting climate of English public opinion—which go far to account for the other pessimistic elements of Ricardo's vision. The country's businessmen—the many successful ones among them—were indeed flourishing, as participants in and beneficiaries of the on-rushing industrial revolution. But as a class they knew some uncertainties and fears about the long-run prospects of their (the country's) expanding economy and their own respective enterprises and profits; for in their small island-country, with its fixed and limited area of land and supply of native natural resources, its fast-growing population, and its supply of new capital needing profitable investment outlets, there seemed to be in prospect in the long run an inevitable, progressive exhaustion or preemption of the better opportunities, and a decline of the rate of growth of the national output, and of profits.

There was indeed a realization that all that would be alleviated in some large measure, and through some considerable period of time at least, by expansion also *beyond* the home country's limits, by the growth of imports of food and raw materials, the growth of exports of English manufactured products, and the growth of exportation of English capital to aid in and profit by developing other less-crowded and already developed countries. But it seemed inevitable too that even this wider expansion, or progressive using up of the power of the external or foreign world to support expansion of the English economy, would eventually reach or approach a limit. And in the meantime, full use of this way of escape from the more imminent and confining limitations imposed by those of the home country's own area and resources, was being prevented by a national policy which was maintained by a hard-to-overcome factor in the existing domestic political situation. The growing business and middle class was only beginning to break down the traditional monopoly of political power, and the controlling influence of the vested interests, of the older, nonbusiness, "landlord" ruling classes of landed aristocrats and country gentlemen. Those "higher" classes in the English hierarchy were maintaining the Corn Laws—protective tariff against food imports—in order to maintain the high domestic price of food or agricultural produce and the resulting high rental and selling values of the country's farm lands. And this was maintaining at high "artificial" levels the cost of living for the country's industrial workingmen and the wages their employers must pay them, as well as increasing the share of their remaining profits which the businessmen must pay away in ground-rents to the landlords. The high cost of food and therefore of labor, and therefore of producing manufactured goods, was reducing the competitive advantage of the latter in the foreign or world market, and thus hampering the growth of the country's exports, required to pay for its needed growth of imports and provide the net surplus of foreign exchange which must be available if there was to be exportation of capital. In short, the businessmen were involved in a two-sided struggle to maintain their own (profit) share of the national income or aggregate value of the national output—a struggle with labor, to hold down the share absorbed by wages, and a struggle with the landlords, to hold down the share absorbed by land-rents—and they tended to foresee or fear an eventual shrinkage of their profit share, for the reasons already indicated. All or most of this was spelled out in Ricardo's system of economic theory,[3] and gave it the main part of its pessimistic tone or cast, thus to a great extent reflecting the current, real situation and prospects and prevailing viewpoint of the national business community, of which he was a member.

Let us not leave out of sight, however, Ricardo's adherence to economic liberalism, his heritage from Adam Smith, and the inclusion also in his total theoretical vision of a good deal of the normal liberal-optimistic view of the potential functioning of competitive capitalism. On the power of continuing "free competition" in all markets to bring about all the proper adjustments and readjustments (to changing conditions) of the relative prices of the economy's different products, and of the allocation of its total manpower and resources among different employments, to ensure maximal efficiency in all production and an optimal balance of responses to all market demands—on all this, which

[3] Ricardo did not hold that high wages due to high food prices hampered English exports; his theory of international trade (not discussed in this book) ruled out such an influence.

always has been the *main* theme of liberal-optimistic economic theory, Ricardo fully agreed with Adam Smith and stands entirely in the line or tradition of that kind of theory. Agreeing in this field with all the other theorists in that tradition, he never doubted that the liberal capitalist or business economy would be self-adjusting and perform admirably *as regards* efficient production, maximization of the aggregate of all production, and appropriate matching of the balance of the outputs of different products with that of the public's demands for them. It was only in the other respects already touched on above that he thought the economy's functioning-and-growth would proceed less favorably. In the field or process of the distribution or division of the national income into the rent share of the class of landlords, the wages share of the laboring class, and the profit share of the capitalists or businessmen, he saw the interests of the three classes as not in harmony but in conflict. He thought that as this division would work out in the long run, the wage earners would get only "subsistence" (and their capitalist-employers would find it increasingly costly to themselves to provide even this). The landlords would get a great and growing, unearned share of the national income by merely charging and getting, in the growing economy with a fixed supply of land, rising rents for rights to use the lands owned by them while not *personally* contributing to production; and the profits left for the capitalists or businessmen would over time decline toward zero.

The impression, however, of *predominant* pessimism in Ricardo's theoretical system as a whole, is due to the fact that he gave his main interest, attention, and emphasis to just these problems, on which he reached these pessimistic conclusions, about income distribution and the effects of economic growth upon it. Adam Smith had mainly emphasized (1) the question how a nation could best foster growth of its total national output or income, and (2) the processes of adjustment in the liberal economy through which it would best serve this purpose. But Ricardo, while agreeing with Smith on the need for such growth and for the liberal economic policies and system as best fitted to achieve it, held that the full range of all the variables capable of affecting the size and rate of growth of the total national output or income, made up a subject matter too broad and complex, heterogeneous, and lacking in stable or reliable regularities, to be the appropriate subject matter or domain of economic science. Instead he conceived of the latter as properly concerned primarily with just the "laws" or principles controlling the division of the (growing) national income into the land-rent, wages, and profit shares, and the *effects* of economic growth *upon* that division of those shares. And in developing and modifying Smith's subordinated and less than fully worked out theory of *this* subject, into his own emphatic and full-blown theory of it, Ricardo evolved the latter along the more starkly pessimistic lines, reflecting the situation and outlook prevailing in the England of his time, which I have already outlined.

SOCIAL PHILOSOPHERS VERSUS ECONOMISTS; UTOPIAN SOCIALISTS

In Ricardo's time and world there were still—chiefly among builders of all-embracing social philosophies, not specializing as he did in technical economics—those who retained all or much of the optimism and utopian tendency which had been so prevalent in the preceding century. As we saw in a former chapter, there was much of that even in the utilitarian-liberal philosophy of Bentham and his followers, a group with which Ricardo was associated in a measure and which tended to claim him as a member. Since he and the Utilitarians alike were liberals, advocating the same public economic policies and often acting together politically, he was highly respected among them, despite his more pessimistic outlook. But Ricardo himself, as I have said, was no broad philosopher, and I think his system of economic theory owed little or nothing to any of the ideas of Bentham, though perhaps his economic liberalism had at least mainly, like Bentham's but in a looser sense, the social-utilitarian ground or motive—the simple pragmatic belief in the expediency, for national economic progress and prosperity, of the system of free private enterprises and competitive markets. At all events, his lack of active interest in the Utilitarian or any all-embracing social philosophy—his exclusive preoccupation with just the problems of economics which he worked on—may further help to account for the more than half-pessimistic "realism" of his thought. For the current economic situation and apparent prospects of the people, or even of the business and middle class, in the early part of the nineteenth century—in that disturbing and distress-producing stage of the industrial revolution and all its concomitants—were not of a nature to suggest a utopian, optimistic theory of the current or the potential working and development, in all respects, of competitive capitalism, *to* minds engrossed in close study of the economic scene as such.

Only minds that were engrossed rather in developing all-embracing speculative social philosophies, and hence were less fully and acutely aware of the gloom-suggesting features of the economic scene, could in that time easily and fully retain the high hopes prevalent in the just preceding time of the Enlightenment, about an impending and already beginning approach by mankind to attainment in the near future of a happy world of happily self-ordering, free societies. And the *fullest* continuation of that hopefulness and faith was no longer to be found even in such a philosophy as liberal Benthamism, which advocated a *laissez-faire,* competitive capitalism along with political democracy, *and* was only moderately optimistic, i.e., relatively realistic. Instead, the full measure of such optimism was henceforth to be found only in the more radical and very different "philosophies" or visions of such diverse "utopian socialist" thinkers as Robert Owen, Fourier, and others. The spreading social disturbance, distress, and discontent arising from the industrial revolution was breeding hatred of capitalism or the business economy, and *dividing* the seekers of a new utopian or perfect society *from* the adherents of the classical liberalism, which sanctioned (liberal competitive) capitalism and sought only moderate reforms or changes —to greater freedoms for all individuals—away from the ages-old, traditional European form of social order. Though there had been in the eighteenth century, among its advocates of social change, a few socialists along with the countless liberal individualists, the program of the latter had then seemed sufficient, to most such idealistic minds, to realize the dream of a world of "perfected" institutions, policies, people, and human relations, and great and ever-growing, universal welfare and happiness. But in the early nineteenth century, when it seemed that the moderate liberal program was well on its way to full realization in practice and yet the state of the real world was extremely disappointing, the liberals were generally becoming less optimistic and utopian; and the still numerous, full-fledged utopians—heirs and continuers of that eighteenth-century dream—were in most cases becoming socialists.

The *utopian* socialists, however, not only were, but also *seemed* utopian in the derogatory sense to those of their contemporaries and immediate successors who surpassed them—and they were easy to surpass in this!—in realistic knowledge and understanding, both of the current and immediately prospective working and development of contemporary capitalism (and its mixed good and bad results for the people generally), and of the inevitable slowness, difficulty, and necessary method or strategy of a change or transformation of the social order as radical and profound as that from contemporary capitalism to a future, realized socialism would have to be. And the outstanding socialist thinker who soon emerged within this category of the better realists, or with more realistic knowledge and understanding of all that, was Karl Marx. It was he who first applied the disparaging adjective "utopian" to his socialist forerunners, and set out to make socialist thought "scientific" instead of "utopian," i.e., to create a real social "science" *about, mainly, not* the ideal socialist world to be realized in the future *but* the "historical process" and course of action *through* which it would be realized. Yet there were in the strange mixed pattern of Marx's thought, besides the one relatively realistic and scientific component which he fashioned from or with the aid of Ricardo's economics plus his own historical research, two other essential components which in fact were and remained utopian or purely speculative and expressive rather of his ideals, wishes, hopes, and dreams, than of any solid knowledge capable of being established as such through empirical-and-logical research.

One of those two radically nonscientific and unrealistic components of Marx's thought and all Marxism was and is the vague socialist vision itself, of the future, perfected, socialist society, which Marx took over essentially unchanged from his more purely utopian socialist forerunners. In criticizing the mode of thought of those forerunners *as* "utopian," he did not intend any criticism of their goal itself as fantastic and forever unattainable on earth. On the contrary, he fully shared and retained their extremely visionary, wishful, and hopeful faith that "some day" all men would live in complete or absolute freedom and harmony, as spontaneously, perfectly cooperating members of ideal communities of workers, collectively owning all "means of production" and individually contributing to the collective output or income "according to their abilities" while sharing its use or enjoyment "according to their needs." Only the ideas of his utopian forerunners *about the process of attainment* of this utopia seemed to Marx "utopian" or unrealistic. They expected simply, through preaching and argument, to persuade the public of the wisdom and attractions of their program, and thus to bring about its adoption and execution by general agreement. They did not realize that in the current state of the existing capitalistic societies, the circumstances and resulting interests, attitudes, and power of the members of the dominant class made that impossible; nor did they (the socialists) realize that they must wait for and through, understand, and cooperate with the impending historical process of social evolution which would in time "ripen" the existing societies for easy transformation into socialist societies—and then complete the transformation through well-prepared and well-timed revolutions. But involved in Marx's own theory of this historical process of social evolution, to be completed at its future end by the socialist revolution, was *the second* visionary-philosophic, not scientific or realistic, component of his own scheme of thought—the conception of all human history as a "dialectical" process working its tortuous way to a preordained goal, which Marx carried on (with a revision of his own) from the philosophy of Hegel. Thus it was in the enveloping context of his dreams of the future, harmonious, socialist world, and the necessary road of struggles leading to it, that Marx incorporated the more solid core of his intellectual system—the analysis of the current and prospective functioning and evolution of capitalism as an economic system, which he fashioned from Ricardo's economics together with his own researches into facts of earlier and contemporary economic history.

The degree of "pessimism," then, which characterized Ricardo's theory of the current and prospective working and development of the business economy of the early-industrial-revolution time, was far surpassed by the utter grimness of Marx's only partly similar theoretical picture, and forecast of the future, of that economy. For in Marx's mind his visionary faith in the socialist-utopian destiny of mankind set up a standard by contrast with which the contemporary capitalist world and system appeared to him as an intolerable "mess," which surely would (he wishfully believed) bring about its own destruction, through its malfunctioning and self-induced degenerative evolution. Ricardo on the other hand, although he was a liberal and thus favorably disposed to the existing or emerging order which Marx hated, had a mind that was *not* too much influenced by the usual liberal visionary faith in the liberal utopia; and he achieved, simply, a rather highly objective and realistic understanding of what in fact was going on in the economy around him. But by no means all later liberal economists were to do as well in this respect.

It is remarkable that Ricardo's system of economic theory, with all its realistic, relative pessimism about the "natural" working and development of competitive capitalism, became and remained through several decades the cherished, dogmatic creed of most of the economists, businessmen, and politicians who wanted to uphold that regime or system and the public policies most favorable to its "free, natural" operation and development. Of course, the "grim" results of the real system's working as depicted in this theory or creed, were all attributed to "natural laws" which, it was held, public action could do little about. And perhaps the very fact that even this creed or theory represented the real system's working as not much better than barely endurable for the people generally—together with the fact that in that harsh era most potentially popular alternative theories or even limited revisions of exactly this one, were likely to represent the real system as *un*endurable and issue in demands for public action to reform it—perhaps all this explains *why* the Ricardian-classical scheme of theory tended to become for its adherents a sacred orthodoxy, to be preserved and taught as it stood, with vigilance against all new interpretations, revisions, and developments which might be or become dangerous heresies. But as the early and middle decades of the century passed, the gradual rise and spread of prosperity, and of democracy, brought a new growth of social stability, security, confidence, and optimism. The (multiplying) supporters of the liberal economy and economic policies, including the (also multiplying) liberal economists, became less timorous; and the latter and their public became ready for both the new advance of economic theory in the last three decades of the century and the change of outlook in that field away from the Ricardian-classical pessimism to renewal of the economic-liberal optimism which had flourished in the eighteenth century and as then, so now again, often verged too nearly upon utopianism.

In the appropriate later chapters we shall study both sides of that later development—the real and substantial advance of technical, theoretical, or analytical work in the science as such, beyond Ricardo's achievements, and (owing to the stronger influence of the more confident liberal ideology) the swing away, not only from Ricardo's pessimism, but also from any "realism" or "sense of reality" equal to his, into new excesses of unrealistic optimism. But we must now, in the next chapter, go beyond all the broad, general, and peripheral topics that have occupied us in this one, and take up direct study of Ricardo's "technical" theoretical work in economic science itself. It will be necessary to confine our attention almost entirely to just the main part of his work—the views that he worked out in what he held to be the main, central, or general field of economic theory, as distinguished from the several appended, narrower, special fields.

In other words, our concern is to be with his theory of "value" or the relative prices (exchange values) of the different goods produced in the economy, and theory of the division of the national income into the land-rent, wages, and profit shares, and theory of the effects of economic growth (growth of the country's population, supply of labor, and supply of capital, in its fixed land-area) upon that division or those income shares. But the fact must be stressed that Ricardo also produced, besides his system of general economic theory dealing with those topics, important contributions to knowledge about other problems, in the special fields of study of money, banking, and monetary policy, international trade and finance and commercial policy, and fiscal policy or public finance, especially taxation. Ricardo had much to do with establishing the practice, continued by all subsequent economists, of dividing the total field of economics into the central or main field of general theory and those (and other subsequently added) special fields. And his own great contributions in his special fields, especially that of monetary theory and policy, in fact were largely made *before* he created the scheme of general economic theory which is now about to receive *nearly* all our attention. But in approaching my treatment of that scheme I must begin by explaining the view which dictated Ricardo's sharp *separation* of "monetary theory" and "general economic theory" from each other; for this view, which made that separation seem essential, was itself a primary principle of his economics, and must be understood at the outset if we are to understand the point of view and structure of his scheme of general theory.

CHAPTER 8

Ricardo: The Ricardian Theory of Exchange Values, Income Shares, and Economic Growth; and the Underconsumption Heresy

ECONOMICS VERSUS MONETARY THEORY; RICARDO'S THEORY OF "VALUE"

As was said at the end of the last chapter, we must now first glance at Ricardo's theory of the role of money in the economic system, and the reason why he regarded study of that role as a separate specialty and not a part of general economic theory. Money, according to Ricardo and his followers, has no other function or significance except that of serving as a "medium of exchange" which obviates "barter" or direct exchanges of different "real" goods for each other, *but only replaces literal with virtual or indirect* "barter" in that sense, or enables *the same results* to be attained in a more convenient and economical way. Any sale of anything for money is only one and not the final step toward the seller's goal—a means to the end of obtaining the other things he will buy with the money. The money itself can be of no benefit to him until he spends it, hence in every case he will certainly soon spend all of it, for consumers' goods or/and investment goods. Thus what really goes on, in and by means of all commerce or selling and buying, is a process or network of exchanges, of the outputs of the products of the economy's different industries and enterprises, and of the inputs of labor-time and means of production that go into them, for each other: exchanges among owners of these different items, forms, or elements of "real" (nonmonetary) wealth, *by way of* their intervening acquisitions and spendings of money, which at once facilitate and disguise the real process but do not essentially alter or affect its character and outcome.

Changes of the economy's supply and flow of money can indeed raise or lower all money-prices, and—because when that happens some money-prices change more quickly than others, and the normal relations among them all can be reestablished only in the long run—such monetary changes *temporarily* change the exchange ratios among the different, "real" goods which men are disposing of and getting in return. And it is the task of monetary theory to explain, and the task of monetary policy to control and minimize, these fluctuations and transitional disturbances. But general economic theory needs to *abstract from* all the monetary phenomena as such, in order to avoid confusion in performing its different task of explaining the relations and behavior of the "real," nonmonetary variables which over the long run control the economy's functioning.[1] The question of the validity of this idea will concern us only in a much later part of this book; here the student should not accept or reject or judge it, but only understand it as a basic tenet of Ricardian theory. If he does so, he will understand that—and also why—Ricardian "general" theory begins with the problem of "value," not in the sense of money-value or price but in that of the value-in-exchange of any one for any other one of all the goods that are being produced and exchanged in the economy. What is, with respect to any good, the basis of its value *in terms of* each other good—the cause, determinant, or regulator of the physical quantity of the (any) good acquired, which a unit-quantity of the good exchanged for it "is worth" or equivalent to or would just exchange for in the long-run normal equilibrium of the fluid, free, competitive economy?

Now in developing his theory to explain exchange values in that sense, Ricardo agreed up to a certain point with Adam Smith's discussion of the same problem, but diverged thereafter to a different conclusion. Thus at the outset he agreed with or followed Smith in assigning only a limited role or significance to a good's utility or value-in-use, and the resulting demand for it, in helping to account for its value-in-exchange. As Ricardo in effect put this proposition: if a thing

[1] Although I am sure that students of Ricardo's writings on monetary and other economic subjects will agree that he held the views I have attributed to him thus far in this chapter, this cannot be documented by specific references to specific passages.

The further exposition of Ricardo's theories, in the bulk of this chapter, is all based on or refers to the first six chapters of *Principles of Political Economy and Taxation: The Works and Correspondence of David Ricardo,* Piero Sraffa (ed.) (London: Cambridge University Press, 1952), vol. 1. Again, footnotes referring to particular passages are generally omitted below, because the entire series of Ricardo's chapters must be read as a connected whole if his views on particular points are to be understood.

has no utility for anyone and there is consequently *no* demand for it, then of course it will have no exchange value; existence of (some) utility and demand is a necessary condition for existence of exchange value; but this *necessary* condition generally is *not sufficient* by itself to determine *the amount or magnitude* of the good's exchange value. *Given* the existence of some—no matter how much or little—utility and demand, the exchange value, in Ricardo's general case, can be anything in the long run, depending on a quite different variable which I will for this moment call "cost of production"—deferring the required explanation and reservations. Now at this point we must proceed carefully, for it was at this point in the Ricardian line of argument that the later anti-Ricardian "revolution" in "theory of value" was to find its point of attack, and raise its significant but confusing issues. The later "marginal utility" theorists, in other words, were to make the full or detailed analysis of utility and demand and their role, which Ricardo failed to make; and the "revolutionists" among them were to attribute entire control of exchange value to just utility and demand alone, and accuse Ricardo of conceding *no* importance at all to them, and wholly deny his view imputing an *independent* importance or role to (something involved in) the good's "cost of production." Hence it is important here to explain Ricardo's real position as fully and clearly as possible.

He in fact granted *not only* that utility and demand are always necessary to give exchange value to any good. He *also* granted that utility and demand do exert complete control *in* the special cases in which "cost of production" either is nonexistent or cannot exert control; i.e., in all cases of goods either not produced by human agency but supplied by "nature" in restricted quantities, or humanly produced but by monopolies controlling and restricting their supplies and thus ruling out the competitive adjustment of supply to demand at the cost value and so of exchange value to the cost-determined level, which he assumed to be operative in the general or most common case, in the kind of economy which his whole system of theory was about. And finally, going still farther, he *also* granted that even in that general (competitive) case, utility and demand always have an immediate controlling importance *in the short run*, when and while supply is out of adjustment to demand-at-cost and until such nonadjustment is replaced by full adjustment. Thus for example, whenever the market's demand for a good increases, and the supply cannot immediately be increased to the same extent, the immediate result will be a rise of the good's price (relative to the prices of other goods not in this same situation); but in the long run, if the Ricardian competitive adjustment mechanism is working, the higher price and reward for production of this good will attract more capital, land, and labor into that employment, and the output or supply of the good will increase to equality with the enlarged demand at the cost price, and this will bring the actual price down to the cost level again.

In short, Ricardo in his argument as a whole quite fully recognized the entire, actual role of the utility-and-demand variable, even though his theory lacked the clear, detailed analysis of this which was to be the primary contribution of his later critics. But he put his main stress on the long-run processes of adjustment of supplies to all changes of demands, in the fluid, liberal, competitive economy, and the long-run control of *the points of balance* of supplies with demands and so of the equilibrium exchange values of the different products, by their relative "costs of production." When his friend and contemporary critic, Malthus, accused him of giving too little study and stress to the role of demand, he replied that he fully appreciated the importance of that role but thought of supply as generally, in the long run, "pressing closely on the heels of demand," and thus making value dependent finally—regardless of the extent of demand—on cost of production as the regulator of supply.[2]

We must next notice, however, how Ricardo's *analysis* of cost differed from that of his later critics, and from Adam Smith's. In considering the components of the cost of producing a good, Ricardo emphasized *not the values* of the required labor-services, materials, use of land and equipment, etc., which the late-nineteenth-century opponents of his doctrines *were to* emphasize and view—in a way entirely consistent, really, with his view *of them*—as *derived from* the values of the alternative, potential products of the same resources, and so as indirectly dependent on—not independent of—utility-and-demand variables. Ricardo's stress here was wholly upon *the quantities* of the input-factors required per unit-quantity of output of each good, precisely because he realized that in competitive equilibrium the producers of all products, drawing on the common supplies of the same input-factors, must pay at the same rates for them, hence the *different* values of the different products must reflect and correspond to the different *amounts* of the input-factors needed to produce them. It was therefore only, so to speak, *this dimension of* the cost of producing a unit of a good—*not* the prices paid for the input-factors *but* the amounts of them required—which Ricardo *meant* or had in mind, *in* treating "cost of production" as a crucial, independent variable, independent of utility-and-demand variables, and playing in the long run the all-important role in determining the relative position of each good in the system of exchange values—in full equilibrium of the fully competitive econ-

[2] The letter from Ricardo to Malthus containing this passage appears in *ibid.*, vol. 8, pp. 300ff.

omy, with mobile labor and resources flowing into all employments to the point of equalizing the rates of earnings obtainable in them.

But if we follow and accept this line of thought, thus far, we now have before us a dilemma. *This* conception of "the cost of production" of a good—in the not-prices-but-only-quantities-of-inputs aspect—*as* the set of quantities of *all* the input-factors needed to produce a given output of the good—is an impossibly awkward, heterogeneous concept, referring to a group of quantities that are incommensurable and cannot be added up: X man-hours of labor *plus* Y acres or square yards of land, *plus* (?) Z units (?) of capital, is meaningless. The best that can be done to get a usable concept, as consistent as possible with the line of reasoning which led us to this one, is to accept the rough approximation of using only the variable quantity of *one* of the input-factors—the one that is generally predominant, and apt to vary in the same direction with most of the others—to stand for all of them. And this, I think, is what Ricardo did in adopting—with careful qualifications, to be explained hereafter—his famous "labor theory of value": that in competitive equilibrium the relative values of the conventional unit-amounts of any two different goods, *tend to be approximately proportional to* the relative amounts (in man-hours) of labor-time directly and indirectly "embodied in" them, i.e., required to produce them (including production of all the produced means or equipment, tools, materials, etc., which enter into them)—under the existing conditions and with the currently used techniques of production in the industries concerned. But now, to test this interpretation of Ricardo's theory and to get a fuller understanding of it, let us turn back to Adam Smith's discussion of the value problem and then follow up the criticisms and revisions of Smith's views through which Ricardo arrived at his own position.

As we know, Adam Smith confined the sphere of valid application of "the labor theory" to the (his imaginary) ultrasimple "primitive" economy in which "laborers" alone produced, received, and owned everything. They specialized in producing different single products and supplied their other needs through barter with each other, had virtually only their labor-time to "put in" to production, and applied that to the best advantage, i.e., chose their occupations with a view to maximizing the amounts of their fellows' products obtained in exchange for the product of each man-hour of work. All those conditions are implicitly assumed in Smith's (and Ricardo's) famous familiar illustration: two primitive hunters go into the forest, the one hunting deer and the other, beaver; the deer hunter needs (on the average) two hours in which to find, kill, and bring back one deer, while the other can "produce" one beaver in one hour; then, if the two are to stay in their respective occupations, i.e., continue hunting the same animals, their products must be and remain exchangeable at the rate of two beavers for each deer. For at any other rate (ratio) of exchange, *not* thus corresponding to the relative labor-time "costs of production," either the beaver hunters would gain more by becoming deer hunters instead, or vice versa; and enough individuals *would* transfer from the less to the more advantageous occupation, to alter the relative supplies of the two products to the point of *making* any unit of each "worth" the amount of the other representing the same labor-time "cost."

Ricardo agreed with and repeated this illustration and argument of Smith's showing how the "labor theory" would work in the "primitive" economy, thus conceived; but he disagreed with Smith's different view of the more developed and complex, real economy around them, in which both men of course were far more interested. Smith, as we know, regarded the "labor theory" as *not* valid *in* application to the latter, on the ground that in the latter the laborers had to "share" (the value of output) "with landlords and capitalists," i.e., the wages paid for the labor-time involved in production of a given output of a good now made up only a part of its full-cost value, and the remaining parts of that went as rent to landlords for the land-use involved, and profit to capitalists on the capital involved. It did not seem to Smith that one only partial determinant of the relative production costs of different goods—the relative labor-time requirements and resulting costs for wages—could be *the* determinant of the relative or exchange values of the goods. His apparent reasoning on this point involved the (quite reasonable) implicit assumption that labor-time, land use, and capital use would or might well be combined *in different proportions* in producing different goods, hence the costs for wages alone would be *different* fractions of the full-cost (money) values of the latter, and their relative values-in-exchange for each other would then *not* be proportional to their labor-costs-in-production, alone. Hence Smith, on leaving consideration of the simple, "primitive" economy and taking up the task of analyzing the complex, real economy around him, discarded the "labor theory" and replaced it with a total-money-costs theory of prices, which said only that, in long-run competitive equilibrium, the prices of products would be equal to the sums of the necessary payments of wages, rent, and profit for the labor, land, and capital required in their production.[3]

Ricardo, however, regarded that mere money-costs theory of prices as insufficient or unsatisfactory, and undertook to show that and how *a somewhat qualified* "labor theory" of exchange values could be made to fit all the real conditions present in the contemporary, complex econ-

[3] See the previous presentation of this part of Adam Smith's discussion of the "value" problem, in my Chapter 4 above, pp. 105–107; and the footnote references there to the relevant passages in the *Wealth of Nations*.

omy, and provide a more profound or thorough explanation of the relative or exchange values of its different products in long-run competitive equilibrium. To Ricardo I am sure the mere global money-costs theory of prices seemed—as indeed it is—superficial and circular. In the competitive economy all prices are interdependent, and it is no full or sufficient explanation of the prices of products to say only—though this is true as far as it goes—that in equilibrium they will equal the sums of the total prices (per unit prices times quantities) of all the inputs of labor-time, land use, and capital use required to produce them. For this set of equalities or equations reflects the influence *of* the prices *obtainable for* the products in the markets, *on* the prices the producers can and in competition must pay (per unit) for all those inputs, *as well as* the influence of the latter prices *on* those they "must" get for their products to cover costs and keep going.

As we saw before, to get outside that circle, to the factor in costs that is independent of demands and prices and, by governing supply adjustments, determines the *relative* prices of different products in the long run, it is necessary to focus solely on *the quantities* of the inputs technologically required to produce unit-quantities of output of the different products. For practical purposes, this means to focus on the best usable approximation to the complete sets of the input-quantities required, viz., the labor-time requirements. Ricardo, then, endeavored to so analyze the relations of the different elements of the total money-costs of producing goods to their exchange values as to establish *the generally predominant role of the labor-time requirements* in determining the latter. And he proceeded toward his goal by way of a series of arguments about *the other* elements of production costs in Adam Smith's sense—viz., land-rents, wage rates, and profits—either wholly or largely *eliminating* them from consideration as part-causes of the values of the products. First he argued that the land-rent elements in the prices of all products *do not at all affect* those prices, but entirely *result from* the latter. And then he went on to argue that although wage rates and profits or capital costs do affect all prices, they *do not as a rule much* affect the *relative* prices or exchange values of the different products—or do affect those significantly only in some special cases. Thus in the end he got down to or had left his labor-time requirements, in the total production processes for different goods, as the principal determinants of their exchange values. Let us now consider, first, his theory about land-rents and product prices.

In the national economy as a whole there exists only a fixed and limited amount of land; and this total supply is made up of lands of various different qualities or grades from the standpoint of producers of each kind of product—e.g., for any branch of agriculture, there are soils of many different degrees of fertility; and generally, for each purpose, the supply of the *best* land is *quite* small, even second-best land is not very abundant, etc. Now if and as long as a new or young, growing country has only a small or sparse population relative to its total land area, and demand conditions call for only small total outputs of the different products, the entire output of each product may all be produced on or from *the best* or most productive land for that purpose; and as on this land the production costs (for the labor and capital required) per unit of output will be low, the equilibrium price of each product also will be low (only covering those costs), and the owners of the land used may be unable to charge and get any net or pure land-rent, i.e., anything more than compensation for the costs they may have incurred *for adding man-made improvements* to the land as such or as "nature" made it. That is, if there is still "plenty" of land of the best grade for each purpose, to more than satisfy all demands for its use in production, there will be no competitive bidding up of rentals by eager would-be tenants for each piece of land, but rather a competitive cutting down of rentals by owners in order to get their lands used. This procedure will continue as long as they are still getting any net returns at all over and above repayment of whatever costs they incur only when they rent out the lands.

But that initial situation cannot last long in a growing country or economy, i.e., one in which all economic quantities *except* the land supply are increasing over time. With continual growth, in its fixed land-area, of the economy's population, labor supply, capital supply, and demands for all products, the outputs of the latter will increase *in two ways, alike involving rising additional labor-and-capital costs of production of the additional outputs*. One part of the increase of production is attained through increasingly intensive use of the best land already in use, i.e., application of more and more labor and capital on that same land, per unit of its area, to increase its output. But *this* process is subject to "the law of diminishing returns," i.e., beyond a certain point the further additions to output which can be made in this way decline relative to the additions of more labor and capital on the land, which are needed to produce them.

In other words, the latter, and hence the additions to producers' costs which they entail, rise relative to the additions to output which they yield. And *because* the increase of production on or from the best land is subject to this "law," the same new conditions (of demand for the product and price obtainable for it), which nevertheless make it pay, will also make it pay as well to bring into use additional poorer land, not used before, on which from the outset the per unit production cost for the labor and capital required is likewise high as compared with that in the original situation on the best land. The growing economy meets its growing demands for all products with increases of output involving *both* increasingly intensive use of its better lands *and* an ever wider extension of production also to less and less good, additional land-areas. And since in both these processes, as they continue, the new additions to producers' costs for the new additions to output rise progressively, the growing demands for the products are met with only such limited increases of their outputs as will keep their selling prices equal to those rising "marginal costs" of the most expensively produced "last" increments included in the equilibrium outputs.

Now in that latter situation, however, of generally increased demands and production, *the greater part* of the total national output of each product is still being produced *on lands that are better, in various degrees, than the poorest* land being used in the industry; and on each such piece of "intramarginal" or "better than marginal" land, the *average* cost of production per unit of its output (for the needed labor-and-capital input only) *is below* the "marginal" cost which the selling price of the product must cover to make total production equal to demand. Hence the sale of the output of each piece of intramarginal or relatively good land yields a "surplus" of total receipts over total production costs (for labor and capital), which reflects and measures the extra productivity of that piece of land, and the advantage of its use, over that of the "marginal" land in use in the industry. And the competition of would-be users or tenants for each such piece of land enables its owner to obtain a rent for its use equal to this "surplus" of receipts over (other) costs which any normally competent user of it can acquire. Thus land-rents arise *as results of* the heights at which the prices of products are fixed by "marginal" labor-and-capital costs and the lower average costs for those factors on the lands concerned, *and are not themselves parts of the price-determining costs* of production. This is not yet the place to take up the other aspects of Ricardo's theory of the land-rent share of the national income, including his (implied) view of it as "unearned" by the landlords who received it. Thus far our task in hand is still that of understanding his route toward demonstration of his "labor theory" of the values of products through arguments eliminating their other supposed determinants; and we have now just completed, with him, the first step along that route, i.e., the argument eliminating land-rents from any role in that connection.

Still, before going on to the next step let me add here, as illuminating the Ricardian theory of the origin of land-rent just presented, an account of the improvement of or upon it which was worked out by the later German economist von Thünen,[4] who devised a simplification of Ricardo's argument that makes the essential point stand out more clearly. Ricardo's presentation, as we have seen, emphasized—though

[4] See J. A. Schumpeter, *History of Economic Analysis* (New York: Oxford University Press, 1954), pp. 465–468.

this really is *not* the essential point—the fact that an economy's total supply of land normally includes lands *of different grades* or qualities for every purpose, and that where this is so, and the growth of demand is met partly by extending production to lands less good than the best, rent arises *first* on the *better* lands and appears to reflect and measure their degrees of superiority over the "marginal" lands—the least-good "pieces" brought into use at all, at a given point in the growth of demands, and of such little worth (productivity) that at that point no rent can be paid or obtained for them. Ricardo indeed *did make* the essential point, as we also have seen, *that it is the rise, on the better lands themselves, of the marginal costs of increasing their own outputs,* above the average or over-all per unit costs of production on them, and to equality with the initial costs on the marginal lands, *which accounts for the coming into use of the latter, and for* the emergence of the rent-surplus on the better lands. But he *seemed* to regard this rise of intensive-marginal costs on even the best lands as *only* explaining the resort to poorer lands also and *to view the latter as the cause* of the emergence of rent on the better lands.

Now what von Thünen later showed was that the true explanation of the origin of rent is only unnecessarily complicated and obscured by assuming (in agreement, to be sure, with the usual facts) a non-homogeneous land supply, and allowing this really irrelevant detail—the differences of different pieces of land—to appear to have key importance. To show this, von Thünen set up instead an ingenious conception under which all the land in the economy he analyzed would be economically alike or uniform. In his imaginary "isolated state"—a self-sufficient, closed economy—there existed a central market town and, all around it, concentric rings, or belts, of farm land, with differences of soil fertility always precisely offsetting differences of distance from the market town and so of transportation costs. The richer soils were just enough farther away to have no advantages—the less rich soils enough nearer to market to have equal advantages—so that on balance all the farms would be just alike and equally profitable. This economy still had, however, like Ricardo's, a fixed total supply of farm land, and over time a growth of population, capital, demand, etc. And as von Thünen rightly argued, as soon as this growth caused cultivation of all the farm land to become intensive, or go beyond "the point of diminishing returns" of additional produce for additional inputs of labor and capital, *rent would emerge*—the same rent per acre, for all land alike. To bring about a given increase of output from the land, the growth of demand would have to raise the price of the produce to equality with the marginal or extra cost of the extra output; and the excess of this cost-and-price over the average cost of production per unit of the whole output of each farm would engender the rent surplus. And finally, it remains as true in this as in Ricardo's own picture that the land-rents do not *affect* the prices of the products, *but result from* these prices as determined by the labor-and-capital costs of production of the marginal increments of or in the equilibrium outputs.

And now let us return to the further course of Ricardo's argument. He has shown us that of Adam Smith's three elements of the supposedly price-determining cost of production of every good, one—the rent element—is *not* price determining at all, but price determined. Now what can be said of the other two elements—wages and profits? As to wages (wage rates), Ricardo could have made his essential argument very simple if he had been willing to go extremely far in the use of unrealistic, reality-simplifying assumptions. Were all labor assumed to be homogeneous, alike, or uniform, *and* mobile into the best-paying employments, it would follow that in the competitive economy in equilibrium, all the labor in all industries or lines of production would get just one single uniform wage rate per man-hour, and the wage-costs per unit of product turned out could vary as between different products only as the amounts of required labor-time varied.

But Ricardo did not ignore the complexity of the real world to *this* extent. He recognized the existence of a scale or hierarchy of grades of labor, or degrees of skill, and corresponding wage rates, and the fact that some products "embody" higher proportions of highly skilled and high-priced labor than do others. He did try, however, to argue that these facts necessitated only a small modification of his (almost) exclusive stress on *quantities* of labor, and this argument took the following form. The scale, he said, of grades or kinds of labor or degrees of skill and of their wage rates is as a whole a fairly fixed or constant structure over long periods. (He was interested above all in explaining *changes* of the relative values of different goods, and therefore inclined to attach only slight importance to any feature of the situation which, being subject to but little change itself, could not greatly contribute to such changes.) Moreover, he went on to say, in comparing labor of any two different degrees of skill and expensiveness, one could well regard the more highly skilled and high-priced labor as in fact representing, in all, correspondingly *more* labor; for besides the *current* labor of the highly skilled worker one had to count also the *previous* labor invested by him in *acquiring* his superior skill. Assuming a wide distribution of all native talents or potential abilities in the laboring population, and opportunities for all youths to choose their occupations rationally in the light of knowledge of comparative costs and prospective earnings, the relative supplies and prices of the different more and less skilled kinds of labor would tend to be self-regulating in the long run in such a way that the amount of preparatory training work and time required to acquire a given kind and degree of skill would be just compensated, afterward, by the higher earnings of those who *had* acquired it. There would thus be a normal, direct proportionality between the hourly wage for current labor of a given kind and grade of skill and the total number of hours (adding in those previously spent in acquiring the skill) really being paid for.

Thus Ricardo felt justified in treating an hour of skilled labor, getting twice the wage paid for an hour of unskilled work, as really equivalent to two hours of the latter, and in working then with these *weighted* labor quantities as his fundamental regulators of the relative values of different products. But it should be said, I think, that this argument is one of the weaker parts of his whole analysis. The assumptions about the distribution of all talents and opportunities, and others about the actual determinants of men's choices of their occupations and so of the supplies and earnings of different kinds of labor, etc.—in short all the assumptions which are needed to support the theory that earnings are in general proportional to the total amounts of work required to earn them—cannot be justified as "realistic" in application to the English economy of Ricardo's time, or to any other. The particular "weights" or multiples used in computing the total amounts of labor-time, supposedly represented by single hours of current labor of different kinds, really had to be derived from the current structure of market wage rates, without any full, valid justification of the kind suggested; and this meant that the argument really was circular or question-begging—a demand-dependent value-phenomenon, the market value of each kind of labor was after all incorporated into the supposedly independent purely quantitative (value-free) labor-time determinants of the relative values of the final products.

Ricardo, then, did not really succeed in eliminating, as fully as he tried and claimed to eliminate, the wage rates paid for the different kinds of labor, "embodied" in diverse proportions in different products, from the list of the elements of production costs which must be regarded as significantly affecting the relative values of those different products. But now let us turn to the further question, raising other problems, of the element of profits-on-capital, in the prices of all products, and the role of the rate or rates of profit in affecting the relative or exchange values of the different products. It was easier in a sense to think of the national supply of "capital" as homogeneous throughout, and fully mobile (in the long run) between or among all fields of investment, than to think of the labor supply in the corresponding way. And Ricardo did assume with respect to capital, as he did not with respect to labor, that mobility and competition would be always tending to bring about, as the long-run equilibrium situation, a single uniform rate of remuneration throughout the economy. The prices of all products would, in the general equilibrium, include profits at the same rate (per cent) on the total amounts of capital "necessarily" invested in producing them. Thus *unless* there were variations, as between different products, *of the ratios of those amounts* of capital *to* the amounts of labor-time "embodied" in them, per unit of the output of each product, the profit elements in the absolute prices of all products affecting or "raising" them all in a uniform proportion *would not affect their relaive* values in exchange for each other.

We shall see below, after first examining Ricardo's concept and analysis of "capital" itself, how he managed to recognize and deal with "exceptions" under the above proposition—i.e., cases in which the profit element *would* especially and greatly affect the prices, and thus *would* affect the relative values, of the particular products concerned. But we need to grasp here, at once, the great significance of this general idea about profits and relative values and how it must affect our interpretation or understanding of Ricardo's "labor theory of value."

In his form the latter asserted no more than a general tendency of the *relative* values of different goods to be, in long-run equilibrium, *proportional to* the relative amounts of labor-time "embodied in" them —*not equivalent to or identical with those* amounts of labor-time, but *only proportional* to them. As long as or wherever they did not disturb that proportionality, the profit-additions to the wage-costs, included in the prices of all goods alike, presented no special problem to Ricardo's mind. The later ideas of Marx asserted that the total value of each good is produced or created by labor alone and must "equal" the labor-time "embodied in" the good, and hence that the receipt by labor of less than all that value in wages, and receipt of the rest instead by the capitalist-employer as profit on his capital, must signify exploitation or underpayment of the labor. *These* ideas, inherent *in the Marxian* "labor theory of value," were *not* involved or implied in *Ricardo's* theory at all. We shall indeed see in a moment how Ricardo left the way open, so to speak, *for* development of Marx's *different* "labor theory of value" *from* his own, by seeming to regard "real capital" itself as only "embodied labor," i.e., by failing to include in his concept of the former any explicit idea of the separate contribution to production by the capitalists as distinguished from the laborers, and thus failing to explain why or for what the profit share of the values of the products, is paid to the capitalists. Although he did leave materials or premises for Marx's theory available, so to speak, in other parts of his own general theory —not of value directly but of capital, production, and the income shares —Ricardo himself, I think, did not, within his own theory of exchange values, draw the conclusions which Marx was to draw. Ricardo's theory of exchange values, if I may repeat this point, treated them not as equal, but only as (usually approximately) proportional to the amounts of labor-time "embodied in" the goods concerned; and therefore in itself his theory was and is entirely consistent with acceptance of the division of the value of output into wages for the workers and profits for the capitalists as in every way legitimate.

CAPITAL AND PROFIT VERSUS LAND AND RENT

We must now go on, however, into these further parts of Ricardo's whole system of economic theory—his theories of capital, and production, and wages, profits, and land-rent as shares of the national income. Of capital, as of everything else, Ricardo of course was bound to emphasize or treat as fundamental, not the monetary form, but the "real" forms or counterparts of the monetary form; not the money-capital invested in or used to finance the process of production, but the produced material factors (goods required and used) in that process, *in which* (the main part of) that money is invested, *and which the investments so made bring into existence, i.e., cause to be produced* in response to the demands for them which are thus financed. But within this category of "real" capital he included and even mainly emphasized another subcategory besides those "capital goods" that come first to our minds, i.e., the produced, durable, material means or instruments of production, such as buildings, machines, equipment, tools, etc. All those items he indeed regarded as *one part of* the economy's stock or outfit of real capital—the "fixed" capital, to which investments are committed for long periods. But he gave the primary place, so to speak, to a different part of the whole as he conceived it—the main part of the "circulating" capital that is continually, rapidly used up and replenished—the wage-goods, or consumers' goods (food, clothing, etc.) which "support" the productive workers—the goods they buy with their money-wages, which come out of their employers' money-capital, and use in their "productive consumption," which sustains, nourishes, or continually renews their productive energies. But let me now present a more complete over-all view of the Ricardian-classical theory of the formation, elements, and role of the economy's supply of real capital.

Excluded from that, of course, was the economy's fixed supply of land as provided by nature, apart from man-made improvements—the latter being included in "fixed capital." Individuals may regard their investments in buying land itself as capital investments from their own points of view; but as such investments bring about only transfers of ownership of already existing assets, and not any increase of the whole economy's equipment and producing power, they are not, in relation to the interests of society as a whole, true capital investments, i.e., real-capital-creating investments. For this and other reasons Ricardo regarded "land" as no part of "capital" but a separate, different "factor of production." He thought of the economy's supply of real capital as including only *produced* aids to further production—produced and used as such *by labor* which, however, is thus employed *because* members of the nonlaboring middle and upper classes, receiving money-incomes larger than their necessary expenditures on their own consumption, choose to save-and-invest (instead of spending on their own consumption) parts of those incomes; i.e., they choose to use those parts to hire and equip labor to produce goods to be sold to their profit. And as conceived in the Ricardian-classical theory, the "real" effects of that saving and investing, or formation and use of money-capital, work out as follows.

1. The "capitalists"—all the persons who do any of this saving-and-investing—are doing less consuming with their incomes than they could be doing; hence they are demanding and causing less production of the specific types of consumers' goods adapted to middle- and upper-class tastes than would otherwise be occurring. And by using one part of the money-capital formed by their "savings" (of money not spent on their own consumption) to pay the wages of all productive labor, *they enable the workers to do their* "productive" consuming—and to demand and cause this volume of production of consumers' goods adapted to the workers' tastes. There is, then—as one effect of any *increase* of saving-and-investing and the corresponding *decrease* of consumption by the "capitalists"—a transfer of some labor and productive resources of all kinds, from use in producing one to use in producing the other class of consumers' goods. And in final, brief summary of all this part of the story—the "capitalists" in effect transfer to the workers (with suitable alterations of specific types) consumers' goods "foregone" by the former. In this way, they "pay" to the workers their "real wages," or divide among them, this part (the real "wages-fund," to be further explained hereafter) of the entire supply of real capital—all produced real wealth or goods of all kinds, produced by labor but owned by "capitalists," and as a total stock owing its existence, volume, and growth to (*a*) nonconsuming by "capitalists" and (*b*) production not of the things they consume but, instead, of those they buy with invested savings. In using money-capital to pay wages to labor which then spends this money for its own consumers' goods, the "capitalists" are in effect buying (investing in) *those* consumers' goods to be "productively consumed" by the workers and thus play their role in the ever-on-going process of production.

2. The workers, then, in return for the real wages they receive from the capitalists or out of real capital, produce for the capitalists new goods of all kinds which belong to the capitalists who will realize their profits when they sell these goods. Some of the workers are producing new instruments (buildings, machines, tools, etc.), and/or more or less "raw" materials, to be used later on, largely in producing finished

consumers' goods (for all classes); while others currently are *using* instruments and materials already produced in the same way in the past, in producing the current output of finished consumers' goods. But *all* these products alike first enter into the stock of real capital, and the only ones which eventually (while still in existence and in use) leave that stock or category, or cease to be capital and become something else instead, are *those* finished consumers' goods that eventually are sold to and consumed by consumers (mainly "capitalists," *qua* consumers) *other than* productive laborers. *These* cease to be capital when they are bought by their final consumers; but all the consumers' goods that go to productive laborers remain, as we have seen, items of real capital (in the Ricardian-classical view) even when they are being consumed. The provision of these goods for consumption by the productive workers is the primary or basic, "real" investment made by the capitalists; and all the new goods produced for them by the workers in return represent, in a sense, *the same* capital in new and different specific forms or embodiments.

Only one part of the capital of each enterprise or firm goes into wages to the workers it employs, or provision for their consumption; the rest goes into or is represented by the equipment and materials they use or work with or upon. But the firm's investments in the purchase of that equipment and those materials only repay, with profits added, to the other firms from which they are bought, the previous investments by those other firms, which were partly in wages to the workers *they* employed—and partly in reimbursing still earlier wage investments by still other firms, etc. In the final analysis, all goods are produced by labor—the current labor involved *plus* the past labor "embodied in" the products (instruments, etc.) being used by the current labor—in return for labor's real wages. Thus the total mass of real capital existing at any time has these two aspects: it is both the mass of products that have been produced by labor in return for the real wages it has received and consumed, and the source of the new real wages it is still to receive for its on-going work of replenishing and adding to that mass of products.

Let us now consider, however, the questions that arise as to what Ricardo may have meant, and whether he was self-consistent, in saying or seeming to say that all those products are produced (entirely or solely?) "by labor" and that, e.g., the machines (real capital in this form) which are used by current labor and of course increase "its" productivity, themselves "embody" or represent (only?) the amounts (in man-hours) of past labor that was needed to produce them. As I said above in discussing the relation of Ricardian to Marxian theory, it was by at least seeming to say just this about the capital-as-equipment used by labor in production—that this capital itself is or represents only so-

and-so-much previous labor—it was in this way above all that Ricardo enabled Marx, later on, to claim his (Ricardo's) authority and support for the Marxian absolute "labor theory of value" and its corollary, that the capitalists' profits result entirely from "exploitation of labor." But I think that, although Ricardo's explicit statements on this matter did invite and appear to justify this (Marx's) interpretation of them, they did so only because he failed to make fully explicit all that was logically involved in his own analysis of the sources and formation of real capital and the role or contribution of the capitalists.

The Ricardian view *of production* can be best expressed, I think, by saying that all production is carried on or performed *on* land, *by* labor, *supported and equipped with* capital. The workers are in one sense *the active producers* of all products, including of course those used to support and those used to equip them, i.e., wage-goods and machines, etc.; they are the active producers of everything involved except the land as provided by "nature." But this statement that the workers are the active producers *does not* mean, of course, that all of "their" output is to be attributed entirely or solely to their exertions as its only cause or required antecedent; the land and the capital (and *everything* involved in the formation of the latter) also are important "factors of production," which we may regard either as themselves "productive" or as helping to account for or enhance the productivity "of labor"—two ways of saying the same thing. Of course, no one, however, not even Marx, ever denied that obvious truism that the physical volume of goods produced "by labor" is heavily dependent on the quantities and qualities of the land and the produced equipment—all the "means of production" in Marx's phrase—with which the labor is equipped. The *real* questions are about the roles in or contributions to production of the other *persons* and "classes" of them, besides the wage-earning laborers—the landowners and the capitalists. It is on *these* questions that I think Ricardo failed to make fully explicit the views that were clearly implicit in his theoretic vision.

In particular, he did not sufficiently elaborate *the contrast between* the relations of his landlords, on the one hand, and his capitalists, on the other, to production and to their respective types of properties and incomes. The landlords, as such, were simply or only the legal owners of parts of the country's fixed supply of never humanly produced but permanent or eternal land, a "free gift of nature." (In so far as landlords saved and invested and/or worked to maintain and improve the productivity of their land, they were acting as capitalists and/or workers and earning profits and/or wages. But their distinctive role was that of owners of the land as "nature" made it. In a crowded and prosperous country with "scarce" land and keen competition for rights to use it, they could charge and get, *in addition* to all such (full) compensation for all their *personal* contributions to production, large pure or net land-rents, *simply* for rights to use their lands.) And as in the nation as a whole its landlord class received as pure land-rent a large or very substantial share of the national income, there was left for all the members of the other classes, together doing nearly all that was done to produce that income, much less than all of it, i.e., less than the full values or equivalents of their contributions to it. Thus in its implications, though never explicitly, Ricardo's view of pure land-rent income was similar to Marx's view of *all* property income, i.e., in effect Ricardo conceived the former as involving "exploitation" of the nonlandowning, productive workers *and* capitalists or saver-investors, as Marx was to trace *all* property income to "exploitation" of the workers. Although Ricardo never sufficiently explained his *different* view of the interest or "profit-income" of the capitalists as distinguished from the landlords in his system, there is no real doubt that he *did* view *this* share of the national income in a *different* light; and this is the point that must now be explained.

Unlike the economy's fixed supply of "land" as such, existing from and to eternity as a "product" of "nature" only and not of any decisions or activities on the parts of its owners or any human beings, the economy's variable, increasable supply of "real capital," i.e., all humanly produced and not forever enduring goods needed for production of other goods, owed *its* existence and size or volume at each point of time to (1) all the previous saving-and-investing done by its capitalist owners *and* (2) all the labor which all that saving-and-investing caused to be employed in producing these capital goods *instead of* the consumers' goods that would have been produced and unproductively consumed if the capitalists had *not* done the saving-and-investing but had spent their incomes entirely on their own consumption. By Ricardo's own explicit account, the capital goods were *not* results or products *of previous labor alone, but joint results* of that labor *and* the thrift, self-restraint in consumption, or "parsimony" (his and the then commonly used word for this) practiced by the capitalists, which had caused the labor to be *so* applied. Thus when, in the other passages which Marx was to build upon, Ricardo allowed himself to indicate that capital goods "embodied" *only* previous labor, he was lapsing into inconsistency with his own analysis. By the plain implication of that analysis, the real, third, distinct or separate "factor of production," distinct alike from all labor and from land but involved in "capital," was the fruitful "parsimony" or productive service of saving-and-investing performed by the capitalists—through which they contributed to growth of the economy's equipment and productivity, and thus *earned* their profit share of the national income.

Various later economists, as we shall see, were to develop *this* element of Ricardo's thought—just as Marx developed the *other* element into his "exploitation" theory—into theories explaining "interest" or "profit" (the return on capital as such) as the "reward" due to the capitalists for their "abstinence" from consumption, or giving up of "present goods" in exchange for "future goods" despite a human-natural "time preference" in favor of the former, or "waiting" for future increases of enjoyment or consumption while in the present using income rather to increase production. Those formulations of the point, however, unfortunately emphasized the dubious, supposed, subjective "sacrifices" by the capitalists, involved in saving-and-investing instead of consuming. However, all that matters in this connection is the plain fact that saving-and-investing which is needed to bring about and does bring about the formation of new real capital, *is a productive service* like work or labor itself, as clearly indispensable and contributory to production as the labor is, and thus capable of "earning" interest or profit in precisely the same way or sense in which labor "earns" its wages. Ricardo, I think, very clearly implied just that, but failed to say it explicitly, perhaps because he thought it too obvious to need saying; but his failure to say it, and his lapse into saying instead, inconsistently, that the economy's real capital represented only previous labor, was very unfortunate in the cue and advantage it bequeathed to Marx.

WAGES—THE "WAGES FUND" AND THE "IRON LAW"

But now, before I say more about Ricardo's theories pertaining to the capitalists' profits and the landlords' rents, let me proceed *from* his theory of the formation and role of capital *to* his theory of the laborers' wages, and how the free-market economy's "natural" working and development would determine the average real-wage income per worker. We have seen already how he conceived the economy's supply of real capital as containing not only the equipment and materials in current use by labor in production, but also the wage-goods or workers' consumer goods obtained by the workers with their money-wages and productively consumed by them. And *this* idea was the immediate basis of one part or side of his theory as to how the real-wage income per worker is determined. The size or volume of this part of the existing supply of real capital—the real "wages-fund"—divided by the number of workers to be paid, would give the average amount which *could* be (and under the pressures of competition would be) paid, per worker. I will not here attempt to go fully into the ambiguities and difficulties of this doctrine which led to a great deal of confused controversy over it and finally to its abandonment, at a later time, by Ricardo's disciples. It was not original with or peculiar to Ricardo; Adam Smith's discussions, as we saw in a previous chapter, had already implied it; and it was widely current in Ricardo's time. It was logically included in his system of theory and had his full support; and its wide, stubborn vogue in the time just after his was due largely to his prestige and influence. It involved an imperfect glimpse of an important truth, but by formulating this in a much too simple and rigid way, Ricardo confused it with illusions and errors. It is true in the business economy that all producing organizations or firms need and use money-capital, not only to buy the equipment and materials they use, but also to pay wages to their employees; hence in the economy as a whole there is a dependence of the outflow of wages, from the firms to the workers, on the inflow of money-capital supplied by saver-investors to the firms (including of course the profits reinvested by the firms themselves). In the terms of the Ricardian-classical theory, just as the "real" measure of the investment in equipment and materials is the (nonmonetary, physical) quantities of the different kinds of equipment and materials themselves, which are actually produced and obtained, so also, the "real" measure of the investment represented by the sum paid out in wages to the workers through a given period is the quantities of consumers' goods the workers obtain when they spend those wages. The true point in the wages-fund doctrine was the point that a capital-poor economy cannot provide at once both full employment of a large wage-earning population and high real wages; a large total volume of real wages cannot be afforded if there is only (in total, real value) a small amount of capital available. Increase of the total volume of real wages requires a prior increase of saving-and-investing, or capital formation—a decrease by the well-to-do of their own consumption, and use or investment of their increased savings by producing firms to hire productive labor and pay its wages, and transfer of the consuming power, not used as such by the well-to-do, to the productive workers.

But the doctrine ran into trouble with the great complexity of the total, imperfectly analyzed process it referred to—the pattern of all the relevant variables and relations among them—which it oversimplified. Above all it too closely assimilated to each other, and confused, the two different parts of its over-all conception of the economy's supply or existing stock of all real capital: on the one hand, all the productive "plant," machinery, tools, etc., and materials, produced and used by labor; and on the other hand, the wage-goods, bought by the wage-earning class or population with its money wages, paid to it out of the (monetary) working capital of the employing firms. As a whole the stock of "plant," machinery, etc., existing at any one time represents, of course, an accumulation, over a very long indefinite previous period of time, of all the fruits of all the production-saving-investing new production, etc., carried on within that time; and the whole amount is so large, as compared with the additions made to it in any one year, that it cannot be quickly or greatly changed by new decisions and actions responsive to new opportunities.

The main error in the "wages-fund" doctrine was the supposition it involved, that the same or a closely comparable short-run rigidity must also characterize the volume of the economy's stock or "fund" and possible outflow of real wages for its labor force. It was not sufficiently realized that (1) if at any time current conditions and profit expectations should make most firms in the economy eager to hire more workers and increase their outputs, they might well be able in most cases to obtain the required new or additional, monetary, working capital rather quickly by offering more attractive interest rates to lenders, and thus stimulating increased new, current saving and investment; and (2) if this occurred the results would be: a decrease of consumption (demand for consumers' goods) by the saver-investors; an increase of demand and competition for labor and rise of money-wages; an increase of consumption (demand for wage-goods) by the labor force; and production of more wage-goods *instead of* so many consumers' goods of the other kind—and hence a rise of real wages, as well as of money-wages. The wages-fund doctrine rightly asserted dependence of the wage income of the labor force on the supply of capital; but it exaggerated the rigor of the constraint or limitation imposed on the wage income by this relation, by not recognizing—clearly, fully, and consistently—that the dependence is mainly on the more quickly, greatly variable *part of* the supply of capital, *and the way of using* the other more enduring, slowly accumulating, and relatively inflexible part of that supply.

I have thus far discussed, however, only one part of the two-sided, Ricardian-classical theory of wages—of the determinants, and process of determination, of the level of real wages, or average real-wage income per worker in the whole economy. This income was held to be determined currently in every *short run* of time simply by the ratio of the size or volume of the wages-fund to the labor supply (total number of workers). But over the long run, with growth of the supply of capital and the size of the wages-fund, there would also be growth (as Malthus had explained) of the population and supply of labor. The rate of *this* growth as compared with that of the wages-fund, and as affected by the current levels of real wages in successive short runs, would be self-regulating in such a way that its persistent "tendency" would be to make the real-wage incomes of working-class families, generally, just equal to "subsistence"—for the parents and enough children to make the supply of labor in the next generation fully equal to the likely demand for it then, at this low wage level. For if the currently prevailing rate of real wages should rise for a time above this level, the increased prosperity of the wage-earning mass of the population would encourage earlier marriages and larger families, and enable more of the children born to be well supported and therefore to survive; the birth rate would rise and the death rate would fall. Thus the population and labor supply would grow faster, absolutely, and relative to the slow growth of the wages-fund, and force the level of real wages down again toward bare "subsistence." And contrariwise, if the wage level should fall for a time *below* that required to support a rate of growth of the population and labor supply equal to that of the capital supply and wages-fund and demand for labor, this opposite disparity also would be self-rectifying in the long run. The extremely low wages and great poverty of labor would lower the birth rate, raise the death rate, check the growth of the population and labor supply, and allow that of the wages-fund and demand for labor to outstrip it and again raise wages to their "natural" level.

In this way, then, the Malthusian theory or "law" of population growth as self-adjusting in relation to economic growth, formed an integral and vital part of the Ricardian-classical theory of economics. This part of the latter—the theory of long-run "natural" wages just described—has been called the theory of an "iron law" holding wages down to "bare subsistence." But that designation is inaccurate; i.e., it exaggerates the rigor and grimness of the theory as developed by Malthus and Ricardo, by omitting the alleviating element made explicit by both of them: that a working-class population which, in a time of relative prosperity for it, had become accustomed to and determined to maintain a better-than-bare-subsistence standard of living, and had acquired the habit of the requisite use of "the preventive check" or regulation of its birth rate, could in this way make, not "bare subsistence," but its somewhat higher, customary, and insisted-upon standard of living, the "natural" or long-run equilibrium wage level.

Even with this modification as Malthus and Ricardo applied it, however, their theory of the determinants and process of determination of real wages was indeed "grim" enough. Not only did the "wages-fund" part of the complete theory, as we saw above, exaggerate the rigor of the limitation of real wages by the limits of the volume or supply of capital, but the "grimness" of the whole was further accentuated by the way in which the population-growth part exaggerated the exactitude of the responsive, long-run adjustment of the size of the population and labor supply to that of the "fund." The adjustment mechanism, thought of as adjusting the supply of labor to the demand for it and its price or wage to a rather low and more or less fixed "natural" level, was just like the mechanism thought of as adjusting the supply or output of any produced good to the demand for it, and its price to its cost of production. The "natural" wage rate was in effect conceived as just covering "the cost of production" of that supply of labor in the next generation which the economy then, with its supply of capital, would just be able to employ and pay at this rate—if by "the cost of production" of this future labor supply we mean the cost of living (including the support and rearing of the children) of working-class families just large enough to provide their quotas of the labor supply in question. The less than entirely valid, severe doctrine, that in this way the supply and price of labor are controlled by a "natural law" quite similar to the "laws" controlling (in a competitive economy) the supplies and prices of produced commodities, was to popular thought in its time about the most "dismal" and widely resented doctrine of Ricardian-classical economics.

PROFIT; ECONOMIC GROWTH; THE INCOME SHARES; AND THE STATIONARY STATE

Now we must work our way back from that theory of wages to the not yet discussed parts of the Ricardian-classical theories about profits, land-rents, the relations and prospective changes of the three income shares in the growing economy, and the trend toward the future end (cessation) of that growth or the arrival of "the stationary state." In again taking up Ricardo's ideas about the "profits" received by the capitalists, let me first explain—what perhaps I should have explained earlier at our first encounter with this topic—what, precisely, the word "profits" meant or referred to in his usage, i.e., the common usage before, during, and well on beyond his time. Comparatively few business enterprises were as yet organized as modern business corporations or (the term that always has been used in England) joint stock companies. Most firms still were either personal proprietorships or partnerships, as a rule managed directly by their owners, who themselves owned and invested the greater parts, at least, of both the permanent and the working capital required, and might or might not borrow additional amounts of both, on good security and at fixed contractual rates of interest.

The term "interest" was applied—by Ricardo, Adam Smith, and others before them, and by most economists until a more recent time—*only* to interest on *borrowed* capital, i.e., "loan" or "contractual" interest, generally at definite, agreed-on percentage rates (the market rates when the loans and agreements were made), and generally on well-secured loans so that those rates were but little enhanced by "risk" considerations. The "profits," then, received by the active "capitalist" who both owned and managed a firm or enterprise and who provided, from his own resources, most of its capital, meant the whole of his net personal income from the business, over any one year, considered as a percentage return on his investments of his capital in that business. The element of this "profit" that would now be called "interest" on the proprietor's or equity capital—the interest that would have been paid for this capital if it had been borrowed, or could have been gotten for it if it had been lent out to others, on good security—was not called "interest," but was included in the category "profit," and indeed was that which as a rule an economic theory of "profit" in those times, and especially Ricardo's theory, mainly meant or was mainly about.

It was commonly recognized that the normal or typical full amount and rate of "profit," as the word was used, included also in addition to this element—the return on, from, or for the proprietor's capital as such—both a "risk premium" (since the proprietor had no secured contractual guarantee of any return or even against loss of the principal or his capital itself) and a "wage of management." But these additional ingredients of the proprietor's composite "profit-income," though frequently mentioned, were as a rule but little considered or theorized about; and in Ricardo's brief, little-developed theory they were not even mentioned. Essentially, his theory of "profit" was entirely, and most such early, rudimentary theories of "profit" were mainly, in more modern terms, rudimentary theories of "interest"—the interest-yield of the capital employed in production. Even contractual or loan interest—for the borrowing proprietors an expense like others, but for the lenders the yield of their parts of the capital employed in production—was probably in those times generally regarded in much the same light as, or along with the mainly considered part of, what was called "profit." The "profit" share of all income or the value of all output was the share that went to the "capitalists" because their saving-and-investing provided or brought into being the "capital" required and used in the economy. The main body of the "capitalists," in a national economy like that of Ricardo's England, were the active "capitalists" who owned and managed its producing enterprises. But despite some recognition of their other roles or functions they were thought of mainly as just "capitalists," providing "capital" and in return receiving "profits."

In this really primitive view of these matters, *the worst* deficiency or lack of sufficient analysis was neglect, not merely of the routine "managing" activities of those active "capitalists" and the "wages of management" included in their "profits," but of the still more important personal contributions to the national output really made by some (the leading ones) among them, in their further roles as "enterprising," inventive or creative, new-ideas-conceiving-and-executing, high-business-policy-making, planning and directing "entrepreneurs." Unnoticed was the fact that the latter earned (extra) "profits" in another sense, over and beyond both mere interest on their capital and ordinary "wages of management," by being repeatedly among the first "operators" in their lines or fields of business to introduce new or improved products or means and methods of production, and through or from each such innovation earning "temporary monopoly gains" until their competitors generally caught up with them. Economic theory in its general development did not until much later—long after Ricardo's time—arrive at this *or any* idea of the "entrepreneur" as distinguished from the "capitalist" function, and of the "profit" reward of "enterprise" as distinguished from the interest (or "profit" in the old classical sense) reward for just providing capital.

It was a very important weakness of most economic theory in, and before, and often long after Ricardo's time—a weakness connected perhaps with its too deterministic, mechanistic character and illusions about its resemblance to natural (physical) science—that it paid very little attention to this human factor, creative "enterprise." Instead it thought of the economy as functioning with—as "factors of production" and sources of income of distinct kinds—*only* (wage-earning plus managerial) labor, land, and capital; and it even thought of the historic and on-going growth, development, or progress of the "capitalist" or business economy as a process propelled by little more than just the automatic "snowballing" of the mass of capital, yielding "profit" of which the greater part is reinvested or becomes new additional capital.

"Profit" then to Ricardo meant essentially the kind of income that in a more modern view is really "interest"; and the little that he said about it must be understood with this fact in mind. Now about this income-yield of capital as such (no matter which word we use to designate it), there are for economic theory *two* general problems. The first one is to explain *the entire phenomenon*—why and how income of this kind arises—or for what, why, and out of what resources, how created, the "capitalist" or saver-investor as such receives an income *in addition to* remaining the owner of his original capital, and a *net* income besides all that is needed for upkeep and eventual replacement of the particular, not-forever-enduring assets originally invested in. And the second, further problem is to explain how *the rate* of this income-yield, per cent per year on the capital itself, is determined—how this rate is connected with, and varies with the changes of, other economic variables (and *what* others are important in this connection) in the working and development of the economy. On the first, the more fundamental of those two problems, Ricardo, as we saw above, failed to offer any clear, explicit theory; in fact he made no attempt to solve that problem, did not even state or raise it, and perhaps did not see or grasp it *as* a problem. And by seeming to regard real capital or capital goods as representing only the labor that "produced" them, he left the road open to Marx's "exploitation" doctrine, that all "interest" or "profit" arises from or through underpayment of labor. Yet as we also saw above, Ricardo's theory of capital formation clearly implied that saving-and-investment is a productive service, through which the saver-investors increase the productivity "of labor" and of the whole economy, and thus "earn" their "profit" incomes. And this I think may be taken to be his real theory of the source and *raison d'être* of all "profit," though he failed to say so explicitly.

On the further problem, however, as to how the *rate* of "profit" was determined and would change with the changing conditions that he saw as in prospect in the growing economy, Ricardo's analysis was more explicit and satisfactory. The nation's labor force, aided by its capital supply, was producing its output (the national income) on or from its fixed land-area. Over time both the population (labor supply) and the capital supply were growing, but the land supply was not; and as new additions were made to the inputs of labor and capital on the limited land, they would make—in the absence of fully compensating technological progress—*decreasing* additions to the national output or income. At each stage or point in this growth process, the last-added increments of the labor and capital supplies would divide between them, or into the wages of the one and the profit of the other, the last-added increment (added by them jointly) of the national output or income. The resulting rates of wages and of profits would become those generally prevailing for all labor and all capital throughout the economy; while the rent-receiving landlords would get the "surplus" of the total output or income over the sum of the wage and profit shares determined in that way. But in the division of the "marginal" joint product of labor and capital into wages and profits, labor must get its "subsistence" wages and the capitalists could get as their profits only the remainder.

That last statement, however, is a little too simple and needs a slight modification, as we shall see in a moment. For the capitalists, their profits are both the source and the incentive for new saving-and-investing; i.e., those already received are the source (the income out of which they save and invest) and those in prospect are the incentive or goal of their saving-and-investing. Thus so long as the profit rate is high enough to support and induce more saving-and-investing, that will go on and the economy's supply of capital will continue to increase. And this will cause a continuing growth of the demand for labor, which will tend to keep the average rate of real wages at a level *a little above* the "subsistence" needs *of the existing or a constant labor supply,* or at a level sufficient to support and cause on-going growth of the population and labor supply, corresponding to that of the capital supply. But as the growth of both goes on, and the slowing growth of the national income and the increase of the land-rent share of that work to reduce both wages and profits, they will finally fall to levels so low as to bring all the growth to an end, or bring into being "the stationary state"—the final, true, or complete "equilibrium" of the system.

In the approach to that state of things, it becomes true that the latest additions to the ranks of the employed workers—and *all* those workers individually or severally—make such small differences to the outputs and revenues of the firms employing them that they earn and can be paid (the firms can afford to pay them) hardly more at all than "bare subsistence" *for* families of the size required to just maintain the existing population. And even to maintain *that* amount of real wages per worker or per family, the level of money-wages, hence the share or fraction of the value of output paid in wages by the capitalists, must rise, because the price of food (the main or a major part of real wages) is rising, due to the rise of the "marginal" cost of producing more food from the fixed and now insufficient supply of agricultural land. One could also add, though Ricardo did not, that like the productivity of additional labor on the limited land, the productivity of additional capital investments, too, is falling for the same reason, in step with the fall of profits which could be viewed as due to this *as well as* to the requirement of a larger outlay on "subsistence" wages, out of the reduced joint output of the additional labor-and-capital together. The profit rate, then, in this growing economy, inevitably falls, eventually to a level so low that all new saving, investment, and capital formation cease. Thus the stock of capital becomes and thereafter remains constant, and so do the population and supply of labor; the "stationary state" arrives, in which the level of wages is barely sufficient to support the stationary population, profits (if any) are so low that the amount of capital is stationary, and the remaining, great part of the nation's continuing total output or income goes in rent to the owners of its land. Ricardo did not say clearly, however, what rate of profit he thought of as the lower limit of the fall. Would this be zero profit, or enough net profit-income for the class of capitalists, above the upkeep or maintenance of the existing capital, to just meet their urgent needs as consumers, or a little more than that but not enough to make new saving and investing seem worthwhile? In the failure to answer those questions, we may again see failure on Ricardo's part to consider the fundamental problem of the nature and necessity of the whole phenomenon of interest or profit—whether it is merely a residual that will wholly disappear when and if the system and all its variables get fully adjusted or in equilibrium, or an essential part of the system which must retain some positive magnitude, not only to keep the system growing, but to keep it in existence.

RICARDO VERSUS MALTHUS, AS TO "UNDERCONSUMPTION"

I have now surveyed in a fashion all the main basic parts of Ricardo's system of economic theory, *except* his argument in reply to a fear expressed by Malthus (and others) about a matter that has not yet been touched on. The prediction or prophecy of the future, dismal, "stationary state" of the economy, in Ricardo's system, was pessimistic enough—indeed too much so as the actual evolution proved. For Ricardo (in company with Malthus) failed to foresee the extent of the continuing triumph of technological progress over their "law of diminishing returns," and the extent to which, in the career of the working class, the rise of its living standards and fall of its birth rate would slow down the growth of its numbers relative to the growth of production, aggregate profits, capital, and demand for labor, and thus allow a self-perpetuating, rising trend of the level of real wages. Although Ricardo and Malthus shared the same too pessimistic vision of the coming stationary state, Malthus had, in addition to that, another fear about trouble of an even worse kind in store for the economy, which Ricardo did *not* share.

The strong bent of the capitalists toward "parsimony"—their great propensity to limit their spending for consumers' goods and do all the saving-and-investing they could, thus continually increasing the supply of capital—not only would, Malthus thought, bring about over time the fall of profits and the trend toward the stationary state; but it also would, he feared, engender in the meantime, recurrent crises of general overproduction and underconsumption, or glutting of the markets. He foresaw depressions during which the market prices of goods generally would be below their costs of production, and there would be a general contraction of investment, employment, and output in all lines, and widespread unemployment. The rapid, immense growths, in normal times, of the economy's supply of capital and consequent producing power, which resulted from the intense "parsimony" of the large and prosperous middle class, doing little consuming and a great amount of saving-and-investing, was certain to lead each time, at a later stage, to a great increase of the output of consumers' goods. But the continuing "parsimony" of the middle class, and the general poverty of the working class or main mass of the people, obliged to live meagerly on "subsistence" wages, would mean insufficient total demand for all those consumers' goods. The result would be a glutting of the markets for them, collapse of their prices, and general depression—until over the period of greatly reduced production, the gradual using up of the surplus goods, and completion of many readjustments in the system, would make possible a new surge of expansion.

The root of the trouble, as Malthus saw it, was too little consuming and too much saving by too many of the wealthy and well-to-do—all the ardent "capitalists" or saver-investors—and a consequent chronic tendency of the economy's capital supply and producing power to outgrow its consuming power. There was a need to reduce saving and increase spending for consumption, and to have a slower growth of production and faster growth of consumption, in balance with each other, that there might be at all times an adequate demand or market for the current output. And the conservative Malthus further built upon this piece of analysis a plea for approval instead of disapproval of the nonparsimonious, free-spending, elegant-living habits of those *other* wealthy and well-to-do classes in the England of his time, the aristocracy and gentry, whose persisting way of life belonged more to the "feudal" past than to the "capitalist" present and was generally not approved by the typical middle-class representatives of the latter. Reversing, as he often did, the more usual applications of the Utilitarian point of view, Malthus appealed for recognition of the social utility of high consumption spending, as opposed to excessive saving by the rich, as an aid to maintenance of adequate demand for the final fruits of all saving-and-investment, and of full employment.[5]

Ricardo, however—and all his loyal disciples—regarded as demonstrably and entirely fallacious, the ideas of Malthus that there could be oversaving, underconsumption, and a general glut in the markets, or inadequate aggregate demand for all that the economy, with full employment, could produce. The basis of the Ricardian-classical argument about this matter—the argument to demonstrate the impossibility of the "general glut"—lay in the analysis already outlined at the beginning of this chapter, of the (limited) role of money in the economy and the "real" nature of all selling and buying as in final effect a method of "exchanging" different goods for each other. Since in the final analysis the supply of every good is disposed of in exchange for other goods, the aggregate supply of all goods together, and the aggregate demand for all goods together, must be the same; all goods are really bought with other goods (that is, with the money obtained from the sales of the other goods, which *qua* money is useless and always fully spent, so this comes to the same thing). Hence every over-all increase of production in the economy as a whole *is* at the same time an equal over-all increase of demand. This general thesis was most fully elaborated by J. B. Say, the French economist contemporary with Ricardo and in agreement with him on this matter, and has come down in the subsequent history of economic theory as "Say's law"; but it was affirmed by Ricardo independently and was an integral part of his system of theory, so I need not here digress to speak further of Say. Rather, let me conclude this chapter with a slightly fuller exposition of the purely Ricardian argument, from this thesis, in direct answer to the fears of Malthus about excessive saving-and-investing and underconsumption.

[5] On Malthus' underconsumption theory, see Keynes' essay on Malthus in *Essays in Biography, passim;* and Keynes' citation of the relevant parts of Malthus' *Principles* and other writings. For fuller discussion of the views of both Malthus and Keynes on this subject, see Chapter 17.

If the people who receive large incomes decrease their consumption spending and increase their saving-and-investing, the results, according to the Ricardian-classical analysis, work out as follows. In so far as the increase of saving-and-investing enlarges the wages-fund and the outlay by firms in hiring labor, there is an increase of consumption spending by the workers which partly offsets the decrease of that by the saver-investors. And the other part of the increase of saving-and-investing, going into purchase by the rich of capital goods (produced by many of those workers), in the place of the consumers' goods *not* bought by the saver-investors, correspondingly alters the balance *in production* of these different things, i.e., brings about more production of capital goods, and less production of consumers' goods (for the rich and well-to-do). Nor is it true, as Malthus thought, that this, in turn, must lead in a limited time to a large increase of the output of consumers' goods, unmatched by increase of demand for them. On the one hand, many capital goods are used in producing other capital goods, which again are used in producing still others, and so on more or less indefinitely; and there is room for choices, responsive to market demands, of the kinds of capital goods produced and the ways of using them; the capacities of the consumer-goods industries need expand no faster than the demand for their products; continuation of a great amount of new saving-and-investing, and only limited consuming by the rich and well-to-do, will mean continuation of production, to a corresponding extent, of new capital goods rather than of consumers' goods. And on the other hand, the same entire process does generate over time a continual growth of the total of consumption by the whole society. Parallel with growth of the supply of capital and (or including) the wages-fund, there is the on-going growth of population including the labor supply; the growth of investment spending includes growth of the aggregate outlay in wages for labor, and resulting growth of consumption spending by the growing labor force; and the capitalist class, also growing in both numbers and wealth, will increase its absolute aggregate amount of consumption spending *as well as* its saving-and-investing, even if the degree of "parsimony" of its members undergoes no change. As the society's total output grows, so do its total flows of income, consumption spending, *and* investment spending; and in the competitive system, with all prices flexible and the supplies of all particular goods adjusting to the changing, particular demands for them, there is no reason why any "general glut" should ever occur.

These matters actually are extremely complex, and the early, simple theories about or attempts to analyze them, whether on the line of Malthus or on that of Ricardo and his followers, did not get to the bottom of them. We shall see in later chapters how the study of them has advanced, but the problems involved have by no means all been fully solved even today. The Ricardian system, unduly pessimistic on the whole, was unduly optimistic—and dogmatic—in this area, but the underconsumption theory of Malthus as worked out by him does not stand up logically; and in the contest with his and all similar views of the matter, the Ricardian-classical view long seemed securely victorious.

CHAPTER 9

John Stuart Mill: Philosophy, Ethics, Politics, and Logic

MILL'S STATURE AND CHARACTER, AND BASIC VIEWS IN PHILOSOPHY, ETHICS, AND POLITICS

John Stuart Mill's place among the "great thinkers" in the history of the Western world is perhaps in not the first but the second rank. But he was and is a very appealing, attractive, lovable, and admirable figure; and his many, voluminous, deeply and widely informed and thoughtful, lucid writings on a great variety of subjects—philosophical, social, moral, political, and economic problems—long exerted a widespread, mainly beneficial influence, and are still worth reading. Ethically a "good" man to the point of saintliness (though he was so faintly and unorthodoxly religious that no church could have thought of canonizing him), he was deeply "idealistic" in the popular-ethical sense, earnest (but not humorless), and thoroughly "open-minded," i.e., determined to be fair to and learn all he could from all points of view. He was transparently, intellectually honest and candid; the uncertainties, confusions, doubts, and limitations in his thought are revealed in his writings and never concealed under any false pretenses. In the course of his intellectual development he was influenced by a wide variety of different ways of thinking, and his efforts to combine the views that appealed to him in a coherent synthesis was never entirely successful; consequently his thought was full of unresolved dilemmas. But they were and are the dilemmas or conflicts of diverse, at least partly true insights, that have always been and remained unresolved, at the core of Western intellectual life in general; and it was more the breadth of Mill's interests, knowledge, and receptivity, than any special deficiency of his analytical powers, which made them stand out as they do in his writings.

The story, told in Mill's autobiography, of his unusual early education by his father, and its effects throughout his life, is well known.[1] The father, James Mill, was Jeremy Bentham's chief disciple and lieutenant, a friend of Ricardo's, and an able economist, psychologist, and political thinker in his own right. He was a rather fanatical heir of the Enlightenment who believed that education of the people at large in the true principles of utilitarian psychology and ethics, jurisprudence, liberal-democratic politics, and classical economics would ensure an unlimited progressive growth of universal human happiness. James Mill, in short, was a crusading dogmatist, and a much less attractive person than his son became; but as a child the son was educated (or indoctrinated) by this father, with incredible thoroughness from an incredibly early age, that he might later continue the work of "enlightening" the general public—which he did, but not entirely with just his father's creed, unmodified. That creed, however—essentially Benthamism plus Ricardian economics—became and remained to a great extent the basis or core of John Stuart Mill's intellectual life; to which in the later course of his own development he made various large and diverse additions of other views from other sources, which at best were imperfectly consistent with it; with the result that his intellectual life as a whole was a never entirely successful struggle to reciprocally adjust, reconcile, and harmoniously combine the several different strands of thought which together formed it.

Besides the ideas of Bentham and Ricardo, "our" Mill absorbed others from the English Romanticists Coleridge and Carlyle, and still others from August Comte's intellectual system, and still others from the visions of utopian socialists; and—with, of course, some conscious modifications in all cases—wove them all together into a by no means wholly self-consistent outlook. He was more, however, than an eclectic "combiner" of the views acquired from others; although his powers of original thought were not of the very highest order, they were good, and he not only developed and revised but added much of his own to each and all of those sources of his thought; hence the whole "body" of the latter is very rich and complex. Its complexity, however, is not the intricacy and subtlety often found in the kind of intellectual work which advances and elaborates detailed analysis of a particular subject matter to a point very far beyond the simple or elementary "common-sense" beginnings of all such analysis. John Mill's search was for a very broadly inclusive or comprehensive global wisdom, about a wide range of the great, general, perennial problems of mankind; hence his attention was spread widely over many subject matters, and he did

[1] J. S. Mill's *Autobiography* is available in many editions. One of the best is that published—with a preface by Harold Laski—in *The World's Classics* (London and New York: Oxford University Press, 1924).

not carry analysis of any one of them *very* far beyond the elementary, "common-sense" stage or level. A kind of relative simplicity, rather than any great complexity, may be said to characterize each of his writings. Only the entirety of his thought is complex, and it is so in the different sense or way resulting from his constant, simultaneous sensitivities to all or many kinds of relevant considerations and the elements of truth that he saw in many diverse points of view.

One of the foundation stones of John Mill's thought was his philosophical empiricism. As a British philosopher he carried on the tradition or line of thought of Locke and Hume—the empiricism which insisted that all truth or knowledge, to deserve acceptance as such, must be derived from and pass the test of agreement with facts perceived or observed with the human senses; that all claims to possession of intuitive-general or a priori knowledge of "self-evident" primary truths, not capable of and not needing support or confirmation by empirical evidence, must be rejected; and that every individual has the right and the duty to do—in so far as he is or can become competent to do this—his own skeptical, critical testing of all alleged truth or knowledge, presented to him as such, i.e., to test it for agreement with his own perceptual experiences, or sense-perceptions. In particular, this empiricist theory of knowledge was for Mill an important part of the foundation of his most central, ethical conviction—his liberalism, or moral outlook demanding full liberty or freedom for the mind and soul of every human individual, and dictating eternal enmity to all authoritarian, dogmatic orthodoxies which had ever sought or might ever seek to impose themselves as obligatory on entire societies. To Mill's mind, every despotism had its source in uncritical mass acceptance of a common creed; and the latter in turn always had its source in acceptance of the claim of the exponents of the creed, that the truth of the premises forming the logical foundation of the creed could be guaranteed by something other and better than the sense-experiences of individuals. Therefore Mill felt that an essential safeguard of the liberties of all individuals must be a general prevalence of the critical, skeptical temper of mind, and proneness on the part of each individual to insist on testing all ideas proposed for his acceptance for agreement with his sense-experience.

Before going further, however, in consideration of Mill's liberalism, we must consider his complex attitude toward his father's and Bentham's creed, utilitarianism—the system of psychological, social, ethical, political, and legal theory which *they* had erected upon the foundation of empiricism and as the more detailed and immediate basis of *their* liberalism, but which John Mill subjected, in both connections, to much revision.

As we know, the utilitarian system aimed and claimed to be, and to some extent actually was, a product of empiricism, but at the same time it was mainly a more or less logical system of abstract ideas with a very limited, inadequate empirical foundation. Its central effort was to derive its norms of "good" human conduct, legal justice, the proper constitution or organization of the state and society, and all right or wise public policies, from experience of the consequences of the diverse possible kinds of conduct, institutions, laws, and policies, for human happiness; *instead of* deriving them from arbitrary premises or moral "axioms"—flat affirmations of "moral absolutes"—thought of either as "self-evident" intuitions of moral "reason," or as contained in the Christian "revelation" of the will of God. This appeal to experience of results for happiness *was* of course in line with the dictates of empiricism; and it was legitimate to include in the concept or category of sense-experience, or all sense-perceptions, not only perceptions of "objective, external" objects and events, but also the sensations, feelings, or experiences of pleasures and pains, or happiness and unhappiness, or satisfactions and dissatisfactions, connected with them. But there was in utilitarian thought no remotely adequate realization of the endless variety and variability, complexity, subtlety, and elusiveness of the latter "subjective" human experiences, and the extreme difficulty of treating them, or this material—through introspection and communication—as the subject matter of genuine, effective, scientific, empirical research. In fact, Bentham and his followers hardly attempted any such research; or rather, what they attempted, and regarded as sufficient, amounted to extremely little. In effect they merely used, as the basic premises of their whole system of doctrines, a few very abstract, general "common-sense" notions of the elements and required conditions of the "greatest happiness" of human beings, universally, and the supposed psychological laws of their predictable, actual behavior (to maximize their net amounts of happiness or aggregate of pleasures) in different situations or sets of circumstances, and the normative laws, observance of which supposedly would lead to long-run optimal results in the way of happiness throughout society at large.

Hence the system, despite its background of philosophical or theoretical empiricism, and its stress on the criterion of experienced results, was mainly a flimsy structure of deductive theory, having as its basis nothing like adequate and/or accurate factual knowledge about human beings, their real motives and behavior-patterns, and the real conditions of their greatest happiness, but only a few general and abstract, superficial, and in many applications highly unrealistic assumptions about those matters. Now it is true that John Stuart Mill did not greatly improve or reform the system in that respect, or even see clearly how to do so or what was needed, but only, in his revision or new version as compared with Bentham's, made it *less* logical or self-consistent *without* making it much more satisfactory in any other respect. But he did at least become sharply, uncomfortably aware of its great deficiencies or limitations, while adhering always to the central idea of ethics as not an effort to impose arbitrary commandments on mankind, but an effort to study and discover the requirements of its greatest happiness. And the improvement of utilitarian theory which he tried to carry out, by combining with it insights of a different kind which he acquired in a different quarter, is of interest and value despite the logical and other objections which lie against it.

Mill's sharpest criticism of the character of Bentham's thought, and the clearest disclosure of the source and direction of the very different line of thought which Mill was to draw upon in the effort to supplement, revise, and improve Bentham's, may be found respectively in his short essays on Bentham and on Coleridge, which appeared as a pair.[2] There is really no doubt that Mill's own outlook, in spite of all its differences from Bentham's, had and always retained much more in common with the latter than with that of Coleridge, the romantic poet and political philosopher who in the latter role had preached a quasi-mystical, anti-Enlightenment, feudal-tradition-loving Toryism or Conservatism, diametrically opposed to all that Bentham stood for and in almost as much conflict, on the whole, with the less clear-cut, consistent, and stable views of Mill. Yet Mill, with characteristic open-mindedness, generosity toward the opposition, and severity on his own party and tradition, not only ranked Coleridge and Bentham together on the same plane, as in British political thought "the two leading, seminal minds" of their generation, but actually expressed more adverse criticism and less appreciation in the essay on Bentham than in that on Coleridge. And he fairly well described the main weakness of Benthamism in political thought, in calling it a system of "political geometry," which tried to deduce, with a precision and rigor like that of mathematical reasoning, the rules or precepts that should govern political life and governmental decisions, from premises in the fields of psychology, the social sciences, and ethics. What I think this must be taken to mean as a criticism is that Benthamism lacked an adequate empirical foundation of factual knowledge about politicians, the people and situations they must deal with, and the real possibilities in political and governmental decision making; that it was an overtheoretical and insufficiently realistic body of doctrine, well developed only on its formal, logical, systematic, analytical side, and evolved from assumptions formed with too little sensitive or perceptive awareness of the relevant human and social realities, and of nuances differentiating the diverse, more and

[2] These essays may be found and read in J. S. Mill's *Dissertations and Discussions* (London: 1859–1867), vol. I, pp. 33ff. (Bentham); 393ff. (Coleridge).

less important values, lumped by Bentham in the one all-embracing, abstract category of "utility" for "happiness."

Now the philosophy of Coleridge—indebted and closely akin to the post-Kantian German romantic Idealism—was *not* in the empiricist tradition to which Mill adhered; but professedly used as fundamental premises—asserted with dogmatic confidence—alleged intuitive-general insights of the German and Coleridgian, higher, synthetic "reason" (not the inferior, analytic "understanding"); in short this was a philosophy of the kind to which, in general, Mill the empiricist was profoundly opposed. Yet in spite of this I think it is true, and the true explanation of the degree of Coleridge's attraction for and influence on Mill, that in fact there entered into the intuitive premises of the former's thought, as compared or contrasted with the too simple and rigid assumptions of Bentham's, a far more adequate, sensitive awareness of the complex and various real make-ups of the souls and behavioral propensities of human beings, and the kind of hierarchy in the realm of values which most good-and-wise men try to grasp. It is an ironic paradox that the humane-liberal thought of Bentham and his followers, with its nominally empiricistic basis, was more deficient in the humanistic insights dependent on full awareness and use of this subtle kind or part of all human experience, than was the romantic-conservative-or-reactionary and more authoritarian thought of Coleridge and his kind. But the Benthamic liberalism did not depend upon, but rather was weakened by, the deficiencies of the Benthamite assumptions and doctrinal system; and the political conclusions or views of Coleridge did not all follow with logical necessity from his basic psychological and ethical or humanistic awarenesses or insights. Mill, in criticizing Bentham's thought and more generously appraising that of Coleridge, in this pair of essays, was groping for a way to repair the faults of the former's "method' of inquiry, and to use or draw upon the latter's richer humanistic insights for this purpose, *without* deserting the former's liberal or accepting the latter's conservative program.

To learn what results that effort on Mill's part led to, we must turn to his essay entitled *Utilitarianism*.[3] Unfortunately, this essay in fact discusses only one part of utilitarianism or Benthamism as a complete system of thought or doctrine—and chooses to discuss (both defend and revise or amend) that part in which the system is weakest and least useful. Mill's *Utilitarianism* essay is only about the utilitarian theory of ethics proper, or ethics in the narrow sense—the proper conduct of their personal lives by individuals. It is not in this field, but in that of all collective or public action, to shape and develop the institutions of

[3] See *Utilitarianism, Liberty, and Representative Government*, by John Stuart Mill (London and New York: Everyman's Library, 1914).

society and the state and all legislation and public policy, that utilitarian principles can be most fruitfully and usefully applied and are least inadequate. In the shaping of legislation and public policies, there is a large place for efforts to "calculate" or predict, from the findings of all appropriate social-scientific research and analysis, the probable effects of alternative policies or measures upon the happiness or welfare of the people generally, and of different groups among them; and to choose the policies most likely to be conducive to something like (in the ambiguous Benthamite phrase) "the greatest happiness of the greatest number." But in an individual's conduct of his personal life, it is generally impossible for him to achieve much in the way of foresight and comparative estimation of the important (remoter as well as more immediate) likely consequences of his different possible actions or decisions, for his own and other peoples' happiness, and "scientific" choice of the actions or courses that will have on the whole the best consequences, or deserve to rank as the ethically best or right actions by this criterion.

No doubt it can be argued that, despite the overwhelming difficulty of such a thorough-going application of it, the general principle is valid; one should try to make his conduct such as to bring about, for himself and for all persons affected by it, as much happiness and as little unhappiness as possible. But it must be admitted that this principle, by itself, is less adequate for the daily ethical guidance of the individual's conduct of his life, than the principle that public affairs should be conducted on the lines most favorable to the general happiness of the whole mass of citizens, is or can be for the guidance of legislators, public officials, and voters as such. Yet it is understandable, although regrettable, that Mill's *Utilitarianism* essay considers only the basic or logically first question of ethical theory as such: the question, what is the proper criterion of "good" or ethically correct conduct or human living—the ground or first principle of the rational ethics or morality by which men should live?

In his discussion of that question, then, Mill first stoutly defends the utilitarian (Bentham's) answer to it, against the common or usual, ill-founded criticisms or objections grounded in misunderstandings, and alternative or rival answers which he regards as either wrong and morally pernicious, or meaningless, or really equivalent in meaning to the utilitarian answer even if their exponents deny that. He then goes on to develop his own measure of dissent from the principle in Bentham's form, and to revise or amend it to make it more fully express his own ethical outlook. At the outset he insists that it is a misrepresentation to interpret the idea of living with happiness or pleasures in view as the goal of life, as meant to sanction the unworthy, not self-disciplined, sole or primary pursuit of the "low" or "vulgar" pleasures of the body, appetites, and senses—or "worldly" pleasures obtainable in abundance by any clever or ruthless rascal through control of great wealth, power, etc. To understand Bentham, Mill insists, one must understand the words "pleasure" and "happiness" as having very broad inclusive meanings, and referring alike to all satisfactions of all possible human desires or aspirations—all enjoyments, or pleasant, agreeable, or delightful experiences, emphatically including those of the intellect, the aesthetic sensibilities, humane sympathies, and satisfactions of the religious desire for a sense of harmony with all life and existence, as well as and no less than the pleasures that signify only satisfactions of the bodily or animal appetites. To try to so live as to be and continue to be as happy as possible in the fullest, all-around sense, *and* contribute as much as one can to the happiness of one's family, friends, neighbors, and fellow citizens and, if possible, of mankind, is the ideal, not of the self-indulgent libertine, but of the truly good-and-wise man and citizen. This is, in effect, what Mill maintains, and rightly as we may grant, especially when he adds or admits the paradoxical but true point that happiness cannot be won by a too conscious, deliberate, intent, and anxious pursuit of it, but only by a more self-forgetful, objectively or outwardly directed conduct of one's life, in a well-balanced pursuit of all the ends, success or progress in attaining which in fact *brings* happiness as an unsought by-product. Mill even holds that the utilitarian ideal, as he thus interprets it, is in fact identical with that of the original Christian ethic, i.e., that of Jesus; but he spurns as an opposite and evil tendency in much historic, official Christianity the perverse, grim tendency to regard all the normal human pleasures as bad and desires for them as sinful, and associate virtue not with joy but with gloom. In short, as Mill—in agreement, thus far, with Bentham—explains the utilitarian ideal or principle, it emerges as indeed wholly acceptable, immune to all objections, and in full agreement with all "other" sense-making and persuasive doctrines in its field.

Yet he goes on to dissent, himself, from a further important aspect of Bentham's version of it, and to develop as his own a different, complex, and hardly self-consistent version or position. Bentham had sought to reduce all "qualitative" distinctions among values or pleasures to "quantitative" distinctions only, and thus to make ethics, in principle or potentially, a simple, exact, mathematical science. Utility-for-happiness was to be the sole and universal criterion; all pleasures, of all kinds alike, could contribute to or be parts of happiness—a person's happiness would mean the sum of all his pleasures or enjoyments; and the only "ranking" of diverse pleasures was to be on the basis of the long-run total net amounts of happiness represented by or connected with them—account being taken of their different intensities, durations, and degrees of "purity" or nonentailment of associated, or prerequisite, or subsequent pains or displeasures, and "fecundity" or fruitfulness in leading to other additional pleasures beyond themselves.

And finally, on all those points or questions about his own pleasures and how to rank them all in his own hierarchy or preference-scale, each individual was to be the sole judge; there were to be no universal absolute standards but only, for each individual, the set of personal standards or relative evaluations of all his own desires and satisfactions, to be worked out by and for himself through reflective examination of his own experience. As Bentham said, if you happen to prefer playing pushpin (a trivial game) to reading poetry—i.e., if the former gives you the greater pleasure—then for you pushpin *is better* than poetry, and that is that. But John Stuart Mill could not accept this point of view; to his fastidious mind and feelings it seemed clear that there are among the pleasures enjoyed and sought by human beings, distinctions or gradations of quality and merit—refinement or vulgarity, nobility or baseness, worthiness or unworthiness—which cannot be reduced to just different quantities of pleasure as estimated for himself by each individual, however ignorant of values, depraved, or deficient in good taste he may be. "It is better," said Mill, "to be Socrates, dissatisfied, than a fool, satisfied." [4] Men should not simply, accepting themselves as they are, seek to satisfy all their current wants as fully as possible; they should first of all and above all seek to develop in themselves worthy wants, desires, or aspirations for the goods or ends or goals worth seeking—those yielding not simply large amounts, but fine qualities of happiness or pleasure. For Mill it was not enough to insist, with Bentham, that *happiness* as a term includes or covers all kinds of pleasures, hence those of the (good) mind and the (noble) spirit *as well as* those of the body; he insisted, further, that certain kinds of pleasures are intrinsically better than other kinds and *should* be mainly valued, sought, achieved, and enjoyed by *all* men, although in fact, for the most part, these finest pleasures *were not* appreciated or desired by the majority of men in their current blindness.

Now it was a matter of some difficulty for Mill to reconcile that conviction of his, about the superior and inferior qualities and values of the different kinds of pleasures, with his empiricism—his equally strong conviction that the sources and tests of all truth lie, not in alleged, intuitive, general insights convincing only to some minds, but in specific experiences available to all. On its face, his belief in the universal normative validity of the class of particular tastes or value-judgments, in fact peculiar to the highly cultivated, relatively wise-and-good minority of mankind, seems to be in line rather with the intuitionist epistemology and aristocratic or elitist, authoritarian political tendency of Platonic and Romantic-Idealistic (e.g., Coleridgian) thought than with em-

[4] See *ibid.*, chap. 2.

piricism, utilitarianism, and democratic liberalism. But Mill, at least dimly aware of this difficulty, tried hard to square his idea of the absolute hierarchy among kinds of pleasures with his empiricism by arguing that there is agreement on the former among all those whose opportunities have been such that they have been sufficiently exposed to, i.e., have had in sufficient amounts, all the relevant kinds of experience. Men with ample experience of both the cheap or common and the finer pleasures generally agree in preferring the latter; the untutored "common man" is likely to prefer or think that he prefers, e.g., inferior "popular" music or art to the best masterpieces, *only* because he has never had the opportunities leading to adequate exposure to or experience of the latter. And as it is in the spheres of music and all the fine arts, so according to Mill's thought it is in the spheres of all kinds of values, delights, or pleasures; only the best-educated, fully and finely cultivated minds and spirits have access to the experiences which engender and confirm knowledge of the superior qualities of the pleasures of the intellect and of the finer ethical as well as aesthetic feelings, as compared with all the ordinary, common, or vulgar pleasures, of which ample experience is readily available to all men.

This thesis, however, involves a faith in the equality or similarity of all men as regards their innate or potential aptitudes, capacities, or sensitivities, which is hardly consistent either with general observation and experience or with modern psychological knowledge (such as Mill of course lacked), and which Mill himself in his other writings by no means always exhibited. His revised-utilitarian theory of ethics, changing Bentham's criterion of utility-for-happiness (all pleasures as diversely ranked by diverse individuals) into that of utility-for-"true"-happiness (involving the particular way of ranking, selecting, and combining pleasures, of which Mill approved) was really no longer utilitarian, or self-consistent, or consistent with his simple empiricist theory of all knowledge or warranted beliefs or judgments; nor was it very clearly consistent with that devotion to democracy and trust in the common man to which he was generally, though uneasily, inclined. Yet I think we can see in this logically unsatisfactory essay, as a fruit of his effort to revise or improve his father's and Bentham's inadequate ethical-and-social philosophy, the enrichment of his insights, as compared with theirs, which came partly from his appreciative study of the views of Coleridge and other English Romanticists, and partly from his own native sensitivity and finer feelings.

Now if we turn from Mill's essay on *Utilitarianism* to his essay *On Liberty,*[5] we again, I think, find in the latter, as the central docu-

[5] Mill's *On Liberty,* like his *Utilitarianism,* is available in many editions, but most conveniently in the Everyman's Library edition, combining both essays, and also that on *Representative Government,* in a single small volume (London and New York: 1914).

ment of his *political* thought, further evidence of the ways in which he was both helped and handicapped, in working out his own exact positions, both by his measure of adherence to his utilitarian heritage and by his departure from it. This famous essay, *On Liberty,* has been justly rated as one of the few great classics in the English-speaking world's literature of at once eloquent and reasoned appeals for public creation and protection of the largest workable spheres of individual liberty or freedom, for all individuals severally, from coercive control by others—by the state, society, other individuals, or groups or organizations of whatever kind; or appeals, in other words, for restraint of all coercion of human beings by other human beings to the unavoidable or indispensable minimal amount. But while this is truly a great essay, it is so, again, in spite of serious limitations and logical defects. There is really no doubt that Mill deeply felt the value of every individual's liberty or freedom to be very great indeed, and the "intrinsic" value of an end or good in itself and not merely or only the "instrumental" value of a means to other (public, social, or collective) ends. But he was precluded by his empiricist and utilitarian heritage from asserting or accepting any doctrine of the "natural rights" of individuals, and was obliged to try to reach his delimitations of their proper freedoms and the proper authority of the state and society by using, solely, the criterion of what would have the greatest social utility or expediency, or discussing what could be expected to work best in the long run for the stability and progress of society as a whole, and for the welfare or happiness of its members generally.

Thus his immediate rule for reaching those delimitations was that society is justified in controlling or restraining its individual members so far, and only so far, as it must "in self-defense" or for its own (society's) protection. That is, society can properly restrain each individual from all acts demonstrably injurious to others and thus to society itself, but not from any acts affecting the welfare only of the acting individual himself. "Paternalistic" control of the (adult, responsible) individual "for his own good" only is never justified; as to all that is, or pertains to, or affects, or concerns his own welfare only, each individual is to be the final judge and have complete or absolute freedom. But this rule obviously fails to imply or ensure clear protection of anything like as much individual liberty or feedom as Mill obviously wanted to defend or advocate. Very few of the possible, important actions of the highly interdependent members of complex, closely knit societies affect only themselves individually, or lack important consequences favorably or unfavorably affecting countless other persons and in that sense "affected with a public interest"; hence a very great extension of public control, reducing the liberties of individuals to very small dimensions, can easily be justified by this criterion which Mill meant to use with an opposite result.

Mill's struggles to make this rule yield the result he wanted appear in his discussions of various concrete cases, problems, or examples, which I cannot here take the time and space to consider; but they were, in general, unsuccessful struggles. He would have done better to take as his guide, or adhere to, the seemingly similar but really different, traditional rule or principle of the classical liberalism, that everyone should have all the liberty that can be consistent or compatible with the same or equal liberty for everyone else; or in other words be subject only to those restraints that are necessary to protect, not the complete "welfares," but only the (equal) liberties of others. But *this* idea involves the presupposition that liberty is a very great good in itself or for its own sake—that it is not merely a *means to* but an essential *part of* human welfare or happiness, and a part so important that all men should have much of it even at the cost of being free and likely to do considerable damage to each other's sums of "welfare" or "happiness" *as* estimated *without* sufficient weighting of liberty itself in that computation. And this presupposition amounts to the essence of that idea of the "natural rights" of all individuals to extensive freedoms, even at a cost to other less important aspects of each other's welfares, which originally was a cornerstone of the classical liberalism, but came to be discarded by Bentham, Mill, and others as being a nonempirical, a priori dogma, grounded, not in the experiences of men generally as to what they most want or value or find to be or yield the greatest pleasures, but in an arbitrary assignment to liberty as such of a high and absolute fixed value which it does not necessarily have, universally at all, in the experiences or for the feelings of particular people.

It is true that liberalism in the classical sense demands a great deal of freedom for all diverse individuals to arrive at and live by their own diverse patterns of value-judgments, to a great extent, but it also demands that all of them shall very firmly, steadily, and consistently value freedom itself, as compared with other goods, much more highly than many of them often actually do. If the members of a society come generally to insist that they must be made to so behave as to maximize the welfare or happiness of all (apart from their freedoms), they will not long retain large freedoms; a society of free individuals cannot be perfect in other respects, or entirely free from internal conflicts, disorders, and harms to other aspects of the welfare of each by the free actions of his fellows. In his essay on *Utilitarianism,* Mill had weakened his liberalism, or come near to deserting it, by "amending" simple utilitarianism through insisting on his absolute, higher evaluations of refined as opposed to vulgar pleasures. Here in his essay *On Liberty,* on the contrary, he even more seriously weakened his intended liberal stand, in the opposite way, by adhering to a straight or simple utilitarian approach to the subject *instead of* insisting on an absolute, higher evaluation of an ample liberty for all severally, as opposed to other goods or pleasures. Although Benthamism originally was meant and appeared to support the classical liberalism, it led more logically and in the long run toward the "welfare-state" ideal of modern democratic socialism and the modern "liberalism" which generally is more socialistic and less libertarian or individualistic than its classical namesake and ancestor was; and John Stuart Mill's was a confused, not clearly self-consistent outlook, in transition from the classical-liberal to the modern-liberal point of view.

Yet this essay *On Liberty* contains much more of high merit than I have yet mentioned. Besides insisting that only necessity for protection of the welfare of society at large *can justify restrictions of* the liberties of individuals, it further goes on to insist, equally, that ample, secure or protected liberties for all individuals severally—emphatically including those nonconforming, eccentric individuals who seem most obnoxious to the popular majority—are in the long run *so important for* the welfare of society as a whole, that the latter in its own best interests must positively establish and maintain them. And the main part of the argument advanced in support of *this* thesis is or consists of Mill's theory of the process and conditions of continuing all-around social *progress*. (Liberalism has always been or meant progressivism as well as libertarianism, and the connection between the two—theory of the dependence of social progress on individual liberties—here worked out by Mill, is of great interest.) All progress—advancement of knowledge and wisdom, and progressive change and improvement of old ways of thinking and feeling and the consequent old behavior-patterns or habits, customs, and traditions—can come about only through free individual dissents and dissensions, innovations at first resisted by inert or conservative souls (who tend to be the majority), and a free competition of all the old and diverse new ideas, creations, things, and ways for eventual general or widespread acceptance on the basis of demonstrated (experienced) superior results for the welfare or happiness of the people generally. In any large mass—society, or group of people sharing old, loved traditions—the strong tendency to insist on conformity and collective unity or solidarity, to repress dissents and innovations, and to tolerate only what all agree with, inevitably works to prevent any progress, and to thwart the creative impulses of all the more able and original minds. Prevailing fear of changes *for the worse* works or tends to prevent *any* changes, growth of variety, and competitive testing of the old traditions and diverse novelties against one another to find out what is best or works best for the general or common welfare and happiness. Extensive freedoms for all so-inclined individuals to dissent and innovate, in all spheres of life, activity, and culture, and in all directions, including those most feared and hated by the conservative, tradition-bound majority, are indispensable for continuing, all-around progress. A convincing presentation of this valid and important thesis, the core of the liberal-progressive outlook, is the core of Mill's essay *On Liberty*.

Recognition of the facts that the able and original or deviant minds whose innovations can lead to progress are or make up an elite minority, and that there is in every large society a large majority of mediocre and normally inert, tradition-bound, conservative minds and souls, did not prevent Mill from supporting *democracy*, but did make his support of it hesitant and carefully qualified. What he supported in this field was emphatically not an all-out, simple, or absolute democracy, meaning simply (with universal suffrage) majority rule, but only a *liberal* democracy—majority rule qualified or limited by firm protections of minority, and all individual, rights and liberties, even as against the governing majority. And he feared the overconservative and often illiberal, conformity-demanding or intolerant or repressive, and rather stupid tendencies of the popular majority, to the point of wanting to further qualify or modify majority rule with such devices as proportional representation to ensure that all significant minorities would also be able to exert some influence. In fact Mill, like many another liberal intellectual in every generation, was torn between his democratic sympathies, or concern for the liberties and welfare of all the people, which he knew could be well protected only by giving "the many" a good deal of power; and his poor or low opinion, on the other hand, of the tastes, intelligence, and wisdom of "the many" or "the common man," who, when personally encountered, offended his own high and fastidious standards. Many a democratic liberal has evaded this dilemma by indulging and cultivating a theoretical, blind, unrealistic optimism about the innate or potential capacities of "the many," but Mill did not generally or consistently do this; in a typical moment of sad candor he exclaimed that "average human nature is such poor stuff!"

Yet he also did not trust any elite group or class to use power for the good of all and not in its own narrow special interest; hence he saw the basic political problem as that of so dividing power among all groups that all would have enough to protect themselves, while at the same time none—not even a large cohesive majority where that existed—would have enough to get its way completely against the desires and rights of any of the others. But this, he knew, even if it could be achieved and maintained, would not by itself be enough to ensure protection of all individuals, and/or impartial and effective government in the common interest of all. The proper liberties and rights of necessarily powerless tiny minorities and lone individuals could be protected only by a very difficult-to-achieve, firm devotion to "enlightened" liberal principles by "the many" and by the members of all potent groups. And a system of divided and balanced powers could work only with general prevalence, in all quarters, of such reasonableness and willingness to compromise as is rarely prevalent *enough* in any great society. Above all, a well-working liberal democracy must have respected, though not invariably or blindly followed, leaders (not rulers), always readily entering into public life, mainly or largely from the ranks of the minority of able, cultivated, wise, and devoted men. All these requirements at once, for realization of a good democracy, have rarely been better fulfilled than they were in Mill's England; and he always steadily, fully exerted his substantial influence in helping to bring about the further progressive development of a sound democracy and all its prerequisites within his own country. But he was never under the illusion that all societies or countries could immediately or soon meet all the requirements, or that a universal spread of democracy should be desired as an immediate goal.

On one point I have still not sufficiently indicated the more pessimistic side or part of Mill's attitude to democracy. He was afraid that, even in his England, the rising and growing, not only political but also extrapolitical, *general* power and influence of the popular majority of the middle and working classes would tend to bring about a dangerous growth of both governmental and other informal social pressures upon or against the liberties and diverse spontaneous propensities and contributions of the country's superior, nonconforming, original, deviant, or creative minds and characters, upon whose diverse departures from the previously most widely popular views and practices, on-going progress would depend. And his "sermon" against this too likely tendency of the democratic majority to try to enforce universal conformity with its own mediocre and merely traditional standards, in all departments of life and of culture, was the most central message of his essay *On Liberty*. Yet in spite of all that was critical and relatively pessimistic or quite realistic in his judgments about "the common people," Mill on the whole was "on their side," and often nearly or quite "radical" as a sympathetic champion and supporter of their causes. For he was full, not only of humane sympathy for and with them, or concern for improvement of their opportunities and achievements of all kinds, but also of a degree of stubborn, long-run hopefulness about them, not clearly, fully consistent with his frequent pessimistic judgments. Particularly on behalf of labor or the working class, he was full of idealistic partisanship, long-range hopes, and ideas of reforms to be developed and carried out for their benefit. He could be a severe critic of his own middle class as well as of the aristocracy and gentry, but he tended to think of the working class as made up largely of individuals—both leaders and rank-and-file members—with attractive, promising minds and characters or traits and attitudes. Yet he suspected that they were so attractive mainly because they were as yet unspoiled by possession and exercise of great power as a class within society; and he feared that with the growth of their power, which he foresaw as inevitable and regarded as just, they would in time become as prone to misuse it in their narrow apparent class interest, and against society's and their own true best interests, as other dominant classes always had been.

It was partly, I think, that sympathetic or humane concern for justice to the working class, and partly his idealistic yearning for a more fraternal and harmonious, cooperative, less fiercely competitive and strife-torn society than the one he lived in, which led Mill to his long flirtation with and eventual loose adherence to the vague "socialism" or vision of a future "socialist" society that was coming into existence as the dream of a new minority movement in his time. We seem here to encounter another one of the many inconsistencies or unresolved dilemmas in his thought: how could Mill, the great advocate of liberal individualism and free, individual innovation and competition as the indispensable condition or method of all progress, and in political economy the final great exponent of the Ricardian-classical principles leading to support or endorsement of *laissez-faire* competitive capitalism—how could *this* author at the same time flirt with socialism and come in the end to call himself a socialist—without ever renouncing any of those other views? But I think that we are *not here* confronted with as great or clear an inconsistency within Mill's thought—one as great or clear as it seems to be. To understand and judge it fairly we must know (1) what he did and did not mean by "socialism," (2) how he envisaged and distinguished what could be hoped for in the distant future and what must be accepted as the best practicable regime in his time and well beyond it, and (3) with what extensive reservations and qualifications he always surrounded his support of *laissez-faire* economic liberalism or individualism, even in and for his time. Much of my explanation of these points and especially of the last one, must be developed in connection with my discussion, in the next chapter, of Mill's economics and political economy. But it has seemed desirable to raise the question of Mill's "socialism" at this point, while I am still discussing, not his economic thought as such, but its general social-philosophic background, and to consider what "socialism" did and did not mean to him.

The early, vague, incipient developments or varieties of "socialist" thought that were burgeoning in Mill's time, and drew his friendly interest, were dreams envisaging a (distant) future, radical reorganization of the economic and general life of mankind, *not* through or under omnicompetent national states as vast public units owning and managing all productive enterprises and resources within their borders, but instead through or in countless, small, informal, voluntary cooperative societies, associations, or communities of people, choosing and agreeing to share or pool their wealth and jointly plan and organize their lives and labors. When the world should come to consist entirely of such (local, small) communities, they would all be loosely linked together, by mutual agreements, in large-area confederations and perhaps a world-wide confederation of all those; but there would no longer be any nation-states, or states of any kind, with coercive governments; for when all men had learned the wisdom of renunciation of their individual private properties and acquisitive ambitions, and the superior attractions of harmonious cooperative living with their fellows in ideal communities, the strife or conflicts which coercive governments exist to control would no longer exist, and the latter could and would be dispensed with. It is not surprising that this, as a vision of the goal at the distant future end of the long road of mankind's progressive moral "enlightenment," appealed strongly to Mill; or that, as a liberal, he not only, from the first, denounced the tendencies of many of its conservative opponents to attack it unfairly, misrepresent it, and try to get advocacy of it legally suppressed. Mill of course demanded that its advocates and their arguments be given a fair and full public hearing and consideration; but eventually also he was led, by his own long, sympathetic study or consideration of *this* socialist vision or ideal and the question of the long-run possibility of its realization, to decide more or less fully in its favor and end by describing himself as a socialist. But he always realized, more fully than most such socialists did, how very long at best the preparatory period would have to be, of gradual progressive improvement of the mental and moral condition of mankind to the point of readiness for and ability to carry out and truly realize the socialist ideal. And instead of giving up and withdrawing from the unready contemporary world and living only to preach socialism and await its realization, Mill put his socialism "on the shelf" as only a hope for the distant future, and devoted his main efforts to the studies and activities through which he hoped to contribute to many of the countless, small, immediate improvements of the society and culture around him, for which he deemed it to be ready in the sense that early realizations of them should be quite feasible.

MILL'S LOGIC AND IDEAS ON "METHOD" IN ECONOMICS AND THE OTHER "MORAL SCIENCES"

Thus far I have described only some of Mill's most basic general beliefs and attitudes: his empiricism, his revised-utilitarian ethics, and his views on liberty and progress, democracy, the future of labor, and socialism. Together all this may be said to have made up the background or wider context of his economics and, along with the latter, the basis of his ideas of the proper public economic policies, or proper relations between the state and the economy. But before going on to describe his study of and main general conclusions in economics and political economy, I must now insert a brief account of still another segment of the wide range of his intellectual work—his ideas on logic, induction, and scientific method, and their proper, special features as applied in economics and the other social (or "moral") sciences.[6] Perhaps not logic but only convenience has guided me in arranging these different general topics in this sequence; but it has seemed to me logical enough, as well as convenient, to survey first the substance of Mill's basic general outlook or perspective on all existence, life, and values, then his theory of logic and the methodologies of the particular sciences of chief interest to him, and finally the substance (again) of his work in the main one of those, political economy. Unfortunately, the little that I can say here about his great treatise on logic and its sixth book, "The Logic of the Moral Sciences," is bound to be extremely superficial and inadequate, owing to the limitations, not only of my time and space here, but of my knowledge. Let me strongly advise every deeply interested student to examine Mill's *Logic,* and especially to study its Book Six, "The Logic of the Moral Sciences," for himself. The *Logic*—a large treatise on the whole subject, but mainly emphasizing the theory and methods of "inductive" logic—may well be rated as perhaps the best one of all Mill's intellectual productions or performances—the one most deeply, broadly, and thoroughly grounded and prepared, most fully matured, most clear and penetrating in its field, and best written. In contrast with it his *Principles of Political Economy* was a hastily produced and, in level of intellectual achievement and distinction, inferior book; and no wonder, for Mill spent ten years in the production of his *Logic,* but tossed off the *Political Economy* book in his spare time in a single year during which he also worked as a clerk in the office of the British East India Company! In its time and for some time his *Logic* was an outstanding classic in its field or discipline and, although it is now old fashioned of course, it is still worth reading.

The work's especially full treatment of the theory and methods of "inductive" reasoning was of course in line with Mill's basic philosophy or theory of knowledge, empiricism, and with that view of the distinctive character of all "modern science," as contrasted with ancient-classical and mediaeval-scholastic efforts in the sciences, which prevailed from Locke's and Newton's (or even from Lord Bacon's) time to and through and beyond Mill's time. The following description of that contrast was generally or very widely accepted. On the one hand, it was

[6] J. S. Mill, *A System of Logic* (New York: Harper & Brothers, 1869), or any one of the many other editions.

said, Aristotle and the ancient philosophers generally, and the mediaeval Schoolmen, had developed and mainly practiced only deductive reasoning, from purely speculative, empirically unsupported, and untested premises, to conclusions merely spelling out the detailed implications of those premises and thus not yielding any novel or genuine discoveries. On the other hand, the secret of the great, on-going progress of or in all modern sciences, from the seventeenth century on, was held to lie in the discovery and use by their builders of a new method of research and reasoning, which began with experimental or observational studies of particular facts (sense-data) in the field or subject matter of each science. And this new method, it was further held, then went on to derive by inductive reasoning from those data the basic empirical generalizations which replaced the old, discarded, speculative premises; and yielded through further deductive reasonings (now of reduced, only secondary importance) from them (the basic empirical generalizations), detailed analyses of their implications, i.e., of the knowledge that was all essentially contained in the prior observations and inductions. For all believers in this theory of the supposed method or procedure of all modern sciences, it was of crucial importance, of course, to develop or work out fully the logic of induction—the logically valid ways of deriving the basic empirical generalizations, principles, or premises, to be used in each science as the foundation of its structure of theory, from the empirical data already arrived at by prior empirical research in its field. Yet, though various earlier writers had tried and had made contributions, no very full or adequate and satisfactory study of the possibilities of inductive logic had been made until Mill's work appeared. The Aristotelian deductive logic of the syllogism, although long widely regarded as terribly inadequate, antiquated, and of little relevance to the fundamental logical problems of the modern sciences, had largely continued to hold the field in the systematic study of logic merely because no adequate successor or alternative to it had appeared. Mill's *Logic* was thus widely and warmly welcomed as at last meeting a long-felt but unmet need. But it did not and could not really have all the great value or fruitfulness which its author and public had hoped for, because its underlying point of view, i.e., that theory of the process of scientific discovery and the primary, all-important role of inductive-logical reasoning therein, was not entirely valid.

As I think most philosophers and scientists would now tend to agree, there is necessarily in the process of inquiry and discovery of truth—a process which cannot be fully defined and prescribed by any uniform, exact formula—a more or less equal or evenly balanced interplay among all the factors mentioned in the following rough account of this process. (1) The investigator's initial fund of already analyzed or clarified or formulated, global, general, gestalt experience of his general subject matter, *suggests* to his mind, in relation to the problem he is working on—(2) a line of imaginative or speculative thought through which he forms a hypothesis that he thinks may be or contain the true solution of the problem—arriving at this no doubt through "induction" in a sense, from facts known to him, but not a kind or process of induction for which any exact, correct, and sufficient logical rules have ever been discovered. Then (3) deductive analysis or explication of the full, exact implications of that hypothesis, turns it into a developed *theory;* and *then* only, (4) *directed,* methodical, empirical research (observational and, where possible, experimental work) seeks to ascertain the exact relevant facts in order to test and improve the theory—either verify it or disverify it or, if (as often) it turns out to be almost but not quite able to satisfactorily fit and explain the facts, indicate or suggest the needed revisions of it. And finally, (5) the new information that has thus been gained improves (1) above and makes it better able to suggest, in relation to another related problem, a new line of speculation leading to a new hypothetical solution of *that* problem—and the process, sequence, or cycle that I have now described, is repeated.

Now in such a process, imaginative speculation and deduction or analysis are fully as legitimate, necessary, and important as observation or empirical research and induction. Moreover, speculation—"thinking up" hypotheses—seems *to be* itself the initial and main "inductive" step or operation—*but* to be, necessarily, rather a free or imaginative than a definable or rules-observing logical operation; proceeding from or out of prior experience *but not* entirely from or on the basis of detailed, exact, definite, empirical facts or observations—as these are mostly to be attained only at a later stage through directed research aided by already previously formulated theories. Speculation and deduction—theoretical work in short—does not only follow after but in part precedes empirical research and gives indispensable assistance—direction or guidance—to it, as well as being tested, corrected, and assisted by it. And the role of methodical or systematic and exact empirical research is not to provide the initial basis or groundwork for all theorizing, but (1) to verify or test already developed theories, and (2) to enrich and improve the mass of experience with the aid of which new speculative and deductive theorizing can develop.

In the light of all this, it should be recognized that the ancient and mediaeval Aristotelian "method" of inquiry in the sciences was not as completely wrong, misguided, or fruitless as the early founders or pioneers, philosophers, and eulogists of "modern science" were prone to think; and that the great improvements, which have made the (or some) sciences so much more highly and securely successful and progressive in modern times, have not consisted of any single, wholly new discovery of *the* correct "scientific method," or of any general, complete, or definite replacement of reliance on speculation-and-deduction by reliance, instead, on observation-and-induction only or primarily. The main definite lack in premodern times was the lack of any sufficient development of exact techniques, facilities, and tools for conducting the amount and kind of empirical research required to verify or test and improve theories, and to enlarge and improve the fund of empirical knowledge available to theorists to the point of enabling their imaginations to conceive the most appropriate hypotheses. They (the theorists and inquirers of earlier times) were not generally deficient in appreciation of the need to acquire and use or build upon experience of facts and make their theories conform to or fit and explain the facts; and their basic thinking or speculation was probably often as largely "inductive" (in the same indefinite way) as that of modern scientists. Nor was their exclusive stress, as far as theory of strict logic goes, on developing deductive logic, mistaken; the rigorous-logical part or component of scientific theoretical work is still as predominantly if not purely deductive as it ever was. The modern development of empirical research in intimate, reciprocal alliance with theoretical work has been and is supremely important, but this has not been to any great extent a matter of developing and applying a new inductive logic.

What is true, however, as regards the logic of science, is that in its best form it is mainly not the Aristotelian, formal, verbal deductive logic of the syllogism, but the different and superior kind of deductive logic uniquely inherent in mathematical reasoning or mathematics. If Aristotle made a great mistake and through its influence misguided the sciences for many centuries, the mistake was not that of neglecting observation and induction or overencouraging speculation and deduction, but that of deriving his basic general ideas about all nature from biology (biological taxonymy) instead of from mathematics, and proceeding mainly by *classifying* things and their properties instead of by *measuring* changes or variations and trying to grasp or conceive and observe the relations among variables and their variations.[7] The basic advances from the Aristotelian to the modern sciences were made possible, jointly, by the progress of mathematics to the point where it could supply the conceptual and logical tools required by the latter, *and* the progress of empirical research, and discoveries or inventions of better techniques, instruments, etc., for use in it—and the inspired or fortunate, basic discoveries in astronomy and physics made in the sixteenth and seventeenth centuries by the geniuses, Copernicus, Kepler, Galileo, Huyghens, Newton, et al., who rightly combined, and showed their successors how to combine, brilliant hypotheses, mathematical-deductive reasonings, and verificatory observations and experiments.

[7] See A. N. Whitehead, *Science and the Modern World* (New York: The Macmillan Company, 1925).

In saying all that about the nature of science I have not meant, however, to say or imply that inductive logic is of *no* importance, or that Mill's stress upon it and effort to work out its principles as fully as possible in his work on logic was not worthwhile. Although logical inductive reasoning is not *the* or a magic key to new scientific discoveries, efforts to develop, use, and improve it are important aids both to the formation, out of experience via speculation, of well-founded and fruitful hypotheses, and, above all, to the crucial work of ascertaining what the raw data discovered by empirical research mean or indicate as regards the validity of the theories to be tested. Mill's work on the principles of inductive logic had substantial value, though not the great value that it seemed to have to minds imbued with that partly mistaken, oversimple, and one-sided conception of the nature of all modern science that was prevalent in his time.

This value—of Mill's particular way of treating inductive logic—was further reduced by his lack of knowledge, understanding, and appreciation of mathematics, including the mathematical theory of probability, which underlies most of the inductive part of scientific reasoning. Not only is the large and important, deductive part of scientific logical-theoretical work in the main deductive rather in the mathematical than in the verbal-syllogistic way; but to a great extent also the inductive part—employed mainly in drawing inferences from the findings of empirical research, in order to test speculative-and-deductive theories—is inductive in a way governed more by the mathematics of probabilities than by Mill's simple methods of agreement, difference, etc. Especially in the more complex and therefore less exact sciences and branches of all sciences, where empirical research cannot consist at all or mainly or entirely of controlled experiments but must be either partly or entirely statistical instead of experimental research—and this alone presents all the really difficult problems of inductive logic—the analysis of probabilities must be the main guide in solving them. Mill's methods of inferring from observed data, which observed events are "causes" of which other ones—by noting that when *a* is present, *b* is present, when *a* is absent, *b* is absent, when *a* varies, *b* also varies, etc.—all presuppose the possibility of conducting the observations under experimental conditions, i.e., conditions in which all other interfering variables are held, or are, constant. Logically correct inductive inferences are indeed to be reached in all such cases by Mill's methods, but these are the easy cases and the normal, intuitive, or common-sense methods generally, correctly employed even long before Mill or anyone so clearly described them. The great difficulties arise only when experimental conditions do not exist and cannot be created—when many variables are changing and interacting at once, and the investigator is obliged to try to discover the relations among them all—and in these cases it is necessary to go beyond Mill's simple principles and to invoke those of the mathematical science of probabilities. Still it is possible and wrong to go too far in depreciating Mill's work on this subject; it had and has the substantial though modest value of a thorough, systematic, clear analysis and formulation of a set of elementary truths or principles of great importance, which able minds generally would grasp and apply at least with rough correctness even if they never had been made so fully explicit, but which it is well worthwhile to have fully clarified.

Nor was Mill's *Logic* as a whole concerned only or entirely with induction, though that received the main, special emphasis. The book included also many useful and in some degree original or novel, clarifying discussions of the classical problems of deductive logic, and of various forms and combinations of inductive and deductive reasoning required in attacking diverse kinds of scientific problems in the different sciences. And in this connection I must now turn our attention wholly to the work's Book Six, on "The Logic of the Moral Sciences"—probably, and of course not surprisingly, the most valuable part of the entire treatise—which deals with special features of the logical and methodological problems of the "sciences" making up Mill's main field of interest, knowledge, and fullest competence. In an earlier form his views on the logic and methodology of economics, his main "moral science," had been included and published in his *Essays on Some Unsettled Questions in Political Economy;*[8] but these views were restated, along with a broader survey of all "the moral sciences," in the sixth book of his *Logic;* and I think the latter as a whole, as well as the *Essays,* should be studied by all students of Mill's thought, i.e., even by those who are interested mainly in his economics.

By "the moral sciences" Mill of course meant substantially what we now call "the social sciences"—all branches of the study of the activities, problems, and behavior of human beings and societies, as distinguished from the "natural" or physical and biological sciences. The continuing, common usage of the older term, "the moral sciences," perhaps carried with it in Mill's time and for him a slight remainder of the old, original *meaning of* this term—the ages-old conception (still in full vigor as we know in the eighteenth century) of these "sciences" of or about human life and affairs as, unlike the "natural" sciences, not

[8] J. S. Mill, *Essays on Some Unsettled Questions in Political Economy* (London: 1844). The essay referred to, on methodology in economics, is essay five in this collection, *On the Definition of Political Economy and the Method of Investigation Proper to It.* When this volume as a whole was first published, in 1844, Mill's *System of Logic* was already out. But the preface (by Mill) says that all five essays had been written in 1829 and 1830, and the fifth—on method, etc. —had had an earlier printing (before the appearance of the five collected essays or of the *Logic*).

purely or only positive but also and equally normative in purpose, i.e., aiming to discover how men and societies *ought to* conduct their lives and affairs, *as well as* how they *do* conduct them. Certainly, Mill, as we have seen already in this chapter, was interested fully as much in ethics and the ethical-normative side of social and political thought and (or including) political economy as he was in the positive-scientific aspects of psychology and the social sciences of economics, politics, etc. Yet, like most present-day exponents of the "social" sciences, and unlike most pre-nineteenth-century exponents of the "moral" sciences, he tended strongly to think of the subject matter of these studies as just the actual courses, causes, and results of actual human behavior and social processes; and to assume that the normative conclusions they would lead to would emerge as corollaries of their positive-scientific knowledge of that subject matter—just as the practical working rules of the arts or techniques directly based on the "natural" sciences are corollaries of the scientific laws discovered in the latter. The progress of knowledge (understanding) of the social processes and results arising from diverse ways of acting on the parts of societies and their members, leads by itself (according to this view) to all needed growth of practical, moral, and political wisdom, by "enlightening" societies of men to the point of leading them to choose, consistently, the ways of acting understood to be those logically required to lead to the "best" results, i.e., attainment of the ends most valued and desired by all.

Unfortunately, this too simple view of this matter involves the untrue presupposition that in general all or most men agree and are right or wise "by nature" in their ultimate or basic value-judgments and desires, or that this would be so if they all knew and understood all the conditions, costs, and consequences of attaining different ends in different ways; that devotions by many men to ends or purposes which many other men regard as evil are always due only to ignorance and mistaken opinions about matters within the realm of potential positive-scientific knowledge, of facts and logic and actual patterns of connected causes and effects. There is no sufficient ground or evidence for this faith that agreement on the true answers to all positive-social-scientific questions, if this were achieved, would be enough to bring all men to any sufficient or tolerable agreement in their ultimate aims, desires, or values. Diversities and conflicts of ideals—conceptions of and convictions about the morally imperative goals of life and civilization—appear to have partly independent roots and persistent lives of their own, and not to diminish notably with the growth and spread of the kind of knowledge and understanding sought in the social sciences as positive sciences. Rather they seem to cause or motivate diverse developments and conflicting uses of the latter in their "applied" aspects, as increasingly potent techniques employed to serve the warring aims of the groups of adherents of diverse and warring "ideologies." Rational inquiry and discussion as to what the controlling aims of human lives, societies, and civilization *ought* to be, is inquiry of another kind, which needs to be pursued in the proper kind of interaction with, but not to be allowed to control or be entirely controlled by, the positive sciences of human life and affairs.

The proper combination of these things would be the properly constituted, dual or bifocal "moral sciences"—including in themselves the social sciences and also an associated but distinguished, and separately and equally cultivated, and not simply dependent or derivative, normative, moral-social philosophy. The old "moral sciences" in times (centuries) now far past were, I think, tending to develop in that way or proper form; but by Mill's time, although the term "moral sciences" was still in use, the prevailing conception already was becoming that of only positive social sciences, with relatively minor and entirely dependent or derivative, normative appendages, or sets of corollaries. And Mill's utilitarian heritage of course made that conception natural for him; since it was the essence of the utilitarian outlook that all normative precepts to guide both private and public action were to be derived from knowledge of the results to which all actions would lead, for or in satisfactions of men's actual desires. Thus there is not in Mill's book or chapters on "The Logic of the Moral Sciences" any discussion of the special, logical or/and methodological problems of inquiries venturing beyond the study of "what is" or also including efforts, of a different and partly independent kind, to seek true answers to questions of or about "what ought to be." But the discussions to be found here, of logical and methodological problems of the purely positive social sciences, are of much interest and value as far as they go.

Serious limitations, however, are imposed on those discussions by the limitations, already discussed here, of Mill's basic views about all sciences and the nature and methods of all induction. He could not bring to his study of the logic of the sciences of human behavior and social processes an adequate vision of the proper character, development, and role, in them, of empirical research and inductive studies to verify or test and improve the provisional conclusions of speculative-and-deductive theoretical work. For as we have seen, his theory of induction embraced only the kind of induction that is usable in the simple, strictly experimental sciences, and he had no grasp of the way of analyzing probabilities and statistics which must play the main role in empirical and inductive research in the social sciences. Here we have, I think, the explanation of the striking paradox that appears generally in the works of Mill and all the early or classical philosophers of empiricism, whose work apart from that in general philosophy was always in the social or "moral" sciences. Whereas in theory they advocated, for all sciences, primary reliance on empirical observations and inductive reasoning, in practice they all relied mainly, in their own work in the "moral" sciences, on deductive analysis or spelling out of the implications of their "common-sense" assumptions, which were not too well grounded or tested empirically. And Mill's treatment of the logic of these sciences is, in fact, largely a defense of this procedure—on the following lines. Like his forerunners in developing the philosophy of empiricism, he recognized as authentic, basic, experiential data, besides the observations or perceptions of physical facts directly involving the use or activity of the external or bodily senses, also the data of "consciousness"—introspective awareness of psychological facts, through what Locke had called "the internal sense." Hence Mill believed that in the social ("moral") sciences, the main and crucial primary premises for theoretical work in them—initial propositions about human motives and the human mental and resulting behavioral processes which impel and direct all social processes—could easily be discovered and established at the outset, through introspection and communication, as generalizations from or of, and directly supported by, this part of everyone's "experience"—his direct "consciousness" of his own motives, mental states, and processes. Deductive development of the implications of these primary, general truths of experience would then yield scientific theories about the processes in or functionings of societies, arising from the desires, thought processes, and behavior of their members. These would not need further empirical verification, since their empirical validity could be guaranteed by that of their initial premises together with the logical validity of the deductive reasoning from those to the conclusions, or "laws" of the social processes, arrived at.

Now of course that argument only rationalizes the general practice of Mill and his forerunners of relying, without empirical research, on deductive theorizing from or upon "common-sense" assumptions; and of course it is vulnerable to a number of serious criticisms. Men's "consciousness" of their motives and other mental states leading to their actions is actually not a very penetrating or reliable source of the psychological knowledge needed as a part of the foundation of the social sciences. Assumptions or premises having only this source or basis cannot be regarded as established, scientific, empirical generalizations, capable of leading through deductive theories to conclusions in the social sciences, so reliable as not to need further, independent, scientific, empirical verification. Rather, all such assumptions or premises should be regarded as provisional, speculative hypotheses—admissible along with or among others suggested, e.g., by psychologists' theories about men's "subconscious, real" motives—and used in developing rival, tentative structures of theory to be tested, eventually, by such developments of social-scientific, empirical research as Mill in his time could not envisage. Moreover, all theoretical work in the social sciences of course requires not only psychological assumptions of one kind or another, but also and equally—as Mill well knew—other assumptions about the objective circumstances or situations in and with reference to which the members of societies decide upon their courses of action. Legitimate, generalizing, and simplifying assumptions, made in such theoretical work, about those situations and their effects upon those courses of action, of course, entail needs for subsequent, appropriate, empirical research to determine the degrees of empirical validity of the theories thus arrived at, and to suggest revisions of the assumptions in question, and thus of the theories, toward greater empirical realism.

But Mill was by no means so foolish or completely unaware of these points as I may be seeming to imply. He could not foresee the more modern developments of empirical research in the social sciences, and did not fully appreciate the need for them; and he greatly exaggerated the sufficiency and security of the kind of informal experiential basis upon which theoretical work in them in his time had to proceed. That work was not empirically so well grounded as he supposed, but was much more speculative or hypothetical in its basis than he knew, and was, as well, mainly deductive in its logical method. But he was right in defending its use of that method; and its value or importance; its on-going, subsequent development has played a necessary part *in leading to* the more modern developments of empirical research in these sciences, which lay beyond Mill's horizons. And finally, although he did not grasp the required nature of advanced scientific empirical research in the social sciences, he did fully feel or sense, and in practice, i.e., in his work in economics act in line with his sense of, the need to supplement and correct that kind of abstract, deductive, theoretical work, very extensively, with observational and descriptive studies designed to get much more of the rich content of experience and empirical reality into his account of them, than got into the assumptions of his logical, theoretical system.

A few words must still be said about his ideas on the proper division of labor among the different social sciences, the place of economics or political economy among them, and its relations with the others. He admired, and was influenced in some ways by important features of, August Comte's intellectual system. But of course, and rightly, he rejected Comte's contention that political economy as a special or partial analysis of human societies and their functionings, attempting to isolate and deal only with the economic subject matter in them, could not be a genuine empirical, as well as logical, science; that the true and only true social science in that sense would have to be his (Comte's) unitary, all-embracing sociology. But it may well be that his study of Comte's critique of political economy helped to make Mill more fully aware than his forerunners in developing classical economics had been of the fact that the latter *was* only a partial analysis of empirical social realities, and needed to be supplemented or complemented by other social sciences, analyzing other elements or aspects of those realities. At all events, he did realize that fact very fully, and this realization accounts, as we shall see shortly, for the character and professed aim of his *Principles of Political Economy*. His aim was to combine with or add to his exposition of Ricardian-classical economic theory a much broader survey of other features, which that theory neglected, of the nation and its people, institutions, customs, etc., in order to build his version of "political economy" as distinguished from pure "economics," i.e., his practical program of economic policy, on a broad foundation.

He was not so fortunate, perhaps, in his chosen definition of the special field of "economics," in the narrow sense, as the science of the consequences of only one of the "forces" (human motives) at work throughout real societies, i.e., "the desire for wealth." It is hardly a tenable notion that there is in men or in human behavior any single "economic motive" which is not derivative from or dependent on a very wide range of other underlying motives, including all or most human motives of whatever kinds. But what Mill meant is perhaps clear and tenable enough: that economic theory is about those "tendencies," in the working or functioning of economic societies or social economies, which result from the "tendencies" of men, in the conduct of their economic affairs and activities, to act "logically" or as they need to act in their situations in order to maximize the ratios of their resulting acquisitions of wealth or economic goods to the costs they incur in their efforts to obtain them. The point is, he fully realized that almost no human actions or social events are in fact determined solely or entirely in that way; economic theory, as thus conceived, yields only a partial explanation and account of what actually goes on, even in the business world, and needs to be supplemented and in a sense corrected or modified by other analyses of the noneconomic kinds of considerations also affecting men's decisions and actions and the resulting developments, if complete and completely true accounts and explanations of the latter are to be attained.

Mill does not give us, however, any scheme or map of all the social or "moral" sciences and their respective fields or tasks and interrelations, or tell us how he conceived, in themselves or as related to those of economics, the provinces and problems of political science and/or other recognized disciplines in this group. But he did express an idea which is of some interest and throws light on his way of thinking, although it is hardly "workable," and neither he nor anyone else has tried to carry it out. He talks about a desirable new social science which should be developed as one important supplement or complement to economics: "Ethology," a science or comparative study of the "national characters" of different nations, which develop on various lines, and diversely modify the detailed-concrete developments and functionings of their economic, social, and political systems, so that no one universal, abstract theoretical account or model of, e.g., economic life can fit all or any of them entirely and exactly. In summary, then, on Mill's logic, methodology, and philosophy of economics and the social or "moral" sciences as a group, it is clear that he took his empiricism seriously, tried hard to be faithful to it, and groped his way fairly far along in the direction of the kind or kinds of research it called for. Though he properly and highly valued precise and rigorous logical, deductive theory, or theoretical work, to fully spell out the exact implications of particular visions of certain aspects of human affairs, or groups or ranges of social-science problems; he also clearly saw the limitations and insufficiency of this kind of work, by itself, and the need to progressively acquire and utilize more and more of the rich material of all relevant experience and empirical knowledge, to improve and combine the basic visions, spelled out into theoretic structures, into an adequate and accurate vision of the real, empirical, human-social world. His imperfect theory of scientific method and inductive logic—imperfect understanding of the necessary roles and reciprocal interplay of speculation and deduction (theoretical work) and observation and induction (empirical research)—did not enable him to achieve the best kind of development of the latter, and effective union or integration with each other of the two kinds or parts of scientific work. But in spite of this handicap, he did rather well; and I must now at last turn to my comments on his work and views in economics and political economy.

CHAPTER 10

John Stuart Mill: Economics and Political Economy

THE AIM, ACHIEVEMENT, QUALITY, AND ORGANIZATION OF MILL'S *Principles*

It would not be quite true to say that Mill, who divided his intellectual labor among so many fields, was even mainly a political economist. He probably gave larger parts of his time, energy, and thought to his work in other fields—philosophy, logic, ethics, politics, and social-reform endeavors of many kinds—than to economic studies; and perhaps did more and better, original or creative work in some of those other fields than in economics. That he has come to be generally or widely thought of mainly as a political economist is a fact to be explained by the proportions, not of Mill's interests, but of those of the world in and since his time in political economy and in the other subjects that concerned him. Mill's achievement in or contribution to political economy was substantial though modest; and its large influence on the subsequent development of the study and teaching of that subject in the English-speaking world was not undeserved. What he aimed to do and did in this field was not primarily to advance the "science" far beyond the stage of development to which others before him had brought it, by making many new, important, original contributions to its body of established principles or theory. Rather, his main ambition and achievement in this field was merely to explain with a new fullness and clarity, to his wide public, all that was known and thought in his time about the whole subject by the best experts on it (including himself), *and* put around their common, limited body or structure of abstract economic theory (to which he did make a number of significant new contributions) a wide, rich context of more concrete descriptive information about the English economy and society of his time, and informed and thoughtful discussions of many institutions and social problems to which little or no attention had been paid by the Ricardian group of theoretical, "pure" economists.

In avowing and explaining that last-mentioned aim, in his preface to his *Principles*,[1] Mill spoke of the diverse merits, which he wanted to combine, of the works of his great forerunners, Adam Smith and Ricardo. Adam Smith, he pointed out, had made the *Wealth of Nations* a very broad and rich, but conceptually and logically rather loose, vague, imprecise, and nonrigorous survey and discussion of most or very many parts and facets of all that went on in the life of the nation and substantially affected the wealth and economic welfare of its people. Then Ricardo and others had improved the logic, or precision and rigor, of the scheme or structure of economic theory which they found in the *Wealth of Nations* as its central core. But in their concentration on improving that, they had greatly narrowed their field of attention and left out of consideration many of the human traits and circumstances, institutions, and social problems which Mill agreed with Smith in regarding as in need of full consideration, as parts of the real, complete, human-social setting within which the economic process as such went on. Thus the declared purpose of Mill's *Principles* was to combine a full, clear exposition of the improved Ricardian structure of theory with a new broad survey and discussion of the (national) social scene or setting, similar to the one that Smith had offered, but brought up to date. And as a whole Mill's book admirably accomplished this purpose, although one general criticism must be made: the two separate components of the book—the structure of Ricardian abstract theory, or theoretic "principles" and the descriptive matter and discussions of institutions, etc.—stand side by side without substantially affecting each other. There is no sufficient integration of the whole, or use of the included body of theory to illuminate and analyze the mass of more "empirical" material, and/or of the latter to improve the former.

The merits, however, of Mill's *Principles of Political Economy,* in my opinion, overshadow that defect and all of this work's limitations; and it is even today a book to be read with profit at least by intelligent "laymen" in its field, if not by professional economists. Only a few features of its treatment of some of its main topics can be noticed here; let me first briefly outline the organization of the book, and then return to the parts to be described and discussed a bit more fully. The first "book" or part is about the "production" of a nation's wealth; the dependence of the national economy's output on the supplies and qualities of its land and basic natural resources, the numbers and qualities, skill,

[1] J. S. Mill, *Principles of Political Economy, with Some of Their Applications to Social Philosophy*. Available in many different editions; a particularly good one is that edited by W. J. Ashley (London and New York: Longmans, Green & Co., Inc., 1909).

etc., of its productive workers of different kinds, and the formation and role of its supply of capital; and the Ricardian "laws" about growth over time of the population and labor force, the supply of capital, and the total output (which cannot grow as fast as do the supplies of labor and capital employed on the fixed supply of land, which yields "diminishing returns" from increasingly full or intensive use of it). Mill's second "book" then is about the "distribution" of the national output or real income, i.e., its division into the class-incomes, the wages going to the laborers, the profits of the capitalists, and the rent-share of the landowners; *and* how this is or may be affected by features of the particular nation's legal and customary institutions, property arrangements, etc.,—on this I will comment below. In Book Three, the first six chapters are about the "exchanging" of the economy's different products in its markets, and the process of determination of their relative values and prices by competition, supply and demand, and costs of production. The remainder of this "book" and the next "books" are on the special subjects of money and banking, international trade, and public finance; and important though they are, I shall have to omit any comments on them. The final "book" is on general (normative) principles which should guide the state in all matters of economic policy, i.e., the grounds and limits of the *laissez-faire* maxim and of proper departures from it. Before saying more about this I must first say something about a few main features and portions of the first three "books."

THE FIRST "BOOK," ON PRODUCTION

The first book's opening chapters, about the importance for an economy's producing power of the quantities and qualities of its land, natural resources, and (in its population) supplies of labor of different kinds, make only obvious points and need not detain us. But the immediately following chapters on "capital" present a full, painstaking exposition of the important and somewhat obscure or difficult "classical" theory of the formation and role of this vital, third, humanly created "factor of production"; and the core of this may be summarized as follows. Like Ricardo before him, Mill thought of the economy's volume of real (in contrast with money) capital as having two parts or being continually created and re-created in two stages, one leading to the other. In (1) its primary or initial form, the new real capital is the real wages-fund, i.e., that part of the just currently emerging output of finished consumers' goods which the economy's capitalists or saver-investors could *but do not* themselves consume, but enable the productive workers (their employees) to consume instead, as the real wages or wage-goods bought with the money-wages which are paid to the workers with or from the money saved and invested by the capitalists out of their previously received profits. Then (2) in its second, resulting, and more enduring form this new real capital is the output of new producers' goods produced by the workers for their employers in return for their wages and consumption. In other words, the formation of all new real capital involves these steps: (1) saving (nonconsuming) by the capitalists of a part of their profit share of the national income; (2) investment of that saved income in wage payments to productive workers, who thus receive it as their wage income and consume it; and (3) production by the workers, in return for their wages, of the new capital goods which replace the consumed real wages or embody, in its final form, the capital obtained by the capitalists for or with their invested savings. Saving-and-investing leads *by way of* the employment and payment of the workers, and their "productive" consumption and work in exchange for and sustained by that, *to* the formation of the economy's equipment (of productive plant, machinery, tools, and materials or goods in process) for on-going production.

Mill's detailed exposition of that theory, in chapters four and five of Book One of his *Principles,* completes his initial discussion of the economy's three basic "factors of production"; and the rest of this book then spells out the Ricardian "laws of the increase," or growth over time in the economy, of its population and supply of capital, and the diminishing rate of growth of the total output it can produce with its growing supplies of labor and capital on or from its fixed supply of land and natural resources. As we know, this vision of economic growth as a process increasingly impeded by land scarcity and "diminishing returns" led to the expectation that all such growth would eventually end in the arrival of a "stationary state," as the reduced ratio of the total output to the number of claims upon it would lower real wages per worker to the point of stopping growth of population, and lower the profit rate almost to zero or to the point of stopping growth of the supply of capital. Now Mill retained this expectation *but* regarded the prospect as a rather pleasant instead of a gloomy one. This he could do partly because his judgments of facts and possibilities led him to revise, in a more hopeful direction, important details of the theory as to how and at what point "the stationary state" would arrive and what the actual conditions in it for the people would or might be. But another part of the reason was that his personal, basic value-judgments caused him to regard as of main importance for the true welfare of mankind, *not* endless growth of material wealth, but rather the improvements of cultural and spiritual life which might well come into their own or be generally, fully sought and won only after the rush and scramble of material progress had done its work and come to its end. As we shall see, Mill had hopes that the laboring population would yet learn to so regulate its birth rate that its growth would end, not with a "bare-subsistence" level, but with a good or adequate level of real wages prevailing. As such good wages, in an advanced stage of economic growth, would absorb nearly all the value of total output and leave very little as profits for the capitalists, the growth of capital too and thus all economic growth would stop at that point. "The stationary state" would then be a state not of prevailing poverty, but of "enough" for all and no more, and contentment with that; there could be a salutary, general turning of men's minds or main interests away from the mad and harsh race and struggle for more and more material wealth, to more important matters. As we look back now it seems apparent that in any form the "classical" vision of the supposedly approaching "stationary state" was a mistaken, wholly unrealistic dream. The progress of natural science and industrial and agricultural technology, infinitely beyond all that was then imagined or thought possible, has kept economic growth going on and on, and made us increasingly inclined to think of it as probably perpetual. But if it can be made truly world-wide, and carried far enough in the now still "underdeveloped" countries to become—with the aid of sufficient checks on their excessive population growths—adequate for the material welfare of all mankind, then possibly the time may *still* come when a "stationary state" of the world economy, of the happy kind envisaged by Mill, may come to be generally desired, be attained, and prove its merits. At all events I think it is to Mill's credit that the supposed prospect envisaged by his forerunners with dread was by him envisaged with hope.

THE SECOND "BOOK," ON DISTRIBUTION

As we move on through Mill's *Principles,* the first book on the "production" of the nation's wealth is followed by the second book on the "distribution" of the national output or real income, i.e., its division into the class-incomes—the total of real wages for the laboring population, the profits of the capitalists, and the rent share of the land owners. The fact that Mill's treatment of this subject immediately follows his treatment of "production," and precedes his treatment of the pricing of the economy's diverse products in the markets for them, significantly reflects the difference of the "classical" from the more modern view of the logical interrelations of these different subjects or parts of the subject matter of economic theory as a whole. In the modern view, the "distribution" of the proceeds from production in payments for labor, use of capital, etc., is governed by the market system's interrelated pricings of the different products produced *and* of the productive services rendered to or in production of them by the workers, pieces of land, equipment, etc., employed in producing them. Hence the modern theory of income-distribution or wages, profits, etc., is logically the sequel or concluding part, instead of the independent forerunner, of the (modern) theory of "value" or the work of the market mechanisms in determining the prices of all products and productive services. But the "classical" view was that the distribution or division of the national income, as it is produced, into the class-incomes, is determined *first,* within the process of production as such, and determines the costs of production of the different products, which in turn determine their (long-run, "natural," competitive) values and prices; hence the arrangement of Mill's treatise was logical, on his assumptions.

The most important feature, however, of Mill's second book, on income-distribution, was the very large place in it that he gave to discussion of the man-made and reformable social institutions—legal property rights and social customs—which affect the actual distribution of incomes and wealth among all the people, and the *smaller* place that he gave to exposition of the abstract "laws" of classical economic theory, as to how the economic process would "determine" the levels of wages, profits, and land-rents *under* given or assumed institutions and conditions. Mill apparently felt that the English capitalism or economic system of his time was giving on the whole a satisfactory performance *as* a system for *producing* wealth, but a morally unsatisfactory performance in the matter of distributing the large and growing output of the country among its people—giving too much of that output to the already wealthy, propertied minority and too little to the still too poor and hard-working majority. And he wanted above all to counteract or remove the impression, which earlier expositions of "classical" economic theory had made on the public mind, to the effect that the current inequitable distribution of the national income must be fatalistically accepted as the unalterable result of "natural" economic laws. Thus he was led to begin Book Two with an introductory chapter expressing his humane attitude and essentially correct insight on that matter, unfortunately in the form of a confused, untenable dichotomy or contrast between the economic "laws" of the "production" of wealth and those of its "distribution," to which he assigned entirely different characters or meanings.

Economic production, he asserted, actually is controlled or governed by "natural" physical conditions and laws (of the connections between physical causes and their physical effects), which human choices or desires and efforts, social arrangements, etc., cannot alter; i.e., with given natural resources, physical production techniques, items of equipment, and applications of human and other energies, a country can only produce, or choose among, just the same combinations and amounts of different goods or products, no matter what kind of social, legal, and economic system it may choose to set up and/or retain and operate. But on the other hand, Mill flatly asserted, the shares of the output that shall be distributed to the people severally is a matter for entirely free, collective, human choice or decision; i.e., a society can distribute its economic output among its members in whatever way it, or the controlling group or power in it, deems desirable, by choosing to create, maintain, and operate the appropriate system of institutions, designed to bring about or ensure the desired distribution of the collective output. In other words, according to Mill, economic theory's "laws of production" really are universal, "natural," physical laws, having the same applicability and validity in all societies alike, regardless of their different institutional or social systems; whereas, in complete contrast, economic theory's "laws of distribution" presuppose and are entirely contingent upon one particular institutional system, i.e., they describe only the special way in which a society's output or income gets distributed among its members *if* its system of property rights and institutions generally is that of free, competitive capitalism or the system of free, private enterprises and competitive markets.

Now, of course, the glaring fault of that view or account of these matters is that its two parts—about production and about distribution of an economy's output—are one-sided or only half true, in opposite ways. In reality, *both* the actual course and outcome of production, i.e., the size and composition of the economy's output, and the actual distribution of it that occurs, are affected *both* by humanly chosen and changeable institutions and practices *and* by the relevant physical facts or conditions and laws of the relations among changes of the relevant variables, which determine what the results of each possible constellation of human, public and private decisions and actions will be. Mill's abstract, physical "laws of production"—e.g., the classical "law of diminishing returns"—say only that *if* men (workers and directors) engaged in producing material goods, with given physical means and under given physical conditions, decide to act thus and so, then such-and-such results will follow. For example, if, with continuing use of unchanging techniques of production on land, men continue to apply increasing amounts of labor and capital to the fixed available amount of land, they will find that the later increments they can thus add to the output of produce will diminish relative to the increments they must add to the inputs of labor and capital in order to obtain them. *Such* general "laws of production" are indeed independent of the variations of institutional or social systems, but the detailed behaviors in production, and the degrees of productivity of the human societies concerned, and the volumes and compositions of their total outputs are not. The production of wealth, as well as and no less than its distribution, can be influenced by all the choices made by or in societies, of the lines on which they and their members will develop all their institutions, policies, and courses of action.

Moreover, on the other hand, the "laws of distribution" sought by economic analysis are just like its "laws of production"; they are "laws" about the results to be expected from particular types of human behavior in particular types of objective circumstances; and they can help us to know *how* a society's institutions will affect the distribution of its output among its members, just as the "laws of production" can help us to know how the same institutions will affect the output itself. Mill was right in stressing the dependence of distribution on humanly alterable institutions, but wrong in contrasting distribution with production in this respect, and in failing to perceive that any institutional reforms designed to ameliorate distribution would have effects on production also and would need to be considered from both points of view. As we shall see later on, Karl Marx's contempt for Mill was provoked in part by what Marx—perhaps inferring it from this chapter of Mill's—took to be Mill's belief that the distribution of income and wealth could be radically altered in favor of the working class, *without* altering the *entire* structure of "capitalism," *including* its way of organizing and controlling production. But we need not agree with the views of Marx—either as to the inevitability of continuing and even deepening, dire poverty for the working class so long as "capitalism" should endure at all, or as to the certainty of both far greater production and egalitarian distribution under the "socialism" envisioned by Marx as the ultimate destiny of mankind—in order to agree that Mill was mistaken in speaking, in this chapter, as though we could and must think of production as entirely controlled by "natural laws," but of distribution as completely changeable by or through institutional reforms, which would somehow not affect production. Mill, however, was not elsewhere as blind, stupid, foolish, or confused as this chapter seems; we may forgive its confused generalities which misstate what he wanted to say, and go on to consider his actual treatment, in the body of Book Two of his *Principles,* of income-distribution in the economy of his country and time, and the institutions *and* economic "laws" which he in fact saw as together controlling it.

Yet we must first notice what immediately follows that introductory chapter, i.e., his still preliminary, general, friendly discussion of "socialism" in the pre- and non-Marxian forms known to him—of the schools of St. Simon and Fourier—and his discussion of the variety of forms, possibilities, and abuses of private property as a basic institution in non-socialist systems. It is of interest that in the successive editions of his *Principles* Mill lengthened and increasingly stressed the favorable parts of his comments on "socialism." No doubt, he did so because his views were developing further in that direction, but perhaps also in part because he had disliked the misdirected praise of the first edition by a conservative reviewer. This reviewer took the work as a whole to be a sound, orthodox demonstration of the merits of the existing English economy and social order, and of *laissez faire,* and the chapters on "socialism" to be intended simply to condemn and refute it. In an angry reply and objection to that review, in the journal that had published it, Mill avowed his opposition to the views or attitudes the reviewer had imputed to him and affirmed the rights of socialists and all others freely to express and agitate for their opinions and proposals, and the duty of all to pay open-minded and fair-minded attention to them. In revising the subsequent editions of his *Principles* Mill made it plain that he did not regard the economic system and social order of his country in his time as by any means ideal, or regard the socialist ideal as one to be either fought as evil or dismissed as foolish.

He did, however, regard the socialist vision of pure cooperation for the common good and no competition for private gain as realizable, if at all, only in a far-distant future. Its attainment, he felt, required far higher prevailing levels of popular or public intelligence, wisdom, and virtue than the slow progress of civilization had yet brought about or could bring about for a long time to come. And he looked for all earlier or less-distant improvements of the lot and lives of the main mass of the people to come, not through the radical or total reorganization of economic life and all life envisioned by the socialists, but through a great number of small reforms of the concrete details or detailed features of the system of private properties and contracts, and private enterprises competing for gains through service to the public in free markets. As he pointed out, the institution of private property is no simple or fixed thing, but a mass or maze of variable legal rights and customary practices, which can undergo countless and in time and sum far-reaching changes, for better or for worse, depending on whether the evolution of the mass of law and custom is controlled by a progressive enlightenment of public opinion and prevailing attitudes, or by an unresisted growth and multiplication of abuses, contrived by narrowly selfish men and groups, and put over on an apathetic public. Much could be accomplished, without waiting for the ideal new order conceived by the socialists to become workable, to realize, through suitable reforms, the best possibilities—best possible development or set of modifications—of the existing order.

Most of the large part of Book Two, which follows that discussion of socialism and private property, is about the (in Mill's time) important agricultural or agrarian parts of the English and other European economies: specific forms of property in land and land tenure, and other related institutions which were important therein; and the effects of the different, detailed varieties of all those institutions—legal and customary rights and duties and relations of landlords, tenant farmers, small owner-farmers, and agricultural laborers—upon the efficiency and output of agriculture and the distribution of the proceeds from it to or among all those participants. That most of Mill's detailed description and discussion of the institutional framework around and affecting economic activities and relations, and largely controlling the distribution of income and wealth, is concerned with institutions important mainly in the agricultural, rather than with those important mainly in the industrial, part of the economy is probably to be explained in several ways. It was in the agricultural or agrarian sphere that old, not fully modernized or reformed institutions and customs, retaining traces of the heritage from feudalism and not fully in accord with Mill's liberal and progressive ideals, were mainly to be found; and he was always primarily interested in the study of things that he felt to be in need of criticism and reform. But also, the institutional setting of the industrial and commercial or nonagricultural part of the economy was probably so much more familiar to Mill and his forerunners (the classical political economists and liberals generally), and to most of his readers, that they tended to take it for granted, and feel little need to study and discuss it; and above all, as it more fully or more nearly conformed to economic-liberal ideals and thus to the institutional assumptions or presuppositions of Mill's abstract, Ricardian-classical economic theory, he doubtless felt that the latter alone was substantially adequate to explain the distribution of the income derived from industry and commerce, whereas that derived from agriculture was distributed *less* in accordance with the expectations of such theory and in a way more influenced by peculiar institutions which therefore especially needed separate consideration. Mill was almost asserting the decisive importance of that last point for him, in asserting generally and repeatedly all through Book Two this basic proposition about income-distribution: that it is determined, in all parts of the economy, in various proportions, partly by the influence of "competition" and partly by that of "custom," and that the role of the former is less and that of the latter is more pronounced in the agrarian as compared with the industrial and commercial worlds. For example, the land-rents actually paid by tenant farmers and received by landlords are seldom the full theoretical economic rents to which complete or perfect competition in the land-use market would lead, but are generally, largely controlled by "custom" and kept by it at lower levels. It could be of interest here to say more about Mill's lengthy discussion of the agrarian world's institutions and resulting income-distribution, but my space limitations will not allow me to do so. I turn now, instead, to the other, not "institutional," but "theoretical" part of or chapters in Book Two—Mill's exposition, applications, and discussion of his Ricardian-classical, abstract "laws" or principles about the shares of all income or the value of all output which competition, supply and demand, etc., tend to cause to go respectively into wages, profits, and land-rents.

Mill's basic theory of wages was Ricardo's—that the average real wage per worker is determined jointly by (1) the size (in "real" terms) of the wages-fund, i.e., that part of the economy's volume of existing capital or accumulated savings which is available for investment in paying wages, and (2) the size of, or number of workers in, the working population or labor force. The wages-fund, as we know, was conceived to be or govern the demand for labor; and the population of people needing employment for wages in order to live was the supply of labor. Hence the theory was that the level of wage rates in the labor market was always being so adjusted, under the pressures of demand and of the competition of the workers for the available jobs, as to just enable the existing wage-capital to hire and pay all the workers. If any workers remained unemployed, the lack of employment for them would indicate that the current rate of wages was too high or made the available amount of wage-capital insufficient to employ and pay all the workers at that rate; and the competition of the unemployed for jobs would lower the market rate of wages for all labor to the point of equalizing demand and supply, or the size of the wages-fund and that of the labor force times the average wage rate or wage per worker. Growth of the amount of capital endeavoring to hire labor would tend to raise wages, whereas growth of the population and supply of labor would tend to lower them; hence whether wages would rise or fall would depend on which was growing faster, the amount of capital in the economy or its population. The population-growth theory of Malthus and Ricardo led in this context to the pessimistic thesis that population growth was sure in the long run to win the race and force wages down to a "subsistence" level, barely sufficient to enable the workers to support themselves and families large enough to keep the labor force, in the next generation also, equal to the demand for labor (as determined by the then available supply of capital) at that wage level. Now Mill's humane desires and hopes for the welfare of the working population were, of course, in conflict with that Malthusian element of his theory of wages, but he remained always deeply impressed—and oppressed—by what seemed to him the weight of the argument and evidence in favor of the latter. He came to believe, however, in a possible "way out," which must now be discussed.

The real basis of the Malthusian pessimism lay in the judgments of Malthus that, whereas all men and women (in the working class and every class), as husbands and wives and as fathers and mothers of children, *should* sufficiently restrain the indulgence of their sexual desires so as to bear no larger numbers of children than their economic resources, earning powers, and prospects would enable them to support and bring up in health and comfort, educate, and provide with good opportunities or a good start in life; the great majority of parental couples—especially in the working class where the need for such "prudent restraint," the amount of it required, and the difficulty of achieving that, were greatest—*would not* fulfill that ideal obligation and could not be taught or led to do so. The strength or ardor of the sexual desire and the fertility of normal, healthy, human animals were too great, and the typical human capacities for rational or prudent and moral behavior in this matter—for exercise of all the self-control required—were too weak, to make it possible to expect that any human population would in this way reduce and hold down its birth rate to so low a level that, with only a normal death rate not increased by widespread serious poverty, etc., the rate of population growth would be and remain no greater than the expectable long-run or indefinitely continuable rate of growth of the output of food and all means of adequate support for the growing population, so that a high or good standard of living for all could be both achieved and permanently maintained. Now it was not in John Stuart Mill's nature to be resigned to a sad belief in the permanent inability of human beings to achieve or do anything which they manifestly ought to achieve or do as an imperative or necessary condition of their individual and common or collective welfare or happiness. Human nature at any given time, or the characters and capacities of men as they were, might be full of sad faults, weaknesses, and limitations, and many imperative moral achievements could be terribly difficult; but he held that men could make and remake their own characters, and learn by experience and become more enlightened; and he refused to believe that the future progress of advancing and spreading enlightenment and virtue need have any fixed limit, or that any of the grim evils that had so far always afflicted mankind were forever unconquerable.

Thus, for Mill, the great practical corollary of the Malthus-Ricardo theory of the "tendency" of the population and supply of labor to grow excessively, and force and hold real wages down to a meager "subsistence" level, was simply that the working-class people *must* learn or be taught to lower and hold down their birth rate or the sizes of their families to such a point that the aggregate demand for labor could grow even faster than the aggregate supply of it, and thus bring into being and maintain a really adequate level of real wages. Then further, his hope or faith that eventually this would be achieved drew support or assistance from several sources. He became one of the early supporters of the "birth-control" movement, which sought to spread the knowledge and use of contraceptives and make "planned parenthood" universal; but, sensibly, he did not regard this alone or its prospects for early, complete or sufficient success as *the* adequate, entire solution of the problem. The nonprosperous, toiling millions must become enlightened to the point of *wanting* to limit their families enough to practice a good bit of Malthus' "moral restraint" *and* make intelligent supplementary use of contraceptive methods as and when satisfactory ones could be made generally available to them. The basic need was to change the motives, desires, or values of the people. And these were so connected with their economic circumstances, experiences, and conceptions of the possibilities and values of better living standards for themselves and their children—or lacks of the experiences that alone could make them determined to achieve and maintain those better standards—that the economic improvement (of the generally prevailing level of real wages), which in theory could be expected only as a *result* of the new behavior of working-class parents and the slowing down of population growth, must in practice somehow be achieved in some measure first to aid in bringing that about.

Malthus and Ricardo had already reasoned that their "subsistence" level of real wages, to which population growth and "pressure" would reduce them in the long run, was not a wholly definite or rigid level but was subject to the influence of the "habits and customs"—the accustomed and firmly desired as minimal or necessary standard of living—of the working-class population of each particular country and period of its history. They had only supposed that the working-class people everywhere would probably forever remain resigned to, and prone to multiply up to the point of being barely able to maintain, living standards on the verge of real poverty; lacking knowledge or experience of anything better, they would never be strongly enough moved by desires and hopes for real prosperity to so change their behavior as to achieve and maintain it. But Mill believed that this vicious circle must and could be broken; by pushing economic progress ahead of population growth, and by doing everything possible to give the working class a little better share of the benefits of such progress, the subjective minimal standards of living of the working people can be so improved that they *will* learn to so reduce the rate of growth of their numbers that they can maintain their improved positions. Mill was never too clear as to just *how* it could all be done; but I think the Western world since his time clearly *has* been moving ahead in this matter in the general way that he preached and prophesied.

It is too bad to report no more of all that Mill had to say about labor and wages than that bare outline of the most central, general theme in it. But we must get on to the rest of his theory of income-distribution, and turn, next, to capital and its "profits." Mill thought of the "profit" or proprietor's net income from a year of operation of a productive enterprise—the proprietor's net income as a percentage return on his own capital invested in the enterprise—as a composite income made up of three components: interest (at the current market rate on good loans, generally well below the full rate of profit in the composite sense) on the proprietor's own or equity capital; plus a wage of management or superintendence for the proprietor's work as owner-manager; plus a "risk" premium to induce investment *not* in loans guaranteed as to payment of interest and repayment of principal, but in a "venture" of one's own with all its possibilities and hazards. Yet the two additions thus made to the idea of "interest" on equity capital, or ideas of the other elements of "profits," were not much elaborated or analyzed by Mill. He took "interest" in that sense—the return on, to, or from capital as such—to be the core of "profit," and sought mainly to explain or understand what factors or variables and relations among them generate that return and determine its rate.

As we know, Mill retained the Ricardian expectation that the growth or accumulation of the economy's supply of capital would eventually force down the rate or level of its net return to its owners, over and above mere amortization or replacement, either quite or virtually to zero. Given the fixed and limited supply of land and natural resources, and "diminishing returns" of additional output from increasingly intensive use or exploitation of them, the additions to output made by further additions to the amounts of labor and capital employed, would decline eventually to the point of bare equality in value with the necessary real wages of the labor (counting both the labor required to operate or use, and that required to produce, maintain, or replace, the real capital involved). This view involved the presupposition that capital yields a net income to its owners only because, and while, there is still a general "scarcity" of capital relative to the amount required for any full development of the economy's productive possibilities; and hence a scarcity-value of the use of capital to aid production, which gives rise to payments to or incomes for its owners, which enable and induce them to save and reinvest large parts of those incomes and thus increase the supply of capital and reduce its scarcity-value, which they will go on doing as long as they continue to receive any net incomes at all. In other words, although there was implicit in the Ricardian theory the idea that saving-and-investing as such is a productive service (so long as the economy has still unsatisfied needs for more capital)—a service or activity helping to increase production, or the productivity of the economy or its labor force—there was *not* present in the theory any idea that the rendering of this service involves any "sacrifices" by the capitalists or saver-investors for which they should be or need to be compensated, either in justice to them or to induce them (make it worth their while) to undergo the "sacrifices" (of fuller satisfaction of their wants as consumers), i.e., to continue to save-and-invest.

At least, there was no idea of a (some) definite, minimal but substantial positive rate of interest or remuneration as the "necessary" or "equilibrium" rate, such that at any lower rate the supply of new capital would fall short of meeting the demand, and the rate would rise. On the contrary, the Ricardian theory implied that only while the economy was still in a dynamic state of "disequilibrium" in this respect, or capital shortage, would any positive income in return for saving-and-investing continue to exist; and that the long-run "equilibrium"—the stationary state—would be reached only when the rate of interest fell to, or very nearly to, zero. Moreover, the idea seems to have been that interest or profit was needed (to keep the capital supply increasing) less as the inducement for than as the source of new saving-and-investing. So long as the incomes of the capitalists *enabled* them to satisfy their needs or moderate wants as consumers and have anything left to save-and-invest, they would "automatically" continue to save-and-invest that remainder. Ricardo imputed to the capitalists generally a strong disposition to practice "parsimony" or restraint of their consumption for the sake of future or further increase of their wealth—so long as any of that could be thus achieved—and did not think of them as needing to be motivated to that restraint by the prospect of gains "sufficient" to repay their "sacrifices." Between Ricardo's time and Mill's, however, other inquirers had developed or suggested various ideas about these matters, which Mill was aware of and took into account or considered in developing his own views, which thus were not purely or entirely Ricardian.

William Nassau Senior had expounded his idea of "abstinence" from consumption by the capitalists as precisely the "sacrifice" on their part requiring compensation. And a very different writer, John Rae, in a long, as much sociological as economic essay on the nature and historic origins and growth of capital and the human motives, etc., involved therein—a book of which Mill thought highly—had gone well beyond Senior's oversimple and dubious idea, somewhat in the direction of the view that Mill developed.[2] Mill used the phrase, "the effective desire for accumulation"—substantially, the willingness to practice the "parsimony" of Ricardo or the "abstinence" of Senior, i.e., limit current consumption for the sake of future income and wealth and power to more fully satisfy future wants, foreseen and weighed against present or current wants with full, forward-looking rationality and self-disci-

[2] John Rae's book was originally published in 1834, and entitled *Statement of Some New Principles on the Subject of Political Economy*. It included criticisms of some things said by Adam Smith in the *Wealth of Nations;* but the core of it was its new ideas and material about "capital," etc. The most available edition of it now is perhaps a modern reprint with a changed title, *The Sociological Theory of Capital,* C. W. Wixter (ed.) (New York and London: The Macmillan Company, 1905).

pline—and he came to think of this "desire" as historically a gradually achieved and growing human capacity, or product of accumulating experience and advancing enlightenment. Primitive peoples were highly deficient in it, and so far even the relatively most civilized peoples had developed it only partially or still insufficiently. But in time all or most men would learn to do all the saving, or abstaining from current, immediate, transitory gratifications, needed in order to make adequate provision for their own and their children's future. The supply of capital was everywhere still so limited as to yield on the average rather high returns or profits, not only because the growth or progress of production had not sufficiently enriched many people to make the ability to save very widespread, but also because "the effective desire for accumulation" was still weak in most men; they would not, even if rich enough to be quite able to do so, save as much as would be wise in both their own interests and the public interest; nor would they save much at all unless lured by the prospect of large gains.

The capitalists of Ricardo's theory had already fully developed this virtue in which men generally, in Mill's view, still were deficient. Hence the views of Ricardo and of Mill as to all that would be involved in the future growth of the capital supply, decline of the profit rate, and evolution to the stationary state were not quite the same. Ricardo envisaged all this as merely a matter of on-going growth of abilities to save and resulting savings, until the capital supply should become fully equal to the needs of the economy, and abolish profits, and stop the process. But in Mill's theory the process would be complicated by the presence and role of an additional factor—the growing prevalence and strength in men of "the effective desire for accumulation," which would play its part in leading to the same results. With reference to the current situation, Mill had a theory of the *raison d'être* of existing profits, which Ricardo lacked. Profits currently were and had to be what they were, not only because the economy still needed more capital, and the service it could render in raising productivity was worth its price, but also because the potential saver-investors generally undervalued their future or prospective as compared with their current wants and satisfactions, and required the bribe of substantial profits to induce them to provide in any adequate measure for the futures of their own families and for meeting the economy's needs for capital.

Thus, Mill largely retained but also modified the Ricardian theories about the wages share and the profit share of the national income. His theory of the remaining, land-rent share was substantially, purely Ricardian, but he drew from this a practical conclusion or corollary for public policy in the field of taxation, which Ricardo had not drawn. Apart from that corollary, which I will speak of in a moment, the one "addition" that he made, if such it can be called, to the theory of rent itself was not too fortunate. Mill continually or frequently spoke of the class of owners of land as having a "monopoly" of the nation's fixed and limited supply of land, and so as receiving rents not limited to normal competitive profits on any productive investments made by them, but capable of being raised by the pressure of growing demand and scarcity to any levels, i.e., as in this respect just like the monopoly profits of the sole producers and suppliers of particular products who are not compelled by competition to sell at prices only slightly above their production costs or yielding only moderate profits on their investments. This, of course, is not a valid comparison or extension of the concept of "monopoly." The restriction of the supply and elevation of the price of a monopolized product is achieved through ownership or control of the entire supply by a single person, organization, or unit, and deliberate refusal to increase the supply or allow others to do so. But the fixity of the land supply of a country with set frontiers, and the tendency of land-rents to rise with growth of the country's population and wealth, are independent of the number of, and degree of competition or lack of it among, the country's landowners. In the production of a product the competition which makes "necessary" production costs the governors of selling prices is the competition of those producers who will increase the supply on the market if the demand increases, and who will continue to do so as long as their production costs are a little more than "covered" or repaid. But the nonexistence of such a regulator or limiter of land-rents is due only to the fact that land (as defined by Ricardo and Mill, i.e., the pure "gifts of nature" in the land, excluding all man-made additions or improvements) is not a product at all or cannot be produced but exists in a fixed supply which cannot be increased. Hence the only kind of competition which could keep supply adjusted to demand at a cost-plus-normal-profits price does not have to be prevented by the formation or existence of any monopoly, but is impossible in the nature of things.

Mill's "error" in this matter, however, was only the perhaps trivial one of slipping into a loose, vague usage and misapplication of the word, "monopoly"; he, of course, fully and correctly understood the substance of the matter, exactly as Ricardo did. At the same time, it may be that his application of this word—always opprobrious in the economic-liberal tradition—to the position of the landowning class reflected an attitude or animus on his part toward them, going beyond Ricardo's in the direction of more hostility or adverse criticism. Ricardo, though envisaging the landlord class as gaining from the country's growth without having to contribute to it, did not apparently consider that any social injustice was involved; and he did not propose any public action in the matter except abolition of the Corn Laws which *further* increased agricultural land-rents in England by restricting importation of food produced abroad on non-English land. But Mill saw the rise of land-rents and land values with the country's growth as giving to the landowning class an "unearned increment" or increase of its wealth, which in justice should not be retained by it, but should be taken by the state and used for the common benefit of all the people; and accordingly he included advocacy of a tax of this nature, or for this purpose, in his recommendations about taxation.

THE THIRD "BOOK," ON EXCHANGE AND VALUE

Having now surveyed the main parts of the first two books of Mill's *Principles,* on the production and the distribution of the national income, I turn to the first six chapters of Book Three, on "exchange" and "value," or the processes of adjustment of the supplies of particular products to the demands for them in the nation's markets, and of their prices to the levels determined by their costs of production. Significantly, Mill's presentation of his theory of this subject is short and simple as compared with either of the two preceding books. The theory of "value" or the working of the "price system" was not elaborated into the extensive, dominant, and highly complicated part of all economic theory, which it came to be in the later, "neo-classical" economics of the late nineteenth century, by any of the old, original, "classical" economists—Adam Smith, Ricardo, Mill, or any of that group. Although in a way the "classical" theory of the functioning of the competitive economy's market mechanisms, to allocate all parts of its total supplies of land, labor, and capital into their most productive-and-demanded uses, adjust the outputs of all products to the public demands for them, and adjust the mutual or reciprocal exchange values or the relative prices of the different products into correspondence with their relative production costs—although in a way this all held a "central" place in the over-all pattern of all "classical" economic theory, it was never regarded as the most difficult nor as in all ways the most important part of the entire, far broader structure; nor was it given the main or a very large share of all the space and attention in such comprehensive treatises as Mill's.

To some more modern economists, trained in the "neo-classical" tradition, this means that the early "classical" writers had only a rudimentary or as yet largely undeveloped theory of value, prices, etc., and failed to see or recognize the real complexity and full importance of this subject or all the problems involved in it. And Mill has been much criticized and ridiculed for the judgment, expressed in his Book Three, that the theory of value as presented therein by him had been substantially completed and perfected; all the problems of any importance connected with this subject had been fully solved; and there was little new or further work on it still to be done. That indeed rash statement was made not long before the great "neo-classical" development or its first beginnings arose and began to "revolutionize" all economic theory, primarily by greatly expanding and radically revising this part of it for which "theory of value" is the common and convenient, short, but inadequate label. There is no doubt that that later development significantly enlarged and improved the understanding of the economic world by economists; or that Mill's complacent belief in the finality of the "classical" theory of "value," as "completed and perfected" by himself, was mistaken and foolish. At the same time, I do not fully agree with the modern views attaching very great importance to the "neo-classical" expansion and improvement of this part of economic theory, and holding the old theory as presented by Mill to have been radically defective or inadequate. The question is partly one as to how economists should allocate their time and intellectual efforts to or among the different parts of the very broad field of diverse problems demanding their attention. The great elaboration and refinement of "value" theory in "neo-classical" economics had merits and made contributions, but it involved comparative neglect of other, arguably more important branches of the study of economics; and Mill's brief and simple treatment of this "central" subject, though it left a good deal to be desired, was and may still be viewed as roughly adequate for many purposes. It made possible what seems to me the better balance of his treatise as a whole, or its shares of attention to different subjects, as compared with many more modern works.

Mill's theory of the competitive economy's "natural" working as regards the pricing, etc., of its different products, as presented in Book Three, was by no means merely a reproduction or good exposition of Ricardo's theory, but considerably improved or advanced beyond that. Like most economists before and after him, he divided price theory into a theory of the immediate determinants and determination of current "market" prices of brief duration, and a theory of the "long-run" adjustments that determine the "normal" or "natural" levels around which those prices fluctuate and to which they "tend" to return. And like Ricardo and others, Mill regarded "supply and demand" as regulating "market prices," but thought of the "cost of production" (per unit of output) of each product as "tending" in the "long run" (under competition) to control its selling price—*by* controlling the "long-run" relation of the supply or output produced to the demand in the market. But Mill improved on Ricardo's theory of "market price" by introducing, in the place of the vague, inadequate notion of this as depending at each moment on the current "ratio" of the supply to the demand, the better idea of an "equation" (equalizing) of those two quantities to be brought about at each moment by the appropriate price. A price in a market could have even the most temporary stability only if, in response to that price, the supply of the good (amount of it offered for sale on the market) and the market's demand for the good (amount of it demanded, i.e., salable at the price in question) would be equal or the same. Any price that would draw into the market either more of the good than could be sold at that price, or more demand than could be satisfied by the supply attracted by the price, would thereby create a situation that would cause the price to change immediately in the direction required to make the amount offered and the amount sought equal. This—Mill's theory of market price—came near to being the same in substance with the fully modern, correct theory of prices in competitive markets as always subject to the changes required to fulfill the conditions of "equilibrium" of the demand-and-supply "forces" acting on them, though much has been added, in the way of more detailed analysis, to Mill's brief, general account of the matter. But we must now turn to his consideration of the "long-run" problem.

Over any "long run" of time, how lavishly or scantily the markets for a good are kept supplied with it will depend not merely on the attitudes of dealers holding the existing stocks—attitudes in the range between eagerness to sell at current prices all they have or can get of the good, and reluctance to sell at current prices or tendencies to withhold their stocks from the market and wait for better prices to become obtainable; but the situation will depend also on the volume of production of the good and that of production (either maintenance, contraction, or expansion) of the means, facilities, or "capacity" of the industry concerned. And the steady continuance, contraction, or expansion of the total output of a good by a competitive industry (all the competing firms contributing shares of this total output) will depend on profit prospects as determined by comparisons of market prices with production costs. If the good is selling at a price far above the cost of producing it and thus yielding high profits, and this state of things is widely known *and* generally expected to last for some time, and the following reactions to it are possible, the existing firms will tend to expand their outputs and "capacities" to take fuller advantage of their good opportunities, *and* additional producers will tend to enter this profitable industry and further enlarge its total output. And all this will tend to go on *until* the total output or supply of the product has been increased to the point of lowering its market price so nearly down to the cost of producing it, that all incentive to produce still more of it has disappeared. Conversely, of course, when the market price is so low in relation to the cost of production that the business is unprofitable, production ultimately (if that situation persists) contracts as people transfer their investments and efforts, when and as they can, out of this underpaying and into other better-paying activities; and this will go on until the reduction of the output or supply of this good raises its market price again to the level of its cost of production plus a "normal" profit. Thus all "long-run" adjustments of supplies to demands work toward the point of correcting the departures of market prices from the levels determined by production costs or bringing them back to those levels.

In other words, expansion or contraction of the public's demand for a good will raise or lower its price *temporarily, until* the resulting behavior of producers expands or contracts the supply enough to make it again equal to the changed demand at the near-cost price, and thus restores the price to that level. This simple formula assumes, however, that the production cost per unit is not itself changed by changes of the size of the total output of the industry; that the industry is made up of firms all able to produce at about the same unit cost, and to grow or contract and still in the end have about that same unit cost, and that if new, additional firms grow up in the industry when it is expanding to meet growth of demand, they too will produce at about those same unit costs when the firms get established. Mill, like Ricardo, took this case of production at "constant cost," regardless of variations of the industry's total output, to be the general or most common case in the economy; and it was their assumption to this effect which led them to think of *the* cost of producing a good as controlling its "natural price," and of particular amounts and variations of demand as having only temporary or short-run importance. Of course they did consider also the case of production at rising unit costs for increasing outputs, which would be that of any industry that could expand only in the face of the obstacle of a scarcity of appropriate land and natural resources, and by making increasingly intensive use of the "good" part of the entire supply of them already in use, and bringing into use additional, inferior parts of that supply, and accepting the "diminishing returns" involved in these operations. This "case," however, did *not* figure *as* largely in the "classical" economists' theory *of value* as we might expect, because their much-stressed "law of diminishing returns" had its *main* significance not in this part of their total structure of theory—concerned with single industries and products considered "one at a time"—but in their over-all theory of the whole economy's growth over time. In each given stage of that over-all growth, it would generally or often be possible for single industries to expand (if others were contracting) without encountering land scarcity and diminishing returns. If the changes of demand for particular goods or products were only transfers of demand from some to others, the resulting contractions of the adversely affected industries would release resources including land which might go into use in the expanding industries and enable them to expand at "constant cost." Still there would be cases of branches of production requiring special types of land and resources existing only in limited supplies and not transferable among many industries. For these branches, large increases of their outputs to meet enlarged demands would entail rising additional costs for the additional increments of output, and the expansions would go only far enough to leave market prices still high enough to cover those final extra costs and yield "normal profits" on the extra investments represented by them. And the producers within the industry owning and using the best lands and resources for its purpose and having lower average costs than the final, extra costs just covered by the selling price would have their "profits" increased beyond the "normal" level by inclusion in them of the "rents" of their superior lands and resources. Mill's presentation of the theory of this case was better than Ricardo's; but neither writer apparently grasped the point that this case undermined their general view about the role of demand variations in price determination as affecting only temporary "market" prices, and leaving the "natural" price of each good to be determined solely by its cost of production. Where production cost itself varies with the volume of output, and the relevant cost figure itself depends on the volume of demand that is to be supplied or satisfied, that attempt to separate the two parts of the theory of value in the "classical" manner breaks down.

There remains the question of how fully Mill agreed with Ricardo's belief in the dominant role of the amounts of labor-time required to produce different products in determining their relative production costs and "natural" values. Ricardo, as we know, was not satisfied with Adam Smith's final working theory of (long-run) prices as depending simply on the full expenses per unit of production of each product, but insisted upon an analysis of those expenses and the relations of different parts or components of them to the price of the product, which concluded by eliminating *almost* everything *except* the "quantity of labor embodied" in a unit of the product, as having no effect on the value of the latter. Still, as the reader knows, I think Ricardo's theory of value is best described as *not* a pure "labor theory" but a cost-of-production theory *mainly* (not solely) emphasizing labor quantities as the principal value-determining elements of production costs. Mill's emphasis was a little different, and, though he fully agreed in eliminating land-rents in Ricardo's way, he seemed otherwise to let production costs in the ordinary sense, or expenses, come a little more into the foreground of his picture, so to speak, and let the labor quantities retreat a little into the background. But he did single out and emphasize the latter, essentially in Ricardo's way and on the same grounds; and I think the difference is more apparent than real—a matter of accepting, and presenting more clearly, the real conclusions that Ricardo in fact came to, while getting rid of the exaggerations and obscurities attributable to Ricardo's effort to make his "labor theory" as nearly "pure" as possible.

In fact, as a whole, Mill's theory of value and the economy's processes of adjustment of supplies to demands and of prices to costs, etc., did not sufficiently depart from or improve on Ricardo's theory of these matters to at all satisfy those later architects of the new and different (and superior), modern theory of them which I have referred to as "neo-classical," and will notice again in later chapters. Rather, Mill's views or doctrines in this field and the dominant influence which his total system exerted for a time as the reigning "orthodoxy" made his work, along with Ricardo's, the main target of the critical attacks launched by Jevons and the other "pioneers" of the "neo-classical" movement. And there is some truth in the modern view to which the latter has led, i.e., that Mill did not fully understand the work and functions of a competitive economy's market or price mechanisms; and this is not without its bearing on our next and final subject here —Mill's general standpoint about public economic policies, the proper relation of the state to the economy, or the fields and degrees in which liberal principles should be understood to imply adherence to *laissez faire* or resort to state intervention.

The economic liberalism of the later economic theorists who reconstructed the theory of value and the competitive price system on new lines unlike Ricardo's and Mill's became a liberalism more doctrinaire and stringent than theirs in its general devotion to *laissez faire, especially* in the field of whatever could affect the work or functioning of that price system—in their eyes the all-important, central, and crucial part of the liberal economy's self-regulating mechanism, which if "free" or unhampered in its working, *and* "competitive" throughout, would keep the pattern of all economic activities and resource-uses working at its best for the general welfare. This later view was only a full, detailed, and rigorous development of the view that already was present, though not so fully developed and single-mindedly stressed, within the views or complete outlooks of Adam Smith, Ricardo, and Mill. But because the latter were all as much or more concerned with other phases of the economy's total working—economic growth, development, or progress over time, and the distribution of income and wealth understood as *more* than *just* a matter of the price system's work in the pricing of productive services, and other subjects—they did not sharply concentrate or focus their attention on the price system, and develop their theory of its ideal, logical possibilities to the point of being thus fully armed for thorough, consistent defense of *laissez faire* on every battlefield connected with it.

THE SIXTH "BOOK," ON LIBERAL ECONOMIC POLICY

Mill's later book, then, on these general issues of public policy, is not the clearly focused, logically one-track discussion or argument that we might expect. But—like everything else that he ever wrote—it is a many-sided and at times confused, "judicious," balanced discussion of a problem conceived as not single but multiple, and admitting of no fully definite or unqualified solution. He did, however, believe that on the whole, though with many exceptions, the state should allow the spontaneous developments and adjustments within the economy to work themselves out as they would. Despite his lack of enthusiasm for the harsh capitalism of his world and time, and his hopes for a future, better world of friendly cooperation among all and poverty for none, he believed in progress through individual freedom for all, not coercion by or through the state, and trusted the collective purposes and wisdoms of governments, electorates, classes, and parties less than he trusted the free competition of free men for gain through service to the public in free markets, and the liberal economy's impersonal processes of reciprocal adjustment of or among the activities of all of them. It would not, I think, be worthwhile to take the space here to report and discuss Mill's more detailed principles for deciding when or in what cases and conditions the state should adhere to the general rule of *laissez faire* in dealing with particular matters, and when it should intervene; for his effort to work out a set of such principles had reference to a range of then current problems, and the results he arrived at are not of great interest in relation to present-day problems. The important point is that he so limited his support of *laissez faire* by attaching numerous qualifications to it that, although he was the last great exponent of the old classical economic liberalism, he was also, at the same time, an early forerunner of the modern liberalism which seeks to make the liberal-democratic state an effective instrument or vehicle of cooperation among all the people for their common welfare.

CHAPTER 11

Karl Marx and His Intellectual System; Its Socialist, Hegelian, and Ricardian Elements

INTRODUCTORY

Although in other respects Mill and Marx had scarcely anything in common, they were contemporaries and had intellectual interests in almost the same range of subjects and problems. Mill's *Principles of Political Economy* and *The Communist Manifesto*,[1] composed by Marx and Engels and representing the first important exposition of the core of "Marxism," both appeared in the same year, 1848. There is, a bit strangely, no reference to Marx in any of Mill's writings, and no evidence that Mill ever heard of Marx. But Marx knew of Mill and his work and views, and referred to or spoke of them frequently and always scornfully. The tempers and fundamental attitudes of the two men were indeed poles apart; and to pass directly as we do here from study of Mill's to study of Marx's thought is to plunge, with a feeling of shock, out of the atmosphere of serene sweet reasonableness and into a maelstrom of revolutionary fervor inspired by a strange, dogmatic, speculative vision of the entire past and future of mankind. In fairness to the reader I must freely confess at the outset that I do not love Marx and may not be able—though I shall do my best—to describe his intricate, and to me at many points repugnant, system of ideas with that degree of sympathetic understanding which must be included in the basis of a decent objectivity. But today few things are more important than the effort, by all of us who are and will remain opposed to much that is in them or has grown out of them, to gain more knowledge and

[1] For a good modern edition, see *The Communist Manifesto—With Original Texts and Prefaces*, Harold J. Laski (ed.) (London: George Allen & Unwin, Ltd., 1948).

understanding of the ideas of Marx. For they have proved to possess such power, as the ideas of but very few men in all history have had, to inspire or incite a by now immense number of men—the world's present-day Communists—to both violent and persistent efforts to transform the world. And effective opposition to the aims and methods of those efforts is hardly possible without some understanding of the ideas by which they are inspired.

At the same time it also is necessary, of course, to beware of and avoid the error of approaching the study of Marx's own thought with the partly false assumption in our minds that we can regard him as alone responsible for all the follies and villainies which have been and are being committed in his name by his leading, present-day, professed disciples, the so-called "Communists" of our time. Karl Marx "in person" was a complex man, a man of several kinds at once. He was a truly great scholar and thinker, regardless of what or how we feel about him. Also he was on the whole a civilized, humane man, whose indignant sympathy with the miseries of millions of humble toilers in the world of his time, and whose beliefs that "capitalism" was the cause of those miseries and that "socialism" was to be the one true and destined way of salvation from them, inspired his hatred of the one and his zeal to hasten the arrival of the other. And finally, he was a passionate, often violently emotional man, whose emotions became so fused or blended with his intellectual, speculative vision that in that blend the emotions gained an unnatural permanence, fixity, and communicability, and charged the intellectual vision and creed with explosive power. Now such a creed-and-gospel, as construed, developed, and applied by later disciples with less than the Master's true scholarly and intellectual abilities and interests, and often little or none of his civilized humaneness, understandably has been *a* factor *along with* experiences and dispositions of their own not traceable to Marx, in leading them—the modern Communists—into courses, and the production of results, which surely would appall Marx, if he were alive, and evoke from him repudiation. Even so I do think that we can and must hold Marx responsible *in part —though only* in part—for the tragically evil thing or force that his creed-and-gospel, in the hands of those modern disciples, has become. In the state in which he himself left it, his intellectual output as a whole was, I think, a very complex blend or mixture of many more or less fully true insights and real contributions to all "social science" *and* other erroneous, or really unsupported and incredible, fantastic notions bound to have evil consequences.

The purpose of this chapter is to convey at least a beginning of or toward an understanding of Marx's outlook and system of ideas or main doctrines. But there were three different, antecedent sources which, as changed, developed, and combined by him, became components of his thought; and I think it is best to begin with preliminary, brief accounts of them in their several, separate, original forms, and then go on to see what Marx made out of them. One of the three strands that went into the fabric of his thought was socialism itself, i.e., the socialist ideal, or vision of the goal of all human, social progress. This vision had been developing for some time, in various quarters and forms, before Marx came on the stage and became the creator of the special creed of a new and the most important phase or branch of the socialist movement. Another equally important antecedent source of Marx's thought was the great German philosopher Hegel's philosophy of history, which Marx "inverted" (see below) or changed and developed in his own way into his own philosophy or philosophic vision of the general direction, course, and process of all human history, past and still to come—the past, on-going, and prospective evolutions of all human societies—the history and destiny of mankind. And the third antecedent factor in the same sense was Ricardo's system of economic theory, which Marx took over, interpreted, revised, and added to or developed further in his own way to form the very important economic-theoretical part or component of his own all-embracing intellectual system. This part or component of the whole was his elaborate theory of the existing structure and current working, origins, history, and prospective, "inevitable" development or evolution and self-destruction of "capitalism" as the economic system, and the basis of the social order and civilization, conceived by Marx as the successor of feudalism and the forerunner of the inevitable and glorious, realized "socialism" of the future. Although Ricardo's economics has already received much attention in this book, we shall need to consider it again briefly in the aspects important for understanding what Marx made out of it. But first, we need to look at the character of pre-Marxian socialist thought and the relation to that of the Marxian variety, and then at Hegel's philosophy of history and Marx's own in relation to that.

MARXIAN VERSUS "UTOPIAN" SOCIALISM[2]

The search for the earliest beginnings of socialist thought, activity, agitation, etc., can be pressed as far back in history as one chooses; but socialism in this sense first took on both fairly definite and seriously important forms around the end of the eighteenth and beginning of the nineteenth centuries, and has had or undergone its main developments since then—all through the nineteenth century and down to the present. In part, I think, the oldest historic roots of the general socialist outlook

[2] On the subject of this section, see the relevant part of any standard history of socialist thought, e.g., the first several chapters of Harry W. Laidler, *Social-Economic Movements* (New York: Thomas Y. Crowell Company, 1944).

or perspective lay in ancient classical and Christian ideals of harmonious, fraternal, cooperative human societies, to be achieved through abolition of the individual, group, and class egotisms and excessive, selfish, or acquisitive ambitions, and power-lusts, and achievements, institutionalizations, and abuses of power (of men over other men), which result in oppressions, injustices, rebellions, and conflicts within actual societies. But also another, no less essential "root," I think, was the later, post-Renaissance and chiefly Enlightenment ideal of applied-scientific-rational reorganization of all human societies and redirection of all human conduct to ensure fulfillment of the (to be ascertained) conditions of the greatest or best possible, all-around welfare or well-being of all persons, simultaneously and all the time, and a rationally planned, effective, and smooth cooperation among all for their common welfare. The socialist vision—as well as the different, liberal vision—of the ideal goal of on-going social and moral progress has grown out of ancient Greek plus Christian ethical ideals, plus the Enlightenment's optimistic faith in the power of advancing (social-and-moral as well as natural) science and "reason" to end the reign or sway of all irrational traditions and to redesign and rebuild all human societies as rationally required in the real, best interests of all their members.

The *main* branch of the eighteenth-century Enlightenment's social-reform movement, to give human societies their "rational" and "natural" potential forms, adapted to the needs and capacities of the "human nature" in all men and the conditions of their greatest welfare—was the evolution of the classical liberalism, described in earlier chapters of this book. But there grew up also besides that, among some of the intellectuals associated with the French Revolution, a more radical, left-wing fringe movement, generally at once anarchist and socialist in character, which had already attained an importance second only to that of the classical liberalism in and just after the French Revolution. In a sense the aims of the two movements really were quite similar, but they differed widely as to the extent and the character of the institutional changes, away from historic precedents, that were thought of as needed for realization of those aims. The liberals saw as needed the abolition only of some features of the old, traditional, European social order, such as the remains of feudalism and of absolute or unchecked monarchy and aristocracy; the tendencies of nation-states or their central governments to try to act as omnipotent, "paternal" regulators of all the affairs and actions of their subjects; denials to individuals of their rightful intellectual and civil liberties; and the economic policies of mercantilism, and the guilds or closed corporations and monopolies or exclusive privileges of all kinds; or in sum, all "excessive" restrictions of the liberties and spontaneous propensities of most (all not specially privileged) individuals. In other words, as we know, the exponents of the classical liberalism believed that if any society would give and guarantee equal and generous amounts of freedom to all its individual members alike, the latter would then spontaneously develop the cooperation, order, and harmony required, so that all would live by a mutually beneficial exchange of their diverse products and services in open, free, or competitive markets, or serve their own by serving each other's ends or interests; and the greatest welfare of each and all would be thus achieved. Retained or carried over from the old order, with the extensive revisions indicated, would be rights of all to private property, private enterprises and free trade and competition, and governments with important though limited functions and coercive powers.

The anarchist-socialists, on the other hand, believed in the need for a far more radical transformation of social arrangements, away from all existing or historic patterns. To their minds the "rational" and ethically "good" society would have to have collective or communal instead of private ownership and management of all substantial wealth, means of production, and producing enterprises, and a fully, centrally or jointly planned pattern of cooperative work and living, and egalitarian distribution of all products for consumption. No members must be allowed to have any income-yielding private property; there must be no rich and no poor people—no division of the society into upper and lower classes; all alike must be workers only, with hand or brain, for the common good. And there generally or often went along with that socialist vision as such, the anarchist vision also, of a society without any coercive government, or coercive control of any of the members by any others. For, it was argued, the needs of existing and historic societies for coercive governments have resulted from the institution of private property and the resulting inequalities, oppressions, discontents, and conflicts. The state has had to exist, essentially, to protect the properties of the rich against or from the poor. But when all men learn to renounce or give up their private properties and acquisitive ambitions, and join together in willing, cooperative labor for their common good, the need for coercive government will disappear and it, too, will be abolished; and the new "enlightened" societies of men will practice an entirely voluntary, free, or spontaneous, and harmonious cooperation.

Now it may seem that my "sketch" here, thus far, of the origins and characters of the classical-liberal and the anarchist-socialist visions has been controlled by a point of view at the opposite pole or extreme from the Marxian "economic interpretation" and "class-struggle theory" of history, which will have to be examined later on in this chapter. I have seemed to trace the classical-liberal view *and* the pre-Marxian socialist outlook *only* to antecedent spiritual-cultural sources or "roots" in Western history, and to describe only the pure philosophies, or patterns of ideas and ideals, that emerged, without referring at all to the earlier and contemporary, economic and social conditions, and attitudes, interests, and desires prevalent in different social classes as results of their various relationships to or experiences of those conditions. But the point of view that is more usual or common today—i.e., which not only is included in a special, "strong," and dogmatic form in Marxism, but also in a general way is widely prevalent in modern thought far beyond all Marxist circles—would "explain" the classical liberalism as simply an expression of the desires and resulting views, responsive to their circumstances in the eighteenth and nineteenth centuries, of most businessmen and other middle-class people, who were in revolt, in the earlier part of that period, against the remainders of feudalism, autocratic government, and mercantilism, and in short all restraints of their freedom to do the things they most wanted to do, and who at a later time had to defend their achieved freedom from the efforts of advancing political democracy and aggressive, organized labor, etc., to impose other, new restraints upon them. And the same point of view about historic causation in all such cases would likewise "explain" the development of the socialist outlook and movement as a product of established capitalism, its oppressed proletariat or working class, growing discontent and rebelliousness in that class, and the growth among its members of the desire for and vision of a new regime of joint ownership and equal sharing of wealth by and among all worker-citizens, and fraternal harmony.

My own real point of view, however, is neither of the two that have just been described. Both "monistic" theories about the historic causation of social and political philosophies and movements—the one ascribing them entirely to previous developments within intellectual history, and the other entirely to previous developments within "objective" economic and social history—seem to me to be extreme or one-sided half-truths. Surely it is more reasonable to suppose that the evolutions of "ideas," and of the conditions of life and the "interests" of large groups (not always entirely just the Marxian "classes") of people, are semiautonomous, coordinate (in importance), and interacting phases of history or social evolution, which *jointly* produce or engender social and political movements and philosophies, party programs, and new institutions. And I think it generally can be shown in reasonably objective studies of actual historic cases that the basic, novel developments of the *ideas* involved in new social movements *do not spring originally, simply from* the circumstances, experiences, and desires of the large groups or numbers of people who are not "intellectuals" but have more purely "practical" mentalities and orientations, and react more impulsively than thoughtfully to the environing conditions that impinge on them personally. The *ideas* that count are *first* developed—as new modifications of older, culturally "inherited" ideas—by "intellectuals" and groups of them, who engage in the search for wisdom, pointing to the true or right or best solutions of the problems confronting the societies and times in which they live. No doubt the ideas developed by the intellectuals are always more or less affected by the conditions they observe or experience, and their sympathies with some and antipathies toward other larger groups and classes of their contemporaries and fellow members of the same societies. But they (these intellectuals) generally or at least often have, as compared with typical businessmen or workingmen or others, wider horizons and relatively more detached or "objective" attitudes, keener interests in the intrinsic merits or rational persuasiveness of ideas themselves, and more proneness to engage in thorough and honest, inquiring and reflective pursuit of truth and wisdom about the real conditions of achievement of the greatest welfare of mankind at large. Such thinkers, with such motives, normally make the best—which often are among the first—contributions to the philosophies of new social movements. *Then* the circumstances and desires of the larger groups or classes, of less intellectual or more practical men, play their part, mainly (1) in helping to determine *which* philosophies or intellectual visions, theories, and programs will "catch on" or become widely popular and thus potent in the world of action, and (2) in causing those "taken up" to be more or less modified, revised, or reinterpreted to suit the common understandings and desires of the large bodies of men who take them up, and develop the practical applications actually made of them.

Thus the classical liberalism *was not originally* a business-and-middle-class creed shaped simply by the usual circumstances and desires of the members of that class in the period of its origin. Instead it was at first a high-intellectual, social-moral philosophy, evolved by various, justly eminent, seventeenth- and eighteenth-century thinkers, chiefly out of ancient classical and early modern intellectual sources. It *became* a widely prevalent, business- and middle-class creed, with many modifications and distortions—in the nineteenth century. Nor is there anything surprising about this—it could hardly have been otherwise; for in general the nonintellectual, "practical" people—the far greater number of people—need the "guidance" or "light" of already, previously formed philosophies or theories, presented to them, to enable or help them to discover what they want and believe in, or what changes of social arrangements and public policies appeal to them as called for by their circumstances and desires or values. And all this is clearly true also of the history of the socialist movement, which here concerns us. Its early beginnings were not in "proletarian," labor circles to any great extent, and in fact a majority of its leaders, including Marx, have always come and continued to come from upper- or middle-class, not working-class, backgrounds, and above all from the ranks of "intellectuals." The movement was under way and had largely formed its philosophy *before* there was any great growth of the modern, industrial or factory capitalism which in its own early development engendered the widespread labor discontent and radicalism, which in turn caused socialism to *become* a working-class movement. Pre-Marxian socialism in its main varieties was mainly of middle-class complexion, as to both the leaders and their (small) groups of followers; and it was an almost purely "idealistic," not very "practical," affair. Growing up first, as I have said, within the Enlightenment, as a minor current in that and factor in the French Revolution, socialism then had the largest and most important part of its early-nineteenth-century development in France; and it was in France, where he went to study, that Marx absorbed his early socialist ideas. The industrial revolution that was then going on mainly in England was to play an essential role in helping to bring about the full development of socialism into a really potent, mass movement, but as yet that role and result were mainly in the future.

Marx, then, first acquired the ideas or beliefs which made him a socialist from earlier socialists; and he retained or continued, as one integral part of the new system of thought which he created, much that he learned from them. Yet he called them all, half scornfully, "utopian" socialists, and set out, himself, to make (his) socialist thought "scientific" instead of "utopian"; and it is of first importance, in the study of his system of thought, to understand exactly what he did and did not mean by this. He did not mean to condemn as "utopian" *the aims or ideals* of the earlier socialists—their vision or visions of the new good society of the future, to be sought or worked for as the goal of the movement—or mean to imply that anything in *this* part of their thought was "utopian," i.e., incompatible with permanent, human-social realities and real possibilities and thus destined to remain forever impracticable or unrealizable. In fact, to those of us who *do* regard the dream of the anarchist-socialist "heaven on earth"—the perfectly harmonious, cooperative society of entirely or absolutely free, ungoverned (uncoerced) individuals, all spontaneously and happily working together with ideal efficiency and wisdom for their common good, and achieving universal and steadily continuing, abundant prosperity and happiness—to those of us who *do* regard this dream or vision as "utopian," in the sense meaning forever incapable of being realized, the Marxist vision of the final goal to be attained is "utopian" in the same sense, for it is the same. Marx took this over from his forerunners, and never altered it or meant to criticize it. What *he* regarded as "utopian" —unrealistic and impractical—in their outlook and resulting behavior was only the character of their ways or methods of working for attainment of the goal, and of their underlying views or presuppositions as to how great social changes are and can be brought about.

True, full sons or heirs of the Enlightenment, the pre-Marxian socialists generally were naïve "rationalists" who thought it would be sufficient (1) to work out in exact details, or "blueprint," the required organization of the ideal society and plan for the activities, relations, work, and behavior of its members; and (2) by persuasive, rational argument in public for the plan, to convince and convert, gradually, more and more people, of all kinds and classes; and so (3) eventually to bring about adoption or enactment and then execution or realization of the plan—reorganization of all actual social life in accordance with it—by general, common consent or agreement. One other step had indeed been inserted and emphasized by various leaders and groups, or in much of the movement; the first small groups of converts or devoted socialists were to found or construct actual, small, ideal communities, in more or less remote, previously unsettled or unoccupied areas, and so organize and conduct them and all life in them as to demonstrate by successful example, to the wider world, the real possibilities and merits of the plan. A good many such experiments were tried in widely separated places and under diverse auspices and conditions in the first decades of the nineteenth century. Most soon failed and collapsed; a few had longer lives and some success in the eyes of some members at least, but none brought stunning success or vastly impressed any great, wide public. But for the more typical, pre-Marxian socialists—those among them who went in for it at all—this kind of activity was to be only one part of the process of using "reason" to work out, and then to persuade mankind to agree and act to realize, the "true" vision of the ideal society and way of living.

To Marx, however, it seemed preposterous—clearly contrary to all realistic knowledge and understanding of human beings, societies, and history—to suppose that a radical transformation of all long-established institutions and all the familiar features of whole great societies and the situations, habits, and lives of all their members could ever be brought about in that simple way, through reliance solely on "rational" formulation of the plan or pattern of the new society and "rational" arguments for it, addressed to the minds of members of all existing classes alike or indifferently. For to his mind it was clear and certain that those ideas and beliefs which can effectively exist in or enter the minds of any large mass or class of men and control their actions must necessarily arise from, or at least agree or correspond with—be made convincing to them by—their own real, objective environments, circumstances, conditions of life, and experiences. Therefore they can change or be changed radically only if, when, and as those underlying "material" causes of their mental states *first* undergo the changes required to make their minds really receptive to the other, new, or different ideas and beliefs. The prosperous, comfortable classes, mentally conditioned by their environments, circumstances, and experiences to believe (sincerely) in the general excellence of their existing societies, could never—as long as those causes of their views or attitudes remained the same—be led intellectually, by any amount of argument or reasoning, to become socialists or to accept the changes proposed by the socialists. There could be no real communication with them, or mutual understanding of each other's ways of thinking between them and the socialists; "reason" could not bridge the gulf, because the most basic assumptions reasoned *from* in the two camps respectively—and formed in the case of the typical rich man by his economic situation and interests—were utterly different and incompatible. In existing societies the only people to whom, in large numbers, the philosophy of socialism could be made intelligible and convincing were the poor and distressed workers or laborers, who lived in the midst of and knew and felt the mass of evil in the existing societies, and were therefore mentally receptive to the idea of and arguments for a radically different kind of society. And even the workers would not become in really vast numbers fully interested, informed, convinced, and militant socialists—no matter how much they were preached to or reasoned with—until, as would happen in time, the evils in the existing capitalist societies became far *worse* than they were as yet, and made the lot of the entire working class humanly intolerable, and thus really opened the minds of all its members to the truths of socialism.

All history, Marx thought, proved that radical or far-reaching transformations of old social systems always have come about, and that the new one sought by socialists will in time come about, in this, the only possible way. There is always a dominant class of creators, beneficiaries, and defenders of the old system, and an oppressed class of sufferers from its faults or evils. The system, too faulty to be able to last permanently, grows worse and more unworkable and indefensible through its own spontaneous, natural evolution and degeneration, while at the same time its changes prepare the way or foundations for the new and better system destined to supersede it. Then finally the oppressed class (always the larger of the two) becomes fully conscious of its true interests and the true conditions of their satisfaction or fulfillment; it becomes organized and militant, and prepared to initiate and carry out an intelligent, effective revolution. By this time the dominant class and its system have become so weak and discredited that the revolution succeeds easily, and the formerly oppressed but now triumphant class proceeds to create or build up a new social system, adapted to its needs, in the place of the old one which it has destroyed. In every *past* revolution of this kind the revolting class had had or had come to have beneath itself in the social scale, a still lower class which it could in its turn control and exploit for its own ends; and so it had made its new social system one establishing itself as the new dominant class, and repeating or renewing with variations some of the worst features of the old, destroyed system—until this in its turn should degenerate and be overthrown by the now oppressed class. But the future socialist revolution to be carried out by capitalism's working class or proletariat would be the *last* one of the historic series and would have a *different* outcome, because this working class was at the very "bottom" of society and could have no still lower class to rule over and exploit. In overthrowing the rule and system of its oppressors and bringing them down within its own ranks, the victorious mass of workers would forever end all class divisions in society, and make the new system, socialism, a classless society of equals—all workers only—in which no oppression, injustice, or internal conflicts ever would develop.[3]

I have been running ahead of my story, however, or anticipating much that will have to be spelled out more thoroughly hereafter. I could hardly bring out the issue of difference between the earlier "utopian" and Marx's "scientific" socialism or form of socialist thought without doing this. The point is, Marx held that his socialist forerunners, while in general more or less rightly conceiving *the goal* of mankind's social progress, had lacked any true or realistic understanding of *the route toward* that goal, i.e., of the ever-on-going historical process of social change and the practical, effective way of working within and with that, to help it along toward the goal of the socialist movement. And so in setting out, himself, to make socialist thought "scientific" instead of "utopian," he was setting out to create or found a "science" of all (past and future) human history or social evolution, and of the proper, effective strategy and tactics to be used by the socialist movement in each stage or phase of that unfolding process, to accelerate and guide it. Now the basic part of the intellectual equipment which he brought to this task or undertaking, and changed in his own way to make it suit or serve the purpose as he went along, was Hegel's philosophy of history, which Marx had learned or absorbed as a young German university student. I must now try to convey as briefly as I can a real glimpse or glimmer of understanding, first, of Hegel's, and then of Marx's changed or different philosophy or theory of all human history.

[3] As the source of all I have said in this paragraph, see *The Communist Manifesto,* by Karl Marx and Friedrich Engels. Originally published (in German, of course) in 1848, there are many modern English editions. One of the best is Harold J. Laski, *op. cit.*

HEGEL AND MARX—PHILOSOPHIES OF HISTORY[4]

It is probably *especially* difficult for most *American* minds to grasp or understand such intellectual constructions as these—the Hegelian and Marxian philosophies of history—because American culture is almost devoid of the kind of feeling for or sense of history—of the human past as the all-important and intelligible source of the human present and the human future—and devoid *also* of the bent toward and faith in philosophy as the effort to understand everything through an intellectual system of abstract, general ideas or principles. Both of these factors are prevalent and deeply embedded in European culture and were combined in their special ways by Hegel and by Marx. First let me speak briefly of the difference of American and European attitudes to history. In a sense the typical American outlook tends to be "unhistorical." This, I think, is itself in part a consequence of one of the key facts of American history, viz., that our society and culture have been created by ex-Europeans intent on leaving the European past and everything past behind them, forgetting it all, and starting afresh in this "new world" to build here, "from scratch," a new and different, not tradition-bound but forward-looking, progressive, and self-sufficient civilization. American thoughts when ranging at all beyond present or current preoccupations have generally tended to be concerned with the future *only, and not* with the past. The future is conceived *not as* a continuing outgrowth from the past, inevitably determined or conditioned by it, but as something to be shaped at will by the collaborative efforts of living, free men, all unwedded to and uncontrolled by any compelling historic past. And it is really a part of all this, not a contradiction of it, that the always-thus-far dominant American social, moral, and political philosophy was first created by the late-colonial American participants in the eighteenth-century European Enlightenment. This was, in its own way, an unhistorical or ahistorical intellectual movement, endeavoring to understand or grasp in theory and realize in practice, *not* what the future must be as a product of the past, *but* the timeless or eternal, right or rational, general way or plan of human living, which had never yet been truly realized in practice anywhere, but could and should be conceived, agreed upon, and established once and for all, by all "enlightened" men, emancipated from the follies of the past. In the

[4] There is a voluminous literature on the subject of this section; but I know of no one item, or few items, in this literature, covering the ground that I cover in this section in a comparable way, or relevant enough to my entire discussion to make it useful to cite it (or them) here. But an interesting, brief discussion, supplementary in a way to mine, may be found in the chapters on Hegel and Marx in G. H. Sabine, *A History of Political Theory* (New York: Henry Holt and Company, Inc., 1950).

development of European culture the ahistorical, rationalistic Enlightenment was a transitory episode soon overwhelmed by reactions after and against it, and new developments leading away from its point of view. But the United States of America was largely formed within and by it, and has retained that point of view in a unique degree, to the present day; for the subsequent, opposing or divergent, European intellectual movements have all had only limited amounts of influence in or upon this country. And America has been able, so far, to continue its own "progress" for the most part happily along or within the lines foreshadowed in the initial vision of its founding fathers. And while remaining loyal to that vision, it has felt little need to develop or change the vision or philosophy itself much further, or to continue much of the kind of intellectual activity which first created it—*or* to think consciously of the American future *as* one to be determined by the American past, or to think much about the past at all.

Then too another factor of a different kind in the production of the unhistorical American mentality has been the simple fact that the mobile or migratory American people, living in newly settled and developed areas and continually, rapidly changing all their artifacts and physical surroundings, have thus far accumulated no great mass of ancient monuments, cities, houses, furnishings, art works, etc., to remind them constantly of age-old customs, feelings, and beliefs and so make history, for them, a vivid, real, living, continuing affair or process. Europeans live in and with their entire history all the time and do not only learn about it in schools or from books, but absorb it through all their senses, inevitably, daily, throughout their lives. Thus it is understandable that in most European thought about social problems there generally has been and continues to be a strong tendency to make the study of history or of the past and its continuing influence the main foundation on which to build an understanding of the present and programs for the future. The temporary, partial departure from that practice during the Enlightenment, induced by the early flood tide of confidence in the power of the then new "modern scientific" method of inquiry in all studies, to equip "reason" for discovery of the permanent, general pattern *of* all nature *and for* all "rational" human societies and conduct, soon subsided in Europe. There was a return to—even newly intensified and more systematic—studies of history and the historically conditioned, on-going process of social change, or efforts to discover not any permanent or timeless pattern of what ought to be, but rather the pattern of the (past and continuing) historical process itself.

The "age of reason" was immediately followed, in Europe, by the golden age of history as a study or discipline; and "historical schools" or movements advocated "the historical method" in all social sciences, which came to be widely regarded as in fact the one true "scientific method" in or for them. Hegel's philosophy of history played its part in or influenced much of that general development; and Marx with his revision or variant of the former also became a strong participant in or contributor to the latter. The feeling that only those who first equipped their minds with full knowledge and understanding of the past would be able to foresee and influence the future became prevalent not only among conservative scholars and thinkers (Hegel on the whole was one of these) who loved much in the European past and wanted to see it perpetuated, largely or with only moderate changes. It prevailed equally among even the most radical intellectuals, who thought of immense changes away from the mainly evil past and present as necessary for the welfare of mankind, but felt, as Marx among them felt, that all realistic, practical, or effective efforts to bring about the required changes must be guided by understanding of the processes through which great changes had been brought about within the past. For Marx, as we know, the fidelity of his new form of socialist thought to this point of view was the essence of its "scientific" character, as opposed to the "utopian" character of the earlier socialist thought which instead was faithful to or exemplified the earlier, common point of view in the Enlightenment. And it has been, in part, because Marx in this respect moved with the general movement of European thought, away from pure "rationalism" and into "historicism"—which has never occurred to any comparable extent in this country—that the system of thought created by Marx has commanded widespread, ready understanding and respect among European—but not among American—intellectuals and scholars.

American efforts, however, to understand such things as either Hegel's or Marx's *philosophy of* history tend to be still further handicapped by the common American lack, not only of the general European, all-pervading, and profound concern with history, but also of the kind of interest and faith in ambitious, systematic, philosophical inquiry that has always been and remained prevalent in European culture; and Americans lack, above all, the combination or union of those two great interests or intellectual passions, which produces philosophies of history. The relative feebleness of the typical American's interest in philosophy, as well as that of his interest in history, may also be due in part at least to the peculiar, continuing influence of the Enlightenment upon or in all American culture. For although the cosmic, social, and moral philosophy—the classical liberalism—which was dominant in the Enlightenment, and has remained the foundation of traditional American thought-and-feeling about all public affairs—although this was and is a philosophy, it has been from the outset a simple, limited, supposedly complete and final, self-satisfied philosophy to end philosophizing. It has been an almost positivistic outlook, tending to dismiss, as insoluble and unimportant, the profound riddles that all more ambitious systems of philosophy have striven to solve.

Moreover, whereas in Europe the Enlightenment was followed by revivals or new movements of philosophical thought of that other, more ambitious or more boldly and profoundly speculative kind, the strongly prevailing trend in the subsequent development of American culture has continued or gone on further, from the starting point of the Enlightenment, in the positivistic, antiphilosophical direction. The romantic movement produced in Germany, above all, and to some extent in Europe generally, a great renaissance of visionary, speculative efforts of all-embracing, philosophic thought, and was as a rule contemptuous of and hostile to the simple mode of thought of the Enlightenment. In America the same movement produced only such results as the essays and homilies of Ralph Waldo Emerson, still in the main in tune with the Enlightenment and only tingeing the outlook carried on from the latter with a bit more of romantic fervor or enthusiasm—and asserting only, without arguing for them, collections of *aperçus* or insights, and hence not really amounting to philosophical thought in the systematic sense. And the greatest and most typical of American's later or more modern philosophers, William James and John Dewey, have carried the *not* all-out speculative *but* applied-scientific-practical bent of most American thought into the very citadel of philosophy itself. Meanwhile, in general, American public thought about public affairs, while continuing a certain amount of ritualistic use of or appeal to moral-philosophical ideas of the kind carried on from the Enlightenment, has ceased long since to include any fresh or living, philosophical endeavor to further develop, modify, or add to that old fund of such ideas, or adapt and apply them in new, creative ways to the novel elements of contemporary problems. But I have said enough about the American as opposed to the European attitudes to philosophy per se and to history per se, and must now conclude this digression or detour with a word about the American lack of readiness to understand the kind of *union* of the philosophical and historical interests which led Hegel and Marx to work out their philosophies of history.

Despite the general prevalence in American culture at large of relative indifference to history, American scholarship and education have, of course, continued to include a certain amount of development of historical research and teaching or cultivation of history as an academic discipline. But in general the American professional historians have been in the vanguard of the general trend of thought among professional historians in all countries, in recent times, toward extreme caution, skepticism, or modesty about developing or accepting any large generalizations purporting to *explain* historical events and their interconnections and the over-all movement or course of history. The study of history, within our culture, has increasingly been thought of as a matter of establishing the true, complete, detailed record of actual past events, but of doing (almost) nothing more than that. One may play cautiously with tentative theories as to why and how particular events or developments came about as they did, but the confident, ambitious search for "historical laws" or any sovereign key to the whole course of history is frowned on or smiled at by historians of this way of thinking, who dominate their guild, above all in this country. There is much to be said for this attitude, and I am not arguing in favor of the opposite point of view of a Hegel or a Marx, but only trying to open the minds of American readers to it or suggest that it may be understandable and worth considering. In their different ways, Hegel and Marx each tried and claimed to open up a way *to understand or explain* the human past —how and why all human societies and civilizations have developed, thus far, as they have; and through understanding of the past-and-continuing processes of social change, they tried to *foresee* much of the human future in its general outlines. With the aid, moreover, of all such knowledge, understanding, and foresight, they hoped *to participate in* the detailed shaping of that future, intelligently and effectively. Now let us try to see first how Hegel, and then how Marx, went about creating and using the intellectual master tools supposedly required and adequate for this ambitious undertaking.

In this connection we must try to understand (1) the aspect of Hegel's philosophy—"idealism" in the technical, philosophical sense —which Marx rejected and replaced with its opposite, "materialism" (and thus to understand the latter also), *and* (2) the other aspect of Hegel's philosophy—the idea or theory of the "dialectical" nature of the historical process—which Marx retained, with the adaptations required to make it consistent with his "materialism" instead of with Hegel's "idealism." The Hegelian philosophy of history was "dialectical idealism," and the Marxian scheme is "dialectical materialism." Let us first consider "idealism" and its antithesis, "materialism," and then try to grasp the all-important (in both philosophies) idea of the "dialectical," historical process. Here I shall boldly skip or evade the deeper philosophical issues and difficulties, and not try to present more than a, doubtless, very superficial account of these matters, which I think may be sufficient for our purpose here. Crudely stated, the question at issue between "idealism" and "materialism" is that of whether, in the world of all that is or can be experienced by human beings, the physical part or the mental part has the prior and more fundamental "reality" and causal efficacy, or which of the two parts or components of the whole (the experienceable world in its entirety) "essentially" precedes and engenders the other. Is the material or physical universe only a panorama of results or products of an underlying, all-pervading, indwelling, creative, mental, or spiritual activity, for the most part divine but in a small part human, which develops systems of ideas *and* gives them material embodiments of exemplifications? Or is the material universe, on the contrary, the fundamental reality or set of realities existing from and to eternity, and a self-developing system, which engenders all human, mental life as merely one of its results or by-products? To many of us this seems a both unanswerable and unnecessary question. In all human experience both the physical and the mental "realities" seem to be "there" from the outset, together, and to act reciprocally upon each other; and the two kinds of monistic, speculative systems, "idealism" and "materialism," seem equally unprovable and improbable and to be rejected. But to understand the ideas of Marx we must understand what "idealism" meant to him, why he rejected it, and what lay behind his insistence on the viewpoint of "materialism."

For Marx, I think, "materialism" in philosophy was associated with all modern science and all intellectual and social progress, or advancing, realistic, and practical understanding and mastery of the material world, and resulting growth of the power of mankind to improve the material or mundane welfare and happiness of all human beings. And for him "idealism" in philosophy was associated, on the contrary, with religion and all ancient, antiquated superstitions and forms of unrealistic dream-thinking. To his mind, it served the purposes of intellectually and politically "reactionary" people in the upper and middle classes, who wanted to maintain or restore a ruling climate of opinion throughout society which would divert the minds of the poverty-stricken millions away from their material miseries to concentration on "spiritual" matters, and thus keep them contented, docile, and easy to rule and exploit. The sociological function of religion, Marx held, is always that of helping to buttress the position and power of the dominant class, by acting as "the opiate of the people," or by deluding the subjugated and exploited millions with dreamlike false beliefs which keep them happy and undisposed to rebel and make realistic efforts to improve their own situations or act intelligently in their own real interests. In the Middle Ages, the Church and the religion taught by it to the people had in that way supported the feudal lords and their regime. In the more recent past and the current (Marx's) time the insurgent *bourgeoisie* had first come near (in the Enlightenment) to general rejection of Christianity and all religion and adoption in their place of a modern-scientific, "materialistic" philosophy or outlook. But in the process of destroying all that was left of feudalism and its civilization and creating in their place the new economic-and-social system, capitalism, and the bourgeois civilization going with that, the new dominant class had later begun to revive Christian, religious, and idealistic, "spiritual" beliefs, in new or modified forms, and had begun to work to indoctrinate or reindoctrinate "the masses" with them, in a more or less conscious or unconscious effort to buttress their class power and regime by supplying "the masses" with an effective "opiate." And the German idealistic philosophy, of Hegel and his forerunners, appeared to Marx —in this aspect, as idealism—to be just an aid to that reactionary revival of religious faith, i.e., a sophisticated, philosophical version of religious thought, attractive to advanced intellectuals and serving to swing many of them into line with, and thus give prestige to, the reinvigoration of popular religion which served the interests of the capitalist class.

Now there is, I think, alas, although by no means complete truth, an uncomfortable degree of truth in this Marxist view of the historic social and political role or effects of organized religion and philosophies, such as the "idealism" also condemned by Marx, on the whole related and friendly to it. The churches and many religious thinkers, leaders, preachers, and teachers of the people have too often made religion, as represented by them, an unduly conservative force or influence in society, too fully or uncritically sanctioning and "sanctifying" existing and traditional institutions and the current mores of the upper classes. Exaggerating and twisting the proper religious stress on spiritual or high, unworldly values or ideals as opposed to the mere pursuit of material wealth and worldly pleasures into the view (affecting the poor as an "opiate") that wealth *and* poverty have no importance anyway, they have often tended to confuse ethical virtue, for the mass of the people, with docile obedience to their social superiors. Although this class of perversions of Christianity (and of other religions, too) has been much too common in history at large, and the Marxist attitude in this matter is thus understandable, still this has never been, by any means, the whole, true story. Christianity at least, in its truer, purer forms, has repeatedly shown its power to act in a quite opposite way as the inspiring source of a practical, high ethical-social idealism leading to sustained, effective work for progressive social reforms of countless sound kinds, and endless progressive advancement of mass-popular welfare and toward full justice from and to all members of society. Also there have been many Christian or Christianity-inspired "radical" movements with creeds and programs which one may question or criticize as regards their wisdom or soundness while fully respecting their adherents; e.g., much non-Marxian but genuine "socialism"—much of British socialism especially—has drawn its main inspiration directly and unmistakably from simple Christian ethical convictions.

The great error of Marx and all his strict disciples in this whole connection has been to regard the historically too common or frequent, extremely or purely conservative, or existing-regimes-supporting role of organized religion as arising necessarily from the essence of all religious (and "idealistic" philosophic) thought. In fact this has been merely a matter of *perversions* of religious-moral teachings attributable to the connections of churches and their clergies with existing regimes and ruling classes and resulting absorptions of the moral-political prejudices prevalent in the latter into their official teachings. There is really no logical or other necessity whereby every religious faith, or religiously inspired philosophy, *must* lead or issue into conservative or antiprogressive social and political attitudes and precepts. The belief that the ultimate "reality," and that which has the primary causative power throughout all nature and all human life and history, is "spiritual," and that the "material" world is merely the procession of its transitory products, creations, or manifestations—this general basic belief can be developed, with equal ease, in all kinds of ways and directions, and lead to moral-political "conclusions" of any degree of conservatism or radicalism. Nor do modern science and "progressive" thought really have any logical or other necessary connection with philosophical "materialism." Still, it is possible and worthwhile to understand the origins and surface plausibility of these basic tenets of Marx's thought, even while rejecting them as false.

But I must now return to Hegel and take up the other "dialectical" part or aspect of his idealistic-and-dialectical philosophy of history: the idea, in his form, of the "dialectical" nature of the onward movement of all human history. In its original or first usage, in ancient Greek philosophy, the idea of "dialectics" was the idea of the intellectual process of argument, debate, or controversy between two persons. They start as exponents of mutually opposed or opposite or antithetical doctrines, but in the course of the debate, they learn from and make concessions to each other, or correct or modify each other's views by the convincing power of logical reasoning. They finally converge into agreement in a third view, distinct from the initial views of both disputants, but representing a superior "synthesis" of the valid parts or elements of both of those initial views—the "thesis," at first asserted by one party, and its "antithesis," at first asserted by the other.

Now Hegel as an "idealist" believed that within all human history as an on-going process, the history or development of thought or ideas underlies and produces all the rest of the process. He also believed that this fundamental or primary causative part of history, i.e., intellectual history or progress, all proceeds in the "dialectical" way in that ancient Greek sense, and gives to *all* history the same "triadic" form or pattern or law of movement—progressive resolution of the conflicts of opposites through achievements of syntheses of the original theses and antitheses, with the syntheses becoming new theses which provoke and conflict with new antitheses until still newer, broader, and higher syntheses result, etc. Hegel, in other words, built his philosophy of history upon his view of the history of philosophy. Philosophy (and all intellectual life and achievement) advances through controversy or (in the literal Greek sense) dialectical discussion: a first school of thought develops a highly imperfect system of ideas, containing some true insights but also much of ignorance and error; then its defects provoke opposition and the formation of a school with the opposite beliefs, and the two are in conflict. The debate between them results in a synthesis, superior to and contributed to by both the first and the second systems; but this is still imperfect and provokes new opposition and the process is repeated. And as this is the method and pattern of all intellectual progress, that of history or social evolution or progress, being all created and controlled *by* intellectual progress, has a similar pattern. In one epoch, one people, nation, or society develops a culture, ethos, ideology, or set of controlling ideas and beliefs and ideals, and imperfectly realizes or embodies them in its actual institutions, practices, and material creations. But the faults of this special civilization, and the underlying defects of the intellectual vision it is based on, cause a neighboring nation to develop a culture, etc., antithetical in spirit to the first one, and there is conflict—perhaps including war—between the two. This culminates, through conquest of one by the other, or otherwise, in a synthesis of the good insights and achievements of both cultures—and the process goes on in this way. Hegel had a vast knowledge of European history and construed or explained it all on lines of this kind, with much plausibility and real insight. But we need still to look at other backgrounds and facets of his basic, general idea of the "dialectical" movement or law of all history.

What I have thus far suggested is only a partial explanation of that idea, arrived at by considering only Hegel's view of all human history and ignoring, for the moment, the rest of his broad philosophic system —or view of *all* existence and *all* process, i.e., the natural universe and its evolution as well as human civilization and *its* evolution. Now to glimpse the meaning of his all-embracing, basic, *general* idea, that *all* process, history in that sense, or evolution is "dialectical," we need, I think, to glance first at an older, pre-Hegelian, common or prevalent belief of most earlier philosophers, which Hegel revised or modified. This older belief was or may be called the metaphysical "rationalism" which supposed that rationality, or logical consistency (among all the parts of the whole), is a necessary characteristic not only of any valid system of human thought about the universe, but also of the real, objective universe itself. Reality is rational; whatever does or can really exist or occur is necessarily consistent, compatible, or in harmony (not in conflict or "contradiction") with all other realities or real occurrences. The first "law of logic," that no two mutually contradictory or inconsistent propositions can both be true, was thought to presuppose or involve an underlying "law of nature" to the effect that incompatibles —things naturally bound to destroy each other—cannot coexist.

According to Hegel, *this is true about* the final, permanent system of all fully realized or perfected "realities" which is (are) in process of progressive realization in the cosmic-temporal process of evolutionary change of all temporary actualities; but the premise of consistency or absence of contradictions or conflicts *is not true about* the temporary actualities or the parts or elements of and factors in the on-going process of evolutionary change, itself. On the contrary, within that process as distinguished from its goal or destiny, conflicting opposites are always everywhere at work compelling changes in each other, and this is precisely the basic cause or explanation of all process, change, or evolution. Human thought evolves toward discovery of the internally consistent system of all perfect truth or knowledge through a "dialectical" process in which conflicting views of partial truths compel (with evidence and logic) revisions of each other and unite their contributions. And in the same way all changeful existence evolves toward realization of the self-consistent, harmonious universe of perfected beings through a "dialectical" process in which the conflicting, imperfect, temporary parts of all current existence in each passing time compel each other to change toward compatibility or harmony and union with each other. The goal or destination of the evolutionary process is achievement of full rationality, consistency, or harmony; but the cause of continuing change in that direction is precisely the long-run instability or non-viability of each new state of the world that is still convulsed with internal conflicts.

Now Marx retained that basic, general, Hegelian idea of all evolutionary change as impelled by conflicts but toward a final harmony; but he disagreed in two respects with Hegel in working out its application to human history or social evolution. In the first place, his "materialism" as opposed to Hegel's "idealism" entailed, in this field, a reversal of Hegel's view of the relation between developments in the mental or subjective sphere of prevalent ideas, beliefs, and attitudes, and developments in the objective sphere of actually existing social systems and conditions. Hegel stressed the dependence of the latter on the former; Marx, the dependence of the former on the latter. On this question Marx said he had found Hegel standing on his head and turned him over and set him upright on his feet. To Marx it seemed an "upside-down" view to suppose that the ideas, beliefs, and feelings within the minds of men in great numbers first change, somehow, by themselves, and then cause the millions, newly animated by those ideas, etc., to change or reshape their societies. The "right-side-up" view, he thought, was that as actual social systems and conditions change or evolve (in the way that he set out to explain), this causes changes of the experiences and, in consequence, of the ideas, beliefs, and attitudes of men in their millions. Their new or altered outlooks "reflect" their new or altered, real situations in their real, existing, and changing societies. Although their changed beliefs, etc., do affect their behavior and thus affect or react upon the objective social change or evolution, still this role of the mental or subjective factors in the latter process is derivative and secondary; they count or are effective only as intermediate links between earlier and later states of the real societies, and never as the original or primary fundamental causes of change in the latter. Men's mental states react upon, but are first formed by, their "material" environments and circumstances; man's consciousness does not determine his existence—on the contrary, his existence determines his consciousness. But now I must speak of the other, second, important difference of Marx's from Hegel's theory of the human-social, past and on-going historical process.

The social groups or units emphasized in Hegel's theory were nation-states (in modern times) or their nearest equivalents (in more remote past times)—entire societies, in their areas or habitats, internally united and divided from other such societies by their special languages, cultures, traditions, etc. And for Hegel, accordingly, the conflicts of main importance in the "dialectical" evolution of all civilization were the conflicts of or among these units—international rivalries, wars, etc. Antitheses between, and syntheses of, rival national civilizations were impelling world history toward production of an eventual, single, rich, and harmonious world civilization. But in Marx's theory of the history or past and future of mankind, the groups or units emphasized were social classes, internally dividing all nations alike, or the world as a whole without regard to national frontiers and distinctions. And the main conflicts through which the "dialectical" evolution had gone on and would go on to its destination, were "class struggles" between the ruling or dominant and the submerged, oppressed, and exploited classes of successive epochs—slaves *versus* masters in antiquity, peasants and burghers *versus* feudal lords in the Middle Ages, and wage-earning workers *versus* capitalists in the modern epoch.

MARX'S SOCIOLOGY, OR "ECONOMIC INTERPRETATION" AND "CLASS STRUGGLE THEORY" OF HISTORY[5]

It is now time, however, to pass on beyond this outline of Marx's basic, but only very general and speculative philosophy of history—

[5] This section is heavily indebted to J. A. Schumpeter's chapters on Marx, forming part I of the former's *Capitalism, Socialism, and Democracy* (New York: Harper & Brothers, 1950); and also to M. M. Bober's *Karl Marx's Interpretation of History* (Cambridge, Mass: Harvard University Press, 1950).

his "dialectical, historical materialism"—to consideration of his further and connected, but different, social-scientific work and theories—his far more specific and fully detailed, systematic, logical elaboration of his views, and efforts to support or confirm them through much scholarly, historical research. And within this part of his work or system I take up, first, the core of what may be called his "sociology"—the thesis, principle, or doctrine of his "economic interpretation of history." This needs, I think, to be distinguished from, although it is related to, his philosophical thesis, "historical materialism," which has already been described. The latter was, on its very high level of abstraction, his broadest, general, heuristic principle about, or guide to the understanding of, all human history; and his "economic-interpretation" thesis was, on its somewhat lower level of abstraction, his particular and more detailed application of his "materialistic" point of view in the work of trying to explain all kinds of historic developments or changes of the institutional set-ups, cultures, "ideologies," politics, and policies of human societies. The ground for assigning this "economic-interpretation" thesis to the field of "sociology" rather than to that of "economics" is that, although it relies on "economic" factors to explain the extraeconomic or noneconomic, institutional, sociocultural, and political developments which it is about, or concerned to explain, still it is concerned with explaining the latter—phenomena that we generally think of as within the subject matter of "sociology," and not those within that of "economics." It is true that Marx would have objected, and his followers do object, to this distinction within, or way of dividing, the whole body of his social-scientific work and doctrines. For Marxist orthodoxy the whole system is one single, "seamless" whole—a fully unified social-economic or at once economic and complete social "science." But I think it need not at all distort, and may help, our understanding of the system to divide it, in accordance with the now (for most non-Marxists) more usual and familiar, modern habits of intellectual specialization and resulting categories, into the part that is "sociology" and the part (to be taken up last in this chapter) which is or belongs to "economics" proper. It is, then, as the core of Marx's "sociology" that I now take up (1) his theory affirming an "economic interpretation" or explanation of all other-than-economic developments in human history, and (2) his closely connected, subsidiary theory of the "class struggles" through which, according to his views, changes of economic systems and conditions have caused or led to all broader social and cultural changes.

Now the first step toward understanding of the Marxian "economic-interpretation" thesis must be to clear out of the way a common but unfounded misconception. Marx did *not* hold the theory that the economic (or acquisitive) *motive*, so-called—the desire or greed for wealth or economic gain—is the dominant "force" in all "human nature" and the main underlying cause of all human feelings, thoughts, beliefs, and deeds. This cynical theory that "the profit motive" in the members of societies accounts for everything that they do and bring about in the working and development of their societies and civilizations *is not* the authentic Marxian "economic-interpretation" theory, at all. According to Marx, the peculiar, excessive development and strength of the economic-gains-seeking-and-accumulating motive, *in* the members of the class of capitalists or businessmen, *in* the part or period of history dominated by the special, transitory, capitalistic economic and social system and civilization, is an abnormality or aberration peculiar to that epoch and class and culture, and *not* a universal and permanent, inherent trait of "human nature." His "economic interpretation" was meant to explain *all* history, *not* the "capitalist" part of it only, and hence the basic reference is to something else, *not* this economic "motive." His fundamental idea in this connection was, in fact, that the objective economic *conditions,* situations, or circumstances in which people live so strongly affect or color all their experiences, thoughts, and desires or motives as to play the main role in forming their outlooks, characters, and conduct. The diverse economic lives and situations of rich men and poor men inevitably cause them to develop widely diverse and mutually contradictory ways of understanding and reacting to all occurrences. And, in more detail, all the different, historic, upper and lower social classes of men—ancient slaveowners and their slaves, mediaeval lords and serfs, and modern factory-owning businessmen and hired factory workers—all in their different times and worlds have been made into the different kinds of people they have been or are, and caused to think, feel, and behave as they did or do, about all matters of all kinds, mainly by the effects upon them of the economic or "material" environments, circumstances, and conditions of their lives. Then furthermore, Marx held that within the historical process, and as the part of that which engenders the rest of it, there goes on a largely autonomous evolution or progress of the techniques, methods, and organization of every society's processes of production of the material, economic goods its members live on. As this economic development goes on, it continually changes the roles, relations, and situations of the social-economic classes of men and the economic conditions basically affecting their lives, and thus changes them as people and causes them to change their beliefs and actions and all parts of their societies and cultures.

Within the complete structure of every society and its civilization, according to Marx, in each period of its history or stage of its evolution, the part of the whole which is the "foundation" of all the rest is the society's then existing "mode of production" of the economic, material goods which its members live on. But the "mode of production" itself has two components: (1) "the forces of production" that are used or exerted in it, and (2) "the social relations in production" of or among all the human agents having any roles in or connections with it. Accepting the usual and probably correct or adequate translation or explanation of this terminology, we may identify each level of development of the "forces" of production with that of the techniques or technology of physical production employed in the economy. "Social relations" would mean the entire complex of institutions—the special system of property rights, and all other features of the social-economic system or organization of the statuses, roles, and relations of the different classes and groups of men having different functions in or relations to the process of production as carried on with that set of techniques, in that society in that stage of its development. The idea is that as progressive change and improvement of the technology of production goes on—the older, less efficient techniques or methods get supplanted or replaced, gradually, with newer, more efficient, and different ones—this creates needs for, and tends to bring about, appropriate or adaptative changes of the institutional set-up, social organization, or pattern of roles and relations of the human agents, to enable the new techniques to be used most effectively. But the entire, complete society and civilization includes, besides its economic part or "foundation" (its "mode of production" of material goods, involving both the technology and the institutionalized human relations)—a complex, variegated, extraeconomic or noneconomic "superstructure," i.e., the political and legal system and the entire intellectual, spiritual, artistic, and moral culture—the society's sciences and arts, philosophies, religion, morality, etc. Now the system of the social relations making up one aspect of the "mode of production" is related not only to the technology also included in the latter, but also to the "superstructure" or culture, ideology, morality polity, and legal order.

In every nonsocialist or presocialist system or "stage" of evolution, the social-economic, organizational, institutional, or human-relations structure is above all a class structure or hierarchy, with a dominant owning and directing class at the top and a much larger but wretchedly poor, subordinate, toiling and producing class at the bottom. There is pressure from the progressively evolving technology for adaptive change of the social relations in organized production; but the anxiety of the dominant class to maintain its power position unimpaired becomes a source of counterpressure or resistance on its part to the evolutionary social reforms or institutional changes which come to be needed for full realization of the rising, potential productivity of the advancing technology. And from the standpoint of the dominant class, the "superstructure" or culture, ideology, morality, polity, etc.—which has all been created essentially by and for the dominant class and expresses the outlook of its members which results from their circumstances and experiences—has the function of sanctioning and supporting the existing institutions and social relations including the power position of the dominant class; i.e., of implanting and nurturing in the minds and hearts of all the people the beliefs and attitudes conducive to their loyal acceptance and support of the existing order.

The upsetting effects of technological progress upon that order, the growing needs for institutional changes, and the growing fear of them on the part of the dominant class as a threat to its power position make it increasingly, intransigently conservative and inclined to use its power to prevent such changes. But this in turn causes the evolving economy or "mode of production" to work or function ever more badly, or develop increasingly severe "internal contradictions," frictions, or maladjustments and malfunctionings. It intensifies the poverty and misery of the submerged toiling class or main mass of the people, and/or intermediate classes, to the point of bringing on a revolution. *Then* the accumulated needs for institutional reforms or changes, to reshape the "social relations in production" into full harmony with its technology, are all met in or by the revolution and its aftermath, the reconstructive work carried out by the class that has won the revolution and made itself the new dominant class. Thus the first, early part or phase of the life-history or life-cycle of each kind of economy, society, and civilization that arises in the course of history, is a phase in which that new, young system has as yet a good degree of internal harmony and ability to function well and achieve or undergo a good deal of free and balanced all-around progress. But in time the continuance of technological and economic change and disturbance, and the institutional changes required in adjustment to it all, build up new internal frictions; threats to the power position of the dominant class; fearful conservatism or resistance to further change on its part; resulting, intensifying evils within the system, etc.—and the formerly "new" system, in its old age, deteriorates again toward another necessary revolution. The historical process as a whole is a series of long waves of at first progressive and later on degenerative evolution, with widely separated (in time) revolutions at the critical turning points of transition from each long epoch's general kind of social system and civilization, to the next, radically different one.

There is much that should be said in critical commentary on this general Marxian "sociological" theory of the historical process; but we must get on to consideration of the other and main part of the entire structure of Marx's social-scientific, theoretical work—his structure of economic theory—which in a way is the central core of Marxism as a whole. The whole, however, was left by Marx, and has remained, unfinished or incomplete in a way, or two ways, somewhat obscuring the relations of its "economic" and "sociological" parts to each other and to history as a whole. With respect to the precapitalist, ancient and mediaeval epochs and systems, the Marxian line of inquiry as far as I know has never come to offer more than a bare, general, sketchy outline of the supposed exemplifications of its "sociological" theory in the facts about them and their evolutions—and virtually no analysis of the structures, workings, and evolutions or internal histories of their economic systems, or "modes of production," as such. Substantially all of Marx's great and impressive structure of economic theory is about "modern capitalism" only—the economic system that Marx thought of as still fairly new or young in his time, and as destined to be the penultimate one in the historic series—the immediate forerunner of the final, perfect one, the realized socialism of the future. Most of the little that appears in the whole body of his writings, about the ancient and mediaeval, precapitalist societies and civilizations and their evolutions, pertains not to their economic but to their extraeconomic or noneconomic, "sociological" aspects. In his far more extensive and detailed analysis of the epoch, economy, and civilization of "modern capitalism," the converse is almost (though not quite) as true—i.e., in this main part of his work his economic analysis, of the economic system as the "foundation" of the whole and of *its* past, current, and prospective evolution, is heavily predominant and alone fully elaborated; and his vision of the consequences of this evolution, for or in that of the bourgeois societies, states, and culture, is much less fully spelled out, or is only suggested. But I must now conclude this chapter with a summary—which must be all too brief and inadequate—of Marx's theory of the economic system of evolving "capitalism."

MARX'S ECONOMIC THEORY OF EVOLVING CAPITALISM[6]

Whatever estimates may be made of Marx's intellectual work in his roles as philosopher, sociologist, and historian, he was, I think, beyond doubt an economist of considerable stature, although by no means without his failings and errors. He was a keen, able, and industrious scholar and investigator, and he attained a wide and deep knowledge both of the works and ideas of most other economists of his own and earlier times, and of the real economic world around him in his time. And he largely mastered and accepted, made his own, used, and built upon or added to the insights of his great forerunners in the study of economics —Adam Smith, Ricardo, and others—although he changed some of their ideas or doctrines, in some cases for the worse, to fit them into his

[6] See the excellent modern restatement—by a true Marxist *and* first-rate economist—of Marx's system of economic theory: P. M. Sweezy, *The Theory of Capitalist Development* (New York: Oxford University Press, 1942).

own system. His bias, of course, was of a kind opposite to the bias which may in a measure be justly charged against Smith, Ricardo, and the entire, main, "orthodox" line of nineteenth-century economists, who as liberals in the classical sense in their social-and-moral philosophies or outlooks, tended to be friendly or favorable to the liberal or free and competitive *form of* "capitalism" or the business economy. Marx as a radical, revolutionary socialist was a bitterly hostile, adverse critic of that economy or economic system in *every* form. He therefore constructed, as compared with that offered by the liberal-orthodox economists, a rather different theoretical picture of the (same) economy's "natural" working and development. But I think his hostile and their favorable bias led mainly to different insights and discoveries, and different blind spots or limitations of insight, and made the resulting visions and analyses of the system in some ways mutually complementary. The liberal-orthodox economists in general far excelled Marx in discerning, analyzing, and describing the better possibilities or best potential functioning of the business economy; but he excelled them in discerning, analyzing, and describing its defects or flaws, its possible and frequent internal maladjustments and malfunctionings, and its capacities to go wrong and make serious trouble for itself. With his extreme bias against the system and his desire to prove it a thing so evil that it must inevitably destroy itself, he exaggerated all its flaws and discordant tendencies and falsely claimed to prove that they were inherent in the system, and incurable within it, and bound to grow worse and destroy it, and thus open the way to the bright future of socialism. But I think that even liberal-orthodox economists can, without accepting any of his exaggerative nonsense of that kind, learn much from his work in economics, which can improve their own realistic understanding of the business economy and its internal problems.

Marx's system of theory about the economics of capitalism or the business economy was framed within the wider context of his theory of all human history or social evolution, and endeavored to explain not only its structure and current operation in his time, but also and above all its past (previous) and current and prospective evolution as an unstable or dynamic, growing, and changing system. His prophecies about the direction of its evolution and its fate were biased and in essential parts have been and are being disproved by actual events; but there was much truth in his vision of its dynamic, evolving nature, which few other economists have grasped and analyzed as well as he did. More clearly than anyone before his time, he saw this fact about capitalism as an economic system: that by its nature it is bound or at least strongly tends to be not a static, fixed, immutable system, but a very dynamic, growing or expanding, and perpetually self-changing and world-changing affair. And to explain this fact, Marx offered a not uninstructive comparison or contrast of capitalism with a different, simpler kind of commercial or exchange economy—half-historic (precapitalist) and half-hypothetical—which he called "simple commodity production."

In the latter system there would be division of labor, or specialized producers of different products, private properties and enterprises in a sense, and markets for the selling and buying of the different products; but the crucial feature of capitalism as conceived by Marx would be absent; that is, there would be no separate class of owners or proprietors, investors, and employers, and no dependent class of hired workers owning only their abilities to work. All members of this economic society would be self-employed workers or producers, owning their own premises, materials, tools, and products, and simply earning their livings by producing goods to sell to each other for the money they would use to buy from each other all they would need to live on. In this simple system, said Marx, the formula describing the pair of market transactions continually repeated by each individual as both producer and consumer, would be *C-M-C;* one would sell his product or commodity, *C*, for money, *M*, in order then to spend the latter for the other commodities, *C* again, entering into his consumption and having in all a total money-value equal to that of his output and sales of his own product. And the gain or advantage would lie simply in getting the other goods you want more urgently, i.e., those having more utility or value-in-use for you than the good you sold in order to be able to buy them. No physical, quantitative increase of your wealth over time would be needed, in this system, to give meaning, point, or purpose to economic activities.

But in the capitalist system, the central figure in it—the investing, owning, and labor-employing capitalist—starts with a sum of money to invest at or for a profit, and the formula that describes the sequence of *his* transactions is *M-C-M′*, where the *M′* needs to be bigger than the *M* to make it all worthwhile. The capitalist invests his money, *M*, in hiring and equipping workers to produce an output of a good or commodity, *C*, which he expects to sell for *M′*, more money than he started with. And Marx imputed to all typical capitalists a very powerful "passion," urge, or drive toward gaining the largest possible profits, *and* reinvesting most of those profits to enlarge their amounts of capital, in order to get still larger profit-incomes in the future, *and* again reinvest the bulk of them, and so on forever. And he held that the resulting, snowballing accumulation, growth, or expansion of the mass of capital employed in the economy, and the constant and growing need or pressure to keep on finding or creating ever new, profitable investment opportunities or outlets, and markets for more and more new products, accounted for the inherent tendency of the capitalist system to both grow and change or evolve in the course of time.

Moreover, Marx recognized a good or beneficial side to that, for mankind, at least through the early, progressive phase of the life-cycle he assigned to the system. Though he hated capitalism as compared with his vision of the socialist heaven-on-earth that would some day supersede it, he could still praise capitalism as compared with older or earlier and worse systems in past human history—the slave economy of antiquity and the feudal system of the Middle Ages. And there is in *The Communist Manifesto* a famous passage that has been called his "hymn of praise" to the businessmen as the builders and operators of progressive capitalism—a passage that might have been written by any Rotarian. There Marx says that in a few generations of modern European history the *bourgeoisie* or capitalist class brought about a greater advance of all economic production and wealth than had been achieved in all previous history, and thus made possible a great growth of population, and of cities, drawing masses of people out of rural stagnation into urban civilization and progress. And yet this giving of credit to the profit-gaining-and-accumulating, investing, and enterprising capitalists, for economic progress or rising productivity, was hardly consistent with his central economic doctrine (still to be examined here) that all profits and property incomes result entirely from exploitation or underpayment of hired workers, who alone produce or create the "value" of all output, but get only bare or meager living wages, while all the surplus of the total value of "their" (the system's) total output over the total wage income of this working class, goes into the profit, interest, and rent incomes of its capitalist masters, the owners of all "means of production." Marx's capitalists seem to be at once, through their profit-retaining, investing, and enterprising activities, great developers or increasers of the productivity of industry and labor, and yet also mere parasites on the working class, which alone is productive but is forced to surrender a great part of its output to its capitalist masters.

Only a brief account will be given here of that mass or labyrinth of mystery and folly, Marx's "labor theory of value," and its corollary, his "theory of surplus value," i.e., of the source of all capitalist or property incomes. I could not in any case present a really clear, full explanation of this in-a-way central but weakest part of Marx's whole structure of economic theory, because to my mind it simply is not, in itself, fully clear or intelligible. But some light may be thrown upon it, and upon the errors in it, by considering briefly its relation to and difference from the half-similar but relatively more intelligible and defensible theories held by Adam Smith and Ricardo, which Marx drew upon, but went beyond. As the reader will recall, Adam Smith explicitly regarded *his* "labor theory of value" *as valid only under the special conditions* imagined by Smith as having prevailed in a prehistoric, ultrasimple, primitive economy, and recognized by him as *not* present in the kind of economy—of chief interest to him and to all economists—which Marx called "capitalism." That is, Smith held that the relative values of different, regularly produced goods would be (in equilibrium) strictly proportional to the amounts (in man-hours) of work or labor needed to produce them, *only in* the primitive economy of his conception, in which there had not yet occurred the later "appropriation of land and accumulation of capital stock in private hands," and the laborers therefore did not yet "have to share" the value of all output "with landlords and capitalists." If the laborers were self-employed producers, owning all the simple "means of production" used in their work and the products turned out, and receiving as their own incomes the full values (in each other's products) of their outputs, *and* were all fully "mobile" laborers, ready at all times to move into the most remunerative employment or branch of production; under *these* conditions, according to Adam Smith (and the logic of this argument is faultless), the relative or exchange values of the different products would be stable only when proportional to the amounts of working time and effort needed to produce them. For that would be the condition of equilibrium in this kind of economy or situation—the only set of those relative values consistent with a stable distribution of the labor force among the different employments, or equality of reward for equal time and effort in them all. But in the more developed, real economy of his own time and country, Smith decided, where the values of the outputs of goods had to yield the rent incomes of landlords and the profits of capitalists as well as the wages of the laborers, and where labor, capital, and land might well be used in differing proportions or relative amounts in producing different products; here the equilibrium (or "natural") prices of the different goods *no longer would be* necessarily proportional to the labor-time inputs or costs, alone. Thus for this case—of "capitalism"—Smith abandoned his "labor theory," and instead presented simply a theory of the "natural," competitive, equilibrium prices as equal to the full costs or expenses of production of the different products, or the wages plus the profits plus the rents which the product prices must yield or "cover," to enable all the industries to attract and retain the amounts of labor, capital, and land required for production of the outputs equal to the amounts demanded by the public at these "natural" prices. On the whole, Smith's "theory of value" yielded only a little of the material for that of Marx, and contained much more of a very different tenor. Even the "labor theory" applied by Smith only to his primitive economy was (as we shall see) unlike Marx's theory. Smith asserted only that (even in that primitive economy) the "market mechanism" or processes of adjustment would work to bring about proportionality or correspondence of relative values with labor-time requirements —*and did not* assert at all, as Marx was to do, that "embodied" labor-time and real "value" *are the same thing,* regardless of whether the actual price brought into being by market forces corresponds to that real "value" or not.

Ricardo, however, as we have seen earlier, revised Adam Smith's analysis and went a few steps nearer—but still not all the way—to that of Marx. Ricardo also, like Smith and unlike Marx, was mainly interested simply in the "mechanical" problem of explaining how the actual exchange ratios among goods, or their relative prices, get determined by the working out of the adjustment processes of the free and flexible, competitive economy in which all things flow to their best markets or into their most remunerative uses or employments. But Ricardo, as we know, disliked Smith's theory which saw as the causes of (equilibrium) product prices, only the sums of the prices of the amounts of all the productive services (of labor, capital, and land) required to produce the products. He probably regarded this simple theory as superficial and circular, or as relying on prices to explain other prices when in fact the general mobility and competition would make all prices reciprocally interdependent, and necessitate attention to some underlying, nonprice variable or variables as the basic cause(s) of all prices alike. Thus Ricardo tried to revive or reinstate Smith's "labor theory," *for* application also to the existing "capitalist" economy—but found that he would have to, and did, "qualify" it considerably in this application, or treat it as only *approximately* valid. As we know, he eliminated the land-rent elements of product prices, in his way, as being really results only and not contributory causes of the latter. Then he argued that in general the wage-costs, per unit of output, for the different products, would vary directly with (simply) the amounts of labor-time required; since labor mobility and competition would equalize the wage rates for similar labor in all employments, and the scale of permanently diverse wage rates for labor of different kinds or degrees of skill could be viewed as consistent with his (almost) pure labor-quantities approach, since the more highly skilled and paid labor really represented correspondingly *more* labor, when account was taken of the previous labor "invested" in acquiring the skill, in addition to the current labor, involved in exercising it. Finally, as to the element of profit in all prices, here again the mobility of capital would work to equalize the profit rates in all industries, and they would as a rule affect all prices about equally, hence *not* affect the *relative* prices, or exchange ratios among the goods themselves, which were to be explained. Here, however, a major "qualification" entered into Ricardo's theory: where the production of particular products required the use of exceptionally great amounts of capital, relative to the amounts of direct or current labor also employed, the profit element *would* increase the prices of *those* products as compared with others produced with the aid of less capital or more largely with direct, current labor simply.

Thus the final result of Ricardo's analysis was his doctrine that, in the equilibrium state of the competitive system and on his assumptions about it, the relative values of the different products continually produced in it would be—with perhaps some exceptions even to this statement—at least approximately or nearly proportional to the total amounts of labor-time needed (per unit of output) to produce—at the margins of land-use, where rent was eliminated—(1) the produced means of production of the final products, *and* with their aid, (2) the final products themselves. Let me stress the point, however, that this doctrine, unlike the "labor theory" in the different, special, absolute form that Marx was to give it, asserted as even "tending" to be brought about, approximately, by the market mechanisms, *only* values *proportional, not* values directly *equivalent,* to the labor-time quantities. Ricardo never said that the total value of the total output of each, or any, product, was either all produced solely by, or equivalent to, the input of labor-time in its production; or that the profit shares included in the values of the products were created by the workers, though retained by the capitalists. The Ricardian thesis was only that the profit shares, in so far as they merely raised the prices of all products alike, by equal percentages, above their wage-costs, would not affect the *relative* values of the different products, but would leave those *proportional* to the relative labor-time costs or requirements. And *this* thesis is entirely consistent, at least, with a view of the profit shares as "earned" by the capitalists, i.e., just compensation for productive services rendered by them, and not as "stolen" from the workers.

Moreover, it seems to me far more likely than not that Ricardo did think of the capitalists as, unlike the landlords, "earning" their incomes through active, personal contributions to economic growth or progress. The landlords merely collected rents as payments for rights to use a factor of production provided by "nature" in a fixed supply but legally belonging to them, and without personally doing anything to increase that supply or the economy's producing power. But the capitalists through their saving-and-investing activity continually increased the economy's supply of capital, and so increased its productivity, and the national income, their own *relative* share of which—the profit share as a percentage of the whole—progressively declined as growth went on. The Ricardian system of economic theory *needed,* for its own self-consistent, full development, an explicit theory of this productive service rendered by the capitalists, as the source of interest or profit—the return on capital. But it is true that Ricardo failed to make this explicit, or to offer any explicit theory to explain the existence, as distinguished from the variations of the rate, of profit; and that he even committed the worse, positive "slip," which directly opened the way to the doctrines of Marx, of describing "real" capital itself, or the "capital goods" (e.g., machines) used by labor in production, as representing or "embodying" *only* the previous *labor* by which it (or they) had been "produced."

Marx, then, was able, in consequence of that omission and that slip or error on Ricardo's part, to make it seem, and probably he himself thought, that the Ricardian and his own—the Marxian, absolute—"labor theory of value" were the same, in spite of what I have brought out here to the contrary. In the Marxian theory, the "value" of a good in effect *means* the amount of labor-time "embodied in" the good or required to produce it. There is simply a dogmatic, arbitrary, absolute "equating" of these two concepts with each other, which leads to or becomes the assertion that, whatever other factors or variables may also affect the economy's *physical* productivity and output, all of the *value* of all output is created entirely or solely by the labor of (hired!) workers, and therefore all non-wage incomes—shares of the value of output going as interest, rent, profits, dividends, or whatever, to persons other than wage-earning laborers—result entirely from "exploitation" or underpayment of those laborers, who produce all but get only a part of the value of all output. That real exploitation of hired workers can occur and has often occurred, where the owners of the other factors of production and employers of labor have had and abused positions of monopoly power or one-sided bargaining power in the labor markets and products markets, to control wages and prices, is of course true and just ground for indignation and humane reform efforts. But all this has little to do with the different, far more extreme, and nonsensical Marxian dogma, that *all* income or value of output is due exclusively to the wage-earning workers, and as long as *any* of it goes to anyone else, they are being "exploited."

Moreover, as to *what* share of the value of output the economic "laws" of the "natural" operation of the "capitalist" system allow those workers, who create it all, to receive as their wages, Marx had another dogmatic theory which must now be examined. As the "values" of *all* commodities are the costs, in labor-time, of producing them, so too the "value" of labor-time itself—of the hour of work sold by the worker to the employer for his hourly wage—is the cost of enabling the worker to live and work through that hour, i.e., the amount of other labor "embodied in" or represented by the amount of consumption of food, clothing, shelter, etc., required to engender or support the energy expended in that hour. The workers, in other words, get only "bare-subsistence" wages—and the fact that they can and do produce more than enough to support themselves is the source or cause of the "surplus value"—

excess of the value of output over the value (cost) of the labor that produces it—which goes to their "exploiters."

Now here again we must notice both a point of agreement with, and a point of divergence from, the Ricardian theory on this topic—the "natural" level of real wages. In the Ricardian theory, as we know, the alleged tendency of real wages to fall to and remain at a "subsistence" level was explained with the aid of the Malthusian theory of population growth. Higher real wages would lower the death rate, raise the birth rate, and speed the growth of the population and supply of labor to the point of forcing real wages down again to the level that would just maintain continuing equality or equilibrium of the labor supply with the economy's demand for labor as conditioned by its supply of capital. But Marx rejected the Malthusian theory, calling it "a libel on the human race"; and had therefore to find a *different* cause, in the "natural" working and evolution of the capitalist system, which would operate to hold real wages down to the minimum necessary to support the labor force required in the system. And he thought he found this cause in the tendency of the capitalists to foster and utilize technological progress; continually, increasingly mechanize production, and react to all temporary upward movements of wages or labor costs by introducing new laborsaving inventions; and thus continually create and re-create enough technological unemployment to depress wages back down to the "subsistence" level, through the competition of the workers displaced from their previous jobs by new inventions or machines for the jobs of the still employed workers. He admitted that technological progress and rising productivity would in the long run cause expansion of total production, income and consumption in the economy as a whole, and eventual reemployment elsewhere in the system of the workers displaced by each new invention. But as newer inventions and displacements would keep on occurring while the lagging readjustments to the earlier ones were still in process, there would always be in existence a fluctuating but substantial "reserve army of the unemployed," exerting its downward pressure on wages in the labor markets.

Let me for an instant defer the critical comment obviously called for by that last "reserve army" theory, to say that we are now at least beyond the worst nonsensical part of or spot in Marx's whole system of economic theory, i.e., his absolute "labor theory of value," and moving on into consideration of further parts of his analysis in which, again, he displayed real insights, however mixed with errors and exaggerations. And so our comment on even this theory of "subsistence" wages maintained by effects of technological progress must be mixed, or must give the credit that is due as well as make the adverse criticism that is called for. Of course there is a process of that kind at work in a progressive capitalism—displacements of workers, creation of transitional but ever-renewed unemployment, and some degree of depressing influence exerted by the latter on the level of real wages, making their advance lag a bit behind that of productivity. But there is no reason to expect this to work so strongly as to maintain a "bare-subsistence" level of real wages, generally and permanently, in spite of ever-rising productivity; and the predictions of Marx in this matter have been disproved long since by actual developments. He actually predicted even, in the later part of what he thought would be the whole, rather short, life-history of capitalism, a progressive worsening of the lot of the working class, or an intensification of its poverty and misery. But, in fact, there has been and continues to be a pronounced rising trend of the level of real wages in all progressive capitalist countries.

There remains a good deal, however, in the further parts, still to be summarized here, of Marx's over-all theory or forecast of the evolution of dynamic capitalism, which logically depends not at all upon his false dogmas about labor and value, the origin of all "surplus value" in pure "exploitation" of labor, and the forces certain to perpetuate (even increasingly) meager "subsistence" wages. Much of his general forecast depends only upon his valid, obvious points that the total value of the economy's output would normally include a substantial "surplus" over and above the total income and consumption of the workers; and that this "surplus," going first into profits and other property incomes, would then go in large part into new investments, increasing the volume of capital and leading to continual growth and change of the economy. Now one further important part of his general theory of that process of growth and change was about its fluctuating course and character, or what later economists were to call "the business cycle," and Marx called the succession of "crises" to be expected in the career of evolving capitalism. This all refers, of course, to a very complex set of phenomena, in the study and understanding of which a good deal of progress has been made since Marx's time, but about which, even today, economists still do not know enough to be able to agree, either upon a full, true explanation of them or upon the best public policies for alleviating them or coping with them. Naturally then, Marx did not by any means achieve any full or adequate, unified theory to explain the "cycle" or the "crises" which he thought of as inevitably, periodically recurrent in the career of evolving capitalism. But he was among the first economists to begin to understand the sequence of alternating "booms" and "depressions" as resulting "naturally" from the "natural" working and development of the unstable, dynamic, business economy; and he achieved a number of more or less valid and penetrating insights into this problem. In a way, whereas most efforts by other economists to explain "the business cycle" have been mainly concerned with "depressions"—the common tendency of minds with "friendly" attitudes to the system is to assume prosperity or approximately full employment and good incomes as the "normal" state of the system, and to puzzle over how to explain the recurrent departures from that—for Marx, with his general view of the system as a wretched one, the chief problem, one may say, was to explain "prosperities."

Marx envisaged the majority of the people as never getting incomes sufficient to enable them to buy and consume very much, and the rich minority of capitalists as so eager to reinvest the bulk of their profits in acquiring ever more capital and power that they would never be lavish consumers either; but the continual growth of the system's total mass of capital and producing power would thus strongly tend to exceed the growth of total consumption or final demand, and eventually glut all the markets for consumers' goods, and cause chronic depression. "Prosperities" would occur, in the Marxian picture, only in the periods or intervals of preparatory expansion of plant capacity for future production of more consumers' goods, with new, improved machines and methods and thus with lower expected costs. Every such expansion, not immediately yielding any great increase of the current output of consumers' goods, but bringing a temporary near-approach to full employment and rise of wages, and good profits for all the capitalists selling new machines, materials, etc., to the other capitalists eagerly investing in them in the expectation of good future profits for themselves from future sales to ultimate consumers—would thus bring about a period of prosperity. But the strong demand for labor, materials, and machines would bid up costs and cut down the prospective profits on further new investments; and the emergence in time of a new flood of consumers' goods would bring to light the inadequacy of total, final demand, and again glut the markets and bring on a depression.

This is only one part, and perhaps not the best or most impressive part, of all that Marx had to offer to explain the "cycle" or recurring "crises"; but I think I have not unfairly summarized an important, central, and characteristic part of his view of the matter. There is one more feature of that view, however, which must be emphasized. Marx was sure that, as the system went on evolving, each new "crisis" would get worse or increasingly severe, and the final one would be the utter, catastrophic breakdown of the system which would ignite the revolution and ensure its triumph. It is not surprising that the Great Depression of the 1930s, which was or seemed the worst one yet and so bad that it might well be that final breakdown, gave intellectual Marxism at that time a tremendous boost or growth of influence in the Western world. But there is no clear evidence of a general historic trend toward increasingly severe economic depressions in the capitalist world. And there is no reason, today, to doubt the ability of the governments, businessmen, and workingmen concerned to learn progressively to master, control, and moderate these fluctuations, and enable capitalism to endure and go on correcting its faults and improving its performance for the economic welfare of all the people.

There is still one more part, so important that I must describe it, of Marx's theory of evolving capitalism: his theory that along with its fluctuating growth or expansion it would undergo an eventually fatal structural change, from the early competitive capitalism of very many small or moderate-sized competing enterprises, to a latter-day "monopoly capitalism" dominated by a few giant firms and combinations or industrial and financial empires. Competition among business firms would progressively destroy itself, as the few winners would ruin or absorb the many losers in the game, and the growth of the mass of capital in use in the system as a whole would be accompanied by a growing concentration of the ownership or control of it all in the hands of a diminishing number of increasingly rich men and small cohesive groups of them. In part this prophecy rested on Marx's oversimple and exaggerated notion of the economy or efficiency of bigness in producing and business organizations or units—his assumption that there was no limit to the rule that the bigger the firm, the more efficient it would be, so that continual growth of the average size and shrinkage of the number of successful or surviving firms would be the natural law of business development. Today all competent, objective students of this matter know that it is less simple; bigness has advantages in many fields, up to some point in each case, but there seem to be limits, though not rigidly fixed ones; and smaller enterprises in many fields continue to be numerous and flourishing. Whether there is a trend of declining prevalence of competition, or growing prevalence and power of monopolies within the economy, is still uncertain. The biggest firms now are much bigger than any that existed fifty or a hundred years ago, but the market areas throughout which firms of all types compete with each other are also much bigger than they were then, and the monopoly powers of firms depend on not their absolute sizes but their sizes relative to those of their markets. Marx showed foresight in predicting the growth of modern big business, but went, as usual, to a false extreme in predicting that the giants would become *so* big and few and all-controlling that the structurally, radically altered system, consisting merely of those few giant "outfits" and their few enormously rich owners, and the starving mass of rebellious workers, would be ripe for inevitable and easy transformation into the socialist or communist system.

I will not take up here—as this would lead beyond consideration of the ideas of Marx himself, the exclusive subject matter of this chapter—the further development by his modern Communist disciples, out of his false vision of a latter-day "monopoly capitalism," of their twisted theory of "capitalist imperialism," or aggressive pursuit by the advanced capitalist nations, at the demand and for the benefit of their own rich capitalists, of control of the resources and populations, markets, and investment opportunities of or in the underdeveloped nations in the world. Nor will I here discuss the small part of Marx's own system of thought which went beyond his vision and analysis of evolving capitalism and prediction of its "death," and dealt, very briefly and vaguely, with the question of how, beyond or after the revolution, the new and glorious socialist system was to be constructed, operated, and developed. The extremely little that Marx ever said about this is of no importance as compared with what the modern Communists where they are in power are doing about it; but perhaps the glaring contrast is worth a few words. Marx did envisage a destruction, by the victorious working class in its revolution, of the states and governments which he regarded as, in all capitalist countries no matter how nominally democratic their political systems might be, mere "executive committees" of the capitalist class as represented within those countries. He foresaw the creation by the revolting workers, to replace those states and governments, of temporary ones of a new kind—"dictatorships" of or by the "proletariat" or working-class population of each country—which would build and perfect the new socialist system in each, get it working perfectly, and then go out of existence or "wither away," leaving just the workers to cooperate in perfect freedom thereafter under no governmental coercion or control. But the dream of perfect order, harmony, and cooperation, unmarred by any dissents and conflicts, has (in the practice of the modern Communist regimes) naturally swallowed up the dream of perfect freedom for all individuals, and become a recipe for total despotism, since among free men there will always be conflicts if they are not suppressed. The element of utopianism in the thought of Marx was its greatest weakness, and the professed builders of his utopia are in fact building a hell. But apart from the streak of madness in the genius of Marx, which has fatally affected the character and results of his vast influence, there were in his intellectual output, as I have tried to show, many insights that are worth the efforts required to grasp them, and are of potential value to all inquiring minds regardless of their political views.

CHAPTER 12

Victorian Conservative Liberalism and Neo-Classical Economics

THE LATE NINETEENTH CENTURY'S RULING CLIMATE OF OPINION

The intellectual scenery now changes, abruptly and radically, as we turn our attention away from Marxism to the main new developments in our field of interest in the last few decades of the nineteenth century: the resurgence of the classical liberalism, which again became (with some new modifications), the ruling climate of opinion in the Western world; and the associated new advances of the main-traditional, liberal-and-scientific kind of economic theory. In fact the outlook that prevailed most widely in this final part of the nineteenth century—and on into the present century, down to the First World War—was not only extremely unlike the outlook of Marx. It was also, although less markedly, considerably unlike any of the diverse outlooks that had been widely prevalent, in different quarters, in earlier parts of the nineteenth century, and expressed or reflected in such diverse intellectual productions as the political economy of Malthus and Ricardo, romantic-conservative political philosophies, early (pre-Marxian) socialism, and the composite pattern of the views of J. S. Mill. And the changes, from the early and middle parts to the latter part of the century, of the background of prevailing, real economic and social conditions and popular attitudes undoubtedly helped to produce this change of the intellectual climate.

Until rather late in the nineteenth century, industrial capitalism, the bourgeois civilization, and democracy were all still young or incipient, immature, raw or crude, at once promising and disturbing, distress-laden, and diversely received, controversial affairs. Hence the times produced a wide range of rival philosophies and programs. At about the center of that range stood the classical liberalism—expressed as a whole most fully in Benthamism—and the liberal, classical political economy; but they were under strong and widespread, hostile, critical attacks from both sides—from romantic-conservative or reactionary critics to the "right" of them, and from the early radical prophets of socialism to the "left" of them. Moreover, even the liberal economists—Malthus, Ricardo, and their followers—presented a rather largely and deeply pessimistic view of the current operation, tendencies, and prospects of the liberal capitalist economy, and the current and prospective state or condition of society and the people. They thus expressed a sense of the existing and prospective evils, or widespread miseries, which was not entirely unlike the impressions that underlay and motivated those other rival creeds and gospels, even though the liberal economists alone regarded those evils as resulting from unalterable "laws of nature" and not from the liberal system or institutions, which they favored as the best attainable.

But later, when time and the further evolution of the modern Western societies had moved on into the last few decades of the nineteenth century, industrial capitalism and the business civilization and democracy had become well established, mature, successful, and much more generally or widely accepted. Prosperity was unmistakably both rising and spreading to more and more of all the people everywhere. The old European-conservative kind of opposition or resistance to the liberal-individualistic outlook and regime had declined or moderated to the point of making its peace with the latter and, so to speak, entering into a kind of synthesis or symbiosis with it, which modified it in a measure only. And the socialist outlook, although still flourishing and developing in its own circles, was now, for the time being, a less widely prevalent and potent, not immediately menacing, rather small minority affair. Thus the (slightly modified) classical liberalism as a general outlook or point of view not only was resurgent but attained the greatest degree of prevalence, secure predominance, and practical influence it has ever had. Moreover, the tone of most liberal thought was now again more optimistic, as it had been in the time of its origin, the late eighteenth century; the element of pessimism, which had been introduced by the views of Malthus and Ricardo, faded away. This again may be explained by the background change of real conditions. Population pressure was being relieved by the results of the opening up of great new areas of fertile land as sources of food for the European peoples, a rate of continuing technological and economic progress such as Malthus and Ricardo had by no means fully foreseen, and a falling birth rate. Thus events were *not* fulfilling Ricardo's gloomy forecast; the real wages of labor were rising generally, the rates of profit on new capital investments were not falling seriously, and the land-rent share of the value of output was not growing relatively or at the expense of the other income shares; and there was no sign of the approach to "the stationary state." Most important, in this new and more comfortable (for most people) state of the Western world, the earlier prevailing sense of the pervasive presence of inevitable, grim class conflicts over income-distribution tended to decline, and allow a full or nearly full renewal of the still earlier (eighteenth-century) faith in "the economic harmonies" in the "natural" operation of the liberal economy, that is, in the full conduciveness of a universal "free play" of individual self-interests (within the limits of liberal legal justice among all) to the economic and general welfare of all the people.

Furthermore, the liberal outlook in this period was optimistic in another way, which had not been fully paralleled in the eighteenth century: the idea of ever-on-going, all-around, inevitable, automatic, human-social *progress,* which had been "born" but not fully developed within the Enlightenment, and had been hardly able to develop freely or win general outright acceptance amid the troubled conditions prevalent in the earlier parts of the nineteenth century, now came into its own. I speak here in particular of the simple liberal theory of progress in that sense, which was unlike the Hegel-Marx theory of a tortuous, fluctuating, eventual progress through a series of alternating phases of improvement and deterioration, grim struggles or conflicts, wars or revolutions, new forward surges, and so on. The simpler and different liberal theory involved merely the idea of a rather steady or continuous cumulative growth and advance of all knowledge and wisdom or "enlightenment," and of application of that to all social problems, and hence progress in solving the latter or improving institutions and practices in all the ways shown by advancing knowledge to be needed to make them bring about the best results for human welfare. There was failure to realize the great limitations within which progress of that kind is confined; that it always has been clear-cut only in a restricted range of fields—the strict sciences and the techniques based on them, economic, "material" production, medicine and public health, etc.—and depends, even in these fields, on the presence of the right social and cultural conditions, thus far prevalent in human history only in the last few centuries of Western civilization, and by no means certain to become universal or endure forever. It was not realized that in the even more vital fields of aesthetic and ethical insight and achievement—prevailing discernment or appreciation, pursuit, and realization of the highest values, or wisdom in the choice of ultimate ends and thus in the use of all progressive knowledge or the knowledge that is power—that here such "progress" as there has been in history has been at best only occasionally recurrent through brief intervals, or highly fitful, and subject to frequent, long, disastrous declines or reversals; or in short that the chances of widespread and enduring achievements in this most vital sphere are always highly precarious.

Moreover, the much too simple and absolute, overoptimistic, late-nineteenth-century liberal theory of progress greatly exaggerated the power or ability of the best intellectual and spiritual achievements to control the actual conduct and course of practical affairs and the evolutions of societies. The dynamics of objective social evolution or history are extremely complex and still by no means fully understood by anyone; certainly they were not fully or correctly understood by Marx, though he had some insights absent from the liberal theory in question here. The effects of intellectual progress on social reality are subject to much counteraction and complication by developments running in the other direction, i.e., effects of changes of "material" conditions, through consequently prevailing attitudes, upon all intellectual and cultural life and achievement. The nonrational, emotional factors in all human behavior, and the power struggles among groups, classes, nations, etc., play important and often antiprogressive or progress-reversing roles which the liberal theory of progress never sufficiently allowed for. This phase of the optimism that was prevalent, to an extent now hardly conceivable, in the late nineteenth and very early twentieth centuries, has been rudely shattered since then by two world wars, and we live now in a world pervaded by a mood of pessimism verging on despair that I think is equally, in the opposite direction, excessive and unwarranted. In spite of all that I have said and all that needs to be said in adverse criticism of that confident, hopeful, progressive outlook, it is easy now to despise it much too completely and respect it much too little. It inspired much steady, intelligent work to help along all the progress believed in, and thus much progress was achieved.

THE CONSERVATIVE TINGE IN THE RENASCENT "LIBERALISM"

But now, having compared the renascent liberalism of this epoch with the original, late-eighteenth-century liberalism, with regard to the optimism that was present in both but made even more pronounced in the later version by its inclusion of the fully developed liberal theory of progress, I am going to compare and (in a measure) contrast the two in a different respect, in a way which may at first confuse the reader or seem to be in conflict with a part of what I have just said. As compared with the original eighteenth-century form of the classical liberalism, the revival-and-revision of it which was the late nineteenth century's ruling climate of opinion was, I think, in a not great but significant degree, less "radical" or more "conservative"—in a sense now to be explained. The liberal vision of the good society of free individuals was now (in the later period) less a vision of a new order still to be achieved through emancipative reforms or a throwing off of still existing and strong, old, traditional restraints; it was more nearly or largely just a favorable, theoretical depiction and celebration of an order thought of as already largely achieved or existing, or well on the way to full realization, and an armory of arguments in its defense, against new, incipient threats to it, arising from the advance of democracy and expanding activities of democratic governments, the growing strength and demands of labor or the working class, and the continuing socialist movements. But to clarify, explain, and defend all that I have in mind about this, I must say more about the historic meanings and relations of "liberalism" and "conservatism."

The expression "conservative liberalism" can seem self-contradictory only if one thinks, in the far too simple but common way, of "liberal" and "conservative" as words with simply, directly opposite meanings, i.e., of the "liberal" simply as the "progressive" person, favoring reforms or changes (of just any kind, or all kinds?), and of the "conservative" simply as the standpatter or opponent of all changes away from whatever is the *status quo* in his particular time and country. But the absolute relativism to which this leads makes little sense; e.g., it implies that, in a Communist country, the orthodox Communist is the true "conservative." And of course it has long been abundantly clear to the reader of this book that "liberalism" in the classical sense cannot be equated with reformism or progressivism of just any or every kind. Throughout its history or development, "liberalism" in this more definite sense has always been a particular vision of "the good society," mainly stressing its ideas of the proper liberties or freedoms of all individuals, which for everyone must be extensive but limited for the sake of the similar freedoms of all other men, and an equitable balance of the freedoms of all; and a scheme of institutions harmonizing the free activities of all, in pursuit of their own ends, with the requirements of their common welfare. Indeed, an ideal of progress also has always been inherent in this liberalism—but progress, first (from all older, nonliberal starting points) *to* the fullest possible realization of that vision; and then continuing progress mainly through free, private efforts and innovations by all in all departments of life, and competitive selection of many among those for general or widespread adoption and continuance; with later, new, institutional reforms or changes only as made necessary by emerging new conditions, for continuing realizations of the old, enduring, liberal ideals. This liberalism, then, was relatively "radical" in the contemporary setting when it first appeared as a fully formed and articulate "vision," in a still very nonliberal actual world, and implied or called for a sharp break with or away from the dominant nonliberal traditions; and the same liberalism became, in the altered setting of a later time, relatively more "conservative," when its "vision" was, or was being, largely realized. All this, however, still does not fully bring out my meaning in referring to "Victorian conservative liberalism"; let us look, next, at the also not very simple historic meaning of "conservatism."

The old European conservatism that was dominant most of the time through long ages before the Enlightenment, and resurgent for a time just after it, was rooted in the nonliberal conviction that extensive freedoms for all individuals would be certain to prove incompatible with, and would destroy, any good or tolerable *order* in society. For this outlook stressed the inequality or diversity or unlikeness of men, i.e., the existence, in many grades, of naturally superior and inferior kinds of men—as regards all kinds of intellectual, practical, and moral capabilities; and the necessity of control of inferiors by superiors, as the *sine qua non* for a well-ordered society. There must be firm government by an elite of the wise and good, a definite and (by all) accepted social hierarchy, fixed statuses and roles for all men, and strict subordination of all private individual desires to a common conception of "the common good" and the duties of all in relation to that, imposed by the ruling elite; in short, in this sense, an "organic" society. From Plato to Burke, this outlook in different forms had many great exponents. There is a clear contrast between its basic assumptions and those of liberalism, which stress the near-equality or similarity or "common human nature" of all men, and attribute to (nearly) all alike innate, potential capacities for adequate rationality and decency, or wisdom and virtue. Obviously the liberal assumptions lead to the liberal belief in the possibility and desirability of achieving and maintaining all needed order and harmony in society, through a free agreement and collaboration among all in developing and supporting the necessary institutions to make secure the freedoms of all, and justice among all, and the growth of a system of exchanges or mutual services aligning their private with their common interests. At the respective foundations of the two outlooks lie, above all, liberal optimism and conservative pessimism about the native mental and moral capacities of most men—all ordinary men—or "the many."

Now by no means all eighteenth-century liberals—advocates of a great enlargement of the individual liberties or freedoms of "the many," or a general abolition of most of the old conservative restrictions upon those—were *conscious* "radicals" in like degrees. Many did not at all fully realize how "radically" or greatly the old order might be transformed in the long run by the results of the carrying out of their program; for they tended to suppose that when all became "free," their behavior in most respects would change but little from what it had been under the traditional controls, which they regarded as simply unnecessary. In particular the structure or hierarchy of the social classes, and the roles and relations of and attitudes between the upper and lower classes, were not expected by many to be greatly changed. Even under the new conditions, of absence of the old compulsions, and freedom of all individuals to follow the dictates of their own interests or desires, there would still be leadership by those best qualified to lead, and sufficient, voluntary deference to them by the majority; for as intelligent and decent individuals, all would see their own interests as best served by these relations. The liberals in any case were not complete, extreme, all-out, or absolute libertarians in the manner of the anarchists; nor were they (generally) egalitarians like the socialists. The most moderate among them envisioned continuing, general, "free" acceptance of a social order on the whole more like than unlike the old familiar one, or involving only a few limited departures from it.

But in the early nineteenth century, the state of things became, in fact, greatly altered. Partly in consequence of the new individual freedoms and the uses made of them by growing numbers of self-made captains of industry, and workingmen, and others, and partly in consequence of changes of conditions which would have occurred to a great extent in any case, there appeared to most observers to have been a great growth of widespread distress, disorders, and disharmonies in the working of the "free" societies—new tensions and conflicts, and so on. Hence there were, in different quarters, the strong resurgence of the old conservatism, the growth of radical, utopian socialist dreams and agitations, and the tendency of even liberal thought to become strongly tinged with unwonted pessimism. The still later improvement of conditions, already described above, toward the latter part of the nineteenth century, brought about the revival of very widespread acceptance of the liberal outlook, and of its confident optimism; but the trial it had gone through, and the lasting effects of the earlier, renewed preaching of the old conservatism, left a mark upon it. The body of liberal-individualistic belief in the late nineteenth century, in the upper and middle strata in Western societies or among all the most influential people in them, was a liberalism that had absorbed and been modified by a little of the outlook of the old conservatism, so that it was a *relatively* conservative liberalism, *more consciously* than that of the late eighteenth century had been. The composition of the really governing class or classes had changed. The men of business and wealth, more than those of high birth, were now dominant; but they tended to imitate the old aristocracy or take on many of its attitudes and views, to believe in the right and duty of their class to exert the main influence in society and the state, and to consider it the duty of the members of the lower classes to accept subordination to them. At the same time, the growth of political democracy was transferring potential, predominant political power to those lower classes; hence the *laissez-faire* maxim of economic liberalism became primarily a demand that democratic governments be not allowed to enlarge their spheres of authority and activity, and invade or restrict the spheres of the independent authority of businessmen and organizations over their affairs and employees or subordinates, and/or do things contrary to their strong desires.

THE VARIETY OF VIEWPOINTS, ESPECIALLY AMONG "INTELLECTUALS"

Yet I must now immediately "qualify" that too simple or single account of *the* liberal outlook of this era, which rather describes the relatively most conservative variant, or part of the rather wide spectrum of differing "shades" that in fact coexisted in different quarters. The variant just described was indeed widely prevalent, especially among the rich and the men of business, but never universal even among them. In other quarters there were many exponents of other outlooks considerably unlike that—often much more universally and impartially humane-liberal, and progressive or reformist on various lines, and in some cases quite "radical." The very stability, security, confidence, and optimism that prevailed favored tolerance of dissent, and there were many viewpoints and much free discussion. My whole effort in the first part of this chapter, to portray the general climate of opinion of the era, is designed only as a prelude to discussion of the new developments, within it, of liberal-and-scientific economic theory, which were influenced by and related to that climate. But there were important differences, as I will hereafter indicate more fully, of the (varying) political views of the eminent economists who carried out those new developments, from the views or sentiments predominant in the business community and already generally characterized here. Nor were the economists alone in "deviating," in various ways and degrees, from the standpoint of just *that* body of conservative-liberal opinion. It is, for my purpose here, an awkward fact that systematic, broadly comprehensive, articulate, social-philosophical thinking and writing, or political theory in that sense, was already declining in this era, which produced few important political philosophers and, among them, fewer still who had much knowledge or understanding of or interest in economic problems and affairs as such. The on-going growth of intellectual specialization was further separating the newer developments of economic analysis, on the one hand, from those of political reflection, on the other, in some ways to the detriment of both. Hence most of the writings, by noneconomist intellectuals, in the broader field of general social, moral, and political philosophy, that I might refer to here, did not in fact have much clear relevance to the problems of main interest to us. But it may be worthwhile to refer very briefly in passing to a few such writers and their points of view.

Herbert Spencer's extreme individualism and antistatism, and "social Darwinist" theory of all social "evolution" (identified with "progress"), glorifying the unmoderated competitive struggle among men and groups and societies as "nature's" method of producing progress through innovations, conflicts, and "survival of the fittest," had a wide vogue among the successful and especially conservative, conservative-liberal businessmen and other people in this period. But Spencer went, in these matters, to an extreme position far beyond the views of most economic-liberal economists, and his outlook must not be confused with theirs. How far "liberal" thought, within this same era, could diverge or differ from Spencer's variety is well shown by the example of the Oxford political philosopher, T. H. Green, a humane-idealist reformer who wanted the state to do a great deal, to create and maintain for all men the conditions—involving many restrictions of their "freedoms" in the simplest, ordinary meaning of the word—under which all would be enabled and helped to develop in themselves the good human characters that would make them "free," in a deeper sense, from the inner compulsions of their evil passions, and from the frustrations the unwise run into. But Green's interesting philosophy, also, had little relevance to or connection with the liberalisms of the era's liberal political economists.

And the same must be said even of the different political ideas of the essayist, Walter Bagehot, despite the fact that Bagehot was himself a respectable economist in his way and on the side. His *Lombard Street,* a study of the workings of the London money market, deservedly became a classic in its field; and his short essay on *The Postulates of Political Economy* gave an excellent statement of the conditions and limits of the empirical validity of the traditional assumptions and resulting "laws" of economic theory. But Bagehot's social and political philosophy expressed a point of view and an array of insights which lay (alas!) beyond the mental horizons of this era's leading economic theorists. His political outlook was conservative-liberal (with the main accent on "conservative"), in a way or sense which meant that he and they had little in common. He had a fine blend of two different visions, not often combined. On the one hand, he had the Burkeian and romantic-conservative vision of the socially useful and necessary, though nonrational, emotional, and imaginative foundations of social unity or cohesion, order, and voluntary deference and loyalty from below upward, and responsible humaneness from above downward in the social hierarchy. And with that he combined the liberal-individualistic, rational and practical (economic and utilitarian) vision stressing free pursuits and fulfillments of and adjustments among the self-interests of all, in the competitive economy and in the political system of the democratic state, as they could work within the limiting, modifying, and protecting milieu of that other part of the spiritual, cultural, or moral, social order. Adam Smith could have understood Bagehot—indeed these two had much in common—but the fields of awareness of the liberal economists of this later time did not, I think, generally extend far into this other area. It is time now to turn to what can be said about *their* social philosophies or outlooks.[1]

THE POLITICAL AND POLICY IDEAS OF THE LIBERAL ECONOMISTS VERSUS THOSE OF THE BUSINESSMEN

Here the difficulty is that as a rule the social philosophies of the liberal economists were not made at all fully explicit in their writings. "Political economy" was already beginning to change—become contracted or narrowed down—into "economics"; economists were becoming more strictly specialized, or concentrating their efforts, with a new intensity, on just working out a full, precise, and rigorous development of their own body of abstract theory of the potential working, or processes, of the "free" and competitive business economy. Many of them indeed also made contributions to the kinds of empirical research connected with that, which were beginning to advance beyond the early rudimentary stages to more modern scientific forms or methods and achievements. But the main emphasis was still on theoretical research in economics; and the social-institutional ideals and assumptions or presuppositions of liberal-and-scientific economic theory tended as a rule, in the new development and expositions of the latter, to be more latent than explicit. But a glance at what generally *were* their explicit views on some particular issues about proper governmental economic policies will serve to bring out the rather wide distance separating their (more consistent) liberal ideals from those which were then dominant in the business community and generally in the ruling climate of opinion of that era.

The business community's and general public's form or version or understanding of economic (*laissez-faire*) liberalism was naturally not really self-consistent or fully in line with the authentic tradition of thought of the liberal political economists. For of course "practical" men have always tended to demand, simultaneously, ample freedoms

[1] For excellent short accounts and discussions (appropriately documented) of the varied "liberal" political philosophies of Spencer, Green, Bagehot, and other English writers of this period, see Crane Brinton, *English Political Thought in the Nineteenth Century* (Cambridge, Mass.: Harvard University Press, 1949), chap. 4.

for themselves, from public control of or interference with *their* acquisitive activities, *and* restrictions, for their protection or benefit, of the freedoms *of others* to invade their markets or fields of opportunity as new competitors on even terms. Hence the spread among the Western world's businessmen, after the age of mercantilism ended, of inclinations to support *laissez faire* in general never made them all supporters, e.g., of international free trade—or made this part of the consistent program generally popular among them, outside of mid-nineteenth-century England, where the special, local, and temporary situation of the English manufacturers of that time did lead them to support this also, in their own self-interests. But in other countries and very generally in this slightly later time of which I am speaking, tariff protectionism was, inconsistently, a part of the program of public policies strongly supported among businessmen devoted in (some) other respects to *laissez faire.* Nor was there in the business world ever a prevailing, full, consistent awareness of the fact, and the implications for public policy of the fact, that within each national economy there could be a real harmony of all private business interests with the common or public economic interest of that whole community only if the economy in question had in it no monopolies, and no impediments limiting the mobility of labor, capital, and resources of all kinds out of the less and into the more productive and demanded and rewarding fields of employment for them. Public policies designed to foster and maintain full prevalence of real, complete "free competition" in that sense, throughout each national economy, have always been included in the policy programs of the liberal economists, but were *not* generally supported by businessmen in this era. On the contrary, the latter generally wanted the governments of their countries and localities to not only tolerate but actively assist their efforts to achieve and maintain more or less monopolistic power positions for their enterprises, and put obstacles in the way of their would-be competitors. In short, they really wanted the state to be active in all the ways seen as helpful to their own business interests; and *laissez faire* to them meant only a ban against all the kinds of reform legislation or state intervention that were beginning to be demanded by spokesmen for labor, social service workers and reformers, discontented agrarian groups, etc.

Now the views of the leading "orthodox" economists of this same era, as to what public policies should be, were in almost complete opposition, on all these points, to the views prevailing in the dominant business and political circles. The economists continued, with virtually complete unanimity, to argue for complete freedom of international trade, or free development, and full use of the benefits, of the international division of labor. Also, they all realized and stressed the need for either nonexistence or public control of monopolies, and full mobility and "free competition," as the precondition of realization of "the economic harmonies." Hence, all at least opposed public policies or measures seen as aiding growth or maintenance of private monopolies; while many, especially in the United States, where governmental "antitrust" or antimonopoly legislation began to develop in this era, saw its consistency with the spirit of true economic liberalism, and strongly supported it. Nor did the economists *only* thus, in these two areas, of foreign-trade policy and policy with respect to domestic competition and monopolies, uphold the full, consistent, *laissez-faire* tradition and oppose the tendencies of business-community sentiment that were inconsistent with its applications in these areas. The economists or many of them also, in varying degrees, themselves departed from adherence to strict *laissez faire* in some of the other fields or directions in which the businessmen most strongly insisted on it, and supported many of the reforms most vigorously opposed in the business world. Among these were inspections of factories and mines and enforcement of laws to safeguard the health and safety of the workers; restrictive regulations of female labor and child labor, and compulsory education; workmen's compensation for industrial accidents and diseases; and legalization of previously illegal labor-union activities. Also they generally favored public regulation of the services and charges for the services of such both publicly essential and naturally monopolistic enterprises as the railroads and (later) light and power companies; and monetary policies that would allow adequate expansion of the supplies of money and credit along with the growth of production and trade, and be just to debtor as well as to creditor classes. All these and many other such issues found the leading economists, more often than not, aligned with the democratic, popular, and progressive reformist elements, and against the conservative businessmen. Thus, all in all, there was already in that time a tendency among the latter to regard the academic economists generally as "subversive radicals."

A few among the economic theorists of the time, moreover, gave still more ground for that charge against them by giving favorable theoretical consideration to the possibilities and possible merits of thoroughgoing socialism as a regime or system alternative to free and competitive capitalism. But these were exceptional; although the range of differing political views among the economists was fairly wide, the majority were firm believers in the liberal capitalist system and the program of liberal public economic policies already indicated here. Whether and how far my term "conservative liberal" applies to them is perhaps an open question; certainly they were as a rule much less "conservative" or more "progressive," perhaps even "radical" in many cases and on many issues, than were most of the businessmen and upper- and middle-class people of the time. But I think that on the whole the greater number of the eminent theoretical economists of this era *can* be classified as tending to be in slight degrees at least "conservative" liberals in their over-all social, moral, and political outlooks. They were adherents of the traditional liberal vision, of the good, "free" society and economy with its limited role for the state and large role for the "free play" of private interests and initiatives, competition, voluntary adjustments among individuals and groups, etc.; and adherents of that vision who thought it was on the way to progressively fuller realization in the world around them. Thus they viewed that world with considerable optimism, and argued for preservation of its essential features and against all really radical, socialist, and other programs for change away from them. There was often too little realization, by these economic theorists, of the real width of the gap between their ideals and those that were dominant in the business community and were exerting more influence than their own on the current evolution of the real, existing order. But I have said enough about all these matters; it is time to turn to the new developments, in this period, in or of economic theory itself.

"NEO-CLASSICAL" ECONOMIC THEORY; "MARGINAL ANALYSIS," OR "THE REVOLUTION" IN VALUE AND DISTRIBUTION THEORY

As I have said, this era (1870 to 1914) witnessed, along with renewed prevalence of the liberal ideology, a great renaissance, and array of new, further advances of economic theory of the main-traditional, liberal-and-scientific, general kind. There had been, as regards the progress of such theory, a relatively sterile interlude of about two decades after the first appearance of Mill's *Principles*. The Ricardian-classical theoretical system as expounded and improved by Mill had become, for all concerned with it, substantially a finished, static body of doctrine, repeated in the textbooks but no longer undergoing much further progressive growth and improvement. Outside the circle of its "orthodox" exponents, a good many other economists were dissatisfied with it, and various minor, scattered, and isolated theorists did produce, within that otherwise sterile interval of time, little-noticed studies which in various degrees and ways anticipated or resembled the new developments that were to conquer and dominate the field after 1870. In fact, the list of forerunners of those later developments runs much farther back, into the quite early nineteenth century. Diverse scattered writers in various countries, unconnected with the early classical school and unknown, until much later, to most economists, had done bits of work on the "mathematical" and "psychological" lines (see below) and had already made some of the same "discoveries," which were later independently renewed and more fully developed in the big theoretical "revolution" of the era that I speak of. Probably Von Thünen, Gossen, and Cournot[2] were the most important of those earlier forerunners; but the "revolution," i.e., its impact on the whole profession began when, in 1870–1871, W. S. Jevons in England, Karl Menger at the University of Vienna, Leon Walras in Switzerland (University of Lausanne), and (though he did not *publish* any of his work until much later) Alfred Marshall[3] at Cambridge, England, all about simultaneously, and independently of one another and of those forerunners, struck out on their differing individual variants of the new lines of economic-theoretical research involving, centrally, what came to be known as "the marginal utility theory of value."

As it appears now in retrospect, the total movement which thus began exhibits as a whole a striking unity-in-variety. In all it produced or included a large "family" of similar-and-different systems of economic theory, created in different countries and centers by different economists and "schools" or groups of them, as schemes of analysis differing among themselves in many important detailed respects, but all involving, in a broad sense, the same general theoretical vision. Although in the following classification which in part is rather arbitrary, some of the groupings make less sense—have more internal diversity and less distinctive characters *as* entire groups—than others, one may perhaps speak of the Jevonian, Austrian, Walrasian, Scandinavian, American, and Marshallian "schools," or varieties or variants of the "new" kind of economic theory, of this era.

W. S. Jevons led the way in England, and the later English theorists whose styles and views most nearly resembled his and who may perhaps be grouped with him or called "Jevonian"—even though these two were in many ways unlike each other and unlike Jevons, and though all three were equally brilliant, original, and independent—were Philip Wicksteed and F. Y. Edgeworth. Meanwhile, in Austria, at the University of Vienna, there came on the scene at the same time with Jevons, but of course independently—these men and Jevons at first knew nothing of each other's work or ideas—the trio of first-generation leaders of the famous, still continuing, "Austrian school" of economists, Karl Menger, Eugene von Böhm-Bawerk, and Frederick von Wieser. Meanwhile again, at Lausanne, Walras—at the same time with Jevons and

[2] If any curious reader to whom those three names—Von Thünen, Gossen, and Cournot—mean little or nothing, will take the trouble to look them up in J. A. Schumpeter's *History of Economic Analysis* (New York: Oxford University Press, 1954)—using the "index of authors" at the end of that work, to find the three names and the page references under them to all the passages giving information about the three men and their works and ideas, and then reading the main passages cited—he will learn a good deal about all three, and their relations to the later developments of theory I discuss in this chapter.

[3] For fuller information about these four men—Jevons, Menger, Walras, and Marshall—and their works and contributions, see *ibid.*

with Menger et al., but again in complete independence and isolation from them all—was producing *his* unique and impressive system of economic theory which, however, was to gain any wide vogue or influence only in a later time and slowly, because it was fully "mathematical" in substance *and* expression, and intricate and difficult, and hence was at first and long remained beyond the reach or ready comprehension of most economists. "Walrasian" theory did fairly soon begin to spread among Continental European economists of diverse nationalities, and find here and there among them various able adherents and exponents who went on improving it and adding to it or developing it further on their own lines; and the ablest of all these later Walrasians was the great Italian figure, Vilfredo Pareto. In the English-speaking world, Walrasian (and Paretian) economics have only quite recently begun to be really widely studied and appreciated. But we are only halfway through my list of six general "groupings" of the great economic theorists of the last decades of the nineteenth century.

In the Scandinavian countries, two Swedish leaders became most widely known and influential, beyond as well as within those countries: the earlier and greater of these two was Knut Wicksell, and the later and less original, Gustav Cassell; but there have been many others in that able group. In the United States, the important theorists in the era that I speak of were fairly numerous and diverse and do not all belong in any single "school." J. B. Clark, F. W. Fetter, T. N. Carver, H. J. Davenport, and others developed systems considerably resembling that of "the Austrian school" and somewhat indebted to it, though each had much originality. F. W. Taussig remained, as a theorist, closer than others to the old, classical, Ricardo-Mill tradition, and only half absorbed or accepted the "new" ideas of his generation; but he had great wisdom, produced much good work, and taught and formed a great many younger American economists of outstanding merit. Irving Fisher stood out as the one great American *mathematical* economist—on his own, not Walrasian, lines. And now having glanced at all these groups I circle back to England and speak last of Alfred Marshall (of Cambridge University) and his pupils, admirers, and followers, the "Marshallian" school. This makes sense because Marshall, though he started to form his own system back in the time of the first appearance and impact of the work of Jevons, and included in it ideas similar to those of Jevons though arrived at independently, did not publish any of his main work or make his system as such known beyond the small circle of his Cambridge pupils until much later—1890—so that all the other "schools" I have mentioned were already flourishing before his emerged, so to speak, onto the world's stage. As we shall see hereafter, the Marshallian system was in some ways a broad "synthesis," combining elements or features of several of the other "new" ones of this era *and* of the old

Ricardian-classical tradition generally, more fully discarded in the other "new" schools.

Now I shall adopt here a doubtless arbitrary and criticizable, but fairly common and convenient, usage of the terms *classical* and *neo-classical* for designating general types of economic theory, and use these terms as follows. By the "classical" theory of economics I mean the old, early-nineteenth-century theoretical structure which was created mainly by Ricardo, and given on the whole its best full formulation or elaboration, with his own (Mill's) revisions and additions, in J. S. Mill's *Principles*. And I use the term "neo-classical" in two different senses: in a very broad sense, *all* the diverse, late-nineteenth-century theoretical structures, that I have referred to, can, I think, be called "neo-classical"; whereas the Marshallian system, alone or uniquely, was "neo-classical" also in a narrower, special, strict, and emphatic sense.

The Jevonians, Austrians, Walrasians, and Americans (with the exception of Taussig), and generally the Scandinavians (partially excepting Wicksell) were prone to lay exclusive stress on their disagreements with and departures from the Ricardian-classical tradition, and regard their innovations or new concepts and analyses as making up a complete intellectual "revolution" or "new economics," having very little in common with the old Ricardian-classical economics. But this I think resulted in all these cases from a too narrow or exclusive concentration of attention on the (indeed important) issues, questions, or matters of relatively detailed and technical, conceptual and logical significance, involved in all the innovations or new advances; and from a tendency to "take for granted" and not fully realize the large amount of continuity that was there at the same time, as regards the broad, basic, underlying *general outlook* that was—with some changes even here indeed, but largely—carried on. All (in the broad sense) "neo-classical" economic theory had in common with the old Ricardian-classical type of theory, in the first place, the economic-liberal outlook and hence the same general conception of the province or field and over-all task of economic theory as such, i.e., to develop a full understanding or explanation of the abstract general "laws" or "principles" of the operation, functioning, or processes of the liberal economy, or system of "free," private, producing enterprises and consuming households and competitive markets. And this carried with it, also, continuing work on much the same range of theoretical problems, concerning the "determinants" and modes of "determination," in the working of that system, of the exchange values or relative prices of the different products, the changing allocation of all productive efforts and resources into different employments and resulting outputs or supplies of the different products, and the "distribution" or division of all income, or the value of all output, into the "shares" going as wages, profits, interest, rent, etc., to the contributors of the different kinds of "factors of production" or productive services. In all the varieties of "neo-classical" theory, new and different and generally superior *analyses* of these problems were developed, with the aid of new "conceptual tools" and reasonings, which led to largely or partly new and more "correct" and fuller "solutions" of the old problems. But there was to a great extent retention or continuation of the early "classical" vision of the general character, structure, and mode of operation of the liberal economy, and of the array and the interrelations of the main problems which should be investigated. Among all the "neo-classical" systems in *that* sense, the Marshallian system was "neo-classical" *also in the special sense that* it retained or carried on, and combined with (Marshall's version of) the "new" ideas, important elements of the old Ricardian-classical, distinctive *analytical* scheme, which the other "new schools" either wholly or more largely discarded.

All of the "new schools" together achieved a very considerable advancement or improvement of the science *on* its abstract and "technical," conceptual and logical or theoretical side; an advance beyond the primitive or rudimentary, Ricardian-classical theoretical analysis of economics, which had achieved little more than a relatively clear and systematic formulation of "common-sense" ideas about the subject matter, to a much more truly or fully "scientific" kind of analysis. The latter, in other words, was more fully precise and rigorous, thorough, penetrating, and logically unified, and could yield many insights *not* readily evident or available to the "common sense" of generally informed and intelligent but not specially trained or mentally equipped observers of and reasoners about economic affairs. There was still not very much truly scientific *empirical* research in economics, or effective work toward making the inquiry an empirical as well as a logical science; but the advances made in this era in theoretical research were also required and useful steps toward making more scientific empirical research possible later on. Yet along with all the real and important gains or advances that were achieved, there was I think a partly offsetting loss of some of the somewhat greater or relative "realism" in a meaningful sense, which Ricardian-classical theory, with all its crudity and deficiencies, had possessed. Although the latter had not spelled out so well, with full precision and logical rigor, all the implications of its basic insights; it had embodied on the whole a better intuitive grasp of the most important factors and connections in the real processes of the operation and development of the real economy. The "neo-classical" systems, in the process of improving theory as such, made it more abstract; and the new preoccupation with the work of perfecting the conceptual and logical details of the analysis, and working out all the exact implications of various possible sets of assumptions, or conceptual visions of imaginable situations, entailed a partial withdrawal of attention from the effort to form and adhere to a realistic vision of the real world.

Moreover, there was also, in neo-classical as compared with the old classical theory, an increased and excessive concentration on just "value and distribution" theory, or analysis of the competitive market system's way of determining the relative prices of the economy's different products, and productive services and resources, and allocating the latter among different industries. There was no adequate continuing development of "aggregative" theory, of the whole economy's total output or income and the places and relations within that of total consumption, saving, investment, etc.; and theory of economic growth or development. Perhaps, however, all these limitations of "neo-classical" economic theory were or made up only the unavoidable and not excessive "price" of all its new, real, and great achievements, which on the whole outweighed them. And it would be futile to deplore the fact that the new advances made economic theory, as it had not been in earlier times, too intricate, "technical," and esoteric to be readily intelligible to a very wide public; although this change probably reduced its influence on public opinion and actual governmental economic policies. For of course the "science" still did not gain enough prestige to make the public willing to accept the recommendations of economists *without* understanding the analyses behind them. Economics had to go through this phase of its development, which was of more value for its still later, further progress than for its current usefulness within this era.

Now I turn to consideration of the two main aspects of the innovations or novel elements in neo-classical as compared with Ricardian-classical economic theory. In a sense all these innovations were mathematical in form, i.e., in their conceptual and logical nature—even when expressed in ordinary language, not in the special "language" of mathematics. And in substance the most important substantive innovations were in a sense "psychological," i.e., were comprised in the new analysis of "utility" or all the human wants and satisfactions, subjective feelings, and comparative estimates of the amounts of "utility" of different goods or goals or gains, or in short "motives," thought of as underlying, producing, and directing human economic behavior. In other words, on its formal side, all the "new" economic theory systematically carried out—although often entirely or mainly in ordinary verbal language—applications of the concepts and logic of integral and differential calculus to the task of analyzing the relations among the changes of variable economic quantities—"inputs" of work and of other resources in production and "outputs" of products, and market supplies, demands, prices, costs, incomes, spendings, savings, investments, etc. And with the help of this new conceptual and logical apparatus, as applied in this particular field, the attempt was made to analyze fully

—as Ricardian-classical theory had not tried to analyze—the psychological or subjective backgrounds of consumers' demands, and evaluations of products, and the backgrounds in the same sense of all economic choices or decisions and actions; *as well as* greatly to improve on the older "classical" analysis of the other, not human-psychological, but physical or material part of the economic subject matter—the relations among the changes of the "tangible, objective" economic quantities or variables.

THE MATHEMATICAL ASPECT

On its formal side then, all "neo-classical" economics represented an early stage of the long, slow development, which still is going on today, of "mathematical economics" or what may be called a gradual "mathematicization" of economic theory. Yet in a sense the real origins or "roots" of this development are very old; only the "fruits" have been slow to appear and "ripen." To a great extent many of the central problems of all economic theory always have been, in one aspect, mathematical in kind or nature, i.e., problems *needing* to be studied with the aid of mathematics. Thus there were already gropings and anticipations in this direction in quite early times and by economists with no command of any mathematics beyond arithmetic. To go no farther back, the Ricardian-classical "law of diminishing returns" of additional produce from more intensive cultivation of agricultural land was an insight which really needed, for its proper statement, a simple use of differential calculus; though Ricardo and the Ricardians could only explain it clumsily, in words and with the aid of arithmetical illustrations. And in fact *that* "law of diminishing returns" was only a special case of a much more general principle, the elaboration of which in all its bearings came to pervade, and make up a great part of, all "neo-classical" economic theory. Moreover, another indication of the real shortness of the distance separating "classical" economic theory from the later growth of "mathematical" economic theory, is the fact that Malthus, of all men, foresaw the latter and expressed his belief that "fluxions" (as the branch of mathematics that is now called "calculus" was called then) would someday come into use in economics, as it already was in physics and other sciences. Nor were the first steps toward the fulfillment of that prediction long in coming, though they came in other circles unknown to Malthus and Ricardo. In all a good many scattered mathematicians and economists produced significant pieces of work in mathematical economics within the first half of the nineteenth century. The most important of them all, probably, was the French mathematician Cournot, whose *Mathematical Theory of Wealth,* published in 1830, was later to influence Marshall and others. But the modern growth and general spread, among all economists, of the vogue of this kind of work, to the point of causing most young economists to feel that they must become equipped and able to take part in it, was long delayed and has been slow.

Thus there were great differences among the various leading late-nineteenth-century theorists already mentioned here as regards the senses and degrees in which their works were "mathematical." Jevons strongly urged his view that the science was inherently mathematical in nature and must become so overtly, or be developed with full use of all the relevant mathematical aids to both research and exposition; and he tried in his own work to make full use of his rather limited knowledge or command of mathematics. Although he was a brilliant economist and theorist, his limitations on the mathematical side were such that—so a competent judge,[4] with a high opinion of his work, has said—a skilled reader of his writings can see that he evidently had to do his economic-theoretical thinking "in English" (not in mathematics), first, and then "translate" it, or a few parts of it, rather painfully and awkwardly, into mathematical formulations. On the other hand, the same authority has said that the converse of that procedure was the practice of Alfred Marshall. A first-rate mathematician and a great economist, Marshall *thought out* his system mathematically, but then expressed or presented it mainly and as far as possible—wholly in his main text—in ordinary verbal language, "hiding away" all his supplementary mathematical formulations in footnotes and appendixes, in order to avoid "scaring away" otherwise qualified but not mathematically equipped readers, and to make his work attractive and intelligible to a wide public of businessmen and other "lay" citizens as well as economists and scholars of all kinds.

Nor does this contrast between Jevons and Marshall indicate by any means the full range of the variety of attitudes, abilities, and practices among the "neo-classical" economists. The members of the Austrian school completely avoided any overt use of mathematics, and performed extraordinary feats of complete, thorough, lucid exposition of their analyses in ordinary verbal language; although in essence their ideas and reasonings were mathematical, and could have been presented in mathematical "language" with far greater economy as compared with the prolix or repetitive verbal expositions needed to fully clarify and "drive home" their points. Again in complete contrast, the work or system of Walras was uniquely and fully mathematical in both conception

[4] I am referring to Allyn A. Young, who, during the 1920s, was a Professor of Economics at Harvard and at the London School of Economics (where he died, though still only in his late fifties in age). I was a graduate student under him at Harvard, and remember these statements about Jevons and Marshall in his lectures to us then; as far as I know they appear in none of his published writings.

and development, and presentation—using sets of simultaneous equations to display the general forms of the relations of interdependence among all economic variables. The Walrasian system long stood almost alone as representing "mathematical economics" par excellence, and in consequence the system long had, among economists in general, a quite limited receptive "public." Apart from it, some works by Irving Fisher, a very few other economists of this era, and the "real" Marshallian system as fully understood only by the few fully, mathematically equipped students of it—most of the literature of economic theory produced in this era was not, or hardly, on its face, "mathematical" at all. Simple graphs—demand, supply, and cost curves, and the like—appeared in all or most theoretical treatises and textbooks, but that as a rule was the only "mathematics" used in exposition or presentation. However, the common, prevalent body of "conceptual tools" and reasonings was, to repeat this point, in real essence mathematical all the same—a set of applications of those used in differential calculus—even though they were generally expressed only in verbal language.

Since that era, down to the present day, the continuing development of mathematical economics in countless newer forms has gone far beyond all that was known or conceived in the time of the "neo-classical" systems. But because the latter did represent the virtual beginnings—in the bulk of the literature—of this kind of work or economic thinking, and do need appraisal in this aspect or respect, among others, I venture to present here a few words of comment on the value and limitations of mathematical economics, as I see it. I am sure that this kind of work does have an important place and value as *one* of the kinds of investigative work to be carried on by economists. It is the best way of doing the useful things it does do—with intellectual economy and full precision, rigor, and thoroughness; and no doubt in many of its more advanced developments, it is the *only* way of dealing at all with the problems therein considered. Some of the deficiencies that are often present in such work only reflect the still transitional state of the profession in this matter, or the fact that not all economists who try to work in this way or field are adequately equipped as *both* economists *and* mathematicians. Too often, those who are really good mathematicians are not very good economists, and vice versa. Able mathematicians generally, it has often been noticed, "mature" as such or reach the "peak" of their powers as mathematicians while still quite young—since this is purely a matter of developing and exercising intellectual ability, and not at all a matter of acquiring experience and knowledge of "the real world." But mastery of economics—of its real subject matter—requires accumulation of experience and knowledge, and growth of personal maturity and wisdom through the greater part of one's lifetime. The good, mature economist, who did not become a good mathematician in his youth, generally finds it extremely difficult or impossible to do so by starting late in life. On the other hand, the brilliant young mathematician and mathematical economist may in some cases never become in all respects a really good economist, because for him it may be easy to attain high prestige without ever learning much about the real economic subject matter. It can be easy and fascinating to play all kinds of intellectual games with arbitrarily devised and chosen sets of postulates and reasonings having little relevance to any social-economic realities and real problems; and within a profession in which many of the members are easily overawed by such mathematical-intellectual performances, they may bring a false prestige resulting from the human tendency to confuse exact knowledge of the implications of ideas or propositions with exact knowledge of substantial truths about the real, empirical world.

The developments, which are going on today, of scientific (mainly statistical) empirical research in economics, and fruitful unions and reciprocal interactions of these with mathematical-theoretical research hold greater promise. But in my opinion even this kind of work can never become more than one small part of all the investigative work and thinking which should be carried on by economists. Aside from the transitional difficulty already mentioned, there are permanent or inherent limitations of or around the important value of all mathematical economics, even when it is combined with or includes statistical research and is thus in its own way or sense empirical as well as theoretical. All good work of this kind helps to meet important real needs and I do not mean to belittle it. But I think there are and will always be other equally great needs for studies and reflections of quite other kinds, concerned with the nonmeasurable and not even conceptually quantitative, intangible, elusive "human elements" of the economic subject matter and the complete human-social contexts within which it always occurs; and with all the values, of all kinds (aesthetic and ethical as well as economic) which are at stake in all human, private and public, action or conduct. These very extensive and supremely important parts of the subject matter that should properly concern all economists are of such a nature that they necessarily elude the grip of all mathematical and indeed all strictly scientific, intellectual machinery; but the tendency to exclude them, on that ground, from the field of the economist's interests is I think a radical and tragic error.

Achieving in the study of economics and political economy a well-balanced union of all of the appropriate mathematical and statistical work, with all the appropriate work of other kinds—in economic psychology and sociology, economic and general history, and general and social, moral, and political philosophy—achieving this is not easy. It never has been done ideally well, and the modern trends in intellectual life lead mainly away from it, but I think it remains the supreme need and proper ideal of the inquiry.

THE PSYCHOLOGICAL ASPECT

In a sense the "neo-classical" phase of the history or development of economic theory involved not only the beginning of the still continuing, progressive "mathematicization" of much economic theory, but also the beginning of the trend, which I have just been deploring, toward general prevalence of the mistaken view or supposition that *all* economic theory could be made mathematical in nature, or reduced entirely to precise and rigorous, logical theorizing about, only, the relations among economic quantities or variables and among their changes. And this I think was responsible for the limitations (as well as the achievements) of the so-called "psychological" part or aspect of all neo-classical theory—the new "utility analysis" which played so great a role within it. There is almost a paradox in the dual contrast between Ricardian-classical and neo-classical economics. The former, although it lacked the latter's calculus-born conceptual tools, gave most of its attention to the related changes of the objective, physical-quantitative, economic variables and, though in a general way recognizing and assuming the existence and roles of the subjective-value or "utility" variables, had very little to say about them. The neo-classical theory, on the other hand, applied its new conceptual tools first of all to the task of analyzing the behavior of those subjective variables, and stressed this part of its work as its most fundamental new achievement and the very basis of its renovation of the science. It often tended even to reverse the Ricardian-classical one-sidedness or go too far toward the opposite extreme, i.e., give insufficient attention to the purely objective part or side of the subject matter—although the new conceptual tools were really more fully adequate for study of the latter. It is true, however, that the new (calculus) concepts were also needed for achieving, and in this use did achieve or yield, a systematic, general, abstract, or formal analysis of the "quantitative" variations of experienced "utility" or want-satisfactions with the physical quantities of desired goods or services acquired and enjoyed; and the general forms of the patterns of the economic choices and behavior of all human actors in the economy, in their various situations, which would maximize their satisfactions; and the effects of such human behavior on the "behavior" of all market demands, prices, supply adjustments, etc., or the functioning of the economy. And all this "utility analysis" had real validity and a substantial though limited significance and value, as far as it went. It was a real gain for economic science to be thus enabled to resolve the old, false "paradox of value," or to discover and establish the real relations of dependence of exchange values or prices on use values or the relations of the things priced, to human wants and satisfactions; and to get some new light on not only the effects of human actions on the physical variables, but the responses *to* the latter, the motivation, and the likely directions of the human actions themselves. But the narrow limitations of the real significance of the new "psychological" part or component thus introduced into economic theory must be fully recognized, as they generally were not in the heyday of neo-classical theory.

As "psychology" this merely formal, abstract analysis of the diminishing intensities of "wants" as they become more nearly satisfied, and the patterns of allocation and use of incomes or resources required to maximize men's total satisfactions of their constellations of "wants" of all kinds—as "psychology" it is all very superficial. It is only an extremely simple and abstract schema which conveys virtually no information about or insights into men's specific psychological make-ups and processes and behavior-patterns, or the sources and likely developments and changes of particular "wants," etc. Moreover, the ambiguous notion of "rational" behavior involved in that of "maximizing satisfactions" made it too easy to confuse the "psychology" with the logic involved in the analysis, and either falsely impute a real and significant, ideal "rationality" to all actual economic behavior or else, as the one sure way of avoiding that error, so define the terms and construe the analysis as to make it simply tautological, and hence "true" about all possible behavior, and entirely devoid of information about any actual behavior. Too often, the neo-classical theorists did both of those things at different points in their discussions. First, they carefully used the safe or neutral, tautological version of this theory about human wants, behavior, and satisfactions, as long as they were engaged only in "explaining" (not evaluating) the operation of the economic system. But then, in arguing the case for economic liberalism or faith in the virtues of the "free" competitive system, they slipped into the assumption that all actors in it would behave with perfect, real "rationality" in their own best interests. Thus they reached the conclusion that the system would work perfectly to maximize the economic welfare of the population. Nor is the normative interpretation of this formal theory of "rational," utility-maximizing conduct any more useful than its positive interpretation as a formal analysis of actual behavior. The positive economist needs to make real psychological studies, and the "welfare" economist needs to work out real, reflective, and consistent "value-judgments." Both need to go beyond the mere introduction to these provinces afforded by the utility calculus, on further into these provinces themselves, where in great degrees the logical security but empirical (experimental) emptiness of mathematics must give way to vague, insecure gropings for more substantial and specific though unavoidably less precise knowledge and wisdom.

SPECIFIC CHANGES OF ECONOMIC "DOCTRINES"

From all these general comments, however, on the achievements and the limitations of the "mathematical" and the "psychological" aspects of all that was "new" in neo-classical as compared with Ricardian-classical economic theory, I turn now, finally, to a different, over-all comparison of the old and new systems of economic "doctrines." In trying to discover the general "laws" and results of the "natural" operation or functioning of the free and competitive business economy, Ricardian-classical theory had started with considerations about the national economy's aggregate supplies of land, labor, and capital, including the fixity of the supply of land and the tendencies of the labor and capital supplies to grow as long as the resulting growth of output and the real wages and profit shares of that enabled them to do so. Attention was fixed primarily on the physical production of material goods, the ratios of the outputs to the required inputs of labor and capital, and the tendency (with given techniques of production) of those ratios to fall (in agriculture) as the land became more crowded; and this basic vision yielded, together, a theory of production and a directly connected theory of income-distribution or the wages, profit, and land-rent shares of the national output. The theory of "exchange" and the relative values or prices of the different products then appeared only as the final part of the analysis. Here again, as the magnitudes and changes of the public's demands for the different products were merely assumed, with no effort to explain or analyze them or their "psychological" backgrounds in consumers' wants and subjective evaluations or utility estimates, the stress was all on the adjustments of the supplies of products *to* the market demands whatever those might be, and—as in the end controlling these adjustments—the *physical* determinants of production costs ("costs" considered as inverse to physical efficiency in production), i.e., the required inputs of labor-time and real resources represented by the final or last-added units of the equilibrium supplies or outputs of the different products.

Now in contrast with all that, neo-classical theory of the economy's functioning began with consumers' wants for and evaluations of and demands for the final products—the "utility analysis" of the subjective backgrounds of market demands and market-or-demand prices, not attempted in Ricardian-classical theory. And from this new starting point, the neo-classical theory proceeded in the opposite direction, or reversed the field. From the demand prices (for given supplies) of the different products, the new analysis derived the demand prices for the productive services, in the production of those products, of the workers, capital, and land employed, and thus moved from the subject of "value" into that of income-distribution, instead of doing the reverse. This also led to the view that all "costs of production" are in their main aspect "opportunity costs," i.e., the payments which the producers of each product have to make for the productive services, of all kinds, which they hire and use, depend upon or must equal the alternative opportunities or possible earnings of the recipients, in other industries, which in turn depend upon the demand prices, in the markets, for the other products. The competitive equilibrium adjustments of the outputs and supplies of the different products to the demands for them would, it was said, indeed make their selling prices equal to the costs of producing them. But the latter, made up in each case of the payments for productive services, made necessary by the selling prices of the other products, could not be regarded as independent causes or determinants of the selling prices of those particular products. The demands in the economy for all its different products, and the resulting, rival demands for the productive services of its limited supplies of all factors of production, would determine both the prices of the products and those of the productive services, hence also the costs of producing the products.

This argument, however, though of course valid in its own field of reference, and implicitly recognized in Ricardian-classical theory, was no argument against—did not join issue with—the real thesis of the latter's value theory, which in its view of the price-determining role of production cost had reference not to the prices but to the quantities of the productive services "embodied" in a unit of each product. The two theories or views on this general question were really not inconsistent but complementary—each stressed the part of the complete answer which the other "took for granted." But neo-classical theory did lead to a better logical unification of "value and distribution" theory, or theory of the working of the price system in the "pricing" both of products and of the services of the different factors of production. And in the latter field, by generalizing the old "law of diminishing returns" into a law of decline of the "marginal productivity," and demand price for the services, of *any* factor whenever the supply of it increases relative to the available supplies of the other factors, the neo-classical analysis in a sense ended in the area in which Ricardo's started, but with a more symmetrical and flexible or, in short, general view of the problems in that area.

Yet here again the one-sided stress on productivity and demand, in contrast with Ricardo's stress on cost and supply conditions, led to a different delimitation of the field of inquiry. In Ricardo's theory of income-distribution, the supply of labor was expected to increase to the point of reducing its real wages to the "subsistence" level—the "cost of production" of that labor supply—and the supply of capital, likewise, was expected to increase until the rate of profit or interest would fall so low that no more accumulation would occur; only in the case of land-rent would the changes of "demand" have the decisive influence, since the supply of land is fixed and without any cost of production. But in neo-classical theory the tendency was strong to ignore or rule out the problems of the ultimate "supply prices" for labor and capital, and extend Ricardo's view of land and rent to all the factors and income shares, i.e., to regard the aggregate supply of every factor in the whole economy as simply "given" at each point of time and not to be explained by economic theory, and to consider productivity and demand conditions only, in "explaining" income-distribution. This in a way corresponds to the contrast, at the other "end" of the entire route traversed in opposite directions by the two types of theory, of the Ricardian neglect of, and the neo-classical stress on, the foundations of demands for the final products; as the neo-classicists added what Ricardo omitted at that "end," they omitted what he mainly emphasized at the other "end." But my generalizations in this chapter about "neo-classical" theory have referred to all its varieties *except* the Marshallian one—which largely retained many of the Ricardian elements omitted in the others and was thus a "synthesis"; and to this I now turn, in the next chapter.

CHAPTER 13

Marshallian Economics

INTRODUCTORY

Among the great late-nineteenth-century economic theorists who were mentioned in the last chapter, Alfred Marshall emerged or stood out finally as perhaps the most eminent and widely influential single figure, at least within the English-speaking world. Hence it seems not inappropriate to present now, after the merely general survey of the whole, broader movement that has just been offered, a more detailed examination of the particular system of economic theory erected by Marshall—England's, if not the world's, greatest economist of his generation. In the entire historic line of the great British economists, moreover, Marshall, I think, belongs in the company of Adam Smith and John Stuart Mill; that is, the qualities and merits of his work were more or less equal, and in some ways similar, to those of their works. The more advanced and technical or esoteric nature of Marshall's work as a theorist meant that it could not directly reach and influence so wide a public as had been directly impressed by the *Wealth of Nations* and Mill's *Principles*. But along with his new, more intricate, theoretical analysis, evolved with the aid of higher mathematics, Marshall had also, in common with Smith and with Mill, a similarly wide range of interests and knowledge, great breadth of outlook or vision, and depth as well as breadth of knowledge and wisdom; and he strove, with no little success, to communicate it all to as many other professional and "lay" minds as possible.

Marshall's family forebears were substantial businessmen and dissenting or nonconformist men of faith and piety, and he retained much of the special kind of ethical outlook or convictions that derived from that background. He believed in both the economic and the ethical merits or virtues of a civilized, free, and competitive capitalism or economic "system of free enterprise"—that is, he valued such a system not only for its superior economic efficiency but, still more, for its healthy, disciplinary, moral influence on the characters of all the human individuals at work within it. And in his writings he continually mingled much "Victorian moralizing" with his positive scientific theory or analysis of the economy's functioning.[1] But he also brought to his work a wide knowledge of philosophy, the natural and "moral" sciences, history, and mathematics; and he achieved in his work in economics not only his great theoretical system and insights, but also a large amount of detailed empirical and realistic knowledge of the English industrial and business world of his time. He was also very well versed in the history and historic literature of economic theory, including especially both the earlier "classical" political economy and all the newer advances beyond that which were maturing in his time and to which he made his own contributions.

Along with Jevons, Menger, and Walras, Marshall was the fourth independent originator of "the marginal utility theory of value" and the entire "revolution in value and distribution theory," though he delayed the publication of his version of those new ideas for almost two decades, and was meanwhile developing and circulating them only in "the Cambridge oral tradition."[2] Unlike the other leaders in the new movement, he did not regard it as a complete intellectual "revolution" in the science, or a complete new theory of economics which should or could entirely displace or replace the old Ricardian-classical theory; instead it seemed to him to lead, properly, only to some revisions of and additions to that. There was also one other respect in which he differed from both his forerunners and his contemporaries among economic theorists, in his outlook as a theorist, or in his conception of the proper nature and role of theory as one part of the work of economists: more distinctly than others, he introduced the idea that a system of theory should be thought of as only an "organon"—an apparatus of conceptual and logical "tools" for use in continuing, both theoretical and empirical, research—and not as a system of fixed and final doctrines or established truths.

I shall attempt no more here than a review of some parts of Marshall's *Principles*—the book that presented by no means all, but the most important part of, his work.[3] At the outset of that book he defined the

[1] I put the phrase "Victorian moralizing" in quotation marks because it was used —with strong overtones of disparagement and protest—by the late Professor J. A. Schumpeter, in characterizing and discussing Marshall's work. See his extensive half-laudatory and half-adversely critical treatment of the latter in his *History of Economic Analysis* (New York: Oxford University Press, 1954), *passim.*

[2] See the memorial article on Marshall by his distinguished pupil, J. M. Keynes, in *Memorials of Alfred Marshall,* A. C. Pigou (ed.) (London: Macmillan and Co., Ltd., 1925), and also in Keynes' *Essays in Biography* (New York: Harcourt, Brace and Company, Inc., 1933).

[3] Alfred Marshall, *Principles of Economics,* 8th ed. (London: Macmillan and Co., Ltd., 1922).

field or "scope" of economics, as he thought of it, very broadly and rather vaguely: economics, he said, is not only the science of wealth, but a science of the activities of "mankind in the ordinary business of life." [4] Going on to explain this, he insisted that economists should include in their province, or the field of their keen interests, study of the effects of men's economic activities, surroundings, relations, and lives on their human characters as well as on their earnings, wealth, and standards of living. And in the short sketch of the economic and general history of Western civilization, which became an appendix to this introductory chapter of his *Principles,* Marshall made clear his own view of the way in which the historic and on-going evolution of the prevailing pattern of economic life had been and was making that, on the whole, progressively "better" in its effects on men's characters as well as on their economic achievements. What he saw in this history was a gradual progressive growth of the freedom, independence, and rationality of the economic activities and behavior of individuals; a tendency of more and more of them to come to be, in successive epochs, less and less controlled by arbitrary, blind, and rigid customs and traditions; or to be increasingly free, disposed, and able to manage or conduct their own affairs through independent, informed, and rational personal decisions on their ends or goals and the most efficient ways and means for attaining them, available to them, in their situations. Although he recognized, and on the whole approved also, as one part of the further consequences of all that, a historic growth of competition or competitiveness—rivalry or "racing" by men against one another, for economic gains won through efficient service in the markets—he insisted that there had been and was going on along with that a more or less equal growth of voluntary cooperation among men and groups, for common ends of all sorts. And he denied the charges, made both by socialists and by the lovers of more ancient ways, that a "greedy," selfish competition, antithetical to and inconsistent with cooperation for the common good, was really the or a distinctive or essential feature of the long-emerging, modern, individualistic or libertarian, private-enterprises-and-free-markets form of economic society.

Aware that to many people "competition" was a "bad word," signifying strife in contrast with cooperation, and holding it to be untrue that the business system which he believed in was especially or necessarily strife torn or unsocial, Marshall preferred, in describing that system—which was for him an ideal that had been in process of slow realization throughout Western history—to emphasize mainly, as its most important features, not competition or competitive acquisitiveness, but individual freedom, independence, and rationality. Further, he saw in it a multiform blending of much harmless, healthy, and socially beneficial,

[4] *Ibid.,* book 1, chap. 1, *passim.*

tempered or sportsmanlike competition with as much, in many forms, of spontaneous cooperation; basic cooperation among all in the exchange of mutual services, through the system of markets; and flexible adaptations of the activities of all as producers to the wants and demands of all as consumers, and to the possibilities of using resources in the most efficient or productive ways, and an all-around progressiveness —all this, resulting from the growth and spread of individual freedom, independence, and rationality, and of many alternative opportunities available to everyone for him to choose among. Nor was it only, to repeat this point, the resulting economic efficiency and progressiveness of a system of this kind that appealed to Marshall. Even more important, in his view, were the wholesome moral effects, on the characters of individuals generally, of the greater responsibilities for their own behavior and success and welfare, and decisions on and fulfillments of their social duties, going with their greater freedoms as free, independent, rational individuals, not fully or strictly controlled or guided by any complete and rigid mass of collective customs and traditions, or of collective or public rules and regulations of a more modern kind.

Seeing the past evolution or progress of Western freedom-and-order in those terms, Marshall *hoped* that the same progressive evolution would continue indefinitely in the same direction, in the future beyond his time. It would, he hoped, in due course bring about, through advancing productivity and the spread everywhere of ever-improving employment and earning opportunities, eventual, complete abolition of all life-stunting poverty; make good lives possible for all men; and continually increase the freedom, the variety and richness, and the relative harmony, of the lives of all. But he feared to some extent, as the one evil development that might prevent the realization of those high hopes for mankind, a possible growth of too much organization and centralization of control of economic life, in either or both of the forms of excessively large private business firms or organizations, or/and state socialism or excessive control of national economies by national governments. His judgments ran against both socialism and "big business," on the same grounds: in any gigantic organization, public or private, of the working lives of vast numbers of men, there would be the same inevitable curse of a vast, elaborate bureaucracy with its deadening routines, injurious both to efficiency and to the freedom, independence, initiatives, and morally healthy responsibilities of the individual. On his conviction, however, that efficiency would suffer, he based his hope that in the long run the too enormous units would prove self-defeating and would not prevail; in a competitive world the winners and survivors would be not the supergiants but the firms, in all the various industries, which managed to grow up to but not beyond their optimal sizes, at once large enough for the best use of the most efficient technologies available in their fields, and yet small enough to enable the human beings who must together manage and operate them to function at their individual and collective bests, and have the right incentives, opportunities, manageable and agreeable tasks, and harmonious relations, conducive to their most efficient personal performances.

Also, Marshall further fortified his hope by stressing, as variables affecting the efficiency of the firm, not only its size but also its youth or old age as a firm, and matters likely to be connected with that. The able, enterprising founder of a new firm, though it might be small at first, would often bring to it new ideas and a fresh vigor that would ensure success and growth, even in competition with older and larger established firms in the industry. Growth up to the new firm's optimal size would react favorably upon, as well as result from, its successes; and so would, for a time, the concurrent process of maturing, mastering the problems of the industry and the firm's situation in it, and achieving the best relations with the best suppliers, customers, etc. But in time the firm, growing old and perhaps too big, would come to be less vigorously and progressively managed; the founder or founders would be succeeded in the top directing posts by less able and/or less personally concerned men, who would only carry on the business in a routine way and rely on the firm's established reputation. And this old firm would decline and eventually yield up its place in the industry to a newer, younger, initially smaller one, again brought into being by another creative entrepreneur of a new, young generation. The whole economy, and each of its great industries or sectors, would be like a forest, made up at each point of time of many individual firms (trees), of all ages and sizes or positions in their individual life-cycles. The largest and oldest units would be declining toward their deaths, while in many cases the youth and vigor of the smaller firms would more than offset the disadvantages of smallness; and these firms would grow and lose those disadvantages and take the places of the decadent or dead. In this way, Marshall hoped, the economy would remain permanently and adequately competitive, or free from the enduring, gigantic monopolies which he viewed with disfavor on both economic and ethical or humanistic grounds. He envisaged a system of many independent, rival enterprises, among which the majority would be of moderate sizes, and with enough long-run turnover to preserve enough room and opportunities for many new, small men and firms.

Marshall's system of economic theory, then, was about the functioning—the operating and self-adjusting processes—of an economy or economic system of that kind. But it was not about an unreal, ideal world of "pure" and/or "perfect" competition—concepts that are now familiar among economic theorists but have been developed since Marshall's time. That is, Marshallian theory was *not* about a world or system in which the individual firms were assumed to be *so* numerous and small in all cases that each one's decisions and actions would be strictly determined by external, general, market conditions which it could not in the smallest degree control or influence; *nor* was it about a world conceived as having in it no impediments to the prompt, immediate achievement, by all firms and all individuals, of the ideal or "optimal" adjustments of their activities to their situations and opportunities in each current interval of time; nor did Marshall in any manner "assume away" all disharmonies between private and public interests. The now familiar, very modern, refined concepts of the purely imaginary and (in any real world) impossible conditions that would have to exist in an economic system to make it one of "pure" competition (devoid of any elements of "monopoly power" or "market power" in the hands of any individual firms or units in the system)—and of the other conditions required to make the system "perfectly" competitive (devoid of any "frictions" preventing or retarding transfers of men and resources out of old into new employments, or transfers of patronage to other sellers, or readjustments of men's doings to their changed, best opportunities—such "frictions" as deficiencies of knowledge of the available alternatives, or deficiencies of mobility, obstacles to movement or change, etc.) —these modern, logically refined ideas of the logically required assumptions in a theory of an absolutely ideal or perfect "liberal" economy, which if it could and did exist would function with entire perfection on the lines of Adam Smith's economic-liberal ideals—were as yet unknown to Marshall and his contemporaries, as well as to all still earlier economists. And there is no validity in the now too common notion that, because the "liberal" economists of past generations, from Adam Smith to Marshall inclusive, often had tendencies to be in some ways relatively optimistic about the "natural" functioning of the "competitive" economic systems they envisaged and theorized about, they must have been, in effect, unconsciously assuming the prevalence in those systems of "pure" and "perfect" competition, as we now understand these concepts. Let me explain this matter a bit further, and then go back to Marshall.

The older economists generally tried to develop not absolutely precise and rigorous theories of a purely abstract, absolute utopia, but rough, approximate, and much more realistic theories of the main, broad, general "tendencies" in the operation of what they thought were or could be, in the real worlds around them, *relatively* well-working, real, or realizable economic systems characterized by the general internal prevalence of *enough* competition, mobility, etc., to make them "tend" to operate or function in substantially the indicated way or manner. And they generally had, I think, more awareness than they fully expressed of the imperfections, from their standpoint, of the real conditions and results occurring in the real-world systems they were analyzing. They tended to accept the inevitable imperfections as a matter of course and say little about them, because their standards of comparison were not any fully and precisely spelled-out conceptions or figments of the "perfect" system from their point of view, but real or potentially real alternatives viewed as markedly *worse* than the kind of best-really-possible system they were trying to describe, analyze, and advocate. But in any event, in the case of Marshall there can be no doubt that he at least strove to make his system of theory as realistic as possible, as a theoretical account or analysis of the actual working of the real economic world around him; *and* there is no doubt that he was quite fully aware of the prevalence in that world of the phenomena which we now call those of "monopolistic" (in contrast with "pure") competition, and others which we call those of "imperfect" (in contrast with "perfect") competition. And with his own conceptual tools he did what he could to designate and analyze those real phenomena along with others; although he did not possess—as no one did until after his time—the modern, precise concepts and theories of those real phenomena and their unreal opposites, which were in fact developed in the next generation, *by* students of Marshall's work, precisely through further study of the logical problems that were not satisfactorily solved within his system, and could not be with just his set of conceptual tools.[5]

Marshall's theoretical work aimed at realism, but his method was to start with simple, avowedly not fully realistic—reality-simplifying—sets of assumptions about, or conceptions of, situations in parts of the economy; suppose single variables within those situations to change in particular ways, and all others capable of affecting the results to remain constant; "reason out" the consequences of those provisional assumptions; and then in subsequent, successive steps, introduce more and more of the complex, likely, real conditions and occurrences into the assumptions, or modify and complicate the latter *toward* full realism, and at each step again "reason out" the consequences of the changed assumptions. He was keenly aware of the almost infinite complexity of the real economy; of the endless number and variety and variability of the variables in it, and relations of interdependence among them all; and of the artificiality of his procedure of mentally "isolating" one part of the economy (e.g., one industry) and one small group of variables important in and for it, at a time, "impounding" everything else in the "pound" of *coeteris paribus,* and asking how, on these unreal assumptions, a particular change of one of the "isolated" variables would affect

[5] My statement that Marshall lacked the "conceptual tools" needed in the more modern theories must be qualified in view of the passage in his Mathematical Appendix (Principles, 8th ed., pp. 841–850) about a seller's "marginal revenue."

the others. But he held this method of piecemeal or "partial" analysis, and progressive approximation toward a more realistic and complete analysis, to be the only route to an at once richly and accurately detailed, and comprehensive understanding of the functioning system.

There remains one more introductory topic on which a few words must be said: how Marshall conceived, and sought to understand, the motives and behavior-patterns of the human actors in the economy, or the general forms of their reactions to and upon the changes of the external "variables" in their economic situations or environments. He held that in the universally money-using business economy, "the measuring rod of money" serves to "measure" and record or register, in market prices of all kinds, the strengths or intensities of the "motives" or psychological, subjective motive-forces of all kinds, (1) which cause individuals to be just willing to pay those prices for, *and* buy the amounts they do buy of, the particular goods or services concerned; or (2) which, in the cases of the sellers, make it necessary and sufficient to pay the prices in question to them, to overcome their *other* desires or the attractions for them of their other opportunities, and induce them to contribute their quotas to the available supplies of the goods or services in question. "The measuring rod of money" could thus serve the economist in a role analogous to that of "the chemists' balance" in the latter's science. Economics could be the relatively most exact of the social sciences, *not* because the human motives included or involved in its subject matter could be thought of as peculiar in any way, or divided off from another part of the range of all human motives and regarded as having peculiar, measurable properties, *but* because market prices, in a money-and-markets economy, provide uniquely exact "measures" of the motive-forces, of all kinds, which are at work in it. Marshall denied the existence of any special "economic" motive or motives; money and economic goods are not ends but means, and they are means to all kinds of human ends. Hence economic activities and decisions reflect or involve desires or motives of all kinds; but the relative strengths of all the rival desire-forces impelling men to different actions in the markets get "measured" for the economist by the relative market prices which prove necessary and sufficient to bring about the actions that he can observe there.

UTILITY AND DEMAND; AND COST AND SUPPLY

Of the six "books" or parts of Marshall's *Principles of Economics,* the first two are introductory or concerned with preliminary topics, including those I have now discussed here. The "body" of the work begins with Book Three, on "Wants, Consumption, and Demand"; and this, significantly, is quite short—a series of six very short chapters. The theory of this subject was the part of economic theory that was undergoing the most vigorous development in Marshall's time, and he himself was an important contributor to that new development, and might have been expected to share the common enthusiastic view of his fellow workers that they were building the all-important, entirely new foundation of the entire science—the basic part of it all, and the part needing the most extensive treatment. Yet Marshall in fact regarded this analysis of consumers' wants, demands, and satisfactions as a simple, small, and minor part of all economic analysis—in a way the least important part of the whole, and capable of being fully presented, briefly, though having its logical place as the first step in a logical presentation of the whole. He did not concur in the view that this new part of economic theory, added by his generation of theorists, should dominate and "revolutionize" the whole. For him it was only an addition of substantial but limited importance to Ricardian-classical economic theory, leading also to a measure of revision of the latter, but not replacing it, and leaving that older body of theory, as improved, still the main part of all economic theory—the part dealing with the more extensive, difficult, and fundamental parts of the entire field or subject matter.

In other words, in Marshall's view the new analysis of the psychological or subjective backgrounds and the shapes and changes of the consuming population's demand-price functions for the economy's different, particular products—the effects, with given demand conditions (functions), of changes of the prices of products on the quantities demanded or salable, and the effects of changes of the functions themselves (determined by the numbers, tastes, and incomes of consumers) on sales volumes at given prices, or prices obtainable with given sales volumes—all this filled what had been a serious gap in the older body of economic theory. Now that the new theory of this part of the subject matter was available, it was logical to start with it in presenting the entire theory of economics, since all production went on in response and adjustment to consumers' demands, and study of the behavior of the latter was therefore a logical prelude to the study of production and the economy's functioning. But Marshall agreed with Ricardo in believing that, although demand conditions and their changes played the main role *in the short run*, in determining the relative prices of the different products, and the profitabilities and expansions or contractions of the different industries; still the main big task lay in the study of the processes of response and adjustment of production and the supplies of products *to* the public's demands for them, and the behaviors or variations, in those processes, of the physical variables—ratios of required inputs of labor-time and other resources to resulting outputs of products—involved in the cost-supply functions, and of main importance *in the long run* in determining the points of equilibrium in the adjustments of supplies to demands, and the relative equilibrium prices or values of the different products.

Thus after presenting the new theory of consumers' demands, briefly, in Book Three of his *Principles,* Marshall went on to lay the other, second, and more important part of the foundation of his theory of prices and incomes, or the market system's pricing of all products and productive services, and the economy's functioning, in a much longer Book Four. This book considers the factors, organization, problems, and processes of production, and the physical efficiency or "real-cost" elements of the cost-supply or supply-price functions for the economy's different industries and products. The treatment, in the main group of chapters (9 through 13), of the last-mentioned topic—the cost-supply functions of different types, for different types of industries and products—is the core of this book, and the logical sequel to Book Three completing along with that, the foundation for Book Five, on "value" or the prices of products; and I shall here concentrate attention on this. Book Four as a whole contains also, in the chapters about the different factors of production, some preliminary, partial suggestions of the corresponding parts of the theory of income-distribution, which is later resumed and more fully developed only in Book Six: but I shall defer consideration of all this material until we get to that final book.

In the central or "core" part, then, of Book Four, the questions taken up concern the effects of growths or expansions of whole industries (in response to enlargements of the markets or demands for their products) upon efficiency and therefore upon production costs within the industries, and so upon the eventual amounts of the expansions of the industries and their outputs, and eventual levels of the prices of the products, which given demand increases would "tend" to bring about in the long run. Each "industry" within the economy is conceived as made up of a more or less large number of independent, competing firms or enterprises or producing units, all contributing to the aggregate supply of one kind of product. And the different "industries" are held to fall, as regards the forms of their cost-supply functions, into two main categories: on the one hand, the agricultural and, more generally, all primary or raw-materials-producing industries, and, on the other hand, manufacturing or processing industries and perhaps all those in the fields of transportation, merchandising, etc. The primary industries, which are especially dependent for their efficiencies on the amounts and qualities of usable land and natural resources available to them, have their cost-supply functions affected *mainly though not solely* by the "law" of or "tendency" toward "diminishing returns" in the old Ricardian-classical sense of this term or concept. That is, as these industries expand toward the limits of their abilities to produce more from the limited available supplies of their required types of land resources, their expansions must sooner or later pass points beyond which the further increments they can add to their outputs will "tend"—so far as the effect of this one most important feature of their situation is concerned—to diminish relative to the required additions to their inputs of labor and capital; in other words, the additional costs of producing the additional increments of output "tend" to rise. Even in these industries, however, this one "tendency" alone is not, as we shall see in a moment, the whole story, but is more or less modified or partially offset by *other* consequences of expansion—"economies," or improvements of the organization of production and efficiency of use of all factors, made achievable by and likely to be achieved with growth of these industries and others serving them and the producing units in them. On balance, Marshall thought, expanding primary industries would have rising additional costs of producing further additions to their outputs, but the steepness of the rise of these costs would be lessened or moderated, more or less, by the contrary effect of the "economies" contingent on growth. And conversely, in the industries of his *other* type in this matter, though here again both kinds or modes of influence of expansion on efficiency and cost would be at work, the outcome "on balance" would be the other way.

Thus in any manufacturing industry—or *any* industry—the effects of land scarcity and "diminishing returns" in the classical sense are never absent. The best or most advantageous locations or sites for factories in any particular manufacturing industry are limited in number and in their sizes or areas. As the industry expands, both the increasing intensity of use of those best sites—"crowding" them with more or larger and higher buildings, to use more labor and machinery and produce more output on them—and the resort also, by the same or/and additional new firms in the industry, to other, inferior sites or locations —both of these developments will, of themselves, "tend" to increase the additional costs incurred in the industry relative to the resulting additions to its output. But in every case of this kind, Marshall thought, those effects of expansion on costs would be *more* than offset by the contrary effects of all the "economies" of various kinds—improvements of the organization, methods, and efficiency of the industry's production process resulting partly from the growths of individual firms and their increasing realizations of the economies of large-scale or mass production, and partly from the growth of the industry as a whole and the associated growths of all others serving or aiding it and its member firms —developments of the common, external environment around the latter, helping them all alike regardless of their sizes, to reduce their costs per unit of output. The "economies" resulting for a firm from its own growth—those of large-scale production as such—Marshall called "internal economies." But these, he thought, generally had limits in the sense that a firm's efficiency would be increased by its growth only up to some "optimal" size—generally small enough to leave it still a rather small part of its entire industry, or leave room in the latter for many or at least several other firms also at or near *their* "optimal" sizes —and that further enlargement of any one firm *beyond* that size would work to make it *less* efficient. Hence Marshall's belief, that continuing growth of any *whole industry* in this general category would continue, without limit, to lower the prevailing, average, per unit cost of production of its product, depended heavily on the importance of what he called "external economies"—the cost-reducing effects, for all individual firms within the industry and for all "scales" of production by them, of the growth or enlargement of the industry as a whole (with new firms entering it), and all the associated, favorable changes of or in the environments of the included firms.

With the growth of a whole industry there would tend to go a growing regional specialization or concentration—most of the firms or their main plants would come to be located near each other in the region or part of the country affording the best facilities of all kinds for efficient production of the kind of product or products involved. Apart from the initial or "natural" advantages of the region for the industry in question, the very concentration and growth of the industry within that region would draw into it, or stimulate the development of, everything required to enable the industry and its member firms to become more efficient: ample supplies of labor with the special skills required in the industry, supplies of capital, business ability, and the needed professional skills all provided locally by people attracted to and familiar with the industry and region, and expanding and improving auxiliary industries and services of all the needed types. Some "external economies" realized by the firms in the particular industry might depend on "internal economies" of large-scale production realized by other firms in other industries, supplying those in the first one with "parts" for their products, or items of equipment. But the whole Marshallian concept of "external economies" is a very broad one, as has now been indicated.

If we return for a moment to consideration of the (on balance) increasing-cost industries, e.g., branches of agriculture, we find a passage of Marshall's showing how he "put together" the effects in their expansions of the classical "law of diminishing returns" or rising cost due to growing "pressure" on the limited land supply, and the contrary effects of the "economies"—particularly "external" ones—brought about for even these industries by their growths or expansions. In the passage referred to, Marshall envisages the long process of gradual settlement and growth of an initially, very sparsely populated and little-developed, "frontier" farming region. As more and more of the region's arable land is brought under cultivation, and the more fertile soils are cultivated with increasing intensity, the region's whole output of agricultural produce increases but at rising, added costs for the added units of output —in so far as simply the input-output ratios on the farms themselves are concerned. But the total process entails also growth of towns in the region, more and better roads, more and better and cheaper equipment and farm supplies, and marketing facilities available to the farmers, or in short many "external economies," all tending to lessen the rise of cost with output. The possibility of important "internal economies" of large-scale farming, by large business units operating with great areas of land, masses of mechanical equipment, the best scientific farming techniques, armies of wage-earning field labor, and the most efficient business methods—this possibility was not within the field or range of Marshall's theoretical vision, as its practical realizations have only begun to appear in the world in our present time. But even this is entirely consistent with his points and only adds to them another one which may perhaps, where it too is operative, "tip the balance" that he talked about the other way, or make even the affected parts of agriculture subject to not increasing but decreasing cost with increase of demand and output.

It is necessary, of course, in considering Marshall's "laws of cost," i.e., of the directions of change of cost with growth of output for different kinds of products, to understand that they necessarily "abstract from" or leave out of account all technological advances in or affecting an industry which occur in the course of time and may accompany, but cannot be explained as simply results of, growth or expansion of the market and the industry. To draw a "cost curve" for, e.g., an agricultural product, showing rise of cost with growth of output, does not imply that, if the growth goes on over a long period of time and the relevant technology is revolutionized in the meantime, the cost (per unit) of producing the product will be higher at the end than it was at the beginning of the period. The "curve" means only that, with a given, unchanging technology—or one changing (improving) only in so far as expansion per se brings about improvements—expansion in the face of land scarcity, etc., will of itself tend to increase, progressively, the additional costs of successive new additions to the total output. If while the expansion is going on other events, independent of it, occur and lower the industry's production costs—as they might have done in any case, even with no expansion—their effect as far as the "cost curve" is concerned is not to alter its slope but to "shift" all of it downward, or make it necessary to redraw it at a lower level throughout. And the concrete, historical "trend" of the relevant costs—or "supply prices" for the different outputs properly adjusted to demand conditions at the different dates—through the time interval concerned, will then be a separate line, reflecting the composite or resultant effect of the two sets of causes—a "time series" of "cost" figures, declining through time in consequence of the technological advances (downward shifts of the "cost curve" or cost-supply function), but showing a *rate* of decline *reduced or moderated* by the influence of the "tendency" of cost to rise with the increase of output as such, as indicated by the form of that "curve" or function. And so also, of course, in the other case of Marshall's "law of decreasing cost" for an expanding manufacturing industry: here again the cost decreases referred to include only those brought about by the expansion as such, and the "economies" contingent on or resulting from it, and do *not* include any others brought about in the meantime by other independent causes, such as new inventions, which again would "shift" *this* entire cost curve downward, and not be in any part responsible for its downward slope.

In this connection, however, Marshall introduced a distinction between two types of technological advances or improvements. What I have just said would apply, in his view, to and only to all "substantive new inventions" representing truly novel achievements of advancing science or applied science, and not any predictable results of the growth of this market and industry. But growth itself would often be necessary and sufficient to bring into use in the industry, adaptations and applications of previously existing knowledge or ideas capable of leading to cost-reducing improvements of parts of the industry's equipment, methods, and production processes, but only when the industry attained a sufficient size. Thus Marshall *did* include in his categories of the "internal" and "external" economies through which the growths of firms and industries would reduce their per unit production costs, all *such* improvements of their actually used technologies, involving not any "substantive new inventions" but only the adaptations and applications of existing knowledge which would become profitable for and be carried out by the growing firms and industries as they grew sufficiently.

Throughout his discussion of the effects of growths of markets and industries of different types on the costs of production of the different products, Marshall did not strictly, mentally "isolate" one (each) single industry at a time and assume it *alone* to be growing within an economy of an unchanging, aggregate size, or with only transfers of demand and of resources to the growing industry. Instead—as I have already implied at various points—he was really, throughout, envisaging (as Ricardo had done) on-going growth of the entire economy; not of its territory, land-area, or basic supplies of natural resources, but growth of population, of the "national income," of the flow of saving-and-investing and the stock of accumulated wealth or capital, and of the flow of aggregate consumption spending. And as parts of all this or in this setting, he envisaged growths of (presumably) most of the many diverse, particular industries, not necessarily in any steady or particular proportions or *without* (also) transfers of demand and of resources, back and forth, among them, but always within or as parts of the growing, whole economy. Only with this "background" assumption of *general* growth in mind can we understand why, in his theoretical scheme or picture, the "tendency" of a growth of the demand for and output of any primary product (raw material) to raise its cost is never neutralized or made inoperative by events releasing for this use enough additional, suitable, good, or highly productive land—i.e., offsetting contractions of the demands for and outputs of other products "competitive" with this one for this land. And with regard to his "decreasing-cost" industries, Marshall's broad account of the "external economies" likely to be realized by or in each one of them as a growing industry again involved the assumption of a growing, whole economy, in which each single industry would be made increasingly efficient not only by its own growth, but also by the associated growths and improvements of all others forming useful parts of its environment.

Thus the general conclusions that emerge from the entire discussion may be summarized as follows. In the growing economy, increasing pressure on the limited supplies of land (space) and natural resources, and the working of the classical "law of diminishing returns" in exploiting them, by itself makes for rising costs with growing outputs. This "tends" to be of predominating importance in the agricultural and other primary industries producing raw materials; hence the outputs of the latter generally tend to be increasable only at rising costs—costs rising at least gently along "curves" which may, however, be continually or recurrently shifted downward by technological advances. On the other hand, apart from the growing pressure on the land, the other effects of economic growth—growth of population, aggregate and per capita income and wealth, consumption, and investment, and so of markets, industries, and firms—all contribute to growth of increasingly elaborate and efficient division of labor or economic specialization in all its forms or aspects, and improving coordination, reciprocal adjustments, and organization of all activities, and abilities fully to utilize the most advanced and efficient available techniques and the often very large and expensive indivisible units or blocks of equipment required by them; and so to progressive reduction, in all these ways, of per unit production costs for most kinds of products. These favorable effects of growth on efficiency tend to be of predominating importance in all or most manufacturing or processing industries. Whereas raw-materials costs tend to rise, in the growing economy, the costs of processing the raw materials into finished products tend to fall; even apart from the new major technological advances which, again, may repeatedly bring downward shifts of *these* "cost curves" also. And now finally, if we combine the costs of raw materials and costs of processing for the different finished or complete products, and ask what happens to the full costs of the latter, we get a range of possibilities that includes a new, third category. In the cases in which the increases of raw-materials costs and the decreases of processing costs happen to just about offset each other, the outputs of the finished products will increase at constant, full costs of production per unit. And in other cases, where the raw-materials costs are of main importance and/or increase more sharply than the processing costs decline, the full costs rise, for increasing outputs; and where the "balance tips" the other way, they fall. But we shall encounter all these propositions again, and more fully explore their implications within Marshall's theory of "value" or the system's determinations of the relative prices of all products, in Book Five, to which we now turn.

SUPPLY AND PRICE ADJUSTMENTS OVER DIFFERENT LENGTHS OF TIME

In Book Five, Marshall "puts together" in a rather complicated way, his analysis, carried over from Book Three, of the psychological backgrounds and the forms and changes of consumers' demands for different products, and the analysis made within Book Four, which I have just summarized, of supplies and costs of production as affected by growth of output in response to growth of demand. But the complexity of his dual, demand-and-supply analysis, or utility-and-cost analysis of the "value" problem is due chiefly to another feature—his division of the whole problem into a series of subproblems concerned with the different modes and degrees of response and adjustment of supplies to demands which "tend" to occur and complete themselves over different lengths or periods of time. In this matter, he went beyond the early "classical" division of "value" theory into only two parts—theory of the immediate causes of the temporary "market price" of a good in each current, short interval of time, and theory of the ultimate causes tending to control its "natural price" or the central, "true" value around which the more volatile "market price" would oscillate and toward which it would be always tending to return "in the long run." In Marshall's theory there were not two but three different "stages" or parts of the long process of fully adjusting the supply of a good to a given state of the demand or market for it, and thereby adjusting the market price of the good to the "normal" level, just fully sufficient to induce or evoke continuing, steady production and marketing of the right supply, equal to the amount demanded at that same level of the price. All this involved the (fully conscious, deliberate) unrealistic, artificial device of assuming or supposing the demand situation to change only at long intervals and, after each change, remain constant throughout the time required to complete all three of the successive but overlapping "stages" of the process of fully readjusting the "supply" of the good to that new fixed state of the "demand" for it. Thus, it must be admitted, in the real world the changing, actual prices of things never, or rarely ever, arrive at—much less remain or continue at—Marshallian "long-run normal" levels. Usually if not always, long before the supply of a thing can become so adjusted to any recently established and temporary state of the demand for it, as to bring its price to the "normal" level, the demand situation changes again, and the process of readjustment begins all over again.

But this serious deficiency, or lack of full realism, of Marshall's theory of these matters was not his fault, so to speak, and does not mean that his theory was or is useless or irrelevant to the understanding of what does go on in the real world. What it means is that whatever can be done in the way of analyzing or explaining demand conditions and their changes cannot by itself—as Marshall insisted—take us more than a small part of the way toward a full understanding of the processes of price determination and the economy's functioning. In a fast-changing world the public's demands for particular products are in most cases subject to either continual or frequent, rapid, erratic, and often great or drastic changes, which economic analysis can at best only partially explain, and cannot predict. In themselves the potential processes of adjustment of the outputs and supplies or market offerings of different goods *to* any given, stable demand situations—the supply adjustments possible in time in a competitive business economy with all factors of production "mobile" in the long run, out of the less and into the more remunerative employments—are amenable to much more nearly full and satisfactory, scientific analysis than are the erratic changes of demand conditions. Hence there is no better way of working toward the fullest possible understanding of real economic changes and adjustments than first to do what is possible in the study of demand and then "suppose" demand conditions to change at intervals but remain stable through sufficient intervals, and thus fully to explore the more understandable potentialities or inherent "tendencies" of supply adjustments. And those "tendencies" have real significance even though they are seldom allowed to proceed all the way to their final, logical destinations. Economic events, developments, or changes can be thought of, usefully, as of two kinds: the unpredictable, *originative* changes, and the much more predictable (in principle) *adaptive* changes in adjustment to them. Economic analysis can be little more, and should aim to be nothing less, than full analysis of the internal logic, so to speak, of the adaptive changes and all their potential consequences, or the processes of adjustment to initially existing, basic conditions including the results of past originative changes. And this can be worthwhile even though it can be only a partial analysis of the concrete, real developments—not the whole truth and hence not wholly true about them—since they are affected also by the "interfering," new originative changes which prevent the attainment of complete adjustments by redirecting the processes of adjustments toward new goals before the old ones are attained.

Let us then, with the true Marshallian understanding and acceptance of its imperfect realism, examine the Marshallian theory of the types or degrees of adjustment of the relations of demand, supply, and price attainable over his three different orders of lengths of time after the establishment of the demand conditions being adjusted to. Only in the final part of this discussion, pertaining to complete adjustment or the longest of those time intervals or "the long run," will we again meet those "laws" of production of increasing outputs at increasing, constant, or decreasing cost, which were discussed above. We have first to start at the other end, with theory of "market" price in the "very short run," or the kind of immediate, provisional adjustment or "temporary equilibrium of supply and demand" which "tends" to become established very quickly. This "run" of time is defined as too short to allow any change, within it, of the current volume or rate of production of the good. Hence the "supply" that can vary within this time interval is or means *not* "output" or new production, but the amount being offered on the market by the holders of the already previously produced, existing "stock" of the good, who may either be eager to sell out their complete holdings quickly at the current price, or be inclined to withhold them and wait for the price to rise, or be of varying minds in the range between the two extremes. Hence also, *no* production costs are capable of influencing the selling price or its movements within this interval; producers' costs can affect the prices at which the products can be sold, only as they bring about adjustments of the amounts produced to or toward equality with the amounts demanded or salable at cost-covering prices; and within time intervals, immediately subsequent to demand changes, which are too short for any such adjustments, market prices are entirely independent of or unaffected by producers' costs.

Thus, the "supply curve" used in study of the interactions of supply, demand, and price over the very short run is not a "cost curve" of any kind; what affects the "supply" put on the market by the dealers holding the existing stock is not any costs that have been incurred, but two factors together determining the dealers' decisions to sell now or wait—their guesses as to whether the now-ruling market price will rise or fall, or persist unchanged in the immediate future, and their needs to sell quickly or abilities to wait as determined by their needs for or reserves of "cash" or "liquid" assets. In general, the higher the price prevailing at any moment, the larger will be the supply attracted by that price, so to speak, onto the market for immediate sale. This "supply curve," then, is drawn to indicate simply the tendency of supply to vary with price in this direction—to become the greater, the higher the price obtainable, and the smaller, the lower the price attainable. The "demand curve," however, runs as always in the other direction, i.e., price increases reduce the amounts demanded on the market, and price decreases increase them. Hence the two "curves" intersect at the only price that equalizes supply and demand and is therefore able to endure —as long as the demand and supply situations or sets of possibilities described by the "curves" remain unchanged. Any price higher than this one "equilibrium" price will make the supply greater and the demand less, or will cause the amount offered to exceed the amount wanted; and this will cause the price to fall back toward its "equilibrium" level. Any price lower than this appropriate one will reduce the supply and increase the demand, or cause more to be sought than is offered, with the result that the unsatisfied demanders will "bid up" the price to its "equilibrium" level again.

Now let us move on to consideration of the further adjustments which tend to occur in the next longer "run" of time—a longish "short run," intermediate in length between the *very* short run and the "long run." Here we meet some of Marshall's most original, unique, and important contributions. This order of time duration is defined as long enough for readjustment, by the industry producing the good or product under consideration, of its current output of the product, within the limits set by the existing "capacity" of the industry, but *not* long enough to allow any change of the latter also, in adjustment to a changed state of the demand for the product. Hence we now have to consider some but not all elements of the producers' costs as exerting an influence on, and sure to be at least "covered" by, the product's selling price, within this period. The two kinds or groups of cost-items, all included together in the total costs incurred by a producing firm, were respectively called by Marshall, in his English terminology, the firm's "prime costs" (for a given output) and its "supplementary costs." In the terminology more familiar to American businessmen and economists, the Marshallian "prime costs" are called "operating" or "variable" costs, and the "supplementary" costs are the firm's "overhead" or "fixed" costs. That is, the former category consists of the outlays or expenditures such as the wages bill which decreases or increases along with current output, the payments for materials, fuel or power, etc., which do the same, and in short *all* the items that (as totals) are thus variable, fairly promptly, with or according to the current volume of production. And the other, "supplementary" or "overhead" or "fixed" costs are those such as the interest which must be paid on the firm's permanent or long-term debt (bonds), the depreciation of buildings and machinery, property taxes and all taxes independent of the current volume of production, the salaries of the more permanent, nonvariable part of the staff of employees, etc.—in short, all items that, as totals, remain "fixed" or constant obligations of the firm over extended periods, regardless of the variations, within those periods, of its output or volume of production, even if that varies over the entire range between zero and "full capacity." The location, however, of the line between the two categories varies with the length of the time interval that is being considered; the shorter the interval, the more of all the costs are "fixed" through its brief duration, and the longer the interval, the more of all the costs become variable or adjustable. "In the long run" *all* costs are variable, i.e., a long continuing, increased, or great demand, enabling the firm to sell and continue selling at a high price a greater output than it was previously equipped to produce, will lead it eventually to increase its "capacity"—add to its "plant," permanent staff, capital debt, etc.—and in so doing also increase its (for shorter periods) "fixed" costs. And a long continuing "slump," or loss of business, making its former "capacity" and "fixed costs" decidedly and enduringly excessive, will lead it eventually to sell, lease out, convert to other uses, or abandon idle plants or machines, etc., retire or pay off a part of its debt, reduce its entire staff, etc., and thus reduce all its costs or outlays. But over any period of, say, more than a few weeks but less than a year or two, there is likely to be a fairly clear and definite division of the cost-items into the two categories that have been described.

Now let us suppose that there occurs a large decrease of the public's demand for the good or product being produced by an industry or all the firms composing it; a decrease such that, even if they reduce their selling prices to very low levels, the firms cannot sell more than fractional parts of their "capacity" outputs; and that this lowered demand remains in effect for a considerable time. In this situation, what will the firms do—if they act "rationally" in their own interests, i.e., to minimize their losses—and what will happen to their costs and outputs, and the supply and price of the good on the market? Clearly they will, to some extent or other, reduce their outputs and thereby reduce, in more or less nearly the same proportions, the totals of their current operating, variable, or in Marshall's word, "prime" costs, as such. For each firm this kind or part of cost *per unit* of output will perhaps not be greatly changed; though as we shall see in a moment, there are reasons why *per unit* variable cost is unlikely to be constant throughout the range of all possible (within "capacity") outputs. The total of the "fixed" costs will remain "fixed"; hence this part of the cost *per unit* of output will rise sharply—and the more sharply, the farther output is reduced.

In the situation, however, of a greatly reduced demand for the product and excessive totals of "capacity" and "fixed costs" throughout the industry, it will be impossible for the firms, whatever they may do, to obtain prices and sell outputs, or realize receipts, sufficient to cover their fixed as well as or in addition to their variable costs. Even if they combine or agree to eliminate competition among themselves, act together as an industry-wide monopoly, and try to maintain the price of the product at a level high enough to cover the full per unit cost of production; the effect of the high or maintained price will be to so reduce the volume of sales and output, and increase the amount of unused or idle, expensive "capacity," as to raise the *per unit* fixed cost to a level above that of the price agreed on. Every attempt to raise the latter, further, to the level of the former, will, by further reducing sales and output, only push the *per unit* fixed cost to a still higher level. In a situation of this kind it is the better—less disadvantageous—policy to give up the impossible effort to cover or recoup the full cost of production and, by lowering the price of the product, sufficiently maintain the volume of sales and production to prevent an inordinate rise of the full cost per unit, and make the excess of total receipts over the total operating or variable cost as large as possible. But in order to analyze this case more fully, as Marshall did, we must consider the likely shapes and relations of the demand and variable cost "curves," and the likely or loss-minimizing behaviors of the firms, (1) if they are in full, mutual competition for the available business, and (2) if the competition among them is restrained or limited in a measure, in the way or on the grounds—to be explained below—which Marshall thought would generally prevail.

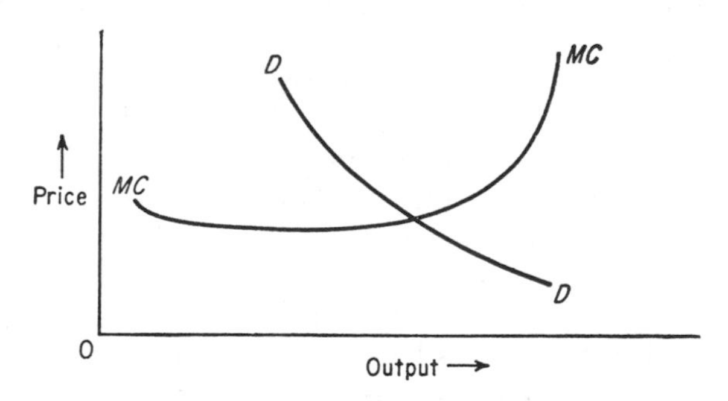

It is perhaps safe to assume that as a rule, with variations of the output of the industry, the typical "prime cost" per unit of output would remain about the same—at least for all outputs within a middle range, all well below the industry's capacity, but all large enough to avoid the "diseconomies" of the extreme reductions of the employed personnel or working forces that would make it impossible to maintain the normal patterns of division of labor or specialization of roles required for normal efficiency. Were the slump of demand to be *so* severe as to oblige each firm to discharge all but a small fraction of its normal number of employees, and cut down production to a very small fraction of its capacity output, its operating cost per unit for that very small output might be raised in the way just indicated; and a partial recovery of demand, sales, output, and employment might again reduce this per unit operating cost to its "normal" level. And near the *other* end of the possible range of outputs, with demand so increased (again) as to cause the firms to try to produce nearly to the utmost limits of the capacities of their plants, etc., per unit operating cost would rise steeply, with overtime wage rates, day and night shifts and the extra costs of the latter, and "diminishing returns" of extra output by the extra labor etc., with the limited, fixed amount of equipment. But over a large middle part of its whole length the "curve" of per unit operating cost may be "horizontal." And if so, the all-important (for our problem here) "curve" of "marginal" cost—additions to total cost, entailed by successive unit additions to output—will be identical with that of per unit operating cost throughout this part of the latter. Since the total "overhead" or "fixed" cost will be fixed, the whole or sole increase of total cost when output increases is the increase of total variable or operating cost; and if this is varying in direct proportion to output, the additional cost of producing an additional unit is the same as the per unit operating cost for any output in this range. With the near-approach to full capacity output, however, and rise of per unit operating cost as explained above, this "marginal-cost" figure—extra cost of each new extra unit of output—rises *more* than, or to levels increasingly *above* the simple average or per unit (operating) cost figure. Still the "curve" of "marginal cost" as a function of output—*MC* in the diagram on page 357—has the same *kind* of shape as that of per unit operating cost, on the assumptions made here; or it is, where the latter "curve" is "horizontal," identical with it, and where the latter rises, *MC* also rises, though even more steeply.

Now let us, for the moment, concentrate attention on the situation of considerably depressed demand and operation by the industry in the range of outputs for which per unit operating cost and marginal cost are constant and identical. The reason for the importance of the concept of marginal cost is that, as long as a firm can increase its volume of sales by (if necessary) reducing its selling price, and can still in this way increase its total receipts or revenue *more* than its total costs will increase, it obviously "pays" the firm better to get the additional business in this way—by price cutting—than not to get it. In other words, so long as the (low) price which must be quoted in order to sell a bit more of the product is still at all above marginal cost for the slightly increased output—or the additional cost of producing to fill the additional orders

—the additional business will add more to income than to outgo, and is worth going after. Thus under conditions of all-out competition for business among the firms in a temporarily depressed industry, each firm would be led to continue to cut the price down *to* the level of its marginal cost for the resulting output; and this as we have seen would be the same as per unit operating or variable cost in the assumed situations. The latter then is the only "floor" under prices, or lower limit of price cutting, under such conditions; all "fixed" costs are without influence on the price which "tends" to prevail during the time over which they are "fixed"; the "tendency" is toward a price equal to marginal cost and thus, when demand is far below the industry's capacity, to operating cost per unit, only; and equality of supply with demand at this low price. Such situations indeed cause competitive pricing to be called "cut-throat" competition; i.e., it leads to a price below the full cost of production. These situations also stimulate efforts to bring about industry-wide organization and an enforceable agreement among all the firms to restrict their outputs and the supply on the market, and maintain the price at a level at least more nearly covering per unit full cost. But the possibilities of success for such efforts are likely to be limited. The basic cause of the inadequate price, or price below the full cost of production, is not simply interfirm competition but the insufficient total demand for the product in any event, or excess of capacity and of total fixed costs in the industry relative to the demand situation; and as raising the price would further reduce the demand and further raise the per unit fixed cost, as was said above, even an effective monopoly would be unlikely to be able to find and set any full-cost price. It might however, be able to make the surplus of total revenue over total operating cost a maximum (the largest possible in the situation) and more or less *nearly* equal to total fixed cost, or equal to some more or less substantial part of that, instead of allowing this "surplus" to be dissipated by unrestrained competitive price cutting, or efforts by each firm to increase its share. But further, preserving adherence to the required agreements is apt to be very difficult in such a situation, because each single firm has a strong incentive to violate the agreements if it expects the others to adhere to them.

Thus Marshall's final conclusion about this case was that the most likely outcome would lie in the range between the extremes of entirely unrestrained competition and a price barely equal to marginal and per unit variable cost, on the one hand, and a fully effective monopoly or formalized and fully observed agreement leading to the best possible combination of price and volume of business for the industry, on the other hand. Price cutting by each firm would be restrained somewhat by its fears of forcing the other firms to more than match its price cut each time, and in turn being forced to undercut them again, and so on. And these deterrent fears would be the more effective in the absence of any formal and supposedly binding agreement, or impediment to prompt retaliations by all in response to every price cut. At the same time they would not entirely prevent all price cutting. It would still be true for each firm that every additional order it could get at any (reduced) price still above the additional cost of filling it would improve the firm's position; and this would still "work" to some extent even if all the other firms "matched" the price in question, i.e., made it the one prevailing market price. The deterrent force of the mutual fears among the competitors would only make their price competition moderate or cautious, and tend to check it at some point that would allow the market price to become uniform and stable at a level still somewhat above that of the firms' per unit operating costs. The common "fear of spoiling the market," in Marshall's phrase, would make all firms cautious, and lead them to avoid a demoralizing "price war" that would get out of hand—and cause the customers to expect and wait for even lower prices. A tacit, not overt, agreement among the firms would in effect come into being to halt competitive price cutting at a level of the market price still leaving all at least a slight margin or excess of revenue over and above operating costs. Marshall's theory on this point—about this force and effect of "fear of spoiling the market"—reveals the fact that he envisaged his "competitive" industries *not as* of the type we now would call *purely* competitive, but rather as characterized by what is now called "oligopoly" (competition among rivals few and large enough to have significant amounts of power, individually, to affect the whole market and each others' fortunes, and thus be impelled, by fears of each other's powers, to compete or use their own powers only with restraint or caution). Though Marshall did not have these more modern concepts, of "pure competition" and "oligopoly," his "realism" led him at this point, in effect, to recognize the prevalence of the realities or real conditions that we now designate by the latter word, and to analyze acutely this part of their consequences.

I must now, however, conclude my account of this whole part of Marshall's theory of adjustments, over different lengths of time, of supplies and prices to demand and cost conditions—his theory of the adjustments "tending" to occur within his "intermediate short run"—and get on, very soon, to his theories of the "long-run," full adjustments "tending" to work themselves out eventually in the different types of industries subject to constant or increasing or decreasing (full per unit) production costs for increasing outputs. But a little more must be said about the "intermediate short run," before we leave it. As we have seen, over this interval too short for any change of an industry's "capacity" and "fixed costs" but long enough for adjusting its current output, within the limit set by its capacity, to the current demand at a price related to the firm's variable and marginal costs—the latter "tend" to control the price of the product; though if the demand and the adjusted output are so low that the marginal cost price would barely cover the per unit operating or variable cost, there is likely to be a slightly greater reduction of output, and maintenance of the price at a level a little above that of operating (and marginal) cost, caused by "fear of spoiling the market." We have not yet considered the other possible demand conditions and supply-and-price adjustments over this "short run." Suppose the demand to be so great (even at relatively high prices) that the industry's capacity is fully utilized, or even insufficient; what part of production cost then governs price, and to what extent and how does it do so?

As I explained above, as the output of the industry and that of every firm in it approaches the full or utmost capacity output, the per unit variable or operating cost rises, and the marginal cost (extra cost of each new extra unit) rises *more* sharply and thus to levels increasingly above that per unit operating cost. And it is marginal cost which governs price; the firms will accept and try to fill additional orders if and only if the price, and thus the additional revenues they will get, will at least fully cover the additional costs they must incur. The minimal "supply price" of additional output is the marginal-cost price. And this, for the industry's full capacity output, is far above the per unit operating cost, and may well equal or exceed the per unit *full* cost, including all "overhead" or "fixed" costs. Of course, if the demand even at a very high price calls for a greater output than the industry can possibly produce with its existing facilities, then the price will rise still higher, to the point of reducing the amount demanded to equality with that supplied, and this price may be any distance above, and is independent of, production cost in every sense. But for any output that is both within the industry's capacity, and equal to the amount demanded at the marginal-cost price, the latter rules.

There is one more topic still connected with Marshall's theory of these "short-run" adjustments which I must touch on; namely, his famous, original, and important theory of what he called "quasi-rent"—elements of incomes which, over "the short run," are determined just as Ricardian land-rents are even in "the long run," i.e., they are not elements of price-determining production costs, but variable, demand-and-price-determined "surpluses" *over* the costs (for *other* factors of production) which *do* make up that other category. In Ricardo's theory of land-rent, as we know, the supply of land available for use in growing "corn" is permanently fixed, and every increase of demand for "corn" is met by using more labor and capital (seed, fertilizer, cultivating tools, etc.) on some or all of the available land. Only the wages which must be paid for this labor and the profits which must be earned on this capital—only the costs *of working* the land—count in affecting the price of "corn," by so regulating the amount produced that it can all be sold at a price "covering" them. As long as the demand is so small that only the best land is used and even it is not intensively used—the output can still be varied at a constant cost per unit—none of the land will yield any rent to its owners. But when demand becomes so great that "diminishing returns" come into play, in meeting it—marginal cost rises above average or per unit cost, and the price which must cover the former more than covers the latter—there emerge for landowners rent incomes equal to the "surpluses" of the values of the outputs from their lands over the costs (for labor and capital in tillage, sowing, cultivating, harvesting, etc.) of producing those outputs. And the amounts of these land-rents depend on or vary with the demand for and price of the product, and do not affect that price.

Now in the same way, in Marshall's theory of the possible fluctuations of the fortunes of any industry and its member firms within the (intermediate) "short run," the income-yields, to the firms, of the factors of production ("plant" and equipment, managerial staffs, etc.) making up their temporarily fixed "capacities," are the "quasi rents" earned by those factors, i.e., the variable "surpluses" of gross revenues over total operating or variable costs. The "fixed costs," connected with these factors existing in temporarily fixed supplies, do not as such affect the price at which the product will be sold. And the currently realized returns (if any) on the investments represented by those "fixed-cost" factors, depend on the current state of the demand for the product, and the latter's selling price as determined by the marginal cost of the output adjusted (as well as possible) to that demand, and the excess (if any) of that price over the per unit variable or operating cost. Only over "the long run" do long-term capital investments, in the purchase or production of durable producers' goods or factors of production, "tend" to yield returns or incomes (net over the costs of *using* them) equal on the average to depreciation plus interest at the going rate on the original investments. Over any "short run" these returns or incomes may be of any magnitude from zero to sums far greater than mere normal interest, etc.—depending on the demand for the product and its selling price, which they do not influence. More will be said below about Marshall's theories of land-rent, capital's quasi rents, and interest, as parts of his theory of the distribution of income in the economy. Here we have seen only that his important theory of quasi rents grew out of his theory of the "short-run" effects of demand changes, and the supply and cost and price adjustments possible within the "short runs" in question. And now I move on to his theory of the "long-run normal" prices of all products, i.e., the prices that would go with *complete* adjustments of the industries concerned—adjustments not only of their current outputs, but of all elements of their "capacities"—to the states of their markets, or the demands for their products.

Let us briefly consider first in this connection, as the simplest case, that of an industry which can, in the long run, produce its product in whatever quantity the market calls for, at a constant or unchanged, full per unit cost of production; expansion or contraction of the industry does not, in the long run, either raise or lower this full per unit production cost. In this case, the fully adjusted, normal, or long-run equilibrium *price* of the product is determined by and equals this production-cost figure (including in this "cost" the "normal profit" required to reward the capital and enterprise of the firms in the industry as well as they could be rewarded in alternative employments, and to induce continuing production of this product in the amounts demanded). If the industry has once become fully adjusted to its market, and has been selling its product at the "normal" or "cost" price, but then the demand (at that price) increases—the immediate temporary effect of the latter event, of course, will be to raise the price above the normal or cost level. But in time this extra profitability of the industry will draw new firms and factors of production of all kinds into it, and increase its total capacity and output, or the supply of this product on the market, to the point of again lowering the market price to the (unchanged) normal or cost figure.

This simple case reveals in the clearest light the independent role of the (physical) efficiency and cost of production, as distinguished from that of the utility of and demand for the product, in the process of determining its price or value. It also reveals why Marshall—like Adam Smith, Ricardo, Mill, and all the early classical economists—regarded utility and demand and their changes as importantly affecting price or value, only or mainly temporarily or in the short run, and treated efficiency or cost as the more important determinant of value in the long run. But even in the more complex and important cases, as we shall now see, of production at increasing, or decreasing cost (per unit for increasing outputs), the same principle applies in the sense that, while in these cases the changes of demand change the relevant efficiencies and costs themselves and thus change the long-run equilibrium prices of the products; still it is the effects of the eventual supply adjustments on efficiencies and costs, and not the direct effects of demand changes per se on market prices, which determine those long-run equilibrium prices.

Let us consider next the case of the (any) increasing-cost industry or product; a good example might be coal mining. Here the industry is likely to consist of diverse producers with various efficiencies and per unit over-all production costs. The few fortunate companies, owning the few best mines, with ample amounts of excellent and easily or cheaply extractable coal, can produce up to certain amounts at low production costs per ton; and if the total demand is no more than they alone can easily produce, they alone will operate, and the price will depend on and equal their low costs. But if demand increases far beyond this, (1) these lowest-cost mines will increase their outputs to the point of raising their per unit and, still more, their marginal costs—the latter up to the level of the price obtainable, i.e., well above the former; and (2) additional, inferior or higher-cost mines will also operate and contribute to the total supply on the market. The long-run "tendency" then will be to make the supply such, relative to the demand, as to make the price equal to the marginal cost of this equilibrium output, i.e., both the initial, per unit, production cost for the marginal mine or producer—the least efficient, highest-cost one from which a contribution to the total supply is required, if the demand is to be met—and the marginal costs of the more efficient mines or producers, which for them are in this case greater, by various amounts, than their average or per unit costs. And so incidentally, in this long-run equilibrium situation for any industry with these characteristics or this kind of supply-cost function, the industry's intramarginal producers—all those more efficient than the marginal producer—realize "producers' surpluses" (essentially or mainly Ricardian "rents") from their superior natural-resource factors, equal to the excess of the marginal cost and selling price of the product over their average or per unit production costs, times their volumes of output.

Quite different, however, is the Marshallian theory of the decreasing-cost industry, where growth—of the demand or market for the product, and so of the industry, and (up to some point, i.e., its optimal size) each individual firm—in the long run lowers the cost of production per unit of output, for every firm, and the price at which the enlarged demand can be profitably satisfied. A large number and variety of "external" and "internal" economies of greater volume production are brought into effect which, combined, more than offset the effect of any increase of "pressure" upon any permanently "scare" factor or factors of production required in the industry. Here not marginal but average or per unit production costs count in affecting the selling price, since where average cost is falling, marginal cost is lower and falling faster, and production at a price covering only marginal cost would be unprofitable and would not continue. And in this case the differences in the efficiences and per unit costs of the various firms in the industry have not the same significance as in the increasing-cost industry. Where the more efficient can expand only at rising cost, a great increase of demand must be met with the aid of less efficient producers also, with the result that the selling price must rise and remain high enough to cover their costs and keep them in business. Where the final effect of growth is not to raise but to lower costs generally, the firms that fail to lower and keep down their costs sufficiently are eliminated in the long run by the competition of the others which succeed in doing so.

Thus, while at any time the different firms that are currently in being and in operation in a decreasing-cost industry are likely to differ among themselves in efficiency and per unit production cost, the firms which have not yet expanded, fully, to their own optimal sizes, and are able to survive and grow and realize new "internal economies" and reduce their costs, will be tending to expand at the expense of, and cause an offsetting contraction and decline of, the firms that have excessive costs and fail to reduce them, for whatever reasons. At the same time, on Marshall's assumptions, the few both rather large and very efficient firms cannot expand so far as to alone meet or satisfy the entire demand for the product, without in the process becoming overlarge and less efficient. In fact the group of the too inefficient, too high-cost, declining firms may include one or more that already are *too* large and *therefore* inefficient—and the group of the highly efficient and/or still growing and increasingly efficient firms may include some small "newcomers" in the industry, which manage to be efficient in spite of their smallness, or to "hang on" until growth makes them efficient. And costs are being reduced quite generally, although not universally throughout the industry, by realizations of "external economies" by all or most firms consequent upon growth of the industry as a whole, largely through entries of new firms into it. The decisive cost figure, then, which the product's selling price must cover to maintain an industry output equal to the amount demanded at this same price, is per unit production cost not for either the most or the least efficient member firm currently in the industry, but for a "representative" or typical, average, or modal firm. More precisely, the long-run equilibrium price in this case is a price that results in equal or offsetting amounts of growth of some of the firms and their parts or part of the industry's output, and contraction (toward extinction) of some other firms and *their* combined share of the industry's output, while just enabling the "middle," typical firms to continue as they are—and so keeps the industry's output as a whole in balance with the demand at this price. It is a peculiar, complex, dynamic, statistical "equilibrium," of opposite and offsetting disequilibria in different parts of the whole.

Many, indeed, most, *more* modern economic theorists have been strongly dissatisfied with or critical of and inclined to reject this Marshallian theory of competitive long-run equilibrium prices of the products of decreasing-cost industries, because it lacks the kind of logical simplicity, clarity, and indubitable rigor which they demand in all economic theory. But I think that Marshall's entire discussion of this most important class of modern industries, and the "long-run tendencies" to be expected in their growths, was a very valuable, broadly and deeply and richly informed, perceptive, and illuminating discussion, even though it fell short of solving, satisfactorily in a logical sense, all the problems that it raised. But now I must conclude this overlong chapter, quickly, with a necessarily very inadequate account or sketch of some of Marshall's ideas in the remaining field of theory of the distribution of income in the economy, or the processes of determination, by demand-and-supply conditions for the productive services of the different factors of production, of the shares of the value of output going respectively into the wages of labor, land-rents and the quasi rents of factors the supplies of which are "fixed" over considerable intervals of time, interest on capital funds, and business profits.

THE DISTRIBUTION OF INCOME

Here again, in the field of distribution of income, Marshall's general position differed in a measure from that of most of his contemporaries, i.e., his views agreed in a measure with the older Ricardian-classical position or point of view, in the same way as in the field of theory of value, or the processes of determination of the (relative) prices of the different products produced in the economy. We have seen that, in the latter field, whereas the other leaders in the new forward movement of economic theory in Marshall's time tried to make the new analysis of utility and the demands for products the entire basis of an entirely new theory of value, Marshall insisted on retaining, and combining with that new analysis, much of the Ricardian-classical stress upon production cost (efficiency) and supply conditions. In the same way, in theory of income-distribution or the pricing of productive services and determination of the income shares, the prevailing "new" tendency was to base this entirely upon analysis of the "marginal productivities" of the existing supplies of the productive factors, and the consequent demands for and "demand prices" of their services; but Marshall insisted, here again, that fully as much attention should be paid, in something like the Ricardian-classical way, to long-run adjustments of the aggregate supplies of productive factors (apart from "land") and the "costs" requiring to be counterbalanced by the "supply prices" of their services. But all this needs a somewhat fuller explanation, for the benefit of readers not familiar with the "marginal-productivity" theory of the income shares. Let me first briefly outline the essence of the latter, and its relations to the Ricardian theories of land-rent, wages, and "profit" (interest) or the income-yield of capital, and then return to Marshall and his "synthesis."

There were two fundamental achievements of the general advance of economic theory in this period: the first was the "marginal-utility" analysis and resulting theory of the pricing of products, and the other, second, new achievement was the "marginal-productivity" analysis and the theory of income-distribution based upon it. But unlike the "marginal-utility" analysis, which was wholly new as compared with Ricardian-classical theory, i.e., it had not been at all anticipated—even partially, in any measure—within the latter, the "marginal-productivity" analysis involved a wider generalization of, from, or beyond the Ricardian-classical "law of diminishing returns." It led to a theory of income-distribution related in one way to Ricardo's theories in that field, and especially, most nearly and fully related to his theory of land-rents, but generalizing the latter in a way that deprived it of its special significance, and discarding elements of Ricardo's theories of the other income shares (especially, wages), which Marshall was unwilling to discard so completely. As we know, Ricardo envisaged only one application of his "law of diminishing returns"—in the one context, of use of increasing amounts of labor and capital on the economy's fixed supply of "land," in the effort to increase the outputs of products, and with the result of increasing them only in decreasing ratios to the required additional inputs of labor and capital. In the later terminology, this amounted to a "law" asserting that, as more and more labor-and-capital came to be employed in productive operations on the fixed available amount of land, the joint "marginal productivity" of the labor-and-capital would fall to lower and lower levels; that is, the higher the ratio of the number of workers, and that of the amount of capital invested in paying their wages and equipping them with tools or machines, etc., to the amount of land, the smaller would be the differential contribution (difference made) to the output by employing, as against not employing, any one worker and the increment of capital investment associated with his employment. Now the later, fully developed, "marginal-productivity" analysis simply generalized that special "law" into one that (1) assumed continuous variability of the proportions or relative amounts in which all the different factors of production could be combined in any productive enterprise or operation; and (2) assumed the potential existence, in every enterprise or operation at any given time, with its given technology, etc., of some one optimal combination or proportion of all the factors, from all standpoints, i.e., one that would maximize the ratio of the amount of output to that of each and every factor employed; and (3) concluded that *every* departure from that optimum, through use of more (beyond that point) of any one factor along with fixed amounts of the other factors, would always entail a declining marginal productivity of the "increasing" factor.

The Ricardian "case" of adding new increments of labor and of capital on the same land and getting diminishing additions to output came to be viewed as only one special case of or exemplifying a far more general principle. A factory could, within limits, vary the number of workers employed, with the same plant and equipment—and beyond some point, successive further additions to the labor force, if nothing else was changed, would result in declining additions to output, i.e., a declining marginal productivity of labor. Or a constant labor force could be equipped with more and better machinery, through investment of more capital—and beyond some point this would bring into view a declining marginal productivity of capital. Or with labor force and produced means of production constant, a farm or other enterprise could use more land, and the marginal productivity of land would emerge and obey the same "law." Finally, this all-around generalization of the old "diminishing-returns" principle was made the basis of a new theory of income-distribution, or the market values of the productive services of all the different factors of production, in the following way.

The difference that would be made to the output, sales, and gross receipts of any enterprise, by its employment at any time of one more unit of any single factor of production, with the amounts of all other factors in use held constant, would determine or be the value or benefit to that enterprise, at that time, of employing that or any equivalent unit of that factor. In a competitive economy, all enterprises would be competing not only to sell their products in the product markets, but also to hire all the factors of production in the factor markets; and endeavoring to combine all their factors in the most advantageous or profitable proportions, in view of (1) their potential productive contributions and (2) their currently prevailing, market, hire-prices. At the same time, in every factor market, all units of the existing supply of that factor would be competing for employment. So long as any enterprises could employ more units of any factor, profitably, at its current hire-price—i.e., by doing this add more to output and value of output or receipts than to outlays—they would do so; and by so doing, they would add to the demand for this factor, or tend to "bid up" its hire-price. But if, when all enterprises were using the largest amounts of any factor which they could with any advantage use at its current hire-price, i.e., using enough of it to make the value of its marginal product (the differential contribution to output of one unit of the factor) barely equal to that hire-price; if at this point a part of the existing supply of the factor was still unemployed, the competition of this part for employment would lower the market hire-price, and then some enterprises would hire more of the factor. Thus the competitive-equilibrium hire-price, or rate of payment for the productive service, of each factor of production, would equal or measure and be determined by the marginal productivity of that factor, in the equilibrium situation of full employment, together, of the entire existing or available supplies of all the factors.

There is no reason to question the validity, as far as it goes, of this general theory, as an account of the "tendencies" of competition in the factor markets, or the "natural, competitive" rates of payment for all productive services—in an economy with static, "given" supplies of all factors of production. But it deals only with "the demand side" of the general problem, and does not answer or even raise or consider any questions about long-run effects of high or low rates of payment for productive factors on their aggregate supplies, and return effects of the possible responses or adjustments of supplies (of course via resulting changes of marginal productivities) on the rates of payment.

Now in Ricardian-classical theory, as we know, only one of the factors of production—"land"—was thought of as "fixed" in aggregate supply, so that only changes of the volume and intensity of demand for its use could alter its income-yields to its owners. Thus Ricardo's theory of land-rent was the only part of his theory of income-distribution which fully resembled, in a way, the later "marginal-productivity" theory of *all* income shares. But this resemblance can be seen clearly only if we now bring into view another aspect of the latter theory. Supposing the amount-in-use of any factor to be varied, with the amounts-in-use of the others held constant, would lead to "explaining" the share of income (of the value of all output) received or paid for the use of this factor, *as* the value of the increment of output dependent on employment of the last-added unit of this factor, times the number of units employed up to that point. *Or* the same results could be reached in another way, by supposing use of a fixed amount of this same (any) factor and varying amounts of the others, and regarding the income-yield of the "fixed" factor as the "surplus" of the total value of total output *over* the sum of the shares paid for *the others* in accordance with *their* "marginal productivities." It was in this latter way, as we know, that Ricardo arrived at his theory of land-rent—as the "surplus" of the value of the output on or from each given piece or area of land, over "the cost of production" of that output, i.e., the sum of the necessary payments for the labor and the capital employed; and the rates of the latter payments would decline, and the rent surplus would increase, as more labor and capital came to be employed on each piece of land. According to the later theorists, Ricardo's view of the situation was too limited; his land-rent surpluses were that in one (his) view, but they also were at the same time the values of the marginal products or productive contributions of the pieces of land as such; and the wages of the farm workers and the profits of the tenant farmers, while corresponding to the productivities of the labor services and the capital investments, could also be viewed as rentlike surpluses, over the productivity payments for the land services.

Now of course Ricardo's special theory of land-rent did not involve or imply any denial of—but was entirely consistent with—recognition of the productivity of the land. His theory treated "land" and its "rent" as "peculiar" among the factors of production and income shares, only in respects beyond the purview of the "marginal-productivity" theory of them all. That is, he held that of bare land as such—the pure "gifts of nature" in or associated with it, as distinguished from all man-made "improvements"—there is in the world or on the earth, substantially, a fixed supply; although of course technological and economic change can alter the amount of it that mankind is able to use. Above all, the essential point in the logic of the Ricardian view about this is that the supply of "land" in the sense indicated—bare land, free gifts of nature, apart from improvements—does not respond and adjust to the growth of demand and rise of rent-yields; the rise of the latter does not cause production of more land and a consequent fall of the rent-yields back to levels only compensating the producers of new land, or returning to them its production cost, with interest. Ricardo thought "land" in his sense a "peculiar" factor of production, not humanly producible, having no cost of production, but existing in a fixed supply, and hence yielding to its owners incomes that, with economic growth, could rise indefinitely and permanently, or would have no "natural" or "normal" levels, determined, through supply adjustments, by production costs. And he further implied, I think, that those incomes (rents), while paid for the productive services of land as such, were *not* paid for any *personal* productive services rendered by the land*owners*—full compensation to them for all their costs for improvements, etc., were first deducted from the gross business rentals, in computing their pure or net economic "rents," received by them simply as legal owners of "free gifts of nature," in positions to charge for rights to use them. Still, whether all this really makes "land" and "rent" peculiar at all depends on whether any contrasting things are true about the other factors and income shares.

In Ricardian theory the clearest contrast appeared to be there in the case of the labor supply and the "natural" long-run adjustments of that and so of the level of (real) wages. The Malthus-Ricardo theory of this matter, as we know, held that temporary, high, real wages would always spur population growth and cause the labor supply to increase to the point of again lowering real wages to a "subsistence" level. This theory of wages, let us notice, was entirely consistent with the later "marginal productivity" theory, but added to that its thesis that the supply adjustments would over the long run tend to make and keep the marginal-productivity wage itself equal to that just covering the cost of support and reproduction of the needed, or equilibrium, labor supply. There was, however, the loophole of recognition of the possibility that a sufficient "temporary" rise of real wages, sufficiently prolonged, might so raise the prevailing subjective standard of living of the working population as to lower its birth rate or make "the preventive check" more strongly active, and thus limit the increase of the labor supply and set the long-run equilibrium wage rate at a new, higher level. The unexpectedly full realization of this possibility in the modern Western world has made the old Malthus-Ricardo theory no longer very relevant or significant in this area. Some validity must perhaps be granted to the view of some of the later neo-classical theorists—the Austrians especially made this point—that as population growth and the long-run determination of the aggregate labor supply in that sense is really not controlled by economic variables alone, but is a broader, sociological, not a purely economic problem, the marginal-productivity theory of wages represents about all that economic theory can do with this topic (wages). But I shall touch, below, on Marshall's views on these matters—efforts to analyze cost and supply, as well as productivity and demand, variables affecting wage rates and the earnings of labor of different sorts.

As to capital and interest, Ricardian theory unfortunately left the basic questions in this special field for the most part unanswered and even unrecognized. One can say I think that Ricardo's capitalists, or saver-investors, were clearly, unlike his landlords, paid not for rights of use of "free gifts of nature" legally owned by them, but for the personal, productive service of saving-and-investing and thereby increasing the economy's supply of capital and producing power; in this sense they "earned" their "profits," as the landlords did not "earn" their "rents." But Ricardo, alas, did not spell this out or make it explicit; and further, by treating real capital or capital goods, e.g., machines, as only "embodied labor," he even appeared to deny the existence of this separate factor of production, distinct from labor and from land, i.e., the service of productive saving-and-investing; and thus he opened a door to the false doctrines of Marx. Nor did Ricardo clearly suggest that the capitalists needed to be paid interest to induce them to do enough saving-and-investing—that this service of theirs to production involved any "cost" or "sacrifice" on their parts which required to be compensated, or which would so limit the supply of the service as to ensure this compensation. He expected that with economic growth, the growth of the capital supply, in the fixed land-area, and "diminishing returns" (declining marginal productivity of capital, in the later terminology) would lower the rate of "profit" or interest, perhaps eventually to zero. At what point this decline would check the growth of the capital supply and all economic growth or bring about the "stationary state," he did not clearly say; but he seems to have thought of "profit" or the net incomes of the capitalists mainly as the *source* of new savings, and not also as a needed incentive or "supply price" for them.

It is in a way unfortunate, I think, that most of the subsequent developments, after Ricardo's time, of capital-and-interest theory failed to stress the productivity *of the service* of saving-and-investing; and exclusively stressed either or both the productivity of capital in the sense of capital goods, e.g., machines—letting this appear to involve nothing different from the productivity of land—or/and various theories of the psychic or subjective "cost" or "sacrifice" involved in saving (and investing), and the necessity of a "normal" or minimal "return" or rate of interest or net income, to "reward" or compensate and induce it. The idea of the latter kind that eventually became most prevalent—being most elaborately developed by the Austrian theorist, Böhm-Bawerk—was that decisions to save and invest parts of incomes instead of spending them entirely on current consumption, involve "exchanges" of "present goods" for "future goods," and have to be compensated or induced or paid for because it is human nature to "undervalue" future as compared with present wants and goods. The saver-investor gives up command over present or current satisfactions for future repayment and power to command satisfactions only at the later time. He is willing to do this only if, not merely repaid, but also paid a "premium" (interest), because he appreciates future wealth less highly than the present wealth (consuming power) he is giving up, and must get more of the former to make it equal, in his present estimation, to the latter. Any fuller account here of Böhm-Bawerk's whole, much more complex, theory, is impossible and unnecessary. Marshall, as we shall see in a moment, had a similar, independent theory, and called the subjective "cost" of the service of saving-and-investing, "waiting"—the saver-investor "waits" to be repaid and compensated, and the compensation (interest) is the reward or incentive for his "waiting." But now let us turn back to Marshall's theory of all income-distribution.

With regard to "land" and rent," Marshall largely adhered to the Ricardian special theory on this topic. He endeavored to clear away misunderstandings of and misplaced objections to that special theory, and also to revise or improve it, and as modified, to defend it. He improved especially on Ricardo's statement of the distinction between "bare land" or the "free gifts of nature" connected with land, and all man-made or at-costs-produced-or-maintained additions to or features of good-land-in-use. Thus, for example, soil fertility, as Ricardo did not explicitly recognize, can be increased and/or can become depleted if not maintained by proper farming practices. But as Marshall insisted, there are purely "natural" endowments of land—as portions of space or room on the earth, in more or less advantageous locations, and with their "annuities of sunshine and rainfall" in Marshall's phrase—which do make up a "factor" of production that is not produced in a variable output by human industry but is supplied in an ultimately fixed amount by "nature," so that parts of this supply yield incomes to their owners which depend on or vary with demand conditions, only, with no long-run supply adjustments operating to return them to cost-determined, "normal" levels. But Marshall went on to add that "land" in this sense or aspect is only the extreme or limiting case of a much larger class of productive agents, all existing at each point of time and through at least considerable intervals of time in supplies so "fixed" as to make their production costs, if any, irrelevant to their current income-yields; and thus we come back to his concept of "quasi rents." "Land" in the Ricardian sense is *permanently* "fixed" in supply, and has no production costs that even in the longest run affect the rent-yields, through supply adjustments. But all produced aids to further production which are durable and of which the supplies respond and adjust to the demands for them only with marked delays or over quite long runs, yield incomes which within shorter intervals of time "behave" or vary like Ricardian land-rents, or as pure results of current and changing demand conditions—the variable "surpluses" of the values of outputs over the costs of using or operating them, or the other, more quickly variable costs connected with production of those outputs. "Returns" from long-term investments in production of buildings, machines, and the like—also from investments in acquiring, through education or training or experience, business or professional or technical and industrial skills—are not continually held at levels representing return, with interest, of the original investments. They only "tend" toward such levels, on the average over quite long runs; and over shorter runs they may currently be anything from zero (no return even of the original investments, to say nothing of any interest on those) to indefinitely great amounts far in excess of mere recoupment plus "normal" interest. Marshallian "quasi rents," then, are all such elements of incomes, of whatever kinds, which because of delays of adjustments of supplies to changed demands, and so of the payments-for-use to cost-determined "normal" levels, are in the meantime determined in the same way in which Ricardian land-rents are determined even in the long run.

At the other end of his spectrum or continuum from "land," with all quasi-rent-yielding factors ranged *between* these two extremes, Marshall placed "free or floating capital," i.e., new savings and all capital funds not yet committed to any specific long-term investments; and he connected "interest," as distinguished from "rent" and from "quasi rent," especially with this "free or floating capital." The latter, that is to say, is what always commands simply interest at the going rate—no more and no less. For on the capital-funds market there is always, from business firms, a demand for more new capital—and for a greater amount, the lower the interest rate—as long as the expected benefits (from borrowing and investing more) to their outputs and earnings exceed the interest they must pay. And there is always a supply coming onto this market, from lenders and investors—a greater supply, the higher the interest rate—as long as the promised returns (of interest) appear to the suppliers to be sufficient compensation for the "waiting" they undergo. Hence the opposite variations of the demand and the supply with the interest rate keep the latter at its equilibrium level, and equalize the demand and the supply. Unlike the supplies of particular capital goods, which get adjusted only more or less slowly to demand changes, to the point of returning their income-yields to "normal" (depreciation plus interest) levels, the supply of "free or floating capital" adjusts very quickly to the demand at the equilibrium interest rate, and hence always commands just that rate of return. Though it would be desirable to say more about these theories of different types of property income, I must now turn to the subject of wages for labor, and briefly notice a few of Marshall's ideas in *this* field.

That in competitive labor markets, at given times or with given available supplies of labor of different kinds, the market rates of wages for them, set by demand conditions, would be determined in accordance with the "marginal-productivity" principle—this proposition, advanced by other leading theorists of his time as the complete, true theory of wages, seemed to Marshall valid enough as far as it went, but only one part of an adequate theory. Even in its own field he insisted on a minor "qualification" in the interest of "realism": employers generally could not, in practice, hire additional workers without also in some degrees increasing some of their other investments; hence the added workers would earn only their marginal *net* additions to the employers' revenues. So long as more labor of any kind was available, and any firms could, by hiring more of it at the current wage rate, increase their outputs, sales, and revenues by more than the entailed increases of their costs or outlays, they would do this; and the demand would thus equal the available supply at a wage rate equal to the marginal net value-product of each worker of this kind, when all of them were employed; and the competition of firms for workers and of workers for jobs would move the wage rate to this level. But all this was true on the assumption of "fixed" or "given" available labor supplies of all kinds; and Marshall held that, in this field as in others, a complete theory must include a further, separate analysis of the likely long-run supply adjustments, responsive to and reacting upon the prices—in this case wage rates—in question.

He did not, of course, endeavor to revive, for the aggregate supply of all labor and general level of all wages, exactly the Malthus-Ricardo theory of increase of the former through population growth, and reduction of the latter to "subsistence"; nor did he maintain that this theory in this simple form, without extensive revisions, could claim continuing validity in the Western world of his own time. But he did include as one of the many parts of his broad discussion of diverse influences affecting wages a critical review of, and effort to revise, this old theory. He noted that it had been substantially valid in its time, and was still valid in many parts of the world; and he endeavored to revise it suitably for application in the more modern Western world, or reanalyze the changed and changing situation in the latter, with regard to the rates and the interactions of population growth and economic progress, and *reciprocally interconnected* improvements of the (marginal) productivities, real earnings, and living standards and ambitions to maintain and improve the latter, of the mass of working people. Of perhaps even greater interest, however, are his discussions not of that problem, but of other problems relating to responses and adjustments of supplies, and supply prices, of labor of different kinds—how prospective earnings, and costs of entry and training, etc., and other considerations affect young workers' choices of their occupations and the relative numbers going into different ones; what influences affect the choices and mobility of workers generally among jobs and parts of the economy; and how "supplies of labor," not only in the sense or aspect of numbers of workers available, but also in that of their degrees of eagerness to work and the quantities and efficiencies of work offered by them, may respond to improvements of their wage rates and other incentives. Under that last heading, for example, Marshall noted the fact that while in "backward" (we now say "underdeveloped") countries, where working people generally are accustomed to low fixed standards of living and are not ambitious to improve them, the response of work offered to a rise of wage rate may be *negative,* i.e., people will work only enough and long enough each day to earn their accustomed daily income and then "quit," or they will work fewer hours, the higher the hourly pay. In the advanced and progressive countries, on the contrary, where the people are ambitious, the response generally is positive, i.e., they will do more and better work, the better they are paid.

As to choices and movements of workers among jobs, Marshall stressed the point that relative financial rewards alone are not always decisive. Workers tend to balance or "weigh up" all the attractions and disattractions, to them, of the different available jobs—the earnings prospects *and* the working and living conditions, congeniality or the reverse of the environments and associates, foremen, and fellow workers, neighborhoods to live in, schools for their children, etc.—and choose the jobs which they feel offer on the whole the greatest "net advantages," all things considered. In other words, the levels of the wage rates that any particular employer or firm, as compared with others, may find it necessary to offer to attract adequate numbers of workers of different kinds may be affected—raised or lowered—somewhat, by all sorts of features of or incident to working for that firm, *besides* its wage rates. This of course is obvious, but easily overlooked by economic theorists; Marshall's stress on and detailed discussion of it was typical of his constant efforts to make all his theories as realistic as possible, and suggestive of all problems in need of further empirical as well as theoretical study. He had still much more to say about labor and wages which cannot be considered here. I must now turn, finally, to his unique treatment of the abstract factor of production, "organization" (as distinguished from all the particular factors, land, labor, capital, etc., combined and organized into business enterprises)—and the activities of businessmen as such in creating and developing effective organizations —and their rewards for or earnings from or through those activities, i.e., "profits" as returns distinct from and additional to ordinary interest on their equity capital, and wages for their routine work as managers of or within already established organizations.

The treatment of *this* topic within Marshall's *Principles* is somewhat especially diffused, vague, and difficult, and the little I can say about it here must be *very* inadequate. He conceived as a very important aspect of human-social life, and within that, of all economic life, the "organizing," and the resulting "organizations"—in the broadest sense—of the "undertakings" of all kinds that arise, develop, and function in societies, and of the interrelated activities and the resources of the groups of people who jointly carry them on or come to have various roles in or relations to them. Within his very broad and diversified vision of all the organizing and organizations occurring in societies (not "economies" alone but "societies" in all their aspects), the included vision of all (primarily) economic "organizing" and "organizations" and the latter's internal structures and external relations and performances or functionings had its place as only one part of the still more vast and varied whole. To a large extent, he thought of the origins and growths and functionings of "organizations" to produce or do things needed or wanted within societies as "natural" developments, responsive to existing or potential or anticipated demands, and the discoverable or sensed conditions of meeting, satisfying, or serving those demands as efficiently and profitably as possible. But the chief "organizers" of all economic resources and activities, in the economic world and system which Marshall's economics was about, were the active businessmen; and the "organizing" done or carried out, by them, with their "business ability in command of capital," figured in his thought as their distinctive role or function in the economic system, and the source of their special rewards or incomes, business profits.

CONCLUDING COMMENTS

It is hard, at the end of this survey of some of the contents of Marshall's *Principles,* to pull what has been said into focus, and conclude with any worthwhile assessment of the work as a whole. The student who wants real understanding and appreciation of Marshallian economics must of course read and study the *Principles* for himself, and not rely on what I have said about it. My attempt to survey, in the latter part of this chapter, some of the material in Marshall's sixth book, on the distribution of income or the value of output among the contributors of different productive services or factors, has been perhaps the most inadequate and unsatisfactory of all parts of this chapter. Marshall's own treatment of this part of the whole subject matter of his theoretical system is in some ways the least well organized part of the latter and the most difficult to summarize, and my summaries here are much too brief and randomly selective to be of much value. But I felt unable or unwilling to omit this part of the whole work entirely from consideration here, because this subject—theory of income-distribution in this sense—was a major preoccupation of the leading economists of Marshall's time, and was important to him; and his contributions in this field were important. Although in more recent and now current times, this traditional part of economic theory has been falling into relative neglect, I think it continues to deserve and need more attention than is now generally given to it, and the study of Marshall's work in this field is still worthwhile. But the more important, main core of Marshall's *Principles* lies in—together with its third and fourth books, leading up to this—its vital fifth book, on the processes of adjustment of the supplies and prices of the different products produced in the economy to the demands for them and the costs of producing, as efficiently as possible, the supplies adjusted to those demands—the processes of adjustment of this kind which "tend" to be accomplished, in stages, over short and long runs of time, in a fluid, free, competitive economy. The partial account of this which I have given here is also very inadequate; but a few final comments on it may be offered in conclusion.

As we have seen, in Marshallian theory of the pricing of products etc., the focus is upon whole "industries," each made up of many independent firms all contributing to the aggregate supply of one kind of product; and the demand, cost, and supply conditions for the product as that of the entire "industry"—with but little attention to the special situations and behaviors of individual firms. In the more modern development of this branch of economic theory, since Marshall's time, there has been a marked change in this respect. The newer theory of "monopolistic competition," thought of now as the generally prevailing, real form of business competition, stresses the degrees of market power of individual firms and their freedoms to choose, within limits, their own price and output policies; and thus shifts the main focus of attention away from whole "industries" to individual firms. The concept of "industries" is seen to be vague, arbitrary, and full of difficulties, and tends to be abandoned. Now this on the whole is undoubtedly an advance of price or value theory and leads to, in some ways, a more realistic, detailed, and accurate type of analysis. But I think the older, Marshallian, broader and more unified though rougher, theoretical "picture" of main general "tendencies" in the economy as a whole and its major parts still has a value of its own. It is true, on the other hand, that Marshall's theory of these matters, with its way of focusing on one "industry" and product at a time, lacked the logical completeness and neatness of the Walrasian "general-equilibrium" theory, which kept the whole economy in view throughout, stressed the interdependence of all prices and all economic variables, and expressed the abstract general forms of the relations among them all in a system of simultaneous equations. But as compared with *this* kind of price theory I think Marshall's "one-industry-at-a-time" analysis gets beyond the very limited, abstract, formal achievement of Walrasian theory to a somewhat fuller, more detailed, and realistic understanding of each major part of the whole system of all economic processes. And I think this more than compensates for its failure to bring out as clearly the over-all general pattern of the whole.

In much present-day economic theory there is again, besides tendencies to prefer other kinds of price theory to the Marshallian kind, an even more important tendency to attach less importance than all or most nineteenth-century economists attached, to all price theory, and turn more attention to other tasks and problems of economic analysis. This is somewhat connected, as we shall see in the next chapters, with a recent widespread change of the general outlooks—the social, moral, and political philosophies—of many modern economists. The centrality of price theory in all classical and neo-classical economic theory was in a part a result of the influence of the old economic liberalism—the idealizing vision of the system of free enterprises and competitive markets—on the views of economists as to what were their main scientific tasks. Near the top of the list of the merits ascribed to the free and competitive economic system, was the role ascribed to its system of flexible relative prices as reflections of demand conditions and incentives and guides to production, in bringing about an efficient deployment of all productive efforts and resources toward a full and balanced satisfaction of the peoples' demands for all kinds of products. Hence to all economists sharing this outlook, analysis of the processes of adjustment of the relative prices and supplies of all products appeared to be the central and most important task of economic theory. Other outlooks now more in vogue lead to greater stress on other groups of problems, and other directions of main effort in developing economic theory and research. But as the reader knows, I personally believe that the old economic liberalism has in it much enduring wisdom, and accordingly believe that a good deal of emphasis on the task of understanding the potential working of a free price system is still appropriate. There are other important tasks of economic analysis, and the nineteenth-century economists, including Marshall, did much useful work on many of them, which it has not been possible to notice sufficiently within this book. But I think there is wisdom, for today, in an attitude toward Marshall similar in one way to his attitude toward Ricardo. As Marshall held that the "revolution" in economic theory in his time was not really so complete a "revolution" as it claimed to be, making Ricardo's achievements wholly obsolete, but a limited advance or range of advances which needed to be combined with the enduringly valid elements of Ricardo's system, so I would say, the theoretical "revolutions," claiming to be such, of our later time, are again only limited advances beyond the range of Marshall's insights, which also contained much that is worth retaining and combining with them.

CHAPTER 14

From the Last Heyday of the Classical Liberalism to the Mid-twentieth-century World's Ideologies, Regimes, and Conflicts: Communism and Fascism

INTRODUCTORY

In the on-going general development of economic theory, the period of full dominance of just the neo-classical (including the Marshallian) type of theoretical work and doctrines lasted through about the first two or even three decades of the present century. Various new developments were beginning to emerge in the 1920s; but it was not so much in that decade immediately after the First World War as in the next decade, dominated and profoundly influenced by the Great Depression, that the big changes got under way. And before considering the "big changes" since that time, in the character and state of economic theory, it may be well to consider what have been the concurrent "big changes" in the state of the world in all respects—far-reaching changes of prevailing, real, economic, social, and political conditions—of the relations, within nations, between their economies and their states and governments—assumptions by the latter of new, enlarged roles and new policies in dealing with the former—and growths of new ideologies and climates of public opinion about all public affairs. The world of today has become very different from the world in which neo-classical economies flourished, in the late nineteenth and very early twentieth centuries; and the world's "big changes," over these recent decades, have not been wholly without influence upon those of the state and character of economic theory, or the interests, lines of inquiry, and ideas of (most) economic theorists. I do not mean to suggest that there have been clear, simple, direct, or in all cases important connections between the recent new developments in the state of the world, to be surveyed in this chapter and the next, and the recent new developments of economic theory which will later engage our attention in the final chapters. But it does seem worthwhile and not inappropriate to look at the former before we take up the latter.

In a way this procedure is the best available substitute for that which has hitherto been followed throughout this book, of dealing in alternating segments of the whole with developments of formal political thought—political philosophies—and then with developments of economic theory for which those political philosophies have been the relevant, wider, intellectual "backgrounds" or "contexts." The declining importance and growing "scarcity," in all recent times, of philosophical political thought, and the movements of both modern economic theory and modern political life or practice away from or beyond the reach, so to speak, of the influence of any new, modern, political philosophies make it impossible to continue exactly the same procedure in dealing with the most recent period. We found this situation emerging in the late nineteenth century, and in trying to grasp the character of "Victorian liberalism" as the ideological background of or context around neo-classical economics, had to rely only partly on a few, slightly or doubtfully relevant, contemporary bits of articulate political thought, and partly on impressionistic generalities about the general climate of opinion of the epoch. And now we come to the fully modern time in which the situation above described is fully present, and there is nothing for it but to try to describe and discuss the several diverse climates of opinion (and the closely associated, actual regimes and social systems, types of public policies, etc.) which have recently arisen in the world: Communism, fascism, democratic socialism, and the newer, modern, modified, nonclassical "liberalism" which has been important mainly in the United States from the New Deal onward. I shall in the end, I admit, treat only the last two, and for the most part only the last one, of those four "isms," as having any very significant relations or connections with the modern developments of economic theory to be taken up in the final chapters. The Communist world, ideologically dominated by its revived and distorted Marxism, has of course contributed nothing—thus far—to the development of modern economic theory, which has gone on only in the non-Communist world, and has been affected or influenced, if at all, only very slightly and indirectly by Communist thought and practice and some aspects of the "free world's" struggle with the Communist world. And the fascist episodes, arising after the First and leading to the Second World War, had no direct significance for economic theory and will engage our attention only briefly.

Essentially, as we shall see, among all the various new developments of economic theory, the ones that remain at all fully in the "political-economy" tradition, and will alone receive consideration in this book (in the final chapters), have all grown up within and had importance for only the still more or less "liberal" part of the world; and have been interacting with the main "ideologies," important within the latter, chiefly in the sense or way of playing a (small) part in its groping search for "middle-way" policies, between the extremes of adherence to *laissez faire* and the leap into all-out or full-fledged socialism. Still, as the "liberal" world's internal tendencies and problems have not been by any means entirely unaffected by its external struggles with the "totalitarian" systems, creeds, and menaces, it seems not amiss here to begin with some remarks about the latter.

THE RISE OF COMMUNISM

Just before the end of the First World War, as we know, the Russian Revolution brought Lenin's group of radical Marxists to power in Russia and started the development of what has become the now vast and challenging "Communist" world or movement and "bloc" of countries ruled by "Communist" regimes. It is probably the most significant single fact about those regimes that all of them, so far, have come into existence in what were previously, by all modern Western standards, more or less extremely "backward" or "underdeveloped" countries, which had never known either well-developed and well-functioning economic systems of private "capitalism," or political democracy, or in any sense "liberal" cultures and societies. On the eves of their Communist revolutions all those countries were—to use these categories in this Marxist manner—in various early stages of emergence out of "feudalism" into "capitalism," and in early stages of industrialization, or of the industrial revolution—always, everywhere, in world history, highly productive of social disturbance and unrest, and especially so in these countries, given their special internal situations and the great disparities between them and the advanced Western countries. Living then under both cruel and weak, decadent despotisms and landlord ruling classes, and having only small and weak middle classes, businessmen too few and despised in their societies to have any influence, vast illiterate peasant masses, small groups of generally discontented and radical industrial workers, and small but highly influential groups of native intellectuals full of patriotic shame about the conditions of their countries and zeal to revolutionize and modernize them; all those countries were indeed "ripe"—though *not* in accordance with the recipe of Marx!—for revolutionary Marxism.

There is, I think, every indication, in the history of the world since

Marx's time, that he was in complete error in his expectation that the revolution which he prophesied would occur in each country only when that country had first gone through the full course or all the stages of capitalist evolution, maturation, and decline; that it would be, everywhere, the final stage of the life-cycle of capitalism which would engender the worst prevailing conditions, and open the minds of the masses to socialist truth, and so produce, for the first and only time, "the revolutionary situation" in which the socialist revolution could and would occur and triumph. On the contrary, as matters have turned out, everywhere the *first* stages of the growth of modern industrial capitalism have been its most precarious, distress-filled phase, either nearly or quite conducive to the occurrence and success of socialist revolutions. And in the countries where industrial capitalism went on developing through and beyond that phase, it has evolved into a persistently progressive system, gradually improving the lots and lives of more and more of all the people, and turning even most socialistically inclined workers and intellectuals into mild reformers instead of violent revolutionists. The successes of Communism in our present century, exclusively in "backward" countries, and its failure everywhere in the advanced and still progressive West, prove or at least very strongly suggest that Marx's views of predictions on these crucial matters were exactly wrong. Yet this of course did not appear to be the case in the 1930s—the decade of the Great Depression in the capitalist world. The latter then appeared to be confirming the prophecies of Marx; the Great Depression itself seemed to be the "final breakdown" of capitalism which he had predicted; hence Western Communist or neo-Marxist intellectuals had a transitory "field day" of great influence with or over many really non-Communist "liberals" and socialists. Of this and more recent Western developments I shall speak later; for the moment I am still concerned with what the story has been in the now Communist countries.

Another point about the attitudes of many of the native intellectuals in those countries, on the eves of their Communist revolutions, may have been important. Not only were those intellectuals commonly, as I have said, full of patriotic shame and zeal to bring about radical and rapid over-all improvement, but they were also commonly full of or addicted to vague, visionary, and enthusiastic modes of thought and feeling. Although deficient in practical experience and skills, they were educated in various products of Western thought, among which Marxism, with its visionary and impassioned quality congenial to their minds, made a special appeal to them, despite its limited relevance to the problems confronting them. In old Czarist Russia where the modern rise of Communism started, a large number and variety of revolution-minded intellectuals had long been at work in conspiratorial and agitational efforts through various parties and sects, with revolutionary Marxism, in several variants or interpretations, as the creed or creeds of the more important groups. And when the strains imposed upon that old Russia by the First World War and its part and experience therein—strains upon the strength of its regime and the loyalty of its people—brought "the revolutionary situation" fully into being there; and the first, Kerensky, moderate, middle-class, liberal-democratic revolution failed, as it was bound to in that society, to produce a strong, effective, solidly based and supported, new regime; Lenin and his Bolsheviki emerged as the strongest group of all, and successfully seized power and began the work of transforming Russia into what it is today.

In the Western world at first and for a time, a great many liberals, who thought of old Czarist Russia and all Oriental despotisms as the last, worst strongholds of all ancient evils, and were still full of the naïve optimism which looked forward to a destined, world-wide spread and progressive realization of their own ideals, hailed the Russian (Lenin's) Revolution with enthusiasm and expected it to lead on in that direction. But as the actual sequels have occurred, the Russian Communist regime and the others later added to it have merely developed into new despotisms, indeed far more efficient and progressive in many ways than the ancient despotisms replaced by them, but also even more thoroughly despotic, illiberal, brutal, unscrupulous, and inhumane. They have been succeeding, however, in rapidly industrializing their countries, increasing their economic outputs, modernizing those countries and their cultures as far as science and technology are concerned, and educating their vast populations, though on lines severely cramped, distorted, and weighed down with Communist indoctrination.

No doubt they have been achieving more rapid progress of the economic and related kinds than it would have been possible for those countries to achieve under or through any such systems of capitalism or of private enterprises, and more liberal or less despotic governments, as they might conceivably have been evolving if their Communist regimes had never arisen. By driving their peoples into making immense efforts and sacrifices; swiftly advancing their techniques of production from initially primitive to the most advanced, modern levels; fully utilizing abundant resources of all kinds that had previously been either unused or much underutilized; and planning, organizing, and coordinating, more or less effectively, the patterns of productive activities which previously, in those societies, never had been, as in well-developed, modern and efficient, private capitalist economies, efficiently planned and organized in all or most of the separate enterprises involved, and coordinated as whole patterns through adequate networks of well-organized markets; by doing all these things with furious energy, the Communist regimes in those formerly backward countries have brought about spectacular progress in a short time, without allowing and waiting for the slow, natural evolution of efficient systems of spontaneous, private activities, which those countries, with the best helps and encouragements and under the best conditions, probably could have achieved only in the course of one or two centuries.

Even when and where good, modern, liberal societies, with economic systems of efficient, free business enterprises and free markets, are highly developed and enabled to function well, they are perhaps not necessarily superior, by the sole criterion of economic efficiency and progress, to compulsively ordered and hard-driving systems of the Communist, despotic type. It has always been a mistake among purely pragmatic or utilitarian liberals to lay exclusive stress on the alleged, purely economic superiority of the liberal system, and feel certain of its necessary superiority in that respect simply, to or over all possible alternatives. The real, decisive, superior merit of the liberal system lies in its unique ability to combine *good* economic performance or achievements *with* realization by and protection for all of the human or humane freedoms which are ends of supreme value in themselves, and the freedom, integrity, and richly varied and progressive achievements of all intellectual, spiritual, and cultural life. It is not at all necessary to depreciate the indeed impressive economic or material achievements of the Communist regimes and countries in order to regard the price which those peoples have paid and are paying for them as excessive and tragic, and to remain fully convinced of the ultimate, universal, humane and ethical superiority of liberal civilization, and the duty of all who share in the latter and its benefits to defend and preserve it, and resist the spread of Communism.

THE ROLES OF INTELLECTUAL MARXISM AND OF OTHER FACTORS IN SHAPING THE MODERN "COMMUNIST" SOCIETIES

In considering the nature of modern Communism it is important to realize that, almost surely, its intellectual creed as such—Marxism—has played no more than a rather limited, small role as one among the many factors helping to shape the actual Communist regimes and social systems and determine or produce their characters, institutions, policies, achievements, and (to liberals) morally abhorrent features. That the influence of intellectual Marxism cannot alone have produced all that has been done and brought about in the now Communist countries is in fact a conclusion that already follows simply from knowledge of what is and is not contained in intellectual Marxism. For as we know, that system of thought as created by Marx did not include any blueprint, or anything more than a very few, very vague, general directives, for construction and operation and development of the new ideal social order.

Nearly all Marxism is about "history" and the evolution of "capitalism" and the "struggle" of the "working class" and its leaders within and with "capitalism," *up to* the triumph of their revolution and *the beginning*, only, of the work of building up or realizing the ideal new order. As to what the latter should and would be in its detailed structure and working, or how to design and build or realize it, Marx had in all extremely little to say, and that little was too vague to afford any very significant guidance to his followers. Hence his modern Communist disciples have had to improvise their actual regimes and policies as they went along, with very little help from their bible, the writings of Marx.

That has been true perhaps most clearly and fully in the important central field of economic theory and policy or "planning." Marxist economic theory is by its nature almost completely irrelevant to the problems that arise in the effort to build, operate, and develop a socialist "planned economy." It is an economic theory exclusively about the functioning and development of capitalist (*not* socialist) economic systems; and it is also, as economic theory, quite primitive, rudimentary, or crude, and contains no analysis of the requisites or essentials of true or good "economy" in the use of the available resources to attain any set of objectives—such "economy" as all good business managers try, and as planners and managers in a socialist economy must try, to practice. Hence Marxist economic theory is not convertible from its primary use for explaining how capitalist economies function and develop, to the different use of serving as a guide or aid to socialist planning. Modern economists, since the time of Marx, have developed much, far more advanced economic theory which, though also developed primarily for use in explaining how capitalist economies work or function, *is* thus convertible to that other use, and *could* be of far more assistance to economic planners in the Communist countries than anything in their Marxist heritage is or can be.[1] But this non-Marxist, modern economic analysis is—or at least has been until very recently—beyond the pale, or forbidden, in those countries, as "bourgeois economics," developed by economists reputed to be friendly or favorable instead of hostile to capitalism. Thus the Communist regimes have attained their impressive economic achievements not with the aid of Marxist econom-

[1] There is an extensive literature of good, purely economic-scientific, theoretical studies and discussions—by distinguished modern, non-Marxian, and in many cases politically and ideologically nonsocialist economists—of the theoretical problem of how a socialist economy would need to be designed and operated, to bring about the most "economical" pattern of uses of all productive efforts and resources in it, to maximize the satisfaction of the wants of its people. See, for example, the small book *On the Economic Theory of Socialism*, by Oskar Lange and F. M. Taylor, Benjamin E. Lippincott (ed.) (Minneapolis: University of Minnesota Press, 1938); and the summary of this literature and discussion of the problem in J. A. Schumpeter, *Capitalism, Socialism, and Democracy*, 3d ed. (New York: Harper & Brothers, 1950), part 4, "The Socialist Blueprint."

ics but in spite of being encumbered with it and reluctant to use the more useful modern intellectual tools of this kind, which they could be using.[2]

I shall argue in a moment, however, that if we consider not the economic systems, policies, activities, and achievements which have grown up under the Communist regimes, but the characters of the latter in their noneconomic or broader, social, cultural, moral, and political aspects, we may view their main traits of this other kind as *in part* results of the ideas of Marx; though *not* such results as he most probably intended or expected, i.e., not realizations of his ideals, but instead the inevitable actual results of all-out efforts *to* realize those ideals. But before I elaborate or explain that point, let me first remind the reader of another feature or element of intellectual Marxism itself, which in another way suggests the likelihood of only a limited role for it (Marxism), and a more important role for other factors, in the shaping of the modern, actual, Communist societies in *all* their aspects. Not only did Marx's system of thought *not* contain any detailed design for the new social order; it *did* contain, as its own most basic positive tenet, the proposition that the fundamental causes of men's actions and the social systems they create are not their ideas and beliefs, but the "material" conditions or circumstances, environments, or backgrounds of their lives, and the pragmatic necessities thereby imposed upon them. According to this basic tenet of their creed itself, the modern Communists in Soviet Russia, China, etc., have been most fundamentally impelled and directed, in all that they have done and created in those countries, not by their creed, but by the former, old, historic characters of and conditions in their countries, by the emerging, newer conditions they have been creating, and by the practical exigencies and necessities arising in the course of their endeavors. And I think there is little room for doubt that to a great extent that has been true in fact, though I don't think we can suppose that the causal factors (including the creed) and their roles and relations, or the process, have conformed exactly to Marx's theory, or dynamics, of "historical materialism."

That theory, as we know, asserts that the "material" conditions of life in which great masses of men live somehow *generate* in their minds, *via* their experiences, the desires, ideas, and beliefs, *through* which (not apart from or independently of which) the aforesaid "material" conditions *indirectly* bring about their actions. Thus the Marxist creed would have it that in the now Communist countries, all the features of their

[2] Professor Wassily Leontief, however, has recently returned from a visit to Soviet Russia and reported to his fellow economists at Harvard University that adherence to Marxist economics and unwillingness to study and use the best modern developments of economic analysis and research, have been abandoned, now, in the highest quarters in that country; and they are fast "catching up" with the West in this, as in all branches of pure and applied science.

actual regimes, social systems, policies, etc., have grown up as results of a spontaneous generation of the entire Marxist faith or outlook in the minds of "the masses" of the people in those countries, by their past "material" environments and circumstances, and resulting experiences. But this idea of course cannot be credited with more than a tiny fractional amount of truth. The poverty and ignorance in which those "masses" were immersed before the new regimes arose, and out of which they are beginning to be lifted, have no doubt facilitated their indoctrination with, and dispositions to believe, such elements of the Marxist creed as they could dimly understand. But in the main their nominal acceptance of the creed has been imposed by the compelling authority of the new, small, ruling groups. That "the masses" would have to be thus indoctrinated—that the theory of spontaneous generation of the "right" beliefs and attitudes in the mass mind, simply by "material" conditions, would not work—was in fact virtually admitted by Lenin when he said that if let alone the main body of the industrial workers would never develop the true socialist "consciousness" or view of their real class interest, or anything beyond their trade-union "consciousness" or outlook, which he described (of course correctly) as bourgeois in character. There would have to be, said Lenin, a strong "leadership" of the "proletariat" by its enlightened "vanguard," the Communist party—i.e., authoritarian indoctrination. And that of course has been going on in all the now Communist countries; and the actions of the rulers and those of the peoples directed by them, though undoubtedly in a vague way inspired and influenced by the Marxist vision, have been mainly directed, in all specific details, by the largely otherwise formed, particular purposes of the members of the ruling groups, by the practical exigencies confronting them, and by their improvisations of means and routes to their ends in their situations.

Somewhat more truth may be credited, however, to the theory of spontaneous generation in men's minds, by their environments, of devotion to the Marxist (Communist) beliefs and aims, and so of the resulting actions, if we think of this as applying not directly to "the masses" but only to those leaders among the builders and rulers of the Communist regimes who have been or become both able and trained Marxist theoreticians and also able planners and executives. As I said earlier, the "material" and general conditions which prevailed in the now Communist countries before they became that (in their revolutions), and which affected the outlooks or attitudes of the intellectuals who became leaders in developing their Communist movements, undoubtedly did much to make or turn those men into Marxists, i.e., those conditions made Marxism attractive and convincing to them, *and thus* impelled and directed them on their courses of action. But this also points somewhat away from the supposition that exactly the Marxism of Marx himself has been the main immediate cause of all that has since been done and brought into being in those countries. For the particular old environments or backgrounds, traditions, and experiences which must have formed or greatly influenced the minds, characters, beliefs, and dispositions of the great, early Communist leaders in Russia, China, etc., caused them not only to embrace Marxism but also to construe it in their own special ways. Their old environments helped to make them, in their ways of attaining and using power as men of action, ruthless, cunning, and unscrupulous tyrants, in ways and measures beyond any ever fully envisaged by Marx, who expected that the builders of his utopia would be fully civilized and normally humane "leaders of the working class" in fully developed, modern capitalist, industrial countries.

Yet I do think that to a considerable extent we can attribute the monolithic and ruthless, totalitarian, despotic nature of the Communist systems to the influence of the Marxist ideal of achieving completely unified or solidaristic, harmonious societies, with no (allowed or overt) internal conflicts. The actual result of adherence to this aim is bound to be ruthless despotism, since the dream of a genuine, spontaneous, perfect harmony or cooperation among all the members of any vast society of diverse free men never has been or can be anything but a foolish, utopian, unrealizable dream. Where men are free there are bound to be conflicts, and where the goal is to eliminate all conflicts, the result is bound to be suppression of all freedoms. "Emancipating" the toiling "masses" from the limited powers of control of many separate, diverse, and rival employers, and striving to make them all work together with complete solidarity and high efficiency for the common good as defined by their "leaders" or rulers, has necessarily meant subjecting them to the far more despotic authority of the all-powerful state as the sole employer, owning all resources and all output or income or means for the support of life, and hence also in effect owning the bodies and souls of all its people. Yet the fact that the new regimes of this type have been built up in countries which always had had despotic regimes, and under historically created conditions that imbued the new leaders with despotic tendencies, and the masses of the peoples with submissive tendencies, undoubtedly has still further accentuated those results of the influence of the ideas of Marx.

MARXISM AND OTHER FACTORS IN FOREIGN POLICY AND RELATIONS WITH THE WEST

Moreover, if we now consider not simply the internal policies of the Communist regimes in their own countries, but their common attitude and behavior toward the rest of the world, and the development of the "cold war" or conflict between them and the Western capitalistic and democratic countries; here again we may see at work both the Marxist creed and some other accentuating factors. The Marxist prophecy and program demands extension of the revolution and the subsequent creation of the new order, eventually to or over the entire world; and there is no doubt that in this way their creed inspires in all ardent Communists—both in the countries which already have established Communist regimes and in all others—a fervent, genuine, "missionary" zeal to assist, foment, lead, and control potential revolutions wherever they may emerge, and progressively to add more and more countries to the Communist bloc. This of course means that the foreign policies of the already Communist countries are in effect committed to this program of world conquest. The West, however, has perhaps been slow in learning, after its recent experience with enemies of a different kind in the Second World War, that the Communist powers, in so far as their Marxist creed inspires and guides them, are committed to a program that is *not* primarily one of extensive, outright, military conquest. It is, rather, a very (indeed indefinitely) long-range program of patiently persistent, gradual, bit-by-bit expansion of their sphere of influence, to be accomplished mainly by exploiting local "revolutionary situations" within other countries, as and when and wherever they appear, that is, by infiltrating and capturing, assisting, leading, and directing local movements or strivings of discontented groups for radical change of any kind, which can be turned in the Communist direction.

According to the Marxist creed, all or nearly all significant, attempted, or potential revolutions emerging anywhere in the modern world are similar, "inevitable," and laudable developments within a uniform world-wide pattern, or on-going world-historical process, of progressive decay and self-intensifying evils and mass-popular revolts against the latter in all parts of the "capitalist" (non-Communist) world. And it is held to be predestined that eventually the revolutions will multiply and spread and succeed everywhere, and the entire world will become Communist, with provision only of some aid and guidance to each local revolt, as it occurs, by Communists on or sent to the spot and by the already established, major Communist regimes. The aid provided by the latter, however, of course can always include whatever military aid or pressure is judged to be at once feasible, reasonably safe, and necessary or expedient; and the Marxist theoretical predictions, program, and criteria for deciding where, when, and how to undertake each new campaign are vague enough to allow much room for each new actual decision to be governed largely by whatever other motives and considerations, external to the creed, may come into play. The Communist powers are impelled by *more* than *just* the ideological "missionary" motive, as I shall explain in a moment, into efforts to extend their power over more and more of the world. They *may* try to use the method of outright military conquest to almost any extent if all else fails and this promises success; and their great on-going build-up of military power and their recurrent use of military threats and forays as parts of their program, of course, make military preparedness and alertness in the West necessary. But the even greater, supreme necessity for the West, in view of the nature of the central and main challenge offered by the Communist powers, is to maintain and continually improve the virtues, vigor, health, viability, and progressiveness of the economic, social, and political systems of the advanced Western countries themselves, and the welfare, loyalty, and morale of their peoples; and also to help all the still non-Communist, "underdeveloped" countries to achieve their needed and desired modernizations and reforms as rapidly as possible by advancing on lines as consistent as possible with Western liberal ideals, and so to become and remain immune to the Communist revolutionary virus.

Let me now speak briefly, however, of the other factors, apart from the Marxist creed or fervent vision, which also help to make the Communist regimes belligerent and aggressive in their foreign policies. One additional factor is, of course, the consequence of Western hostility, which their own hostility toward the West has evoked and made necessary, but to which they do in turn react. Having, as a menace to the West, compelled the West to menace them, they feel menaced, and respond with a further intensification of their efforts to overtake and surpass the West in power, and to press their offensives as, in part, one form or method of defense. Then also a second, additional factor of a different sort *may* be involved: in so far as their internal policies, of suppressing all internal conflicts and freedoms within the Communist countries themselves and of pressing their peoples for unending, strenuous efforts and sacrifices, tend to strain or weaken the loyalties of those people to their regimes, the latter may find it convenient to go on intensifying the conflict with the outer world and the popular sense of the external menace, in order to bolster the mass-popular, patriotic loyalties which they require. And finally, I think it may be that still another factor is at work, i.e., a continuing carry-over or revival, in these Communist despotisms, of the ancient militaristic and imperialistic tendencies inherent in the old, not only pre-Communist but even largely precapitalist, feudal bases of the former despotisms in those same countries.

Despite all that the Communist theoreticians maintain—and this I will consider in a moment—about advanced "capitalism" as the source of all modern "imperialism," I think there is far more historical truth in a very different theory about the real origins of most true "imperialism" in all human history, which traces it to cultures, outlooks, attitudes, and behavior-patterns bred originally in and by old feudal and despotically ruled societies, in which the ruling classes were made up of war lords, and the military virtues and war and conquest were exalted or glorified. These static, primitive economies could be made to support growing populations and provide the upper classes with substantial wealth only with the aid of recurrent, predatory seizures of additional lands and resources; while at the same time the natural primitive reactions to the disliked, alien cultures, creeds, and habits of neighboring peoples ran toward militant crusades to conquer, subjugate, and convert or "civilize" them. In the main the long, progressive evolution of modern Western capitalism and its bourgeois culture has been *away from* all that underlies and breeds imperialistic attitudes and policies; and the once whole-heartedly imperialistic Western powers have long been growing less and less inclined to try or want to enlarge or even retain their old inherited colonial empires, and increasingly willing to prepare the native peoples for successful self-government and gradually to relinquish their own powers of control over them.[3]

But such evolutions of more liberal, nonimperialistic ideals and policies had never gone so far, to say the least—just as the evolution of capitalism and its civilization had not—in the now Communist countries, before they became Communist; and I think it is likely that a good deal of the old imperialistic spirit or mentality of the former ruling groups in those societies has been carried on by their Communist successors. The element of pacifistic idealism that is present generally in socialist thought as such, including one part of Marxist thought (its vision of the ultimate, future, ideal societies), is nullified in the Marxists (Communists), as far as their current behavior is concerned, by their much stronger, warlike, revolutionary, and revolution-spreading ardor, and their hatred of the capitalist world; it serves them mainly as a cloak or disguise to conceal their aggressive, real purposes under constant protestations or professions of their "peaceful" intentions. The aggressive, imperialistic temper inherited from the pre-Communist despotisms agrees with and reinforces that arising from their Marxist creed and gospel; and although their achievements in developing the economic systems and potentials of their countries *could be* removing the ancient economic, supporting causes of or reasons for imperialistic designs and policies, there are, I think, clear reasons why that is not occurring. They are forcing their economic development efforts ahead so fast, with such great priorities for heavy industry and all that contributes to military power, and so high a rate of saving and capital

[3] For the most brilliant, original, and convincing exposition and support of the "theory of imperialism" that I have summarized in this paragraph, see J. A. Schumpeter's essay, "The Sociology of Imperialisms" in his *Imperialism and Social Classes* (New York: A. M. Kelly, Inc., 1951).

formation as opposed to production of consumers' goods to raise the current living standards of their populations, that they are beginning to outdo or outstrip even the richer Western capitalist countries in generating surplus amounts of capital and capital goods of various kinds, which they can export to underdeveloped countries, invest in aiding them and gaining power over them, and use also in types of foreign trade serving to alleviate the pressures on the living standards of their own peoples, without slowing the pace of their own accumulations of new capital and basic industrial power.

THE COMMUNIST THEORY OF CAPITALIST IMPERIALISM

Yet I must now speak, finally, of that special part of or outgrowth from or addition to their Marxist creed—the theory, held by all Communists, of or about Western capitalist "imperialism"—which serves the rulers of the Communist countries as their most potent intellectual or propaganda weapon in the cold war, and appeals strongly and persuasively to people in the "underdeveloped" countries which are or were parts of the colonial empires of the Western powers. This theory enables the now really most aggressive, expansive, and imperialistic Communist regimes to pose as the sole defenders of the world's peace and the freedoms of all countries, from or against the alleged imperialistic and war-engendering designs and policies of the Western capitalist countries. The germs or rudiments of this theory about how "imperialism" grows out of the nature and internal dilemmas of advanced "capitalism" were present within Marx's theory and forecast of the evolution and degeneration of capitalism; but these ideas have been developed by various latter-day disciples of Marx, including Lenin and his successors, the modern Communist theoreticians, into the full-blown theory which goes far beyond all that Marx suggested.

Lenin's main use of the theory, in the form which he helped to give it, was to explain and justify the occurrence of the first successful Marxist revolution in Russia, a comparatively backward country, in the face of the contrary prediction of Marx that the first such revolution would occur in some previously, fully developed capitalist country. The reader has already had *my* explanation of this discrepancy—that Marx was fundamentally mistaken—that the earliest, not the latest, stages of capitalist evolution are generally the ones most likely to engender socialist revolutions; but this simple view of the matter was of course not available to Lenin. He instead derived from some of Marx's other economic-theoretical ideas—about the expected world-wide consequences of the final stages of the evolutions of the economic systems of the most advanced capitalist countries—a way of making the Russian Revolution appear to harmonize well enough with the general, main tenor of the prophecies of Marx. The evolving capitalist countries or national economies, according to Marx as interpreted by Lenin, were bound to become increasingly "imperialistic," and to form or become linked together in a "chain" of "imperialist powers," jointly and severally oppressing and exploiting the rest of the world, as well as the working-class members of their own populations. And according to Lenin, Czarist Russia was already a "capitalist" country although not one of the most advanced, and so was a member or part of—and the "weakest link" in—that "chain" of the "imperialist powers." The growing, revolt-engendering pressure on the world's "masses," although caused by developments originating mainly in the most advanced Western capitalist countries, was felt throughout the world, and naturally produced the first effective revolt in weakly governed Czarist Russia—the "weakest link" of the "chain" was the first to break. But now let us look more closely at the theory which not only thus served Lenin's original immediate purpose or "rationalized" the Russian Revolution in the context of Marxist thought, but has ever since so well served to "rationalize" and aid the subsequent spread of Communism's power over other, still more backward countries, and the entire developing program of the Communist bloc and movement.

In each of the advanced (Western) capitalist countries, according to this theory, the on-going evolution of its national economy or economic system includes the following "inevitable" developments, which have the over-all result of causing the country and its government to become, in foreign policy, increasingly "imperialistic." Within each such national economy the growing accumulation of new capital is accompanied by a growing concentration of it in the hands of increasingly few but, individually, increasingly rich and powerful capitalists and/or small united groups of them, with expanding, gigantic enterprises and centrally administered groups or chains of them under their control and dominating the economy. In other words, the earlier competitive form of the economy, of many small or moderate-sized competing enterprises, disappears and is replaced by the form of a latter-day "monopoly capitalism." The few gigantic outfits in this economy that together control the greater part of the economy's manpower and resources are no longer obliged by competition to practice moderation or restraint in exploiting workers and consumers; they have and use great monopoly powers to extract high prices from the latter, and pay very little for labor and materials; and they limit the supplies of their products offered on domestic markets, and their investments in production for those markets, to match the limitation of demand therein, arising from the high prices and the low incomes of most of the people.

But further, according to this theory, as all this increases the profits and new capital accumulations of the great monopolies, but makes them unable to invest the latter at all fully in their home economies without glutting their domestic markets and having to reduce their prices and profits; they are impelled, by the dilemma arising for them from their own business policies, to use their great political power and push the governments of their countries into "imperialistic" foreign adventures, designed to gain and hold great areas in the economically underdeveloped parts of the world and make those areas, as colonial dependencies, exclusive or protected outlets for the surplus capital and products of the great business monopolies within the mother countries. As another concurrent part of the same evolution, the advanced capitalist countries increasingly restrict international trade among themselves, i.e., they raise protective barriers against imports of either goods or capital from each other in order to reserve for their home producers their increasingly inadequate domestic markets and investment outlets. In this way, all these countries oblige each other to try to build up empires in the underdeveloped regions, as the only areas to which their capitalists can freely export the goods and capital that are "surplus" at home and not allowed entrance to the other advanced countries; areas in which their capitalists can invest, can employ and exploit cheap native labor and resources, and can create new markets, to some extent, in spite of the poverty of the native populations. The latter are supposed to be, by the results of the entire process, *only* oppressed and exploited, not benefited at all; and the rival efforts of the Western countries to expand their empires are alleged to have been the primary causes of all modern wars.

Now I cannot here devote to this use the amount of space that would be needed for an adequate critical discussion of that mainly false and outrageous theory.[4] It contains, indeed, a few grains of truth and has, as a whole, a superficial plausibility—and in its general tenor a broad agreement with and great power of appealing to the prejudices of too many Western liberal intellectuals—and has therefore long been widely, much too fully accepted or influential, far beyond Marxist circles. At the same time, it consists mainly of extreme oversimplifications, gross distortions, and outright falsehoods; it mingles together and confuses absurdly, ideas or views of two entirely different things—on the one hand, the mainly beneficial flow of Western capital and enterprise into underdeveloped countries, making needed contributions to their economic development, and on the other hand, "imperialism" in the only true or proper sense, i.e., political-and-military conquest, subjugation, and oppression. Although an adequate discussion here is impossi-

[4] For a full statement—by a writer who is both an able modern economist and a thorough convinced Marxist adhering fully to the Communist "party line"—of this theory, see P. M. Sweezy, *Theory of Capitalist Development* (New York: Oxford University Press, 1942), part 4.

ble, I must conclude the part of this chapter concerned with Communism with a brief "reply to" this Communist theory of capitalist "imperialism."

The basic errors, of course, grow out of the false theses of Marx about the alleged (for "the masses" everywhere) purely oppressive and exploitative, not at all beneficial, nature of all capitalism as an economic system and the economic activities of all capitalists, *and* the alleged complete control by the latter, wherever they and their "system" flourish, of political and military power, assuring invariable, ruthless use of all such power, always, solely in the service of the economic interests or ambitions of the capitalists. I shall come in a moment to the crucial questions concerning political and military power and the degrees of connection of their imperialistic uses with business interests; but we must notice, first, the purely economic-theoretical nonsense in the theory before us. "Nonsense" is the only right word for the notion that all capitalism as an economic system is wholly a system of oppression and exploitation (underpayment) of "labor" or "the masses" by investing capitalists, whose profits allegedly represent nothing but unpaid-for labor and not at all, even in any part, earned rewards for productive services performed or rendered by capital and by the capitalists, increasing the productivity and earnings of the working people and in net results still benefiting them even after the profits of the capitalists are deducted and allowed for. And in the theory of "imperialism" which we are examining, this nonsense appears twice or plays two roles: first in the account of the internal economic processes in the Western economies, leading to their exports of capital to underdeveloped countries, and then again in the account of the alleged results within the latter. Let us consider these two parts of the argument, successively.

We are asked to believe that within the Western economies, as time has gone on, the growing, total accumulations of new capital out of business profits have become excessive in relation to all domestic, profitable investment opportunities *because* the oppressed and exploited working-class majorities or "masses" have been so held down in poverty that the domestic markets have become inadequate. The outflow of capital to the underdeveloped countries is depicted as resulting entirely from capitalist extortions and mass poverty within the West; *not* (as in reality has been the case, in the main at least) from progress of Western economic development (with benefits very widely shared by most of the people) to the point of creating conditions under which further increments of new capital often can be invested more productively and hence more profitably—in ways filling more urgent needs and rendering greater, widely beneficial services, hence also yielding higher returns—if invested in new enterprises in still underdeveloped countries. As the real case can be explained in the terms of neo-classical economic theory, in the Western countries with their relatively abundant supplies of already invested capital, the "marginal productivity" of capital has fallen to lower levels than those still obtaining in the underdeveloped countries where, in view of their great shortages of capital, additional new investments resulting in the use of modern techniques and equipment along with some of the abundant native labor and natural resources can often make immense new contributions to production, and thus earn very high returns.

Beyond any question this account of the matter has far more truth—to say the least—than can be credited to the notion that within the Western economies, there has been a persistence of mass poverty and hence a failure of total domestic demands or markets for consumers' goods, and so also of demands for capital, to grow along with supplies of the latter. It is possible that the rate of increase or improvement of the real incomes and living standards of "the masses" in the Western countries has been less rapid than it should have been—in consequence of imperfections in their economic systems—and that a resulting insufficient growth of domestic markets and investment opportunities has in some degree accentuated the growth of capital exports to underdeveloped countries. But it is hard to believe that this factor can account for more than minor additions to the latter, which certainly would have been occurring in any case for the other main reason already given. And in any event this possible limitation of the West's internal economic progress by lack of fully adequate participation of all the people in its benefits, is a hypothesis very unlike the false, Marxist, grim picture of entire persistence of universal, dire, mass poverty, and a silly, self-imposed necessity obliging all Western capitalists to go on "exploiting" their laboring populations to the limit and thus ruining their domestic markets, with the result that as they (nevertheless) continue to reap profits and accumulate new capital, they "must" increasingly use the latter only to "exploit" the native labor and resources in the underdeveloped countries. Nor does the theory that Western capitalism has become "monopoly capitalism" add much to the cogency of that "explanation" of the rise of "imperialism." There have been some growths of monopolies and some decline of competition in the Western economies, but the real extent of these developments has been nothing like the grossly exaggerative portrait drawn by the Communist theoreticians. It would be impossible to prove and seems unlikely that their real effects have included any very pronounced adverse effects upon Western levels of real wages and mass living standards—which in fact have undergone their greatest advances precisely in this same recent period.

Moreover, were it true that within the Western economies domestic mass poverty and inadequate markets have been the cause depriving new Western capital of profitable domestic investment opportunities, and forcing it to flow out to the underdeveloped countries; then through the same logic it would seem to follow that the latter, with their far worse mass poverty and more restricted internal markets, must have even still much less to offer in the way of such opportunities. And were it true that the Western capitalists, establishing new enterprises in the underdeveloped countries, simply practiced pure and all-out exploitation of the native populations and did nothing at all to alleviate their poverty, the possibility of high profitability and great growth or expansion of this operation would seem rather difficult to explain. Initially, the prevailing, dire poverty in these countries does in fact of course severely limit their power of attracting Western capital for use in producing, within them, new goods to be sold within them. Only as incoming capital and enterprise succeed in increasing the productivity of the native labor and resources, *and* by sharing the benefits of rising productivity with the native populations, improving their living standards, can the markets and opportunities for further profitable investments in those countries be made to grow.

The picture of the profit-hungry, invading Western capitalists as unmitigated oppressors and exploiters is absurd. Of course they have not all been entirely benign and wise, pure benefactors, either—never in any cases giving grounds or occasions for growths of native hostility against themselves. But it makes no sense to think of this on the whole mainly beneficial process—consisting simply of all movements of Western private capital and enterprise into non-Western, underdeveloped countries, in efforts to earn profits by developing productive enterprises within the latter—to think of all this as *in itself* "imperialistic" or deserving to be tagged with that opprobrious term. And it is a quite separate historical fact that much of all this "economic penetration," over the several centuries during which it has been going on, has been concurrent and often in considerable measures interdependent with the very different, political-and-military foreign adventures undertaken by the governments of Western countries, and alone constituting real imperialism—adventures which, again, it is grossly oversimple and false to regard as having all been solely caused or instigated by, or designed simply to serve, business interests.

The extensions of the ruling powers of European national states over non-European territories and populations, which began to occur in the main early cases in the fifteenth, sixteenth, and seventeenth centuries, and went on in recurrent waves or bursts at irregular intervals through the nineteenth century, always had mixed causes and motives of various kinds. The business interests or ambitions, and shares of political influence, of the interested businessmen and groups in the European countries concerned played generally more or less important, but rarely the *most* important, causal roles. Ambitions of political and military leaders, governing groups and classes, and "patriotic" people of all classes for increments of national and/or personal or group power and "glory"; sheer adventurism; ideological missionary or crusading fevers to conquer and "civilize" regions and populations living in "darkness"; and above all, the rivalry among the great powers, always threatening to break out in war, and the imperative needs of each one, for the sake of national security, of wealth-and-power-in-the-world superior to that of its likely enemies, and prior acquisition, ahead of them, of strategically vital areas—all *these* "forces" have surely conduced even more strongly to the creations or growths of the colonial empires than has that of the desires of interested businessmen, as such, to have conditions in the colonized or controlled areas made more favorable for the success of their business ventures therein. Of course the latter "force" has often counted for much as one contributory factor; but it is ridiculous to ignore all the others, or treat them as somehow entirely derivative from this one alone, and this as the sole "fundamental" cause —and as itself arising uniquely and inevitably from the nature and internal working and dilemmas of *advanced* "capitalism" within each "imperialistic" country.

Let me at this point again refer to historical facts about far-past times. In general, the economic, social, cultural, and politico-military causes of imperialistic behavior on the parts of societies or their ruling elements—their proneness to engage in conquering, ruling, and exploiting neighboring or distant societies—were at their strongest, everywhere, in old, precapitalist, feudal and despotic societies. The modern European national states which have had or acquired extensive colonial empires in Asia, etc., in the main cases first acquired the larger parts of them back in the sixteenth and seventeenth centuries, when the domestic societies of those European states themselves were full of survivals from their still recent feudal pasts, and their (mainly commercial, preindustrial) "capitalisms" were still "infant" affairs. That was an epoch or time of transition *before* the full development of modern Western, progressive, "free-enterprise" capitalism, and before the rise to prevalence in the Western world, in the eighteenth century, of the classical liberalism, idealizing freedom or independence for all human beings and all peoples, peace and mutually beneficial commerce or exchange among them all, and limitation of the use of coercive power to its use by governments to maintain peace by enforcing justice among the governed, i.e., to prevent the latter from using power to coerce each other.

In the epoch just before modern capitalism began to be really, fully ascendant or predominant and to show its own maturing nature, and before the liberal idealism began to be a widely ruling climate of opinion—in the just previous epoch, in which the "imperial" nation-states of Western Europe laid the foundations of their empires in other continents, the prevailing climate of moral ideas affecting the conduct of all national and international affairs was still harsh, "realistic," ruthless, and warlike. The governing groups in those nation-states—their ruling oligarchies—consisted mainly of aristocratic or noble landlords who were descendants and heirs of feudal war lords, and continued to practice statecraft in the ancient spirit which took the inevitability of recurrent war among states for granted. They aimed at continuous maximization of the relative wealth and power of one's country as compared with its potential enemies, through all available means including, as a matter of course, all or any feasible and expedient conquests of weakly governed and poorly defended, distant, alien territories, populations, and resources that would add to the wealth and power of the conquering country and forestall growth of or reduce the wealth and power of its unconquerable and dangerous nearby rivals. It is true that commercial capitalism was already flourishing and growing; the larger capitalists or "merchant princes" were gaining positions as junior partners in the outer fringes of the governing circles, and their business interests in trade within and with the distant coming-to-be colonial or dependent areas played an important role in the building up of the colonial empires. But even this fact is not consistent with the modern neo-Marxist or Communist theory, which regards "imperialism" as a by-product of advanced, mature, or fully evolved capitalism, not the infant capitalism that was then in being. And the role which the latter played, in that age of the first foundings of the now old empires of the European powers, was, though important, subordinate to the role that was played by the statecraft mainly carried on by aristocratic statesmen. The essential spirit of the general kind of economic thought and national governmental economic policy which prevailed in that epoch—mercantilism, of which colonial imperialism was an integral part—was subordination of economics to international power politics.

At a much later time, the natural fruit of the emergence of full fledged industrial capitalism, and of prevalence of the spirit of the classical liberalism, first appeared in mid-nineteenth-century England in the anti-imperialism or "little Englandism" of Cobden, Bright, and company—the chief political spokesmen of the English business community of their day. They preached, as desirable for England on both moral and economic grounds, the kind of long-range program that modern England has now long been practicing, i.e., gradual withdrawal from its empire or release of parts of the empire into independence, with prior preparation of them for that, in the faith that as friendly independent countries they would become far better customers and suppliers for the English economy, and England would be spared the unprofitable, great cost and strain of ruling them. And it is significant that in Victorian England, the last important, small, transitory resurgence of imperialistic sentiment or the spirit of active imperialism occurred under the leadership of Disraeli and his Tories, who had their main base of political support in the landed aristocracy and gentry with their ancient feudal traditions; and who hardly bothered to try to reply to the economic arguments of the anti-imperialists, but relied mainly on romantic appeals for preservation of the traditional grandeur and glory of England, and talk about her world-civilizing mission. Among the businessmen as well as among the laboring men of England, desires to enlarge or even to maintain the British Empire as such have long been dying. And the renewal of imperialistic tendencies and efforts among the European powers in general, in the late nineteenth century and on into the twentieth, was not due mainly to Disraeli's England, or to economic pressures arising within and from advanced capitalism. It was due to the arrival on the scene or entry into the game of Imperial Germany, a belatedly unified and belatedly, rapidly self-modernizing country or society, full of strong remnants of the spirit and traditions and social and political structures of feudalism and despotism, and with a becoming-advanced capitalism and business class imbued with no spirit of economic and general liberalism, but instead with that of willing dependence upon and subservience to their national state and its ambitions for greater power in the world. When this new challenger entered into the power rivalry among the Western powers, and sought to build up a colonial empire, the other powers were obliged in self-defense to renew their efforts to retain and if possible enlarge their empires. And although of course there were businessmen and groups within them, who sought advantages for their business interests in the colonial areas and joined in supporting imperialistic governmental policies toward the latter, these were more often band-wagon riders than prime movers in bringing about the adoption and execution of those policies. The main general trend in the West has continued to be that of a gradual decline of national wills to build up and maintain colonial empires. And the Western countries, such as France, in which this trend has gone less far than in England, are precisely the less fully advanced modern capitalist countries, less fully, internally reformed in line with the ideals of the classical liberalism.

Yet I do not wish to claim more for the theory that (most) imperialism is a lingering, old, historical result of ancient feudal institutions and traditions than a full survey of all the relevant evidence would warrant. Nor do I wish to leave uncriticized the too common American, naïve and self-righteous kind of anti-imperialist idealism, which today hampers the defense of the "free world" from the aggressively expansive Communist part of the world by creating frictions between America and its still empire-laden allies. American history contains its quota of past manifestations of an "imperialistic" national spirit inconsistent with any claim to complete innocence in this matter, and owing nothing to any feudal inheritance, of which this country has none. The record of our treatment of the American Indians, and our aggressive wars with other countries (e.g., Mexico) in the course of our expansion over what is now our continental domain, shows that our nation was long inspired by a sense of its "manifest destiny" to gain control of and spread over this vast territory, and did not allow itself to be much inhibited by humane consideration for the rights of others; in other words, the record shows that our nation had a good deal of the "imperialistic" spirit. And later on we took Cuba and the Philippines away from Spain, and became in the strict sense one of the "imperial" powers. Nor are Latin Americans in general entirely without grounds for their conviction that our businessmen and national government have often shown tendencies to behave "imperialistically" toward them. In this whole American case, of course, the impetus toward imperialistic behavior *has* sprung in the greatest measure from the business ambitions of Americans in general (without regard to any class distinctions), *together with* the popular patriotic urge toward national greatness; though *not* from our economy's evolution into a domestic-market-restricting "monopoly capitalism," with a consequent growing need for a colonial empire as a field for investment of its accumulating surplus capital. No feudal inheritance has played here the role that it *has* played in the creations of the old, great empires of the European imperial powers. Peoples and national states *can* be made imperialistic by many kinds of causes; but the Communist theory of all imperialism as a unique, necessary, and vicious product or expression of advanced capitalism is in conflict alike, as I think I have now shown, with the general mass of the historical evidence, with rational analysis, and with common sense.

Yet in the present world situation, the real falsity and absurdity of that theory do not seriously reduce its great potency as propaganda, on the Communist side, in the underdeveloped countries which were until recently or still are parts of the empires of the Western capitalist countries, and are full of grievances against the latter which the Communist regimes exploit with ease. Nor do the ironical aspects of the situation do much to alleviate those grievances and the Western handicap in dealing with those countries. Historically, the latter, when they first came under imperial rule by Western powers, generally were not and never had been self-conscious nations of free people. They had lived under despotisms, native or alien, generally worse or more oppressive than the regimes built up by the Western powers, which in general gradually improved the conditions of life of the native populations, and made them into nations that eventually acquired, from contact with Western culture and education, growing desires and more belatedly and slowly growing abilities to become self-governing or independent national states. The benefits conferred by the Western ruling powers have on the whole outweighed the injuries inflicted by them; but the benefits equally with the injuries have stimulated growth of the spirit of revolt against and hatred of the Western powers, by teaching the native peoples to conceive and desire still greater benefits, and feel not grateful for those received but only injured in not receiving greater ones. And among the injuries suffered, the worst and most keenly felt have been not the cases of degrees of brutal oppression and real economic exploitation of natives by Westerners, but the "color" or "race" prejudices and discriminations displayed and practiced by the latter, and their general attitudes of haughty superiority.

Of course the movement toward independence for all these countries is both morally right and inevitable; imperialism—of the Western kind—is dying, and rightly so. But the now necessary effort by the West, in its defense of all free civilization against the Communist menace, to hold or gain and hold the friendship of all these underdeveloped countries, and aid and speed their evolutions into modernized, prosperous, educated, democratic, and strong, free countries, is immensely hampered by the lingering hostility toward the West left over from the heyday of Western imperialism, and the advantage thereby given to Communist propaganda and the lure of the Communist alternative. But I have now said all that I need to say on the subject of the Communist part of our twentieth-century world and its development over the decades since the Russian Revolution. It is time to turn to consideration of the other developments which were mentioned near the beginning of this chapter: the fascist systems which arose before, and brought about, and perished in, the Second World War.

THE NATURE, AND THEORIES OF THE ORIGINS, OF "FASCISM"; THE GERMAN CASE AND OTHERS

Those fascist developments or episodes belong, even more clearly than does Communism, in the category of pathological developments; they are, as objects of study, of but little interest in themselves, having scarcely developed any ideas or realized achievements of any positive value or enduring viability. But the world's inevitable and healthy, morally indignant, and finally victorious reaction against them (the main ones) in the Second World War; and the various, popular theories that arose therein, about the nature and origins or causes of the evils they embodied, and what must be done to prevent new, future, similar developments anywhere; these things—the reaction against fascism and the associated theories about it—have had more lasting and significant effects upon other modern intellectual and social movements;

and it is mainly in this connection that the following comments may be of interest. But any discussion of theories to "explain" the fascist developments must be preceded by a characterization of them (the latter), indicating *what* is to be "explained."

A fascist regime, I think it may be said, arises when some large part of the people of a nation, confronting what they feel to be, for their nation, desperately severe, hardly surmountable crises in its domestic and foreign affairs, and intolerably severe internal class or group conflicts unresolvable by reason, compromise, etc., become ready and eager to follow and obey an emerging, fanatical, ruthless, and cunning demagogue "leader" and dictator, who makes himself the voice and instrument of the passionate desire of the frustrated multitude for a forcible creation or achievement of national unity or solidarity, order, and vigor, and a strong assertion and great aggrandizement of national power, which relieves or compensates the feelings of individual and group weakness, inferiority, and humiliation, or inflates the depressed ego of the average individual supporter of the movement by enabling him to feel "great" as a member or part and servant of a regenerated, powerful, and glorious nation. The ideal of submergence of all otherwise separate, conflicting, and frustrated wills in a single, unanimous, collective, "general will" of the nation as a unit, expressed and carried out by the hero-leader; and the paradoxical achievement of a sense of "freedom" through renunciation or surrender of all freedom in the ordinary meaning of the word—all this is in complete antithesis to the liberal ideal of the fullest possible, equal and mutually consistent or adjusted freedoms (in the ordinary sense) for all individuals, who as reasonable or moderate and social beings achieve all necessary agreement, order, and cooperation through voluntary, limited, mutual concessions to each other; and who, within the framework of agreed-on rules which limit and impartially protect the rights of all, may freely differ and compete as rivals in all spheres of life, and develop a rich variety of lives, characters, outlooks, and achievements. The antithesis in which fascism stands to liberalism is in fact far more complete than that in which it stands to democracy in the sense of the sovereignty of the will of the majority. Any fascist regime is of course opposed to formal, rational, and liberal parliamentary democracy; but it always has, requires, seeks, and gains mass support—with the aid, it is true, of much manipulation of the minds and emotions of the people with irrational propaganda—and it expresses and carries out the passionate will of what may well be even a large majority, for complete suppression of all hated, dissident minorities and all internal conflicts and disorders, and achievement of national unity, order, vigor, power, and "glory."

A few more points may be quickly made in further characterization of the fascist movements and regimes. Their gross immoralities, or violations of normal humane ethical decencies, are, I think in the main, results of the temper of fanatical extremism in the assertion and enforcement of their own horribly twisted but in a sense, at bottom, genuine kind of ethical or moral idealism. Their "innovations" in the sphere of political or state institutions—the one-party state or party dictatorship and the organization of the ruling party itself under its personal dictator-leader and his henchmen; the paramilitary bodies serving (helping to enforce) the will of the party and its boss, the propaganda machinery and methods, the system of secret and political policemen, spies, or informers, prison camps, and tortures, and the denial to accused persons of any judicially protected legal rights; and "totalitarian" extension of this "state's" authority over all aspects of life—these features are really only adaptations of the ancient devices of all absolute despotisms, or of those of Communism. And on the economic side, the fascist mode of organization and control of a national economy, to make all economic activities subservient to "national" ends as determined by the ruling group, and to ensure subordination of all private ends or interests to those—through the imposed social-economic structure of the "corporative state" with its organizations of the industries and occupational groups, controlling their members and controlled by the state—all this may be said to represent an effort to revive a mediaeval pattern and adapt it to modern conditions.

On its face, and to a certain extent in reality, this kind of social-economic order differs from the Communist system, in leaving private property rights and property incomes intact in a sense; and so it appears to preserve private "capitalism" as opposed to Communism or any form of true, thoroughgoing socialism. But the extreme restrictions of all private economic freedoms, the subjection of the management of all properties and enterprises, and decisions on the uses of incomes and resources, to arbitrary control by state authorities, who are not bound by any fixed or reliable body of law but make and change and enforce their *ad hoc* rules as they see fit; all this takes most of the meaning, reality, or substance out of private property and business rights, and makes the contrast with Communism or authoritarian socialism more nominal than real. Yet there is a different point of real contrast both with Communism and with free or liberal private capitalism, i.e., a lack of the effective, concentrated drive toward, and systematic provisions for, progressive economic development and high economic efficiency, which in different forms are present in both of the other systems. The economic theories and policies typical of fascist systems can scarcely interest economists as such, for they have almost no consistency or rationality from an economic point of view. The essential aims of fascist regimes are not economic—to cause the resources and productive energies of the people to be used or applied as efficiently as possible for the sake of abundant, all-around satisfaction of all their ordinary human wants—but are really non- or extraeconomic, political, military, and sociocultural aims—to make the economy or system of all economic activities and resource-uses subservient to the state machine and its military machine and the vague, variable ends pursued by the authorities in the name of the national will to power and grandeur.

Now as I have said, we may find it more rewarding to consider mainly not the detailed ideas and features of the fascist movements and regimes themselves, but the question of the origins or causes of their evolutions, characters, and deeds, and the kinds of answers to this question which became prevalent in different non- or antifascist quarters during and after the Second World War. And in this general connection it seems best to consider and get out of the way, first, certain views about the special case of the German Nazi or "national socialist" movement and regime and its development, nature, over-all significance, and deeds, including the external aggressions which were the main immediate causes of the war. For although fascism in the original and strict sense was Italian, and the Nazi phenomenon was different in some ways or had uniquely German features, and of course every instance of this general kind of development has borne the special marks of its own special milieu and origins; the uniquely great importance of the German case and the world's reactions to it led to a widespread special interest in it and conflict of views specifically about it, which it may be well to examine briefly, *before* we take up the *general* question about all developments of this type.

The Nazi movement, as we know, arose in a deeply wounded and disturbed Germany, ridden by unmanageable problems, crises, and internal divisions. The state of the nation and its problems were due to the combined results of: the nation's defeat and humiliation in the First World War, the postwar settlement or Versailles Treaty with its punitive reparations clauses, the Kaiser's abdication and exile and the replacement of the country's previous regime by the Weimar Republic, the latter's failure to win and hold the full loyal support of the entire nation, the destructive extreme inflation of the 1920s, and then the Great Depression. Rising in that situation, the frenzied and violent Nazi movement under Hitler's leadership attained power, with the aid of some much more respectable conservative nationalists, some big businessmen or financiers and industrialists, the deceived senile President, General von Hindenburg, and the millions of distressed and angry "little" people who made up the rank and file of the movement itself, all the criminal elements which rose to power in and with it, and a passive, acquiescent, general population. And having attained power, the leaders of the movement—Hitler and his aides—while at first putting into effect a few somewhat constructive measures to alleviate the depression, unemployment, etc., and thus win wider popular support, at the same time imposed on the country a totally ruthless and unscrupulous despotism. They manipulated the national mind with a flood of insane propaganda into a mood of violent hatred of the Jews and all different, disliked, and possibly disloyal, and convenient-as-scapegoat, domestic minority groups, and hatred also of foreign nations; and then they embarked on the external aggressions to revenge and reverse the defeat of 1918, enlarge the "living space" of the German people, and expand the nation's and regime's power in the world as far as possible—which precipitated World War II.

Now it is of some interest to consider and try to evaluate with common sense the diverse theories about the supposed causation of that entire development, which became popular in different quarters during and after the war. To some non-German and (for various historic reasons) easily anti-German, European, English, and American minds, the matter presented hardly any problem; their conviction was that all this mass of horror was simply the newest and worst-yet manifestation of an old and constant, evil, German national character; aversion in the German people to the individual political responsibilities entailed by freedom and democracy, German love of order and regimentation and readiness to submit to any German despotism that would inflate the average German's ego, and German militarism and love of war and ruthless imposition of German power upon other countries. Even some scholars and intellectuals, philosophers, political theorists, intellectual historians, etc., have more or less fully embraced this "theory," and pointed to various old writings influential in the history of Germany's intellectual life and culture, as alleged expressions and reinforcements of that alleged evil national character: some early-nineteenth-century expressions of old German Romanticism—exaltations of passion and visionary dream-thinking as productive of a higher wisdom and nobler way of life than could result from adherence to common sense and sober, rational, mental life; and elements of Hegelian and other German political philosophies, exalting the state above its human subjects and above all obligations to conform to ethical or moral standards, i.e., justifications of *realpolitik* or amoral "political realism"; and other old ideas long widely influential in Germany, all said to exhibit the same national tendencies most fully realized in the mental life and behavior of the Nazis.

Now I don't think it is possible *either* to accept this line of thought in answer to the question before us as wholly true and the whole truth, *or* to dismiss it entirely or be sure that there is nothing in it. A "national character," if there is a reality corresponding to this concept, is in every or any case and certainly in the German case a vague, elusive, and very complex and *not* wholly permanent, stable, or unchangeable affair, full at any time of very many diverse and mutually contradictory elements and as yet unrealized potentialities, and highly mutable or variable as a whole through long periods of time. For it is made up only partly of the diverse biologically hereditary or "innate" characters or sets of character traits or dispositions of the many elements of the national population, of which some in some and others in other periods may exert the predominant influence on the "national" behavior. It consists in another important part (at any time) merely of a mass of habits, traditions, customs, beliefs, and attitudes, formed under the influence of temporal, environmental conditions and historical events and experiences. And although all these elements, once formed, may have much durability, persistence, inertia, or momentum, they are certainly subject to eventual changes consequent upon those of the causal factors responsible for them. Historians know that over recent centuries, the at different times apparent and reputed "characters" of all the Western nations, severally, have changed repeatedly and greatly; and the notion of a really fixed, immutable, simple, definite, and wholly evil German national character is a product of unjust, "fanatical," wartime enmity, which cannot stand up under either rational or historical examination. At the same time, a nation can be or become and long remain especially difficult for other nations to trust or live with, and the needed reformation of the national character can be a profound affair not capable of rapid or easy achievement; and this I think has been true in the case of modern Germany.

The Nazi episode, then, was *to some extent* an outgrowth from fairly old and durable elements of the German national character and "spirit," and the resulting, somewhat special reactions of some large percentage of the German people to the events and conditions that plagued them and their country in the period just before and during the rise to power of Hitler and his party. In a sense the opposite, one-sided, partial, oversimple "theory" to the one just considered is that which sought to explain (and excuse) the entire episode as merely the natural, inevitable result of the events and conditions of that period in German history —the outcome of the First World War and the harsh Versailles treaty, the inflation, the depression, and so on. Here again, while these "causes" undoubtedly played an important contributory part or role, and would or could have produced severe disturbances and drastic political changes of some sort in any nation had it been subjected to them; it is wrong I think to deny the responsibility or guilt of the German people (the predominant or mainly influential part of them) for the specific reactions to their provocations which produced the Nazi movement and its triumph, character, and deeds, and World War Two. The entire outcome was a *joint* result of the German "character" in its then existing state or stage of evolution, *and* the conditions and events or stimuli that impinged upon it, and cannot be validly imputed to *either* set of causes *alone*. But I now turn to consideration of still another and again quite different "theory," about *not only* this German case or the Nazi development *but all* the so-called "fascist" developments, which is of even greater interest for our purpose here.

I refer now to the "theory," widely popularized during and after or since the war by all leftward-leaning commentators, to the effect that the Nazi development and all the fascist developments could be understood simply as results of the efforts of "right wing" or "reactionary" big capitalist or business groups to protect their own interests and positions from the menaces of Communism and all socialism and social-reform movements, by setting up or embracing and supporting dictatorial or authoritarian regimes amenable to their control and favorable to them, and suppressing democracy and all civil liberties, and redirecting toward or against other "safe" targets, the popular discontents and angers underlying the feared "radical" movements. In its most extreme, clear-cut, and simple form, this has been from the outset and remains Communism's theory of or about this other, opposed or rival kind of aggressive, totalitarian despotism—fascism—at once enemy and twin in some ways to Communism itself. But also in other slightly differing, looser versions—generally without the Communist insistence on the absolute "inevitability" of the trend to fascism in all "capitalist" countries as their deteriorating "capitalisms" approach the verge of the Marxist revolution—substantially or nearly this same theory has been espoused by most socialists and anticapitalist liberals, or adherents of any of the various political groups making up "the non-Communist left."

Now it is true that in the developments of the fascist movements and regimes, generally, roles of considerable importance *have* been played by alarmed business groups which, out of their fears and hatreds of really or supposedly impending socialistic revolutions in their countries, or of political trends viewed as intolerable from their standpoints, have gone into action as financial and political supporters of the fascist movements, when the latter came to seem to them their only possible "saviors," or when all the alternatives looked *worse* to them from their points of view. And I do not wish to say anything here that would seem to minimize or in any measure excuse the parts played by such business groups or interests, afflicted with cowardice, myopia, and utter selfishness, in helping those evil and disastrous movements into power. But I think it is an untenable, extreme oversimplification of the facts to regard the businessmen and groups concerned as in all or any of these cases the sole important prime movers, and attribute all that occurred to them; and it is a wholly unwarranted extrapolation to suppose that tendencies to engender and support fascist movements are universally or generally inherent in all capitalist societies and classes, and sure or likely to appear everywhere if and when the latter come to feel severely threatened politically. The real fascist systems have been "capitalist" or "procapitalist" only in a very limited, relative degree or highly qualified sense—not systems that businessmen as such could ever be entirely happy with. And the complete, real, complex, social and political situations causing many of the affected businessmen to choose to support *such* systems in preference to all or any available alternatives have all been special situations, of a kind not likely to arise universally in the world, simply from or in the development of capitalism and of political movements to subvert or modify it.

I think it is a fact and a very significant fact that all countries which have so far had or produced real fascist regimes have been countries whose nontypical capitalisms evolved within or amidst extensive and important, surrounding, surviving relics of feudalism; countries in which the business and middle classes never achieved full spiritual and political independence and dignity or learned to stand entirely on their own feet, but always tended to lean for support upon the heirs of the old, aristocratic, ruling classes and the national governments and state bureaucracies; countries that never were fully imbued with the ideals, or acquainted through long experience with the values and the conditions of achievement and successful operation, of liberalism and democracy; and countries with intellectual and moral cultures still containing, along with modern developments, much in the way of decadent survivals of mediaeval ideas and attitudes. Thus all those countries, or national societies, have had social class structures and interclass relations—traditions of hierarchy, or social stratification not simply as to levels of income and wealth but also as to ranks of relative, social superiors and inferiors, with the former tending to feel entitled to be domineering, and the latter to be allowed only limited rights and opportunities—social systems of this antique kind, carried on and preserved from feudal times, more fully than in any of the modern world's more fully modern capitalistic and democratic countries. Now as modern developments of industrial capitalism went on within *such* societies, there naturally grew up in them also, both especially radical, revolutionary, and militant labor and socialist and communist movements, *and* reactionary-authoritarian responses to them; and in the lower-middle classes, hatreds of both big business and big labor and demands for national-state control of both, compulsory cooperation of all for common national ends, and suppression of all the conflicts of class and sectional and private interests. In short, the fascist developments have occurred in national societies sufficiently far advanced on the way to becoming fully modern capitalistic and democratic countries, to escape the fate of becoming Communist countries, but still in some ways sufficiently "backward" in that sense to fall victims, instead, to this other half-similar kind of ruthless despotism. But now let us drop this subject, and turn to consideration, in the next chapter, of the two modern movements or trends which alone are really important within the Western, long fully modern capitalistic and democratic countries: democratic socialism, and the modern revised liberalism that is groping vaguely for its goals and methods in the middle ground between socialism and the *laissez-faire* tradition of the older classical liberalism.

CHAPTER 15

The Mid-twentieth-century World's Ideologies, Regimes, and Conflicts: Democratic Socialism and Interventionist Liberalism

THE SOCIALIST AS COMPARED WITH THE CLASSICAL, LIBERAL OUTLOOK; AND THE UTOPIAN, MARXIAN, AND MODERN VARIETIES OF THE FORMER

It is a relief to turn our attention away from the nightmare of fascism, and the frighteningly efficient inhumanity of Communism, to the entirely ethically decent or civilized, and relatively rational, though I think mistaken beliefs, ideals, and program of the modern Western, democratic socialists. Though I cannot here survey this in any detail, a few things must be said about the historical background—the history of socialist thought and movements from the early nineteenth century to the present—to bring into view the main constant and variable elements and the general trend of the still on-going evolution of the pattern of socialist thought and practice. As I said in an earlier chapter, the philosophy of socialism and that of the classical liberalism alike had their origins chiefly in the eighteenth-century Enlightenment, and have always had a good deal in common, really, as regards their ultimate objectives. The opposition between them has been chiefly as to means or methods. There has been the liberal effort to limit, narrowly, the role of the state and of all organized collective action, and to rely mainly on the competitive market mechanism as a "harmonizer" of the "self-interests" of all individuals. And in contrast, the socialist effort has been to make the democratic state or community the vehicle of fully organized cooperation among all in the direct service of their common welfare. The common central aim—of the liberals no less than of the socialists—has been to make the activities of all members of society, through all their consequences, as far as possible, never injurious and always maximally beneficial to the common welfare of them all. And they have sought to achieve this through (1) the functioning of institutions designed and developed for this purpose through free public discussion and agreements, and (2) the voluntary actions of all individuals within the framework of those institutions. But the two philosophies have always had somewhat different ideas of the meaning or the contents of "the common welfare," and radically different ideas of the character of the required scheme of institutions.

The classical liberalism has always had or involved, as compared with socialism, *not* less concern for, *but* a more limited, less all-inclusive conception of that "common welfare," which all should be concerned to protect, contribute to, and enhance or maximize. For a basic element of liberal thought has been its stress upon the diversity of the minds, characters, desires, and abilities of different human individuals, and the legitimacy and importance of much freedom for everyone to develop and realize, to the extent of his abilities, his own independent, individual vision of the good life, though subject to the obligation to make that consistent with the necessary public order in the community and the equal rights or freedoms, of the same kind, of its other members. Hence the liberal conception of "the common welfare" has included, not by any means all of everyone's, or anyone's, complete "welfare," but only the truly common, basic essentials or prerequisites of the differing "welfares" sought by all severally; i.e., the necessary freedoms, opportunities, minimal initial means or resources, educations, etc., required to enable all severally to achieve by their own efforts and rewarded services to each other, the kinds and amounts of "welfare" suited to their widely differing individual natures, desires, and abilities. It would be unfair to socialist thought to suggest that it necessarily or generally goes all the way to the other pole, and thinks of "the common welfare" as a uniform or standardized, complete "welfare" to be delivered or guaranteed to all alike by the entire community; but it does I think tend to go much farther in this direction than liberal thought can go with it.

But the other major difference and issue is only in part a result of that one, and concerns the choice or question of the kind of institutional set-up best suited as means to the ends of the social order. The classical liberalism envisioned as the main part of the best set-up, a system of "free," private, producing enterprises and consuming households, and open, free, or competitive markets, with a high mobility of all into the fields of their best opportunities, and a general maximization by everyone of his private gains and satisfactions, *through* maximization of his services to others in the markets. And it wanted so to restrict the roles of the state, and (even more) of all large groups organized for collective action, that the former would concentrate mainly on and fully accomplish its main task of preventing (with legal prohibitions and deterrent penalties) all or any acquisition of private gains through actions either injurious to the public or to anyone, or *not* rendering beneficial services commensurate with the gains acquired. But socialist thought has been always hostile to these ideas of the economy of private enterprises and competitive markets and the merely or mainly "policeman" state. It has always insisted that people and their activities could not be made adequately "social," or contributory to the common welfare, by anything less than common or collective ownership and management of all or most substantial wealth, resources, or "means of production," and entire replacement of competition by fully organized and planned, deliberate cooperation among all for the common good of all, and a more or less egalitarian, not market-regulated, distribution of economic output or income to or among all the people.

To the socialists, the classical economic-liberal vision of the *liberal* "capitalist" economy of free private enterprises, competitive markets, and so on, has seemed nothing more or other than a highly unrealistic, "prettified," false portrait of evil "capitalism"—their enemy and the antithesis of their own to-be-realized ideal, socialism. That the ideal conception of the special liberal form of "capitalism" could be taken seriously as something potentially realizable in practice through adequate reform efforts directed to this end, and something which if realized would be quite different from unregenerate, ordinary "capitalism," has seemed to socialists no more than a silly illusion. But I think some deeply foolish illusions of their own have been the bases of both their unshakable belief in the uncurable, total depravity—unsocial and antisocial, "greedy" nature—of *all* capitalism, and their dream of replacing it in time entirely with their radically different alternative, socialism. One of their basic illusions has been the belief that only acts of "labor" are productive—that "capitalists" or saver-investors, private owners, and active businessmen in their roles as such do not produce or contribute anything, but acquire their incomes entirely by "exploiting" the hired "workers" who alone produce all wealth.

Another basic socialist illusion is the belief that the institution of private property and the resulting unequal distribution of wealth—ownership of most of society's wealth by the minority of its members and ownership by the majority of nothing or little beyond their abilities to work—that this is *the* source and the only possible important source *of power* in the hands of some (the rich) to oppress and exploit others (the poor), and of all the main conflicts within society. In other words, there has been the notion that if only all the people collectively or jointly owned all important wealth—and the state managed the economy, i.e., the government or group in office and power at any time controlled the jobs and livelihoods of all the people?—there would be no problem or possibility of oppression through concentration and abuse of power (!), and no serious disputes or conflicts within such a society (!). And finally, there have been the illusions involved in conceiving all economic competition as simply and necessarily the full opposite of cooperation—as meaning wholly un- and antisocial, all-out strife or the "war among all"—and never considering competition in its other aspect as the opposite, only, of monopoly, i.e., as meaning for everyone a multiplicity of alternative opportunities for him to choose among, and hence no subjection to any one center of unchecked power. Thus the socialists rejected as absurd or impossible of realization the liberal ideal of an ethically restrained or tempered competition among all which would mean *only* a full system of checks and balances, dispersing and neutralizing all potentially oppressive powers, and would be consistent and combined with an adequate cooperation among all as producers and exchangers, through the market, of mutual services, and joint supporters of all proper exercises of the state's police powers. The socialists have instead cherished a confident belief in the real possibility of achieving in the socialist society a pure and perfect cooperation among all, unmixed with any competition.

Yet in pointing out as such what seem to me the basic illusions present or involved in all socialist thought, I do not mean to characterize it as a pure mass of illusions only, or immediately dismiss all its diverse, historic, and modern forms as entirely devoid of real insights or wisdom, and worth no further serious discussion. In the main, different, general phases of its long evolution, the socialist ideology has I think embodied different, and differently mixed, attractive and (other) not so attractive features. It may seem injurious to the modern, sober, democratic socialism, which it is my ultimate purpose here to illuminate in a measure, to compare it with the early, pre-Marxian, utopian socialisms of Fourier, Owen, and the rest, and indeed the differences, of course, are great; but I do not think they are all entirely in favor of the modern product, or that the similarities are entirely to the discredit of either. The early utopian dreams *were* that—extremely visionary and impractical—but they did express some very attractive, noble, generous, humane-idealistic, high, or fine aspirations. And they were in one respect set far apart from *all* modern socialism—i.e., from both Communism and modern democratic socialism—by a very important, distinctive trait which I think deserves high admiration in one sense, even though it was this above all which made them utopian, i.e., impractical or unrealistic. To state this point first in its negative aspect, those early utopians did *not* advocate any form of state, or *statist* socialism, transferring the ownership of all important wealth to national states, and control or management of the national economies to national governments; whereas modern socialists *are* stuck with *that* program and its liabilities, or are obliged to stand for only partial or fractional socialism or a "mixed economy" retaining much capitalistic private enterprise, if they don't want to make the state omnipotent.

The more attractive, but impractical, early utopian dreams were of a world of countless small, autonomous, voluntary, local communities and/or associations of productive workers, with the members of each community or association pooling or uniting all their assets and agreeing to live and work together in accordance with a jointly worked out, ideal plan, each member giving his best service to the group and all sharing the results or benefits according to their needs. Nation-states and their governments would do no more than before the change, and perhaps even in time go out of existence when, as many of these early visionaries thought, the ending of all poverty and discontent and quarrels over property etc., would end the need for coercive government, or bring about a universal, purely voluntary, perfect, happy cooperation within all the small, ideal communities and producers' cooperatives, and among them all. In becoming more realistic and practical, socialists have had to abandon that fantasy and turn to statism or statist socialism; but this is a comedown and has its drawbacks, as they are coming to realize—of this more later. But finally, in spite of that great contrast, modern democratic socialism has one very important, praiseworthy feature in common with the early utopian variety, which sets them both apart from all the strict followers of Marx, who played his big role in the intermediate period immediately after that of the utopians and before the rise of the modern socialism we are speaking of, and has since been resurrected and exceeded on his own worst lines by the modern Communists.

What I speak of now as the un-Marxian merit common to the early utopians and the modern democratic socialists is this: adherence to the simple, straightforward plan or method of trying to formulate or spell out the vision of the movement's goal—the to-be-realized, good, socialist society—as fully and clearly as possible, and to persuade as many people as possible, with rational arguments, to decide in favor of it and become workers for its gradual, progressive, peaceful realization. Marx, in his effort to make socialist thought about the effective way to attain the goal "scientific" or realistic instead of utopian, led his followers onto a wrong and disastrous path, with his dogmas that the economic circumstances and class interests of the different social classes in "capitalist" societies determine their points of view and make them impervious to rational persuasion which cannot reach across the gulf between them. In consequence, the socialists would have first to await the fulfillment of his prophecies, i.e., wait for the long, automatic evolution and deterioration of "capitalism" and intensification of mass poverty which would turn "the masses" into an army of militant socialists and weaken the capitalists and their system to the point of final collapse of the latter. The socialists would then destroy the collapsed enemy in a violent revolution, and build up the new socialist society with, in the early stages, as much coercion of the people by the new rulers as would still be necessary. What, above all, makes the modern democratic socialists in a vital way unlike the strict Marxists, and more like the early utopians, is the fact that, although they now assign the major role to their national states and not to thousands or millions of independent small communities and associations, they have recovered or returned to full faith in or reliance on rational persuasion, or the method of achieving socialism entirely through free and honest public discussion and majority agreement.

THE FABIANS AND ENGLISH SOCIALISM

The first important creators of modern socialism on this basis, in the period following that of the first flood tide of Marxist influence, were the English "Fabian" socialists—a small group of middle-class intellectuals led by Sidney and Beatrice Webb, George Bernard Shaw, and others, who flourished in the last decades of the nineteenth century and poured out a great mass of attractive, informed, and reasoned essays, articles, books, and lectures, and in spite of their small numbers greatly influenced a large part of the English public.[1] Their simple social philosophy was little more than a new, quite logical development of Benthamism or utilitarianism: democratic, rational planning, legislation, and administration to reshape the nation's social order, bit by bit, into the realization of a new design which would bring about "the greatest happiness of the greatest number"; and public ownership and efficient operation and expansion of the nation's assets and economy, and a new, more equal distribution of all goods and services which would ensure the economic and general welfare of all the people. Basic in their outlook was belief in the inevitable on-going progress of democracy—an evolutionary process then already well advanced in England and much of the Western world and destined, they thought, to occur and triumph everywhere eventually—the progress of democracy to full self-realization in states that would be the ideally competent, efficient, rational, ethical, and reliable agents or servants of all the

[1] The reader can easily acquire a good idea of what the "Fabian" socialists and their ideas were like by reading the old, quite readable and interesting, small book of essays by leading members of the group: *Fabian Essays in Socialism*, 1931 ed. (London: Fabian Society, 1931); or 1948 ed. (London: George Allen and Unwin, Ltd., 1948).

people in them, or agencies to which the latter would, voluntarily and with happy results, entrust the management of their assets and economies, for the general and equal benefit of all of them. The gradual achievement of democratic socialism would simply complete or perfect the achievement of democracy. The Fabians were full of what I think was a much too optimistic faith in the possibility of entirely rational, democratic governmental management of all economic activities, resources, and affairs for the equal benefit of all the people.

Some fairly sound, substantial pieces of research were carried out, by the Webbs and a few other leading members of the group, into such matters as the layouts of data relevant to, and the problems of, industrial management of some particular enterprises thought to be suitable for early transference into local or national public ownership and operation. Much study and thought were given to problems of governmental administrative organization and programing for the proper handling of socialist enterprises. But the Fabians had only a superficial knowledge and understanding of economics; in *this* one of the fields of inquiry of crucial importance for their purposes, their intellectual attainments were much too limited. Their principal and best "economist" was the playwright George Bernard Shaw. With his first-rate intelligence, he acquainted himself to some extent with the works and ideas of Jevons and other eminent, contemporary English professional economists, and accepted their leading ideas, understood them reasonably well, and employed them in his own thinking and writing with some effectiveness.[2] Taking nothing from Marx but a little from Ricardo (chiefly the latter's theory of land-rent) and the "marginal-utility theory of value" from Jevons, Shaw produced some eclectic, sketchy, and superficial economic theory for the Fabians, as a minor part of their equipment. In the "marginal-utility theory of value" and the associated idea that as peoples' incomes increase the importance to them of adding new increments to their incomes diminishes, Shaw thought he found solid support for his absolute egalitarian belief that justice and economy alike required a complete equalization of all family incomes. To him, the extreme inequality of income-distribution under capitalism entailed immense waste in the sense that resources and productive efforts needed to satisfy the urgent, vital needs of the many poor people were instead devoted to sating all including the most trivial wants or whims of the rich.

At the same time another part of this Shavian economics was indebted to Ricardo and/or the American reformer and amateur economist

[2] A good idea of G. B. Shaw's "economics" can be gained by reading his—of course readable and interesting, and oddly or perversely titled—book: *The Intelligent Woman's Guide to Socialism and Capitalism* (London: Constable & Co., Ltd., 1930).

Henry George, who visited in England with the Fabians and impressed and influenced them considerably, though Henry George himself was no socialist and the idea they took from him had to be transformed or extended in their hands to make it a part of their socialist creed. The basic ("Georgeist" and Ricardian) idea in question was that all land-rent incomes (net over and above due compensation of the landowners receiving them, for all improvements added to their lands by their labors or investments) were incomes engendered not by any productive services on the parts of the landowners, but solely by all social progress, growth of the world's and every country's population and wealth and demands and needs for the use of scarce, well-located, and good land, and the consequent, ever-growing power of private owners of the latter to charge and get rising payments of rent for rights to use it. This appeared to Henry George and to the Fabians to be a proof that private ownership of land and the resulting private appropriation of its rent-yields (created by and rising with all social-economic growth and progress) was profoundly unjust and contrary to good social economy; all "economic rent" of land should be taken by the state—through George's "single tax" or the nationalization of all land, which would both amount to the same thing—and used for public purposes, for the benefit of all the people.

Henry George held this view about land-rent *only,* but Shaw and the Fabians went beyond him and took the same or a similar view, also, of the interest or profit income-yields of all real capital or producers' goods (buildings, industrial plants, machines, etc.). Not only landlords but all capitalists appeared to them to be simply property owners "levying tribute" upon society for the uses or productive services of what under existing law were their properties; without themselves, as persons, performing or rendering any productive services, or in that sense earning the incomes created for them simply by society's demands and needs for, and the limited supplies of, all the goods and services producible only through uses of the means of production owned by them. That the required acts of saving and investing, which bring about production of new means of production (other than land) or increase the supplies of them and thus increase a society's or economy's productivity, *are* productive services on the parts of capitalists (other than landlords as such) through which they *do* earn their interest or profit-incomes in a sense or way in which economic land-rent incomes are not earned by their recipients—this view or distinction, implicit in Ricardo's and explicit in Henry George's thought, made no impression on Shaw and the other Fabian socialists. In their view *all* property incomes were like land-rents, unearned, or created solely by the public's demands and by scarcities, and all ought to be redistributed to the entire public through public ownership of all means of production. Thus in spite of their initial adoption of not the Marxian "labor theory" but instead the Jevonian "marginal-utility" theory of value, in the end they reached virtually the same position to which the former would have led them.

About a problem in another field, Shaw had already proposed what long afterward in fact became the English Socialist way of financing gradual, one-at-a-time nationalization of the ownership of the country's industries, with fair compensation to the former private owners at each step or in each case, and yet with the eventual result of nationalizing, finally, not only the particular industries but all once private capital. The state would need only to use, and gradually increase the rates of, progressive income and inheritance taxation, and use part of the proceeds or revenues to buy up one industry after another. Presumably, in the more advanced stages of this process, the state's profits or net revenues from the already nationalized industries would take the place of the earlier tax revenues from them or their then private owners. In this way, while the state in taking over each industry from the capitalists who previously owned it would at the time pay them its market value and thus still leave them in possession of their capital, which they might reinvest in the still private sector; still, over time the continual rise of the tax rates would reduce, eventually to zero, the amount of private-capital wealth remaining in the nation.

That when this ingenious or devilish scheme became established and understood, it might operate to drive English private capital abroad, and reduce the incentives of the capitalists and businessmen in the still private sector to keep up and enhance the efficiency of the enterprises soon to be nationalized—these obvious objections to the scheme were not met or discussed by Shaw, and I think have not been by later English Socialists since they began, in effect though perhaps without a clear, conscious intention, to put the scheme into practice. Nor is it only with regard to the economic consequences of such a process of gradual nationalization that Shaw displayed, and most English Socialists have displayed, incompetence in economic analysis. With regard also to the requisite method and conditions of economically efficient planning in a socialized or nationalized economy—the latter's need to have and use a real system of markets and market prices in order to be able to compute or measure and compare the costs and benefits of using labor and resources in different ways, and achieve the most efficient set or pattern of uses of them, throughout the economy—with regard to this whole vital matter, Shaw in spite of his glimpses into neo-classical economic theory showed no awareness, and most English Socialists have continued to show at most very little awareness, of the problem or the mass of problems in this field. The Fabians were informed and intelligent in most other fields important for their purpose, but weak in economics. However, they made socialism respectable in England, or accustomed the English public to regard it not with fear and horror but as a very interesting, attractive, reasonable, and perhaps desirable goal and program.

Of course the Fabians did not alone, however, create all modern English socialism, though they made a major contribution to it. Other earlier contributions had been made even long before their time by various developments of thought and effort in diverse quarters within the country: Owenism, Chartism, the vague "Christian socialism" of Kingsley and a few others in the Anglican clergy, and the human-brotherhood ethical fervor of the Methodist movement, to name only these. And in the same period with the Fabians there were two or three other, less important, little socialist societies of (as with the Fabians) mostly middle-class intellectuals. Marxism has never had much strength in England but has never been entirely without any adherents or influence among English socialists. Not the whole Marxist creed in its full orthodox complexity and rigor but a few elements or notes picked out of it, and modified or moderated more or less and blended in with other more dominant ideas or views of other kinds alien to it, have played a fairly important role in the general development of the English movement. But what has in the long run perhaps counted for as much as or more than the special work and ideas of the Fabians, and all similar groups, has been the largely independent, spontaneous growth of socialistic sentiments, ideas, and attitudes within the ranks of the English labor or trade-union movement, with which the Fabians and their peers in their time had little or no contact. By no means all English wage-earning industrial workers and members of their big and strong labor unions ever have been or become socialists, nor have all the leaders of the unions ever embraced the socialist outlook and program. But socialist convictions and ardors have for generations had a great and growing prevalence within many unions and throughout a great part of the country's wage-earning population—a prevalence in strong contrast with the almost negligible degree of influence of anything like a socialistic outlook in the American labor movement.

It would be easy, but would take us too far afield here, to explain that contrast as a result of the differences between the United States and Great Britain, as to what have been the social structures of and traditions in the two societies, social-class divisions and barriers and interclass relations, economic conditions and the opportunities of wage earners and their children, and so on. Many features of the British social-and-economic structure and its functioning and evolution, in the late nineteenth and early twentieth centuries, worked to turn most or very many British wage earners into socialists. Yet at the same time the highly successful, loyalty-of-all-inspiring development of the modern British democratic state or political and governmental system, the growth of great political power in the hands of the wage-earning part of the electorate, and the wide prevalence of generous sympathies with labor in the country's middle and upper classes, have all worked to make the socialism of its socialistic wage earners nonrevolutionary. Instead it has been a confident and patient, gradualistic, moderate, democratic-political affair of working through (without wanting to change) the existing political and governmental system to transform the social-and-economic order in the socialist direction. In short, although this working-class socialism has had its own independent roots and growth, apart from the measure of influence exerted by the middle-class intellectual socialism of the early "Fabians," the former in its own way has developed and retained a character in broad agreement with that of the latter, and has therefore been more easily and largely influenced by the latter than one might suppose.

The story of the rise and growth, composition and organization, etc., of the modern British Labor party—officially and predominantly a socialist political party with a mainly working-class but partly middle-class membership—can and must be omitted here. I will say a little at a later point about the most recent development and changes of that party's program, achievements, and ideology. But here for the moment I must turn aside from the entire special history of British socialism to touch on the modern (recent) evolution of most central, northern, and western Continental European socialism—in spite of continuing or lingering, nominal adherence to its Marxian traditions—away from real adherence to Marxian orthodoxy and into varieties of a moderate liberal-democratic socialism essentially or broadly like the English variety, although independent of that and never much influenced by it. The development of British socialism, only minimally influenced at any time by Marx and always mainly a very un-Marxian, native British affair, has been unique; it has been a very important and complex, special development, needing and worth the relatively full account of it which I have tried to give here. But the story of the development of the other kind or kinds of modern democratic socialism from or out of Marxist origins or backgrounds, though this has its own fully equal importance, can now be described here only very briefly.

THE "REVISIONIST" TREND AWAY FROM MARXIST ORTHODOXY IN THE SOCIALIST PARTIES OF ALL WESTERN EUROPE

This development, with its distinctive features, has been due I think to the following factors. The first condition behind it all has been the existence of a degree of real ambiguity or ambivalence within Marxism, allowing growths of—within limits—diverse interpretations or variants of the creed, in different environments. In the second place, impelling causes have arisen in the evolutions of all the more successful, modern, Western, capitalistic and democratic nations or national societies on lines diverging away from those predicted by Marx, and have produced, for their initially Marxian socialist movements and parties, changing real environments and situations, prevailing popular attitudes and desires, and pragmatic political needs or necessities, which have impelled these parties to develop *not* the kind of "hardening" of Marxism which modern Communism represents but on the contrary, a progressive "softening" of it—at first to and then ultimately far beyond the limit, in this direction, of arguable consistency with the real, original doctrines of Marx. But finally, in the third place, certain attractions, for those brought up in it, of the Marxist intellectual system and "language," have tended to cause professions of adherence, or lip service, to it to linger on, even after the real aims and methods of the socialists concerned became in fact decidely un-Marxian.

The entire development can be best illustrated and illuminated through a brief account of one crucial episode in the history of the German social democratic party, in the late nineteenth century—the famous "revisionist" movement that was led by a man named Bernstein, and the background and outcome of this, the hostile reaction to it at the time of the party's Marxist leaders, the controversy over it, and its nominal defeat but eventual victory.[3] This affair—which occurred in the same period with the work of the early Fabian socialists in England—was the most clear-cut and important open outbreak, in any of the Continental Marxian-socialist parties, of the kind of trend away from real or genuine Marxist orthodoxy which thereafter went on in all of them, on lines both parallel with and influenced by the trend in the German party, which came thus early and briefly to the surface there, in this episode. The official leaders of the German party at that time—Karl Kautsky and his fellows—were orthodox Marxists, of their kind; but their Marxism already had been subtly modified, somewhat, in the direction of becoming relatively moderate, liberal-democratic, and in reality more "evolutionary" than "revolutionary." Their own real outlook, in other words, was considerably unlike that of the modern Communists; by no means, to the same extent, of *that* grimly visionary and impassioned flaming character.

They still clung, in theory, to all the doctrines, and expected eventual fulfillment of all the prophecies of Marx, about the on-going deterioration and increasingly severe malfunctioning of the capitalist world's economic system and societies and civilization, intensifying misery and

[3] Accounts of the "Bernstein revisionist" movement and controversy in the German Social Democratic party can be found in many different histories of socialist thought and movements; there would be little point here in citing any one account in particular.

increasing militancy of the proletariat, etc. Looking forward, in theory, to the future, inevitable and glorious, heroic revolution, they held preparation for that to be, in the meantime, the main task of the party or movement; and they were rather severely inhibited in the matter of working for immediate, feasible, limited reforms, within capitalism, to improve the lot of "the masses," by the Marxist feeling that all conditions must rather first become much worse in order to bring about real improvement later on. They were inhibited also by fear that the effect of achieving current small reforms or ameliorations would be to lull "the masses" into relative contentment or decrease their militancy and delay the revolution and the real, great improvement which it alone could make possible. Yet all this was already more a set of theoretical than of entirely heartfelt convictions; and when Bernstein openly proposed that the party should throw away all this mass of Marxist doctrine, and frankly embark on the different course of working to realize socialism gradually through a progressive series of mild reforms—the party leaders vigorously opposed this shocking heresy, and to all appearances at the time defeated it, and kept the party nominally on the path of Marxist orthodoxy; but the subsequent evolution of its real outlook and program and activities went increasingly in Bernstein's direction.

And so, too, have the modern evolutions of the outlooks, programs, and endeavors of most of the Western world's (non-Communist) socialist parties, gone steadily in that same direction; of declining real interest in the doctrines of Marx though with long continuance of more or less lip service to them, and convergence to agreement with the Fabian temper and character of British socialism. Increasingly, they have turned to working through the normal democratic political process to achieve and accumulate a growing mass of varied reforms; public ownership and operation of some industries, imposition of various forms and degrees of public control upon the still large "private sectors" of the national economies, public encouragement of labor unions and collective bargaining and efforts to increase the wages of the working populations and add all kinds of "fringe benefits" to their wages, public subsidies for food, housing, medical care, etc., increasingly heavy taxation of the well-to-do and expansion of free public services, and so on. Whether in or behind all this, however, there is still a fully serious, unwavering determination of all democratic socialists to go all the way to the goal of full, eventual realization of complete socialism in the classical sense—complete abolition of all private enterprises and property incomes, or public ownership of all means of production and distribution of wealth, conversion of all citizens, with no class distinctions, into workers cooperating for the common good, and planned distribution of income or goods and services to all according to their needs—whether in general these modern socialists still are really marching, and mean to march all the way, to *this* goal, is I think very doubtful, to say the least. For there is a plain difficulty or dilemma—surely insurmountable I think—to which most socialists were long made blind by the element of naïve, utopian idealism in their tradition, but which is beginning to be recognized and faced by those among them—and this I think includes most modern Western democratic socialists—who are sincerely and strongly devoted to liberal-democratic ideals, *and* are acquiring, through practical experience and responsibilities, a more realistic grasp of the realities of politics.

THE DECLINE OF INSISTENCE ON COMPLETE SOCIALISM AS THE GOAL; THE "MIXED ECONOMY" AND "WELFARE STATE"

That dilemma is the surely predictable incompatibility in practice between any such complete, realized socialism as I have just described, and liberal democracy—political democracy with the freedoms for all which are required to make it real. With the state—or society as a unit, through the state—owning all substantial wealth or economic resources; and (necessarily) the government or group of men in office and power at any time, in full control of the entire economy or the jobs and livelihoods of all the people; it would be impossible for an opposition party, lacking the support of any independent economic resources, to exist and function freely, and for all those among the people—all being state employees—who might prefer the opposition party's candidates and program, to join that party and work for it openly without risking economic reprisals by the government in power. "Collective" ownership of all wealth, and management of the economy, would necessarily mean in practice, complete control of all resources by the government in power, and possession by it of the power to perpetuate itself in power. This full union of political and economic power would entail complete power to control, also, all education, communications, and intellectual, spiritual, and cultural life—which all require the support of economic resources. Surely it would be absurdly utopian to suppose that any human, not angelic, governing group (and all its members) could be safely trusted to practice, constantly, all the (purely voluntary) self-denial that would be involved in never making any undemocratic or illiberal misuse of such absolute power. The intellectual, spiritual, and moral civil liberties for all the people severally, which real democracy requires, themselves require the support of the economic liberties or freedoms, which are in turn impossible without very widely distributed private property, and private incomes in excess of their minimal material consumption needs for at least a very large part and complete cross section (as regards diverse value systems and political views) of all the people.

"Democratic socialism" is thus really a self-contradictory concept, *if* "socialism" retains the meaning of "collective ownership" of all or nearly all wealth, and "collective" (governmental) control of the entire economy. It is true that, in the past, capitalism has generally involved a degree of concentration of economic power, or wealth and income, and therefore also of an undue share of social, cultural, and real political power, in the hands of the members of a more or less limited, distinctive, and homogeneous social "class," which also is in practice less than fully consistent with ideal liberal democracy; and this is the element of truth in the convictions of the democratic socialists. But the greatest typical degree of concentration of control of wealth and power, existing within any modern Western capitalist society, is as nothing when compared with the complete or absolute concentration or monopoly of power which "total" socialism would necessarily put into the hands of the group of high officials making up "the government." The real road toward realization of ideal liberal democracy must lie in just the opposite direction, of change of the structure of economic society toward realization of the economic-liberal ideal, of moderate but substantial private properties and incomes for (as nearly as possible) all the people severally, and real existence of a system of not too imperfectly competitive markets, and high mobility of all people and resources into the most useful and rewarding locations and employments for them. All this would mean the operation, throughout the economy, of a system of "checks and balances," restraining all exertions of private power, and underlying and giving real substance to political democracy's necessary system of intragovernmental and intra- and interparty "checks and balances."

Today's Western democratic socialists still do not of course generally realize or grant the truth of all that I have just been saying; but I think there has been spreading among them, for some time, a dawning realization of the danger, from the standpoint of their own generally sincere and strong, liberal-democratic ideals, of going anything like all the way to complete socialism or "collective ownership," etc., and thus making the national state, and the government in power at any time, all powerful. At all events, they are clearly becoming disillusioned, wavering, or decreasingly enthusiastic in support of the program of "nationalizing" more and more and eventually all industries; they are veering toward acceptance, for an indefinitely long time ahead, of "the mixed economy" with a still quite large "private capitalistic sector," and a variety of measures of limited or partial public control of that, and the many features of "the welfare state." Whether *this* kind of system or compromise is really wise in the long-run true interest of all the people, or instead defeats its own purposes by hampering economic progress—destroying the progressive dynamism of unfettered capitalism without gaining that of all-out authoritarian socialism or communism—is another, different, grave question. But we can as well discuss this latter question, along with others, in connection rather with our next general topic—the modern or twentieth-century "liberalism," now generally so-called in political discussions especially in the United States, which is the now current successor, or modification, of the classical, late-eighteenth- and nineteenth-century liberalism. For between this newer "liberalism" and the kind of compromise or halfway house that "democratic socialism" appears to have settled into, the difference is not very great. There has been a convergence from both sides toward a common, middle ground—a "watering down" of democratic socialism in the liberal ("libertarian") direction, and a trend of "liberal" thought and practice away from adherence to its old *laissez-faire* tradition, into advocacy of what might be called "humanitarian big government," i.e., in the direction of a semisocialism. There is need, however, for a separate consideration of this development from or on the "liberal" side, which must focus largely though not exclusively upon the American part of this story and its backgrounds in past and recent American history.

THE UNIQUE PERSISTENCE, IN THE UNITED STATES, OF PREVAILING DEVOTION TO NONSOCIALIST, LIBERAL IDEALS

In most "old world" countries, but very little is left or remains alive today of the outlook of nineteenth-century liberalism, *in either* its original, pure state *or* any modification of that very similar to what is called "liberalism" in this country now. For today, as a rule, in the old (many-centuries-old) national societies, the main mass-popular, reforming or progressive movements are socialist and more or less radically anticapitalist in character or in their immediate (recent) antecedents and traditions; and the main, large and strong, more conservative bodies of opinion are still "conserving," in significant degrees, not merely nineteenth-century but far older, pre- and nonliberal ideals and traditions of organic-hierarchical societies led and governed by their propertied and cultivated upper-class minorities, which generally at least would like to govern in a more authoritarian-paternalistic than true liberal-democratic spirit. But in various ones of these old countries there do also exist small minority groups of intellectuals and cultivated bourgeois persons standing for a nostalgic and doctrinaire "liberalism" (under that name), which is often theoretically of a very pure and strict, unmodified, classical variety and which idealizes the economic system of free private enterprises, free competition, and international as well as domestic "free trade," and the entire regime of liberal individualism and *laissez faire* or very limited government. These "liberals," however, as a rule retain actually, in relation to present-day conditions and problems, very little if any of the once genuinely strong and ardent, universally humane-idealistic, and at the same time highly practical, progressive or reforming spirit of the original classical liberalism in its heyday. Naturally *these* tiny groups of exponents of *this* kind of "liberalism," though they are intellectually alive and quite active in various Continental countries, are generally without or unable to exert important practical influence.

The story has been and continues to be somewhat different in England, where *in* the nineteenth century the classical liberalism had its earliest, longest, fullest and best development and influence, and always tended to be less rigidly doctrinaire or more pragmatic, flexible, and realistic than its Continental European imitations ever have been. In England also, it is true, the modern growth of the Labor party and English socialism on the one hand, and, on the other, the continuing strength of a Tory or Conservative party which has shown unique abilities to blend together and reciprocally adjust, in changing proportions, its own very ancient traditions and nineteenth- *and* twentieth-century ideas and tendencies of various sorts—these rivals together have entailed, for the English Liberal party over recent decades, a drastic decline or shrinkage to the status of a tiny minority or third "in-between" party, with little prospect of regaining power and with little influence. The bulk of the old or former membership or clientele of the Liberal party has long since divided and melted away into the other two English parties—the more conservative or classical English liberals, averse to socialism, going over to the Tories, and those with enough of both the universally humane-idealistic reforming spirit and the pragmatic, flexible readiness to turn that in a new direction, going over to the Labor party. But the reduced, small, continuing Liberal party has remained lively; it has retained a few quite able leaders and adherents, and continues to be hopeful—perhaps not entirely without reason—of an eventual, future renaissance. And in outlook today it differs widely from the Continental "liberal" group above referred to, in that its "liberalism" is now not purely classical but has shifted "leftward" considerably, not all but part of the way toward agreement with the Labor party's moderated "socialism"; it does also, in a general way, somewhat resemble the far more important, modern, modified, American "liberalism" which, with its own different American background and independent American development, is now to be discussed.

The salient special features, relevant to our story here, of American history, society, and culture may all be largely explained, I think, by two related, general facts: (1) the nonexistence, in American civilization, of any important feudal inheritance and continuing traditions still living on and bearing the marks of that origin; and (2) the failure of any American socialist movement to develop and retain important strength. Of these two very important, "negative" features of American life, the former, I think, largely accounts for the latter. Though all modern socialism has always regarded capitalism as its enemy and antithesis, it has really developed mainly in reaction against the carry-overs from feudalism embodied in or mingled with the thus impure forms of capitalism to be found in most very old societies. The social-class structures and interclass relations in old, formerly feudal societies—the lingering traditions of real, rigid, social hierarchy, or rule by social superiors over their social inferiors, and a sense of the normality of arrogance in the former and submissiveness in the latter; this, in its clash with developing, modern (post-Enlightenment) ideals of equality, democracy, and freedom for and reciprocal justice among all, has been everywhere the real, main cause of the rise, growth, and persistence of fully and militantly socialistic labor movements. Socialism, that is, has flourished in countries where modern capitalism has developed within, and while modifying, also continued to be modified by, the social milieus of that kind carried on from feudalism. The members of the class of capitalist employers, emulating the true heirs of the feudal barons, have tended to treat the members of the working class as their inferiors and dependents, to be held down in their place, and have been supported in this attitude by all the conservative elements in the societies around them; and there has continued to prevail throughout each such society, including its working class, the habit of thinking-and-feeling more in terms of the classes as units than in terms of individuals and their opportunities. In complete situations of this kind, the socialist vision has naturally made its strong appeal to the working class (and middle-class idealists in sympathy with it) as the only adequate answer to the really semifeudal kind of capitalism alone existing and familiar locally. But in the United States, from the outset, there has developed an almost uniquely pure form or kind of capitalism, evolving along with American liberal democracy, and in a social environment devoid of carry-overs from feudalism. Also the exceptionally great "mobility" in every sense, including "vertical social mobility," of the American people, the great and multiple opportunities generally available to most of them as individuals, the less substantial nature here of class distinctions and barriers, the widespread sense of the essential equality of all Americans as regards their essential human rights and dignities; all this has worked to make the creed of liberal individualism including economic liberalism in (roughly) the classical sense, the prevailing outlook here not only in our business community but throughout American society.

It is only an accidental fact in the history of uses of political terminology, and a fact of no great importance, that the *words* "liberal" and "liberalism" were *not* in constant, general use in American political life in the nineteenth century. No major American political party or faction or movement ever called itself "liberal" or its program "liberalism," *until* this term—with attached connotations of the kind it now has in our political life, more than of the classical nineteenth-century (English and

European) kind—began to come into use here among reform-minded intellectuals early in the present century. It then got applied to all that the New Deal stood for, and thereafter became or remained the accepted "name" for the vague, confused ideology of the "liberal" wing of the Democratic party. In obvious minor ways this bit of American terminological history *is* significant, but the main real fact, obscured by it, is that the older, main American tradition of political and economic thought and practice (now identified with "conservatism" or "reaction") always has been substantially identical with the Western, classical, eighteenth- and nineteenth-century "liberalism," even though in this country it has never generally borne that "name" or label. The classical nineteenth-century liberalism was, everywhere in the Western world, the main, continuing fruit of the eighteenth-century Enlightenment; and American civilization—the American national state, society, economy, and culture—has been *more* fully and lastingly influenced, throughout, by the Enlightenment, than has the civilization, in the same all-embracing sense, of any other country. The American "founding fathers" were all typical men of the Enlightenment, and were enabled by the conditions and prevailing popular attitudes existing in this country in their time to shape our Federal Constitution and infant nation on the lines of the ideals of the Enlightenment, to a unique extent—to achieve much more in that sense than their contemporary European peers were able to achieve in their more resistant, less plastic environment. And in nineteenth-century America on the whole the main conditions affecting the experience and attitudes of most Americans were and long continued to be favorable to a uniquely great degree of continuing prevalence and progressive realization here of the liberal-democratic and economic-liberal, Enlightenment ideals. In Europe to a much greater extent, the Enlightenment, and its main product, the classical liberalism, was a passing phase of the evolution of the civilization of the European nations—a phase which could have only a partial and eventually declining success in its conflicts there with older surviving and later reviving and other, newer ideologies. But in this country the same bright vision, of the good society to be developed through continuing free discussion and agreement among its free, individual members, became and remained "the American dream," and continued to flourish here as such, in a free field, without ever having any important rivals to contend with.

THE PATTERN OF THE HISTORY (EVOLUTION) OF AMERICAN SOCIETY AND POLITICS

Of course this account, so far, is oversimple and needs to be qualified in a number of ways. There was in the northeastern part of the United

States, in the late eighteenth and early nineteenth centuries, a set of somewhat antidemocratic, quasi-aristocratic or oligarchic, federal-power-exalting, and (in economic thought and policy) semimercantilistic rather than pure economic-liberal tendencies in or of the region's leading businessmen and statesmen, which found expression in the "Hamiltonian" philosophy of the "Federalist" party. As the main opposition to that in the same early period, the "Jeffersonian" liberalism—the purest, ideal classical liberalism in our history—appealed mainly to "enlightened" southern country gentleman (like Jefferson himself), and farmers throughout the country, and urban workingmen. *This* outlook was *not* generally popular in its own time in any part of the national business community as such; for there went along with Jefferson's radical libertarian and democratic and economic-liberal (minimal-government, *laissez-faire*) ideals, a tinge of something like or near to anticapitalism—distrust of big cities and big commercial and industrial capitalists or businessmen and groups of them. Full or all-out political democracy was then still generally conceived not as a means of enabling all the people or the popular majority to control and use a big and widely active central government as their instrument for achieving all their ends; but rather as a means of enabling all the little people, or members of the great popular majority, to veto all ambitious governmental plans, which were felt to be too likely to be shaped in practice, in spite of the nominal existence of democracy, by and to suit the aims of rich and powerful business minority groups.

Then too of course, despite the considerable influence of the Jeffersonian tradition in some ways in its southern homeland, the South did not on the whole become and remain a very "liberal" part of the United States, but on the contrary, with its plantation-slavery economy and quasi-feudal society, developed a pattern of ideals and customs in considerable conflict with liberalism and democracy, and half-resembling, in some respects, old European conservative traditions. Thus there were in early America—which as yet was all mainly "eastern," i.e., much developed and settled only in the region east of the Alleghenies—both a northern, capitalist center and a southern, quasi-feudal center and kind of resistance to development of full-fledged liberalism and democracy.

But a new set of factors soon came into play with the growth of "the West"—then the region between the Appalachians and the Mississippi—and the rise and triumph of "Jacksonian Democracy," which expressed and fostered a nation-wide spread or extension of the influence of the spirit of frontier democracy, making more or less the whole nation, socially and politically, more radically or fully democratic than it had been earlier. The gains for "democracy" in every sense, from this development, were substantial; but for "liberalism" in important aspects, the results were more equivocal. Any democratic populace always has illiberal tendencies to impose its own majoritarian tyranny and to suppress unpopular dissenting individuals and minority groups or unduly restrict their proper rights and freedoms; and there has continued to be always in American life a vitally necessary role for members of the small class of truly cultivated or enlightened, generally well-to-do, quasi-aristocratic leaders, and occasional public figures to play, in so influencing public opinion as to keep the ideals of true liberalism alive and effective. In the epoch and flood of Jacksonian Democracy there was a partial eclipse of such leadership, which had been more plentiful and strong in the previous, earliest period of our national history than it ever has been again, and a trend toward the other, worse kind of leadership by opportunistic and demagogic politicians. But all this generally remained within fairly tolerable limits, which have again been further narrowed, at least from time to time, in subsequent periods; and the advance into fuller democracy—effective participation by all the people in the nation's political life and the shaping of its institutions, society, and culture—was, in spite of its hazards, good, and has continued.

I must skip over the Civil War and its prelude and aftermath and all that was involved in or went with it, in spite of the relevance to my theme of all this, and jump down to the new, broad, economic, social, and political developments of the last decades of the nineteenth century, in or from which *modern* America and its main, continuing, ideological, and political divisions and conflicts were first born. The industrial revolution really got under way in this country only in the middle and late nineteenth century, and went on to its first culmination only toward the end of that century. The building of the transcontinental railroads and completion of the country's network of railroads, the growth and multiplication of great factories and manufacturing industries equipped with power-driven machinery, and of business corporations of all sizes owning and operating all such enterprises, and new financial institutions and centers, and large cities, and so on—all the aspects of full-grown industrial capitalism or capitalist industrialism—in a few decades radically changed the face and character of what had been a nation of family farms, small towns and villages, handicraftsmen, and merchants as the only or main group of "capitalists" or "businessmen." The flood of immigration of former peasants and laborers from most parts of Continental Europe, forming a great part of the labor force of the new industrial America, and bringing over with them in some cases Marxian-socialistic ideas and attitudes which their early hardships here kept alive for a time—this too made its contributions to the new America. The new millionaires of this era—great fortune builders and industrial empire builders—in many cases tried to live like and be like feudal barons, dazzle and rule and exploit the country and the people with their wealth and power, unite their powers in great monopolistic trusts, control and use the organs of government at all levels, national, state, and local, to gain assistance of all kinds to their business interests and prevent interference with them, and impose their often crude notions of high culture and morality upon the nation. It was in this era that *laissez-faire* economic liberalism, in a very distorted, one-sided, not at all self-consistent form, first became the dogmatic creed of the national business community. And in other, nonbusiness, mass-popular quarters—agrarian and some labor circles, and among reform-minded intellectuals—there began to develop in opposition to that twisted *laissez-faire* creed of the business community, the American "radical" movements, seeking to use the democratic state and political process to control the latter, which were the earliest forerunners of the present-day American, nonclassical "liberalism."

In a sense, the opposite deviations of political thought, in the business community and among its opponents, from the authentic, classical liberal outlook, were alike, in being group-interest-biased views of the proper and improper fields and forms of governmental intervention in the economy. The main attitude in each or in every group tended (and still tends) to be: the state should not act to benefit our opponents at our expense and restrict our freedoms and opportunities, but it should give us all the forms of protection and assistance that we "need." On many a specific issue, special variations and confusions of the views adopted in diverse quarters, and strange, particular alliances and conflicts, could (and can) arise from the varying ranges and admixtures of perceptions and nonperceptions of the interrelations of group interests and the likely indirect results of the public policies or measures being advocated or opposed. Also in various quarters, on some issues, motives or value-feelings of other kinds, not arising simply from the real or supposed economic self-interests of those concerned, often have come into play. Let us glance briefly at some of the ways in which, in the last decades of the nineteenth century, the growths in the main, diverse, interest-group segments of American society, of their respective, in some cases agreeing and in others conflicting, views and attitudes on various specific issues began to shape the complex pattern of our national politics and actual policies *toward* production of the present state of things.

First let me again stress the importance of the rise in that era, in the main, "conservative" part of the American business community, of what has tended to remain its devotion to a glaringly one-sided, not really self-consistent conception and cult of *laissez faire* or "free enterprise," and the importance of the points of contrast or disagreement of that with the authentic, classical, economic liberalism. The aim of the latter has always been: no public favors to any one set of private interests, to the detriment of the interests of any other part of all the people; or in other words maintenance of equal freedoms, rights, and opportunities for *all* the people. But the business community's twisted version of this has rather been: no governmental actions adverse to the interests of the dominant business groups, or to benefit other, nonbusiness, broader popular groups at their expense, or restrict or limit *their* freedoms, rights, or opportunities, *but* all obtainable governmental actions to protect, facilitate, and assist their undertakings, restrict other's opportunities to their advantage, and enhance their profits. As a first example of this discrepancy, on a specific issue that was very prominent all through the latter part of the nineteenth century, the positions on the question of free or unimpeded foreign trade versus tariff protectionism may be cited. "Free trade" has of course always been an essential part of the true economic-liberal program; but the main groups of American businessmen in that era (even more than now) were staunch protectionists—in unconscious conflict with their professed devotion to the system of "free enterprise." For of course the number and political weight of the spokesmen for the domestic industries competing with imports and "needing" tariff protection greatly exceeded the combined number and weight of the importers and all others directly advantaged by a free flow of imports, and the exporters and producers of industrial goods for export in that era (most American exports then were still of farm products). Moreover, the few industrial producers for export were not always aware that restricting imports indirectly reduced opportunities to export.

Now the real effects, further, of the high tariff barrier against imports of a great variety of manufactured goods, were in general injurious to the interests of the then vast number of American farmers. It raised the prices or costs to them of the manufactured goods they had to buy, while the prices of the main staple farm products were determined in the world market, and depressed by the tariff's effect of curtailing the ability of foreigners to earn dollars in the American market, and thus curtailing the foreign demand for our farm products. Also the tariff worked on the whole rather against than for the interests of American labor (industrial wage earners), by raising the cost of living without correspondingly raising wages, since it caused most of the labor force to be employed in the country's less efficient industries (the ones dependent on tariff protection, and least able to afford high wages), and hampered the growth of other industries in which, otherwise, the productivity and earnings of labor could have advanced to better levels. On this whole issue, however, the protectionist businessmen were highly successful in deceiving American farmers and wage earners with fallacious arguments as to where their interests lay. The farmers were won over with the "home-market" argument, alleging that the tariff, by speeding the growth of the economy's industrial sector and population, cities, etc., would end the dependence of American agriculture on foreign markets and replace those with an enlarged domestic American market more profitable for the farmers. And the wage earners were convinced by the "high-wages" argument, alleging that the high level of American wages as compared with foreign wages meant correspondingly high costs of production of American products as compared with foreign products, and made the tariff necessary to prevent a reduction of American wages to the low foreign level. (Actually, of course, the higher level of American wages was and is due to a generally corresponding higher level of the productivity of labor—output per man-hour—with American resources, technology, abundant capital per worker, industrial management and labor skills and industrial relations, attitudes, etc., and therefore consistent with no higher level of production costs per unit of output, in all but the less than normally efficient ones among all American industries.)

At the same time, it is probably true that the success of those false arguments in leading American farmers and wage earners to think of the tariff as in line with their self-interests was not the *only* cause of the popularity of protectionism in that era with a large majority of all American voters. A sense of the truth—always recognized by classical-liberal economists—of the argument for (temporary) protection of potentially though not yet highly efficient "infant industries"; patriotic pride in a policy of fostering rapid American industrial growth; and aversion to all things foreign, the wish for national self-sufficiency or independence of foreign supplies and markets, the spirit of "isolationism" —all this, too, was probably involved. But the net result was general support of a national policy inconsistent with complete, true economic liberalism, and biased in favor of or mainly benefiting the main mass of members of the business community, and against the true, current, economic interests of a far greater number of Americans outside that community. And this was one part of the prelude to, and later became one contributing cause of, a growth of tendencies on the parts of those other, broader, American groups to regard as due from their government to themselves, not simply or mainly denials of special favors to business groups at their expense, but rather additional, compensating, special favors to themselves at the expense of business.

Nor was it only through espousal of protectionism as opposed to free trade in foreign-trade policy, that the business community itself in that era, or great numbers of its leading members, helped to initiate developments contrary to the ideals of true economic liberalism. The latter has always idealized not only international free trade, but also domestic, national economies kept thoroughly competitive throughout, or "free" *from* controls of any of their parts by any private monopolies. But in many American industries in those last decades of the nineteenth century, the groups of businessmen concerned strove, with much success, to build up great monopolies, "trusts," or "combinations in restraint of trade." In this matter, however, the reaction of the public (including the other businessmen disadvantaged by and opposed to the "trusts") did develop on a true economic-liberal line, and brought about the first steps in the creation and development of our uniquely American body of federal "antitrust" law and policy. The latter in its whole career thus far—with its later, further developments and varying applications—has probably had on the whole a significant though limited measure of success in keeping our economy a little more competitive than it would now be otherwise, or limiting the growths, degrees, and prevalence of great concentrations of business power. But in a good many fields the latter have triumphed to no small extent—perhaps inevitably and not improperly; and this has helped to stimulate the growth, in more recent times, of great power-organizations of other kinds, e.g., labor unions, to "balance" the powers of the giants in the business world. Thus the structure of our whole economic society, in many large and important areas at least, has evolved rather far away from anything like a realization of the classical-liberal, competitive ideal. It is now by no means that highly decentralized and fluid system of many very small, independent, competing units on each side of every market; with an unimpeded, high mobility of all labor, capital, and enterprise out of all depressed and contracting and into all of the more rewarding and expanding parts of the economy; and the resulting control of the economy's functioning not by the powers and to the advantage of the strong, but by the demands of the people in the markets and a set of impersonal, automatic market forces, generally harmonizing all private interests with the public interest. In our modern, no longer atomistic-competitive society, the centralizations of power and the conflicts—in the markets and in politics—of the interests of diverse, big, strong, organized interest groups, have made inevitable a great enlargement of the role of the state, as the only superior power able to preserve order and any approach to all-around justice. To arrive at any satisfactory, in any meaningful sense "liberal," nondespotic solutions of the resulting maze of problems, is terribly difficult, and I do not pretend to know what the right or wise solutions are or would be; but continuing adherence to the *laissez-faire* maxim has become impossible.

The first inauguration, in the late nineteenth century, of the "antitrust" effort was itself an extension of "state interference," *but* was at the same time in line with the classical-liberal ideal, as an effort to preserve the competitive, not by-monopolies-controlled character of the economy, and thus enable it to go on functioning, as a largely self-adjusting or self-regulating system, well enough in the public interest or for the general welfare, to make an endless growth of other extensions of "state interference" of other kinds unnecessary. And the same may be said of the first inauguration, in that same era, of the program of public regulation of those few, peculiar, private enterprises—the start made then was with the railroads, and other "public utilities" have since been brought under similar regulation as they have developed—the enterprises which are at once "naturally" monopolistic and vitally necessary to the public. Either outright public ownership and operation or, as a minimum, public regulation of these special parts of the economy is required according to the classical economic-liberal point of view, or in pursuance of the aim of impartial protection of the equal freedom of all men from any oppression or exploitation by any arbitrary power either public or private. The method, plan, or expedient of regulation, by special public commissions or administrative agencies, given general legislative directives and a measure of discretionary authority to construe and apply them through administrative rulings, regulating the services to be produced or rendered and the prices or rates to be charged for them, to ensure appropriate service to the public and a "fair" and only a "fair" return or profit to the private owners or investors—this is a typical American compromise or mean between the extremes of "socialistic" public ownership and unregulated private monopoly. Making it effective regulation in the public interest, not really regulation by the regulatees, and not, through the piling of a governmental upon a private business bureaucracy, unduly hampering to all individual initiative and enterprise in these fields of activity has proved very difficult, and the measures of success achieved have probably always left much to be desired; but it is doubtful whether any better path or line of attack upon these problems has been available.

Still another very different, general field in which there were late-nineteenth-century developments which must be mentioned here as having played parts in the evolution toward the present state of this country and its problems, ideals, and policies is the field or world of agriculture and the farmers and their hardships and political tendencies. Back in that era the situation in agriculture was very unlike what it is today; but the situation as it was then had results which we need to notice, mainly in connection not with "the farm problem" of today, but with other more general phases of the evolution of our national political life and public policies. One manifestation of the Western agrarian "radicalism" of that time was in the field of ideas and policies relating to money and the national economy's supply of money. The entire period was, in the world generally as well as in the United States, one of the rare periods in modern history to be marked by not a rising but a falling general level of all prices. The rapid growth of production of most kinds of products—of the flow of goods to markets, throughout the Western world—was not fully matched by growth of the stock and flow of money, so prices generally were drifting downward. In the industrial (manufacturing) sector of the American and Western world economy, technological progress and rising efficiency was lowering production costs, so that wages and profits did not generally fall with the fall of prices. But in agriculture the modern technological revolution had not yet begun; and the expanding area of cultivated farm land, and farm labor force, were turning out a growing flood of farm products, which continually depressed their prices without any corresponding decline of their production costs. Farm incomes were thus declining and, moreover, many American farmers were burdened with heavy debts, which became increasingly burdensome as their real costs rose with the rise of the general buying power of money. There was therefore much agitation for national policies with regard to money or the currency which would make money more abundant and "cheap"—adherence to bimetallism (free coinage of silver as well as of gold) instead of adoption (favored by eastern bankers and financial experts) of the single gold standard, and issuance also by the national government of a large supply of "fiat" paper money.

Detailed discussion here of the issues in those controversies is impossible and unnecessary, but a word must be said about the main general question that was really at stake. There has always been a tendency of many strict adherents of the old classical economic liberalism to regard as a necessary integral part of that philosophy of all appropriate governmental economic policies, the principle that with regard to money—though the regulation of this must be, without any question, a governmental function—the government must adopt and adhere to a simple, definite, and fixed system, "the gold-standard" system. The essential virtue of this was felt to be that it made the real value or general buying power of the money unit, or the general price level, dependent *not* upon continually new or changeable governmental or political decisions subject to manipulation by the varying relative political strengths of different interest groups in the economy and society, *but* upon the "natural" conditions and events, not subject to political control, which would determine all the changes of the world's, and every country's, supply of gold and, if the total money supply everywhere was kept strictly tied to that, the supply of money. If the supply of all other goods grew faster than the supply of gold and gold-based money, the general price level would fall, and if new gold discoveries turned the balance the other way, the price level would rise—a perfectly stable price level could not be assured; but at least these fluctuations would have only "natural," not political, causes, and manipulations of the money supply to the advantage of some interest groups and the disadvantage of others, would be ruled out. In that sense "the gold-standard" system formed a logical part of the economic-liberal ideal of letting all things economic be controlled or governed, as far as possible, by "automatic, natural" forces, not political controls.

But the entire modern trend away from all that, into increasing governmental efforts to regulate economic events and relieve or alleviate the hardships of all large groups, has everywhere included, as one prominent and important part of itself, a trend in the field of policies concerned with the supply and flow of money, away from adherence to anything like the gold-standard system. It has become the more prevalent view that governments should have much discretionary power and freedom to continually "manage" that supply and flow, ideally (according to much present-day economic theory—see Chapter 17) in the way required to keep the aggregate demand for all goods and services at a stable price level, continually equal to the aggregate supply of them all, under conditions of continuous full employment of the available labor force, resources, and productive equipment in the whole economy, and of steady and fairly rapid economic growth. The vogue of "cheap-money" ideas in western rural America in the late nineteenth century was of course by no means a full anticipation of this whole modern development, but it was significant, as we can now see in retrospect, as an early stage in that development. And it is of interest that some of the leading American economists of that time, although they stood generally in the classical economic-liberal tradition, did *not* stand strictly with the stern "sound-money, gold-standard" advocates in the Eastern business and financial community, but saw justice in and expressed sympathies with the demands of the Western agrarian "radical" elements for currency policies that would halt the fall of the price level and alleviate the hardships of the farmers.

The discontents of the latter also had other results or led to much prevalence in the rural western America of that time of other "radical" politico-economic ideas, besides "cheap-money" ideas. The "Populist" political party and movement, the main carrier of all the diverse ideas and demands in question (including those for "cheap money"), had a general outlook of hostility to all northeastern "big-business" and financial interests, "Wall Street," the railroads, the "trusts," etc., and a general vague idea of working to make state governments and the Federal government the protectors and benefactors of "the people," i.e., of the great majority—all relatively poor people—as against the supposedly wicked, predatory, rich, and powerful capitalists. To a certain extent, this movement or the saner part of it played a part in helping to support the sound developments in national policies already reviewed here—the antitrust law, regulation of the railroads, etc.—and moderate revisions of currency legislation in the needed direction of allowing some increase of the supply of money. And the depressed state of agriculture which lay behind the movement helped to motivate the first steps taken, a little later, by the Federal government, toward development of the great program of subsidized research and education to make farming more efficient or productive and to reduce production costs in all branches of agriculture. The latter program eventually became immensely effective, and a main source of the new, modern "farm problem" of our time, of chronic overproduction, operating to reduce the free market prices of farm products even below the greatly reduced costs. But the Populist movement also had a more "crazy," demagogic, and ephemeral, vaguely semisocialistic side. In the end this movement became merged with or into the national Democratic party (mainly or largely, though another part of it contributed rather to the subsequent rise of the "progressive" faction of the Republican party); and it was an early "radical" phase of the development of what has become the new American "liberalism" of today.

In still another different area of American life—that of the labor movement, or growth of diverse types of labor unions, etc., among the nation's wage earners—there were also various developments in that period, which I must here allude to. There had been important unions in various skilled trades or crafts from the very beginning of the nation's history, and a slow growth of various newer or younger ones all through the earlier and middle decades of the nineteenth century. A somewhat loose, vague, ineffectual, and ephemeral, broad or general organization, "The Knights of Labor," did not at all confine its efforts to the narrow, practical business of "collective bargaining" but toyed with a great variety of nebulous ideas of social reforms to be achieved through mass education and in part at least through political action. But the "Knights" and the type of thing it represented died early in that period and had no great importance. The main mass of the rapidly growing, largely foreign-born, industrial wage-earning population was without any enduring unions or organizations within this period, and lived and worked under rather wretched, harsh conditions—very long working days, meager wages, grim living and working conditions. There were various bitter strikes and violence-filled dramatic struggles of groups of workers led by militant "radical" leaders against self-righteously tyrannical, hardfisted employers who often got too much public and governmental support. And as might be expected, from that background, there grew up partly then and partly somewhat later, for a time, some truly radical minority movements within the entire, varied, general, American labor movement. A few violent "anarchist" leaders were active for a time in a few industrial struggles and short-lived unions; a partly Marxian, socialist movement arose and grew to considerable strength a little later, for a few decades; and the syndicalist I.W.W. and Western Miners Union became prominent for a time in the very early twentieth century. But the *main* development which emerged, toward the end of the nineteenth and on into the twentieth centuries, had a very different character; the pure-and-simple, nonpolitical, business unionism, dominant in the American Federation of Labor, under the leadership of Samuel Gompers and others, fostered growths of memberships, effective, durable organizations, and skilled bargaining techniques in a growing array of unions, mainly in all skilled trades or crafts. These unions generally accepted the existing economic system and social order as permanent and had no ideology beyond devotion to collective bargaining with employers, backed up by threats to strike if necessary, for continually higher wages, shorter working days, and all kinds of small improvements of working conditions.

If this country's capitalism, or business economy and social structure, and the ruling attitudes in the upper-income strata, and its not too effectively democratic political and governmental institutions (as they actually operated or functioned then)—if all this had persisted, unmodified, far into the twentieth century, with all the garish and harsh or inhumane features that were there in that "gilded age" of newborn, booming, raw, industrial capitalism—the eventual result might have been a growth of a full-fledged, radical, American socialist movement to predominant strength, and a real mass-popular struggle for radical political and social changes, on lines similar to those pursued in so many other countries. But instead, in the first two decades of the twentieth century there emerged here, under Theodore Roosevelt and then under Woodrow Wilson as Presidents and leaders, a kind of renaissance of American liberalism in, substantially, the old or classical sense of the word, which quietly accomplished a good deal toward making American capitalism, in its form and spirit and main practices, more consistent with democratic and humane-liberal ideals, and making American liberal democracy as such more real and effective. More vigorous enforcement, and much strengthening, of the antitrust laws reduced the concentrations and abuses of power in the business world and partially restored the classical competitive form and functioning of the national economy. Protective tariff barriers were sharply lowered for a short time (under Wilson), and this, though short-lived, was beneficial while it lasted. The national monetary and banking system were also much improved in the Wilsonian era.

More important, there occurred a great moral improvement in the nation's political life—a marked reduction of the abilities and tendencies of special business interests to control or manipulate elections, and obtain great, improper, governmental favors. This beneficial change was helped by such specific reforms as direct popular elections of United States senators, instead of continuance of the system under which the state legislatures, too often easily controlled by business interests in the states, elected the Federal senators and made them mouthpieces of those special interests and a barrier able to block most reform legislation for the benefit of the majority of the people. Also the Federal income tax came into being in this period, and this, with the subsequent trend to increasingly "progressive" rates, has made possible the great modern growth of the Federal government's revenues and welfare spending programs, and the resulting effective redistribution of income and wealth among the people in the direction of equality. Though the sum of their tangible achievements was relatively modest, the differing, healthy moral crusades, led respectively by "Teddy" Roosevelt and by the scholarly idealist Wilson, to break or reduce the monopoly powers and the undemocratic, unsocial temper of the very rich, and to enlarge the real freedoms and opportunities of the main mass of the people, were, I think, very beneficial and important.

Yet in the 1920s, in the aftermath of the First World War and the national mood of disillusioned reaction from the high but naïve liberal-democratic idealism which the people had carried into the war itself, there was a less noble interlude of renewed excessive power and greed in and abuses by many rich businessmen, groups, and organizations; and mass-popular political apathy—absorption of most Americans in their private pursuits of wealth and pleasure. Among reform-minded intellectuals, there grew up a range of new trends of thought and feeling, away from full adherence to the individualistic, limited-government ideals of the classical liberalism and the old, main American tradition, into gropings for ideas of new ways in which a national government, controlled by and serving the not-rich popular majority and entrusted with new additional powers and functions, could more strictly curb the possessors and abusers of great wealth and power, and enhance and protect mass-popular welfare. In other words, that decade of the 1920s did much to prepare the soil and the seed, so to speak, for the growth of the new, modern American nonclassical "liberalism," which in the next decade, of the Great Depression, rose suddenly to power, in or with the New Deal. This was and is, or has remained, an amorphous, variegated tide of democratic-humanitarian feeling and generally rather vague or nebulous, fluid and variable ideas, not a movement with a clear, definite philosophy and program. It was and is a movement generally "partial" to labor and the farmers and all really or supposedly handicapped, not adequately prospering groups, and somewhat hostile toward capitalism and the business community; it has sought to achieve its wide array of ill-defined ends through whatever expedients may come to hand, and has aimed generally toward not socialism but some halfway house between that and *laissez-faire* capitalism.

In its earliest phase it lacked not only a clear political philosophy or ideology, but also any clear-cut, useful tools of economic theory. To the latter initial deficiency or lack a contribution was made by the anti-theoretical tendency which had grown strong in much of American intellectual life, including the insurgent, "institutionalist" branch of American economic thought, in the period culminating in the 1920s. The neo-classical type of economic theory, as represented in this country by such economists as J. B. Clark and T. N. Carver, quickly became unpopular with most new-style "liberal" intellectuals inside and outside the circles of professional economists, because it struck them as too nearly an apologetics for the existing business world's "free-enterprise system," and as unduly abstract, formal, unrealistic, and barren of suggestions of any practical measures of public policy for correcting the main evils in or malfunctionings of the economy. Empirical and impressionistic social-economic studies and writings, making little or no use of economic theory in the strict sense of that term generally familiar among economists, and vaguely more or less socialistic or "liberal" in the new unclassical sense in ideological tone or cast, had much more vogue for a time, beyond the body of professional economists and within the part of it composed of young economists in revolt against the discipline's old main tradition. And some of these unorthodox "economists" were among President Franklin Roosevelt's advisors in the early New Deal days, and reinforced his own ignorance of and aversion to real, precise and rigorous, formal, logical, economic analysis. But all that was soon to change considerably as the development among the professional economists of the new, modern revisions of neo-classical theory, to be taken up in the next chapter, became available for use by or in American "liberal" thought in the modern sense, as parts of its equipment. Let us now turn back from the entire survey of political developments, in this now completed pair of chapters, to the history or development of economic "science" through the last three decades.

CHAPTER 16

Recent Developments of New Economic Theories Relevant to Problems of Public Policy: A New Analysis of Competition and Monopoly

TYPES OF RECENT WORK IN ECONOMICS—ONLY SOME CONTINUE THE POLITICAL ECONOMY TRADITION

By no means all the important new developments of the studies, ideas, and knowledge of economists can be said to have any clear connections with ideological and/or political developments. And even in the cases—to be considered hereafter—of those new, modern structures of economic theory which do or may have such connections in a sense, the latter are not as simple, direct, definite, close, and/or rigid as "laymen," who hear reports or receive impressions about them, tend to suppose them to be. Let us here first briefly look at the over-all pattern of what has been going on in the recent progress of the study of economics, *without* having in mind, while we do this, any reference at all to the ideological and political developments in the modern world at large, which we have been considering.

An important feature of the over-all development, through this recent period, of the studies carried on by economists, has been a marked growth of the number and variety of the different, specialized, and separated kinds of work being carried on by different groups of economists. The production, by single economists, of comprehensive treatises on "the principles of economics" has virtually ceased, and perhaps it has become or is becoming impossible. Even in the field or on the level of elementary or introductory textbooks—though the number and variety of these has grown immensely—inclusion in single texts of anything like really, both comprehensive and well-balanced surveys of the entire field has become increasingly difficult and rare. And in its work at advanced levels, the profession as a whole has been dividing into a large and growing number of groups of workers specializing in diverse kinds of investigative work, in different fields, or concerned with different arrays of problems; and increasingly few members of any one group know much about, or are even fully able or equipped to understand, all the newest developments and fruits of the kinds of work being done by all, or many, of the other groups.

Prominent among the diverse lines and types of work and progress going on are various new developments of mathematical-theoretical work, and statistical, empirical research, and unions or combinations of those two things, as in work in "econometrics." Much of the new mathematical-theoretical work has been going into the building of structures of—in various exact senses—"dynamic" theory, in contrast with the mainly "static" character of most neo-classical theory. That is to say, roughly, the builders of these modern "dynamic" theories have been trying to go beyond merely formulating the general conditions of an "equilibrium" of "economic forces" or the "equilibrium" relations among economic variables, and to work toward full detailed understanding of processes of change of the related variables and their relations, through transitions between different "equilibria." And among other, different, more "applied" types of work, studies concerned with the problems of "economic development," especially in hitherto and currently still underdeveloped countries and regions, have lately been gaining a new, special prominence. But it would be pointless to attempt here any complete listing of all the different kinds of studies that are and have been going on; though this very partial list, already offered, may perhaps tend to give unwary readers a not only inadequate but misleading, unbalanced impression of the many faceted, complete, "real picture."

Then also, another and different, vague or elusive but important, general line of division or differentiation of economists, "cutting across" all or most of the many special divisions or groupings of the kind just indicated, has been developing. On the one hand there have been declines of varying degrees, in the cases of (in all) a good many economists absorbed in research work in their various fields and/or of their various kinds—declines of their interests in "political economy," i.e., the old *combination or blend* (really) of economic-scientific investigations *with* broader and different, over-all social, moral, and political reflections, in the effort to work out one's informed and reasoned but necessarily in part subjective, personal views *as to not only how but how "well"* the economy or economic system of one's country or the world is functioning, for the economic and general welfare of all the affected people; and what if any *reforms* of the main, relevant, currently existing institutions, practices, and public policies are needed *to improve* the system's functioning and effects on the welfare of all concerned, either generally or in some held-to-be vital respects. Economists generally have long been becoming increasingly aware of the fact that to be concerned with "political economy" in that sense is to carry on what is really a "mixed" kind, or mixture of two unlike kinds, of intellectual work or activity: economic-scientific analysis and research, and social-moral philosophic thinking or reflection. And of late a considerable and perhaps growing number have been tending to develop negative attitudes toward (against) participation in the latter, and to devote themselves more narrowly or single-mindedly to just their various special kinds of investigative work in all or parts of "economic science" only. With some it has even become a matter of high principle to renounce and avoid all interests in political philosophies or in any ideas or problems in that area, and try not to allow any views of their own, of that kind, to find any expression or place in, or exert any effects upon, their work and utterances in economics. In other words, those who take this position try to make themselves entirely detached and objective, nonpolitical, morally and politically neutral, purely scientific economists, seeking solely to contribute to knowledge and understanding of current, actual, economic conditions, events, and processes, and never to advocate, or criticize, or judge or evaluate anything, or design their inquiries to aid or influence—unless in purely technical respects—any decisions upon or about any public policies.

My own critical commentary on that point of view has already been presented in my introduction or preface to this book and will not be repeated here. Here I want to say only two more things about all *those* recent contributions, of different kinds, to economic science which have been produced by and bear the stamp of economists with strongly dominant scientific interests and little or none of the added or further and different, social-philosophic interest shared by all "political" economists. In the first place, *these* new developments within modern economics have grown up in no clear, definite, or specifiable relations, connections, or interactions with any of the widespread ideological and political "trends" of "our time" in the world at large which have been and are involved in the reshapings of the institutions and policies of nations. And in the second place, notwithstanding their (in many cases) great values (which I do not at all disparage) as contributions to economic science, none of *these* new modern studies and intellectual productions are to be considered in this book which is solely concerned, throughout, with patterns of ideas produced by political philosophers and/or political economists and affecting (as well as, generally also, in part reflecting) widespread changes in public opinion and in actual public policies.

Besides, however, all those modern economists whose interests, studies, and achievements I must set aside as not within the field of attention of this book, because not in the field or tradition of "political economy," there have continued to be at least as many or more of the other type still working on lines entirely in or continuing that tradition. And within this category the main, recent, new developments of economic theory still to be considered in this book have been: On the one hand the new modern theory of "monopolistic competition,"[1] and on the other hand, the "Keynesian" body or kind of theory and ideas or proposals of public policies. These have developed as revisions of different parts or aspects of neo-classical theory and especially of the Marshallian system. The modern theory of monopolistic competition is a revision of the old main-traditional body of theory about the structure and working of the business economy's system of markets for different products and productive services, and the situations of and decisions by firms which determine their outputs and selling prices, and demands and payments for labor, capital, etc. And its general result is to undermine or lessen, to some extent, the old economic-liberal "optimism" about the social beneficence of the "natural" functioning of the (real) competitive business economy under *laissez faire,* by showing that the prevailing kinds and degrees of real competition among the private organizations or units acting within the economy do not in fact fully align or harmonize their private interests with the general, common, or public interest, or cause the latter to be as fully, efficiently and well served by the "automatic" working of the economic system as the liberal political economists of the nineteenth century in general tended to believe that it would be. Hence there is at least a vague general tendency, inherent in this new theory, to suggest that there may be needs for some new departures from *laissez faire,* i.e., reforms and public control policies of some kind or kinds to cause the economy and all the unit-actors in it to serve the public better than it is being served in consequence, merely, of the existing forms of competition. But as we shall see later on it is very difficult if not impossible to see what reforms and control policies would be likely to accomplish the desired results; and this modern theory has not led to any real program or new philosophy of what public economic policies should be.

A very different and much greater impact has been made in that sense, within its own field, by the new, modern, developing "Keynesian" body or kind of theory and directly appended policy proposals. This, as com-

[1] My omission of any treatment of the "companion" theory, by a different author, of "imperfect competition," is explained below, on p. 450.

pared or contrasted with the other new theory that I have just mentioned, is a revision of the other part or side of the classical and neo-classical tradition or type of theory—the part concerned with the inter-relations, as variables, of some of the economy's over-all aggregates, i.e., the total national output, and stock of money and flow of money through the system, the population's total money-income and con-sumption spending, saving, and investment spending, the total "effec-tive demand" for the national output, and the general levels of all prices, wage rates, interest rates and business profits, and the volumes of employment and unemployment of labor and productive resources. In other words, here the focus of attention is not upon the questions of how and how well the economy functions in the matters of "allocating" its manpower and resources among different particular industries or employments, adjusting the supplies or outputs of different products to the public's demands for them, or adjusting "the structure of produc-tion" in that sense, and the structure of the *relative* prices of different goods and services, or attaining and maintaining socially desirable "equilibria" among *these* variables. Instead the focus of attention—both in this part of the old main-traditional body of theory and in the Keynesian revision of it alone—is solely upon the questions of how and how well the economy functions with regard to attaining and maintain-ing, in the sphere of its over-all aggregates, an appropriate volume of flow of money through the system, or "effective demand" for all prod-ucts together, and a consequent over-all stability or steady growth ensur-ing both a stable general price level or buying power of the money-unit, and continuous, approximate "full employment" of all labor and pro-ductive resources or equipment. The general effect of the Keynesian revision of the older body of theory about the economy's "natural ten-dencies" in these respects has been to destroy the former "optimistic" faith in the ability of the system's "automatic" processes to correct its own thus temporary "maladjustments" in this sphere; or in other words, to bring into full view and emphasize the system's liabilities, under *laissez faire,* to *not* self-curing depressions and inflations. Keynesian theory has thus delivered a severe blow to the old *laissez-faire* economic liberalism and has been coupled by its originator and adherents, from the outset, with a fairly definite program or set of proposals of new "interventionist" governmental policies, to maintain in the economy's markets at all times an appropriate level or volume of total demand by varying, at need, the government's tax rates and revenues, borrowings, and expenditures, so as to offset or correct all otherwise occurring or impending harmful fluctuations of the totals of private consumption and investment spending and demand.

Now in some degrees the developments of these modern structures of economic theory, or revisions of parts of the old main-traditional body of liberal-and-scientific economic theory, have been both affected by and contributory to the modern widespread ideological and political trends in this country and throughout the Western capitalistic and democratic world, away from adherence to the principles or precepts of the old classical economic liberalism, and to or into replacement of those by either modern (new style, interventionist) "liberal" or modified "socialistic" governmental policies. But careful discrimination is needed in describing the really quite loose, vague, tenuous, and variable interconnections or interactions between the developments in the two different spheres of public opinion and actual public (national governmental) policy on the one hand, and the economic theory-and-policy thinking of the professional economists concerned on the other hand. The main causal factors behind the growths of new attitudes in broad parts of the electorate and widespread demands for new public policies, and growths of new actual policies, designed by politicians to gain and hold the support of their constituents—the main factors at work in all this are the changing circumstances, experiences, and discontents of the members of large interest pressure groups, the ingenuities of their leaders and political spokesmen in devising expedients for controlling economic developments to their advantage, the amounts of political influence the groups are able to exert, and the compromises worked out among them. And the results of all this are too often medleys of conflicting policies having little rationality or relation to what would be best for the general or common welfare of all the people, and making little sense to the minds of good, able, accomplished, humane-and-wise political economists. Hence the latter are seldom full or typical adherents or supporters of the creeds or programs of any broad political parties or movements in their countries, and seldom do or can exert great amounts of influence on the evolutions of the actual policies of modern governments.

Moreover economists, like other citizens, differ widely among themselves in their political views or outlooks, throughout the range from "conservative" to "radical"; for even those who are most fully, in the old sense, political economists are primarily economists, who largely agree within economics, but on the noneconomic questions also involved in all political issues have types or patterns of views attributable mainly to their diverse personal temperaments and backgrounds, ranges of experience and of sympathies, etc. The culture of the Western world of today does not have in it any one uniform, widely dominant, complete, clear, definite, and self-consistent or coherent political philosophy or ideology able to serve its economists and/or other citizens as the general background of their thinking. The decline of the classical liberalism—the common outlook of past generations of the spiritual heirs of the eighteenth-century Enlightenment—has left us with, so far, nothing else of that kind to take its place. The developments of the modern economic theories now to be considered here—the theory of "monopolistic competition" in the business economy and the Keynesian theory of the latter's lack of an automatic mechanism able to ensure continuous "full employment"—these developments have reflected and made contributions to the decline of faith in the classical economic liberalism. In different ways and degrees these theories have fitted in with, and helped to supply with more rational ideas of means to their ends, the modern political trends growing out of the general public's groping search for new governmental policies able to improve the economy's functioning in the service of the general welfare of the people; but the connections with political trends have not been strict or close. Let us now turn our attention to those economic theories themselves and endeavor to grasp their essentials, and return only at some later points to problems in the sphere of public policy and politics.

THE MARSHALLIAN BACKGROUND, AND MODERN THEORY OF COMPETITION AND MONOPOLIES AND THE SUPPLIES AND PRICES OF ALL GOODS AND SERVICES

The present chapter is perhaps unduly restricted in its scope; it deals with only one of the two similar-and-different, mutually complementary theories and books which it might well be expected to deal with: Joan Robinson's *Economics of Imperfect Competition*,[2] and E. H. Chamberlin's *The Theory of Monopolistic Competition*.[3] My omission here of any account and discussion of the former means not that I regard it as "inferior" to the latter, or less worthy of attention; but only that (1) inclusion here of appropriate discussions of both works would make this chapter and book too long, and (2) my many years of personal friendship with E. H. Chamberlin, and my close familiarity with his work and thinking, have equipped me more fully, I think, for dealing with his contribution, than I am equipped to deal with the only partly similar one that was made at the same time, but independently (as his, too, was wholly independent of hers), by Mrs. Robinson. Both of these works grew out of the background of Marshallian economics, and the struggles of these two (and other) younger or later economists initially "brought up on" that, with the logical difficulties or dilemmas that were left unresolved within it. The source of those dilemmas lay in Marshall's not entirely successful effort to combine theoretical rigor with adequate "realism" and his own great knowledge of the various

[2] Joan Robinson, *Economics of Imperfect Competition* (London: Macmillan & Co., Ltd., 1948).

[3] E. H. Chamberlin, *The Theory of Monopolistic Competition* (Cambridge, Mass.: Harvard University Press, 1933–1948).

and complex conditions existing in the real economic world. Marshall, like the other great economic theorists of his own and earlier times, used or worked with theoretical constructs which in their clear and simple forms involved or required assumptions that Marshall (even more fully than most of those other theorists) knew to be by no means wholly in accord with facts. And Marshall, in the effort to be as realistic as possible, presented his theories with many appended qualifications, which in all made them at some points internally and mutually inconsistent. Hence his successors were obliged, in order to straighten out those muddles, to construct new systems and come to terms more thoroughly with some relevant aspects of the real economic world, by revising basic Marshallian and traditional assumptions and evolving their new theories from the new (revised) foundations.

In the old main tradition of all economic theory, the usual practice was to conceive the economy as indeed containing a few exceptional firms or enterprises having simple or outright "monopoly" positions—properly subject to public control in the public interest—but as made up otherwise and mainly of quite thoroughly "competitive" industries and markets. And the character and effects of the "competition" thus thought of as prevalent all through most of the economy were conceived in a way which involved imperfectly realistic assumptions *of two kinds*. There were in the first place the assumptions that, in all "competitive" industries and markets, there were generally prevalent among or available to the persons concerned both adequate knowledge of and about all opportunities available to them anywhere in the economy, and full or unrestricted "mobility," i.e., ability and readiness at all times to sever any or all previous, no longer most advantageous connections, and take advantage of the best new opportunities for them arising anywhere in the economy. Thus on these assumptions, if in the market for any product any seller should offer the product at a price below the prices charged or asked by his competitors, all the customers would promptly try to shift their patronage to this lowest-price seller, and the competing sellers to hold any business would all be obliged to reduce their prices to the same low level immediately. Competition of this type—involving perfect knowledge and "mobility" by all the customers—would result in a uniform lowest-remunerative market price throughout any market for any product at each moment of time. And again, further, if the buying public should change its habits and begin to buy much more than before of any product and less of some other products or product, there would soon enter or arise in the expanding industry an appropriate number of new additional firms (producers and sellers of the now more largely demanded product). Enough entrepreneurs and workers of all needed types, and capital, land, etc., would leave the contracting and less remunerative industries or employments and transfer into the expanding, more rewarding industry, to restore the balance of the relative volumes of production of all products with those of demand for them, at prices (for the different products) in the end equally remunerative to all suppliers of each type of productive service, in all industries and to all firms. In sum, *these* old standard assumptions, of universal prevalence of full knowledge of all opportunities and full "mobility," made up the essence of *one side of* the old ideal conception of all "competition" or the "competitive" economy. The latter was (in theory) conceived as so fluid throughout that every special advantage briefly appearing anywhere in it for the few people already on the spot would quickly attract or draw to that spot, and be destroyed or "leveled down" by, *new, entering competition from the outside*—from people and resources drawn away from other places and/or activities in the system, now made less advantageous for them or their owners.

In addition, however, "the classical competitive model" of the economy, as it has been called, also involved the further assumption—though this was never made so fully explicit—of complete absence, for any single firm or individual or group-acting-as-a-unit, within any ("competitive") industry or part of the economy, of any "monopoly power" or "market power," i.e., power to control or significantly influence the supply and price of anything to the public or the customers concerned. The individual firms and other unit-actors within the system were severally thought of as able only to respond, and adjust their decisions, to market conditions beyond their control—not to affect significantly those market conditions themselves through their own actions. Every price would always be, although a resultant of the actions of a multitude of actors, yet for each one of them singly, a given datum, beyond his control, for him to react to. Every firm would be obliged, by the competitive pressures it would have to meet, to work simply to maximize its output and efficiency and minimize its costs per unit of output, and to sell at the market price and pay at the market rates for all things and services bought or hired. In other words, any firm would be able to maximize its profits only by maximizing (in order to match or excel its competitors) the quantity, excellence, and cheapness of its service to anyone having dealings with it.

Now at the same time, however, the old generations of economists in fact "knew better" than to mistake their theoretic vision, based on these assumptions, of the functioning of an ideally competitive economy, for a literally exact, accurate, and full description of all that went on in the real economic world. They only regarded their "competitive model" as, for their purpose of analyzing the real system's main "tendencies," a good-enough approximation to reality. Thus the valid way of describing the deficiencies or limitations of their work or accomplishment is to say, not that they were blind to or unaware of the difference between their "model" and reality, but that they did not analyze it—or analyze those features of the real system that were not reflected in their "model"—in sufficient detail. They knew that the real economy's markets were "imperfect markets," made such by the "imperfections" of the knowledge and "mobility" of all those acting or participating in them; but they did not analyze the detailed characters, degrees, and consequences of those "imperfections." Nor did they analyze and come to understand in clear full detail the further required conditions besides prevalence of full or adequate knowledge and mobility for a total absence of "market power" for single firms and other unit-actors in the system; and the differences, and effects of the differences, of actual conditions from those further required ones, or all the causes, kinds, degrees, and consequences of such "market power" in fact prevalent in the real economy. Thus the modern "Robinsonian" and "Chamberlinian" theories can best be understood as endeavoring to fill, respectively, those two "gaps" left unfilled by the old classical and neo-classical theories. At least the main emphasis in Mrs. Robinson's new analysis of the interrelations, forms, and roles of the monopolies and the competition together prevalent in the real economy and jointly affecting its processes of determination of the supplies and prices of goods and services, was an emphasis on the "imperfections" of peoples' knowledge of their opportunities, and of their mobility and that of their resources—their abilities to leave old, declining fields and enter new, rising fields of opportunity—and the consequent "imperfections" of real-world competition, or abilities of (complete or partial) monopolies to exist and endure as such. Her analysis did *not* bring out, in a degree or manner comparable to that achieved in Chamberlin's analysis, the further and different points involving not those "imperfections" of knowledge, mobility, markets, and so on, but the forms, degrees, and effects of "monopoly power" or "market power" that would still be ubiquitous, as they are in the real world, even if the old traditional assumptions about knowledge, mobility, and so on were universally valid. In other words, the Chamberlinian analysis, now to be explained and discussed here, had as its starting point the more radically new conception of "monopolistic" elements *inherent in* most actual business competition, *even under* the main conditions traditionally assumed in economic theory.

THE "CHAMBERLINIAN" THEORY OF "MONOPOLISTIC COMPETITION"

This starts, in other words, with the new idea, or recognition of the fact, that "competition" and "monopoly" are really not simple, absolute (either "all" or "none"), and mutually exclusive phenomena, but variable aspects of market situations, each capable of existing in a great variety of forms and degrees; and aspects which can be and in fact usually are *both present together,* in various relative degrees or proportions, *in the same situations.* Classical and neo-classical theory had thought of the (any, generally or roughly speaking, "competitive") economy as containing only a few monopolies, standing alone in their respective special fields and having *no* competitors; and as, apart from them, made up of many, simply "competitive" industries, in each of which no one of the included firms had any degree at all of the kind of power in or over its market that is signified by the word "monopoly." But Chamberlin's new analysis revealed that (1) *all* monopolies are more or less limited by at least some real competition which they have to meet (from other firms producing different, but in some uses substitutable, products), and (2) throughout the entire economy *most* single firms, even if reasonably classifiable as members of highly competitive "industries," at the same time have or may have substantial though limited amounts of real "monopoly power" to control (increase) the prices they obtain for their products by controlling (restricting) the amounts of the latter which they produce or make available.

Nor does the existence of "monopoly power" in that sense, in the hands of firms which must and do compete with others, depend at all, in Chamberlin's analysis, upon the existence of any of the market imperfections, or "frictions," or impediments preventing or restricting entry of new competitors and competition into the fields of activity concerned. In fact, to bring out this point—i.e., to "isolate" in thought or for attention, and distinguish from all results of those "frictions," the phenomena of "market power" which concerned him—Chamberlin retained or used throughout his analysis the old, classical, unrealistic assumption of "free entry" (of new firms into existing "industries" or fields of activity), and showed that even if that condition prevailed, then even in the "long-run" situations of complete adjustment of the numbers of competitors to the volumes of demand in their common general markets, the individual firms would still possess and use or exercise "monopoly power," and the main (not in all ways socially ideal) results of that would persist. "Free entry" of more competition and the resulting adjustments of supplies and prices would indeed eliminate the "monopoly profits" or "extra" profits initially sought by the firms, or reduce their profits to the "normal competitive" level, *but* the "long-run" results would include inefficiency and high costs and prices and (in quantity at least) limited total production or satisfaction of consumers' wants, as compared with the results in these respects to which "pure" competition (competition unmixed with any monopoly powers in the hands of the competing firms) would lead, if this could and did exist in (otherwise) the same situations. But I have been running ahead of the story that is still to be told or more fully explained; let us return to the starting point, which is Chamberlin's initial, clear spelling out of the required conditions for existence of "pure" competition, that is to say, total nonexistence of power-in-their-markets in the hands of the competing firms.

A firm would be unable to exert any significant (nonnegligible) influence upon the general supply-and-demand situation in its selling market, and thus upon the price it could obtain for its product, only if (1) this firm was merely one of *a very large number* of similar firms together making up the whole "industry" concerned, and (2) *all* these firms were producing and/or offering to the buyers *exactly the same, uniform product,* in all respects, so that (in the absence of price differences) all the buyers would be indifferent as to which firm they would patronize. Hence the individual firm (any one of the many in such an industry) could by itself contribute only an insignificant or negligible fraction of the total supply of the same good on the market, and thus could not, by varying the quantity of this good supplied or offered by itself, noticeably affect that total supply and the market price. The previous generations of economic theorists had generally reasoned "as though" *all* "competition" was or worked as would *this special and rare kind* of competition first defined by Chamberlin as "pure" or unmixed with "monopoly" in the sense of (more than negligible) "market power" in the hands of the competing sellers individually; but they had not realized what the conditions must be—a very large number of competing sellers, negligible size of each one relative to the total market, and perfect uniformity, in the eyes of all buyers, of the products or offerings of all of them alike—to make the resulting competition completely effective in controlling the actions of the individual firms, producers, or sellers. "Competition" in a loose, general sense, or considered in all its various forms and degrees, does generally prevail throughout any modern business economy; but as soon as the required conditions for existence of "pure" competition are rigorously stated, it becomes clear that *this* exists in only a few cases or examples. Some branches of agriculture, e.g., wheat growing, may be examples, or would be in the absence of cooperative marketing and/or joint control of (total) supply and price with governmental assistance. Given millions of wheat farms, all producing one single uniform kind and grade or quality of wheat for the world market, even the largest single farm's or farmer's largest crop would be "a drop in the ocean" of the total supply, and no single farmer could affect the market price of wheat. But in almost every branch of industry or commerce, nearly every firm is able to exert a more than negligible influence on its market, i.e., exercise at least a small degree of "monopoly power," even though it is likely, at the same time, to be involved in keen competition with more or less numerous rivals or competitors.

Now from the fact that two different conditions must both be fulfilled if "pure competition" is to exist—the number of competitors must be so large that each one can contribute only a minute fraction of the total supply of the product, *and* that total supply must be perfectly uniform or homogeneous—it follows that "impure" competition can be of two different kinds—though in fact these are generally combined in the same situations. Hence the analysis, from this point on, divides into two branches—(1) the theory or analysis of "oligopoly" (a term invented by Chamberlin), or the competition of a few rival sellers of the same good, *each* offering a *substantial* fraction of the total supply; and (2) the theory or analysis of the competition among all the producers or sellers (no matter how numerous) of at least slightly "differentiated" or different but easily substitutable, hence rival, products, or "varieties" of "one" general kind of product. In any situation of that second kind, each one of the competing sellers is *the only* seller of exactly *his* product or complete special offering, and persuades some of the customers that what he alone can offer them is superior, for their tastes or purposes, to anything else on the market. Thus he acquires a somewhat special market or clientele of his own, which he as a monopolist—the one and only seller of just what this group of customers most want or prefer—can exploit to some extent, in the manner of any monopolist. In other words, any survey, on these lines, of the whole economy would find in it both many a case or example of "oligopoly" —existence in all of only a few suppliers of *the* product in question in each case, with each one contributing a substantial part of the total supply (and in fact often, in addition, somewhat "differentiating" his part of that)—and also many a case in which, regardless of the number of competing suppliers (of similar but not identical products), each one of them is, quite strictly speaking, a monopolist, although each must compete with all the others.

Now in the field of his theory of "oligopoly" as such, Chamberlin, though he was the first to develop this fully and to grasp the entire set of phenomena involved and bring out their prevalence and importance, and give them this name, had a few much earlier, eminent forerunners in a sense—nineteenth-century mathematical economists, chiefly Cournot and Edgeworth—who had produced theories of "duopoly," or the to-be-expected results in any case of competition between only two rival suppliers of a product. Those earlier theorists, treating that problem differently, with different assumptions, had reached different solutions of it; and Chamberlin, after studying their works on the matter and arriving with their help at his own resolution of their differences and his own solution of that problem, went on to adapt and generalize it into his broader theory of "oligopoly"—every case of sufficient "fewness" of the rival suppliers of any one good, and "largeness" of each one relative to the size of the entire group and its common market, to make the decisions of each one as to its output and selling price of serious moment to all the others. "Oligopoly" is quite common or prevalent in every modern "capitalistic" or business economy. Examples include all the "industries" dominated in each case by a few very large firms—steel, automobiles, and many others—and also many types of local "small" business enterprises serving limited local markets—grocery stores, garages, restaurants, etc., in a town or neighborhood; in short all kinds of cases in which, individually, the *relative* size of each one of the rivals, as compared with that of the market in which they all compete, is sufficient to make each one's decisions on its output and selling price matters of serious concern or moment to the others.

In any such case, no one firm may be or have a "monopoly" in any usual sense, or control more than a minor part of the total supply; yet each single firm in the group may have a quite serious degree or amount of "monopoly power" or "market power"—the power to influence, by its own actions, the entire supply on the market and the market price, which is the economic "essence" of monopoly. There is likely to be among the members of such a group of firms, much of the time, some measure of real competition for greater shares of the available total volume of business in their field and market; and at times their competition may become ferocious and destructive. But this kind of competition is very different, in its character, methods, potential danger to all concerned, and usual limitations, from the "pure" competition that would prevail if the rivals were immensely numerous and individually so very small and impotent in their vast common market that each one could ignore and be ignored by all the others, and simply react on the lines of best advantage for itself to the market conditions and developments which neither it nor any of its rivals could significantly influence. Where the rivals are few and each one has important power as a factor in the common market, any competitive price cut, for example, by any one member of the group, will force the others to retaliate (cut the price still lower) in self-defense. Every such move and the resulting countermoves will seriously affect the fortunes of them all; and the general predictability and normal foresight of all this will commonly restrain, or induce great caution about, aggressive competition of this kind, in the first place.

The situation is less like "pure competition," or business competition as traditionally envisaged in economic theory, than it is like the mutually dangerous and normally circumspect or cautious rivalry among the world's "great powers" or large, strong, national states; and in some degree of analogy with the latter, there may be, in "oligopolistic" business competition, occasional, for-all-destructive "price wars," but a more common avoidance of them through mutual fears and self-restraint by all parties, tacit agreement to live and let live, or uneasy stalemate. Here are of course the main fertile fields for the formation of cartels, trusts, and "agreements to restrain trade" or competition, if these are not forbidden and prevented by law or state intervention. But even if formal organizations or agreements do not develop, purely tacit agreements, or even purely independent, similar, single-firm decisions by each or all, dictated by foresight and fear on all sides, may produce results, for the public, or as to the total supply and the price or prices of the good or goods in question, more or less similar to the results that a cartel or merger, combining all the units into one with an outright full monopoly, would lead to. The possibilities are various and intricate, and there is in one sense no single general theory of the working and results of "oligopoly" applicable alike to all specific cases; rather every special case requires its own special modification of the theory. But the over-all conclusion is that "fewness" of the rivals, and their importance to each other, generally work to restrain or moderate competition, more or less, and produce results departing more or less far *from* those that "pure" competition would produce, *toward* those to be expected from simple, complete, or outright monopoly.

Now let us turn our attention to the other branch of Chamberlinian theory—the theory of "monopolistic competition" in the second, narrower, strict, or special sense, or the competition of or among competing monopolists, where each one is the sole supplier of his somewhat unique product, or special variety, variant, or "brand" of the general kind of product, of which the others offer other variants. Here again, this general category of groups of competitors—competing monopolists—is exceedingly common or prevalent "in the real world," especially if we include all groups in which the members' offerings to the public differ in any ways and degrees sufficient to divide the customers into groups each even slightly preferring the offering of one to that of any others. In business competition, a common procedure is to bring out a novel and unique product or a product with some novel and unique features, vigorously advertise its real or alleged superiority over all alternatives or substitutes, and persuade as many potential customers as possible to feel or develop a strong preference for it and become and remain patrons of its seller exclusively even if he demands a high price, and even if other similar goods can be bought at lower prices. This is both a very important, common way of competing for business, and a way of escaping in a measure from competitive pressures or of acquiring a real though limited and precarious kind of monopoly position, which can be exploited as such to a limited extent. Price competition—competing only by underselling your rivals, or offering exactly the same standard thing which they all also offer but at an especially low price—is by no means the only or the main form of modern business competition. Product competition, or quality competition—making not the price but the product more attractive than any rival's—is generally the preferred or more emphasized way of competing, wherever it can be practiced successfully. And its success lies in so manipulating the desires of the buying public or a part of it, as to create for the special product offered by the innovating-and-advertising seller a both large and somewhat "inelastic" or less than fully "elastic" demand (a demand not too highly sensitive to price comparisons); so that after establishing this strong demand and preference for his special product, the seller can raise his price somewhat above the level of the current prices of "inferior" substitutes without fear of losing too much of his volume of sales.

This broad category of phenomena includes both many examples of real and important, publicly beneficial, competitive product improvements—entirely new, highly useful products, and significant improvements of old products—*and* countless examples of trivial and many of more or less fraudulent, deceptive, or misleading, alleged "improvements"; mere, slight changes, for better or worse (according to one's tastes), or of no real consequence at all, of styles, forms, colors, ways of packaging and displaying the most ordinary products, or little "services" or "conveniences" offered along with them—anything at all to create preferences in multitudes of perhaps foolish or gullible consumers, for the "special" offerings of the particular sellers concerned. And it is not as simple a matter as it seems to many who in this connection make quick, casual snap judgments favorable or unfavorable to the monopolistic-competitive "free-enterprise system," to appraise in a well-balanced, fair, or just way the entire range of its contributions to enhancement of the satisfaction or economic welfare of the people as consumers, and its creations or manipulations and exploitations of their wants and whims. To a great extent, despite the power of advertising, the ultimate responsibility for the system's results remains in the hands of the people as consumers. In so far as they are or become informed and intelligent, "rational," discriminating, and able to choose the products that will yield, for them, the richest satisfactions in proportion to their costs—the competition among business enterprises for their patronage will lead to genuine economic progress or rising living standards, as it should. And if most consumers are foolish or gullible and remain so, they will be abused, and the fault will lie less with "the system" than with them.

Apart, however, from that very difficult matter of appraising the qualities or "real values" of the system's products—or the tastes of the consumers as affected by advertising—there is the different, more readily and firmly answerable question of the effects of monopolistic competition simply on the efficiency of production in the purely physical, technological, or quantitative sense—the volumes of production of all the actual products, with the amounts of manpower and resources of all kinds employed in producing them, and the effects of these "input-output" relations, or degrees of productivity, on the costs and prices of the products, the earnings of the people, and the quantities in which they can buy the goods which satisfy their actual wants (whether artificially created and unwise or not). And the central and main part of the Chamberlinian theory of the consequences of product differentiation and the resulting, competing monopolies, is the analysis leading to its answer to this question.

In this analysis, moreover, an essential role is played by the assumption of "free entry" of new, additional competitors or firms into each general field of activity, or (nonhomogeneous and not very clearly defined or bounded) "industry," or "group" of producers of diverse but, especially, closely similar or competitive products—"free entry" into every such "group" of additional members whenever and as long as those already in it are obtaining, and newcomers can expect, any "monopoly profits" or (in the economy as a whole) unusually high profits. To isolate the effect of the "monopoly" elements (market power due to product differentiation), Professor Chamberlin assumes that on the competitive side the competition is "perfect," i.e., there is throughout the economy full prevalence of knowledge of all opportunities, mobility, etc., and so in the long run, in each field or sector, a full (in one sense) response and adjustment of supply (the sum of the supplies of all products of this sector) to demand or the relevant set of demands, at "cost" prices (yielding no especially high profits). Although, for this reason, his competing monopolists in each sector cannot, by exploiting their monopoly positions, continue to enjoy monopoly profits, they do bring about instead, through their *efforts* to obtain the highest possible profits, overcrowding of their sector with too many firms, all individually too small to be maximally efficient, and, consequently, prevailing inefficiency or low productivity, high costs and prices, limited earnings for all connected with the firms as employees or suppliers of any of their "inputs," and restriction of the sector's total output, from or with the resources employed in it, of satisfaction of the wants of the consumers.

In essentials, the series of "adjustments" leading to those results is described as follows. Initially, each firm in a sector or "group," having an advertised, unique product and a special market or body of customers who more or less strongly prefer this product to all rival products and will buy it even at relatively high prices, charges the price deemed likely—with allowance made for its effect on the firm's volume of sales

—to be most profitable; i.e., the firm tries to so adjust its interdependent price and volume of business and output as to maximize its profits. Then, so long as the firms in the group, by doing this, are making profits above the level of those generally prevalent in the economy, the number of firms in this group will grow, as newcomers enter it. The latter—producers of still other, newer varieties of the species of products represented in this group—will lure away some of the previous customers of the older firms in the group, or so reduce the demands for *their* products as to oblige them to make new decisions in the range between lowering their prices enough to maintain (or regain) their old volumes of business, and reducing their outputs to the amounts now salable (to their most loyal customers only) at their old prices. They will again try to find and choose the quantity-and-price combinations that will, under the new conditions, maximize their profits; this generally will mean cutting the prices somewhat, but also accepting some reductions of their sales and outputs. Further inflows of new competition, and further adjustments of the same kind, will continue until the prevailing rate of profit in the sector is no higher than it is in the rest of the economy. But on the way to this "equilibrium," the growth of the number of firms in the sector and the shrinkage of each one's sales, output, and size—because of its own monopolistic, profit-maximizing policies of sacrificing volume to high price maintenance—will have reduced its size below that required for most efficient operation and raised its cost of production per unit of output. The elimination of "monopoly profits," by the growth of competition, is accomplished only in part through the limited price reductions, and for the rest through this rise of unit costs as the firms in the sector become more numerous, small, and inefficient. The proliferation of increasingly numerous, differentiated products and competing monopolies, and the splitting up of markets, and restrictions of output to maintain high prices result in an inefficient organization of the economy's supplies of all the factors of production, in an excessive number of diverse enterprises, individually not large enough fully to realize the potential economies of large-scale production.

It is arguable that the degree of inefficiency in physical production thus brought about may be more than compensated, in the final reckoning with regard to the economic welfare of the people as consumers, by the great variety of specific products that is made available, and the resulting ability of each consumer to choose the ones—the exact varieties of all general types of products—which exactly suit his special tastes. Perhaps the higher costs and prices are worth paying for things precisely suited to the wants of their buyers. An economy that practiced thoroughgoing standardization, and produced only a limited number of standard, uniform products, each turned out by a small number of highly efficient, large-scale producers, might be able to make all *those* products very abundant, at very low unit costs and prices, and at the same time yield high incomes to the people. But the latter, if they could choose either system, might prefer the one giving them, though in lesser abundance and at higher costs (relative to their incomes), the wider range of choice and better opportunities to satisfy their different personal desires and tastes. In some conflict with this suggestion, however, is the one that was mentioned earlier: that product differentiation and the concomitant advertising artificially create much of the great variety of fancied, special wants and tastes or preferences, in order to exploit them; and the usual further implication of this thought is that creating new wants in the people and then satisfying them does nothing to make the people better off or to enhance their welfare. But this too is open to dispute and doubt; perhaps to speak of "creating wants" is to exaggerate what advertising does. It may only stimulate the people to discover and develop their previously latent but inherent and real, potential wants; and perhaps by gaining a more full and exact awareness of, and satisfying, all the nuances of all their wants, they do gain a real enrichment of their lives. We are here again back in the field of discussion of peoples' "subjective" experiences and judgments, about which few statements can be made with justified, full confidence. But on the subject of advertising—most of which is closely connected with product differentiation and monopolistic competition—there is a further question, still rather about its relation to efficiency, or the purely "objective" aspect of "economy," as opposed to "waste."

In a system of enterprises each monopolizing the business of supplying a differentiated product competitive with many others, and striving, through advertising, to increase and maintain its share of the public's patronage or the demand for its special product, which its rivals are trying to change into demands for *their* products—expensive advertising and "selling effort" in general inevitably plays a very important role. Although no firm can accurately measure or gauge the effectiveness of its advertising outlays, no firm dares to dispense with or reduce them, since all its rivals are advertising their products lavishly and vigorously, and obliging it to do the same in self-defense. A substantial part of the potentially productive manpower and resources of the entire economy are thus employed not in producing products in response and adjustment to a stable existing set of demands for them, but in efforts and counterefforts to change, divert, or shift those demands in opposite directions. And in so far as these rival efforts counteract or neutralize each other—as they must to some great extent—the over-all result, it seems, must be a great, pure, social-economic waste, or wholly, in every sense, unproductive use of the mass of manpower and resources employed in this struggle.

I venture to think, however, that *this* conclusion of Chamberlinian theory probably is not entirely valid, or must be qualified to some extent, for the following reason. It *would* be entirely correct *if* we could assume the total volume of business (demand) available to all enterprises taken together, to be fixed or constant, or unaffected by their rival advertising and selling efforts. But I think it is likely that advertising as an aspect of all modern, competitive, enterprising, and progressive capitalism has played an important role as a contributing cause of all economic progress in societies having or developing economic systems of this type, by stimulating growth or expansion and multiplication of the economic wants and ambitions of the people and causing them to become increasingly industrious, thrifty, enterprising, and productive, in consequence of their rising and proliferating wants and desires to enlarge their earnings and improve their living standards. In all ancient, unawakened, undeveloped, and unprogressive societies, accustomed and resigned to mass poverty, the demands or desires of the people for all economic goods are (or were) as restricted as their earnings; hence their often abundant economic resources and potential productive powers have remained unused. Stimulation of the growth of wants is one of the activities and achievements needed to bring about economic progress; and in the measure in which advertising fulfills this function, it is indirectly productive, for or in the whole economy, and so does *not* represent *pure* "waste." Moreover, we may in this connection see at least a partial validation of the standard defensive claim of people in the advertising business or profession, that effective advertising does not add its costs to the costs and prices of the goods concerned but, by enlarging volumes of sales and production, lowers per unit production costs (through the economies of large-scale production), so that the additional costs of the advertising as such are thus offset or absorbed. And in seeing that there may be truth in this contention, we may see reason to abate or lessen the charge against monopolistic competition that, where there is "free entry" of new competitors into group fields of enterprise, and the existing firms in each group use their monopoly power (built up and maintained by product differentiation and advertising) to try to maintain high prices and profits, the firms become too numerous and small and therefore inefficient, high-cost producers. In so far as advertising has at the same time also this other effect, of enlarging each firm's volume of business as a part of a not static but growing total volume of business for all firms together, in every group and in the whole economy, there is here a counterprocess at work, in some degree counteracting that process described in monopolistic-competition theory, of shrinkage of firms to inefficient sizes owing to growth of numbers.

In sum, then, it seems to me that *the purely economic* case against advertising, or charge that it is economically unproductive or wasteful, remains unproved; its results in this regard are so mixed or complex that the full net sum of them all cannot be known. The clear evils in the phenomena of advertising are not economic but aesthetic, ethical, and cultural evils; the flood of assaults upon the eyes and ears, attention, minds, and emotions of the people, with lurid, tawdry, and ugly appeals, often to their lowest, least worthy motives, and the flooding of all the mass media of communication and culture, or all mass culture, with deplorable cultural junk. There is nothing to be said in extenuation or palliation of the very severe indictment that is justly directed, on this score, against this set or range of the results of aggressively enterprising and competitive capitalism or business enterprise, except that the latter's role in the matter is only to develop and magnify, in the process of responding or catering to and exploiting for gain, many of the most unadmirable, generally or widely prevalent traits of most "human nature." There is no doubt I think that "the system" in this aspect does foster economic progress—at this cultural cost. Perhaps the cost is too great; but I can conceive of no other promising way of working to reduce it than through efforts to more fully and truly educate or civilize or acculturate the people generally and the businessmen and admen, or to imbue them all with higher cultural standards or truer perceptions and appreciations of all real values. To change "the system" or move far away from *laissez faire* or "free enterprise" into public control—beyond the desirable stage of prohibiting and preventing demonstrably fraudulent, untruthful, or dishonest advertising, making false claims for the advertised products and insinuations against rival products—could not be relied upon to improve the situation. In a democracy this would merely change market competition into political competition to control or influence the public legislation and administrative controlling agencies, and replace the not-allowed forms of commercial advertising with political propaganda having the same objectives; and this would hardly be a real improvement. A system of nonpolitical, i.e., undemocratic, control measures would mean giving to a dictator, or group of dictators, absolute power to control the tastes or values of the people and/or the over-all pattern of all economic activities—the allocation of society's manpower and resources into different employments. A progressive socialist regime or economy would need and be certain to carry on extensive and intensive advertising or propaganda to develop and enlarge the wants and demands of the people in harmony with the growth and balance of production; and the cultural effects of this absolute monopoly might well be worse, and could not be counted on to be any better, than those of monopolistic competition.

Let me now, however, drop the special subject of advertising, and turn to an interesting and important criticism which has been made, by a greater and very different modern economic theorist, the late J. A. Schumpeter, of Chamberlin's entire, basic, theoretical appraisal or assessment of "monopolistic" as opposed to "pure" competition; this criticism involves a defense, from the standpoint of the public interest, of competing monopolies. The Chamberlinian analysis, which has now all been summarized here, is in the field or on the plane of "static" analysis, concerned only with the processes of adjustment, or changes or movements into "equilibrium," of the volumes, costs, and rewards or attractions of activity in different fields, under assumed-to-be given and (over time) unchanging basic general conditions in the economy as a whole. Within that context or frame of reference or upon its "static" assumptions, the analysis demonstrates that the possessions and uses of degrees of monopoly power by individual firms, together with the formations of new, additional, competing monopolies in especially profitable fields, make the finally resulting ("equilibrium") adjustments less beneficial to the economic welfare of the consuming public than would be those to which "pure" competition would lead. As the competing monopolies become unduly numerous, small, and inefficient, the public has to pay high prices to cover the high costs of inefficient production (though not in the end to support "monopoly profits"), and its wants in general are less fully satisfied.

Now Professor Schumpeter's main theoretical work was in the different field of not "static" or "equilibrium" theory, but theory of the "dynamic," historical, and on-going temporal process of progressive "economic development" within or under "capitalism." He conceived this as a process in which (some leading) firms or enterprises do not merely adjust or adapt their plans and activities to existing general conditions, but by changing and improving their products, organizations, and means and methods of production, help to bring about, over time, progressive changes of those very conditions *to* which all adjustments within the system must be made. Thus, while granting the validity of the Chamberlinian thesis within its own "static" frame of reference, the "Schumpeterian" view insists that precisely the phenomena of monopolistic competition above all others need rather to be analyzed in the different context of theory of economic "development" or progress if they are to be adequately and properly understood and appraised. Firms, by introducing new or improved products, *or* more efficient ways of producing any products, at first gain temporary positions of more or less monopoly or special advantage, *until other* rival "innovators" match or surpass their "innovations"; it is thus that progress, under capitalism, comes about, and the fact that now some and later some other firms have limited monopoly powers and make extra profits while they last, is an essential feature of the process. Moreover, Schumpeter argued, from the public standpoint this very feature is not at all regrettable, but is useful or beneficial, because progress depends upon it. Investments in research and development and "pioneering" with new products and ways of producing products entail risks of capital loss, and would not be made to the same extent without the incentive of the prospect of a period of monopoly and extra profit in the event of success. The first takers of each step of progress exact high prices and profits from the public while they can, i.e., until the competition they must meet acquires equal or superior advantages, and grows in volume to the point of forcing their charges down to the level of their costs, or eliminating them; but the public's gains in the long run from all the progress that is thus rewarded, stimulated, and induced are more than worth all that it pays for them. At least a good deal of validity and weight must, I think, be granted to this argument.

But I must conclude this chapter with final comments pertaining to two general questions. How important are the new discoveries, in Chamberlin's theory, of the differences of all such competition as actually prevails in the business economy, from the ideal competition which generally tended or appeared to be assumed in most nineteenth-century economic theory? And how far, if at all, do these new discoveries logically oblige the modern political economist to move away from adherence to the old economic liberalism into advocacy of new public controls, in the place of reliance on market competition, to proect the public interest? My answer to the first of those questions will lead into my answer to the second. I think the over-all difference between the old classical and neo-classical view and our new modern view of the "competitive" economy can be characterized as follows. The old view was like the result of looking at the system from a remote distance, through a telescope; it brought into clear focus, and mainly emphasized, only the main general "tendencies" in the working of the system—the results (mainly beneficial adjustments for the public) which "competition" as such generally "tended" to bring about; though it was realized in a general way that in the real world with its detailed crudities these "tendencies" did not go all the way to exact, complete attainment of their own logical end-results. In contrast, the new modern view of these matters is like the result of looking successively at all the small parts of the system from "close-up" positions, through a microscope; the detailed characters and results of all the "flaws" or "impurities" in real-world competition are made fully evident.

What is thus achieved is a quite substantial advance into a more complete and accurate analysis. But it is too easily possible for this new view to carry with it a degree of loss of perspective, or of a true sense of proportion—an exaggerated sense of the importance of even the most minor "flaws," and partial failure to keep in view and duly emphasize the main, broad, general "tendencies," described in traditional theory and still now, as then, really operative to no small extent in the real economy, even though not so fully as may once have been supposed. I do not mean that *all* the "flaws" are by any means of *negligible* importance, in all connections. "Oligopoly" is in many industries and markets a quite important, serious phenomenon or set of phenomena, giving rise to results often very considerably unlike those that a misapplied theory of "pure" competition in these fields would predict, and in some ways less ideal from the standpoint of the public interest. And the seriousness of the degrees of monopoly power, of competing monopolists, achieved through product differentiation, varies I think from trivial in many cases to fairly great in the limited number of cases at or near the other end of this spectrum, i.e., the cases in or nearly in the old familiar category of simple outright "monopoly"—the one-firm "industry," or sole supplier of "a product" as "products" are commonly, not finely, classified, where there is competition only with other quite different, though in some uses substitutable, products. But on the whole, I do not think the complete, real picture is by any means so black as it is often painted by those who conclude that no modern business economy is really at all like the (tolerably well, in the public interest) self-adjusting or self-regulating, competitive system of the Adam Smithian vision. It is foolish utopianism to expect any real system *not* to be full of more or less serious "flaws," and to condemn it wholly for being so; or to conclude at once that because it has these "flaws," it must and can be replaced by or transformed into some very different and much better system. But this brings me to my final question, of the relevance of all this for the public-policy thinking of economists.

Chamberlin, let me say at once in passing, has never leaned at all toward the utopianism and radicalism that I have just been criticizing; but, retaining as his personal outlook what I also personally regard as a sound perspective or sense of proportion, he has kept his political stance relatively conservative, or liberal in the classical sense. He conceived his new structure of economic theory simply as an advance beyond traditional theory, into a more detailed, complete, and accurate analysis of the realities of business competition, and not as a wholly new vision and analysis pointing to a need for a sweeping, radical program of reform. But let me, without further involving him in this discussion, try to indicate the basis of my own relative "conservatism" in that sense.

It is one thing to find that most real-world competition is "impure," or mixed with elements of monopoly power in the hands of the competing firms, and therefore does not fully or perfectly protect the public interest or common welfare; and it is quite another thing to decide that something, and decide what, should and can be done about it. In the American environment, pervaded by much popular belief in the need for governmental action against all monopolies and for preservation of a competitive economy, the discovery that monopolies exist not only in industries entirely controlled by single firms or by "combinations in restraint of trade," but are ubiquitous throughout the economy although generally combined with much competition has tended to introduce confusion into public and judicial thought concerned with developing and applying "antitrust" policy. Should the legal definition of "monopoly" as a legally forbidden thing be revised and broadened into agreement with the new economic definition, with the result of exposing most business firms to possible prosecution in the courts for having and using monopoly powers? Or should the public policy against monopolies be abandoned as impractical in view of the universality of what it seeks to prevent? Somewhere in the range between these extremes—though just where is still unclear—the sensible answer in the development of "antitrust" law and policy will probably be found. Though at its potential best this body of law and policy is certain to fall a long way short of complete effectiveness, it need not be by any means useless. The worst abuses—generally falling within or near the old familiar categories—can be prevented or at least kept limited, and through appropriate, limited extensions of the scope of the legal prohibition in some directions, a useful, more widely deterrent influence can be exerted against socially undesirable developments of the business policies of many firms. But the exposure, by the new economic theory, of the limitations of "antitrust" has been viewed in some quarters as indicating that public policy should turn rather toward regulation of the investment, output, and price policies of all firms having significant degrees of monopoly or market power. This I think would be extremely unwise, for reasons that I now wish to indicate.

Even with all its "flaws," the market competition that is still generally prevalent is a real system of "checks and balances," *limiting* the powers of all unit-actors in the markets to control or affect conditions there and gain at others' or the public's expense or without making productive contributions to the common wealth more or less nearly proportionate to their gains. It is well to know in full detail just how imperfectly the actual "checks and balances" work, or serve the public interest; but it does not follow from all such knowledge, and I do not believe, that any system of public controls could, in practice, work *as* well in the public interest. For the public agencies that would have to exercise this great extension of governmental authority in or over the economy, and the interest pressure groups that inevitably would influence the required legislation and the policies of those agencies, would represent *greater* concentrations of power, *less* subject to control by any good system of "checks and balances," than can be found in the economy or market system, in the hands of any (the most potent) unit-actors there, with the "checks" imposed on them by competition. The contrary view involves, I think, both excessive pessimism about the ability of the market competition that is actually prevalent to (largely) protect and serve the public interest, and excessive optimism about the ability of political democracy to make legal public controls serve the same purpose better or as well.

Nor is it possible, I think, to have much confidence in another control "mechanism" which has been described and praised as an alternative to both market competition and direct public regulation of supplies and prices. Another modern economist, J. K. Galbraith, holding that modern market competition is nearly nonexistent or of little value, has developed a theory that it is being superseded, with generally good results, by the growth in the American economy of a system of "countervailing power"—a counterbalancing and checking of the power of every powerful organized group by that of an opposing group, *on the other side* of the same market or markets, *not on the same* side as in market competition. Big business begets big labor, and big farm organizations, etc., and they all checkmate each other; the state can and should aid the weaker against the stronger parties, and make all these balances of power really balance. Though indeed these "tendencies" also do exist and Galbraith's analysis of them is of much real interest, I can see no assurance of a good set of results for the public, emerging *simply from them, necessarily*. Group power does not always or reliably engender a neither less nor more than equal opposing power; and the interventions of a democratic state in these power struggles are more likely to throw its support to the groups with the greatest political power, than to those that on an impartial view most need and deserve it. (Surely political power at least often varies directly, rather than inversely, with economic power.) Moreover, the consuming public as a whole is too large and amorphous to be able to unite and develop its own share of "countervailing power"; and the potent groups all tend to find alleviation of their mutual conflicts in or through joint exploitation of the consuming public. Finally, even a truly comprehensive and well-balanced system of this kind, if it could be achieved, would tend to produce not a continuous practice on all sides of the adequate, mutual concessions or accommodations needed to generally maximize the wealth and welfare of the entire community; but rather alternations of situations of tense, uneasy stalemate or deadlock and truce, with recurrent outbreaks of destructive warfare. That is, such must be the result *if* each group simply pursues its own narrowly selfish collective interest, with no other scruples or restraints than those dictated by cold calculations of advantage or expediency. But the mention of that "if" brings me to my own idea of the direction in which we should look for the best, perhaps attainable "solution" of this set of problems, posed by the deficiencies of both real market competition and the real phenomena of "countervailing power."

The assumption that all actors in an economic society always act on the lines of their own "self-interests" or so as to "maximize their gains," has always been and I think must remain a basic assumption of all economic theory. But in many applications it is or becomes a "tricky" assumption, open to a range of differing meanings or interpretations. In a "purely" or ideally competitive economy, with the "checks and balances" all working perfectly, there would not be this ambiguity; the completely effective competitive pressures around and against every actor in the system would impel him at each moment of decision to choose the single, uniquely determined course of action clearly of greatest advantage or least disadvantage to him. But possession of a degree of monopoly power or market power gives freedom to choose, within a certain range, among different business policies as to output, price, etc., none of which is sure to be defeated by such competition as must be met; and to aim at "gain maximizing" in one or another of some different senses and ways. Possession of power also entails responsibilities to all who will be affected by its exercise, and tends to engender a variety of social pressures tending to enforce those responsibilities. And it may thus come to be in the truest, long-run "self-interest" of any powerful organization or group, *not* to maximize its *current* gains in the simple and obvious sense and way by fully exploiting its power position or always driving the roughest possible bargains with all with whom it has dealings; but instead, to develop or cultivate the best possible "public relations" with all and sundry, earn general good will from all, and thus most truly in the long run maximize the gains resulting from appreciated services. Though there is much cant in the common talk of American businessmen about being in business to serve their fellow men (and thus earn profits), and managing their firms as socially responsible "industrial statesmen," and the like, I do not think this is all pure cant. It is a partly true, though overidealized description of widespread, genuine attitudes and actual practices, resulting from the economic-and-sociological facts that I have just mentioned. And I think an evolution into fuller, more consistent practice of this kind of behavior by firms and all organizations or groups having power positions—limited but left significant by either or both the market competition or/and the "countervailing powers" they have to contend with—is an evolution which can be hoped for, and be aided by advancement and diffusion of appropriate "education" or "enlightenment" of all into better understanding of the ultimate harmonies of their true self-interests and those of their organizations or groups with the requirements of the public interest or general welfare of society, and their social or civic responsibilities. Of course, no utopia is attainable on this road either—as none is attainable at all; but I think that private freedoms and the public welfare can be reconciled and advanced together, only if and in so far as progress can be made along this road.

Our attention will now be turned, however, to the problems of economic theory and policy, and the new, modern system of theory or analysis, body of knowledge, and policy program, pertaining to these other problems, which have been developed by the late Lord Keynes and the numerous economists advancing further on the lines of study and reflection which he opened up.

CHAPTER 17

Recent Developments of New Economic Theories Relevant to Problems of Public Policy: Keynesian Economics

INTRODUCTORY REMARKS ABOUT TWO FIELDS OR PARTS OF ECONOMIC THEORY: THEORY OF "VALUE," ETC., AND "AGGREGATIVE" THEORY

The reader may perhaps welcome a restatement at this point of the distinction, which was indicated earlier, between the fields, or parts of the total field, of economic theory in which the new modern advance that was discussed in the last chapter and the one to be discussed in this chapter respectively belong. The theory of "monopolistic competition" improves the part or branch of main-tradition economic theory concerned with "value and (income) distribution"; i.e., with *those* processes of adjustment, in the "automatic" working of the economic system of private enterprises and (more or less) competitive markets, which involve and affect the interrelations and interadjustments among the many diverse, limited, particular parts of the entire system; the particular demands for and supplies and prices of all its diverse particular products—adjustments of particular industries and firms to their markets—and demands for and supplies of and rates of (income) payment for the productive services of all the different "factors of production," in all their different employments, and local or regional parts of the economy.

In contrast, Keynesian theory is a new development—revival, radical revision, and extensive further development—of another part, side, or branch of "classical" or main-tradition theory, which is commonly described as "aggregative" theory or analysis. This deals with the entire system's over-all performance as affected by the interrelations and inter-adjustments of a small number of variable, *total* quantities emerging in the system as a whole: its total output (the aggregate supply of all products taken together); the total demand for them all, or flow of money in the system in all sales or purchases; the general levels of all product prices, wage rates, interest rates, and profit rates; and the population's total money-income, consumption spending, saving, investment spending, and the volumes of employment and unemployment of labor and productive resources.

Now there was already within the early "classical" economics of the first decades of the nineteenth century, a limited, rudimentary development of its own "aggregative" part or aspect, about the over-all working of the system and the interrelations, etc., of some of those total or "aggregate" variables. But in most of the subsequent further development of "orthodox," main-tradition economic theory, through a century and more—from the 1820s to the 1930s—that originally included structure of "aggregative" theory generally received but little attention or development.

The other field, or part of theory, about "value and distribution" or the relations and adjustments among the prices of the system's different particular products and different kinds of productive services, and so on, almost monopolized the attention of most "orthodox" theorists throughout that long interval. That situation came about largely because it was mistakenly believed that the early "classical" theorists had already fully and finally solved the main, central, or key problem in the field of "aggregative" theory, or rather shown it to be no real problem at all. Lord Keynes, however, in his final masterwork, *The General Theory of Employment, Interest, and Money,*[1] dispelled that illusion and brought "aggregative" theory, in the new, formidable shape which he gave it, again into the foreground of attention. But before I take up or say more about that "central problem" and the early, false disposal of it and the new view of it that is centrally involved in the Keynesian system, let me first speak about another aspect of the historic background or antecedents and genesis of the latter.

[1] *The General Theory of Employment, Interest, and Money* (New York: Harcourt, Brace and Company, Inc., 1936). Though the ideas in this work by Keynes had great originality and novelty within the English-speaking world, there had been important, much earlier, partial anticipations in the works of various eminent Continental European economists, especially Wicksell and his Swedish followers. See J. A. Schumpeter, *History of Economic Analysis* (New York: Oxford University Press, 1954), p. 1085.

THE ANTECEDENT BACKGROUND OF KEYNESIAN THEORY IN TRADITIONAL MONETARY THEORY

The brilliant English economist, John Maynard Keynes, who became "Lord Keynes" only in the last years of his life, was at first a leader among the pupils and successors of Alfred Marshall, and a specialist in the field of monetary theory, or the study of monetary and financial systems and affairs. Now that specialty, monetary theory, was traditionally regarded by most economists as a thing wholly outside or apart from the field of all general and fundamental economic theory. For the early classical economists, in their reaction against mercantilist thought with its tendencies to confuse the money-values with the real amounts of wealth produced and acquired in the economy, had tried to erect, and their successors generally had tried to maintain, a watertight partition, so to speak, between the special theory of the causes and effects of variations of the economy's supply of money and the value or buying power of the money-unit or the general level of all money-prices, on the one hand; and on the other, the general, main body or system of economic theory, conceived as properly concerned not with the monetary but only with the "real," nonmonetary, economic variables—amounts of labor-time and material resources employed in producing goods, physical volumes of the goods produced, and "values" of the latter (per unit amount of each) *not* in the sense of absolute money-prices *but* in the sense of the *relative or comparative* prices, only, of the different goods, or in other words their exchange values among themselves or in terms of each other; and the "real" (not money) incomes of the people, in terms of quantities of goods obtained.

I shall very soon return to this matter and more fully explain the considerations and views which led to that insistence on rigidly separating the special theory of the money-system and the general theory of the "real" economic system; and the results it led to in the developments of both. But first let me say in the present connection, that for the monetary theorists in their work as such, it narrowly circumscribed the "authorized" field of their interests and inquiries in a way which prevented adequate study of many matters *relevant to* their allotted task, and which Keynes found intolerable. Hence in the development of his work and thought, though he was at first only and long mainly a monetary theorist, he in time broke through and beyond the traditional barrier between that field and general economic theory, embraced them both together in or as his field of interest, and in a sense reunited them. And incidentally, this led to some degree of rehabilitation, in Keynesian thought, of some old elements of mercantilist thought which the classical tradition too sweepingly rejected.

But let me now first briefly notice a few further biographical facts about Keynes and his career, down to the production of his final great work, *The General Theory*—which inaugurated the "Keynesian Revolution"—before taking up in detail the classical tradition and Keynes' work in monetary theory. In the early years of his adult life he was a distinguished young Cambridge don, who quickly became noted for both his wide-ranging and impressive, scholarly and theoretical attainments, and great, practical business and financial abilities. For a time in charge of the finances of his college, he greatly increased its income by skillful and wise investments of its capital funds; and in the course of his life he built up a modest but substantial private fortune of his own by shrewd investments of his own savings. And soon—though always primarily a devoted scholar and brilliant theoretician—he moved beyond purely academic life into expert, advisory, or consultative work for his country's government, its treasury department, and the other agencies. Before going far into that field of work, however, he produced his first important, brilliant and solid, book in the field of pure research and analysis—his study of *Indian Currency and Finance*,[2] which earned for him his wide fame among or with the world's professional economists. Later, after the First World War, he went to the Versailles Peace Conference as one of the expert advisors of the British delegation; but in the decisions on the reparations clauses of the treaty concluded there with Weimar Germany, his advice was rejected, and he strongly disapproved of those provisions of the treaty. Soon afterward, he leaped into world-wide fame with the general public as well as with economists, when he published his book, *The Economic Consequences of the Peace*,[3] severely criticizing those decisions made at Versailles, and generally predicting the serious, unhappy consequences which in fact ensued. And there was in that book, besides its direct treatment of those specific issues, a very broad and penetrating analytical survey of the past and current and prospective state of the "capitalistic" world-economy and its main general problems, which in a measure anticipated some of the basic elements of his much later *General Theory*.

Through the 1920s and well into the thirties, however, Keynes continued or resumed his more restricted lines of work on English and international problems of monetary theory and policy. One of his published writings in this period was a critical pamphlet on England's (1925) restoration of the prewar "sterling parity," [4] which he held to be a mistake and a serious, contributing cause of the British depression

[2] J. M. Keynes, *Indian Currency and Finance* (London: Macmillan & Co., Ltd., 1913).

[3] J. M. Keynes, *The Economic Consequences of the Peace* (London: Macmillan & Co., Ltd., 1920).

[4] J. M. Keynes, *The Economic Consequences of Sterling Parity* (New York: Harcourt, Brace and Company, Inc., 1925), also published in England as *The Economic Consequences of Mr. Churchill* (London: L. and V. Woolf, 1925).

and severe unemployment all through that decade, which was in the world at large a highly prosperous one. Another was his richly suggestive little tract on *Monetary Reform*,[5] which further revealed the growing divergence of his views from traditional monetary and financial "orthodoxy." His crowning work in this whole field—his monetary specialty—was his large and impressive *A Treatise on Money*,[6] produced at the beginning of the 1930s; which even today a few good economists, too conservative politically and otherwise to relish the later "Keynesian revolution" which stemmed only from the subsequent *General Theory*, prefer to the latter and regard as Keynes' greatest work. But Keynes himself was radically dissatisfied with his *Treatise*, which did have serious defects as well as great merits, and turned away from its lines of analysis to the new and different ones—more boldly ranging beyond monetary into general economic theory—which he worked out and expressed in *The General Theory*. The latter, appearing in 1936, in the middle or depths of the Great Depression, and addressing itself directly to the problems posed to economists and to governments by that dire event, made an immediate impact on both professional and public opinion, such as very few works by economists have ever made. But now I must return to the background of Keynes' earlier work as a monetary theorist, struggling with and gradually diverging from the "orthodox," traditional views of and in that special field.

Behind those older views lay, as I said before, the continuing inheritance from the early classical determination to keep monetary theory and general economic theory strictly separate and apart from each other. Now to a considerable extent there was good sense in the ideas which motivated that determination. One part of the ground for it lay in the fact, of which antimercantilist, early-classical theorists were so keenly aware, that because the value or buying power of money itself is variable, the money-values of things are variable, unreliable, and deceptive as measures of the amounts of wealth they really represent; and any *confused* union or blend of thinking about money and about wealth in general would always lead to confused, unsound economic theories, and arguments about and decisions upon public policies.

But a further, second, less fully valid part of the basis of the classical position was the doctrine that money's *only* role or function in the economic system is that of serving as the "medium of exchange," or facilitating the process of "exchanging" all the different "real" goods or forms of wealth for each other. Money as such or in itself, this view insisted, is not really "wealth" at all, i.e., it has no use value or utility

[5] J. M. Keynes, *Monetary Reform* (New York: Harcourt, Brace and Company, Inc., 1924).

[6] J. M. Keynes, *A Treatise on Money* (New York: Harcourt, Brace and Company, Inc., 1930).

of its own. It is wanted not for itself but only as a means of obtaining other things; and hence the sale of anything for money is only a first step on the way to getting the other things which the money will be used to buy, which are more wanted by the seller than the thing he is selling, and will be his final and real "payment" for that. All commerce is "really" a process of "exchanging" goods for other goods, through the "medium" or intermediation of money-sales and purchases. Money is nothing but a set of "tickets," obtained by selling goods or services and useful only for buying other goods or services.

Moreover, from that view the conclusion was drawn that, since no receiver of money gets any real benefit from it until he spends it, everyone receiving money will always pretty soon or promptly spend all he gets, either on consumption or on investment goods; any tendencies that any of the people may have to retain and accumulate or "hoard" money are irrational and must be, in extent, negligible. Money then, according to this classical outlook, was merely a "lubricant" for the wheels of the "real" economic system or machine and process, concerned with the production, exchanges, distribution, and consumption of all the diverse goods making up the stock and flow of all "real" wealth. And the main body of general and fundamental economic theory should be a theory of the "real" components, structure, operation, and results of the system; whereas the theory of money and everything essentially connected with it should be merely a separate, special theory of the system's "lubricating" system, and the possible disorders in or malfunctionings of that system which could cause abnormal developments in the working and results of the main, "real" system, and the needed policies for prevention thereof, or proper control of the supply and value of money, to keep it playing only its appropriate "neutral" role.

Now in monetary theory as developed in line with those views, the central doctrine came to be "the quantity theory" of what governs the value (in other goods) of the unit of money (dollar, pound, franc, or what not), or the converse or reciprocal of that, the general level (generally upward or downward changes) of the prices (in money) of all other goods. According to the "quantity theory," the wholly or almost wholly controlling variable in this matter is the amount (number of units) of money "in circulation" in a country or community; substantially or more or less exactly, the general buying power of the money-unit varies inversely, i.e., the general level of prices varies directly with the quantity of money in existence. This familiar doctrine needs to be distinguished from, not confused with, the equally familiar and associated "equations of exchange"—variant forms of a simple, general, comprehensive, mathematical equation—which came into use as expository devices to explain and demonstrate the doctrine.

Consider the *most* familiar "equation of exchange": $MV = PT$, where

M represents the quantity of money; V, the (transactions) "velocity of circulation" of the money (the frequency with which, through a given period of time, the average dollar "changes hands" or is spent and re-spent by new owners in new transactions); P, the general price level; and T, the "volume of trade" or "size" of the "flow" of goods and services sold, during the period, for MV or the money-flow in the other direction. That MV *must* equal PT is obvious; for MV is the sum of the spendings of money or money spent in all the transactions during the period, and PT (all the quantities of things sold or bought times their prices) is the total money-value of all that is sold or bought during the period; the expressions on the two sides of the "equation" represent *the same thing* in different ways, and it is therefore really an identity, truism, or tautology. But it does not by itself at all prove "the quantity theory," which asserts—if we take it literally, without any qualification—that changes of M are always the sole and fully effective cause of all changes of P; that P is bound to vary directly and correspondingly with the variations of M.

Actually, the exponents of "the quantity theory" did always "qualify" it somewhat, or hold it to be only approximately true. But their conviction that it had to be very nearly or substantially true involved, in addition to the truism expressed in the "equation of exchange," a set of weakly grounded and not in fact reliably or even generally true assumptions about the more specific relations among the "behaviors" of the individual variables. The causes of M's changes were thought of as lying exclusively in events *not* indicated by or within the "equation," e.g., in gold discoveries or international gold movements—changes of the world's, or a particular country's, supply or stock of the money metal or metals—or new or expanded issues or creations (or retirements) of paper money, or bank credit money, on the independent initiatives of governmental or central-bank authorities. In other words, M was considered as the independent, active, and primary causative member of this group of variables; there was no recognition of the possibilities that M might be changed *because* T was growing and/or there were upward pressures on costs and prices (P) already, independently at work, and the *need* for more money to "finance" more transactions at a constant or rising price level would be met by decisions in the right, authoritative quarter to increase the money-supply, *in response to* other developments.

Then there was a second, crucial assumption that V was virtually or nearly a constant, depending simply on the community's relatively fixed or stable institutions, customs, and habits, as to the frequencies and timings of people's paydays or receipts of installments of their money-incomes, and those of their purchases and payments for them, which would determine the sizes of the balances of cash they would need to keep on hand, and the rates at which they could turn over or spend and replenish these balances. Everyone's money was useless to him until it was spent; hence the volume of spending would always be as high as the people could afford and in constant ratio to their financial or monetary resources. If they acquired more money they would spend proportionately more, not disproportionately increase their useless, idle money-holdings; thus, V would be virtually constant. And finally, as regards T, the quantity or number of things being offered for sale per unit of time on the economy's markets, this was thought of as depending essentially on the economy's output or volume of production, which in turn was thought of as generally at or near the "capacity" output of its labor force, productive equipment, and "real" resources, and hence not subject to any marked, quick changes in response to those of the supply of money and flow of spending or demand, which therefore would exert their full effects simply on the level of prices.

The deficiencies of "the quantity theory" were in fact results of the artificial isolation of monetary theory from general economic theory. It was a too simple and rigid, wooden, or mechanical theory of the supposed relations of monetary changes to or with other economic changes, because it was constructed without sufficient study of or thought about all the likely relevant changes of people's economic circumstances, attitudes, and actions, and because too much of this broad subject matter was excluded from the specialty or field of attention of the monetary theorists. Thus Keynes, in the development of his work as a monetary theorist, got to the point of finding it necessary to break over into the most nearly related—the "aggregative"—branch of general economic theory, and to refashion or improve that also—at first, primarily in order to improve monetary theory.

It was obvious, of course, that what, in the working of the economy, would *directly* affect the level of prices—and might well also affect many other things—was *not simply the quantity* of money existing and "circulating" (more or less actively), *but the rate of flow* of the money in or through or as the interconnected money-incomes and spendings or outlays of the people—the flow of money spent in efforts to buy things, which as "demand" for them would, along with their supply conditions, affect their prices. And it clearly was not an adequate analysis of all that could affect this all-important magnitude, *the flow* of money as income and outlay in the whole economy, to simply multiply the stock of money by a supposedly more or less fixed multiple, the "velocity of circulation," and thus throw all the emphasis back upon the quantity or stock of money. An early starting point of the development of Keynesian thought in fact lay in the early departure from the notion of the constancy of money's "velocity of circulation," into emphasis rather on the variability, and study of the causes of variations, of this variable, which already characterized the English-Cambridge,

Marshallian development of monetary theory, even before Keynes went on far beyond its standpoint. When he did go beyond that he eventually came to dislike the concept of "velocity" all together, and the entire approach through any "equation of exchange" associated with the (or even a modified) "quantity theory"; he worked out instead his own quite new and different analysis of the ways in which the changing economic situations, prospects, and expectations of the people as consumers and of the economy's business firms and investors, would cause them to change their decisions on their amounts of spending, in or for consumption, and in or for production—and thus change their contributions to each other's incomes, and abilities to spend. But let us, in passing, glance for a moment at the old or early, Cambridge or Marshallian variant and modification of "the quantity theory" and "equation of exchange" approach, from which Keynes started.

In that, a special stress was laid on study of the causes and effects of variations of the shares or fractions of their annual incomes which people, firms, and households would try to keep, on the average through each year, in their "cash balances," to ensure their abilities to do their buying or spending at the necessary or most advantageous times, regardless of the timings of their receipts of new money-income. Now this variable, as a little reflection will make clear to the reader—the fraction of one's income represented by his usual or average cash balance—*is the reciprocal of* a certain measure of the "velocity of circulation" of the money passing through his hands; i.e., it is not quite the *transactions* "velocity" already defined here, but the slightly different form, aspect, or measure of "velocity" that is called *income*-velocity. If we take (arbitrarily) a year as our unit of time, and suppose that a man's income and outlay over the year is $5,000, and the figure at which on the average he maintains his cash balance is $500; then his balance "turns over" or is spent and replenished ten times in the year—the V multiplier which, when applied to the cash balance that he normally maintains, yields the "flow" of money through his balance or his income and outlay, is currently at the rate of ten per year. And if this individual decides, for any reason, *to increase* his cash balance and for a time at least maintain it at a larger figure *relative* to his income—he will, in executing this decision, necessarily curtail his flow of spending or rate of active use of his money—and will thereby also curtail the contributions which his spendings make to other people's incomes. To be sure, if only this one individual, in the whole economy, changes his behavior in this way, the main effects will be temporary or transitional, only. *While* he is building up his balance to the new higher figure, out of his income, his spendings are reduced; but later he can resume spending at an annual rate equal to his annual income—although maintaining his larger balance, with a decreased rate of "turnover" of it. The story would be different, however, if in the whole economy its members *generally* became inclined to build up and thereafter maintain enlarged cash balances relative to their incomes.

The sum of all the cash balances held as such at a given time by all the members of an economy or community is the entire stock of money then in existence in it as a whole. And if that total stock does not change, the owners of those parts of it *cannot* all or generally, simultaneously increase the *absolute* sizes or amounts of their cash balances. If they *try* to do so, however, through the only possible form this effort can take, i.e., by reducing their expenditures or outlays—they mutually reduce each other's money-incomes. And this does result in a general increase of the *ratios* of their cash balances to their incomes and outlays per unit of time—an increase of which the other aspect is a corresponding decrease of the income-velocity of circulation of the existing quantity of money, i.e., a decrease of the aggregate money-income of the entire community or population, to a smaller multiple of that unchanged, existing quantity of money, in the people's balances. Moreover, *if* the shrinkage of the total money-flow as demand (at the old level of prices) for all things coming onto the markets, results in a corresponding, general decline of prices, the people are not generally in the end worse off as regards their incomes in "real" terms. The real values, or buying powers, of their reduced money-incomes, will be on the average as large as before; and the real values in the same sense of their cash balances—containing on the average the same amounts of money as before, but now representing larger fractions of their owners' money-incomes—will be greater than before. Prevalent efforts to increase cash balances have the effects of reducing money-outlays and incomes and prices, and increasing, though not the absolute amounts (in money) of the cash balances, their ratios to the money-incomes and outlays of their owners, *and* the real values of the balances, hence the amounts of security and other advantages or benefits of whatever desired kinds they confer on their owners.

It was really a stroke of genius which led Marshall and his pupils to all this, their special, "cash-balances" form or variant or modification of the old "quantity theory" about money and the price level. For with that "reversed" or "inverted" form of the (income-) "velocity of circulation" concept, and way of treating it as *not* a near-constant but a very significant variable, and working to study and analyze all the possible causes and effects of its variations—they developed a new and more fruitful form of monetary theory, which initially served Keynes as the suggestive starting point from which he eventually went on to a newer, again different, and still better theory. The merit of the "cash-balances" theory from which he started (in his early work as a monetary theorist) was that it not only recognized the variability, and importance of the variations, of money's "velocity of circulation"; but it opened up a view of the causes of those variations, in the changes of prevalent economic conditions and prospects or expectations, and the resulting desires and behavior of the people; and thus in a great measure it prepared the way for Keynes' eventual "reunion" of monetary theory with ("aggregative") general economic theory.

Before going farther, however, let me point out more fully the contrast between the Marshallian ("cash-balances") view and the early-classical view of money "as such" and its significance (that of their amounts of it, in their balances) for people's desires and satisfactions, and its role in the economy. As we saw, the early classical view insisted that money "as such" could have *no* real significance, or utility of its own, or play any further role beyond that of serving as the "medium of exchange" or intermediate link in the alone-important "exchanges" of items of "real" wealth for each other. No one would ever keep in his "balance" of money on hand any more money than he had to have there—the rather constant, strictly minimal amount required by his needs to be able to make purchases in the intervals between the receipts from his sales. For (as the early classicists reasoned) since no one could realize any benefit from money except by spending it for (or "investing" it in) other things—forms or items of "real" wealth, alone of any real use or benefit to their owners—all monies received would always be spent or "invested" as fully and as soon as possible. But this early classical view was unduly narrow or one-sided—overstressing its valid point and neglecting all others—to the point of being in definite error. It denied or overlooked the important range of facts—later brought into view in the Marshallian "cash-balances" theory—from which it follows that people's (appropriately varying and often substantial) holdings of money "as such" often have for them important, direct utilities or advantages of several kinds. Actual money (cash) "on hand" may be described as *general* wealth, usable at any time for any purpose, in contrast with (severally) all *specific* forms or items of "real" (nonmonetary) wealth, which can yield only their specific or restricted kinds of utility and no others, and cannot always be resold promptly or at all for even the amounts of money previously spent for them, and need if possible to be bought and sold only at the right times, of low and high prices, respectively, for them. In other words, money is "liquid" wealth in contrast with wealth "frozen" in specific forms; and there generally are various valid economic reasons for decisions by people to hold significant, varying amounts, or fractional parts of their total amounts of income and wealth of all kinds, in the "liquid," general or nonspecialized, or monetary form; i.e., not only to be in positions to do *necessary* spending at times of no current money-income receipts; but also to be in positions to await and seize the best opportunities or moments to invest in other assets when they are cheap and their income-yields and money-values promise to rise; and at other times to be or become "more liquid" and secure, when other assets threaten to depreciate (lose money-value) and money per contra promises to appreciate (gain increasing real value or buying power).

In sum, there is here an important general truth, which mercantilist thought in its primitive way recognized but exaggerated and distorted; which early-classical theory in its overreaction against that mistakenly denied all together; which Marshall and his pupils, with their "cash-balances" type of monetary theory, again brought to light in an accurate way; and which Keynes, as we shall see later, eventually made—in the form of his theory of "liquidity preference"—one of the pillars of his final system. And this general truth is, that money *is more than* simply a "medium of exchange" or link in the exchangings of the other things alone making up "real wealth." It *also* is, in the ancient phrase, a "store of value," and so one quite "real" form or part of wealth in general, namely, wealth in its general or nonspecific, "liquid" form, interconvertible at choice with all other forms. And the changing dispositions of economic populations, under the influence of changing economic conditions, to use their incomes in one way or the other—to vary the proportions of their liquid and their nonliquid assets in one direction or the other—exert or produce important effects, through the changes of the rate of turnover of the money-supply or the total flow of spending and income, upon all other economic "aggregates" and the over-all performance of the economic systems concerned.

But enough has now been said about this part of the antecedent background of Keynesian thought, in the previous history of monetary theory. Let us turn, next, to the other part of the historic background, in a certain phase of early-classical thought in a central portion of the field of "aggregative," general economic theory.

EARLY-CLASSICAL "AGGREGATIVE" THEORY, AND "SAY'S LAW OF MARKETS"

In a sense the greater part of most early-classical economic theory—i.e., in particular, the greater part of the Ricardian system—was "aggregative" in its nature. That term of course does not fit Ricardo's, or any, theory of "value" or the detailed working of the causes regulating the relative prices, or reciprocal exchange values, of the economy's diverse particular products. But it does fit Ricardo's whole, no less emphasized theory of the economy's over-all growth through time, as involving the envisaged growths of the population and supply of labor, and the supply of capital, and the output of all products together; the restriction of that last phase of the general growth relative to the former two phases, due to fixity of the supply of land and the law of diminishing returns; and in the course of the over-all growth, the decline of real wages per worker to the "bare-subsistence" level, "checking" population growth; and the rise of the marginal cost of production and price of food for labor, hence of money-wages relative to real wages; and the fall of the profit rate to the point of "checking" growth of the supply of capital; and the increase of the land-rent share of the national income. For our present purpose, however, we need to focus our attention more narrowly upon a particular central part or element of that entire—and every early-classical—system of "aggregative" theory: the included theory of the growths of and relations between the system's total output and the population's total income and outlay and demand in the system's markets; and the effects upon those two aggregate variables—total supply and total demand—of the rate or rates of saving and investment and the formation and growth of the supply of capital.

On those particular matters there was a very important, early, confused controversy between Ricardo and all contemporary "orthodox" economists on the one side, and Malthus and some other "unorthodox" theorists on the other side. The "heretics," including Malthus, feared that "too much" of the total flow of income in the system was being saved and reinvested in expanding production, and, as the other face of this, "too little" was being spent for consumption of the consequently growing output of consumers' goods. If this "wrong" division of the use of income persisted, they said, it would in time bring about a situation of general overproduction and underconsumption, or "glutting of the markets," and a general depression with mass unemployment. In the view behind this fear, the "capitalists," making up the main part of the more wealthy or well-off minority or part of the population, strongly tended—in their avid pursuit of not only profits but ever-growing amounts of capital for later use in gaining further profits—to keep on always reinvesting the bulk of their profits and doing, themselves, only a quite limited amount of consumption spending. And the larger, main, wage-earning mass of the population, in general getting only or little more than "subsistence" wages, *could* do only a limited amount of consumption spending. The *whole* amount of the latter was thus limited; and with continual reinvestment of the bulk of the profit share of the national income in expanding production, the total output would grow and come to include too great an output of consumers' goods, i.e., an output of the latter with a total production-cost value in excess of the buying power of the part of the population's income available for consumption spending.

The "orthodox" theorists of that time, however, developed—with more rigorous logic, from assumptions in fact shared or unquestioned by those "heretics," who thus ruined their case—an analysis proving (on those assumptions) the impossibility of that dire event or outcome, predicted by the "heretics." In explaining this "orthodox" early-classical analysis of the possibilities, I will separate the two questions involved, and deal at first only with the *general* part of the analysis, "proving" the impossibility *in any event* of a "general glutting" of the markets, or deficiency of total effective demand in relation to total output or supply; and defer for a bit the discussion of what was said on the special question of the effects (both on output and upon demand) of saving, investment, and growth of the supply of capital, in whatever amounts.

The "orthodox" classical argument to prove the impossibility of the "general glut," or the necessary equality, under all conditions, of the total supply of and the total demand for the system's products, was most fully developed, elaborated, emphasized, and "sold" to the profession and the public by the French classical economist J. B. Say, and therefore became known as "Say's law of markets." But in substance this same "law" and supporting argument also was held, more or less independently, and was sufficiently and clearly stated, by Ricardo, and by others, and in fact was generally a common element of most economic theory in that period. In its most fundamental and simple form—stressing the view that all products are in final effect "exchanged" for each other, and ignoring the role of money in the system—this argument said simply that, since the supply of every product is or supports or makes effective a corresponding amount of demand for other products—since all the products are exchanged for each other—the total supply of and total demand for them all together must under all conditions be the same. And in the more elaborated form, taking into account the role of money—i.e., its limited, "neutral" role as generally conceived in both the "general economic" and the "monetary" branch of early-classical theory—the argument ran that, since all expenditures in or for production enter into and form the incomes of the people as contributors of work and all other requisites of production, the total income of the population is necessarily always sufficient to buy the output of all products at a level of prices fully covering their expenses of production. Moreover, although my wording of that statement may at first thought appear to leave out this element of the problem, the argument in fact also includes or "takes care of" the "profit" share of the flow of income and the "profits" included in the prices of all products; since all "profits" are spent, either—and it matters not in what proportions—for consumers' goods or for investment goods or producers' goods, which make up one part of total output along with (and currently reducing correspondingly) the current output of consumers' goods; and the part of total demand represented by the spending of profits must offset the over-all effect of profits on the level of prices.

In their further views on the "monetary" side, the adherents of Say's law recognized that, to enable the system to work perfectly smoothly or with continuous, exact maintenance of equality between the flow of money-income and outlay on one side and the money-value of the total current output at the current level of prices on the other side, there would need to be a continuous, ideal regulation or adjustment of the supply of money to keep it growing just *pari passu* with the supply of goods, and to keep the general level of all prices stable and that of all money-incomes suitably related to it, and thus to ensure that there would never at any moment be any deficiency of total demand in the system. But it was generally maintained that even in the absence of such ideal adjustments on the monetary side, though an undesirable behavior of the money-supply and price level and so on would produce temporary, transitional maladjustments, they would all be in the long run self-correcting; since in free competitive markets with flexible prices, the latter would all become so adjusted as to make the real value or buying power of the flow of money-income and outlay equal to the output or supply of all goods, and make any lasting deficiency of aggregate demand impossible.

Now in any effective criticism of Say's law, the central point that requires attention is the all-important role played in the argument, again, by that classical doctrine about money which we noticed before, that as money has no utility of its own, there can be no significant tendencies to "hoard" it. All money-income received by anyone is always promptly and fully spent by him, in either consumption or investment spending, and passes into other people's incomes, who will likewise pass it on, with the results that the flow of money in the system, as the total income earned from production of the output, must all reemerge as the flow of spending to buy the output; and that in both aspects, as income and as outlay, this money-flow is reliably controlled by or controllable through or a nearly fixed multiple of the system's quantity or stock of money. The flaw in Say's law lies here, in the less than full validity of this doctrine or assumption, and the resulting facts that the "transitional monetary disturbances," rather lightly regarded by exponents of the "law," are generally or often much more important than they recognized, and are interdependent with all sorts of other economic changes, and not adequately preventable or controllable simply through regulation of the quantity of money and/or "automatic" and always either appropriate or self-corrective changes of the level of prices. In a time of falling prices and low confidence in the future values of nonmonetary or "real" forms of wealth, there can arise a general pursuit of "liquidity" or enlarged cash holdings, causing a progressive contraction of the flow of spending, income, and further spending, and hence a real deficiency of total demand, a further fall of prices below the level of earlier-incurred production costs, and a possibly serious and not soon or certainly self-curing depression. And the development by Keynes of this point, in answer to Say's law, became, as we shall see, one very important part or element of the Keynesian system.

And now let me return to the other part of the early classical controversy, the discussion of which was postponed above: the effects of extensive saving, investment, and growth of the economy's supply of "real" capital equipment and producing power, upon the amounts and compositions of its output and of demand in the system at a later time. What is now to be said is particularly about the views of Malthus on these matters, and their distant relation to the different, modern views of Keynes and his successors. Keynes paid tribute in his distant retrospect to Malthus for having been, in this general connection, on the right track, when Ricardo and all the "orthodox" theorists of that early time were on the wrong track. Yet I think the degree of similarity of the ideas of Malthus with those of Keynes in this field was really slight. Malthus was prevented from anticipating Keynes in theory of saving, investment, etc., by the former's unquestioning acceptance of the Ricardian and general "orthodox" classical assumption that the amount of saving always controls that of investment spending (which in turn contributes to income and consumption spending), and keeps the second variable (investment spending) equal to itself (the amount of saving). This idea of the relation or bond between saving and investment was "natural" in the early history of economic theory, and probably more true, in relation to the contemporary facts, than it would be today. The savers and the persons using or investing their savings in production were then more often the same persons; and it probably was at least more nearly true then than it is now that all of the part of income saved *for* investment *was* always rather promptly and fully invested, i.e., paid out, in or as expenditures in and for production, and thus returned to the flow of income and outlay or effective demand for the resulting output. At all events, that was generally assumed to be true; and it followed that no amount of saving could lead to any inadequacy of total demand in the system or any violation of Say's law. In contrast, the Keynesian system includes, as we shall see, a new and different analysis of saving and investment, their separate determinants, and the nature and direction of the link between them. From that analysis it follows that, although in a sense the amount of (actually realized or accomplished) saving and that of investment are always equal, the equality between them is maintained not by control of the amount of investment by that of saving, but, on the contrary, by the great influence of the (otherwise or independently determined) amount of investment spending on that of total spending and thus on the volume of income in the system, and thus on the abilities of the people to save, and the amount of saving. And this does open up the possibility—which Malthus was unable to explain, if he had this in mind—that there may be in a society or population or its wealthier part a too-strong *propensity* to save, i.e , a too-weak propensity to consume, meaning that, out of the large total income that would accompany and be interdependent with continuing "full employment" of the society's or economy's labor force and resources, saving, as lack of consumption spending *would* become excessive relative to the field of profitable investment opportunities. And the result would be that the deficiency of investment spending and therefore of total spending and demand would cause a contraction of production, employment, and income in the system, down to the point of making the amount of *realized* saving only equal to that of all profitable investment spending. But this, the core of the Keynesian theory that is still to be more fully explained here, is very different from anything that was said by Malthus. Further discussion here of the latter's views would take us too far afield and be unnecessary; we are now ready to drop all discussion of the antecedent backgrounds of Keynesian theory, jump over the long interval of later-classical and neo-classical preoccupation mainly with nonaggregative theory about particular markets, industries, firms, etc., and take up directly the structure and development of Keynesian theory itself, as a new scheme of analysis created in the middle of and directly relevant to the Great Depression of the 1930s.

THE MAIN ELEMENTS OF THE KEYNESIAN ANALYSIS

The central theme of Keynes' analysis is about the causes and results of variations of the total flow of spending, income, and respending in the whole economy. Hence in our account of it here we may logically take up, first, its analysis of the composition of the income-stream, as considered from two points of view. With regard to its *sources* in the two kinds of spending which together generate it, the population's *income* is composed of the flow of *consumption* spending *plus* that of *investment* spending; or, in the standard symbols introduced by Keynes, Y (income) $=$ C (consumption) $+$ I (investment.) (Y is used to stand for income, because I is needed also for investment.) Then with regard to the two ways of *using* income, it all divides up rather into consumption spending (again) and "saving". The people who do not fully spend their incomes for consumption "save" the remaining parts; "saving" is here defined merely as not-spending-for-consumption. Thus in *this* view of the composition of income, $Y = C + S$ (for saving).

Now from the two equations—$Y = C + I$, and $Y = C + S$—it of course follows that, as $I = Y - C$ and also $S = Y - C$, therefore $I = S$; the part or amount of the national income through any period of time which consists of the flow of investment spending *and* the part or amount of the same income which the people receiving it are not spending as consumers but are saving are always equal. But this result of these equations or formulas, when considered in conjunction with the general theme of the entire Keynesian analysis, seems paradoxical, and is, for students, a difficult, awkward, "tricky" point, or frequent stumbling block in the path to full understanding of the analysis. For as we shall see, despite the necessary continuous equality of *S* and *I* according to the formulas, in Keynesian theory as a whole the immediate, operative cause of the economy's decline from a period of prosperity into one of depression is always the prosperous period's effect of generating an amount of saving *greater than* the amount of investment spending which the profit prospects or expectations of the economy's business firms lead them *to continue* to plan and carry out, in the aggregate. Let me now explain and resolve the apparent paradox a bit more fully.

While or as long as a time of widespread, high prosperity continues, the population's total income, *Y*, is large, and its volume or rate of consumption spending, *C,* though also relatively large, is by no means *that* large. And in fact, as the slightly later, resulting developments prove, *that S* is *too* large to be all used in the economy, productively, and be all or fully conserved, for the savers, as the amount of saved-up or accumulated, enduring, real wealth to which they looked forward. For although the *S* of the period of prosperity is only equal to the *I of the same period,* i.e., to the amount of investment spending *helping to form* the amount of income *resulting in* that amount of saving; this same *S* is larger than the *I of the next, immediately ensuing period,* which therefore does not return all of it back into the income-stream; and the shrinkage of I, and hence also of *Y,* entails also a shrinkage of *S,* which again is equal to this new, reduced *I.* The equality at every time of the current S and the current *I* is continuously maintained, but only because the successive changes of *I* through time immediately cause the changes of *Y* and therefore of *S,* which keep *S* and *I* equal. In the movement through time, each new value of *S* is the surplus of the new *Y* over the new *C,* and is therefore equal to the new *I,* which also is (creates) the part of the new *Y* that is not accounted for by the new *C.* At the same time, the far more important point is that when *I* contracts it does so at least partly because the old *S* has become too large, that is, because the other part of the old *Y*—*C,* the demand for consumers' goods in the economy—and the current and prospective or expected rate of growth of that—are not felt by the business world to be large enough to justify *new* investment outlays equal in their total amount to all those just recently made; though *unless* the old rate or volume of investing *is* thus continued or repeated, there will be failure to return all of the savings that accrued in prosperity back into the income-flow, and thus maintain or continue the old values of *Y, C,* and *S.*

But to get beyond this mere initial account of the component parts of the income-flow, and the obvious relations of dependency among them, and this mere quibble in a sense about the equality, or not, of saving and investment, let us go on into further consideration of the conditions under which, and the ways in which, the several separate components or variables undergo their changes, and play their parts in causing those of the income-flow in its entirety. The next idea, now, to be more fully explained and stressed, though it has been partly anticipated already, is the very important Keynesian idea of "the consumption function": that the amount of consumption spending which the people do is, in this language familiar among mathematicians, always "a function of" the sizes of their incomes, that is, a variable dependent on the latter or sure to vary with them, in a certain way; it is a "function" or covariant relation such that, if the incomes increase, the consumption spending will increase also but *less than* in full proportion to the increase(s) of the incomes, so that at the same time people's savings will increase *more* than in proportion with their incomes. This proposition of course refers or applies only to increases of incomes *above* the very low minimal levels which the people concerned regard as barely sufficient to cover their most "necessary" living costs or expenses.

Initially, only a "common-sense" generalization, from casual observation or experience of the spending and saving habits of people in different income classes, and of those of the same people when their incomes rise, this fertile idea, introduced by Keynes, has since been subjected to a good deal of testing through statistical, empirical research, and on the whole stands up pretty well, but has been modified. Keynes believed "the consumption function" to be a rather *stable,* definite "function" of income, so that, if economists once attained reasonably exact knowledge of its form or character, they would thereafter be and remain able to predict, with reasonable accuracy, by just how much each new change of the people's incomes would change their amounts of spending and saving. But the "function" has been found to be a good deal less "stable" than Keynes supposed it to be. Spending and saving depend *not only* on incomes but also on numerous other variables: habits formed by and carried on from past levels of incomes; expectations, hopes, and fears about likely future changes of incomes from their present levels; people's assets or possessions as distinguished from their incomes; and still other variables. Hence the relations to or with income alone are not very highly stable or predictable. Nevertheless, this simple idea of "the consumption function"—which in its other aspect is also that of "the saving function"—remains a very useful idea or "tool" of analysis. And the *general kind of form* of the function or relation, which alone is vitally important for Keynesian theory, has become established and accepted. When the people's earnings grow, their spendings grow but not as greatly, and their savings grow. And in the other, downward direction, when earnings decline, spending declines but not as greatly, and the main effect of the fall of earnings is a great fall of the rate of saving.

Now one principal, and the most "revolutionary," implication of that idea, that spending *and saving* are in the main simply "functions of" or dependent on the level of incomes, is the implication with regard to saving that—in direct contradiction of most pre-Keynesian "orthodox" economic theory on this question—the amount of saving done in the economy is *not* primarily or very significantly influenced by the extent of the existing, available, and known opportunities for profitable use or investment of the savings, or in other words, the demand for their use in "financing" production, and the inducement offered to savers in the shape of the rate of interest they are able to obtain. Saving is much *more* dependent on people's incomes and *abilities* to save *than* upon the variations of the business world's demand for their savings as new "capital," and the consequent variations of the rather small additions made to the savings themselves by the amounts of interest they will earn. This very important point of Keynesian theory of course helps to explain the vital, central one already noticed above, and to be more fully discussed later on, that saving can become "excessive" in relation to investment opportunities. Instead of developing in response and adjustment to the latter as reflected in the interest rate, as economists before Keynes generally supposed it to do, the amount of saving develops mainly, merely as a result of the existing level of incomes. This in turn depends indeed partly on how much the business firms are investing in production, and thus contributing to the flow of income; but in this way, on their *recent-past* appraisals of their then foreseeable opportunities for profitable investment, and the resulting plans, now being carried out; *and not* on the *now* foreseeable and as yet unmet, *further* opportunities of the near future, which determine the current demand for the people's savings, and may through that affect the rate of interest. Still other implications of this point, that saving varies principally with income as its source and does not adjust well to the demand for capital, will concern us later on when we take up the Keynesian theory of the rate of interest. But now let us pass on beyond our consideration of C and S in relation to Y—the consumption function and its other face, the saving function—to a new range of considerations about I—the flow of investment spending in and for production; what this depends on and how, as a variable, it tends to "behave" as the economy develops.

The second major "tool" concept in Keynesian theory, after that of the consumption (and saving) function, is that of the "schedule" or "curve" of "the marginal efficiency of capital," relating the gains to be expected from using or investing new additional capital to expand production to the point that already has been reached in the growth of the amount of capital in use, as compared with the available supplies of all the other "factors of production." The general idea is that, as the economy, or any or all of the producing firms or enterprises in it, goes on enlarging, through new investments, the amount or amounts of capital employed, the resulting additional gains or benefits, or degrees of profitability of the new investments, normally decline—*if, or under the assumption that,* "other things" or relevant variables, such as the supplies of natural resources, labor, and business ability, and the level of efficiency of the kind of technology or techniques or methods of production in use, "remain constant."

In a very substantial part, of course, *this* "law" or "principle" in Keynesian theory is nothing new or peculiar, but a continuation of the old classical and neo-classical ideas about "the law of diminishing returns," or diminishing "marginal productivity" of capital (or any one factor of production) as the amount of it in use increases relative to the amounts of the other factors in use. But the continuity with these older ideas is not complete; here Keynes did add a significant new stress on a further element of the problem, besides the later-realized, objective, actual results of additions to capital, i.e., the resulting additions actually made, as things turn out, to the outputs, and values of the outputs, and gross and net earnings of the firms making the additional or new investments. Decisions to invest in production are controlled not by the actually resulting gains or benefits, which generally cannot be known or foreseen with any full certainty at the times when the decisions are made; but instead they are controlled by the inevitably, partly "subjective" judgments, estimates, predictions, guesses, or "expectations" as to what those results will or may be, which are formed by or in the minds of those who make the decisions, when or before they make them. And those "expectations" generally turn not only on their knowledge, which may be quite good and reliable, of the physical-production results which can be counted on; but even more largely, in many cases, they are based on groping guesses about how the outputs of products to be produced with the aid of the contemplated new investments will fare on the markets—how great the demands in the markets will be for them, and how good the prices obtainable for them will be.

Now according to Keynesian theory, as we know already, the aggregate demand in an economy's markets for all its products taken together can grow over time only if and as the aggregate income of the population grows. If the latter growth is going on, moreover, the resulting growth of demand for consumers' goods in general will be not in full proportion to the growth of income, but something less than that, with the also growing remainder going into savings. And unless the economy's producers of consumers' goods have, as a group, reasons to expect a good, continuing growth of the consuming public's or population's demands for their products, they will not be inclined to do much new investing to enlarge their plants or potential outputs or their demands for new producers' goods; hence the producers of the latter, as a group, will not be inclined to do much new investing, either. Thus, the economy's producing firms of all kinds, as an entire group, will tend to keep on making, annually, large new investments or additions to the mass of capital in use, only if and while the predominant opinion or expectation in the business community is that the national income is growing and likely in the near future to continue growing at a sufficiently fast rate to make the (associated, lesser) growth of the total flow of consumption spending adequate to justify, or reasonably assure good profits on, these new investments.

Keynes, then, had an additional reason, beyond that in the minds of the earlier "main line" economists, for expecting growth over time of the economy's supply of capital in use in production to tend progressively to lower the generally expectable and expected rate of profit on further new investments. The later would, as compared with the earlier additions to the mass of capital in use, make smaller additions to the economy's output of its products unless in the meantime there occurred discovery of new, good, previously inaccessible natural resources to be exploited, or a growth and/or improvement of the labor supply, or technological advances (needing new capital in order to be carried into practice, and raising the general level of efficiency or productivity) —or changes of some or all of these kinds, sufficient in their total results to "offset" the effect exerted simply by the growth of the mass of capital, as such. In addition, as Keynes saw the matter, the *slowing* growth of the total output and resulting total income in the system, which would be the best result to be expected simply from a *steady* growth of the amount of capital in use, would entail a still more decidedly slowing or decelerating growth of total consumption spending in the system, further accentuating the tendency of the to-be-expected rate of profit on further new investments to fall.

But now we come to still another part of the analysis. The dispositions of producers to make new investments depend not only on their profit expectations as so far considered, but also to some extent on the *costs* of making the new investments, as affected by the rate or rates of interest which must be paid in order to obtain the required new capital. In fact, what matters is the expected or anticipated rates of *net* profit *over and above* the interest payments required to obtain the capital. Keynes held that, in general, expansion through new investments would continue if and while or as long as the investing firms had expectations of resulting benefits in the shape of *any significant* net profits (or additions to their total profits), over and above all costs including that of the required new capital. Thus interest rates appear as the other or codeterminants, along with profit expectations or "the marginal efficiency of capital" in the sense already explained, of the rate or volume of new investment spending undertaken. Hence we now move on to Keynes' theory of the causes of the rate of interest and its variations—a topic on which he again departed rather far from the older lines of thought of the classical and neo-classical economists.

At the same time, the Keynesian theory of interest does not represent a *complete* break with *everything* in the field of the older, traditional "theories of interest." There have been, in fact, *two* traditions of thought in this field, held apart in the past by the continuing influence of the classical separation, discussed earlier in this chapter, of "monetary theory" from "general economic theory." *One* type of interest theory has always been a part of "monetary theory," and concerned itself with the "money-market" rate or rates of interest on "loanable funds," or loans of money or bank credit to business firms by or through financial institutions—the rate or rates of interest studied by monetary theorists, as "prices" playing a role in the adjustments of the supply of money and of funds to "finance" business activity to the demands for them. And *the other* and in a sense main or historically (on the whole) more emphasized kind of "theory of interest," which went through its developments in the nonmonetary field of "general economic theory," was concerned rather with "interest" in the sense of payments for the uses, or productive services, of "real" nonmonetary "capital" as one of the fundamental "factors of production." In *this* tradition, the "savers" in society were thought of as, by holding their consumption spendings to less than their incomes and making their "saved" wealth available for use in production, really transferring into that use not merely money but the "real" productive resources of all kinds (including labor), which the business firms obtaining the use of the saved and invested money would buy or rent or hire with it, and employ in production. And "interest" in this sense was regarded as the "price" which business firms (1) could afford to pay or would be willing and able to pay—really as a share of or deduction from "profits"—for the use of "capital," and (2) would need to pay as the inducement or incentive to bring about enough "saving"—abstinence from or postponement of consumption—to keep a sufficient part of the economy's resources and labor force employed in producing, not consumers' goods for current consumption, but new producers' goods for use in production.

In a sense the Keynesian theory of the "marginal efficiency of capital," already discussed here, continues one part of this older, traditional theory of "interest" on "real capital"; though Keynes in a way at that point reverted to the early-classical use of terms, in associating the "return to capital" in that sense—the net gains from productive investments—with "profit" rather than with "interest." What does not appear in his system at all is the other part of the old traditional kind of "interest" theory in this "real" sense, which regarded payment of the gain attributable to the productivity of "capital," as such, to "savers," for their "savings," as needed to induce them to do enough saving and thus bring into existence the amount of real capital required in the economy. For as we have seen, Keynes held that saving does not occur mainly or to any important extent in response and adjustment to the demand and reward for it, but occurs simply as a result of the existence of large incomes, more than sufficient for all the consumption spending their recipients want or care to do in any case, so that they "save" the remainders "automatically," with little or no regard to any demand or reward for the use of their "savings." And in a wealthy society, Keynes held, saving would often tend to become excessive or redundant anyway, and not a "scarce" service needing to be stimulated or induced, in a barely sufficient supply, by the payment of "interest."

Thus on the whole the Keynesian theory of "interest" (in his use of this term) does not link up with, or have its antecedents in, *the part of* traditional thought about "interest" which had its place in theory of the "real" as distinguished from the "monetary" aspects of the economic world and process. Instead it does link up with the tradition of "monetary-interest" theory, and may be called a "purely monetary theory of interest," though in Keynesian thought as a whole it has its place in not only monetary but all economic theory, since Keynes as we have seen "reunited" the two. And so it is here above all, in this part of the Keynesian system concerned with the rate of interest, that the fruits of his early work as a monetary theorist, and his development of the Marshallian "cash-balances" theory or idea of the variable desire for "liquidity" into something leading away from the simple "quantity theory" of money and the price level—it is here that all this, reviewed already in an earlier part of this chapter, comes fully into play. In this theory of "interest," the economy's owners of amounts or pools of money as such—cash balances—are the potential providers of the capital funds which producing business firms or enterprises may need or want to borrow or "raise" (by issuing and selling new "securities" of all kinds) and invest in production. In one view these pools of money or cash balances do represent the (not yet loaned or invested) "savings" of their owners, or accumulations of the unspent portions of their money-incomes. But the "savers," who have "saved up" these sums of money with little or no regard to any interest inducement for so doing, may want to retain them as "liquid" wealth, not lend or invest them, i.e., exchange them for nonliquid or less liquid properties or assets, which they may later be unable to resell quickly for (even) equal amounts of money if and when they again want the latter, and which may depreciate in money-value. All owners of money in fact generally want to retain at least some parts of their amounts of it in the fully "liquid," actual-money form, and the amounts they want to so retain, and the amounts they may be willing to lend or invest, will vary with their varying circumstances and appraisals of the current and prospective state of the economy and the prospects of the firms or enterprises to which they might hand over the use of their money as capital, in return for shares of the prospective earnings of these enterprises.

In so far as owners of money exchange it for other assets, they surrender "liquidity"; and the rates of interest which enterprises have to pay for the use of capital funds, have to be paid to induce *not* saving *but* this giving up of "liquidity," or willingness to part with the money as such in return for other forms of wealth or claims to money in the future, of less surely predictable value and convenience at all future times. Interest is paid to overcome the variable, and never negligible, psychological force which Keynes named "liquidity preference." Now in this analysis the other factor or variable which, along with or besides the currently prevailing degree or intensity of "liquidity preference" at each time in the history of an economy, also affects the prevailing rate or rates of interest, is the supply of money—the amount of money in existence in the system. Whenever the business outlook is generally felt to be unfavorable or poor, and money-owners are especially reluctant to let their money be invested, the prevalent degree or intensity of "liquidity preference" rises, and producers wanting to use money as capital cannot get it except by offering higher rates of interest for it. But at such a time they are in most cases unable to afford to pay or promise high rates of interest, since the poor business outlook means precisely low anticipated rates of profit. Moreover, at such a time the urge for "liquidity" operates to cause not only refusals to lend or invest without an extra-high interest inducement, but also efforts by people generally, throughout the economy, to build up or enlarge their cash balances by reducing their expenditures. But the cutting down of spendings also cuts down money-incomes, generally, and the demands and obtainable sales volumes and prices for all goods and services; in other words, it *worsens* the business outlook still further. The existing amount of money is "circulating" ever more slowly, as spendings and incomes and respendings contract, because people are "holding on to" their shares of the economy's money-stock, or their cash balances, instead of using them actively in either consumption spending or investment. In such a situation, the only other and better way in which it is possible to satisfy or meet the existing high level of "liquidity preference," and *not* let it produce those consequences, is through action by the state and the central banks to increase the supply and flow of money to the point of enabling the people to enlarge their cash balances, not by curtailing their spendings and each other's incomes, but by putting more into their balances out of enlarged money-incomes, and eventually resuming their spendings and investings on more "normal" scales and terms, when their "liquid" balances have become large enough to satisfy them. The rate of interest can be kept in line with both the profit prospects and abilities to pay interest, of producers needing capital funds, and the "supply price" at which the funds will be made available by their owners, only through public measures to vary the economy's supply of money in the way and to the extent required to offset or counteract the variations of the intensity of "liquidity preference."

We have now gone over all but one or two of the main, central parts of the entire Keynesian analysis of the set of interrelated, "aggregative" variables which together determine the economy's level of over-all performance: the flow of income, consumption spending, saving, profit expectations, interest rates, investment spending, aggregate demand, the degree of nearness to "full employment" of the economy's labor force, resources, and equipment, output, and the general price level. The one vital topic on which nothing has been said yet is the level of wage rates for labor, and its relations to those of production costs, consumption spending and demand for output, prices (obtainable for products), profit expectations, investment spending, and employment. And I have barely touched on the topic of the price level, which of course is strongly connected with that of the wage level, so it may be said that one or two, or one and a half, topics remain still to be considered. But let me now first summarize and bring into sharp focus the general theme of the entire analysis as far as it has been surveyed already, and then fit the remaining points into that context.

The "flaw" which Keynes discovered in the "automatic" working and development of the economic system of "free" private enterprises and "competitive" markets is the system's inability to achieve at need, through its own "automatic" processes, *quite all* of the internal adjustments among its functioning parts required to keep it operating constantly at or nearly at its full "capacity," or maintain continuous, approximately "full employment" of its labor force, resources, and equipment, and the resulting "capacity" output of all goods and services—the aggregate "real" income of the population. Keynes did not question, or concern himself with, what had long been the mainly emphasized part of the "orthodox" theory of the system's admirably effective, self-adjusting processes: the part concerned with the processes of adjustment of the supplies of particular goods to the demands for them, and of the pattern of the *relative* prices of different goods to that required to bring about *the proper allocation of all employed* labor and resources into the most productive-and-demanded set of particular employments, and so on. He only found, in the other sphere of the needed adjustments among the system's over-all "aggregate" variables, several points at which these could not be counted on to come about "automatically."

To provide a growing population with a high and rising standard of living, the system needs to have in it, besides continual growth of the volume and efficiency of its means of production and so of its potential output, also an adequate and steady growth of the flow of income, spending, and demand. But if and when the flow of income does grow at a good rate for a time, there tends to go with that only a lesser growth of the flow of consumption spending or demand for the system's final products, and a growth of saving. *That* is all right *if* and as long as the flow of investment spending, in and for production, continues and grows sufficiently to return all of the "saved" part of the income-flow back into that flow and that of new consumption spending and new saving. But this is the department in which troubles arise—and become potentially the more serious, the more prosperous the society becomes. As prosperity rises, the percentage of the income-flow that goes into spending or demand for consumers' goods declines, and the percentage saved increases; and the amount, and rate of growth of the amount, of annual new investment spending by producers, needed to keep *total* spending or demand adequate to ensure continuing full employment and production, rises. But the field of profitable investment opportunities has limits, both because, as the producing enterprises become ever more fully equipped and mechanized, further investments in new, additional items of equipment (unless they are of newly invented, unprecedentedly efficient kinds) yield only diminishing improvements of productivity or cost-savings, and because the limited growth of demand for consumers' goods in the increasingly prosperous, high-saving economy limits the possibilities or prospects for selling, at rewarding prices, the growing outputs of goods to which ever new and large productive investments must lead if full employment is to be maintained. There is thus a tendency, intensified by rising prosperity in the present, for the profit expectations motivating further new investments to decline. And as they decline and the business outlook darkens, and people with money become more concerned to keep their assets "liquid," interest rates or the costs of obtaining capital for investment rise perversely at the very time when the producers can least afford to pay them. Thus, in all, the system, instead of being adequately self-adjusting, is likely, after it has climbed and briefly enjoyed each new hill in the rising prosperity range, to work itself down into a new wretched valley of depression, owing to underconsumption, oversaving, deficient profit prospects, excessive capital costs, and underinvestment, all adding up to a shrinkage of total demand, production, employment, and income.

Now the remaining point or points concern the "flexibility" or "rigidity" of the levels of wage rates, costs, and prices. Pre-Keynesian economists of the "orthodox" tradition, even if they had been able to follow and accept the argument as thus far outlined here, would still have insisted that if and when the flow of money-income and spending in the system tends to become inadequate to constitute demand, at the existing price level, for a full-employment output, the proper and "natural, automatic" adjustment should and would occur through an appropriate fall and set of readjustments of all prices including money-wage rates and all cost prices for producers, which would restore the population's real buying power and total demand for goods, and the proper relations of producers' costs and selling prices, and their profit prospects, and investment spendings, and the full-employment volume of production. In one special branch of his theory or analysis which we shall omit here, Keynes tried to prove that even on that assumption of complete downward "flexibility" of all prices and wage rates, etc., the system could still at times reach and remain in a state of "underemployment equilibrium." The effects of cutting money-wage rates and other costs and prices generally could not in practice be simple or work out so well as "orthodox" theory had supposed they would, and Keynes tried to show that even if carried out these measures might not prevent or cure the depression. But this little, special part of his argument has not been generally accepted as successful in proving its contention, and was not essential for his purpose anyway, since he could and did in the end rest his case on the simple "fact of real life," that in a modern industrial economy with strong labor unions, radical across-the-board wage reductions as a necessary part of the old "orthodox" prescription for avoiding or curing a depression, simply are not feasible. The alternative way out, which he therefore advocated, was public action to reenlarge the money-flow in the system, restore a sufficient demand for a full-employment output at the old, high price level, bolster up the latter and the profit margins of producers and their ability to continue the full-employment output—and leave wage rates alone. This means in a sense, cutting the "real" wages of the (employed) workers—the real value or buying power, in goods, of the money-wages—below what this would be if, as in historic depressions, the prices of goods or the cost of living fell and money-wages did not, or fell less. Reinflation to support demand at high prices takes from the workers, by way of the latter, what it does not take away by cutting wages; but it is the less resisted, more feasible way of achieving the result of making it possible to maintain "full employment."

As a whole, then, the Keynesian analysis brings out the inability of *laissez-faire* capitalism to maintain continuous, sufficient, total demand and production and employment, or its liability to fall at intervals into depression and mass unemployment—and explains in a masterly way just why and how such "breakdowns" occur. The analysis is not mainly one of "the business cycle" as such, however—the supposedly regular, periodic, or rhythmical alternation of prosperities and depressions, which many economists through several generations have found evidence of and tried to explain. Keynes did include in the structure of theory, which I have been describing much less than exhaustively, some contributions of his own to "business-cycle" theory; but his main emphasis was not on the idea of the regular, periodic "cycle," but simply on the effort to understand and learn how to cure or prevent depressions. His work also suggested, and some of his successors more fully developed, still another idea—beyond both that of just any depression, however timed in relation to others, and that of "the business cycle"—namely, the idea of a long-run trend, in the on-going history of the capitalist system, to or toward an eventual state of full "maturity" or completed progress or development, and "secular stagnation"—enduring, chronic depression in the absence of continuous public support or assistance.

This prediction is in some ways like the early Ricardian-classical prediction of an eventual ending of economic growth in the arrival of "the stationary state." But its basis, unlike that of the latter, lies not simply in the ideas of the fixed supply of natural resources, the law of diminishing returns, and the limits of the possible growth of population and of capital, but in the central ideas of the Keynesian system. Economic development or growth brings rising wealth, saving, and progressive filling up, so to speak, of the total field of profitable investment opportunities, or decline of the profit incentives for and the possibilities of full use of the population's savings. Hence chronic underinvestment as well as underconsumption, and permanently insufficient total demand, must lie ahead, unless growth of public investment in production of non-market goods or services to the population, where the profit incentive is unneeded, comes to the rescue and provides the needed supplement to the flow of spending, income, and demand, which the system of private enterprises by itself will be unable to make adequate. I will not discuss *this* theory here, though I have felt that it should not remain unmentioned. It is a questionable, controversial, not-established, special theory, with strong roots in Keynesian thought but a life of its own apart from the latter as a whole. Its essential weakness is that it tries to ground a "long-run" historical prediction on an essentially "short-run" structure of theory, which assumes "given" techniques or methods of production, i.e., it argues that growth of the mass of capital necessarily diminishes the remaining room for large and highly profitable further investments. All it really proves is that private capitalism or the system of private enterprises needs ever new, great technological advances or industrial revolutions to enable it to go on using, or prevent it from smothering itself in, its ever-growing mass of capital. That the new industrial revolutions are sure not to come or be sufficiently great ones cannot be known.

But this is an overspeculative development of, from, and beyond the more solid part of the Keynesian analysis, and need not detain us here.

I am now almost ready to turn our attention from the analysis as such, to the public-policy ideas or proposals and political tendencies connected with it. But before doing that, let me say a final word about the over-all "scientific" value of the analysis—of the lines of investigation opened up by it, more than of its specific doctrines or initial answers to the questions posed—and the new impetus and direction it has given to much continuing work in the study of economics. The combined theoretical or analytical and statistical-empirical studies of the related changes, through time, of the "aggregate" variables, in national economies, to which Keynes directed or drew the attention of economists—each national economy's annual total output, and flows of income, consumption spending, investment spending, saving, levels of producer's cost prices and final or consumers' prices and business profits, money-supply and interest rates, and volumes of employment and unemployment, etc.—economists' continuing studies and growing and improving knowledge of these matters, today make up a very important part of all the progress that is going on in the study of economics; and it is all due to or growing out of the inspiration of the pioneering work that was done by Keynes. The validity and value of all of this investigative work as such is independent of people's differing views about the wisdom of the public-policy proposals and political ideas of Keynes and his ardent disciples. Many first-rate economists of today, who are personally far more "conservative," politically, than their typical ardent Keynesian colleagues, and by no means unqualified supporters of the Keynesian public policies, fully recognize and appreciate the great value of the Keynes-inspired lines of research and analysis, and participate in them, or use the ideas they involve and the fruits they produce in their own inquiries.

At the same time I think it also needs to be said that, although the value of the new modern Keynesian kind of work and progress in a vitally important part of economic "science" is indeed very great, there is among many more or less exclusive devotees of just this kind of work or analysis and research, only, a regrettable if not censurable "narrowness" of outlook which leads them to overvalue it in a relative sense, or too nearly to identify it with *all* worthwhile continuing work in the whole field of economics, and greatly undervalue and neglect other parts. This myopic tendency often lurks in talk about "the Keynesian revolution," and about its results as "the new economics." Keynes "revolutionized" not all economic analysis, but only one part of it—the "aggregative" part, which should never be mistaken for the whole. Exclusive preoccupation with this part is no better than the opposite, exclusive preoccupation with "value and distribution" theory only, which was too common through so long a period. And as Keynes did nothing to the traditional body of theory on the other great topics, of the causes and effects of changes of *particular* demands, supplies, and prices pertaining to particular goods or services in particular markets or parts of the economy, he created not at all a "new," complete, "economics," but only a new advance in one important but restricted part of the field. In any adequately broad and well-balanced perspective, the other parts of the total field of problems to be studied are and remain as important as the special field which Keynesian economics occupies; and the (now waning) tendency of the latter as a most exciting, novel development to overshadow them, and cause many economists almost to forget about them, has been regrettable. This has bearing also upon the question of the adequacy of the Keynesian analysis as the basis for the public-policy proposals which in fact were and are based upon or derived from it. But I cannot here follow up that point, or attempt to give in any sense an "adequate" discussion of these public-policy proposals.

THE PUBLIC-POLICY IDEAS AND POLITICAL TENDENCIES OF KEYNESIAN ECONOMISTS

Keynes was decidedly not in the tradition of "pure economics," but rather in that of "political economy," in the sense that, like all the great "political economists" of the eighteenth and nineteenth centuries, he was interested above all in the quest for wise decisions on national policies. He directed his efforts toward developing a way of discovering, not only how and how well or ill a nation's economy in any period is working, but also what policies on the part of the nation's government are required to cause or enable its economy to work as well as possible. He aspired to be not only, for the social-economic organism, a physiologist but also a physician, able not only to diagnose its ailments, but also to prescribe the right remedies for them. And his analysis of the mode of causation of general economic depressions led him directly to his recommendations about the lines on which governments should act to cure, or better, to prevent them. (As we shall see, it is always possible, theoretically at least, to throw both the analysis and the program of action or policy into reverse, for application to the other, opposite, unhealthy state of the economy, that of inflationary "boom" or high but unstable "prosperity." As we also shall see, however, the practical difficulties of proper execution of the program called for in that latter case have special, formidable features; and it is not certain that the Keynesian medicine against inflation is "as good," in practice, as the medicine against deflation and depression. In any case, it is best to begin here with consideration of the latter—the first, original goal and product of the work of Keynes.) The immediate cause of a depression is an insufficiently large flow of money in the system, as the population's income and outlay for all goods and services, to constitute, at the existing levels of production costs and prices, an adequate demand for a full-employment output; therefore, the policy problem is how best to bring about an appropriate increase of the effective supply and flow of money, or the flow of spending, and people's incomes and respendings, in the whole economy.

Now the pre-Keynesian, classical type of "monetary policy," based on traditional "monetary theory," had sought to accomplish that result in such situations simply by making more central-bank funds available to and through all ordinary banks, as lenders to borrowing and investing business firms, at lowered interest rates. This was expected to induce the business firms to increase their borrowings and investment spendings, with the further result of also increasing the incomes and consumption spendings of the people; and thus to bring about recovery of employment, income, demand, prices, profits, and production. But the ineffectiveness or inadequacy of this policy or "medicine," in a severe depression, was simultaneously demonstrated both by the Keynesian analysis and by actual experience with the depression of the early 1930s. When in general the profit expectations of business for the near or visible future were below zero, and the thirst of the owners of money for "liquidity" made it impossible greatly to increase the supply and lower the cost of borrowable capital funds for business use, the efforts of the central banks to work in this direction proved unavailing. They could and did enable the banks to lend more freely at somewhat lower interest rates, but they could not lower the latter *sufficiently* or make all lenders in the system follow suit and keep up the active flow of money into business or investment uses, or—the real crux—induce the business world substantially to increase its borrowings and investment outlays, by any feasible lowering of the interest costs, when prospective profits on the required investment outlays were nil or negative. The problem was not how to increase the supply or quantity or stock of money—that was no problem—but how to increase *spending,* incomes, and demand for labor and for producers' goods and consumers' goods. And the only way to do this on a sufficient scale was for the government, as by far the largest and freest-to-act spending agency in society, to greatly increase its volume and rate of spending to a point far in excess of its tax revenues, borrow and spend over and beyond the latter the "created" bank money or central-bank funds which business enterprises were not willing to borrow and invest, and thus pour new additional money into active, general circulation, via the incomes and spendings of all of the initial recipients or beneficiaries of the new additional government spendings. As this remedy began to work, and the increases of people's incomes and spendings became increasingly general all through the economy, and demand and production and employment revived, so would the profit prospects and investment spendings of business also then increase, and the upward spiral, replacing the downward spiral into the depression, would be under way. With renewed growth of the people's incomes, the government's tax revenues would also grow, and at the appropriate point it could begin to taper off the enlargement of its spendings, and allow the growth of its tax revenues to overtake them, and repay some of the debt contracted to finance the budgetary deficit, and carry the rest permanently (meeting the interest charges on it) with the aid of the large tax revenues that a continually, increasingly prosperous society could easily afford.

Now in the United States it happened that the early New Deal administration stumbled or groped its way into doing, among other things, much along this line of the later Keynesian recommendations, *before* Keynes wrote and published his *General Theory*—before he *made* the analysis and recommendations discussed in this chapter, at all.[7] The "blind" responses of a bold, energetic, versatile, and determined government to the actual conditions, popular demands, and practical exigencies confronting it led it onto a path which the brilliant "new economics" of Keynes then came along just in time to "rationalize" or confirm as the highest wisdom, after the event. Understandably then, a great number of the able young American professional economists and advanced students of economics, of that time, received the new "Keynesian" gospel with the greatest enthusiasm, and became its lifelong devotees. They had been feeling severely frustrated by the near-non-existence in the pre-Keynesian economics, which they had been brought up on, of any "light" on the pressing practical problem now confronting them, and their country, as to what the latter could and should do to cure or cope with the terrible depression. Many were already in sympathy with the New Deal government's efforts and expedients, in spite of their violation of all the "sound principles of political economy," which they had been taught; and this flirtation with "heresies" opposed to and by everything in their previous professional educations was at best uncomfortable. But now a great economist of unchallengeable competence and eminence endorsed and advocated lavish governmental deficit spending to engender economic recovery, and showed convincingly just why it was needed and how it would work. Naturally, a very

[7] It is true that for some time before the publication of the *General Theory* in 1936—i.e., in the early New Deal period—many economists knew that Keynes was working to produce that book, and had advance inklings of its contents; and this may have had a slight influence in helping to produce, in this quarter, suggestions toward and support for the New Deal spending-for-recovery program. But I think it is true in the main that the latter had its own independent, nontheoretical, purely pragmatic origins.

large percentage of the members of the then rising generation of American economists quickly became pure, thorough, and ardent Keynesian economists.

Moreover, the prevalent American association of Keynesian economics with the New Deal, which thus grew up and persisted, and the generally reputed "radicalism" of the latter, led also to a prevalent association in American minds—both among economists and among the members of the general public—of Keynesian economics with relatively "radical" or "left-of-center" political views on all or most kinds of public issues; whereas in contrast the other American economists who did not immediately, fully embrace "the new economics" but remained in some ways critical of it and more attached to the older classical tradition of thought in their discipline, were commonly assumed to be in all cases extreme and adamant political "conservatives." These too simple and absolute attachments of political labels to the groups of economists responding somewhat differently to the ideas of Keynes have done no good to the work and thought of the profession as a whole, or to its standing with the public. And it is of some importance here to ask what can be truly said about the real "political philosophies," if any, of these modern types or groups of "political economists."

With regard to Keynes himself, it is on the whole clear to all careful students of his career and writings that his own ideals and aims were relatively conservative, in the sense that he wanted to see preserved, and sought through his own work to help preserve, both "capitalism" and liberal democracy; the economic system made up mainly of largely free, private enterprises and competitive markets; democratic governments serving not the many as against the few but the common welfare and the just freedoms of all as impartially as possible, and enlarging their roles or spheres of authority and activity only to the quite limited extent that he deemed necessary in the interests of the best working, strength, and stability of that economic system; and all the private, individual freedoms for all, of the liberal-democratic and economic-liberal traditions. In advocating that national governments should vary and adjust their programs of taxation, borrowing, and spending in accordance with the changing needs of the national economies, or as required to preserve in the latter at all times the appropriate total flows of money-income and spending and demand for all goods and services, and thus preserve continuous full employment, steady economic growth, and stable price levels; Keynes meant to advocate only this one limited departure from *laissez faire,* or moderate degree and kind of governmental "intervention" in the economic world, *in order to strengthen and preserve* the "free-enterprise system" by curing what always had been its worst defect—proneness to recurrent, devastating depressions, with mass unemployment—and removing the main cause of subversive, radical attacks upon it. This Englishman never supported or flirted with socialism; he disliked the English Labor party as a "class" party, had a very low opinion of the economics and intellectual system of Karl Marx, and was very clearly on the whole an adherent of the individualistic, libertarian tradition of nineteenth-century English liberalism.

At the same time, on topics connected with thrift or saving, interest on loans of money, and traditional canons of "sound" public finance, Keynes frequently uttered radical-sounding remarks and epigrams. His belief that, in economically advanced and prosperous societies, thrifty saving could be and was being overdone, with not beneficial but harmful consequences, made him seem a foe of this central "virtue" in the traditional "capitalist" ethos, and a subversive "radical" in the eyes of all-out conservatives of a certain type. And so of course did his belief —the other side of that same coin—that even the most (by ordinary standards) "wasteful" or "extravagant" spending, both private and public, when or if needed to cure or prevent the far greater economic and human wastes of mass unemployment, should be infinitely preferred to the latter. Then also, his theory that the interest-incomes of those who make "saved" money available for investment in production, are not their deserved and needed rewards and incentives for difficult and virtuous and always socially useful saving, but merely bribes paid to induce them to allow business firms to use or invest the money they would save anyway and simply "hoard" if not paid their interest—this theory of course does seem to have affinities with ancient anticapitalist ideas about all interest as "usury." And in advocating governmental and central-banking policies designed to lower interest rates as far as possible, Keynes in one passage spoke with pleasure of "the euthanasia of the *rentiers*" toward which this could lead. His sympathies lay with the active businessmen or entrepreneurs who got things done, not with the passive capitalists or creditors who merely charge for the use of what they own. And in his *Tract on Monetary Reform,* written long before he produced his *General Theory,* he very significantly expressed the view that the trend, in much of economic history, of gradual inflation or rising price levels and falling real value of the money unit, had the beneficial result of gradually reducing the real burden or retarding drag of old debts and interest charges upon all active business and productive enterprise. It is not surprising that such ideas have helped to cause many more ordinary or typical conservative minds to distrust this "flexible, enlightened," reforming-to-conserve, "conservative" thinker, who in addition had these particular, unorthodox, and eccentric views. But in spite of them, it remains clear that his over-all main purpose was conservative.

The personal outlook of Keynes himself, however, and the possible, long-run institutional results of different, possible, actual developments of Keynesian governmental economic policies, as carried out in practice, may be different matters. Repeated enlargements of the government's budget at times of incipient depression, to enlarge the income-flow in the system and prevent depression, *could* lead gradually into socialism, through growth of the share of the nation's income and wealth taken over, and used in ways determined, by its government. Conservative governments can develop and use the general policy ideas of Keynes on truly conservative lines and with conservative results; but governments or parties-in-power with socialistic or "welfare-state" ideas and purposes can develop and use the same general policy ideas or methods in their own directions also. And the English Labor or Socialist government, of the period 1945 to 1950, did so. What Keynesian economics as such leads to in the sphere of governmental policies is not so much a political direction as a set of ideas or devices which can be used to assist developments in either direction—strengthening and perpetuation of the "system of free enterprise," or gradual change toward socialism—depending on the views and aims, having other sources, of those politically in control.

My final comments, however, in this necessarily very incomplete discussion of the Keynesian public-policy ideas, will be on the different question of their value when adapted and applied to the task of preventing not deflation and depression, but inflation. Viewed in balanced perspective, the Keynesian prescription is: adjust the impacts of the government's finances, taxes, borrowing, and spendings upon the total income-flow in the economy, as required to keep the latter at all times just sufficient to ensure equality of total demand with total supply or the national output of all goods and services, under conditions of approximately full employment of the labor force and resources and equipment of the national economy. If the income-flow is threatening to contract or fail to grow in step with the growth of output under full employment, let the government reduce taxes and/or increase public spending, add more through spending to the incomes of the people than it takes away through taxes, and thus increase the total flow of income and spending or demand in the system to match the growth of output, and keep the price level stable. And if or when, on the contrary, the income-flow threatens to grow *faster* than the full-employment output and cause inflation or a rising price level, let the government *reduce* its spending and/or increase its tax rates, take *more* through the latter *out of* the income-flow than its spendings put back into it, and thus *reduce* the rate of growth of the income-flow to equality with that of output, and so again, stabilize the price level.

But it is not so easy in practice for a democratic government dealing with the kind of economic system and society and interest pressure groups that typically exist today, to carry out that prescription effectively in both directions, as occasions require. Spending to overcome depression is more readily accepted than "austerity" to combat inflation. Moreover—and this is the main point—if the government is committed to a guarantee of continuous "full employment," or maintenance of the flow of total money-income and demand for goods, etc., at whatever level is needed to prevent development of any serious amount of unemployment, this becomes an invitation, so to speak, to labor unions and big business firms and groups to keep pushing wages, costs, and prices upward, relying on the government to so expand the money-income flow that no insufficiency of demand and no unemployment will be caused by the rising wages, costs, and prices. There is here a real dilemma that has not been resolved thus far. Fuller discussion of it here would still be inconclusive.

It is not inappropriate that our survey of a great part of the history of political and economic thought in the Western world over the last few centuries should end "in the air," with no real ending, completion, or conclusion. History is like that—it continues, it does not end.

Selected Bibliography

GENERAL

Bonar, James: *Philosophy and Political Economy in Some of Their Historical Relations* (London: Swann, Sonnenschein & Co.; New York: The Macmillan Company, 1893).

Hoeffding, Harald: *A History of Modern Philosophy,* authorized Eng. trans., 2 vols. (London: Macmillan & Co., Ltd., 1920).

Sabine, G. H.: *A History of Political Theory,* rev. ed. (New York: Henry Holt and Company, Inc., 1950).

Schumpeter, J. A.: *History of Economic Analysis* (New York: Oxford University Press, 1954).

CHAPTER 1

Becker, Carl L.: *The Heavenly City of the Eighteenth Century Philosophers* (New Haven, Conn.: Yale University Press, 1935).

Cassirer, Ernst: *The Philosophy of the Enlightenment* (Princeton, N.J.: Princeton University Press, 1951).

Higgs, Henry: *The Physiocrats* (London and New York: The Macmillan Company, 1897).

Hoeffding, Harald: *A History of Modern Philosophy,* authorized Eng. trans. (London: Macmillan & Co., Ltd., 1920), vol. 1, books 4 and 5.

Sabine, G. H.: *A History of Political Theory,* rev. ed. (New York: Henry Holt and Company, Inc., 1950), chaps. 26–29, incl.

Schumpeter, J. A.: *History of Economic Analysis* (New York: Oxford University Press, 1954), part II (history of all economic thought to about 1790); and especially within part II, chap. 4 (the economics of the Physiocrats, their immediate forerunners, and Turgot).

Stephen, Sir Leslie: *History of English Thought in the Eighteenth Century,* 3d ed., 2 vols. (London: 1902).

Taylor, O. H.: "Philosophies and Economic Theories in Modern Western Civilization," in the author's volume of collected and reprinted articles, *Economics and Liberalism* (Cambridge, Mass.: Harvard University Press, 1955).

Taylor, O. H.: "Economics and the Idea of Natural Laws" and "Economics and the Idea of *Jus Naturale,*" in *Economics and Liberalism, op cit.*

Du Pont de Nemours, Pierre: *De l'Origine et des Progrès d'une Science Nouvelle* (1768) A. Dubois (ed.) (Paris: P. Gehtner, 1910).

La Rivière, Le Mercier de: *L'Ordre Naturel et Essentiel des Sociétés Politiques* (1767) Edgar Déprite (ed.) (Paris: P. Gehtner, 1910).
Oncken, Auguste (ed.): *Oeuvres Economiques et Philosophiques de François Quesnay* (Paris: Jules Peelman and Company, 1888).

CHAPTER 2

Fowler, Thomas: *Shaftesbury and Hutcheson* (New York: G. P. Putnam's Sons, 1883).
Schumpeter, J. A.: *History of Economic Analysis* (New York: Oxford University Press, 1954), part II, chap. 2, sec. 7 (a, b, c, especially b).
Scott, W. R.: *Francis Hutcheson* (Cambridge, England: Cambridge University Press, 1900).
Seth, James: *English Philosophers and Schools of Philosophy* (London: J. M. Dent & Sons, Ltd., 1912), part II, chap. 3.
Stephen, Sir Leslie: *History of English Thought in the Eighteenth Century,* 3d ed. (London: 1902), vol. 2.

Cooper, Anthony Ashley, 3d Earl of Shaftesbury: *Characteristics of Men, Manners, Opinions and Times,* 6th ed. (London: 1737), vol. 2, *An Inquiry Concerning Virtue and Merit.*
Hutcheson, Francis: *An Inquiry into the Original of our Ideas of Beauty and Virtue* (London: 1725).
Mandeville, Bernard: *A Fable of the Bees,* 3d ed. (London: 1724).
Selby-Bigge, L. A.: *British Moralists* (Oxford: Clarendon Press, 1897). (A very convenient book of extensive extracts from the original writings of leading historic British moral philosophers, including Shaftesbury, Hutcheson, Adam Smith, and others.)

CHAPTERS 3 AND 4

Hasbach, W.: *Die allgemeinen Philosophischen Grundlagen der von François Quesnay und Adam Smith Bergruendeten Politischen Ökonomie* (Leipzig: Duncker und Humboldt, 1890).
Hasbach, W.: *Untersuchungen über Adam Smith und die Entwicklung der Politischen Ökonomie* (Leipzig: Duncker und Humboldt, 1891).
Morrow, G. R.: *The Ethical and Economic Theories of Adam Smith* (New York: Longmans, Green & Co., Inc., 1923).
Rae, John: *The Life of Adam Smith* (London: Macmillan & Co., Ltd., 1895).
Schumpeter, J. A.: *History of Economic Analysis* (New York: Oxford University Press, 1954), part II, chap. 2, sec. 7, pp. 126–130; and part II, chap. 3, sec. 4, especially pp. 181–194.
Scott, W. R.: *Adam Smith as Student and Professor* (Glasgow: Jackson Son and Co., 1937).

Selby-Bigge, L. A.: *British Moralists* (Oxford: Clarendon Press, 1897). See the included extract from Adam Smith's *Theory of the Moral Sentiments.*
Smith, Adam: *The Theory of the Moral Sentiments,* 6th ed. (London: 1790).
Smith, Adam: *The Whole Works of Adam Smith in Five Volumes* (London: 1822), vol. 5, *Essays on Philosophical Subjects.*
Smith, Adam: *An Inquiry into the Nature and Causes of the Wealth of Nations,* Edwin Cannan (ed.) (London: Modern Library, 1905).

CHAPTER 5

Albee, Ernest: *A History of English Utilitarianism* (London: Swann, Sonnenschein & Co.; New York: The Macmillan Company, 1902).
Brinton, Crane: *English Political Thought in the Nineteenth Century* (Cambridge, Mass.: Harvard University Press, 1949), chap. 2, sec. 1.
Halévy, Élie: *The Growth of Philosophical Radicalism,* Mary Morris (trans.) (New York: The Macmillan Company, 1928).
Sabine, G. H.: *A History of Political Theory,* rev. ed. (New York: Henry Holt and Company, Inc., 1950), chap. 31.
Stephen, Sir Leslie: *The English Utilitarians* (London: Gerald Duckworth & Co., Ltd., 1900), vol. 1.

Bentham, Jeremy: *The Rationale of Punishment* (London: R. Heward, 1830).
Bentham, Jeremy: *The Rationale of Reward* (London: R. Heward, 1830).
Bentham, Jeremy: *A Fragment on Government,* F. C. Montague (ed.) (Oxford: Clarendon Press, 1891; or reprint London: Humphrey Milford, 1931).
Bentham, Jeremy: *An Introduction to the Principles of Morals and Legislation,* modern ed. (New York: Hafner Publishing Company, 1948).
Stark, W. (ed.): *Jeremy Bentham's Economic Writings,* 3 vols. (London: George Allen & Unwin, Ltd., 1952–1954). (Published for the Royal Economic Society.)

CHAPTER 6

Bonar, James: *Malthus and His Work,* 2d ed. (London: George Allen & Unwin, Ltd., 1924).
Keynes, J. M.: *Essays in Biography* (New York: Harcourt, Brace and Company, Inc., 1933). See the essay on "Malthus."
Schumpeter, J. A.: *History of Economic Analysis* (New York: Oxford University Press, 1954), part II, chap. 5, and part III, chap. 4, sec. 1(a).

Malthus, Thomas Robert, 1766–1834: First Essay on Population (1798), with notes by James Bonar. (London: Macmillan & Co., Ltd., 1926.) ("Reprinted for the Royal Economic Society.")
Malthus, T. R.: *An Essay on Population,* modern ed., from 7th ed. (London: J. M. Dent & Sons, Ltd.; and New York: E. P. Dutton & Co., Inc., 1933).
Malthus, T. R.: *Principles of Political Economy, Considered with a View to their Practical Application* (London: 1820).

CHAPTERS 7 AND 8

Blaug, Mark: *Ricardian Economics* (New Haven, Conn.: Yale University Press, 1958).
Cannan, Edwin: *Theories of Production and Distribution in English Political Economy* (London: Staples Press, 1953).
Edelberg, D. V.: "The Ricardian Theory of Profits," *Economica,* vol. 13 (1933).
Hollander, Jacob: *David Ricardo: A Centenary Estimate* (Baltimore: Johns Hopkins Press, 1910).
Knight, F. H.: "The Ricardian Theory of Production and Distribution," *Canadian Journal of Economics and Political Science,* vol. 1 (Feb. 1935).
Marshall, Alfred: Appendix on "Ricardo's Theory of Value," in *Principles of Economics,* 8th ed. (London: Macmillan & Co., Ltd., 1922).

Schumpeter, J. A.: *History of Economic Analysis* (New York: Oxford University Press, 1954), part III, chap. 4, sec. 2, pp. 469–480.
Stigler, G. J.: *Production and Distribution Theories* (New York: The Macmillan Company, 1941).
Stigler, G. J.: "The Ricardian Theory of Value and Distribution," *Journal of Political Economy* (June, 1952), pp. 195–200.

Ricardo, David: *Principles of Political Economy and Taxation* (1817), 3d ed., 1821 (London and New York: Everyman's Library, 1912, reprinted 1917).
Sraffa, P., and M. Dobb (eds.): *The Works and Correspondence of David Ricardo,* 10 vols. (Cambridge, England: Cambridge University Press, 1951–1955). Vol. 1 contains the *Principles;* vol. 2, the previously unpublished "Notes on Malthus"; vols. 3 and 4, pamphlets and papers by Ricardo; vol. 5, Parliamentary speeches and evidence; vols. 6–9, correspondence, including the full, extensive, and important correspondence with Malthus—many letters by each to the other, discussing all sorts of economic theory and policy questions on which they differed; vol. 10, biographical miscellany.

CHAPTERS 9 AND 10

Brinton, Crane: *English Political Thought in the Nineteenth Century* (Cambridge, Mass.: Harvard University Press, 1949), chap. 3, sec. 1.
Maccunn, J.: *Six Radical Thinkers* (London: Edward Arnold & Co., 1907), chap. 2.
Sabine, G. H.: *A History of Political Theory,* rev. ed. (New York: Henry Holt and Company, Inc., 1950), chaps. 31 and 32.
Seth, James: *English Philosophers and Schools of Philosophy* (London: J. M. Dent & Sons, Ltd., 1925), part III, chap. 1.
Stephen, Sir Leslie: *The English Utilitarians* (London: Gerald Duckworth & Co., Ltd., 1910), vol. 3.

Cannan, Edwin: *Theories of Production and Distribution in English Political Economy* (London: Staples Press, 1953).
Edgeworth, F. Y.: "Mill, John Stuart," in *Palgrave's Dictionary of Political Economy,* 3 vols. (London: Macmillan & Co., Ltd., 1925–1926).
Mill, J. S.: *Principles of Political Economy,* W. J. Ashley (ed.) (London and New York: Longmans Green & Co., Inc., 1909). See the editor's introduction and appendix.
Schumpeter, J. A.: *History of Economic Analysis* (New York: Oxford University Press, 1954), part III, chap. 5.

Mill, J. S.: *Essays on Some Unsettled Questions in Political Economy* (London: 1844).
Mill, J. S.: *Dissertations and Discussions* (London: 1858–1867), vol. 1. See essays on "Bentham" and "Coleridge."
Mill, J. S.: *A System of Logic* (New York: Harper Brothers, 1869).
Mill, J. S.: *Principles of Political Economy, with Some of Their Applications to Social Philosophy,* W. J. Ashley (ed.) (London and New York: Longmans Green & Co., Inc., 1909).
Mill, J. S.: *Utilitarianism, Liberty, and Representative Government,* Everyman's Library edition (New York and London: 1914).

Mill, J. S.: *Autobiography*, H. J. Lasky (ed.) (London: Oxford University Press, 1953).

CHAPTER 11

Bober, M. M.: *Karl Marx's Interpretation of History*, 2d ed. (Cambridge, Mass.: Harvard University Press, 1950).
Dobb, M. H.: *Marx as an Economist* (London: Lawrence and Wishart, 1943).
Hook, Sidney: *From Hegel to Marx* (London: Victor Gollancz, Ltd., 1936).
Robinson, Joan: *An Essay on Marxian Economics* (London: Macmillan & Co., Ltd., 1942).
Sabine, G. H.: *A History of Political Theory*, rev. ed. (New York: Henry Holt and Company, Inc., 1950), chaps. 30 and 33.
Schumpeter, J. A.: *Capitalism, Socialism, and Democracy* (New York: Harper & Brothers, 1942–1950), part I.
Schumpeter, J. A.: *History of Economic Analysis* (New York: Oxford University Press, 1954), part III, chap. 1, sec. 4, pp. 383–392.
Sweezy, P. M.: *The Theory of Capitalist Development* (New York: Oxford University Press, 1942). (This book is the best introduction to Marxian economic theory. Written by an able modern economist, fully competent in modern, non-Marxian economics, *and* a thorough, loyal disciple of Marx, it expounds Marx's system of economic theory with full insight and intelligibility.)

Burns, Émile: *A Handbook of Marxism* (New York: International Publishers Co., Inc., 1935). (A very useful "anthology" of extensive parts of the original writings of Marx and his leading disciples.)
Marx, Karl: *Theories of Surplus Value, Selections*, trans. (New York: International Publishers Co., Inc., 1952).
Marx, Karl: *Capital*, F. Engels, (ed.); E. and C. Paul, (trans.); Intro. by G. D. H. Cole; 2 vols., Everyman's Library (London: J. M. Dent & Sons, Ltd., 1957).
Marx, Karl, and F. Engels: *The Communist Manifesto*, Harold Lasky (ed. and trans.) (London: George Allen & Unwin, Ltd., 1948).

CHAPTER 12

Brinton, Crane: *English Political Thought in the Nineteenth Century* (Cambridge, Mass.: Harvard University Press, 1949), chap 4.
Hutchinson, J. W.: *A Review of Economic Doctrines, 1870–1929* (Oxford: Clarendon Press, 1953).
Jevons, W. S.: *The Theory of Political Economy*, 4th ed., with notes by H. S. Jevons (London: Macmillan & Co., Ltd., 1911).
Knight, F. H.: The article on Jevons in *The Trend of Economics*, R. G. Tugwell (ed.) (New York: Alfred A. Knopf, Inc., 1924).
Sabine, G. H.: *A History of Political Theory*, rev. ed. (New York: Henry Holt and Company, Inc., 1950), chap. 32.
Schumpeter, J. A.: *Ten Great Economists* (New York: Oxford University Press, 1951), chaps. (essays) on Walras, Menger, Böhm-Bawerk, Marshall, and others. (The rounded accounts and appraisals of individual economists in this book are not duplicated in the same author's differently organized *History*.)
Schumpeter, J. A.: *History of Economic Analysis* (New York: Oxford University Press, 1954), part IV, chaps. 5, 6, and 7.
Young, A. A.: "Jevons' Theory of Political Economy," in *Economic Problems New and Old* (Boston: Houghton Mifflin Company, 1927).

CHAPTER 13

Henderson, H. D.: *Supply and Demand* (New York: Harcourt, Brace and Company, Inc., 1922; London: Nisbet and Co., 1926; latest reprint, Chicago: Chicago University Press, 1958). (An excellent, short, and simplified or elementary presentation of the main substance of Marshallian economic theory by a pupil of Marshall's.)

Hutchinson, T. W.: *A Review of Economic Doctrines, 1870–1929* (Oxford: Clarendon Press, 1953).

Keynes, J. M.: The memorial article on Marshall, in *Memorials of Alfred Marshall*, A. C. Pigou (ed.) (London: Macmillan & Co., Ltd., 1925).

Pigou, A. C.: *Alfred Marshall and Current Thought* (London: Macmillan & Co., Ltd., 1953).

Schumpeter, J. A.: *Ten Great Economists* (New York: Oxford University Press, 1951), essay on Marshall.

Schumpeter, J. A.: *History of Economic Analysis* (New York: Oxford University Press, 1954), part IV, chap. 5, sec. 2, pp. 829–840.

Marshall, Alfred: *The Present Position of Economics*. Inaugural lecture at Cambridge University, 1885 (London: Macmillan & Co., Ltd., 1885).

Marshall, Alfred: *The Old Generation of Economists and the New* (Boston: 1897).

Marshall, Alfred: *Principles of Economics*, 8th ed. (London: Macmillan & Co., Ltd., 1922).

CHAPTER 14

Burns, Émile: *A Handbook of Marxism* (New York: International Publishers Co., Inc., 1935). See the several "chapters" which are extracts from the principal writings of Lenin.

Le Rossignol, J. E.: *From Marx to Stalin: A Critique of Communism* (New York: Thomas Y. Crowell Company, 1940).

Sabine, G. H.: *A History of Political Theory*, rev. ed. (New York: Henry Holt and Company, Inc., 1950), chaps. 34 and 35.

Salvadari, M.: *The Rise of Modern Communism: A Brief History of the Communist Movement in the Twentieth Century* (New York: Henry Holt and Company, Inc., 1952).

Wittke, C. F., and others: *Democracy is Different: Democracy over against Communism, Fascism, and Nazism* (New York: Harper & Brothers, 1941).

CHAPTER 15

Beer, Max: *A History of British Socialism* (Older editions, London: G. Bell & Sons, Ltd., 1919–1923; or newer editions, London: George Allen & Unwin, Ltd., 1948–1953, vol. 2). (Vol. 1 surveys mediaeval and early-modern [renaissance, etc.] preliminaries; Beer's history of the modern British movement is all in vol. 2.)

Cole, G. D. H.: *A History of Socialist Thought*, 4 vols. (London: Macmillan & Co., Ltd., 1956–1958). The material of main interest to most readers is in vols. III and IV.

Crossman, R. H. S., and others: *New Fabian Essays* (London: Turnstile Press, 1952; or New York: Frederick A. Praeger Inc., 1952). (Very interesting expressions of the states of mind of some leading reflective English Labor party socialists at the end of their party's 1945–1950 period of power in England.)

Gray, Alexander: *The Socialist Tradition, from Moses to Lenin* (London: Longmans, Green & Co., Ltd., 1947). (A rather unsympathetic, adversely critical history and commentary.)

Laidler, Harry W.: *Social-economic Movements* (New York: Thomas Y. Crowell Company, 1944). (Probably as satisfactory a general comprehensive history of all varieties of socialist thought and movements as any in existence.)

Shaw, G. B.: *The Intelligent Woman's Guide to Socialism and Capitalism* (London: Constable & Co., Ltd., 1930). (The fullest exposition of his socialist views and arguments by this leading exponent of Fabian socialism.)

Shaw, G. B., Sidney Webb, and others: *Fabian Essays in Socialism* (London: Fabian Society, 1931 [5th ed.]; or London: George Allen & Unwin, Ltd., 1948). (The most important source book and "must" reading for study of English Fabian socialism.)

Sweezy, P. M.: *Socialism* (New York: McGraw-Hill Book Company, Inc., 1947). (A rather biased history by a near-Communist, Marxist writer and scholar, doing less than justice to the English and all not-orthodox-Marxian branches of the socialist movement.)

Schlesinger, A. M., Jr.: *The Age of Jackson* (Boston: Little, Brown & Company, 1950–1954).

Schlesinger, A. M., Jr.: *The Age of Roosevelt* (Boston: Houghton Mifflin Company, 1957), vol. 1, *The Crisis of the Old Order, 1919–1933;* vol. 2, *The Coming of the New Deal.*

Schlesinger, A. M., Sr., and D. R. Fox (eds.): *A History of American Life,* 13 vols. (New York: The Macmillan Company, 1927–1948), especially the following:

- Nevins, Allan: vol. 8, *The Emergence of Modern America, 1865–1878* (1927).
- Tarbell, Ida M.: vol. 9, *The Nationalizing of Business, 1878–1898* (1936).
- Faulkner, H. V.: vol. 11, *The Quest for Social Justice, 1898–1914* (1931).
- Slosson, P. W.: vol. 12, *The Great Crusade and After, 1914–1928* (1931).
- Wecter, Dixon: vol. 13, *The Age of the Great Depression, 1929–1941* (1948).

The New Deal—An Analysis and Appraisal, by the editors of *The Economist* (London) (New York: Alfred Knopf, Inc., 1937).

Einaudi, Mario: *The Roosevelt Revolution* (New York: Harcourt, Brace and Company, Inc., 1959).

Fusfeld, D. R.: *The Economic Thought of Franklin D. Roosevelt and the Origins of the New Deal* (New York: Columbia University Press, 1956).

CHAPTER 16

Bain, J. S.: *Barriers to New Competition; Their Character and Consequences in Manufacturing Industries* (Cambridge, Mass.: Harvard University Press, 1956).

Burns, A. R.: *The Decline of Competition: A Study of the Evolution of American Industry* (New York and London: McGraw-Hill Book Company, Inc., 1936).

Chamberlin, E. H.: *The Theory of Monopolistic Competition,* 6th ed. (Cambridge, Mass.: Harvard University Press, 1948).

Chamberlin, E. H. (ed.): *Monopoly and Competition and Their Regulation.*

Papers and proceedings of a conference held by the International Economics Association (London: Macmillan & Co., Ltd., 1954).
Edwards, C. D., E. S. Mason, M. W. Watkins, A. R. Burns, and others: *Readings in the Social Control of Industry,* selected by a committee of the American Economics Association (New York: McGraw-Hill Book Company, Inc., Blakiston Division, 1942). Articles on monopoly, competition, and public policy, including antitrust law policy.
Fellner, W. J.: *Competition among the Few; Oligopoly and Similar Market Structures* (New York: Alfred A. Knopf, Inc., 1949).
Knight, F. H.: *The Ethics of Competition and Other Essays* (New York and London: Harper & Brothers, 1935).
Miller, J. P.: *Unfair Competition: A Study in Criteria for the Control of Trade Practices* (Cambridge, Mass.: Harvard University Press, 1941).
Robinson, Joan: *The Economics of Imperfect Competition* (London: Macmillan & Co., Ltd., 1948).

CHAPTER 17

Hansen, Alvin: *A Guide to Keynes* (New York: McGraw-Hill Book Company, Inc., 1953).
Harris, S. E. (ed.): *The New Economics: Keynes' Influence on Theory and Public Policy* (New York: Alfred A. Knopf, Inc., 1947). (A symposium of essays by many, diverse, distinguished economists.)
Harris, S. E.: *John Maynard Keynes, Economist and Policy Maker* (New York: Charles Scribner's Sons, 1955).
Harrod, R. E.: *The Life of John Maynard Keynes* (London: Macmillan & Co., Ltd., 1951).
Hazlitt, Henry: *The Failure of the "New Economics": An Analysis of the Keynesian Fallacies* (Princeton, N.J.: D. Van Nostrand Company, Inc., 1959).
Klein, L. R.: *The Keynesian Revolution* (New York: The Macmillan Company, 1947).
Pigou, A. C.: *Keynes's General Theory: A Retrospective View* (London: Macmillan & Co., Ltd., 1950).
Robinson, Joan: *Essays in the Theory of Employment* (Oxford: Basil Blackwell & Mott, Ltd., 1947).

Keynes, J. M.: *Indian Currency and Finance* (London: Macmillan & Co., Ltd., 1913, 1924).
Keynes, J. M.: *The Economic Consequences of the Peace* (London: Harcourt, Brace and Company, Inc., 1920).
Keynes, J. M.: *Monetary Reform* (New York: Harcourt, Brace and Company, Inc., 1924).
Keynes, J. M.: *The Economic Consequences of Mr. Churchill* (London: L. and V. Woolf, 1925). American edition entitled: *The Economic Consequences of Sterling Parity* (New York: Harcourt, Brace and Company, Inc., 1925).
Keynes, J. M.: *The End of Laissez-Faire* (London, L. and V. Woolf, 1926).
Keynes, J. M.: *A Treatise on Money* (New York: Harcourt, Brace and Company, Inc., 1930).
Keynes, J. M.: *The Means of Prosperity* (London: Macmillan & Co., Ltd., New York: Harcourt, Brace and Company, Inc., 1933).
Keynes, J. M.: *The General Theory of Employment, Interest and Money* (London: Macmillan & Co., Ltd.; New York: Harcourt, Brace and Company, Inc., 1936).

Index